Wakeful Nights

......it is quite possible that he will someday be acknowledged as the earliest poet of the first rank, writing in any language, to emerge in the national life of Canada."
—Watson Kirconnell, President Emeritus, Acadia University

A beautifully crafted narrative about a turn of the nineteenth-century poet whose life on, and of, the land challenged him to hold to his roots in Iceland while yet wrestling with the vicissitudes of transplantation to the emerging cultures of North America. This book is as much about the transformative particulars of place as it is about the man whose extraordinary poetic record of them reveals a soul torn by alternating turmoil and peace."
—John H. Wadland, Professor Emeritus, Department of Canadian Studies, Trent University, Peterborough, Ontario

...the man who emerges from this portrait is complicated and real. Hreinsson's Stephansson is proud, questioning and sagacious—an Icelandic heir to Emerson, Whitman or Thoreau. /.../ A deferential, unsentimental portrait that ably captures Stephansson's life and legacy.
—Kirkus Review

I thought it would take an awfully long time to read, but surprisingly it did not. It was so interesting and down to earth that I just kept reading and reading. This poet, whether you consider him to be a Canadian, American or Icelandic national treasure, was a fascinating man. /.../

There is so much in this book that I could go on forever. It is well-researched, and written by an Icelandic author who has made Stephan G. one of his main interests in life. There are pictures, maps, and charts throughout, painstakingly obtained, I imagine. It is highly educational and very enjoyable. I came away liking the poet very much. A wonderful book ....
—Judy Sólveig Wilson, Lögberg Heimskringla

I'm only grateful that the book has been written and published. For me, it has revealed and explained many things about my own ethnic community that I have not understood. /.../ One of the joys of Viðar's writing is that it is easy to read.
—William D. Valgardson

Wakeful Nights

Stephan G. Stephansson: Icelandic-Canadian Poet

Viðar Hreinsson

Benson Ranch Inc.
Calgary, Alberta

This biography was supported by:
The Icelandic Ministry of Education, Science and Culture
The Icelandic Ministry for Foreign Affairs
Icelandic Language & Literature Fund, University of Manitoba
Stephan V. Benediktson
Baugur Group, Iceland

English editing: Jane Ross, Kenneth Graham, and Nelson Gerrard
Photo selection and captions: Nelson Gerrard
Book design and layout: Jon Sievert
Cover Painting: Gunnar Karlsson

Copyright 2013 by Stephan V. Benediktson. All rights reserved. No part of this publication may be reproduced, stored in an information storage and retrieval system, or transmitted in any form by electronic or mechanical means without the prior written permission of the copyright holders. Reviewers may quote brief passages in a review. Every reasonable effort has been made to obtain permission for copyrighted material included in this work, and to ensure accuracy at the time of publication, but prices, locations, etc., can change. Any errors that may have occurred are inadvertent and will be corrected in subsequent editions, provided notification is sent to the publisher. The authors and publisher do not accept and hereby disclaim any liability to any party for any loss or damage caused by errors, omissions, or any potential disruption or problem due to application of information contained in this book, whether such incidences result from misuse, negligence, accident, or any other cause.

ISBN 978-0-9733657-3-3

Benson Ranch Inc.
251018 Tower Ridge Estates
Calgary, Alberta T3Z 2M2

Printed and bound in the United States of America

"His intellectuality manifested itself last of all in his mastery of the great literary tradition of the North. Of the Mediterranean, or Graeco-Roman Tradition, he knew nothing at first hand: but his mind was steeped in all of the surviving literature, mythology, and history of the Norse past. The fact makes a full appreciation of his achievement impossible to those not similarly familiar with the legacy of Scandinavia, and will always be an obstacle to recognition by the English or French-Canadian. His most vivid allusions and figures appeal to deaf ears and unseeing eyes. Absolutely considered, however, his breadth of literary knowledge, his historical sense, and his philosophical wisdom, all give him an assured place in modern Scandinavian literature and a permanent claim on the regard of Canadians. Comparative valuation may be premature and unprofitable, but it is quite possible that he will someday be acknowledged as the earliest poet of the first rank, writing in any language, to emerge in the national life of Canada."

– Watson Kirconnell
President, Acadia University
"Canada's Leading Poet Stephan G. Stephansson"
University of Toronto Quarterly
Vol. V, No. 2, January 1936

Contents

Foreword 13
Introduction 14
Preface 17
Overview of Icelandic History 21
Chronology 24

Part 1: Age of Ideals

Chapter 1: Kirkjuhóll and Syðri Mælifellsá 29
   Born in a Cloak of Victory 29
   The Parents 30
   The World Grows Larger 34
   At Home in Kirkjuhóll 37
   In Syðri-Mælifellsá 42

Chapter 2: Víðimýrarsel 46
   The Little Shepherd 46
   Earl Andri and Bishop Balle 50
   The Skagafjörður Academy 52
   The Burden of Poverty 55
   The Long Service 58
   Rough Work at Sea 60
   Going East 62
   On His Own 67

Chapter 3: Mjóidalur 70
   The Errand-boy and the Pauper 70
   The Young Poet 73
   Illness and Pastoral Romance 78
   Hardships 82
   Education and Death 86
   Departure 88
   Revelry in Akureyri 91

Chapter 4: The Journey West..........97
- The Queen 97
- Resurrection from the Manitoban..........102
- On the Train..........105
- In a New World..........109
- Life and Death in Stoughton..........112

Chapter 5: Shawano County..........119
- The Icelandic Settlement..........119
- The Little Colony..........124
- Lumberjacks..........127
- Curly..........131
- Farming, Sex, and Marriage..........134
- A Synod Man or Radical? Exodus..........140

Chapter 6: Gardar..........146
- Pioneers Again..........146
- Winter Journeys..........153
- 'Crossroots' on Stage..........156
- Death, Birth, and Religion..........159
- Grant Us Equal Rights..........161
- Enjoy the House..........165
- Trade and Business..........169
- Self-reliance..........171
- Congregational Fuss..........174
- Meaningful Nature..........178
- A Summer Night in Dakota..........180

Chapter 7: Quest for Knowledge..........184
- Solomon's Temple Speech..........184
- A Conference in Winnipeg..........189
- The Freethinkers..........191
- Struggle, Culture, and Progress..........195
- Daddy, I am Here!..........200
- The Cultural Society and Reverend Jón..........202
- Turning Point..........210
- Work as Prayer..........214
- Bergmannism and Church Gloom..........216
- A Fence in a Churchyard..........219

Chapter 8: On the Banks of the Medicine River..........223
- Settlement in Alberta..........223

On the Train West 225
The Call of the Wilderness 230
Former Servants of the Devil 233
The First Summer, 1890 237
Exploration to Edmonton 240
More Pioneers 243
Disbelief 246
Gestur Pálsson's Bugle 250
No Motherland – At Home 255

Chapter 9: At the Turn of the Century 258
Departure of Friends 258
Old and Irritated 263
Between Calf and Afterbirth 267
The School at Hola 271
Settlement in Verse 274
All Around 280
"The night is … so long." 284
Historical Poems 289
Work and Wakefulness 294
Evening 299

Part 2: Age of Violence

Chapter 10: Busy in a New Century 304
An Icelandic Prostitute in the New World 304
On Par with Zola and Crane 310
Icelandic Identity 314
A Giant Oppressing a Little Dwarf 316
"Go make some coffee, Helga" 319
Colourful Culture 323
Modernity Arrives 327
Heather from Home and Belief in … Life 332
Far Traveller 337

Chapter 11: An Act of Friendship 340
Animals Small and Large 340
Eggert and Rögnvaldur: Ideas of Publication 342
Reconciliation with Reverend Friðrik 347
"I Will Sort Out My Heap of Rubbish" 349

A Reading in Winnipeg 353
Poets Meet 356
Back in Dakota 359
Gestur 361
A Great Event in the History of Poetry 367
The Mirages Disappear Faster 371

Chapter 12: Poetry Against Satan **376**
Mother and World 376
A Rainy Summer 381
Reunion with the Ocean 385
Lost Context of Culture 392
Kolbeinn, the Poet of the Rocky Mountains 397
The Good Shepherd 403

Chapter 13: The War Years **406**
Blood Sacrifice 406
The Spirit of Regression 410
News from the Battlefield 412
Cease-fire 416
Life in Markerville 424
A Good Guest 427

Chapter 14: The Land of Summer **431**
"Dear Poet" 431
Across a Continent and an Ocean 434
The Town of Reykjavík 437
Around the Country 440
The Homecoming 444
Poets Meet in Akureyri 447
Places of Youth 450
Historic Sites 453
A Feast in Sauðárkrókur 454
Building Palaces 458
Homeward Bound 459

Chapter 15: The Memorial **466**
Volatile Atmosphere 466
The Battle at Yankee Bluff 469
The End of War 472
Collapsed Palaces 474
Two Major Issues 477
Multiculturalism – Bread and Stones 479

- Chapter 16: Trail of War 485
  - Malingering and Glacier Walks 485
  - A Late Flare-up 490
  - "The Old Man Sleeps" 495
  - Building on Ruins 497
  - An Aging Revolutionary Poet 500
- Chapter 17: Failing Strength 505
  - Years of Crisis 505
  - Birthday Publication 510
  - Female Trolls Wrestling 517
  - Tidal Changes 522
  - Exaggerated News of Death 526
  - The Eyes of Pleasure 528
  - The Custodian and the Heap 532
  - Memorials 535
- Chapter 18: Moments of Farewell 540
  - Croaking at a Window 540
  - Swan Song 547
  - The Final Hand of Conciliation 552
- **Notes** 556
- **Bibliography** 583
- **Index** 593
- **Image Credits** 606

Foreword

Culture is never quite what it appears to be. At least great culture isn't. The most important Canadian war poetry – or in his case anti-war poetry – was written in Icelandic by an Alberta farmer near Red Deer. For 40 years, Stephan G. Stephansson worked his farm and wrote his poetry, gradually emerging as one of Iceland's most important modern poets – a mythological figure in the country he had left as a teenager.

That he wrote in Icelandic perhaps explains why he wasn't arrested during the First World War. It also explains why he is absent from our anthologies and our conscious cultural memory. And yet his verse, like that of the great West Coast First Nations sagas, is somehow recognizable as the voice of our collective unconscious.

This is one of the secrets of Canadian life – much of our great poetry has been written in neither English nor French. Actually, this is hardly a secret. Many of our greatest poets writing in the two national languages immigrated to Canada in their teens, just the way Stephansson did. And we rightly embrace them with enthusiasm. The difference is not one of experience or ideas or ethics or talent. It is merely one of language.

Even today I can think of dozens of other respected Canadian poets, unknown in Canada, but recognized elsewhere, writing in Chinese or Korean or other languages. Only a translator stands between them and recognition here.

Stephansson is the model for this conundrum. Yes, we have two official languages, one more than most countries. But we are also an unusual country in that our culture has been invented in many languages. The Aboriginal contribution is enormous. And so is that of poets like Stephansson. What matters is the quality of writing and its reverberation in our psyche.

– JOHN RALSTON SAUL

Introduction

It gives me a great deal of pleasure to bring to English-speaking readers a biography of a Canadian poet acknowledged by Watson Kirconnell as "the earliest poet of the first rank, writing in any language, to emerge in the national life of Canada." The poet given such an accolade is my grandfather Stephan G. Stephansson, whose importance is very much circumscribed by the fact that he wrote in the Icelandic language. Also written in the Icelandic language is a major biography of Stephansson by Viðar Hreinsson. This book corrects two linguistic injustices. It presents a biography that introduces us to a world-class poet whose life and works are regrettably little known to English-speakers. It also makes available a story of emigration and pioneering that contributes rich details to the history of the United States and Canada, a story that is well researched and contains a detailed analysis of events and interactions during the late nineteenth and early twentieth centuries's.

I owe gratitude to the many people who seemingly felt compelled to help Stephan G. Stephansson present his works to his Icelandic readers during his lifetime and to those who worked so hard to have his work rediscovered many years after his death; refer www.stephangstephansson.com. A dedicated group in Alberta worked with the Government of Alberta in the 1970's to have Stephansson's homestead restored as a historic site. Icelanders, who regard him as one of the greatest poets in Icelandic history, have been equally busy with the preservation of his memory. Three Icelanders who have been particularly active are Guðmundur Finnbogason (1873-1944), Head, National Library of Iceland, his son, Finnbogi Guðmundsson (1927-2011), former Director of the National Library of Iceland, and Viðar Hreinsson (1956-), the Literary Historian at the Reykjavik Academy. Viðar, an independent scholar who has taught at universities in Iceland, Denmark, and Canada, has authored scores of books and publications, the most comprehensive to date is this biography. Viðar's interest and labour are the chief sources of this publication.

My grandparents had eight children; six lived to maturity. Our family is a diverse lot – people of the land who have worked in a variety of trades and enterprises with average success. A number were dedicated to farming and technical pursuits while a few are dedicated to the arts; personally I am an engineer who worked in the oil business. When I was in my teens it seemed that I had countless cousins living at different places in Western Canada and the United States. Today there are only two grandchildren left, my sister Helga Iris and I, and curiously it would seem that in another generation or so our Stephansson family name will disappear entirely for the lack of male descendents.

Growing up in rural Alberta in an ethnic community, as we did, was not unique, but it was very special; the extended family was supportive and together as time permitted. The principal language spoken was Icelandic. My mother, born in Alberta, knew only two words of English, yes and no, when she started school at the age of eight. Our unique feature was being connected to Stephan G, as he was known. He passed away before I was born but I have a recollection of attending the unveiling of the fine cenotaph that was erected by family and friends at his grave site in our family cemetery near Markerville, Alberta, in 1936. I also remember the speeches at the unveiling of the monument erected in Stephansson Park at Markerville by the Historic Sites and Monuments Board of Canada in 1950 and receiving the telegram at our humble farm in 1953 inviting Mother, who like most people in our part of the world had to that time never been in an airplane, to fly to Iceland to unveil a monument erected at his birth-place on a poor farm in Northern Iceland, 100 years after his birth. Finally I remember attending the opening of Stephansson House near Markerville as an Alberta Provincial Historic Site in 1975.

The legacy lives on; Helga Iris and I were invited to Gardar, North Dakota, in 2003, 150 years after his birth, to unveil yet another monument to Grandfather, erected on the land he homesteaded there in the then Dakota Territory in the 1880's.

When attending high school, actually Grade 10 in 1947, in English class we came to a poem by Stephan G entitled "To Alberta" in our prose and poetry book. Our teacher, Mr. Oakes asked, "Does anyone know who Stephansson was?" I, a painfully shy farm boy, waited hoping someone would say something and finally in desperation put my hand up. Mr. Oakes asked, "What do you know about Stephansson?" I blurted out "He was my grandfather," whereupon I suffered probably the greatest put down of my life when Mr. Oakes asked, "And what else was he famous for?"

It continues; when Mother passed away in 1995, she left a manuscript that has now been published, *Looking Back Over My Shoulder*, that offers an account of her father and of early years in Alberta. An anthology containing a selection of Stephan G's poems, illustrated with photographs from Iceland and Alberta, is being published, a Fellowship for Icelandic Artists has been established in the memory of Stephan G at the Banff Centre in Alberta, and an opera has been written, inspired by the pacifist poems of Stephan G; most notably the poem "Vopnahlé" or "Ceasefire". This biography, however, offers the most thorough account of Stephan G's life and accomplishments.

I sincerely hope the readers of this book enjoy it and that, upon reflection, they will consider the content in the context of the story it tells. Here was a man born of a very humble family from an unlikely background, self educated with no opportunities for schooling, who went on to have an impact on a nation, albeit a small nation, Iceland, through his literary talent and his philosophy. Immigrating to the New World when he was 20, homesteading on the frontiers of the United States and Canada, he wrote over 2,000 pages of poetry and became Iceland's Poet Laureate while a farmer in Western Canada. Stephan G's story and poetry are still being taught in the schools in Iceland. Such miracles do occur.

– STEPHAN VILBERG BENEDIKTSON

Preface

Stephan G. Stephansson first fascinated me in my school years and this fascination increased during my years at university. The powerful language, imagery, and radical ideas of this poet, combined with his involvement with nature, history, and society, prompted me to buy his collected poems and his letters and prose, four volumes of each. From reading his memoirs I learned that Stephan G., as he was commonly called in Iceland, was my great-grandfather's first cousin. That they had met and become friends served to increase my fascination and interest in the work of this poet.

While teaching Icelandic at the University of Manitoba from 1992 to 1994, I renewed my interest in Stephan G. and even initiated some research into his poetry and philosophy of life. Being away from Iceland, I began to recognize how the rural literary culture of his upbringing in Iceland had become integrated with his experiences in the New World, moulding his character as an individual and as a poet. After attending a conference on his legacy in Red Deer, Alberta, in October, 1995, I decided to write his biography and targeted October of 2003, the 150th anniversary of his birth, for publication.

Funding the work on this biography was difficult. I worked at various odd jobs, borrowed money, and finally entered into arrangements with three funding sources: the Icelandic shipping company *Eimskip*, a genetics company, and a bank. At the time, I was heavily involved in establishing the Reykjavik Academy, an institute for independent scholars in the humanities and social sciences. The independence of Stephan G. served as a vital inspiration in our struggle for intellectual independence.

The biography of Stephan G. Stephansson was finally published by Bjartur in two volumes with the twin titles *Landneminn mikli* (The Great Pioneer) (2002) and *Andvökuskáld* (Poet of Wakeful Nights) (October 3, 2003). Insights into the life and ideas of the poet could be gained from his prose and poetry, but writing a biography is more than that. It becomes a kind of dialogue with a past reality, using a variety of sources in order to grasp his life, society, and cultural background, as well as the physical conditions, the immigrant experience, his intellectual and mental development, and his lifelong struggles in as holistic a manner as possible.

For me, this work has been more than a matter of just writing a biography. Stephan G. has kept me company now for two decades. He has not been bad company, and his calm integrity, his warm sense of humour, his loving kindness and self-control – so devoid of religious sentimentality that many of his contemporaries misunderstood and regarded as cold indifference – have been an inspiration and at the same time a subject for scholarly investigation.

In the words of an Icelandic high school principal who met Stephan G. during his visit to Iceland in 1917, "Stephan G. Stephansson was the greatest man I have ever met and likely the only man I have been acquainted with who was calmly ready to... offer his life for his convictions. It was my great fortune to know a man of such abilities, widely read and incredibly broad-minded, endowed with vital serenity and unwavering no matter how others opposed his opinions and political views. I think that I have never met such an ardent socialist, who was as tolerant as he was because nobody understood the standpoints of his opponents as well as he did and he admitted what had to be admitted."[1] Professor Sigurður Nordal, a leading literary figure in Iceland in the first half of the 20th century, thought it would be possible to find at least some flaws in the poet's talent and character. In a biographical introduction to a volume of Stephan G.'s poetry, however, he admitted that this search was in vain and conceded, "I have surrendered to him and sat down at his feet."[2]

I also dreamed of having the biography translated, convinced that the English-speaking world – particularly Canadians – should know more about this extraordinary poet. To me it seemed that Stephan G. would be a much better representative of Icelandic culture than the Icelandic "banksters" who dominated Iceland's public image at this time. I realized that it would be hard to find a publisher interested in accepting a mammoth biography of a little known immigrant poet, particularly one who was a rebel, a freethinker, and a socialist, who was never accepted by the conservative mainstream Icelandic Lutheran community. Furthermore, the biography had been written for Icelandic readers and included much detail that would be of little interest to a non-Icelandic readership.

After writing an abridged version of the biography in English, I remained very concerned with the thought of approaching publishers who would no doubt insist on reducing the length of the book – for me an unacceptable option. My objective was to present English-speaking readers, particularly Canadians, with a comprehensive biography of Stephan G. Fortunately, the poet's grandson Stephan V. Benediktson, who had previously supported some of my work, came forward and offered to manage and fund the project. The resulting process has involved several editing treatments followed by a long process of graphic design, photo and illustration selection, etc., that has involved a team of individuals and a lot of pleasant teamwork.

During the reading of this biography it must be remembered that it was originally written for Icelandic readers, from an Icelandic point of view. Had it been written by a Canadian, it would be quite different. This abridged version is an attempt to present the life and work of Stephan G. in a narrative manner without intrusive authorial comments. The story is an interplay of different voices and various world views, presenting the main actor from different perspectives. In large part the story is also an attempt to convey the immigrant experience, which required newcomers to adapt to the culture of the New World while maintaining elements of their own.

Sources are referenced using endnotes and on a few occasions there are footnotes to explain the text. There is full reference to Stephan G.'s writings, to sources in English, and to direct quotations, but little reference to sources in Icelandic. Readers of Icelandic are referred to the Icelandic version of the biography for a complete description. There is general reference to source material at the beginning of each end note section. Most of the original manuscripts, letters, and various documents used as references are archived at the National and University Library of Iceland.

To maintain the overall style, I personally did all of the translations of Stephan G. Stephansson's works used in the text, as literally as possible, well aware that such prose renderings do no justice to great poetry. The only exception is on p. 338, in honour of my friend, translator Bernard Scudder (1954-2007). The end notes include references to English translations where they are available.

The Icelandic alphabet contains the consonants þ and ð and the vowels á, é, í, ó, ú, ý, æ, and ö, which are not found in the English language. These are retained in names and place names. Icelandic immigrants often changed or "anglicized" their names in the New World and nicknames were commonly used in Iceland. Stephan G. was called *Stebbi* when he was growing up in Iceland, *Stefán* as a young adult in Iceland, then *Stephan* in America. His son Jakob was called *Kobbi* in Icelandic and *Jake* in English. Daughter Jóný was called *Jenny*, etc. There has been no attempt to normalize names in the biography; the lack of consistency is deliberate.

I would like to give a special thanks to Stephan V. Benediktson, without whom this book would never have become a reality, to Stephan G.'s descendants the late Edwin Stephansson, Iris Bourne, and her son Bill, to those who assisted me on my research trips in America, including Magnus Olafson, Dick Ringler, and the Johnsons and Sigurdsons in North Dakota, Douglas Yanke and Ila Hill Moede in Wisconsin, and the staff of various archives in Madison, Bismark, Cavalier, Shawano, Oconto, Green Bay, Calgary, Edmonton, Red Deer, and Winnipeg.

I also wish to thank my editor of the biography in Icelandic, Jón Karl Helgason, as well as those who have in one way or another helped making this book a reality: Robert Berman, Jane Ross, Kenneth Graham, Jon Sievert, Jonnathan Tinoco, Moorea Gray and Birna Bjarnadottir. Nelson Gerrard of Eyrarbakki, New Iceland, did the final editing. With his deep-rooted knowledge of Icelandic culture and language, he always managed to figure out what I really wanted to say. Thanks to my inspiring friends and colleagues at the Reykjavik Academy, and most particularly my family, whose loving humour is always invaluable: my wife Anna Guðrún Júlíusdóttir and my children Egill and his partner Rikke, Auður and her partner Hrafn, Bjarki Hreinn and Gunnhildur. And last but not the least: thanks to the wonderful source of inspiration and joy the last two years, my grandson Þorri Hrafnsson. This is for him and the future generations.

– Viðar Hreinsson

Overview of Icelandic History

Iceland was settled in the second half of the 9th century by Norsemen as a part of a general expansion of the Nordic area that also reached Greenland and North America. It has been estimated that the country was fully settled within 60 years and a new society developed with a general assembly, the *Althing*, established in 930. Christianity was adopted in the year 1000, which is also, according to written sources, the year Icelandic explorers reached North America.

The political order adopted by this new society was based on a system of regional chieftains, but without any central, executive power. This resulted in an increased concentration of control and subsequent power struggles between leading clans, culminating in the 13th century in a state of civil war that resulted in political submission to the Norwegian King in 1262.

The literacy that accompanied Christian traditions and the extraordinary development of a new society in a virgin country produced varied and lively literary activities, culminating with the Eddaic poetry (heroic and mythological) and the sagas, which were prose narratives of ancient Norse kings and heroes, the first generations of the settlers, and contemporary events. A unique contribution to world literature, these literary achievements later became cornerstones of Icelandic identity.

Over the following centuries, Iceland was first under Norwegian rule and then Danish, after the dissolution of the Nordic Kalmar Union in the 15th century. With the arrival of the Protestant Reformation in Iceland in 1550 and the execution of the last Catholic bishop in Iceland (a forefather of all contemporary Icelanders), Danish Royal power over Iceland began a sharp increase through the adoption of a trade monopoly and absolute monarchy during the 17th century.

Although the era of great medieval literature in Iceland is regarded as having come to an end around 1400, literary activities continued and evolved. The medieval sagas were copied and rewritten over the following centuries, even into the early 20th century, and a lively production of romances and new poetic genres emerged, including a rich tradition of *rímur* and ballads. The transcription of law-books was almost an industry, even among self-educated farm-people.

A literary and cultural renaissance followed the Reformation. As the Church monopolized the only printing press in the country, a great variety of original literature flourished in manuscript form. Intellectuals began studying medieval sagas and poetry and writing accounts of Icelandic nature and history, sometimes assisted by avid folk scholars. Poetry and prose were composed by self-educated crofters and farmers on a constant quest for knowledge, and while saga-literature had been more or less anonymous, in the 17th century known individuals emerged as the authors of autobiographies, travelogues, historical accounts, and natural history.

Although prose writing was extensive, poetry and verse-making was perhaps the most important vehicle for a sort of intellectual communication among the common people. A proliferation of occasional verses on every aspect of daily life – news, history, livestock, nature, weather, sexuality, and entertainment – circulated in manuscript form, and a Danish textbook on philosophy was even translated into verse by a prolific rhymester.

The calibre of literacy in Iceland was unusually high compared with that of other European countries, and the nation became semi-literate in the 18th century, with almost everyone able to read. This was in part the result of concerted efforts by the Danish bishop Ludwig Harboe, whose goal was to improve the public's knowledge of Christianity.

The 18th century in Iceland was bleak, with epidemics, climatic deterioration, and disastrous volcanic eruptions (with global effects in 1783) reducing the population to 35,000. In spite of these extreme conditions, the Enlightenment reached Iceland to some extent, and the church's monopoly of the printing press ceased near the end of the century. The resultant journals and books helped educate the common people, who in turn maintained the old literary traditions.

Throughout the centuries Icelandic society was predominantly rural, with the bishoprics at Skálholt and Hólar – and perhaps some seasonal fishing camps – as the only places resembling villages. Conditions slowly began to improve in the 19th century, under the influence of European nationalism, Romanticism, and literary renewal championed by national poet Jónas Hallgrímsson. This trend, largely based on a romantic glorification of the Saga Age, brought free trade in 1855 and launched a long struggle for independence. First spearheaded by national hero Jón Sigurðsson, for many years a scholar in Copenhagen, this gradual move toward a modern society brought lower rates of infant mortality, a greater variety of reading material, and the formation of progressive societies that culminated in the co-operative movement in the last quarter of the century.

When Stephan G. Stephansson was born in 1853, the population in Iceland was roughly 60,000 and the capital, Reykjavík (that he never visited until he returned to Iceland in 1917), was hardly more than a village (established in 1786). Iceland's economy developed slowly, and apart from the northern port of Akureyri, which was even smaller than Reykjavík, a few tiny fishing and trading villages were just forming by the seaside, usually where Danish trading posts had been. The population grew more rapidly, which was one of the main reasons for the wave of emigration to America that began in 1870, stimulated by agents, volcanic eruptions, severe climatic conditions, and impatience with the struggle for independence.

Iceland's development was nevertheless closely followed by many Icelandic emigrants in North America, such as Stephan G. Stephansson. In 1904 Iceland gained home-rule (i.e., a special Icelandic minister located in Iceland) and after the turn-of-the-century progress in trade, business, and communications increased rapidly. A university was established in 1911, the first domestic steamship company in 1914, and sovereignty was eventually achieved in 1918 after fierce political debate over how radical Icelanders should be in their demands for independence. This was a year after Stephan's visit to Iceland, and in the years that followed modernization gained even more momentum. That is another story, however, and whether or not Stephan G. Stephansson would have approved of today's Icelandic society and culture remains an open question.

Chronology

April 15, 1818	Guðmundur Stefánsson was born at Arnarstaðir, Eyjafjörður County.
July 8, 1830	Guðbjörg Hannesdóttir was born at Reykjarhóll, Skagafjörður County.
Oct. 31, 1850	Guðmundur and Guðbjörg were married in Glaumbær church.
Spring, 1852	Guðmundur and Guðbjörg moved to Kirkjuhóll.
Oct. 3, 1853	Stefán Guðmundsson was born at Kirkjuhóll.
July 3, 1859	Helga Sigríður Jónsdóttir was born at Mjóidalur.
Spring, 1860	The family moved to Syðri-Mælifellsá.
Nov. 19, 1860	Sigurlaug Einara Guðmundsdóttir was born at Syðri-Mælifellsá.
Spring, 1862	The family moved to Víðimýrarsel.
June 1, 1868	Stefán Guðmundsson was confirmed.
Spring, 1870	Stefán moved to Mjóidalur, and his parents and sister moved to Mýri.
Aug. 1873	Journeyed to America and arrived at Stoughton, Wisconsin, in September.
Aug. 9, 1873	Stefán's first poem appeared in print.
Sept. 1874	The family moved to Shawano County, Wisconsin.
Aug. 28, 1878	Stefán Guðmundsson and Helga Sigríður Jónsdóttir were married at Green Bay, Wisconsin.
Sept. 25, 1879	Baldur Stefánsson was born.
Summer, 1880	The family moved to Dakota Territory.
Nov. 24, 1881	Guðmundur Stefánsson died.
Dec. 9, 1881	Guðmundur Stefánsson was born.
March 12, 1882	Rev. Páll Þorláksson died.
Spring, 1884	Jón Stefánsson was born.
In 1884	Stefán Guðmundsson changed his name to Stephan G. Stephansson.
June 8, 1886	Jakob Stephansson was born.
Fall, 1887	Jón Stephansson died.
Spring, 1889	The family moved to the Red Deer area in Alberta, Canada.
Oct. 6, 1889	Twins Stephaný Guðbjörg and Jóný Sigurbjörg Stephansson were born.

Chronology

Jan. 23, 1890	The poem "Klettafjöll" (Rocky Mountains) was printed in *Heimskringla*.
May 31, 1893	Gestur Stephansson was born.
In 1894	Stephan's first book, *Úti' á víðavangi* (*Out in the Wilderness*), was published.
Oct. 3, 1899	Stephan composed the poem "Kveld" (Evening).
In 1900	*Á ferð og flugi* (En Route), Stephan's second book of poetry, was published.
July 24, 1900	Siglaug Rósa Stephansson was born.
Jan. 4, 1905	Guðmundur Stephansson married Regína Strong. They had eight children.
Dec. 5, 1905	Baldur Stephansson married Sigurlína Bardal. They had six children.
Nov. 1908	Stephan's first reading tour, traveling as far as Duluth, MN.
July 16, 1909	Gestur Stephansson died from a lightning strike.
1909-1910	Stephan's collection of poetry, *Andvökur* I-III, was published.
Jan. 18, 1911	Guðbjörg Hannesdóttir, Stephan's mother died.
Feb. 1913	Stephan's second reading tour, traveling to the West Coast.
In 1914	The comic "ríma" *Kolbeinslag* was published.
Aug. 1914	WW1 began and lasted until November 11, 1918.
In 1915	Stephan composed "Vopnahlé" (Ceasefire).
May 6, 1917	Fanný Stephansson married Árni Baldvin Bardal. They had one son.
May-Dec., 1917	Stephan travelled to Iceland.
In 1917	*Heimleiðis*, a collection of poems composed in Iceland was published.
In 1919	Furious debate on a war memorial.
In 1920	*Vígslóði*, a collection of anti-war poems was published.
June 11, 1922	Jóný Stephansson married Sigurður Sigurðsson. They had one daughter.
In 1923	Two more volumes of Stephan's collected poems *Andvökur* IV-V were published.
Summer, 1926	Stephan went to Winnipeg for medical reasons.
Dec. 16, 1926	Stephan was struck by a cerebral hemorrhage and partially paralyzed.
Feb.-Mar. 1927	Stephan composed "Þiðrandakviða", his last great poem.
Aug. 10, 1927	Stephan G. Stephansson died.
June 17, 1928	Rósa Stephansson married Sigurður V. Benediktson. They had four children.

July 19, 1936	Cenotaph at Stephan's grave in the Kristinnson-Stephansson cemetery near Markerville, Alberta, was unveiled.
In 1938	*Andvökur* VI was published.
In 1939	*Andvökur Úrval* (a selection with a substantial essay) was edited by Sigurður Nordal and published.
1938-1948	*Bréf og ritgerðir* I-IV was edited by Þorkell Jóhannesson and published.
Dec. 12, 1940	Helga Sigríður Stephansson died.
Dec. 17, 1940	Fanný Bardal died in a car accident on the way home from her mother's funeral.
March 4, 1947	Guðmundur Stephansson died.
June 13, 1949	Baldur Stephansson died.
Sept. 4, 1950	The monument erected by the Historic Sites and Monuments Board of Canada unveiled in Stephansson Park, Markerville.
July 19, 1953	The monument at Arnarstapi, near Víðimýrarsel, was unveiled.
1953-1958	*Andvökur* I-IV, edited by Þorkell Jóhannesson, was published.
March 21, 1958	Jakob Stephansson died.
Sept. 20, 1961	His Excellency Ásgeir Ásgeirsson, President of Iceland, laid a wreath on Stephan's grave.
Aug. 7, 1964	Icelandic Prime Minister Bjarni Benediktsson laid a wreath on Stephan's grave.
June 24, 1969	Jóný Sigurdsson died.
Aug. 10, 1975	Stephansson House near Markerville was opened as an Alberta Historic Site.
Aug. 5, 1989	Her Excellency Vigdís Finnbogadóttir, President of Iceland and the world's first democratically elected female Head of State, laid a wreath on Stephan's grave.
Oct. 1995	Icelandic Connection Conference on Stephan G. Stephansson was held in Red Deer, Alberta.
Dec. 26, 1995	Rósa Stephansson died.
In 1998	*Andvökur Nýtt úrval* (a new selection) edited by Finnbogi Guðmundsson was published. He died in April 2011.
July 17, 1999	His Excellency Ólafur Ragnar Grímsson, President of Iceland, laid a wreath on Stephan's grave.
2002-2003	Stephan G. Stephansson's biography by Viðar Hreinsson was published in Iceland.
Aug. 2, 2003	The monument to Stephan G. Stephansson was unveiled on his homestead near Gardar, North Dakota.

Part 1

Age of Ideals

A typical Icelandic bedstead in the living quarters (baðstofa) of a traditional Icelandic turf, stone, and timber house.

Chapter 1

Kirkjuhóll and Syðri Mælifellsá

Born in a Cloak of Victory

Sources do not agree on which autumn day it was in 1853 that a baby boy first opened his curious eyes in the living quarters of the farm at Kirkjuhóll, in the district of Seyluhreppur in the Skagafjörður region of Northern Iceland. Ministerial records state that he was born on October 4, but when the boy grew up he relied on what his parents had told him, that he was born on October 3, and this has always been considered the actual date of his birth. It was so dark that his mother could not see the brightness in the eyes of her firstborn, but she always said that he had been born in a "cloak of victory", that is, enveloped in the amniotic sac. It was believed that a child thus born was destined to be clairvoyant, victorious in all dealings, and immune to sorcery.[1]

The weather that day was fair. A mild southern breeze followed two weeks of cold northerly blizzards that had left snow on the hay lying in the meadows, forcing the farmers to take their livestock inside to feed them. Most likely Egill Gottskálksson from Vellir delivered the boy. He was considered lucky at delivering babies. Perhaps the grandmother or one of the sisters assisted the mother. The father probably paced in the corridor, no doubt wearing a black vest and trousers of homespun wool, high socks, and shoes of sheepskin – in the fashion of the time. When he came in to see the child, the mother likely spoke softly to him, whereupon the father would have reached for a book of prayers to find something appropriate.

When the fog of birth left the child's eyes and he could focus on his surroundings, there was not much to see. The living quarters were only 4 by 2½ meters, a bit wider in the middle since the old sod walls had sagged. The roof was only 2½ meters high beneath the ridge beam and the wooden rafters and slats were rotten. Tiny gaps in the aged walls acted almost as small windows, letting in a little light and also the cold wind. A lamp fuelled with shark liver oil threw its feeble light on the poor furnishings: a few bedsteads lined with feather or bog moss mattresses, woolen blankets, wool working equipment such as carders, a spinning wheel, and knitting needles, and wooden food bowls. There were a few precious books as well, the edges of the pages darkened and soiled from much handling. Besides *The Bible*, there were some books of prayers and sermons, perhaps a few periodicals containing information on the outside world, and manuscripts of some of the sagas and *rímur** poetry. Some of these books would have been borrowed, however, as this was a home with few worldly goods.

The odds were against a child born in Iceland at that time, as one out of four died in infancy. Those children who did survive, if they were of a poor farming family, had little hope of prosperity or material success. However, an extraordinary fate awaited this little boy. He was to emigrate to another hemisphere, where he would take the name Stephan G. Stephansson and earn a reputation as one of Iceland's greatest poets – the only Icelandic literary figure of such humble origins to achieve such recognition. How could this have happened? What influences shaped him? Why and how did he become such a great figure?

The Parents

The boy's parents were Guðmundur Stefánsson and Guðbjörg Hannesdóttir, whose ancestors included many colourful people, including poets, some clergymen, and even a few sorcerers. Guðmundur, the father, was "of average height, stout of frame, reserved in mind, and quiet."[2] He was born on April 15, 1818, at Arnarstaðir in the Eyjafjörður region, the firstborn of Stefán Guðmundsson and Helga

---

* *Rímur* (plural of *ríma*) were long narrative ballads, often consisting of hundreds of verses in quatrain form, highly figurative, with strict alliteration and end rhyme. *Rímur*, some of which date as far back as the 14th Century, were a dominating genre in Icelandic poetry, and more than 1000 are extant.

Kirkjuhóll and Syðri Mælifellsá

Skagafjörður, birthplace of the poet, on a midsummer night with Mount Mælifell in the distance.

Guðmundsdóttir.* Stefán of Arnarstaðir loved books and music, and his wife Helga was descended from a line of Lutheran ministers and related to renowned poets. Guðmundur's life was similar to that of many others of the time. His childhood had been hard, moving with his parents from farm to farm. His mother, Helga, had died in 1826 after having given birth to her eighth child. Only five of these survived childhood. After her death, Guðmundur's father remarried and had two children by his second wife. Guðmundur was confirmed in the spring of 1832, ranking top in his confirmation class. The church records state that he was "knowledgeable, decently behaved". Guðmundur stayed with his father for some years before moving to the Skagafjörður district.

The little boy's mother, Guðbjörg Hannesdóttir, was born on July 8, 1830. She was "fine-boned, gentle and reserved, warm and cheerful in manner".[3] She hailed from Reykjarhóll in Seyluhreppur, daughter of the farmer Hannes Þorvaldsson, whose mother, Anna, was believed to possess psychic abilities. Hannes, an intelligent man who was skilled at making verses, had once been a prosperous farmer, but he had fallen on hard times in his latter years. Guðbjörg was the ninth of his eighteen children. Her life was similar to that of her husband, Guðmundur.

---

* The Icelandic naming system is patronymic – and in modern times increasingly matronymic as well – so that a last name reflects the father (or mother), but not a family lineage. Thus Guðmundur, son of Stefán, was Stefánsson, and his sister was Stefánsdóttir, daughter of Stefán.

Glaumbær, marriage place of the poet's parents, with the current church and restored turf vicarage and farmstead in the background.

Nine of her siblings had died in infancy. Her eldest brother, Hannes, was someone who would later have considerable influence on her newborn child. His 1831 confirmation records state that he was well versed in his lessons, quick to comprehend, knowledgeable in Christianity, fluent at reading both handwritten and printed books, and well behaved. Hannes was regarded as exceptionally intelligent, skilled at handwriting, talented at making verses*, and capable as a farmer. While these were admirable attributes, he was also known to be "rather dissolute in conduct, not much interested in money matters, but always with a keen eye for women".[4]

The paths of Guðmundur Stefánsson and Guðbjörg Hannesdóttir first crossed during the 1840. By 1839 Guðmundur was working as a farmhand at Víðimýri near Reykjarhóll. Guðbjörg, who had been confirmed in the church at Víðimýri in 1845, with favourable comments, worked for a time as a maid at Reynistaður. Her employer, Einar Stefánsson, was a wealthy and well-respected landowner, rigorous in collecting farm rents but fair with his servants. In the spring of 1849, when Guðmundur turned 31, he was hired as a farmhand at Grófargil in Seyluhreppur, where Guðbjörg, 19 years of age, was by then working as a hired girl. The

---

* Occasional verse making was a very common pastime in Iceland. Single quatrains were made about nearly everything: weather, news, love, horses. Poetry was an integral part of daily life.

two were married in the nearby church at Glaumbær on October 31, 1850. Guðmundur was probably enchanted by this gentle and fetching girl, and it was certainly time for him to marry. At that time love was far from being a valid reason for marriage, and the matrimony of poor servants was not especially favoured by the authorities. Guðmundur, however, was a thrifty man who had already acquired some livestock – 22 sheep and three horses – as was customary among good farmhands. The local authorities were evidently convinced that the couple would not become a burden on the district, as Guðmundur apparently enjoyed the respect and friendship of some of the area's well-off farmers.

No doubt Guðmundur had set his mind on farming and settling permanently in Seyluhreppur. For a poor man such as he was, the best way to attain a stable living and a measure of respect in society was to secure a long-term tenancy on a holding owned by the state, the church, or a wealthy landowner. Such tenancies were difficult to get, however, and most farmers were short-term tenants. As a consequence, despite any dreams Guðmundur might have had, the couple found themselves in the spring of 1851 moving from Grófargil to Reykjarhóll, where Guðbjörg's father was farming. Guðmundur was registered as a tenant on one-tenth of the land, with one calf, four horses, and 40 sheep including milking ewes, lambs, wethers, and yearlings. They stayed at Reykjarhóll for one year before moving once again in the spring of 1852, this time to nearby Kirkjuhóll.

Kirkjuhóll was a very small croft owned by the church at Víðimýri. The wealthy owner of the parish centre of Víðimýri, Einar Stefánsson, regarded Kirkjuhóll as his private property. In addition to the living quarters, there was a pantry and a kitchen whose thick, damp, and crumbling sod walls led into a corridor, four by one meters, that was in a similar state of disrepair. The height to the corridor roof was about two meters, and a tiny window above the exterior door allowed a little light into the hallway. There was also a stable for thirty sheep. It, too, had been neglected. The decrepit walls needed immediate repair and there was no manger. The cowbarn was supposed to house three animals, but could hardly live up to that lofty claim. At least the hayfield was in reasonable condition. Although Kirkjuhóll was among the smallest farms in Seyluhreppur, the annual rent and taxes were high, being 14 Danish rix dollars and 63 shillings. Guðmundur paid his 1852 tax with four wethers and some cash, a high percentage of his annual income. Despite this, by the winter of 1853-1854, he had accumulated a large array of livestock: five horses, a pregnant cow and a heifer, more than 20 ewes that would have lambs in the spring, a few wethers and rams, and 16 yearlings.

The World Grows Larger

> *Child, with the temper woven of*
> *Morning's mild weather and thundering rain,*
> *The weather in which everything grows,*
> *The entire world is so new for you.*

The little boy from Kirkjuhóll composed these lines later in life, suggesting that everything a child sees inspires wonder about the world and its meaning: "from everything, there shines/some deep and urgent meaning."[5] On October 9, 1853, this child was baptized at home by Reverend Hannes Jónsson of Glaumbær. He was given the name Stefán, and the baptism was witnessed by three godparents: the maternal grandfather and grandmother, and Einar Hannesson of the nearby parish centre at Víðimýri.

Before 40 days had passed, the child's mother was "led into church"* by Reverend Hannes Jónsson, who gave her his blessing. The pastor followed the well-being of his congregation closely. He had arrived at Glaumbær as a poor man three years before, but had prospered quickly as Glaumbær was one of the richest parishes in the country. He was small and fair-haired, gentle, gifted with a good singing voice, and very capable as a preacher, but fond of drink.

Ministers were influential members of every Icelandic community. Their theological education was somewhat behind that of their colleagues in the other Nordic countries, but they lived with the common people, sharing their conditions. They visited every household twice a year to survey people's religious education, their spiritual condition, and their morals.

During the first winter, little Stefán lay in his bed in the dark living quarters at Kirkjuhóll. Towards spring he received his first book, Bishop Vídalín's book of sermons, as a gift from his aunt Anna when he cut his

---

* An old Christian ceremony involving the blessing of a mother after she has recovered from childbirth.

first tooth. Apart from the child and his parents, the household included seven-year-old Dagbjört Anna, Guðbjörg's illegitimate niece, as it was common to foster the children of relatives. Guðbjörg taught her niece to read and write, and in return Dagbjört probably tended Stefán and did some light household and farm chores.

The winter weather was harsh and unstable. Although Guðmundur always had his mind on books and learning, he was determined to become an established farmer. Kirkjuhóll offered good grazing for sheep over the winter, but Guðmundur still had to work hard to pasture the sheep outdoors when the weather allowed. He had to use his hay sparingly for the cow and a heifer that calved and increased the family's milk supply.

With the arrival of spring, the light increased and the weather became warmer. The ewes lambed, the sheep grazed on fresh grass, and little Stefán was taken outdoors. His world now grew more beautiful as well as more dangerous. The farm stood atop a hill that overlooked Kirkjuhóll Valley, lying north to Víðimýri. At the foot of the steep hillside lay a rusty coloured bog, and to the northwest of the farmhouses a brook ran into a deep, rocky ravine. Big boulders on the farm led people of later times to claim that little Stefán had played with elves during his childhood, as many people believed that elves inhabited such rocks. A hayfield ringed the farm like a collar.

A 19th-Century Icelandic pastor in Skagafjörður during the era of the poet's youth.

As little Stefán gradually grew bigger and took his first steps at Kirkjuhóll, life on the farm changed little. The old cow died and the heifer took her place, and for a time there were two cows on the farm. The number of sheep and horses increased too. A young farm hand and two hired girls, one with an baby, were hired. The stern Guðmundur took care of the farming, while Guðbjörg, lighter of heart, cheerfully tended their son. In Stefán's memory, she was kindness personified. He portrays the young mother leading her son by the hand to the pastures around the farm, where he discovered a new world. "One summer while we were at Kirkjuhóll, my mother took me south to the farm of Kolgröf," Stefán later reminisced, adding that he must have been very young as she alternately led him by the hand and carried him. On the way back, she had to herd a few milking ewes. She gave little credence to the common belief that elves lived in the rocks and she left Stefán by a large boulder called the Big Dwarf Rock, instructing him not to wander away from it until she returned for him.[6]

Guðbjörg drew her little boy's attention to the beauties of nature, to the neighbouring rocks, and the distant landscape. Stefán's first impressions of the world beyond the hayfield at Kirkjuhóll remained an indelible memory, and they later appeared in a commemorative poem he wrote about his mother. In it the poet captures the interplay between heaven and the mountain peaks, between the light and heaps of snow in the mountains, between the sea and the land – fjords, bays, rivers, estuaries. He writes, "Then I learned all my geography/and could never forget."[7]

Skagafjörður is an impressive region surrounded by high mountains. To the north of Kirkjuhóll is a row of mountains, extending from the rounded Kolgrafarfell above the farm all the way out to rocky Tindastóll, that towers above the fjord. On the fjord are two magnificent cliff-sided islands, Drangey and Málmey. Along the east side of the broad valley is an even more impressive row of beautifully shaped mountains, stretching from Glóðafeykir to Silfrastaðafjall. To the south is the distinctive mountain peak of Mælifellshnjúkur, and south of that is the vast interior of Iceland. Tales and stories are associated with every placename in the landscape.

Little Stefán's mother drew his attention to the beauty of heaven and earth, and his father directed him in tending the animals and working the land. The boy took in everything that happened. In Stefán's first memories, farm work is interwoven with serious religious thoughts, and he combined heaven and earth when his father's best horse was killed. The horse had been injured and was so old that the wound would not heal. His father decided to sell the carcass for shark bait, and little Stefan was shocked by this apparent disloyalty to a faithful servant. He stole the head, dragged it out to the little hill north of the farmstead, and buried it under a mound of stones that he carried from the brook. "Got myself a little piece of wood, stuck a page from an old and worn-out prayer book on it, put a piece of broken glass on top, and erected it

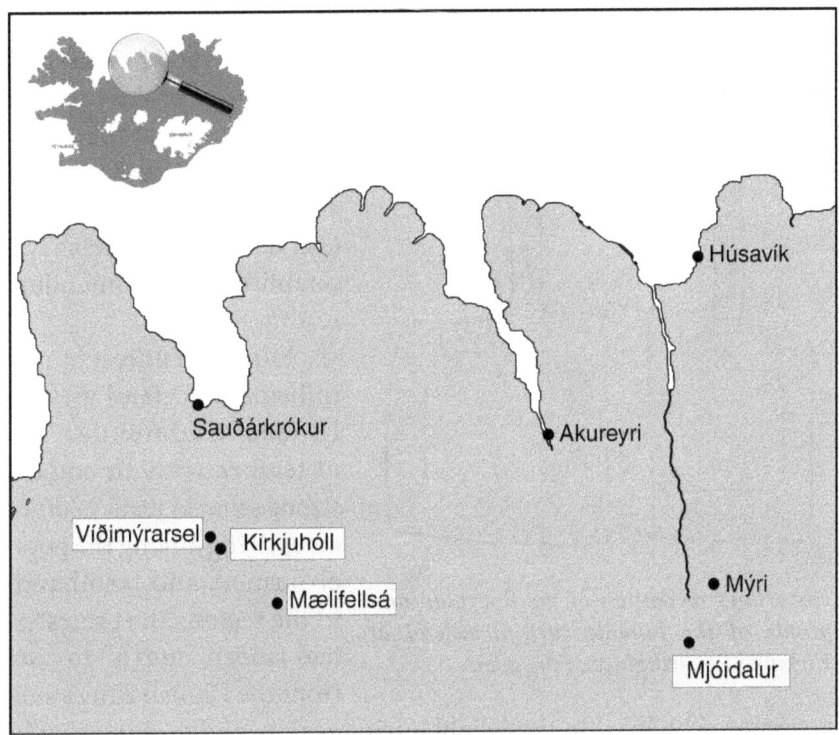

North-Central Iceland, including the Skagafjörður region where the poet was born on the farm of Kirkjuhóll, and the Bárðardalur Valley, where he spent his young adulthood at Mjóidalur prior to imigrating to the new world.

on the mound. I had seen a similar 'tombstone' of wood in the churchyard at Víðimýri. I felt much better after that."[8]

At Home in Kirkjuhóll

According to Stefán's own description, his father was "a serious and proud man, industrious and not self-sparing, faithful and honest, but one who wore himself out on behalf of others far too early."[9] Despite the general poverty and backwardness of the country, books and periodicals that had begun to appear shortly before 1800 received wide distribution throughout Iceland. Guðmundur thirsted for knowledge and despite spending long hours of hard work he followed world events closely by reading every new book and periodical available. He was exceptionally skilled at reading aloud and sometimes people on other farms asked him to read the family prayers on Sundays. "He had a rather low

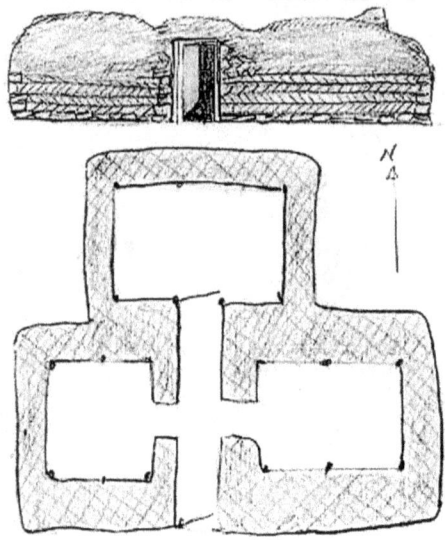

Historian's recreation of the floorplan and profile of the humble turf farmstead at Kirkjuhóll – birthplace of the poet.

voice, but strong, and he read very clearly as if making an effort to press the message into the heads of the listeners," a contemporary wrote, adding that the poetic style later developed by Stefán was reminiscent of Guðmundur's reading style.[10]

European unrest in 1848 influenced Iceland as well. In 1849, Guðmundur, hot of temper with an equally strong sense of justice, joined an uprising among the poorer farmers and farmhands in the region. The protesters had ridden "north" to confront the Danish King's sub-governor, who lived in the neighbouring region, and demand that he step down, as he was regarded a harsh and unjust official. They were lucky that their escapade did not have a serious outcome. Vilhelmína Lever, a Norwegian woman living at Akureyri, was visiting the sub-governor at the time. She was hot-tempered and a renowned shot, who cared little about the consequences of her actions. Rumour had it that she was ready to shoot at the group of protesters, and that it was the sub-governor who stopped her. The leader of this event, dubbed "The Ride North", was a self-educated scholar and poet named Gísli Konráðsson. Among the participants were Guðbjörg's brother Hannes and the noted teacher Sigvaldi Jónsson the Poet. "The Ride North" remained in the memories of the participants for a long time. Stefán often heard about these events and knew many of the participants, whom he judged to be moderate men, not extremists.

Guðmundur's farming operation at Kirkjuhóll improved as the decade wore on. The number of livestock increased and he was able to expand the hayfield. In 1857 he did something that was unusual at the time – he dug a little garden, likely for potatoes. Everything was going well at Kirkjuhóll. The children were learning to read, while Guðmun-

The kitchens of 19th Century Icelandic turf and stone farmsteads were practical but primitive.

Built from natural materials, Icelandic farmsteads blended in with their surroundings and eventually returned to nature. Most homes had small windows covered with stretched animal membrane rather than expensive glass panes.

dur pored over books and periodicals borrowed from neighbours. According to the records of Reverend Hannes Jónsson, four year old Stefán now knew the entire alphabet. His grandmother Rósa was now living with the family. Her husband had died in poverty the previous year and she outlived him by only one year. The small household also included more relatives. The illegitimate Dagbjört Anna was there again, registered as a foster-daughter, though she left the following year. Áslaug, Guðbjörg's sister, was there as a lodger with her four-year-old son, Egill, whose father was Sigvaldi Jónsson the poet, who had taken part in "the Ride North". Sigvaldi had a reputation as a drinker and womanizer. He had sired two illegitimate children by Áslaug, the boy Egill and a girl born in 1852, who died very young. Possibly Sigvaldi wanted to marry Áslaug, but was unable to do so because of their poverty. No doubt he often visited Kirkjuhóll, as he was a friend of Guðmundur. Sometimes Hannes, Guðbjörg's brother, also came to visit.

Little Stefán wanted to imitate his father, so he planted three potatoes in the manure pile outside the cowshed. The potatoes grew extremely well and in his joy Stefán was naive enough to show the thriving potato garden to an older playmate from a neighbouring farm. This boy did not understand much about cultivation and ripped up all the potato plants, even pelting Stefán with the biggest potato. That was the end of Stefán's attempts at potato gardening, but he continued to sow two kinds of grain, rye and barley, in little spots on the farmhouse wall. He even grew a few beans, admiring the stock as well as the fruit.[11]

Guðbjörg had taught herself to read and write, and it was she who taught Stefán the alphabet and the sounds of the combined letters. Once he had mastered these lessons, he was able to teach himself to read. He was soon able to decipher both Gothic and Latin letters, and at the age of six he began to read the catechism. Eventually his father wanted to know how much he knew of the catechism. Although Stefán thought his knowledge was quite good, he was nervous and shy when he began to read. His father, who claimed his people "had always been regarded as intelligent – whatever else became of them," got angry and scolded Stefán, saying that he "would become a disgrace to the family as he was so slow at learning, even mixing up simple words." Stefán later admitted that his father "was actually right – and in the end he promised never to question me again, and kept that promise."[12] Obviously Guðmundur was disappointed with Stefán, but his wrath might actually have aroused in Stefán a need to prove himself and to show what he could do in the field of literature. He took his father's reproach to heart, and when Reverend Hannes came on his pastoral visit in the spring of 1860, Stefán read stutteringly and slowly, but correctly. He also knew five of the commandments.

By this time, life was becoming more difficult at Kirkjuhóll. The winter of 1859 was one of the harshest of the century. It was bitterly cold from mid-January on,

Present in almost every Icelandic home during the 18th and 19th Centuries, Vídalín's Postilla contained sermons and devotional readings for "all occasions and Sundays" throughout the year. These stout volumes, most of them printed at Hólar in Hjaltadalur, were often presented to small children as tannfé (a tooth reward) when they cut their first tooth and later placed in the casket of the owner after a lifetime of service.

and even the first summer months were chilled by cold northern winds that swept inland from across the pack ice that choked the fjords. Hardship followed. Merchant ships arrived unusually late because of the pack ice, and the resulting shortage of provisions pushed up prices on all goods. On the farms, sheep starved and diseases such as the braxy, an intestinal disease, decimated the flocks. By the end of May, 1860, there were still a cow and a heifer and eight horses at Kirkjuhóll, but far fewer sheep. Only 15 ewes with lambs remained, and there were no wethers, no yearlings. Not even a ram was to be found at Kirkjuhóll.

Colourful, ornately woven and stitched bed covers and saddle blankets were a feature of every Icelandic home and were handed down from generation to generation.

There is no way of knowing whether it was these hardships and high prices that forced Guðmundur to give up farming. He was a tenant, and farming at Kirkjuhóll may have depended on who farmed at Víðimýri. In the spring of 1860, Einar Hannesson, Guðbjörg's relative and Stefán's godfather, moved to Ytri-Mælifellsá, where he bought two farms, so Guðmundur may have chosen to move with him, as his farmhand and lodger. Possibly the owner of Kirkjuhóll, Einar Stefánsson, was offered a higher rent by someone else. He had a reputation for being mercenary and hard on his tenants. In any case, on June 9 officials came to Kirkjuhóll to assess the farmstead. Einar Stefánsson was present and Guðmundur's representative was Sigvaldi Jónsson the poet. The assessors examined the interior and exterior of the buildings, measuring them, and even counted the pieces of lumber. They agreed that the cowshed had been repaired and parts of the other buildings had been fixed up somewhat. A platform had been added in the living quarters and pieces of wood had been used to patch the walls here and there. The kitchen roof, however, was caving in and the sheep barn was in worse condition than before. Guðmundur was ordered to pay 40 rix dollars as compensation for the disrepair of the farm. He appealed, pointing out the new garden and the improved hayfields, which were much bigger than they had been when he arrived. The assessors mentioned in their report that Guðmundur was claiming consideration from the landowner for these improvements. They lowered the compensation owing to 29 rix dollars.

In Syðri-Mælifellsá

In 1860 Guðmundur Stefánsson was no longer a farmer. His position in the world was therefore uncertain. Together with his pregnant wife and their six-year-old son, he moved his few animals to the farm of Syðri-Mælifellsá, where he worked for Einar Hannesson of Ytri-Mælifellsá. There, parish census records list him as a lodger one year and as a farm hand the next. It was a short distance down to the church at Mælifell, and there Stefán saw tramps and farmhands among prosperous farmers at services. The view was beautiful, with Mount Mælifell rising just south of the farm, and close to the farm was a gurgling river. On November 19, a daughter was born to Guðmundur and Guðbjörg, and later that day their closest friends and relatives came to visit – probably Hannes from Reykjarhóll, Einar and Sigurlaug of Ytri-Mælifellsá, and Sigvaldi the poet, at that time a lodger on a neighbouring farm. Reverend Sigurður Arnórsson of Mælifell, an energetic character, bustled into the house with the baptismal basin in one hand and the Bible in the other. He baptised the little girl at her mother's bedside. The bond of friendship with the couple at Ytri-Mælifellsá was strengthened when Guðmundur and Guðbjörg named their newborn Sigurlaug Einara. Einar and Sigurlaug acted as godparents, along with Sigvaldi the poet.

Guðmundur and Guðbjörg undoubtedly served the best food in their pantry, smoked lamb with bread, and small measures of "brennivín" for the men. Sigvaldi, a passionate man who was among the leading poets in Skagafjörður at that time, was in a good mood and entertained the guests. His dark, full beard gave his long face a distinguished air and his big grey eyes sparkled when the liquor began to take effect. His wig might well have gone slightly askew during the course of the evening. Reverend Sigurður no doubt appreciated the brennivín, for although he was regarded a decent clergyman, he had a taste for spirits and sometimes became quite unruly. Perhaps his wife, Elínborg Pétursdóttir, recited a poem or two for the occasion, as she and her husband were

Kirkjuhóll and Syðri Mælifellsá

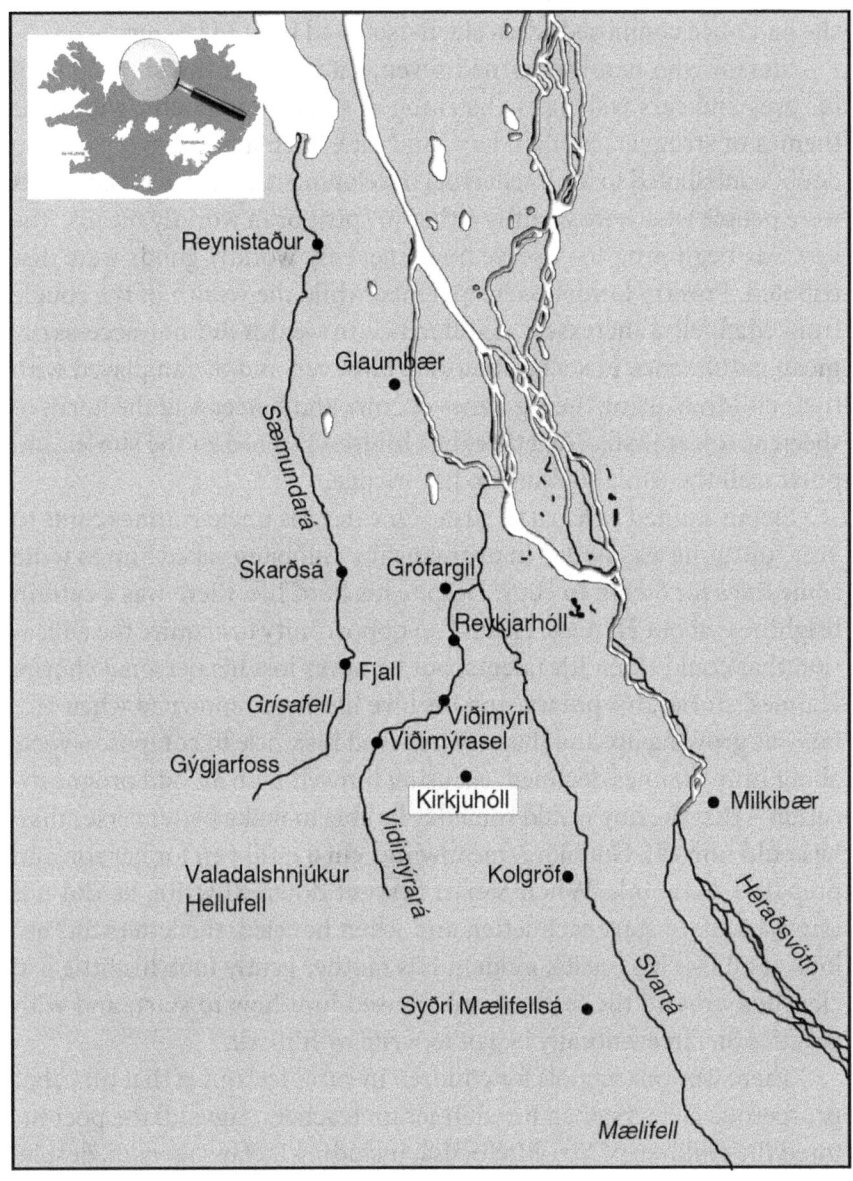

Stephan G. Stephansson was born at Kirkjuhóll in the Skagafjörður region on October 4, 1853.

talented verse-makers. Sigurlaug of Ytri-Mælifellsá, always attentive to those in need, likely sat at Guðbjörg's bedside. An intelligent woman and excellent verse-maker as well, she might well have recited a verse she had once composed when she herself had been in labour.

Stefán, who had just turned seven, sat through the evening with his eyes and ears wide open, listening to stories and poetry with their themes of struggle, conflict, love, and fate. Such a baptismal party no doubt contributed to his intellectual development, as many of the guests were people who were wealthy either in spirit or in worldly means. The boy was beginning to observe how unevenly worldly goods were distributed. Poverty burdened his parents, while the wealth of the couple from Mælifellsá increased. A difference in wealth did not necessarily mean a difference in social standing, however, and Stefán played with their children, using the leg bones of cows and horses and the horns of sheep as toy animals. Together the children listened to the stories and poetry, all the while soaking up knowledge.

Stefán wanted to learn to write. One day his uncle Hannes came to visit, and as he was skilled in penmanship, Guðbjörg asked him to write some lines for Stefán to copy. Despite his hard life, there was a certain brightness about Hannes. He had no opportunity to acquire the education that could ripen his talents, but he never lost his personal charm. Hannes' stories, his poetry, and his love life were renowned when Stefán was growing up, and that day he asked his uncle to compose a verse about him. Hannes declined, excusing himself with an odd prognostication – that the boy would someday be able to make better verses than he could himself. Guðbjörg, meanwhile, cut a quill pen for her son and prepared some ink. When Stefán first sat down to write, he did not know where to start each letter, and when he tried, the letters did not look at all like his uncle's models. His mother gently took his little fist, clenched around the feather, and showed him how to start, and with practice Stefán eventually began to write by himself.[13]

There were no schools for children in rural Iceland at that time, but prosperous farmers often hired itinerant teachers. Sigvaldi the poet tutored the children of Ytri-Mælifellsá, including Stefán. Sigvaldi, despite the fact that he had been raised in poverty and had no formal education, was one of the most remarkable teachers in the region. His thirst for learning was unquenchable and his first attempts at writing had taken place in a barn, on the weathered jawbone of a horse. Later he practiced his writing in the snow, using his shepherd's staff, and it wasn't long before he was an avid reader with artful handwriting. Teaching was his passion. He maintained mild discipline and the children loved him. He could easily step into their footsteps, to see and comprehend things as they did, and he nurtured their best abilities with the understanding that they had the same thirst for learning as he himself. He praised them both for what they could do and for their willingness to work. His insight into the minds of young children was unusual for the time, and his teaching methods may have reflected his exposure to educational theories such as those of Jean-Jacques Rousseau, who maintained that children should be allowed to be children while their abilities were developing. Sigvaldi also took great pleasure in teaching girls to write. At that time, many still held that girls "wrote for their own shame". Perhaps that view was already outdated in Skagafjörður, however, for the level of literacy was exceptionally high in the region. Girls Stefán's age were encouraged to read and write, and most girls in his neighbourhood, even the daughters of paupers, were literate. Sigvaldi also composed poems for the children while teaching. They admired his poetic skills, not least among them Stefán, who at least on one occasion felt the sting of a verse by Sigvaldi:

> *My Stebbi**, *you are clumsy*
> *In forming your letters,*
> *Your willingness to obey*
> *Does not seem too much greater.*

Stefán was disobedient to his father, who often punished him, but he loved his mother, and was very much loved by her.

Guðmundur's circumstances were tolerable during his years at Syðri-Mælifellsá, and he paid taxes similar to those paid by other lodgers in the area. He evidently had ambitions to become a farmer again, however, and eventually he saw an opportunity in the neighbourhood of Kirkjuhóll in Seyluhreppur. In 1857 a dwelling on land belonging to Víðimýri had been made into a croft, called Víðimýrarsel. The little family moved there with their humble belongings and a few animals in the cold, dry spring of 1862.

---

* Stefán's nickname

Chapter 2

Víðimýrarsel

The Little Shepherd

In a poem composed much later, Stefán said that work and poetry were the blessings of Icelandic farmers. His father, Guðmundur, would hardly have agreed with that. He loved books and poetry, but his labour was hardly a blessing.

Conditions deteriorated for the family after they moved to Víðimýrarsel, often called simply 'Sel'. Guðmundur was still only a lodger, working mainly for others. Perhaps God was reluctant to regard him a farmer, as in the parish registers of Reverend Hannes of Glaumbær he was deemed a mere lodger in 1863, although the following year he was registered as "farming". It was not until 1865 that he was registered as a farmer, but even then it was mercilessly noted that he was "without a farm" – merely a lodger. He may have thought that Víðimýrarsel would provide him with the opportunity to gain the independence everyone in his position sought, but this independence would prove elusive. As an indication of the family's worsening state, there were fewer people in the household, and Guðmundur now had only one cow, fewer than 20 sheep, and never more than five horses. The wealthiest farmers, such as Reverend Hannes at Glaumbær and poet Jón Árnason of Víðimýri, who now was Guðmundur's landlord, had ten times more livestock.

The same mountains surround Víðimýrarsel as Kirkjuhóll, but The Sel is higher up in the mountain pass so that the view is even more magnificent, especially from Arnarstapi, a gravel hill just below the farmhouses north of the small river Víðimýrará. Further north, the river Sæmundará runs down from Vatnsskarð Pass and curves to the north. That river has the beautiful waterfall Gýgjarfoss, almost 20 meters

Sheep, the "staff of life" for a pastoral society that subsisted by animal husbandry in Iceland for a thousand years.

high. Near The Sel the main road runs through Vatnsskarð Pass to the neighbouring district of Húnaþing. The long view to the north includes Drangey Island in the fjord so Stefán could envisage the stories of the outlaw-hero Grettir the Strong who lived on the island. Grettir swam to shore to fetch fire and was eventually killed by his enemies by sorcery.

The nine-year-old boy was always busy. In the early summer he had to herd the milking ewes and watch the small hayfield overnight, to keep out the sheep and horses. He often had a little book in his pocket. In Stefán's memory, the life of a shepherd symbolized broadmindedness, freedom, and beauty. "He was born by the manger, fostered in the sheepfold," Stefán began his poem "Smalavísa" (A Shepherd's Verse) much later, comparing the shepherd's path to a king's palace. The highland where the shepherd wandered was the place of "freedom, sunshine, and song."[1] Every spring Stefán and his mother walked up to the mountain Valadalshnjúkur, above Sel, to pick Icelandic moss. He was also sent up onto the distant moors to the south with others for the same purpose. As time passed, he was given more difficult tasks: tending the animals in winter, clearing manure from the hayfield and separating lambs from the sheep in the spring, cutting sod and harvesting hay in the summer, digging manure out of the sheep barn, spreading manure on the hayfield, and slaughtering sheep in the fall.

One day, when the weather was good, Stefán was sent to round up some horses that had run across the river Sæmundará and onto the slopes of the mountain Grísafell. Wearing only long underwear, he ran off with his shepherd's staff and found the horses just as a sudden rain shower began. He bridled one of them and began to drive the herd home. When he came to the ford just above the waterfall Gýgjarfoss, however, he saw a group of prominent men from Skagafjörður and Húnaþing riding toward him. Stefán did not want to meet these dignitaries, for he was not only soaked to the skin, but was not properly dressed. Even his soft sheepskin shoes were tattered. He crossed the ford without saying a word and thought he had made a lucky escape. Then one of the men, Jón Ásgeirsson, a renowned and wealthy farmer, called out to him and told him to wait. Stefán stopped reluctantly as all the men turned back across the river. Jón reached for a huge, decorated drinking horn and dismounted from his horse. He filled the cap of the horn with liquor and gave it to Stefán, who drank it and felt its warming effect. To Stefán's surprise, the wealthy landowner gave him a half a dollar. Stefán heard the district sheriff, who was among the men, say, "This boy has beautiful eyes."[2]

Life was not all work. Stefán and his friends enjoyed horseback riding, running, jumping, and wrestling in the summer, and in winter they played cards and musical instruments. In a letter written in verse to one of his friends many years later, Stefán also recalled skiing downhill, skating, and jumping from huge snowdrifts, as well as teasing bad-tempered hired girls who threatened to give them a thrashing.[3]

It was an everyday occurrence for people to recite lines of poetry or entire poems as they worked. Verse makers composed poems about the seasons, their work, the horses, and newsworthy events. The rhythm of nature and chores were combined in this poetry. With poets all around, young Stefán began to wrestle with words and verses. The sheep roundup inspired his first verses, written in the fall of 1864, during his third year at Sel. He was then nearly eleven years of age. The verse reflects the shepherd's panoramic view when gazing over the Skagafjörður region from a hilltop:

> *I am still allowed to see,*
> *My pretty Skagafjörður.*
> *The flock basks all around in the high mountains*
> *And the grassy mountain passes.*⁴

A second poem composed by Stefán that fall was about a drunkard who fell down as if he was "knocked down dead". Excessive drinking was common among men in Iceland at the time. Stefán continued writing verses that fall, even composing a whole poem about a fierce and heroic fight described in one of the old sagas. He chose a difficult form with internal rhyme and alliteration, and even some kennings, an Old Norse type of metaphor. During the following year, Stefán composed a little verse called "Heiðin" (The Heath), a sincere ode to creation.

> *I love you dearly my old heath,*
> *With brushwood and small brooks.*
> *Swans are singing on the ponds in the morning,*
> *And making their nests on the old ruins.*⁵

It is a Romantic poem. Romantic nature poetry had been introduced in Iceland some decades earlier by intellectuals educated in Copenhagen, and by the 1860s Romanticism had reached young, self-educated, and ambitious poets in rural Iceland.

Stefán wrote poems about nature, the seasons, the weather, the pleasures of life, and the heroes of sagas. Some of the poems are full of *Weltschmerz*; others are cheerful and provocative. In 1866 he composed "Til lóunnar" (To the Plover). In the first stanza, the young poet addresses the plover that arrives when the earth comes back to life after the winter, when the sunshine undresses the earth from its grey cloak. He then asks where the plover goes in the winter "when the severity and blizzards of winter/cover the earth with white snow." Does the plover sleep or has she fled to another country where there is neither winter nor storm? The speaker of the poem wants to do the same when his "period of outlawry" ends and he departs from this world. He wants to sleep "deep in the earth covered with flowers" and then he will be set free "In the summer of eternity/then up to the heaven,/to fly on the strong wings of an angel."⁶ The 13-year-old boy had found a theme for his poetic talent. Stefán's nature poems have a symbolic meaning and in this address to the plover he adopts Romantic ideas of life and death, the material and the spiritual. His enquiry to the plover explores ideas of death and release.

Earl Andri and Bishop Balle

Icelanders were constantly moving and travelling. Farmhands often stayed only a year in each position, and during the fishing season many farmers and farm labourers journeyed across the country. This mobility stimulated creativity and poetry in which everyday events were captured in stories and verse, the best stanzas living on for generations. Storytellers and the chanters of *rímur* who wandered from farm to farm were often rewarded with alcohol and fine chunks of fat smoked meat. *Rímur* were ballads of adventure and romance, meant for pure entertainment. One such poem was Gísli Konráðsson's *Andrarímur*, a long narrative poem about the fictional hero Earl Andri. It had an amazing influence on Stefán. In the winter, during Advent, like most teenagers and farmhands, Stefán was to knit fishermen's mitts to sell to the merchant; four pairs of mitts could buy a small barrel of brandy. Stefán "had been struggling with one mitten for a week, and had to unravel it three times. Now I had reached the thumbholes for the fourth time, and in front of everyone I heard someone say that it was obvious that I would be stuck with it all Christmas if nothing changed." However, when Gísli Konráðsson's *Andrarímur* was chanted one evening, probably

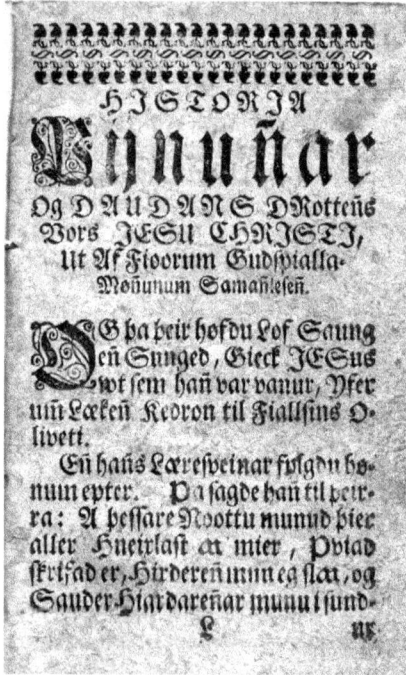

The vast majority of books printed in 18th and 19th Century Iceland were religious in nature – such as this historia *of the torture and death of "our Lord Jesu Christi". Gothic text was used in Iceland from the time printing was introduced until well into the 19th Century.*

by a wandering rhymster staying at Sel, the performance so affected Stefán that he finished his mitts in one night. Stefán was convinced that the adventurous story, in the rhythmic manner of the *rímur*, had greatly stimulated his knitting skills.[7]

Intellectuals and many clergymen had long had a distain for *rímur*, but in Stefán's mind Earl Andri and the colourful traditions of poetry and storytelling evidently merged with the rigorous home schooling supervised by the church. Reverend Hannes Jónsson of Glaumbær thought children should continue studying the catechism two or three years after their confirmation, looking up Bible passages referred to in the catechism, so that Lutheran theology would be firmly established in their minds. Stefán had no problem finding the correct Bible passages, as he read his Bible three times one winter for lack of anything else to read.[8]

The catechism of the day was written in 1791 by the Danish bishop N. E. Balle (1744-1816), son-in-law of Bishop Harboe, who in the 18th century had organized home instruction for Icelandic children under the supervision of parish ministers. Balle was an ardent follower of the religious movement Pietism, that opposed rationalism and atheism. His catechism was soon translated into Icelandic and remained in use until 1877.

The theology of this Danish bishop was difficult for a young farm boy to read and understand. After introducing the Ten Commandments, the Credo, The Lord's Prayer, and the Sacraments, the main text of the catechism begins seductively, especially for the searching mind of a child: "It is extremely important for us humans to learn to know God. Otherwise, we would not be able to understand how the world was created; we would not know what to expect about our state after death; and we would not have unfailing help to rely upon in our troubles." In other words, the catechism is the key to understanding the world. Subservience and confidence balance each other in the individual's relation to his God.

At the beginning of the catechism, redemption weighs more than Mosaic Law; Christ's love is more prominent than God's punishments. In chapter one, a merciful and just God demands categorically that humans obey the commandments as "He wants to reward only those who obey Him, and punish those who are disobedient." The next chapters are about the works of God, how sin corrupts man, the sacrificial death of Christ followed by redemption and atonement, then finally re-conversion and faith, and how sinners can acquire some of the grace and salvation that Christ made available voluntarily with His passion, exhorting us to "avoid evil and strive with all our strength to go forward with good deeds." The sixth chapter of the catechism is about duty, "the fruits of faith in a holy way of life." People were admonished to care for their neighbour as well as their own souls, but to defer to the authority of parents, employers, and governing authorities. However, the authorities could demand obedience only in what served the well-being of the public and did not go against the Commandments of God. The end of the catechism is about the sacraments that strengthen faith and the fear of God, the reading of God's word, prayer, and the eternal life of the just along with the condemnation of the ungodly. It claims that although the world will perish on Doomsday, the "God-fearing will always be with the Lord, and with this hope let us console each other."[9]

Such was the religion that Icelanders were taught. It certainly gave strength in trouble and often there was not much else to rely on in their harsh world.

In studying all this, Stefán must have reflected on the world he knew: a stern father, sensitive poets, and wealthy men who, before God, were no more remarkable than other people. He prepared himself thoroughly for confirmation and compared doctrines with Biblical passages. The children of Skagafjörður must have disliked the message of the sixth chapter, but grappling with difficult texts was a challenge for an intelligent youth. The evident clash between common sense and doctrine, however, troubled 14 year old Stefán. Much later, he challenged in verse: "Do they not make a mistake … those who abandon the child's mind/ on the glacier of doctrine?"[10]

The Skagafjörður Academy

Storytelling and poetry were "a self-acquired education/that sang wisdom and language into one's mind," Stefán wrote later in a poem.[11] These arts flourished among self-taught people as well as the educated, alongside the cultural hegemony of the church, that had dominated the printing press for centuries. A great variety of poetry, lore, narratives, and character descriptions were penned and circulated in all kinds of manuscripts. "It must be said, though, that stories told by common farm people are a great deal more expressive and flawless than the stilted narratives of learned fumblers," wrote the German law professor Konrad

The kvöldvaka, *an evening interlude for reading, singing, story telling, and chanting, as well as every sort of handwork, was a traditional Icelandic social institution that encouraged literacy. As all household members shared the intimacy of the* baðstofa *living quarters, the* kvöldvaka *helped people cope with prolonged confinement.*

Maurer in 1858 when discussing Gísli Konráðsson.[12] The best of those self-educated poets and scholars learned both by constantly recreating texts such as the sagas and writing their own historical works. Foreign intellectuals who visited Iceland were often astonished by the literary activities of common people.

The books that young Stefán read were a mixture of old and new, good and bad. He recalled that he was always in search of reading-material because there were only the most common religious books in his home. Stefán himself owned only *Vídalínspostilla* (*Vídalín's Book of Sermons*),* that his Aunt Anna had given him, an old book of poetry by an eighteenth-century poet who was related to him, and *Njóla*, a long philosophical poem that his Aunt Helga sent him. Though the family owned few books, Guðmundur was a member of a reading society, so

---

*Vídalínspostilla was the most common book of sermons and renowned for its powerful language. This copy is preserved among Stephan's books at the Icelandic Collection in the Elizabeth Dafoe Library, University of Manitoba.

Stefán had access to a wider variety of reading material: sagas, *rímur*, annals, tales of the gifted peasant-poet Bólu-Hjálmar, the biographies of Gísli Konráðsson and others, and periodicals, as well as most new publications. He took books with him wherever he went and read everything from *The Bible* to the semi-pornographic *Bósa Saga*. He read most of the old sagas, tales and poetry in manuscript form, sometimes different versions of each. For most of his life he never owned a printed edition of the sagas, but being endowed with a photographic memory, he remembered these stories all his life. In fact, as a mature poet he composed great poems based on his memory of the sagas.[13]

Young Stefán was on friendly terms with two farmers in the neighbourhood who had libraries. Egill Gottskálksson, who had likely delivered him, lived at Skarðsá, an hour's walk north of Sel. He was a wise and progressive man and a good farmer. Stefán went there once or twice each winter and returned home with a sack full of books. The other farmer who owned a number of books was the poet Jón Árnason of Víðimýri, a cheerful man fond of tippling and able to compose verses as fast as a person could speak. He was known as a good farmer who was helpful and hospitable, and especially supportive of fellow poets who were poor and on their own. A man of many talents, he taught himself Danish, acquired a good knowledge of music, and had a strong singing voice. He was also an exceptionally skilled carpenter and blacksmith. Jón of Víðimýri recognized that Stefán was a promising boy and loaned him every book he asked for.

In a poem written in 1872, Stefán alludes to a cairn on the hill Arnarstapi, near Víðimýri:

> *Cairn, I still remember you*
> *On the wind-blown gravel hill*
> *You, my library*
> *Below the farm!*
> *In your shelter I stole*
> *Many an hour to read*
> *When the wide heaven lit*
> *Its light by the autumn stars.*[14]

The inspiration for this poem dates from 1866. Just before Advent, Stefán heard that Jón of Víðimýri had bought Matthías Jochumsson's new translation of Esaias Tegnér's epic poem *Friðþjófssaga*, which was among the most interesting novelties in Nordic literature at that time. Eager to read this book, Stefán set off down the hillside to Víðimýri one evening, as soon as he had gathered the sheep into the barn and fed them, to ask if he might possibly borrow the book. Jón, a busy farmer, was just as anxious to read it himself. "Well, Stebbi, it is a pity, but I have not begun reading it. I have not even cut it open. I am leaving home early tomorrow morning, however, and I will not be back until tomorrow evening, so I will just lend you the little book in the meantime." Stefán knew that if he went straight home he would have to work some wool. The weather was calm, the sky clear and starlit, and the moon shining, so Stefán sat down in the shelter of the cairn back at Arnarstapi and hungrily began to read. When he saw the lantern being carried from the cowshed to the house he knew it was time for supper and family prayers. By then he had read most of the book.[15]

In 1866 Stefán attended lessons at Víðimýri for two weeks, together with Jón Árnason's children. Sigvaldi the Poet was the teacher. Stefán was impressed by the dealings between the two poets, Jón and Sigvaldi. On one occasion he heard them compose a verse together. Sigvaldi looked out of the window and spoke the first half of a stanza: "Værðum hafnar hríðin jafna,/húss á stafna skín ei sól." (The evenly falling snow disturbs the peace/the sun does not shine on the gables of the houses). Then Jón finished it: "Allir hrafnar ætla að kafna /í þó safnist bestu skjól." (All the ravens are about to suffocate/though they gather in the best shelters). Jón was a humorist, Stefán recalled later, "while Sigvaldi was very God-fearing, and once eagerly began praising God's creation, averring that no link could be removed for fear of the entire creation collapsing." "Well, go and kill all the bloody ravens of creation," Jón retorted, "and let us then see if it goes under!" Sigvaldi fell silent and could not answer. Stefán was amused.[16]

The Burden of Poverty

Stefán made every possible effort to learn and longed to go to school, but that was impossible for the son of a poor lodger. The extent of his yearning for formal schooling became evident on a Thursday in the fall of 1865. Stefán was outside during a storm, when he saw three people ride by the farm, heading towards the mountain pass. His friend Indriði

Einarsson, accompanied by his mother and a farmhand, was on his way to Reykjavík to attend school for the first time. Indriði was a grandson of the poet and scholar Gísli Konráðsson, whose son, Konráð Gíslason, was already a renowned scholar and professor in Copenhagen. Stefán had met Indriði through Sigurður, the son of Jón Árnason of Víðimýri. The three had become good friends, and sometime between 1863 and 1865 each of them began to produce his own handwritten newspaper – the first handwritten local papers known in Iceland.

On seeing his friend leaving for school, Stefán was overwhelmed with grief. He ran out among the tussocks, where in good weather he often sat with a book, and threw himself on the ground in a small hollow, sobbing in the rain. Guðbjörg, meanwhile, was expecting her son to return home, and when he did not, she went looking for him. She called, but he did not answer because he did not want her to see him crying. When she found him and asked what was wrong, he was at first reluctant to answer, but eventually he told her the reason. She was overwhelmed, although she hid it. Never before had the burden of poverty been so painful for her as on that stormy day.[17]

Nevertheless, Stefán continued his self-education. He taught himself Danish from a little textbook with short paragraphs in Danish followed by Icelandic translations. He worked through without a dictionary. Of course he continued to read as much poetry as he could lay his hands on, and one book that undoubtedly had a great influence on him was Björn Gunnlaugsson's *Njóla*.[18] This poem of 518 stanzas in quatrain form was first published in 1852 and was reprinted twice, so popular did it become despite its reputation for encouraging atheism. This book was widely read and discussed in Skagafjörður. The poem was composed at a watershed point in Icelandic culture, when ideas of the natural sciences were challenging church dogma. Björn wanted to establish a new foundation for life by weaving together belief in God with science; the rational order of the world was for him proof of the existence of God. *Njóla* was regarded as blasphemous by the clergy, who wanted it kept out of the reach of children. For Stefán, the poem was like a counterweight to the theology of the catechism.

Njóla begins with praise for the heavens and space that become the basis of the harmony that the poet observes everywhere. The first chapter is entitled "Heaven observed at night" and begins by addressing the Master of the Heavens, asking Him to bend the poet's mind to think of His majesty.

The church at Víðimýri, built in 1835 and protected by the state in 1936, was just over 30 years old when the poet was confirmed there.

> *Now it is a beautiful hour of the night,*
> *The bright decorations*
> *Carry the roof that your hand spread*
> *Across the palace of the moon.*[19]

When the poet observes the myriad of shining stars, his mind praises heaven. Heaven with its stars is the symbol or image of God and harmony. These ideas disturbed the church, as *Njóla* reversed the accepted order. According to the church, God was an absolute reference, the beginning and end of everything. *Njóla*, on the other hand, praised tangible reality and the world order of the natural sciences. By deducing coherence from reality and not merely accepting God as omnipresent, Björn found his God. He saw life as moving toward good; only stupidity was evil and could delay the achievement of that goal. *Njóla* praised diversity, saying that if everyone walked the same path, nobody would see the others and human wisdom would follow a single path into darkness. This idea challenges all forms of absolutism. To young and enquiring minds such as Stefán's, there is much in the poem that must have appealed and raised doubts about Doomsday and reprobation. Goodness over evil and rationalism over church doctrine are themes that later echo throughout Stefán's poetry.

On the other hand, Stefán was familiar with Bishop Jón Vídalín's book of sermons, that he had owned all his life. On the evening of the second Sunday in Advent, he and his mother were alone at home at Víðimýrarsel. Guðbjörg did not neglect the word of God, so she read Master Jón's sermon on the subject of Doomsday. The discourse vividly depicted The Lord as the most rigorous judge: "The fire will burn before His eyes all the way to the lowest hell; in this conflagration the heavens will be torn apart and the primal elements will melt. Around Him a terrible storm will rage. All His great angels will follow Him and His holy thousands will shine around Him. With the terrible trumpet of the Archangel, He will call the living and the dead up unto the heavens and no creature will be able to withstand his coming."[20] This reading came as a revelation to Stefán, but it was not the religious message about the day of judgement that fascinated him. In those matters, *Njóla* likely had a stronger influence. It was the marrow of the rich language, "the imagery and prosody," that ignited in him an understanding of the power of words.[21]

The Long Service

By the spring of 1868 little Sigurlaug had learned to read and Stefán understood the catechism well, according to Reverend Hannes Jóns-

The legendary island of Drangey, once home to the saga outlaw 'Grettir the Strong', was also a bountiful source of seabirds and eggs that helped to ward off hunger in the district. The surrounding waters of Skagafjörður teemed with fish.

Icelandic horses provided the only transport at a time when few roads and even fewer bridges existed. Pack horses carried all luggage, possessions, and provisions.

son. Stefán's confirmation was to take place in the little sod church at Víðimýri on June 1, 1868, and Reverend Hannes rode out from Glaumbær for the occasion. En route, he stopped for a visit with Jón of Víðimýri. Although the pastor was an honest man, he was growing quite old and infirm and was not careful when Jón offered him some liquor. By the time he entered the warm church, Reverend Hannes was quite drunk. He requested a chair to sit on before the altar and was so drunk that he had to kneel in the pulpit. He then demanded a drink from his deacon, who immediately handed him a glass of communion wine. "I do not want any bloody communion wine; just give me some blessed schnapps!" he demanded. When the pastor stepped down from the pulpit, he said to Jón of Víðimýri: "My dear Jón, could you just begin the psalm. I am going to sit down and recover a bit in the meantime." About halfway through the confirmation ceremony, he had to excuse himself to go outside to attend nature's call. Farmer Jón followed him and gave him a little more to drink. When Reverend Hannes re-entered the church, befuddled by the alcohol, he started all over again. The service went like that all day. Some churchgoers wandered out for a while and some even went to visit a neighbouring farm, but others stayed put, curious to know how this comedy would end. The parents of the children being confirmed were offended, and some of the children began crying. Pétur Pálmason, a wealthy farmer, was there with his wife, Jórunn Hannesdóttir, as their daughter Halldóra was being confirmed. Pétur had a hot temper and was about to take his daughter home, but his wife, who had a more subdued temperament, managed to calm her husband. "My dear, this is the last time he is confirming her now. This is just about over. Let us not make any trouble." Pétur sat still, twisting his new woollen mittens in his irritation. When the service was over, after *eight hours*, he had worn the mittens into pieces. So memorable was Reverend Hannes's confirmation ceremony that year that it was long remembered as "The Long Service".

Despite this memorable confirmation service, the lodgers at Víðimýrarsel had reason to be proud of Stefán. Guðmundur could now forgive him for his poor performance in reading some years earlier, as Stefán ranked first among the children being confirmed, just as his father had done 36 years earlier. The girls of Stefán's confirmation class remained in his memory for a long time, as many decades later he compared snow-covered spruce trees in the Canadian wilderness to the girls at his confirmation.[22]

Stefán had begun to write poems about girls. In "Til stúlku" (To a Girl), which might well be from this year, he writes of a girl's strong arms, her fiery eyes that could melt hearts of ice, her morning-red cheeks, lily-white skin, coral-red mouth, and hot tears. The girl dies and the sorrowful poet accompanies her body to the grave with a trembling heart.[23]

Rough Work at Sea

With his confirmation at age 14 in 1868, Stefán became an adult, and he was thus expected to contribute to the family's struggle for subsistence. Guðmundur knew some of the captains of fishing boats on the fjord and he sent his son to the coast to work for one of them. There, Stefán would jig for enough cod to bring home a load of much needed fish. Stefán's first fishing experience was short-lived, for the crew managed only one trip out onto the fjord, between the shore and Drangey Island. The next day there was a cold northerly wind and a dark bank of clouds in the north, so Stefán returned home. The fishing season was better the following year. Stefán noticed that every cod he caught was apparently blind on one side, with a kind of a film covering one eye. An old fisherman told him that fish were attracted by light reflecting from the icebergs and swam around them endlessly, always with the same eye turned to the ice. In the long run, they became blind, but they would continue to swim around the iceberg all the same. Twenty years later, Stefán used this as a metaphor in a polemic against fundamentalist Lutherans.

While sitting in the boat rhythmically pulling at the fishing line, Stefán recited poetry, and he also composed some poems, weighing words, phrases, and imagery on his tongue. Faithful to tradition, he made verses about the captain, about sailing and rowing, and about the boat as it crossed perilous waves with death always lurking, for accidents at sea were extremely common at this time. After a long day at sea, the fishermen hauled their catch up from the beach and retired, cold and wet, to their sleeping huts. There, in the short but happy hour of storytelling, poetry, and singing before bedtime, the young poet recited his elaborate stanzas on seafaring to the entertainment of his fellow fishermen.

During Stefán's fishing forays, the boat sometimes approached the island of Drangey where Grettir the Outlaw of saga fame had lived his last years and met his death. Stefán noticed that sometimes the north wind drove the pounding surf against the shore of the island, while on other occasions the sea was calm and the island basked in the midnight sun in deep silence, except for the cries of sea birds. Nature and history inspired the 15 year old boy to compose a serious poem while sitting on the hard seat of a fishing boat, line in hand. In the six-stanza poem

Most 19th Century Icelandic fishing craft were open to the harsh elements of the North Atlantic. Heavily laden with crew and fish as they returned home, they were vulnerable to rough water and heavy surf on landing.

"Drangey á Skagaströnd" (Drangey off Skagi Coast) he conveys greater symphonies of nature, colours, and human destiny. The first stanzas contain a magnificent image of the island, with its huge waves and rocks, the cold wind, the sunshine, the calls of the birds, and the dark green deep of the ocean. He concludes his poem with the heroic death of Grettir.[24]

Going East

Despite the family's efforts, they found life in Skagafjörður difficult. The weather had become colder over the passing decade. In 1865 it snowed in the middle of July and the cows had to be kept inside for a week. The following winter was cold, and pack ice covered the sea until June of the following year, with occasional flurries until the end of that month. During the winter of 1866-67 there was no grazing at all for the sheep after the middle of October, and the outlook was bleak. Hay shortages would lead to the animals' starvation. A few days' thaw in February prevented disaster, but sheep died in some places, especially near the coast. Pack ice clogged the ocean off the coast of Iceland, the grass grew poorly, and wet weather further hampered haying in 1867. The situation was slightly better the year Stefán was confirmed, but the weather remained extremely unstable.

The deteriorating climate not only affected farming operations, it affected trade. In 1868 the poet Bólu-Hjálmar described unemployment and rising prices, both in trade with foreigners and between Icelanders themselves. He also described the experiences of an everyday person in the struggle for life. In an essay, he pointed out that ordinary farmers, who until now had been able to survive, were in desperate need, while the merchants gouged them, selling the staples at an exorbitant price.

The year 1869 was fraught with adversity. Pack ice remained in the fjords until August. Cold weather meant that the grass did not grow, the sheep did not yield any milk, and haymaking could not begin until late summer. Famine loomed. For some time, the only foods were milk, Icelandic moss, scurvy grass, seaweed, and fresh shark. The trading vessels that braved the pack ice brought damaged goods. One merchant, for instance, sold grain so infested with weevils that people could not eat it and he was forced to take it back. Summer eventually came, however, and the young poet Stefán wrote a poem about abating frost, the divine velvet that covered the ground, sunbeams, and birds on "flowery fields" that "had awakened from the sweet winter sleep."[25]

Guðmundur now decided to give up farming once and for all, and to leave Skagafjörður. Whether the family was denied occupancy of Víðimýrarsel or whether they simply relinquished it is not clear. Such climatic vicissitudes made life difficult for lodgers, and when haying failed, tenant farmers had difficulty feeding the livestock they needed to pay the rent. The number of paupers in Seyluhreppur increased dramatically, and as a consequence the taxes on lodgers, farmhands, and even hired girls were increased. Guðmundur paid the equivalent of 45 fish for the local tax in 1869. He was just over 50 years of age and his situation was precarious. The inhabitants of Skagafjörður now numbered roughly 4500, and it did not make much difference if a small, poor family moved away. For eight years, while herding sheep and fishing on the fjord, Stefán had absorbed the beauty of the scenery on land and sea, and 30 years later he would draw on his memories of the fjord when composing the poem "Skagafjörður". Leave-taking was sad. A two stanza verse, "Kvaddur Skagafjörður" (Farewell to Skagafjörður), is far from cheerful, as Stefán bids farewell to the beautiful fjord, the mountain slopes, the tiny farm, and, most difficult of all, his friends.[26]

In the spring of 1870, the family made the long journey east to the valley of Bárðardalur, where Guðmundur's three sisters lived. Before leaving, they probably auctioned off whatever furniture and animals they could not take with them. What they could take along – clothing, household effects, bedclothes, and books – was packed carefully in trunks and sacks to be loaded on horseback. Sigurlaug was now nine years old and Stefán 16. Guðmundur may have regretted his decision to move, for during most of May the weather was reasonable, alternating between warm southern breezes and a raw northern wind. On Ascension Day, May 26, there was warm southwest wind, and snow was melting in the mountains. This weather held for a fortnight, but the die was cast and moving day arrived on Thursday, June 2, a week before Whitsun. The travellers set off in a warm southern breeze that started the grass growing and made the rivers run deep with meltwaters. The family first rode to Vellir, to cross the glacial waters of the Héraðsvötn on a ferry, then made their way south along the slopes of Blönduhlíð on the east side of the broad valley. Sagas, folk tales, and stories of battles and ghosts were associated with almost every farm. They passed Bóla, where the gifted peasant poet Bólu-Hjálmar had lived, then turned east to follow a rough trail up the valley of Norðurárdalur. After crossing the heath and the boundary of the Eyjafjörður region, they continued down

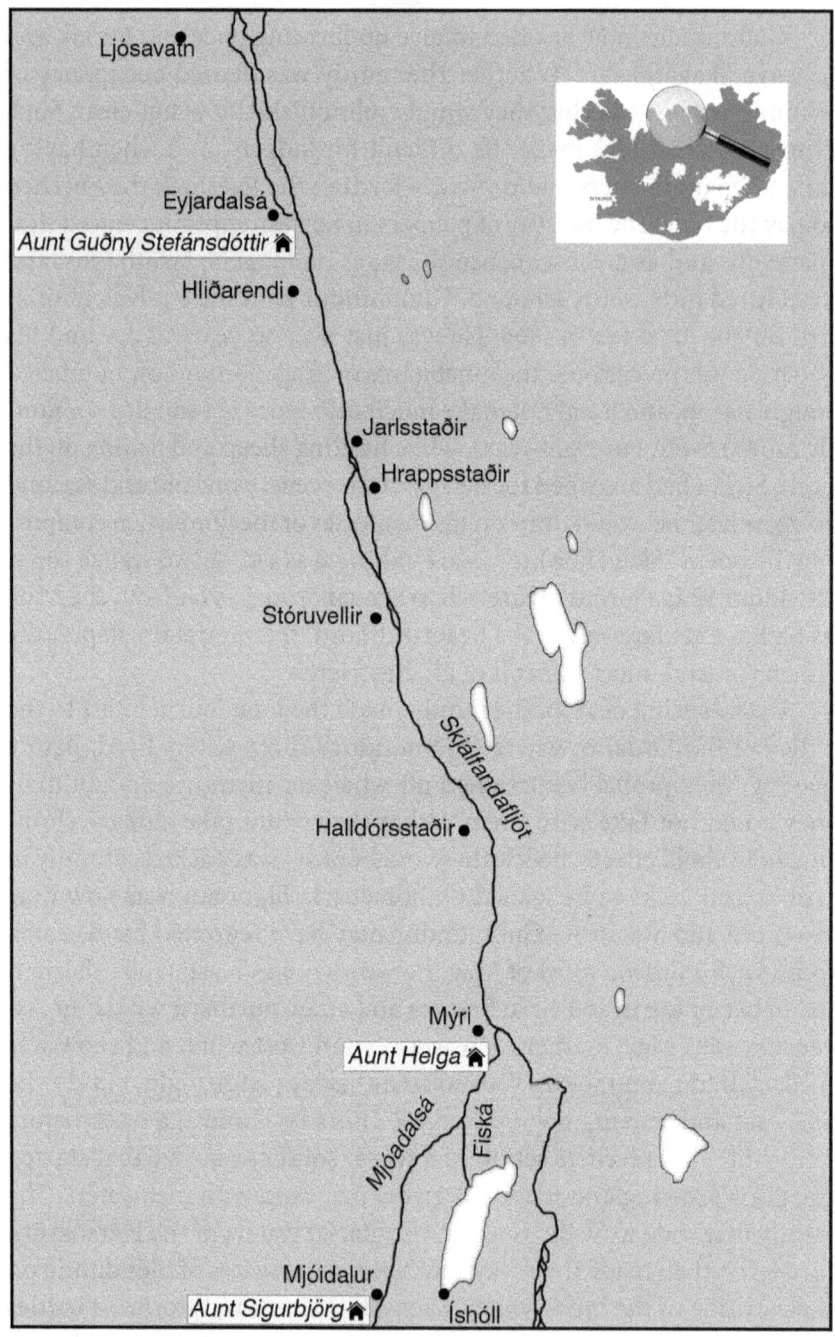

In 1870, Stephan's parents left Skagafjörður and migrated east to the Bárðardalur Valley where his three aunts resided. They took up residence at Mýri. Stephan moved with them and took a position on the nearby farm Mjóidalur.

the Öxnadalur Valley, passing the scenic farmstead at Hraun where the national poet Jónas Hallgrímsson had been born, then the church farm of Bægisá, once the home of poet Jón Þorláksson, who had translated Milton's *Paradise Lost* and had been defrocked twice for getting hired girls pregnant.

Eventually the family arrived at the little town of Akureyri. The warm weather had dried the muddy streets, but the reek of manure and other refuse hung in the air. As the family rode by the headland Torfunef, shark boats were coming in with good catches, and men were busy rendering shark-liver oil in a new factory. Merchant ships had just arrived in the harbour, having been long delayed by pack ice. Akureyri was a wonder to behold, with its big merchant houses and especially the magnificent house of the pharmacist Thorarensen. The siblings from Víðimýrarsel looked around, fascinated by the large mountain-ash trees. At merchant Möller's, they saw an animal they had never seen before, a pig. Possibly the family had some money after selling their things, so they might have been able to go shopping, perhaps buying a few clothes, a book, a little brandy, or coffee. They could even for the first time taste fresh bread from Schiöth's Bakery. Perhaps they stayed overnight at Jensen's or Elín's guesthouse, or possibly at the inn of old Vilhelmína Lever, the lady who 21 years earlier had wanted to shoot the farmers of "The Ride North".[27]

The next morning the family rode south along the shore and out of Akureyri, passing the cottages of tradesmen and lodgers. They then continued a short distance south along the river Eyjafjarðará, to the ferry at Gil where they crossed over. Then there was the long climb up Vaðlaheiði Heath. They had to ride slowly now, as there were still snowdrifts in places and the melting snow made the earth very soft. The warm weather compensated for that, however, and from the top of the heath they caught their first view of the Fnjóskadalur Valley, a great wonder in Stefán's eyes, as the woods of Vaglaskógur were among the last remnants of forest in Iceland. In Stefán's mind, Vaglaskógur would remain the most beautiful of all forests. The river Fnjóská was in flood when they crossed it on the ferry at Skógar. The ferryman was Bessi Eiríksson, a man known to be lucky. He sported a huge beard, looking every bit the part of a saga hero to Stefán. The river was almost impassable as the current was extremely strong, and Stefán worried about the horses having to swim in the wake of the ferry. He need not have worried. The current did carry

The landscape of Bárðardalur ranges from barren lava and eroding hillsides to lush meadows and extensive birch woods through which travellers passed on their way to Mýri.

them some distance downstream, but they managed to reach the other side with no mishap.²⁸

Next the family rode through Ljósavatnsskarð Pass, which was also densely wooded with birch trees. Steep hillsides rose on their left, with Lake Ljósavatn on their right. Finally, when they had passed the lake, they turned south into the Bárðardalur Valley. It was Saturday evening when they arrived at Eyjardalsá to stay overnight. Guðmundur's sister Guðný Stefánsdóttir lived there with her husband, Jón Ingjaldsson, and their children, Helga, Guðni and Stefán.

Guðný had been the first of three sisters to move to Bárðardalur, in 1845. There she had met Jón, whom she married. They first lived on the farm Halldórsstaðir, where Guðný's youngest sister, Helga, joined them in the winter of 1850 to work as their hired girl. That, however, would have consequences. Guðný was pregnant with her son, Guðni, at the time. Her husband, Jón, had difficulty controlling himself and got Helga pregnant. After the birth of a daughter, Sigríður, Helga moved to Mýri the next year, finding employment there as a hired girl. Guðný's other sister, Sigurbjörg, then joined the household, staying until 1857. Little Sigríður was brought up mostly by Guðný and Jón, and it was said that Guðný treated her as if she was her own child. The three sisters were all big-boned, rugged, somewhat temperamental, but noble-minded and good housekeepers. They, like Guðmundur, were strong tempered and kind-hearted.

Guðmundur had not seen his sister often during the 30 years since he had moved to Skagafjörður. Their reunion was no doubt reserved, as they were both rather serious. Jón had evidently recovered from the bout of depression he had suffered during the last months of winter, when he constantly worried that there would not be enough hay for the sheep, even though he had plenty of hay. Now Stefán met cousins his age, all of whom were bright and literate. For them it must have been exciting to have an exceptionally intelligent and poetically skilled cousin from Skagafjörður come to visit.

Late on Whitsun, the family set off south along the grassy lava fields of Bárðardalur with its grey glacial river, Skjálfandafljót, on the left. A steep, wooded mountainside rose to the right. They rode past the prosperous farm at Stóruvellir, one of the two largest in the valley, and to Stefán it looked like a little village with its seven gables. They also rode by Halldórsstaðir, where the well-liked Reverend Jón Austmann lived, then through birch woods all the way to the farm at Mýri – a journey of 26 kilometres from Eyjardalsá. Guðmundur's other sister, Helga, now lived at Mýri with her husband, Kristján.

The people at Mýri no doubt found Guðmundur a good-looking and very intelligent man, and Guðbjörg was both courteous and bright. Sigurlaug, a promising youth, looked more like her father, while Stefán resembled his mother. Hermann, a boy being fostered at Mýri and five years Stefán's junior, thought his cousin looked more like his father, with his thick black hair, high broad forehead, and thick dark eyebrows. "His eyes were dark, calm, and observant, and you could often see a kind of a cold humour in them, and you knew that he would not cave in to anyone. His nose was rather big, but straight. His chin and mouth were also prominent. He had a pale, slightly-jaundiced complexion and his face hardly ever turned red."[29]

On His Own

Stefán was to go to Mjóidalur, a remote farm eleven kilometres south of Mýri. He ended up staying at Mýri longer than he had intended, however, when he accidentally broke the collarbone of Hermann, foster son of the couple at Mýri. Stefán felt so badly about this accident that he remembered it for the rest of his life. The boy, he later reported, "told the truth, that it was his fault, as he wanted to wrestle with me. I felt I could easily get him down as I was used to this kind of tussling. I put my hands in my pockets, and he attacked me fiercely..."[30] Stefán then grabbed Hermann, but lost his grip and the boy fell, landing on his right hand. Hermann then stopped playing around, but Stefán only began to worry when Hermann's shoulder started to swell. He ended up staying for a few more days at Mýri while Hermann lay in bed – reading to him, telling him stories, and teaching him to play chess. At first Hermann thought Stefán was a bit aloof, but as he got to know him better he found him warm and friendly. Hermann had heard that Stefán had poetic skills. Stefán, on the other hand, was reluctant to flaunt his verses and only showed Hermann a little collection of his poems.

Stefán was hired as a farmhand at Mjóidalur. His employer was Jón Jónsson, whose wife was Sigurbjörg, the third sister of Stefán's father. Stefán set off inland for Mjóidalur in about the middle of June, 1870. The weather had changed. A cold north wind, fog, frost, and wet snow lasted until the 20th, so he had a chilly and uncomfortable ride over the grey hills to Mjóidalur. It was too early in the spring to ride straight to Mjóidalur along the west side of the valley, as all the gullies were still filled with snow, so Stefán crossed the river Mjóadalsá and rode south, past the farm of Litlatunga and over the eroded hilltops to Lake Íshólsvatn. There he turned west and crossed the river Fiská, that runs from the lake. A loon on the lake might have been calling and the bushes on the bank were no doubt turning green. This strange remoteness was an unusual sight for a boy brought up with the panoramic view of Skagafjörður. His sense of isolation was only broken by the little farm at Íshóll and its green hayfield, located southwest of the lake. It was hard to imagine a more isolated place.

Stefán may well have stopped and accepted some refreshments at Íshóll before continuing south and up the stony gravel hill to where his path crossed the trail leading south into the vast highland wilderness called Sprengisandur. Many people still believed that outlaws lived there. It seemed unbelievable that there could be any habitation ahead, but as Stefán continued west and reached the top of a hill, the long valley of Mjóidalur came into view. The valley's hillsides were badly eroded, with only a few patches of vegetation here and there, but the bottom of the valley, along the banks of the river Mjóadalsá, was grassy. On the other side of the river, where it curved, was the farm of Mjóidalur, with its many houses and a large hayfield. From there, no other farms could be seen as the valley bends eastward. Stefán urged his horse down the hill to the ford across the river. Because of the cold, the water level was low. He let the horse gallop the last stretch to the farm. Stefán Guðmundsson, no longer in the shelter of his parents, had arrived at his new home.

Chapter 3

Mjóidalur

The Errand-boy and the Pauper

The large farm at Mýri, where Stefán's family remained, had been owned by the same family since the early 18th century, when 20 year old Jón Halldórsson had arrived there as a farmhand in the employ of a rich widow. Later he married her daughter. Jón was exceptionally industrious and became the ancestor of the Mýri lineage. Jón Jónsson of Mjóidalur, Stefán's uncle by marriage, also belonged to the family from Mýri.

Jón Jónsson of Mjóidalur had 12 siblings, most of whom reached adulthood and several of whom emigrated to North America. These included Benedikt and Gísli, who will appear later in this story. Jón Jónsson was a thrifty person. As a young man he began keeping a diary, in which he recorded his expenses and details of the houses and the improvements on the farm, food supplies, livestock and possessions.[1] He was also a bookbinder, weaver, and carpenter. Jón took exceptionally good care of his belongings and became an active member of progressive societies such as the parish reading society, established by 30 farmers and farmhands.

In 1858, at the age of 23, Jón married Sigurbjörg Stefánsdóttir, who was 11 years his senior and no less prudent. She moved in with Jón in the spring and they married in September. In his diaries, Jón writes warmly about his wife, but dedicates more ink to her belongings than to his feelings for her. For a servant, he noted, she was well-off, having saved 50 rix dollars and acquired 10 sheep, some riding equipment, a trunk, a new bed, a feather comforter, books, plenty of clothes, and a variety of small items such as a table service.

The thundering waters and unique basalt formations of Aldeyjarfoss, situated in the lavafields near Mýri, were undoubtedly an inspiration to the aspiring poet during his years at Mjóidalur.

The newlyweds must have been active under the comforter on the wedding night, as fewer than 10 months later, on July 3, 1859, their daughter, Helga Sigríður, was born. Sigurbjörg was in her mid-30's and the childbirth was difficult. Jón had to travel five days to fetch some healing herbs. Two years later, Sigurbjörg gave birth to a little boy whom they named Jón. When Stefán, then 16, arrived at Mjóidalur in June of 1870, Helga was just turning 11 and Jón was 8 years of age.

When Stefán's father moved to Mýri, he publicized his sheep mark in the local paper. He owned a few sheep at Mýri and leased three of them to Jón of Mjóidalur. Although his social status was now reduced to that of a farmhand and his wife was a domestic servant, he probably still dreamed of becoming an independent farmer.

On the other hand, Jón Jónsson had a prosperous farm operation at Mjóidalur. A handsome stone wall surrounded a seven-acre hayfield, and the rather large turf house had an attached cow barn. There was also a potato garden, and even more unusual, an outhouse, a rather rare sight in Iceland at the time. The livestock at Mjóidalur consisted of two cows, nearly 100 sheep, and three horses. Jón Jónsson also noted in his diary that his domestic help had six sheep among them, some of which might have belonged to Stefán. The farm supported 10 people during the first year Stefán lived there: householders Jón and Sigurbjörg and their children, Helga and Jón; a farmhand; two servant women; Stefán, who was listed in Jón Jónsson's diary as an errand boy; and two paupers, Jón's sister Jóna, who was mentally unstable, and Kristján Benediktsson. Apart from taking in paupers, Jón sometimes assumed guardianship of child wards of the poor law, in order to earn some extra income.

Stefán arrived at Mjóidalur in spring, when the lambs were being kept separate from the sheep overnight. After June 20, the farmhands began weaning the lambs. Stefán was appointed shepherd, to drive the sheep to various grazing areas while the children kept the lambs at home. His job soon became routine. He arose at four o'clock in the morning, before the midges began irritating the sheep, sending them looking for shelter in hollows and ravines. Stefán had to drive 50 sheep home to the milking pen every morning and again in the evening. While watching the sheep, he could explore the wilderness, recite summer poems, and compose verses for the hired girls. The weather was cool that summer and the grass did not grow well, so haying was poor. To augment hay supplies, the farmhands cut various flat and grassy areas further up the valley. While helping to cut the hay with a scythe, Stefán made a verse about his heroic efforts to fell the blades of grass like a warrior doing battle.[2]

While at Mjóidalur Stefán encountered some colourful characters. There was the pauper Kristján Benediktsson, who was around 50 years of age. In his younger years, he had been a hardy thug, who had even lived like an outlaw and stolen from the farms. "He was impressive in appearance, with his large head and a huge beard reaching to his eyes. He also had a great deal of coarse grey hair. His forehead was low, his eyebrows heavy, and his eyes deeply sunk. His voice was extremely strong and powerful, sounding rather gruff, except when he spoke to children." He made strange sounds to them: "kalla–stuffa–jaffa–nuff" – hence one of his nicknames was "nuff". His other nickname was "footless", as some winters earlier he lost both feet and all his fingers after almost dying of exposure. Despite his crippling disabilities, Kristján could perform various tasks such as grinding grain and combing, spinning, and braiding horsehair into rope. Stefán noted that Kristján cut hay and sod with the same incredible efficiency. "There he was, with sod divots up to his armpits wherever he crawled on his knees with his scythe," Stefán recalled. If Kristján had confined his amazing energy to slicing off frost boils, all would have been fine. However, he applied the same vigour to the soft hayfield. "With his short scythe, he sliced that much deeper into the soil than others. He once got as far as the home field in front of the houses before he was stopped. A lot of dandelions and sorrel used to grow there, and before anyone noticed, Kristján had not only shorn the weeds, but the best hay – which was half dirt..."[3] Other fodder for Stefán's pen was found at the nearby church. There he found common farm folk, verse makers, storytellers, and artists such as the passionate, poor, peasant playwright Tómas Jónasson – and then there was the self-taught fiddler and painter, Arngrímur Gíslason, who helped people find beauty in everyday life.

The Young Poet

The first snow came in the last week of Icelandic summer, in mid-October, and Stefán composed a Romantic verse depicting clouds covering the mountains.[4] Life remained routine, however, and Stefán took part in the seasonal cycle of farmwork at Mjóidalur – the slaughtering of sheep for the winter and the processing of the carcasses for food. In a society where people sometimes verged on starvation, rendered suet from the slaughtered sheep served not only as a foodstuff, but as a major source of income. Even a lamb that was found dead was rendered for its fat. Jón slaughtered 30 wethers, each of them yielding 12 pounds of suet, and in the fall of 1870 he sold this suet, along with 90 pounds of sheep butter and a large amount of wool, to a merchant. In return he purchased four barrels of grain and 150 pounds of fish for the winter. *Skyr** made from sheep's milk filled 12 barrels and Jón was able to put up three barrels of salted meat. This was the family's winter supply of food.

Autumn was also the time when people began to process wool, and Jón of Mjóidalur began weaving. He also bound several books. Cultural activities started up again and the long winter days were filled with reading, poetry recitation, and lessons for the children. Although Jón had many books, Stefán read less often at Mjóidalur as he had to work more. He tried to keep the sheep pasturing outside as long as possible in the autumn and winter, while snow conditions permitted. First he had to find sufficient grass and then break through the hard crust of snow so the sheep could graze. These tasks did not prevent him from composing poetry, however, wherever he was. Lines came to him with the rhythms of work and occasional verses were inspired by daily life. The content of his long poems, though, reveals strong feelings and profound

---
*Skyr is a special Icelandic milk product resembling yoghurt.

thoughts about life and death, love and sorrow. In the New Year of 1871, Stefán composed poetic greetings to his illegitimate cousin Sigríður at Eyjardalsá. In these verses the New Year sun had risen and the southern breeze and the river were to carry his friendly greetings down the valley.

It is possible that Stefán found the short winter days depressing. In March of 1871, while working wool, he was accused of being lazy. He replied:

> *How boring is Miss Indolence.*
> *Life and cheerfulness wither away*
> *When she, with spread fingers,*
> *Grasps me with her hands.*[5]

Spring brought variable weather, alternating between snow and thaws that allowed for good grazing. April was cruel, with frost through the second half of the month. The people of Bárðardalur, however, had a novelty to distract them from the capricious weather. Tómas Jónasson, an aspiring playwright, had a great passion for books and knowledge, plays and drama. He had taught himself Danish so that he could read the plays of Ludvig Holberg and translations of the plays of William Shakespeare. He wanted to read Shakespeare in English, however, so he bought an English Bible in order to compare the text to the Icelandic Bible – and thereby learn English. He soon realized that he could write plays himself. His first work was a rewritten version of a play by Holberg, transported to an Icelandic setting. The manuscript was circulated to all the farms up and down Bárðardalur, and the young people read it and memorized roles. On the First Day of Summer, the play was performed in the large living room of the farmhouse at Stóruvellir. This was among the first rural theatrical performances in Iceland. It is unlikely that Stefán took part in the play, but he almost certainly saw the performance.

Stefán was busy with his own compositions. "Do you not expect to live long, nephew?" his aunt Sigurbjörg asked him one day. Surprised, he did not know what to say, and asked what she meant. "Oh, I just thought so because of a little note written by you that I found." Stefán then realized that she was referring to a small chest where he kept his writings. On top of the contents he had left a note with instructions that the papers be burned if "the owner should die". Sigurbjörg had found the key, opened the box, and looked at his compositions. In anger, Stefán burned the entire contents of his chest.⁶

No wonder Stefán was angry with his aunt for prying into his personal belongings. He was reserved by nature and found such an invasion of his privacy humiliating. For a long time he kept his poetry to himself, although he "gibbered like hell", as he admitted much later. He composed long narrative poems and wrote half a novel imitating the style and themes of the popular sentimental writers. Before he burned his poems, however, he had given some of them to others.⁷ Some of these early poems are preserved in at least three handwritten notebooks, most of them in a book compiled by his cousin Guðni Jónsson from Eyjardalsá, who collected Stefán's poetry from his earliest scratchings until 1881. His manuscript collection includes poems that the cousins in Bárðardalur sent each other, obviously composed by Stefán as if he were a kind of family poet.⁸

"Mere verse-making does not make anyone a poet," said Níels the Poet, a self-educated rhymster and scholar from Skagafjörður in the 1850s. Certain subjects haunted Stefán and he used all his mental strength to grapple with them. During his first winter in Mjóidalur, for example, he penned tearful lines in "Íslendingurinn erlendis" (The Icelander Abroad). "Hví skal ég lifa lengur" (Why should I live any longer?) is the title of another poem, composed on February 5, 1871, in which darkness surrounds a heart fettered by death: "the breast that is moved by grief/ lacks gentle tranquillity;/why should I live any longer?/I have lived long enough," the young poet wrote. In another poem, written on February 19, Stefán was cheered by a beautiful and starlit winter night and the northern lights. In the following weeks, themes of grief, silence, love, and sorrow dominated his poems.⁹

"Wandering in a churchyard in deep thought awakens in man's soul, more than any reading of books, good feelings, and divine reflections," wrote Reverend Sveinbjörn Hallgrímsson in 1857, in a religious book for young people. It is as if Stefán took him at his word. On Ash Wednesday, February 22, 1871, he wrote a long poem entitled "Í kirkjugarði" (In a Churchyard), in which he explores the intricate paths of human life, finding virtues and vices among a poor scholar, a vile miser, lovers, patriotic heroes, mourners, and murderers.¹⁰ The poem indicates how Stefán was spreading his poetic wings in his choice of subjects and the level of poetic reflection.

As both Mjóidalur and Mýri belonged to the parish of Lundarbrekka, occupants of these farms would have ridden this route to their church, which was considered one of the most beautiful in Iceland at that time. That church and its contents were destroyed by fire in 1878, and the current church at Lundarbrekka was built of local sandstone in 1880.

Stefán's half-written novel is dated at the beginning of December 1872, when he was 19 years of age. Two fragments are preserved in manuscripts. The story is about lovers in the worlds of humans and elves. It begins thus: "Evening was falling, the sun was setting, sweeping across the snowy mountaintops in the evening red; the stars were shining in the east above the mountain peaks that were dark below but lighter ever higher up, as if they wanted to direct the human mind upward in search of what is most pure and sublime." The tale is about an eight-year-old orphan boy who comes to a lawyer's farm where the pillars of society are preparing a feast on New Year's Eve. The lawyer and a greedy and fawning pastor refuse to allow him to stay in the house overnight. The boy seeks the shelter of a rock. There, an elf pastor finds him and leads him into the world of the elves, explaining to the boy the difference between elves and men. Elves are the unwashed children that Eve tried to hide from God. The elves, therefore, do not have immortal souls, but they have more integrity and powers than flighty humans. If love unites an elf and a human, the elf could acquire an immortal soul. The pastor invites the boy to stay among the elves. In the morning, the pastor's daughter comes to the boy. Pure, unblemished children's love blossoms in a poetic setting. In the second fragment of Stefán's novel, the boy has been a knight with the elf king for some time and is now with the king's daughter. The world has become more complicated, however, and the boy desires to return to the human world. The king's daughter wants him to stay. She has a worse temper and is more capricious and vengeful than the pastor's daughter.[11]

These fragments reflect a change in Stefán's world-image as the innocence of childhood disappears. The story is multi-faceted. It is about pure feelings, but also about class distinction and the arrogance of the rich toward the poor. The young poet in Mjóidalur was beginning to explore the complicated world of chaos, instincts, and of conduct – just and unjust.

Despite the Romantic overtones of these fragments, Stefán's writings reveal a challenging and even rebellious mind. He wrote poems about feastings and drinking, and despite his reserved personality he could easily think up witty quips from an unexpected point of view. Sometimes he said things that he himself regarded as frivolous, in order to provoke others, but some of these off-hand remarks later became convictions. For example, one beautiful summer day, while the people from Mjóidalur were riding to church, Stefán was silenced by the beauty of the landscape shimmering in the sun. Perhaps, he was composing verses. A hired girl from Mjóidalur, who loved debate and often had lively discussions with Stefán, all in the spirit of friendship, began praising *The Bible* and then turned her comments to Stefán. This irritated him, as she was disturbing his joy over the beauty of the landscape, so he did not reply. She did not give up, and eventually Stefán replied with a prankish notion that suddenly came to him: "Oh, well, just like other Bibles, for instance the *Edda*." Equating the Holy Scriptures with pagan poetry bordered on sacrilege and the young woman became upset. Stefán was then obliged to come up with an explanation. He had never before heard this comparison made, but he was nevertheless able to defend his novel opinion. "I was quite familiar with both books," he later wrote. "Against every example of hers, I brought up something similar from the *Edda*." The woman had difficulty proving her case and the debate took up most of the long ride to church. Over the course of time, Stefán subsequently came to the conclusion that he was right for the most part – that creation myths and religious ideas are basically similar.[12] He was learning to formulate and articulate his natural insights just as he was beginning to question the Church's teachings. No doubt people were beginning to notice the ideas of this bright and poetically inclined teenager.

It was likely in 1872 or 1873 that Stefán wrote a remarkable poem, "Ég fer mínu fram" (I do what I want), in which he discards the idealism that had characterized his poetry to that point. He evokes familiar images that he then rejects by praising a hedonist life and free will. Hedonism may be a popular theme with teen-age poets, but Stefán goes further. He expresses sharp scorn for wealth and love in down-to-earth images drawn from his immediate surroundings: "When the others chase wealth/and always mourn over the fat sheep/that sadly was caught by death/and died from the worst disease," those who blubber over the pain of love are "like a raven on a mound/in the middle of the night." His own heart is calm when he swills liquor and becomes "the worst drinking pig." The poem ends with a similar denial of piety. The poet delights in the joy of the world: he flirts and drinks while others pin the cross to their flesh, regret their sins, and try to avoid the "snares of the world" that godless men fall into.[13]

Reverend Jón Austmann at Halldórsstaðir, the poet's tutor for one winter, served as pastor to Lundarbrekka for 25 years.

"Grafskrift yfir sjálfum mér" (Epitaph over myself) is the title of another poem born of his turbulent mind. Here, his body is in "the human world", his confused head is in the "world of wine", and his heart is in the "world of love". He even expresses erotic feelings in a verse about an erection in his pants and some unsettling sensations.[14]

Illness and Pastoral Romance

"Illness has been making the rounds. Some have been bed-ridden, but not many have died; one man here lay ill for a week," farmer Jón in Mjóidalur wrote in his diary in July of 1871. He was referring to the errand boy Stefán. The illness, "bilious complaint", was accompanied by pain and a high fever. Stefán had got up on a Monday morning, ready to herd the sheep as usual, but felt very ill. He was sweating and thirsty. After drinking a full bowl of mixed sour whey and water, he passed out.

Mjóidalur

Mýri, the next farm to Mjóidalur and home to the poet's parents during their years in Bárðardalur, was one of the largest and most prosperous in the valley. The head of the household was Jón Ingjaldsson, whose forefathers had lived at Mýri for generations.

Jón sent for Stefán's mother at Mýri and also Reverend Jón Austmann at Halldórsstaðir, as he was a rather successful homeopathic doctor. When they arrived, Stefán regained consciousness long enough to hear Jón say to Guðbjörg, "He's not likely to survive, which is a pity as he is such a handsome boy." Stefán was in serious danger.

By the following weekend, however, he was fully conscious and able to eat. The legless pauper Kristján Nuff had also been ill and lay in the opposite bed. Reverend Jón came again to look in on Stefán one day when the patients had just eaten. Kristján had eaten a litre of *skyr* and milk, a big slice of flat bread, and half a small fish, but had been unable to finish the last and least delicious piece of it. Reverend Jón turned to Kristján and asked very politely, "How are you Kristján? Are you very ill?" The old man was grumpy and complained about his health, claiming that he would never recover because of the lack of nourishment. Reverend Jón asked had he not eaten? "Admittedly, but that was hardly anything," Kristján replied. Jón nevertheless tactfully managed to get him to admit to the enormous amount of food he had just eaten. Stefán, with a keen ear for absurdities and good stories, followed the conversation with amusement. "You can hardly expect a quick recovery under these circumstances," Reverend Jón concluded with a mocking expression. Stefán could no longer contain himself and burst into laughter. Reverend Jón urged him to be quiet lest he have a relapse. His fears came true when Stefán lost consciousness again and had to stay in bed for another week.

Stefán's recovery was slow and he was unable to leave the house. One day, however, when he and his aunt Sigurbjörg were alone at home, he sneaked out and made his way down the slope along the hayfield, all the way to the river, a distance of almost two hundred meters. There he lay down. When the time came to go back, however, he found it more difficult to get back up the hill. "I thought I would die there in the hayfield, in the beautiful weather," he later said. His aunt scolded him for his inconsiderate actions.[15]

Young people in the valley of Bárðardalur led an active social life between the farm chores, visiting each other, entertaining themselves, exploring the countryside on horseback, organizing cultural activities, and even courting. They corresponded, discussed poetry, and wrote poems back and forth.

Judging from his poems from that time, Stefán had begun to look keenly at the fairer sex. His cousin Sigríður from Eyjardalsá now lived at Mýri with her mother, Helga. She and Stefán were good friends and sparks of love were evidently ignited when they met, herding sheep or walking together on the slopes of Mjóidalur on sunny Sundays:

> *I recall a sweet and sunny hour*
> *The dear summer at home.*
> *And in the shadow of a little grove*
> *The small herbs are dreaming:*
> *Your soul is loving, young and pure*
> *Shining in the sunbeams of spirit*
> *That keep a sweeter summer.*
>
> *Below a steep and flowery slope*
> *We both walked together.*
> *Then life had the gentleness of youth,*
> *Only spring and fun.*
> *Poetry, eternity, the beauty of spirit*
> *We discussed –The night touched*
> *The edges of the dark mountains.*[16]

Sigríður Jónsdóttir from Eyjardalsá, the poet's cousin and, perhaps, first love.

For a long time Stefán kept these tender pastoral memories to himself. These stanzas from a commemorative poem about Sigríður are reminiscent of the young love in Stefán's novel fragment.

Four years after this summer romance, Sigríður married a young farmer named Friðgeir Jóakimsson, and in 1880 they emigrated. She was pregnant, but did not let her relatives know as she feared they would then prevent her from leaving. She died at sea after giving birth to twins who also died. Her husband continued to Minnesota, where he later took the surname *Bardal*.

In 1881 Stefán composed two poems in Sigríður's memory, the first one under his own name, including the stanzas above. In it he expresses his sorrow and solitude before he evokes sweet memories. The other poem was composed in the name of his aunt Sigurbjörg. She had taken care of Sigríður as a child and had loved her niece born out of wedlock. The poem is tender, one of Stefán's most beautiful to that time, expressing lyrical grief rather than deep sorrow. They also describe Sigríður's beauty, while revealing a sense of inner, non-superficial beauty as well as a love that is never fully expressed:

> *Now you have fallen asleep*
> *My dear Sigríður!*
> *Sweetly fallen asleep*
> *In calm dreamland.*
> *Your eyes closed,*
> *Lips closed.*
> *The red color has fled*
> *From the beautiful cheeks.*

> *You were beautiful awake,*
> *Yet more beautiful in sleep,*
> *Beautiful in life*
> *But most beautiful in death!*
> *That is the mark of victory*
> *Of an innocent youth.*
> *A beam from the eternal*
> *World of spirits.*[17]

Hardships

It rained a great deal during the summer of 1871 while Stefán was ill. Eventually there was a good hay yield, but haying conditions were poor and when the damp hay was stored, it turned moldy, causing the animals to become sick. The following winter was among the hardest within living memory. As the Icelandic calendar's "Winter Nights" set in, around October 20, a northern blizzard struck with severe cold. Another storm followed a week later. There was almost no winter grazing throughout most of the Þingeyjarsýsla region, though there was less snowfall further inland, in the southernmost parts of Bárðardalur and in Mjóidalur where young poet and farmhand Stefán continued to tend the sheep. His New Year's poem for 1872 is gloomy: the northern lights wrap the heavens in magnetic fires from the wings of the wind. The New Year greets the fierce whine of the wind and the poet predicts that in a year's time his grave will be covered with cold snow.[18]

Stefán wrote less poetry than usual this winter, though one exception was a long poem about a girl who betrayed her fiancé.[19] There were now more important things to occupy his time. During the first months of 1872, he and hired man Björn spent long days breaking the crust of snow to expose some grass for the sheep. The situation was worse in the lowlands, where the sheep faced starvation, and by the end of March farmers in Bárðardalur were driving their flocks up into the highlands, where there was less snow, in the hope of finding some open pastureland. The chores at Mjóidalur increased considerably as Jón took in nearly 100 sheep for tending and treatment.

"Now you should be here... to see the sheep dropping dead from hunger and weakness, to see the thousands of newborn lambs dead from all kinds of incurable diseases, to see even the cows near death

Even hardy Icelandic sheep, adapted to withstanding harsh conditions and scrabbling for every blade of grass on the barren heaths around Mjóidalur, were vulnerable to the increasingly harsh weather of the last decades of the 19th Century.

from lack of fodder, and to see into the homes and hearts of destitute parents," lamented a letter dated June 3, 1872, and published by the regional newspaper *Norðanfari*. Just a few days earlier, a furious blizzard had hit, driving the sheep into rivers or hollows where they were buried by the snowdrifts. A large number of newborn lambs perished and nearly 2000 sheep died in the Ljósavatn district. The situation in Mjóidalur was much better than in the lowlands. Jón of Mjóidalur lost only one sheep and a few yearlings and lambs.

Around this time, emigration to North America was a topic of much discussion. *Norðanfari* carried news from America and some began expressing the opinion that if no justice could be obtained from the Danish government, emigration would be their best option. One of the greatest human migrations in recorded history was taking place as people from all the corners of Europe were flocking to North America. New ideas of progress and independence, first raised around the middle of the century by a few prominent farmers who had established reading and progressive societies, developed among people in the Þingeyjarsýsla region. After 1870, the impatience of the Icelandic people grew because of slow progress in the struggle for in-

These Icelandic emigrants were photographed in Liverpool, England, en route to America in 1872. Included are Páll Þorláksson from Stórutjarnir (at right), Haraldur Þorláksson from Stórutjarnir and his bride, María (centre), and their cousin Hans B. Thorgrimsen (seated at left).

dependence, and added to this restlessness was an overall increase in the birth rate, that strained the ability of primitive farms to support a growing population. Added to these factors was a harsh downturn in the climate.

Farmers from Þingeyjarsýsla were among the first to consider the option of emigration. In the summer of 1872, two sons of Þorlákur Gunnar Jónsson from Stórutjarnir, Haraldur and Páll, together with Haraldur's wife, María, were among those who left the region and made their way to Milwaukee, Wisconsin. Back in Iceland, the winter of 1872-73 began badly. While farmers in Bárðardalur held meetings to discuss the situation, the brothers from Stórutjarnir sent home letters, excerpts of which their father submitted to the regional newspaper, *Norðanfari*. Páll Þorláksson, who was studying theology, had found them jobs, and while inspecting land near Milwaukee he had become acquainted with prosperous Norwegian farmers who had settled there as early as the middle of the century.[20]

Meanwhile, nature continued to wreak havoc in Northern Iceland. A volcanic eruption in the Grímsvötn Lakes, beneath the huge Vatnajökull Glacier, began at the end of December 1872 and gained momentum during the first days of the New Year. "On the 10th so much ash fell, almost an inch, that the snow turned dark brown. In some places thunder was

Halldórsstaðir in Bárðardalur, where Stefán took some schooling for one winter, as depicted by Icelandic artist Arngrímur Gíslason 'málari' in 1868.

heard and from other places fires were seen in the southeast," Jón of Mjóidalur wrote in his diary.[21]

A lesser incident would have inspired a poet. "Veturinn 1873 – um eldgosið" (Winter 1873 – about the volcanic eruption) is dated January 3, 1873. Stefán's poetic visions are powerful. The poem begins with an image of the dark night covering the land and proceeds to the odd creatures living beneath the earth, mythical worms in the soil and "island-whales"* in the dark silence of the sea. Small farms slumber in the valleys. Terror is revived from the depths of the age-old glaciers. Mythical forces hold the ancient power of destruction, the gods of fire and the sea give birth to strange creatures long before flowers in the fields began smiling to the sun. Volcanic fires threaten all life in the lowlands and God's trumpet resounds over the frightened people, heralding what is to come, the poem says.[22] The imagery is tense as Stefán describes the clash of the mythical forces of creation and destruction.

The eruption lasted until spring, convincing several families in Bárðardalur to pack their belongings. Þorlákur Gunnar Jónsson of Stórutjarnir called a meeting at Eyjardalsá, the home of Stefán's aunt, on January 24, 1873, and there some 40 farmers, among them Jón from

---

*Whales resembling islands, a strange metaphor, probably influenced by the travels of Sindbad.

Mjóidalur, discussed emigration. The outcome of the meeting was that a large number made plans to emigrate from the port of Akureyri that summer. In March, Jón of Mjóidalur made the decision to try his luck in the western world, as did others at Mýri and Mjóidalur, among them Guðmundur Stefánsson and Guðbjörg Hannesdóttir and their children, Stefán, who was now 19 years of age, and Sigurlaug, who was 12.

The idea of emigration had been circulating for some time, but now people had simply had enough. Jón Jónsson from Mýri, a young man at the time, wrote in his memoirs that most of the people who left were prudent and industrious. His mother encouraged him to leave, as she "loved animals and found it much saner to earn a living by grain cultivation than this dishonest, risky stock raising." For Guðmundur and Guðbjörg, there was little to leave. Guðmundur was 55 years old, worn out from hard work, with little to show for his labour. Perhaps the idea of emigration ignited a spark of hope for a new life for their children.

Education and Death

Reverend Jón Austmann of Halldórsstaðir was a major educational leader to the people of Bárðardalur. He often took in boys from the parish to prepare them for the Learned School in Reykjavík, and Stefán now had the opportunity to study English with him for a month in preparation for the journey west. After self-study based on his knowledge of Latin, Jón understood English quite well and was regarded as being fluent in the language, but he had trouble with correct pronunciation and idiomatic English. Stefán found Reverend Jón Austmann "an imposing man, handsome, gentlemanly, and politely ironic in his attitude"[23]

There were four other students at Halldórsstaðir at that time, three of whom later became prominent members of Icelandic society – one of them, a member of the Icelandic Parliament. The fourth was a handsome and cheerful boy named Friðrik Bergmann, who later emigrated to North America and would have various dealings with Stefán. Perhaps it was Reverend Jón who suggested that Stefán attend the Learned School in Reykjavík. That was impossible, however, as the family had already decided to emigrate.

The boys read a Danish textbook of one hundred English lessons with such diligence that they lost weight. They questioned each other about grammar and vocabulary, but translated individually. Stefán finished the book when he got back to Mjóidalur.

Schooling was not all work. While others at Halldórsstaðir took a nap, these young men had time to get some outside exercise in the afternoon dusk. They found the wreck of an old sled and together with some female servants and the minister's daughters, they hauled it up the mountain slope above the farm and slid down. They steered with their feet, wearing out their sheepskin shoes. The main challenge was to avoid the manure pile. Stefán once lost control of the sled and all tumbled into the manure pile. It was frozen so no one got dirty, but the following evening one of the girls asked that Stefán not steer as she did not want to go to bed with him in a dunghill. On another occasion, Friðrik Bergmann hurt his leg so badly that he limped for a long time.

While Stefán was at Halldórsstaðir, a young woman visited. Possibly it was Karólína Jónsdóttir, who in the spring married Gísli Jónsson, a brother to Jón of Mjóidalur. This young lady often joined in the sledding, and when she was about to leave, the boys decided to compose a verse which they planned to sing to her at her departure. Three of them shared a bed and stayed awake most of the night composing a long love poem. When the time came for her leave taking, one of them sang it to her. Everyone on the farm came to listen and someone remarked that it was as if all three were in love with her.

A young man named Gunnlaugur Briem had been fostered at Halldórsstaðir. By this time he was a little over 20 years old, a bookbinder and poet, tall and handsome, somewhat melancholic, but always cheerful in manner. He and Stefán became good friends. The playwright Tómas Jónasson came to Halldórsstaðir twice in March, perhaps to discuss drama with Gunnlaugur and Stefán. Gunnlaugur then joined Tómas at Akureyri where his play *Hallur* was performed twice with great success. At Easter, accompanied by two others, Gunnlaugur rode west to Skagafjörður to visit relatives. There was a thaw at the time, and when the threesome crossed the mountain pass of Öxnadalsheiði the Norðurá River was running high. When they tried to ford the river, Gunnlaugur's horse stumbled and Gunnlaugur was swept downstream. His body was not found until the next day.

Shortly after this event, Stefán also travelled to Skagafjörður to say farewell to his friends and relatives before departing for America. On the way, he heard of Gunnlaugur's death. The ride down the valley of

Norðurárdalur was dreary, and when Stefán came to the place where Gunnlaugur had drowned, he composed a quatrain on this ill-fated, last journey. When he returned home, his friends noticed that he was very sad, although he rarely showed his feelings. Stefán's commemorative poem to Gunnlaugur, among his most mature verses to that time, suggests that Gunnlaugur's spirit has overcome death. In this poem, the waves of life break at the dark gates of death, and then Stefán describes the heartbreak felt when the young hero has fallen.

> Free from the heavy burden of the body
> After his life span.
> Now his young spirit lives,
> Above your reach.[24]

This would become a recurrent theme characteristic of Stefán's later memorial poems: instead of expressing overwhelming grief, he keeps the memory of the deceased in his heart.

Departure

During April and May of 1873, Þorlákur Gunnar Jónsson of Stórutjarnir and Tryggvi Gunnarsson, director of the trading company *Gránufélagið*, organized the emigrants' journey west. They could have arranged direct passage from Iceland to America on a ship owned by the Allen Line of Scotland, but instead Tryggvi struck a deal with a certain Mr. Walker, a livestock dealer in Scotland, for the sale of 200 horses and 3,000 sheep. The horse ship was supposed to arrive at Akureyri in mid-July and a ship for the sheep in September. It was estimated that 100-200 emigrants could travel with the horse ship. If the deal was not kept, compensation would be paid. Þorlákur agreed that passage for the emigrants would be cheaper if they travelled to Scotland aboard the horse ship, and besides, the economic situation of the emigrants was dependent upon the sale of their livestock.

While preparations for the journey commenced, some aspects of life went on as usual. On Ascension Day, May 22, Reverend Jón Austmann bade farewell to the people of Bárðardalur. He was moving to another parish, and his last act in Lundarbrekka Parish was to confirm new communicants, among them Helga Sigríður, the daughter of Jón and

Mjóidalur

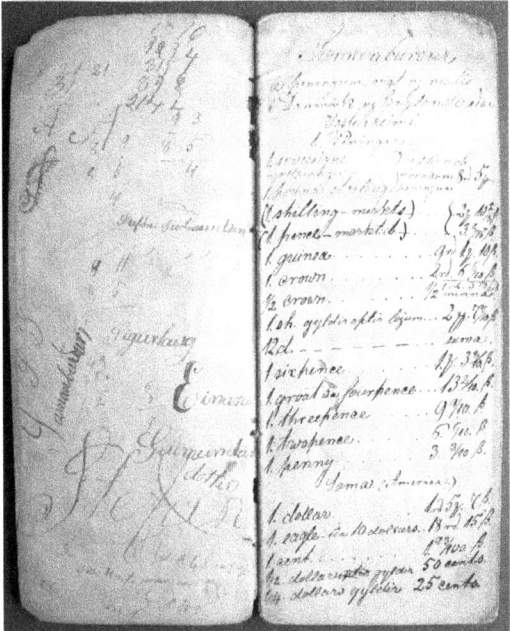

Young Stefán Guðmundsson the emigrant had prepared carefully for the journey, studying equivalents and conversions "of money, weights, and measures in Denmark and England or America" and compiling a record of these in his notebook.

Sigurbjörg of Mjóidalur. The pastor's evaluation of her was excellent and she ranked second among the girls.

The emigrants now busied themselves, preparing for the trip. Jón Jónsson of Mjóidalur sold his farm and livestock. Guðmundur Stefánsson and Guðbjörg Hannesdóttir did not have much to sell, other than a few sheep and horses, and neither did Stefán or his sister. Guðmudur sold his horses to the trading company *Gránufélagið*, for the horse ship. Nevertheless, he still did not have enough money for the entire fare, and he was obliged to borrow 100 rix dollars from Jón of Mjóidalur. Eventually, the emigrants had to select the contents of their trunks – clothing, bedding, a few treasured possessions and household utensils, and most importantly, books, always a priority in the luggage of Icelandic emigrants.

Cold weather brought sleet during the first half of July and there was much illness in Bárðardalur. Everyone at Mjóidalur fell ill and Sigurbjörg, the lady of the house, was bedridden until July 12. The day after, a Sunday, the people of Mjóidalur – Jón and Sigurbjörg; their children, Helga Sigríður and Jón; the farm hand Stefán; and Jón's sister Guðfinna, who had been his housemaid – vacated the farm. First they rode to Mýri, where they stayed overnight. Guðmundur, Guðbjörg, and Sigurlaug joined them the following day, as did the farmer's son, Jón Jónsson, a young man of 20 and a good friend of Guðmundur and Stefán. Approximately 10 people rode slowly down the valley, followed by the pack horses carrying their luggage for the

Akureyri, one of the main ports in Northern Iceland, was little more than a village in 1873.

New World. They slept at Eyjardalsá that night and stayed there the following day, a Tuesday.

On July 16, the group bade farewell to Eyjardalsá. Those who remained felt a deep sense of loss, while those departing had mixed feelings of anticipation and anxiety. Guðný of Eyjardalsá, the lady of the house, was seeing off two of her siblings and their families. She turned to Stefán and told him how hard it was to see him leave – something he still remembered almost half a century later:

> *Surprising as a hurricane*
> *Such a greeting came from her.*
> *Deep is the warmth underneath*
> *Of love expressing few words*
> *The youth best understands*
> *The half words, few but warm.*[25]

Although regret characterized this moment of departure, Guðný did not want to weaken the courage and optimism of the travellers. She had asked her tenant, the poet and playwright Tómas Jónasson, to compose a farewell poem that was sung when the emigrants left Eyjardalsá. The poem is warm, brimming with encouragement. "Forward to victory" is its theme, rather than mourning their departure, the gaps left in the ranks of relatives, and the loss to Iceland. It would be unfair to blame those who left the frost and snow at home for the attractions of the New World. The poet hoped that they would remain Icelandic in spirit and stay their course in the fast flow of time. The travellers were pioneers, "clearing stones from the road." "It is noble to test the ice ahead of others," the second last stanza notes, "so it is easier for others to follow."[26] The poem is a contrast to the accusations of treason that were hurled at emigrants later, and it remained in Stefán's mind for a very long time.

Probably all the emigrants from Bárðardalur rode to Akureyri in one group, past Lake Ljósavatn, silent in the northern chill, where a great northern diver may have swum with its chicks. On a small farm across the lake, there was a five week old boy, Guðmundur Finnbogason, who 44 years later would have a strong influence on Stefán's life. At Stórutjarnir, Þorlákur Gunnar Jónsson and his wife, Lovísa, joined the group with seven children. In all, some 20 people – a large contingent relative to the district's small population – had decided to leave Ljósavatnshreppur for North America, and another 20 were leaving for Brazil. Among those who joined the little group from Mjóidalur and Mýri were four siblings of Jón from Mjóidalur, the newlyweds Gísli Jónsson and Karólína Jónsdóttir, Benedikt Jónsson and his wife, Sesselja, Herdís and her husband, Hallgrímur Gíslason, and the unmarried Guðfinna Jónsdóttir. Two more sisters would emigrate later.

The group spent the next night on a farm in the valley Fnjóskadalur. This time the river Fnjóská was easier to cross than it had been three years earlier when Stefán's family had moved to Bárðardalur. It snowed as they were crossing Vaðlaheiði Heath, and the ground was partially snow-covered all the way down to the fjord on the other side.

Revelry in Akureyri

When the travellers arrived at Akureyri on Thursday, July 17, 1873, it was storming. Stefán, his parents, and his sister went straight to the house where they would stay until their departure. Guðbjörg was quite ill and remained so for weeks.

The ship, unfortunately, had not yet arrived, though more than 100 prospective emigrants had swarmed into the small town of Akureyri. When the group from Bárðardalur arrived, printer Björn Jónsson was working overtime printing an English textbook by Halldór Briem. Jón Jónsson from Mjóidalur and Guðmundur from Mýri found it hard not to have any work to do, but the young people were more easygoing. Helga Sigríður, the newly confirmed daughter of Jón and Sigurbjörg, had her portrait taken by a photographer in town. Stefán and some of the other young men explored the town and had a drink at the Baukur public house, and, as the stay in Akureyri became protracted, they tried to find work. Stefán was able to get a job tending horses for some visitors during the first few days he was in Akureyri, and he then joined some men from Bárðardalur who borrowed a little boat to go out on the fjord to fish. When they returned, they sold their catch to earn a little money. Sometimes Stefán went straight to the pub, tired, his hands sore after rowing and pulling in the fishing line.[27]

Father and son, Guðmundur and Stefán, each wrote a travelogue that was quite different from the other. Guðmundur's was reserved, even bitter, whereas Stefán's showed that he was ready to take on the challenges of the world. His narrative reveals that his ideas and writing skills had developed considerably. His world view was broader than might be expected of a teenager from an isolated farm. Word of this intelligent and poetically talented young man spread through the town, and these reports

Emigrants were faced with packing all their worldly belongings into one or two trunks that could be taken with them. Invariably the items chosen included books and a few small treasures, with the remaining space taken up by clothing, bedding, and food.

reached Vilhelmína Lever, now an old lady, who some 24 years earlier had wanted to shoot the protesters from Skagafjörður when they "rode north" and surrounded the Governor's house at Möðruvellir – among them Stefán's father. Stefán found this amusing and many years later he wrote to a friend: "She had heard about me, was very talkative, but bedridden. She sent for me to come and speak with her. We had a good visit and at parting she wished me well, but all the time I was laughing to myself: So, this is how you are, old lady, you who would not have hesitated to kill the father of this boy."[28]

Near the end of July the emigrants began to feel uneasy, as the ship still had not arrived. Each day a few would walk up onto the hills to look north over the fjord. One day, fog covered the surrounding mountains, but it lifted during the course of the following morning and Stefán and his companions went fishing on the fjord as usual. When they returned in the afternoon, an old government official with whom they had often discussed emigration told them that the *Queen* had been spotted far out on the fjord and could be expected by evening. He had been waiting on the dock for some time just to give them this news and now he also gave them some money, telling them to go to the Baukur pub to drink a toast, as they would not meet again. He thanked them for their pleasant company the last few days and wished them well.

When the ship arrived, Tryggvi Gunnarsson went on board together with his brother Eggert and the shipping agent Lambertsen. News soon spread that the ship could accommodate only 120 passengers and 190 horses. Despite the delay in the arrival of the *Queen*, the shipping company refused to compensate the emigrants and agreed to pay only a very small sum to those who had tended the horses during the long wait. This put the emigrants in a difficult position. Not only were they told they would not be compensated despite the obvious breach of contract, but now they learned that they would perhaps not be able to leave, a shock since they had already spent much of their money. They gathered in the evening to discuss their situation, but dispersed without any resolutions on what to do.

The ship had brought salt, coal, and some passengers, many of whom came ashore. Stefán found all the women homely, he wrote sarcastically in his travelogue. He got a job unloading the salt and found it hard work. When the last boat had been loaded, three of the Icelanders – including Stefán – remained on ship while the others returned to shore. Eventually two sailors were ordered to row them back to shore. They had not gotten very far, however, when the sailors demanded payment from the Icelanders, who outnumbered them and refused. The sailors had little choice but to continue rowing to shore. Their threats fell on deaf ears and when the Icelanders stepped out of the boat Stefán told them to go to hell. The issue of payment was not mentioned again. The following day, Stefán worked at unloading coal until two o'clock in the morning. For his labours he received four rix dollars and four marks. He then penned this philosophical little verse:

> *Dear brother listen to me,*
> *Follow a holy habit*
> *Buy booze but do not*
> *Give a damn about the money.*[29]

During a meeting with the emigrants on Saturday, August 2, Walker demanded that fares be paid to the *Gránufélag* trading company immediately. That was not possible, however, as much of the emigrants' livestock had yet to be sold. Most of the emigrants had planned to pay at least part of their passage from the sale of their livestock. Then, since the ship could not take all of them, there was the issue of who could board the *Queen*. An impromptu committee decided that single men on their own would have to stay behind. Among these was young Jón Jónsson from Mýri, who had accompanied the family to Akureyri. Stefán's father regretted very much that this young man could not go along.

The weather was calm and cloudy on the following day. Walker began to collect payment for the passage, which included the voyage to Scotland and from there to Quebec City, Canada, with the Allan Line. Contrary to the previous agreement, he raised the fares on the *Queen* considerably, arguing that there was too much luggage. The Icelanders felt that their agent, Lambertsen, was doing a poor job of defending their interests. Walker also increased the number of horses to 220.

Passengers were told to report to the wharf at 9:30 on the morning of August 4 and to be ready to board the ship when a flag was run up the mast. The horses and baggage were taken on board at the appointed time, but the passengers, most of whom were now without food, were obliged to wait on shore all day, pacing back and forth with crying children in their arms. Some found shelter in the houses of nearby merchants. It was not until almost bedtime that most were finally aboard the ship – by that time frustrated and angry. One man with a family of 11 was so offended by the poor, overcrowded conditions, which added insult to the injury of Walker's greedy impertinence, that he returned to shore – leaving some of his luggage on board.

Eventually, all 153 Icelanders on board the *Queen* were sent to the lower deck, as English passengers occupied all the first class accommodations. The mid-deck "was a terrible place," Guðmundur wrote, "cramped, hot, and intolerably smelly because of all the horses. They were packed tightly together the whole length of the hold, as well as up on the deck, in pens on both sides of the canvas partition. They were exposed to the force of the open sea and were sometimes knocked over, though they managed to stand up again."[30]

It was foggy when friends and relatives escorted the emigrants on board the ship and bade them farewell. Stefán helped his parents get settled. In his journal he described the accommodations with bitter irony and considerable style: "Now we began to inspect the space intended for humans. You first went down stairs, just before midships, to where the blessed trunks were neatly upside down or on their sides in a large heap alongside the beds, that were in two tiers, upper and lower. People flocked down into these terribly overcrowded quarters with their bags of bedlinen and crammed into the beds, for which they had to compete. This was by no mean feat, as if you were obliged to find a bed on the other side of the hold or were unlucky enough to have settled into a bed that someone else had claimed, you took your life into your hands vaulting across the heap of trunks. I used to leap acrobatically across or used the dog paddle, although I was good at neither. Below these quarters (that I will call Middle) were the horse stalls. There the horses stood, having a bad time of it. Just below the stairs was an open hatchway in the floor of the Middle, which afforded access to the horses. It was adorned with a funnel made of brown canvas designed to expel the stench from the horse stalls, but as the hatchway was wide and the funnel narrow, you could easily get a pleasant whiff from the nether regions. So much about that room. There was another chamber labelled "The Cabin for Ladies", the women's room. Initially, all the ladies were supposed to be there, but there were rather too many, so some of them had to stay in the Middle, among the men, contrary to the custom of the English, who are very well aware of the difference between males and females. Here, however, things had to be different, so women ended up next to unmarried men, etc., though apparently without any harmful effect. These, then, were our chambers. Many of the horses were up on the crowded deck, and it was no small matter getting around there. In short, it is hard to imagine travelling aboard a worse vessel than a horse ship."[31]

Guðmundur lay down near the forecastle when the ship sailed north along the fjord. He felt depressed as he watched all the farms he knew so well disappear one by one. "That was a painful experience," he said. Stefán was also on the forecastle as the ship cut through the fog running in a brisk southeast wind. It was August 5, 1873.

When the ship reached the open seas, the ocean became rougher and people began to get seasick. Guðbjörg was still quite ill and Guðmundur now became nauseous. Stefán did not go to bed until 5 o'clock in the morning and slept until noon. There was a light breeze and cooler temperatures. The men who were not seasick were busy bringing water to the women and buckets for those who were ill – including Stefán, who was a bit seasick. He stared for a long time into the fog and on the evening of the third day he watched the faint blue contours of Iceland's mountains disappear below the horizon.

While at Akureyri, Guðmundur had gone to see editor Björn and handed him a piece of paper with a poem written by his son, Stefán. It was a last farewell, written on Guðmundur's behalf. The poem appeared in the August 9 issue of *Norðanfari*, the first of Stefán's poems to be published. "The moment passes quickly and we must depart," he writes in the first line, and the passage of time initiates each of the following stanzas. The poem expresses stoic calm and deep, painful sorrow over parting with friends and the homeland.[32]

A few days later, the newspaper *Norðanfari* carried a notification publicizing the sheep mark of Kristján Ingjaldsson of Mýri. It was the same mark that Guðmundur had used. The story of Guðmundur's farming career in Iceland was now at an end and the family was on its way to the New World.

Chapter 4

The Journey West

The Queen

The horse transport ship *Queen* cut through the Atlantic waves, heading southeast to Scotland with 150 Icelandic emigrants, including four aspiring poets. One of them was Helga Steinvör Baldvinsdóttir, a 14-year-old girl. Judging from her farewell poem,[1] she was no less promising a versifier than the young Stefán Guðmundsson. He walked around the ship with a long, thin notebook in his pocket. On the first page he had inscribed the title, "Notes written by Stephen Goodmansson", spelling his name in an anglicized manner, ready to deal with the challenges ahead! Already he had jotted down some useful bits of information on currencies and equivalencies, vocabulary about the sea, a few words in French to use in Quebec City, information on Wisconsin, and a list of the English names for domestic animals. En route, he added other notes, comments, and of course, poetry.[2]

Guðbjörg, Stefán's mother, remained ill, but other members of the family recovered quickly from their seasickness. On the third day, the Faroe Islands were sighted on the far horizon. The next morning, Stefán woke up at four o'clock. The Shetland Islands lay ahead and he noted that the coast was rocky on the west side and the weather was foggy. There was a western wind with showers. The islands were "numerous and very rocky, the landscape barren, with little vegetation and no woods," Stefán wrote. "Many of them are inhabited and I saw a number of stately farms, and on one of them I could see hay cocks on the fields. Only in one place did I see some trees. There were many cows and sheep. Once or twice we had to be guided by pilots. It was hard for them to reach our ship as it was stormy, with strong currents in the straits."[3]

Among those awaiting the Queen *was Helga Steinvör Baldvinsdóttir (right), who posed for this portrait at Akureyri with older sisters Friðrika and Jósefína just prior to departure. Though only 14, she was already an aspiring poet and later became known as* Undína. *She would become a friend and neighbour to Stefán and his wife in Dakota Territory.*

Around nine o'clock in the morning, the *Queen* docked at Lerwick in the Shetland Islands. The passengers disembarked. Stefán went ashore with some friends and was surprised to learn that the inhabitants were of Nordic stock and Lutheran. He found the town pretty, with its cobbled streets, and observed that there were restaurants, shops, and banks. He also noticed that the town was fortified. Beyond the town were beautiful fields where cattle and sheep grazed. There were ships and boats in the harbour – a familiar sight – but the houses were strange. They were built out over the water with rowboats hanging on the gables.

Some 15 of Walker's horses were off loaded here, a few of them dead. Guðmundur observed that the horses that had died were beautiful creatures. He was in a pessimistic mood. "I often wished that all of them would die," he said. "Hay was thrown in to them once every 24 hours, and perhaps some got some nourishment, but it was insufficient and the most docile ones got nothing. They were never given water. It upset me terribly to see them straining their necks whenever water was being carried along the deck, but neither I nor anyone else could alter this situation. The crew did not allow us to interfere; they simply left the horses to struggle until they collapsed and died," all of which increased the stench in the passenger quarters.[4]

At noon on August 9, they arrived at Aberdeen. Everything seemed big. The harbour was man-made and the pier was so large that the ship could dock there. The remaining horses were driven ashore in a manner that both Stefán and his father found cruel. Stefán found the crowd more like a mob than civilized people and his father agreed. "There were crowds of people gathered on either side as the horses came up, including a group of rough youngsters armed with staves and sticks and each horse suffered no fewer than two blows on either flank. When the deck had been emptied of horses, those in the hold were hauled up to the mast, lowered onto the deck, and then driven off the ship where they received the same treatment. Finally, they were all driven behind a large building and that was the last I saw of them."[5]

From Aberdeen the *Queen* sailed to Granton, arriving the next day. Many of the emigrants dreaded customs inspection. "Early in the morning, a man came out to the ship, grey-haired and sly in appearance," Stefán wrote. "He began to interrogate the girls about tobacco and alcohol, but as law-abiding citizens they did not have much of that, so the man did not have much luck."[6] While nosing about as people

Granton Harbour near Edinburgh, Scotland, with cranes, trains, and custom houses. Most Icelandic emigrants passed this way.

wrestled with their luggage, he saw a little lump of tobacco in a trunk, and after examining it carefully he marked the trunk with chalk. The Icelanders were certain that he was either a tax official or a thief, so they erased the mark and moved the trunk. A little later another man came along, stating that he was a Customs Officer and that the other man was his colleague. People were told to carry their luggage off the ship. The women and children went ashore, leaving the men to carry the chests and trunks up the steep gangway. It was not easy as the tide had gone out and the gunwales were much lower than the pier. The inspection began, but was less onerous than many had feared. Nothing was found, so the officers soon left.

From Granton the group travelled by train to Glasgow. Astonished by this experience, both father and son described this great wonder: "That was the first time I saw a steam engine," Guðmundur wrote. "It is no easy task to describe this gigantic monster which kills everything that gets in its way. It glistens beautifully, all made of iron with a funnel poking up from it for the steam. Behind the funnel was another pipe, much narrower, with a string attached. When the string is pulled, the pipe lets out a terrifying hoot that can be heard miles away. Anyone who has not heard it before is scared out of his wits. This hoot means "*look out!*" and if the warning is not heeded, the creature that does not obey is death's prey."[7]

The Icelanders kept together as a group as they were herded onto the train. Guðmundur walked slowly as Guðbjörg was still very ill, and little Sigurlaug was sick too. They stopped for a while in Edinburgh, where they saw Sir Walter Scott's monument, which inspired Stefán to compose a verse expressing the idea that in Iceland the mountains were monuments to the poets. After Edinburgh, the trip was a pleasure. "To speed like lightning past cities, fields, and lovely forests," Stefán wrote, and he added a little verse about the contrast between the plains of Scotland and the now-disappeared mountains of Iceland.[8]

It was dark when the group reached Glasgow and the Icelanders found it safer to stick together on the streets of the big city. The street lamps had been lit and the travellers walked quite a distance in a long procession to the guesthouse where they were to stay. A guide walked in front and another at the rear. Indeed, they were force-marched and that created difficulties for those who were ill or carrying children. "We were followed by an enormous crowd of locals; never before have I seen so many people gathered in one place. There were all sorts of ruffians who made fun of us and generally misbehaved, sometimes trying to break up our ranks, but we showed them our tempers and they backed off," Guðmundur wrote.[9] In the midst of this crowd, Stefán observed, the Icelanders were like drops of water in a ladle. The strange caps worn by the Icelandic women attracted the attention of the urchins, who made fun of them.

The emigrants remained in Glasgow the following day. It turned out that a bill of exchange issued by Tryggvi Gunnarsson to pay the fares of those who intended to continue from Quebec City to the United States was not accepted. Some of those bound for the United States therefore had to pay a second time for that part of the trip. Guðmundur was one of them and had to pay another 18 rix dollars, which he could ill afford. Perhaps his brother-in-law Jón from Mjóidalur helped him out. As a consequence, Guðmundur was more careful than ever in Glasgow: "I did not wander far; there are many traps, treachery, and stealing."[10] Stefán, too, found that the streets of Glasgow were traps for the unwary. He studied the currencies carefully and refrained from exchanging money. Some Icelanders made that error. "Men were cheated grossly here," he wrote. On the other hand, a walk downtown proved interesting. "Saw talking parrots, begging Negroes, donkeys pulling wagons, men fighting in the street, drunken girls, hags selling apples, and so forth. As soon as we came out, boys with brushes and blacking gathered around us and offered to polish our shoes for one "penny". These pests followed us all day and it seemed almost as if they were a kind of weed that sprouted in the streets."[11]

Resurrection from the Manitoban

On August 12, the Icelanders boarded the steamship *Manitoban*, a much more dignified vessel than the *Queen*, with room for over 700 passengers and a crew of more than 70. One Icelander missed the boarding while exchanging money. A banker to whom he explained his problem hired a boat and managed with considerable persuasion to get the crew to take the unlucky Icelander on board. The banker did not accept any payment. "Such men exist in England, even among the riff raff and hooligans," Stefán wrote.[12] Conditions on board ship were tolerable and there was plenty of good food. On the afternoon of August 15, 1873, the passengers spotted Ireland, the last they would see of Europe. Stefán composed a farewell poem to Iceland, outlining images of the landscape and saying that his thoughts would drift there, happy to dwell there a little while although other lands were waiting ahead.[13]

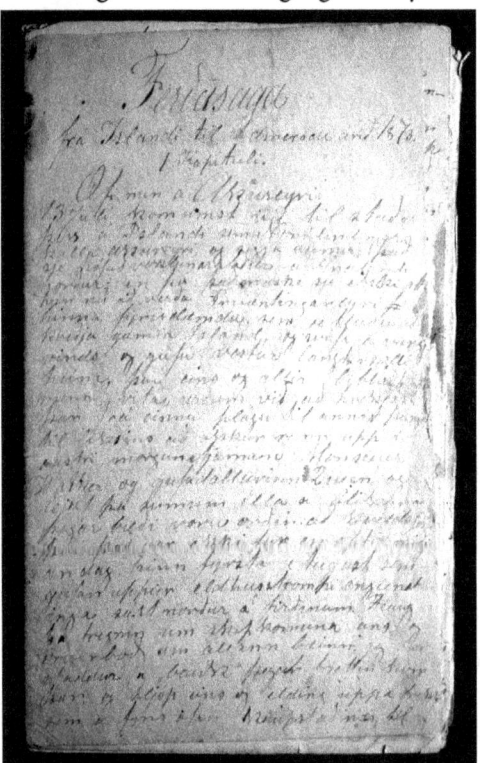

Already an aspiring writer, young Stefán Guðmundsson penned the details of his journey in a notebook under the heading Ferðasaga. *He was both observant and candid.*

The following days were alternately stormy or foggy. On the evening of August 19, Stefán entertained himself by "observing the turbulent sea, running back along the ship in magnificent waves." After retiring, he heard a racket in the next cabin when food containers, in which some Norwegians had hoarded food for the journey ahead, tumbled down onto the heads of the owners. He fell asleep like a child in a cradle.

Earlier that day Stefán had got into a quarrel with a bad-tempered cook. "I approached him with a cup, asking for hot water. When he filled the cup with coffee thick with grounds, I immediately dumped it onto the kitchen floor. The slob then got angry and ordered me to clean it up, but I refused and walked away. He followed and tried to get his hands on me, but could not. I threatened to call the captain." Stefán asked an interpreter for help and the cook also complained. The interpreter told Stefán to clean up the mess, which he flatly refused to do. Eventually he got the hot water. "You are better to steer clear of crew members," he concluded, "they are usually bullies.[14]

On August 21, the ship sailed by some icebergs and Stefán was fascinated to observe how the waves broke against the ice. The following day they saw land. Stefán figured that they must be passing Belle Isle off Newfoundland. "This was the first we saw of America and in fact it was not too attractive as there was a huge iceberg east of Belle Isle, itself rugged and rocky. There was still some snow in the hollows. I saw no signs of habitation except one lighthouse, but there may have been some. Labrador was on our right and Newfoundland on our left."[15] On the night of Sunday, August 24, death took its toll among the Icelanders when a young girl passed away. A sheet was sewn around her body and after the death knell was rung at ten o'clock, people gathered at middeck where the body was carried. A hatch in the gunnel on the side of the ship was then opened and after an American bishop on board read from a book with his hands uplifted, the body was slipped overboard. Stefán wrote a poem about this event.[16] Later in the day he observed an English mass for a while. He found the singing beautiful but lacking in inspiration.

More and more of Canada came into view as they sailed along the Gulf of St. Lawrence. Stefán found the steep, forested slopes on the north side beautiful. He proclaimed August 25, 1873, the day of resurrection of all flesh from the grave of the *Manitoban* when, at seven o'clock, the ship dropped anchor at Quebec City. People got up earlier than usual and had an early breakfast, "quick to swallow the English lumps that were always in the porridge instead of raisins," Stefán wrote sarcastically in his notebook.[17] Then their luggage was taken ashore and transported in wagons into the customs shed, all mixed together with the luggage of the English and the French passengers.

Páll Þorláksson, the son of Þorlákur of Stórutjarnir, had been in Quebec City for five days, peering down the St. Lawrence River in the hope of spotting an immigrant ship full of Icelanders. During the previous winter, he had studied theology at Concordia Seminary in St. Louis, Missouri, where he established contacts with Norwegian farmers and priests and learned about their 30 years' experience as immigrants. He suggested that the Icelandic immigrants should stay with the Norwegians at first, in order to learn farming methods and the ways of the new land, as well as to save some money so they would be able to start their own farms. That arrangement had proven beneficial for the Norwegians, and they responded positively to Páll's request that they receive the Icelandic immigrants. He was expecting 500 Icelanders and had the promise of four Norwegian congregations that they would accept 200 people, some 40 families. On August 12, Páll had received word by cable that 150 Icelanders were setting off from Glasgow so he had hurried to Quebec City. Early on the morning of August 25, a boy reported to Páll's room and told him that the *Manitoban* had arrived. When Páll asked if there were any Scandinavians on board, the boy said there were only Frenchmen. Páll found this odd and hurried down to

The port of Quebec, photographed from Point Levis by Scottish Canadian William Nottman, was the point of arrival for most Icelandic immigrants, including the group of 1873.

the harbour. At first he did not see any Icelanders, so he began calling in Icelandic. He got an immediate reply and soon his tired but happy countrymen, including friends and relatives, gathered around him.[18]

On the Train

The immigrants crowded into large customs sheds where many novelties caught the attention of the Icelandic travellers. Stefán was very impressed by a facility that was "specially for men and another for women, where people could wash off the travel dirt."[19] There were towels hanging on the walls and running water from taps. Some English passengers took off their shirts and washed their whole body. There were many privies too, designated for men and women, with signs indicating which gender was allowed to use which facility.

Páll explained to the crowd on the pier how they would proceed. It turned out that of the 165 Icelanders who had arrived with the *Manitoban* (a woman with 10 children and a maid had joined the group in Glasgow), 115 had decided to go to the Muskoka district in Ontario, Canada. The Canadian government offered free transportation and some of the immigrants could not afford the fare to Wisconsin. Only 50 Icelanders would accompany Páll to the United States. For the first part of the journey, however, both groups were to travel on the same train.

The immigrants then bought their train tickets, marked their luggage, and had something to eat. Stefán, together with some compatriots, went to a liquor store. He bought some cheese and then turned his attention to buying something to drink: "A half mug of what they called brandy, but what we thought was pure alcohol, costs five cents." Stefán bought a few mugfulls from a fellow he found cheerful and friendly, and managed to cheat him by paying twice with the same five cents while they were chatting. The group was then herded onto the train with a great fuss, so Stefán did not even have time to "buy something from the devil who had a sort of restaurant in the middle of the customs hall."

The train was overcrowded, but Stefán was informed that after 50 miles many would get off and that the train travelled "a mile in three minutes." Stefán and another Icelander ventured into a coach where there were only Englishmen, who took exception to the Icelanders. Stefán did not care and sat as long as he wanted, a cocky young man "in the prime of life" – if somewhat "drunk and mindful of the eleventh commandment."[20]

Getting food required some aggressive behaviour and Stefán considered this arrangement uncivilized. Along the railway were houses where a meal was available for 25 cents. A porter went through the train and counted those who wanted to buy a meal and then sent the figures ahead by telegraph so the meals would be ready when the train arrived. People then pushed out of the train and into the restaurant. Everyone had reason to be happy when he was served, "as around here, the Vikings do not obey laws, but each grabs what he can get. When you have just started eating, the money collector comes and shouts into your ear like a raging bull, "25 cents sir!" and then you had better pay, in the hope that you get more on your plate. Once I sat over an empty plate and would have got nothing if an Englishman had not given me a bite, and in the end I never got any tea but had to pay my 25 cents anyway. On another occasion I was given no knife, but then a Danish student loaned me his."[21] Sometimes everything went well and Stefán once got such a fine meal that he had never seen anything like it and did not know how to deal with it. An English girl sitting beside him taught him what to do so he would not embarrass himself.

Later, "aboard an American train speeding like lightning to the Promised Land," Stefán felt even greater than Moses, who only glimpsed the Promised Land in the distance. Sometime after midnight on August 27, 1873, an Icelandic woman gave birth to a boy, Jón, the first Icelander born in the New World. Þorlákur's wife, Lovísa, was a midwife and delivered the baby. The Icelanders collected a few dollars to cover the cost. When the train stopped in Cobourg, Ontario, the couple and their newborn got off to stay for a while. In Toronto, the Icelanders parted ways. Those heading for Muskoka went to the coaches at the front of the train and those bound for Wisconsin sat in the coaches at the rear. The train then split so quickly that they did not even have time to say goodbye. Stefán had many a good friend among those who went to Muskoka. Among those continuing on to Wisconsin were Guðmundur Stefánsson from Mýri and Jón Jónsson from Mjóidalur, together with their families, as well as Jón's brothers Gísli and Benedikt with their wives, Karólína and Sesselja; his sisters Guðfinna, who was unmarried, and Herdís, with her husband Hallgrímur Gíslason; and Hallgrímur's brother Magnús. Þorlákur Gunnar Jónsson from Stórutjarnir and his family also went to Wisconsin.

Stefán was awake most of the following night as he found the next leg of the journey interesting. When the time came to cross the St. Clair

River that forms the border between Canada and the United States, he watched closely as the coaches were unhitched and hauled on board a huge barge that then splashed clumsily across the river. The train was then pulled ashore on the other side, where a customs inspection took place. Those with bed clothes had to pay ten cents each.

The group then continued on, changing trains twice. The second time, they boarded an express train so luxurious that Stefán could hardly describe it, "with upholstered seats and a gilded ceiling!!! I was contemplating all this glory when after all these waking hours I eventually fell into a deep sleep in my seat by the window." [22]

At six or seven A.M. on August 29 Stefán awoke suddenly to a strange mix of stillness and wild confusion. The train had stopped, yet there was complete pandemonium as passengers, some shouting, some praying, rushed to get off the train. It took Stefán a little while to come around, but he then grabbed his hat, shoes, and luggage and rushed to the rear door of the coach. It was crammed with people trying to squeeze through. He therefore turned around and ran forward, but could not get out the forward door either. He began sweating and nearly fainted from the unbearable heat and steam that was so dense he could not even see. In a panic, he threw himself out a coach window, landing on his feet. That

Many of the railway coaches of the day were remarkably stylish, though they tended to become overcrowded and uncomfortable on long journeys.

saved his life, though he was left standing by the tracks with no shoes and no hat, blood on his face and hands. The woollen sock on one of his feet had been singed and he had severe burns on his soles and toes. The surroundings were like a nightmare. Stefán hardly noticed that some people had serious injuries. A few were being rescued from a coach that was all smashed. Someone shouted that the coach was on fire. Páll Þorláksson appeared and ordered everyone to the other side of the train where there were many more people.

What had happened? During the night, a wheel on one of the coaches had broken so the train stopped for repair. Notification of the breakdown had been telegraphed ahead, so everything was assumed to be safe. Many of those who were awake got off the train to stretch their legs. When another train was heard approaching, a man was immediately sent to give a warning signal. He grumbled somewhat and lumbered off very slowly with the result that the approaching train only managed to slow down a little before smashing into the immigrants' train.

Guðmundur had followed the entire course of events: "Guðbjörg just managed to get out before the train smashed into the rear end of our coach and the coach in front. Nothing remained of it except pieces the size of a man's hand on either side of the tracks, and half of the third coach. At the same instant, steam poured into these coaches and immediately began to scorch and burn."[23] Sigurbjörg from Mjóidalur plunged headlong out of the train, scraping herself badly. People were frantically searching for their relatives. Guðmundur saw few of his countrymen except those who left the train when he did. He feared that he would never again see his children or friends alive. After walking along the tracks he soon found Stefán, who was in the woods, in bad shape, bloody and burned, but alive. Guðmundur asked him about his sister, Sigurlaug. Stefán told him that she was nearby, in the trees, safe and sound with some other Icelanders.

Those who were unhurt began throwing suitcases and clothes out the windows. A German woman had been crushed to death with a baby she was nursing. A doctor said that not much could be done except to move the injured into an undamaged coach and continue to the next station, at Muir. When they arrived there, Stefán and a few other Icelanders were taken to a house. A girl came in and asked if anyone spoke English. "No, Madam," Stefán replied, but she nevertheless insisted that he follow her upstairs so he could interpret for a 17-year-old Swedish girl who was seriously injured. Stefán did not know Swedish and could not understand her. Páll Þorláksson understood that she was asking for her father. When the father arrived, the daughter was dying, as were her mother and a ten-year-old sister. A third sister had a broken leg. Stefán was deeply moved by those deaths and the ill-fortune of the father.

After a doctor had bandaged Stefán's wounds and given him a dram of liquor, a young woman nursed him in a motherly fashion. People from the village crowded in, carrying bottles of wine to fortify the injured and making an effort to help in every way possible. The passengers had lost much of their luggage and were received in Muir as if they were lifelong friends. "I did not have a hat like many others," Guðmundur said. "An old English man came to me and pointed at my head and I pointed in the direction of the railway line. He understood where I had lost my hat and told me to come into his house with him. There, he took off his own fine hat and put it on my head."[24] No Icelander died in the accident but several, in addition to Stefán, were injured. The following afternoon, they carried on by train to Grand Haven. Near midnight they took the steamboat *Ironside* across Lake Michigan, arriving in Milwaukee at six o'clock in the morning of August 30, 1873.

In a New World

Milwaukee was a big industrial city serving farming areas that had been settled in the preceding decades by Germans and many other nationalities. A colourful mix of peoples, renowned for its various beers, the city now also became, for some time, a focal point for Icelanders in North America. A few had arrived the year before, and during the summer and fall of 1873 more than 100 joined them, remaining in the city for longer or shorter periods.

Páll Þorláksson, who had become a leader of the Icelanders, approached an attorney as soon as the group arrived in Milwaukee, demanding compensation for losses incurred in the train crash. "We poor wretches had to wait a long while on the steamer while Páll pressed the railway company to assume responsibility for us until we recovered," Stefán wrote.[25] The injured waited a long time, but eventually Páll won his argument and returned with a wagon and a railway clerk. The group was then taken by wagon to the home of Haraldur Þorláksson, Páll's brother, who had just moved into a big house. Most of the newly arrived

Icelanders rested there for a few days, until they were compensated for their injuries and lost property. Stefán received $30 and his father, who waited for him in Milwaukee without work for over a week, $20. Guðmundur was terribly restless and wrote that he had never "seen a place with more temptations. I longed to get out into the country and learn the work methods of the farmers." A doctor, whose first name was Martin, was hired to attend to the injured, but the Icelanders found him inefficient and it was difficult to describe their ailments to him in a foreign language. Stefán wrote in his notebook: "The physician Sir Martin has been here three times, but he has done his duty very badly since we still need medicine."[26] When they eventually received the medicine, however, they found it effective, if slow-working. In his own language, Stefán scorned the doctor in a poem, describing him as fat, like an American pig fed with beans, berries, and herbs from his garden.

On September 6, the couple with the newborn baby arrived from Cobourg, Ontario, and that day Guðmundur received his compensation. Three days later, Páll accompanied 18 Icelanders to the countryside where they were to work for Norwegian farmers. Owing to their injuries, Stefán and another Icelander remained in the city. Guðmundur, Jón from Mjóidalur, and the brothers Hallgrímur and Magnús Gíslason went 80 miles westwards to Stoughton in Dane County, south of the city of Madison. Guðmundur worked for Ole Oftelie, a prosperous farmer who had arrived 25 years earlier when he was 14 years of age.

Stefán remained in Milwaukee for a few more days, absorbing his new surroundings. America was just like he was, young and effervescent, still tied with the Old World by strong bonds, but excited by the seemingly endless possibilities ahead. European settlement of the continent was a gigantic, unstoppable process. Although the country was not yet completely settled, the United States had been through its trials by fire: revolution and the War of Independence against England a century before and a civil war over state rights and slavery in the recent past. The country was now undergoing a 'Reconstruction' that touched all aspects of life. Side by side, progressive ideas of freedom and repressive religious doctrines were evolving and even mixing together into an odd blend. Pioneers and entrepreneurs were looked upon as the economic future of the country, but fundamentalists tried to keep a firm grip on the spirit, and it was not uncommon for the settlers in this new country to adhere to religious ideas that were stricter than those of the Old World. Despite rapid settlement and a burgeoning capitalist market, the economy was in a slump owing to a financial crisis that had begun in New York a year previously. Factories were closed, companies had gone bankrupt, and large projects such as railroad construction had ground to a halt.[27]

Stefán, meanwhile, managed to limp along the streets of Milwaukee, poking about in the shops and dark alleys, or having a pint of beer. It is impossible to know for sure whether it was here that he began acquainting himself with the liberal ideals of Ralph Waldo Emerson, Theodore Parker, and Henry David Thoreau, and the publications of their followers, or whether he later ran across the writings of Walt Whitman, who had captured the turmoil of the times in his poems. Some 18 years had passed since Whitman's *Leaves of Grass* had first appeared, and in the intervening years it had been printed five times, with new poems added to each new edition. "The United States themselves are essentially the greatest poem," Whitman wrote in the beginning of his preface to the first edition, and at the end he stated: "There is no fear of mistake."[28]

The poetry must have surprised Stefán, schooled as he had been in the local, occasional poetry of Sigvaldi the Poet and Gísli Konráðsson and the chilly images of Bjarni Thorarensen, the first Romantic poet in Iceland. Compared to their disciplined verse, this poetry undoubtedly evoked some culture shock. "I celebrate myself, and sing myself,/And what I assume you shall assume,/For every atom belonging to me as good belongs to you." Stefán must have turned the pages in astonishment, reading the poetry with its suspicious lack of rhyme, fascinating licentiousness, strangely long lines, periods, exclamation marks, light kisses and hugs, individualism, and sexuality. This poetry, if it could be called poetry in Icelandic terms, ran like a bearded man in a white shirt and a hat, through open barn doors and out to the field at harvest time, bold yet ambivalent, a happy mother with her firstborn, a travelling salesman with a burden on his back, and a harlot dragging her shawl:[29]

> *I am of old and young, of the foolish, as much as the wise,*
> *Of every hue and caste am I, of every rank and religion,*
> *A farmer, mechanic, artist, gentleman, sailor, Quaker,*
> *Prisoner, fancy-man, rowdy, lawyer, physician, priest.*[30]

Stefán left Milwaukee on September 16, 1873, his head full of new experiences in a New World. He stayed overnight in Stoughton and ar-

Harvest in Dane County, Wisconsin.

rived the following day at the place where his parents were living. Five days later, on September 23, he was hired as a farm labourer. Although young, with strong hands and a willingness to work, he quit after 10 days – without mentioning why. In actual fact he was very willful, and although always ready to work, he did not always accept whatever he was offered.

Not all the Icelanders in Milwaukee were successful. There was little employment and some of them quickly landed in financial trouble. One Icelander died before the end of September, so poor that his countrymen had to pay for the funeral. His widow, Guðrún Grímsdóttir, and her five children left the city and went to de Forest, north of Stoughton, where she worked for Norwegians for a few years. One son, six year old Hjörtur, was a strangely intelligent loner. He was befriended by a teacher, the poet Ella Wheeler, who first became acquainted with the boy when he was playing by a brook with a water wheel that he had made. This family and especially this little boy were to develop a lifelong connection with Stefán.

Life and Death in Stoughton

Thousands of Norwegians had settled on virgin land in Dane County in the 1840s. They farmed and established Lutheran congregations with their inevitable religious feuds. Dane County soon became the most populated and flourishing county in Wisconsin. Grain-growing and dairy-production formed the basis of the local economy, although when the Icelanders arrived there was a slight depression. Most of the Icelanders settled on farms seven miles or less east and northeast of Stoughton, near Utica Post Office. Magnús Gíslason worked for Wetle Fedland, who provided him with an old house and oven, and paid him in raw meat. His brother Hallgrímur did not enjoy the same luxury. He had little work and a poor cottage. He was pessimistic, did not know anyone, did not learn the local ways, and had difficulty asking for anything as he did not speak any other language. Jón from Mjóidalur occupied a house owned by a certain Börtel, but worked for the richest farmer in the area, Jerome Scolen. His monthly salary consisted of bacon and other meat, butter, flour and potatoes – equivalent to $10 or $12. Helga Sigríður, Jón's daughter, went to the Scolens to work as a nanny to their daughter, Kristin.

Guðmundur Stefánsson and his family had a separate house on Ole Oftelie's farm and earned most of their livelihood from him. They lived thriftily in order to avoid debt, as they knew wages would be very low over the winter months. Father and son began working at once, Guðmundur for Ole Oftelie and Stefán here and there. Little Sigurlaug also worked for the Oftelies. They became very fond of her "as she was so efficient at work," Guðmundur wrote proudly in his journal.[31] For her work, she received food and clothing – with new shoes as a bonus. Guðbjörg did not work outside the home, but stayed at home where she soon began reading English books. The Oftelies had no children and Stefán composed a verse about this, indicating that this was due to Mr. Oftelie's parsimony and that Mammon had warned him against having children.

Buildings, livestock, farming, and work methods were all entirely different from what the Icelanders were used to. Here, houses were made of logs or red brick and were much larger and statelier than any in which the Icelanders had ever lived. Some cattle were raised specifically for meat, and dairy cows yielded enormous quantities of milk compared to the production of the small Icelandic cows. Most of the sheep were without horns, with short, tight, curly wool, and long tails, very unlike Icelandic sheep. The horses were enormous compared to Icelandic horses, and Icelanders had at best only heard about grain growing – most having rarely seen a plough slice through the sod.

Guðmundur was impressed by the great progress and the order he observed in everything. Farm work, however, was more difficult than he had imagined. Early one morning he went to a neighbouring farm to help thresh. "That is hard work," he wrote. "Ten horses work with the machine, in twos side by side, evenly spaced around a pillar on which one man stands in the centre and drives the horses. The design is such that they run round the pillar without needing to be steered. The machine spews out the stalks so quickly that three men can hardly keep up with collecting the straw from it. The grain comes out equally quickly but from another opening. There are 12 men altogether working at the threshing. This is done on each farmer's land in turn and they all work together. After two days at this work my armpit swelled up and became infected. A lot of blood and puss came out and I was not able to work for a month."[32] It was Guðmundur's impression that the Norwegian farmers worked harder and did more difficult work than he had known in Iceland, because of the farm machinery "which one cannot do without and they drive one on. I do not think I will ever get used to working here, least of all in the summer heat and quite wish I was back home again," Guðmundur wrote in a letter to his sister Helga from Mýri.[33] Before he completed this letter to her, however, he learned that she had died in childbirth on August 10, 1873.

Autumn and winter followed in succession, with the Icelanders still coming to grips with unfamiliar ways: ploughing the land, working in lumber camps, and tending foreign livestock. Jón from Mjóidalur now had enough means to begin making some purchases, so he bought some household utensils and traded a calf for a few sheep at an auction. Everyone had something to do, even the youngsters, who included Stefán's 13 year old sister, Sigurlaug, called Lauga; Helga Sigríður from Mjóidalur, who was 14 years of age; Jón Jr. from Mjóidalur, 12 years old; and Jónatan, Hallgrímur Gíslason's son, also 12. Meanwhile, the short and slender 20 year old young man whose intelligence had attracted attention in his home parish in Iceland, walked from farm to farm looking for work. He was ambitious, and having learned passable Norwegian and English he was learning to find his way in a foreign land, detecting changes in the weather, understanding a different society, and reading the poems that Whitman had written about America. Stefán wrote stanzas boiling with youthful energy:

> *Let no ties bind you,*
> *Swiftly explore the universe.*
> *My young spirit, swing*
> *Through the entire world.*[34]

He always took his notebook wherever he went, writing down all sorts of details. He recorded the names of the farmers he worked for and how many days he put in. He also penned scornful verses about them, for he found some of them sanctimonious, overly concerned about alcohol and about money to the point of being penny-pinching. He compiled a glossary of terms relating to livestock and farm work, and as a true Icelander he jotted down descriptions of the weather during the first few months, as he tried to figure out the different climatic conditions in Wisconsin. In September and the first half of October, he noted, the days were as warm as the hottest summer days in Iceland. It got colder in the second half of October, with frost at night so it was chilly in the morning. It began snowing on October 27 and Stefán remarked that the "natives" considered this an early start to winter. During this first year in the western world, Stefán roamed across low hills, along winding rivers, through colourful autumn forests, across covered bridges, by riverside mills, along straight roads past black fields and grey hayfields, and past stately farms with neat driveways and red barns – so different from the lowly sod huts of Skagafjörður and Bárðardalur. Having discovered a lack of hospitality among people who generally disliked "tramps" and set their dogs on them, Stefán wrote a verse describing how he would cheerfully rush onward although dogs were barking at him.[35]

On New Year's Eve of 1874, the Icelanders near Stoughton met, no doubt with mixed feelings, missing the old ways but determined to tackle the challenges of a new reality. Stefán read a new patriotic poem with images from Icelandic nature – frost and snow, volcanic eruptions, and beautiful summer nights. The main theme is one of encouragement, the desire to break ties, to fight for victory, and to be a worthy son of the old country.[36]

There was little work on farms during the first months of 1874, but perhaps Stefán found employment at a stone quarry or tile factory. In March and April the Norwegian farmers hired the Icelanders to harrow and seed the fields, jobs that were new to them. Nevertheless, they were more successful in Dane County than elsewhere. Presumably Páll Þorláksson collected some money from the Norwegians to help needy Icelanders in Milwaukee.

During the winter, Stefán had written some melodramatic poems on various subjects, even a patriotic poem in Danish, perhaps to show fellow Scandinavians that nothing was impossible for an Icelandic immigrant with a poetic gift. He also wrote tender letters in verse to friends and relatives in Iceland, asking them to convey his greetings to the mountains, the waterfalls, and the beautiful girls. The name 'S. Jónsdóttir', perhaps *Sigríður Jónsdóttir*, appears as the title of one of these poems.[37] "Parting" (Skilnaður) is the title of another poem in Stefán's notebook. It begins with greetings to a girl whose reply is carried on the winds and whose spirit is born "by flying wings of light beams" to a friend "on a distant shore." The imagery is a tapestry of celestial bodies, light beams, time, and dream visions, as if the poem is an attempt to bridge the distance to this girl back home.[38] When summer came, Stefán composed verses about rain showers and morning beauty.

> *Short interval between showers,*
> *The clouds are spewing water.*
> *Now I think it must be wet*
> *To live in heaven itself.*
>
> *Glowing warm morning beams*
> *Make the eastern skies golden.*
> *In those fires, the flourishing green*
> *Tops of the oak trees are flaming.*[39]

Stefán drifted through small towns and villages such as Stoughton, where there were wagon and harness workshops, tailor and tobacco shops, stores and bars. He explored the entertainment available in the area and composed comic verses about it, for instance about the druggist Frank in Stoughton, who sold booze that he kept in the basement. In this poem Stefán wishes he were a mouse in Frank's beer cellar.[40] In another poem, written in the traditional style of Icelandic *rímur*, he describes a visit to a pub one night in Stoughton, together with an older Icelandic friend, Þorgrímur Laxdal from Akureyri, who was quite drunk. When a Norwegian assaulted the pub owner during an argument, Laxdal felt compelled to take on the Norwegian, who according to Stefán's poem then fled the scene. When Laxdal asked for a reward for this great deed, however, the owner refused, so Laxdal drank a lot on credit that evening. Stefán doubted that he ever paid.[41] Laxdal had a checkered reputation, and once Stefán and his father heard some Icelandic theology students expressing their indignation that Laxdal had been asked to read the Sunday sermon. They thought he was an inappropriate choice, although he was a very good reader. Guðmundur found the hypocrisy a bit too much and commented, "Well, maybe this could be better, but the Scriptures do say, 'In the seats of the prophets are the learned and the Pharisees. Listen to their teachings but do not act like them.'" The young moralists were so shocked that they fell silent.[42]

June of 1874 brought high temperatures just as haying was to begin. The Icelanders, accustomed to cool summers, could hardly endure the unbearable heat as they shovelled manure, dug wells, and worked in the fields. Some of the Norwegian farmers were very demanding task masters, and combined with the heat, humidity, and unfamiliar work, this resulted in some immigrants falling ill. Hallgrímur Gíslason was one of those who suffered from poor health, and on August 3 Pétur Thorlacius died after nine days with a stomach ailment. Many Norwegians attended the funeral. They were helpful and charged nothing for medical aid and funeral costs. Stefán wrote a compassionate commemorative poem describing the exhaustion and the relentless heat, and portraying death as a soothing coolness.[43]

The Icelanders often went to Madison, where they met Rasmus B. Anderson, a young Norwegian who was on a crusade to have the Nordic languages taught at the university in Madison. He had nearly finished his book *America not Discovered by Columbus*, in which he argued that Leifur Eiríksson had discovered America, and he was studying Old Norse, assisted by Icelanders such as Páll Þorláksson and Jón Bjarnason, a young Lutheran minister who had immigrated to Milwaukee in the autumn of 1873. Bjarnason stayed in Decorah, Iowa, that winter, among Norwegian theologians. He was astonished by their old-fashioned, fundamentalist views and expressed surprise that Páll Þorláksson was sympathetic. He felt that Páll even seemed to believe that the sun circled the earth.

On July 4, Stefán went to Madison for the 1874 celebrations. While he was there, Anderson gave him two textbooks he had read in school some years earlier, one on rhetoric and literature, the other on grammar. It was important for Stefán to meet with liberal intellectuals in the New World, and possibly they discussed the idea of Stefán attending school, for at least once after he emigrated he had the opportunity to study.[44] Stefán, however, felt that he could not leave his old and tired parents on their own. He read the books he got from Anderson, wrote comments in the margins, and translated some stanzas.[45]

The Icelanders in Milwaukee celebrated the millennium of the settlement of Iceland. Stefán could not go, but this was the beginning of an Icelandic society in the New World. Ideas of establishing an Icelandic colony were now beginning to develop.

Chapter 5

Shawano County

The Icelandic Settlement

Shortly before the celebrations in Milwaukee in July of 1874, several Icelanders in Dane County urged Páll Þorláksson to search out land where they could settle and form a colony. They did not quite agree, however, on all the details. Ever since Páll had left Iceland and begun studying theology in St. Louis in the fall of 1872, he had reflected on potential immigration, and he had concluded that it would be best for Icelanders to learn from the Norwegians, who were already established. Although many Icelanders feared this would mean that they would lose their language and disappear as an ethnic group, Páll did not share these concerns. He believed that Icelanders in America could "preserve their language with ease if they had their own newspapers, teachers, and ministers, as the Norwegians did, and if they subscribed to papers from their native land" and thereby continued writing in their mother tongue.[1] Páll's vision of the future was of an Icelandic colony where the Icelanders could succeed in the New World while at the same time maintaining their language and culture.

Since employment was hard to get, Páll's father, Þorlákur Gunnar Jónsson, had little success finding work and had spent the preceding winter in Milwaukee. Like many of his compatriots, he wanted to farm and went scouting for land together with Páll and Haraldur. In Iceland he had been a district administrative officer, and in many ways he was more sophisticated than most Icelandic farmers. He and his sons therefore became the leaders of a little group of Icelanders who wanted to take up farming in Wisconsin. Unsettled land was scarce in that state by then, however, so they went all the way north to Shawano County before finding land they liked.

The vision of a pioneer homestead in the new land.

Shawano was a young county and still heavily forested. The first pioneer of European stock had settled there in 1843 as loggers began moving in for the timber industry. Ten years later, there were more than 250 Caucasian inhabitants, enough to form a separate county, and by 1870 the population was over 3000.

According to Páll, the name *Shawano* meant "Bright Lake" in the native language, an exact parallel to the name *Ljósavatn* in their home district in Iceland. As it turns out, he was not correct, as in Menominee and Chippewa *Shawano* means "The Lake in the South". The hamlet of Shawano was located on the east bank of the Wolf River, at the lower end of Shawano Lake. Incorporated as a village in 1871 and as a city in 1874, it boasted guesthouses, blacksmith shops, various stores, and saloons, and new civic regulations were being enacted. For example, the firing of guns was not allowed on Sundays, pigs were forbidden from running loose, and liquor sales required a license. Half a dozen spittoons were purchased for the council room.[2]

As the timber trade expanded northward along the Wolf River, settlement followed, and some 10,000 acres of land had been cleared to the northeast of Shawano Lake by the time Þorlákur and his sons arrived and began exploring an area devastated by a forest fire. Supported by two local Lutheran pastors, Reverend Homme, a Norwegian, and Reverend Dicke, a German who had been involved in building most Lutheran churches in the area, Páll met with the County Board in August. The Board decided that Icelanders could each purchase up to 80 acres of county-owned land for half the regular price. Down payment was 10%, due when the land was settled, and the remainder could be paid off in 10 years with 7% interest. The going price for land was about one dollar per acre. The County Board also decided that the sandy area north of the lake and all sandy land owned by the county could be given to the Icelanders as sheep pasture since they had heard that Icelanders were exceptionally good sheep farmers. This land was seven to nine miles east of Shawano, on the east bank of the Oconto River.

As soon as the Icelanders in Dane County received this news, many began packing, including Jón Jónsson, Guðmundur Stefánsson, and the brothers Hallgrímur and Magnús Gíslason. Together with their families, these settlers said farewell to their Norwegian benefactors and gathered at the railway station in Stoughton on Monday, September 14, 1874. Travelling by train was no longer a novelty, so Stefán had time to read on the way, perhaps the textbook given to him by Anderson or the works of Longfellow, John Greenleaf Whittier, Oliver Wendell Holmes, and other American poets. The landscape did not change much as they passed through forests, fields, and marshlands, and crossed wide, slow rivers. Further north there were more hills. The final leg of the journey, from New London or Clintonville to Shawano, was made by stagecoach. This was a pioneer area and the railway had not reached the village. For a family of four, the trip cost $40.

The Icelanders proceeded straight to the

Þorlákur Gunnar Jónsson from Stórutjarnir and his wife, Henrietta Lovísa Níelsson, were the parents of the large Þorláksson family that settled in Shawano County – including Reverend Páll Þorláksson.

new settlement site and found accommodations with those already living in the area. Þorlákur Jónsson and his family came directly from Milwaukee, as did Gísli Jónsson from Mjóidalur and his wife, Karólína. On Monday, September 14, 1874, Stefán and a few others made the trip to Shawano to purchase the land that Páll had secured. Stefán was the spokesman, as he was by now quite fluent in English. Each settler was entitled to 80 acres, and Stefán and his father shared land costing $54.67, the down payment being $8.90. Jón Jónsson paid only $39 for his land. By the following spring, the market value of land had risen from $2 to $10 per acre.

After concluding the transaction, the little group walked back east along the lake and across the Oconto River to Pulcifer, a tiny village that became their postal address. Stefán sometimes called it *Lucifer*. From there they headed three miles north across forested hills and flats, then stopped northeast of a large bend in the river. Landmarks were of little use, however, as they had to find "Lot 1 of Section 25, Township 28 north, Range 17 east of the fourth meridian."[3] This unfamiliar language meant that they had to come to terms with the land survey system. "Like a chess board, such was the organization/of the cleared, densely populated region," he wrote later in a poem describing a settled area, adding that half of the lines headed for noon, the other half for late afternoon in the main cardinal directions. "Each farmer's property [was] at the beaten track/in fenced rectangular squares,"[4] he wrote, as surveying made artificial borders that did not conform to the contours of the land as in Iceland. Quarter-miles and straight survey lines replaced hills and ravines as markers.

Once the Icelanders found the survey posts, they explored their new properties. The land was mostly forested with spruce, oak, and other deciduous trees. The women and children explored the woods and picked many kinds of edible berries. The soil was loamy, rich with minerals, reddish on top of the hills and sandy in the hollows. In all likelihood Stefán and Guðmundur chose a little hill facing south as the site for the log cabin. All Stefán owned was an axe, a shovel, and $.75 in his pocket. The settlers now began felling trees to build cabins, except Hallgrímur Gíslason who was ill and unable to work for some months, and Jón Jónsson, who temporarily moved into a lumberjack's cabin half a mile from his land. Most of the 10 men in this tiny settlement also planned to work in the nearby lumber camps.

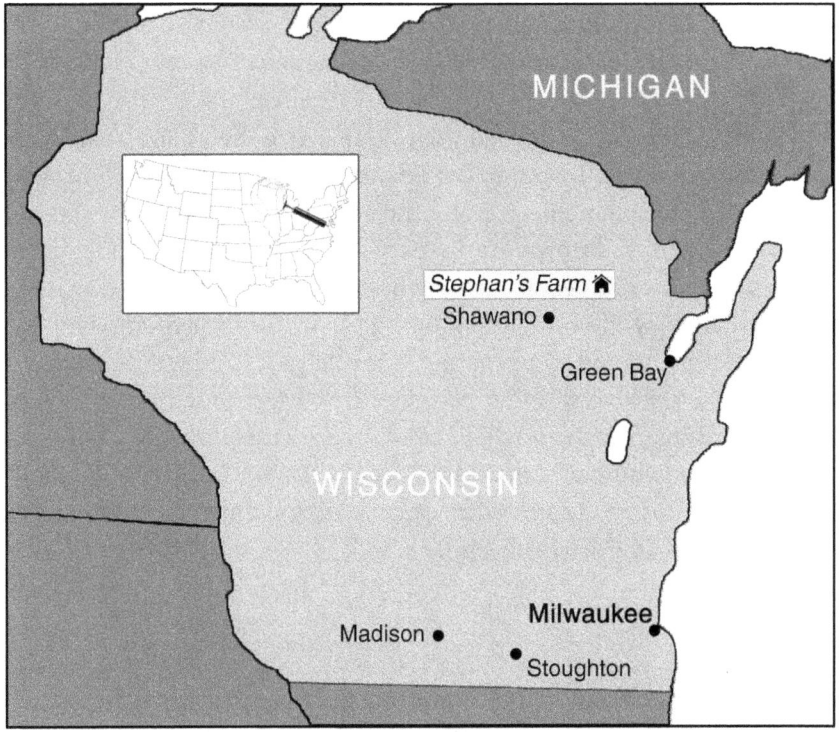

The Wisconsin Years: 1873-1880

Two subsequent trips to Shawano were necessary, the first on October 9, 1874, to sign a contract for the land. Stefán, in accordance with common practice in the new land, adopted his father's surname and signed "Stefen G. Stefensen". A second trip was made on October 26, to swear a declaration that they intended to become citizens of the United States and to renounce "forever all allegiance and fidelity to any foreign Prince, Potentate, State or Sovereignty whatever, and particularly to Kristian, King of Denmark."[5] Those who did so were Þorlákur and his son Jón, the Mjóidalur brothers Jón and Gísli Jónsson, and Guðmundur Stefánsson. Stefán's name was not recorded. Perhaps it was sufficient that Guðmundur took this oath on behalf of the family.

Several Icelanders now went on a scouting expedition, spending a night under the stars. Perhaps that was the occasion when Stefán composed this stanza about Magnús Gíslason, who had a wife called Sigga:

Magnús opens his eyes wide,
He cannot fall asleep,

> *At home, on top of his Sigga,*
> *He would no doubt sleep better.*[6]

A mild November allowed them to improve their cabins and fashion some furniture. Jón from Mjóidalur walked 20 miles to purchase six sheep, one for slaughtering and the others to establish a flock. When not working on their own lands, most of the Icelanders took employment as labourers to earn cash for basic needs. Stefán found work in lumber camps while Jón and Guðmundur worked for themselves and as contractors in road construction. Snow fell and cold winds blew over a Christmas celebrated under poor circumstances in scattered, temporary log cabins. The settlers had cause to celebrate, however, as Reverend Homme, who had helped Páll deal with the County Board, took the initiative to send food – a few pounds of flour, meat, and bacon – to the Icelanders as a Christmas gift.

The Little Colony

Now the Icelanders in Shawano County had to earn a living and organize their little society. During their short training period among the Norwegians, they had learned to build log cabins, clear and cultivate land, and understand an alien government and social institutions. Páll Þorláksson dreamed of a large colony of the descendants of Leifur Eiríksson and even considered the option of getting financial support from the State of Wisconsin.[7]

When frost and snow set in at the end of November, 1874, Stefán and other Icelanders found work in lumber camps, probably those along the Oconto River. They needed cash for food, tools, house utensils, and livestock, and Guðmundur still owed Jón from Mjóidalur $100. The Icelandic lumberjacks stuck together in the camps and gave the Americans nicknames, and Stefán made derogatory verses behind their backs. A beginners's salary was between $16 and $26 a month, with full board. More experienced workers could earn between $35 and $50 and rivermen got double that amount for floating the logs down the rivers in the spring.

By January of 1875 it was very cold and the snow reached the waist of a grown man. In poems that Stefán sent back to Iceland from the lumber camp, he dreamed of summer days back home. On January 24, he wrote a grotesque poem, seemingly about his friend Gísli from Mjóidalur. A sleeper in bed is likened to a newly-buried corpse in a grave under a deep blanket of snow in the dead calm of a silent wood. Allusions to food, beans, and lamb belly, are both American and Icelandic, and the poet speculates that Gísli has eaten too many beans. He dreams of a luscious and desirable girl, but wakes up on his knees on the floor with a bruised face, only to discover that he has fallen out of bed after having wet himself.[8]

Axes resounded throughout the little colony as the settlers cleared future grain fields. After felling and trimming the trees, they dragged the logs down to the river and then tried to burn the branches and roots. As winter passed, they worked more on their land and houses. Collectively, they purchased two draught oxen. Some settlers were more ambitious. Þorlákur Gunnar Jónsson and Magnús Gíslason bought some prairie land for haying, grazing sheep, and even growing grain.

With visions of a new future in America, Gísli Jónsson from Mjóidalur and his wife, Karólína, adopted the surname Dalmann. On April 8, however, their dreams were shattered when they lost their year-old daughter. No longer happy with their lot in Shawano, they found temporary jobs in Green Bay, then returned to Milwaukee where Karólína worked as a seamstress and Gísli as a labourer. He was having difficulties learning English and was both unhappy and homesick.

Early in April of 1875, Jón Jónsson from Mjóidalur moved into a house he had built, before the floor and ceiling were finished. It was cold and uncomfortable and there was not much left of their supplies. By the end of April, they survived by tapping maple trees and boiling the sap into syrup. The Icelanders now each had almost two acres of cleared land ready to break and seed, but when they began sowing the oats and wheat, birds ate the kernels. In May the settlers planted potatoes, corn, and beans. Stefán, who returned from the lumber camps in spring, worked the fields with his father and purchased some livestock. Over the following weeks they had to contend with worms and bad weather, but in July they proudly ate the first products of their own cultivation in the New World – potatoes. These would remain a staple of their diet for some time.

Helga Sigríður from Mjóidalur, now 15 years old, had employment as a housemaid for Mr. Linse. In June, she invested some of her earn-

Reverend Páll Þorláksson graduated in 1875 from the Lutheran seminary in St. Louis, Missouri, and became pastor of the little Icelandic Settlement in Shawano County.

ings in a white cow, in partnership with her father and Hallgrímur Gíslason. The milk was valuable as there was little food in the colony. Nature helped provide for the settlers, however, as by July they could pick raspberries and other berries in the woods.

Late in the summer, Stefán left home to work with a harvest crew. The others stayed home, digging root cellars, laying floors in the houses, and building stables for the increasing number of livestock. Sheep farming was difficult as livestock sometimes disappeared in the forests where there were bears and wolves. In August the diet of the settlers consisted mainly of potatoes, milk, and bread. The grain harvest was meagre, but potato and turnip crops were more successful, and this time they had some animals for slaughtering.

There was also progress in the spiritual realm. Icelandic country folk were accustomed to the spiritual leadership of a Lutheran pastor and the church was practically the only social institution they could bring with them across the ocean. Churches thus soon became the social as well as the spiritual centres of Icelandic settlements in the New World. At the same time, they were a venue for power conflicts.

Páll Þorláksson, having now completed his theological studies at a German Seminary in St. Louis, was ordained by the president of the Norwegian Synod on July 8, 1875. In August, supported by Reverend Homme, he became the minister of four congregations in the counties of Shawano and Oconto. In addition, he established a small Lutheran congregation in the Icelandic settlement, the first Icelandic congregation in the New World, comprising 35 souls.[9]

The colony was not as big as Reverend Páll had envisioned. During the first winter there were only seven homes, mostly those of relatives of Þorlákur Gunnar Jónsson and Jón Jónsson from Mjóidalur. Several single young men were also attached to the colony, among them the cheerful Kristinn Kristinsson, Eiríkur Hjálmarsson, who adopted the surname Bergmann, and his cousin, Friðrik Bergmann, who had studied together with Stefán back in Bárðardalur in the spring of 1873. Friðrik was now studying theology under Páll's guidance, together with Páll's younger brother Níels Steingrímur. Then there was Loftur Jónasson, a carpenter who built good houses for some of the settlers. People came and went, and in 1877 Guðrún Grímsdóttir, the widow of Þórður Árnason (who had died in Milwaukee the first fall), arrived in the settlement with her sons Grímur and Hjörtur and a daughter, Inga. Stefán's friends from the voyage to America found work in various other places, and in a verse-letter to one of them Stefán reveals a cheerful young man working hard at the plough and longing for sunnier pastures, handsome clothes, girls to dance with, and beer and rum to drink.[10]

Lumberjacks

In the fall of 1875 Stefán sowed winter rye and wheat and worked on his house while waiting for winter employment. Soon the lumber crews arrived from Oconto, pulling stoves and supplies on sleighs, setting up camps, and hiring settlers. Lumbering was a huge industry in Shawano and Oconto and Stefán now had some experience in this line of work. This time, he

This tintype has long been regarded an image of the poet and his future brother-in-law, Jón, during their days as lumberjacks in Wisconsin.

A logging camp on the Wolf River in Wisconsin.

and a few other Icelanders went further afield, 50 miles north along the Wolf River.

Life in the lumber camps was rough, comparable to the fishing camps back in Iceland. Logging demanded special skills, tools, and language. In the fall, timber scouts came and selected areas to be harvested and locations for the camps from where it would be easy to haul the logs down to the river. There could be hundreds of men in a camp, but in the smaller ones most of the men lived under one roof. Two axe-men felled a tree, a swamper topped and limbed the tree, and a hauler with an ox team dragged the logs to the road where huge loads were put on sleighs and hauled to the river. When the ice melted, the rivermen used long handspikes and cant-hooks to dislodge log jams and keep the timber moving down the rivers. There was a heroic aura about the lumberjack trade, and sometimes the men drank heavily when visiting the nearest villages and towns.

There were more than 100 lumber camps along the Wolf River and its tributaries, from Oshkosh and to the north of Shawano. Regular stagecoach routes were organized, but there was always the danger of armed robbery. No doubt Stefán walked north to the camp. When he got there, a few shanties of rough lumber came into view: a kitchen and mess hall, bunkhouses, a stable, and a storehouse. The bunkhouses were not too cramped, but two men shared each rough lumber bunk bed. The buildings were heated with wood burning stoves, and after the evening meal the men sat by the fire, talked, played cards, and rested. No doubt Stefán had books to read. Wet clothes were hung to dry by the fire. The food was satisfactory: beef, beans, potatoes, and vegetables.

When Stefán arrived at the camp, there were four or five other Icelanders and about 60 men overall. One of the Icelanders said he was glad Stefán was there. When Stefán asked why, his countryman replied that the language the lumberjacks used about Icelanders was such that they would have to speak up for themselves. The least insulting invective was that they were Lapplanders. Stefán found this incredible but soon discovered that it was no lie, although the men were otherwise rather harmless and even accommodating toward the Icelanders. It did not help matters that one of the Icelanders, armed with the word of God and strict morals, was too pious for this company and often quarrelled with the other workers. Every time he was challenged, he was lost for words, and when he just shook his head and walked away, this further provoked the others. The most foul-mouthed among the lumberjacks was a man named Jack Castelo. Eventually he directed his abuse at Stefán, who replied in like manner. The insults escalated and dragged on, but Stefán did not give in, knowing that words alone could do him no harm – though he added that such language is not worthy of repetition among decent people. The next day, Jack Castelo hurled abuse at another Icelander who was some distance away, but it was Stefán who replied. "Who is answering me?" Jack shouted, asking if it was Stefán. When this was confirmed for him, he concluded, "Well then I will shut up! You are being corrupted more every day." With that the dispute ended and the abusive language tapered off. In fact, Stefán and Jack became good friends and Jack accommodated Stefán in every way after that.[11] Stefán later wrote of his experiences during the winter of 1876:

> *Although the rough quarrels*
> *Increase my disgust and desires of mind,*
> *I fight among rogues*
> *In the mud pools of life.*[12]

Among the Icelanders in the camp were two aspiring Lutheran ministers, Friðrik Bergmann and Níels Steingrímur Þorláksson. Although they were much more learned than he was, Stefán nevertheless often debated with them about everything except religion. Usually they combined forces against him. Then, just as he had once successfully argued with the hired girl on the way to church back in Iceland, Stefán impulsively plunged head first into religious waters. Friðrik and Níels had begun praising the Book of Revelations. Stefán remained silent until they asked for his opinion. "Oh, don't be making so much of the Book of Revelations, boys. It is no holy prophecy, just something written about the author's own times," Stefán replied, comparing it to Benedikt Gröndal's *Gandreið*, a famous satirical play in Iceland. He said this spontaneously, but shocked them completely. They fell silent, but as soon as they could they reported Stefán's comment to Reverend Páll.[13]

Stefán made a short trip home during the winter, accompanied by some German neighbours who were in the same camp. They walked south along the road, then turned eastward to take a shortcut through the forest north of Lake Shawano. None of them knew the way, but the weather was good at first. Then a heavy snowstorm hit and they lost all sense of direction. Stefán felt sure he knew which way to go, but the others did not agree. The cold intensified and they were slightly wet and not well dressed for these conditions. Suddenly they came upon the ruins of a cabin, where they decided to take shelter for a while to see if the weather would clear. The Germans were getting cold and said they would all die if they could not reach civilization soon.

While Stefán realized that they were right, he was nevertheless lost in contemplation about the man who had begun to build this cabin a long time ago. He had obviously not completed it, as there had never been a roof. Perhaps this had been intended as a hunter's cabin with canvas or animal hides for a roof, or maybe it was the cabin of a hermit. While Stefán was musing on the builder, the weather began to clear. He recognised the Pleiades and saw which way was east, which he pointed out to his companions. The Germans had never seen the Pleiades in their homeland and doubted the word of the young Icelander, but they nevertheless followed him and all got home safely. The long ago hut-builder continued to haunt Stefán for many years, and with him in mind he later composed the poem "Ætlanir" (Intentions), which in the first version was entitled "Píónerinn" (The Pioneer).[14]

When Stefán attended a service that spring, probably on the Monday after Whitsun, Páll preached on the infallibility of the Scriptures and the dangers of comparing the Book of Revelations to Gröndal's *Gandreið*. Stefán almost burst out laughing, but managed to restrain himself and even took communion. Páll remained as friendly to him as before and never directly mentioned this incident, but Stefán remained firm in his opinion that the Book of Revelations was merely a reflection of the author's times.[15]

Curly

In the spring of 1876 Stefán left the lumber camp to work in the fields beside his father, ploughing, harrowing, and then sowing in the spring rain. They even tried growing a little tobacco. One evening Stefán wrote a few stanzas, "Vorvísur" (Spring verses), to a cousin in Iceland, reporting on the debauched life of migrant workers, their philandering and drinking until the summer heat was such that they could not even kiss.[16]

When the temperature cooled with the approach of autumn, Stefán worked with a harvest crew nearly 100 miles south of Shawano, near Winnecona and Winchester, not far from Oshkosh where the timber from Wolf River was milled. Travelling by train was expensive, so he preferred to walk. He stuck to settled areas, often

This early photograph of an unidentified Icelandic child is evocative of the poet's relationship with the little girl he called "Curly".

sleeping outside as it was difficult to find lodging. People were afraid of tramps, as they often did some harm. "The region resembles the wild west," Stefán wrote in a poem much later, and he found limited hospitality. He was free to walk along the road, but if he approached any farm he had to reach for his pouch, "Because if you set one foot on the good farmer's ground,/you'll have to pay. We are still/generous regarding streets and political freedom/but God be praised, we are also toll collectors," he wrote.[17]

The districts in the south were prosperous and well established. The dark red barns towered, rather like the lava crags back home. The stately farm buildings and well-cultivated fields contrasted with the rough log cabins and the tiny, newly-cleared fields of the settlers of Shawano County. Stefán sometimes risked stepping through these farm gates to take in a beautiful sight:

> *But if you lift the garden gate*
> *On the driveway to the farm*
> *Then opens the row of beautiful trees like knights*
> *Straight to the farmyard.*
> *The winders crawling up to the overhangs*
> *Up by the front door, a difficult route,*
> *And twigs of grapevine stretch against the sunlight*
> *And wind around windows and balconies.*

Fields and meadows also flourished:

> *But then came spring-grown cornfields*
> *In meadows stripped by the plough,*
> *Like long rows of tongues upwards*
> *The leafy corn was stretching*
> *But the meadow was mostly dark. It acquired*
> *A hue of blue-red buds of clover.*
> *Each clover that opened to the summer sun,*
> *Was a treasure for flying bees.*

Stefán took odd jobs on some farms along the way and earned 50 cents or a dollar for a day's work. Monthly wages were $18, with long working hours from dawn to dusk. On one of the farms where Stefán worked for many weeks, his employers had a little girl who had curly hair and was thus called 'Curly'. She was one of the most beautiful children Stefán had ever seen. Although he was rather aloof, the little girl grew so fond of him that everybody noticed. She followed him wherever he went and stayed with him at every opportunity. This amused her parents because they also liked Stefán. "Of course I grew fond of the kid," he said. Much later, he composed a sensitive depiction of their relationship:

Every morning – I remember – I became your lackey,
At noon your playmate.
Every war and every victory, every conciliation and every pause
Was our joint ownership and kingdom.
In domestic battles, revolt against you,
I bravely carried your flag.

Each evening, when the sea of flaming hot air currents
Was calmly heating the ground,
As if the evening had put the burning sunbeam to sleep
In the black night bosom of earth,
You settled our worlds all around the sun
And all the star-spangled, blue heavens –
You were sitting on my knee, until your blonde, curly
Head fell by the mountains of dreams.

Stefán stayed on this farm until winter when "the low flying December sun/crept along the surface of earth" and frost covered the fields. Dead cornstalks rustled in the wind as Stefán prepared for his trip north to Shawano. He dreaded leaving little Curly, so he got up early, before daybreak, in the hope that she would still be asleep when he left. "You must say goodbye to your little Curly, Stefán," her mother said. "But she is asleep and I do not want to wake her," he replied. That was not so, however, as Curly had got up long before and was waiting for her reserved but warm friend to say farewell to her. He said goodbye as curtly as he could, then set off on foot, clenching his teeth so much that his jaw muscles ached. He looked back once and saw a face in a window:

You were standing in the window, my dear Curly!
Watching me while I disappeared.
You were there, a lonely summer flower,
Alone, unchanged with your six years.
That cold, bright autumn morning, we parted,
You were sad, I was calm and of few words,
Trying to reduce the pain of parting
With a hanging hand in a handshake I did not like.

The pretty face in the window followed Stefán ever afterwards, especially when the "December sun was lowering its flight." The poem "Curly" was perhaps the most beautiful portrait of Wisconsin in the 1870s.

Farming, Sex, and Marriage

While Stefán worked away from home, his parents struggled alongside the other settlers. In March of 1876, his parents began making syrup. Spring was also the time to clear land so they could grow more grain and vegetables. Each settler added one or two cleared acres each year. They had varying success at growing grain since the chickens sometimes ate the seed. Each year they tried different crops – rye, beans, turnips, rapeseed, potatoes, and a little tobacco. As summer wore on, haying and harvesting claimed the days. The number of livestock grew, winter provisions became more plentiful, and life generally improved. Guðmundur reduced his debt to Jón Jónsson to $97 in the New Year of 1876. The women adjusted to the new way of life, learning how to make syrup

During his time as an instructor at the seminary in Decorah, Iowa, Reverend Jón Bjarnason developed a dislike for the extremely conservative religious views that his friend and colleague Páll Þorláksson embraced.

and soap and process the curly wool of the American sheep. They knitted some clothing that Jón from Mjóidalur took on sales trips. The girls, Helga Sigríður and Sigurlaug, worked as housemaids here and there and Jón Jr. earned enough money so he could attend school.

Reverend Páll held some services in his house in 1876 and the settlers considered building a church to help consolidate the settlement. By then a large group of Icelanders had settled in New Iceland, north of Winnipeg in Canada. They also needed a minister, so Páll made a journey north late in the summer of 1876. While there he buried some children who had died of a stomach ailment. He then returned to Shawano, where on November 26 he confirmed six children, among them Sigurlaug, Stefán's sister, who was 16 years old, and their cousin, Jón Jónsson Jr., who was 14.

Reverend Páll spent most of the following year in New Iceland, where he became embroiled in religious controversy when the settlers there called for a minister to serve them permanently. In the power struggle that ensued, some supported Páll while others wanted Reverend Jón Bjarnason. There was strong opposition to Páll's fundamentalist religious views as influenced by the Norwegian Synod, and he also questioned the location of the Icelandic colony. On the other hand, Reverend Jón was very nationalistic and opposed to close ties with the Norwegian Synod. He won favour among the leaders of the colony who insisted upon relative independence.

Meanwhile, Stefán was an active participant in farming and the social life of the settlement in Shawano County as the Icelandic pioneers built barns, increased their livestock, and fashioned wagons and sleighs. In the New Year of 1877, Stefán and Guðmundur were both ascribed to the debt to Jón from Mjóidalur, which was now reduced to $93. Together the three bought a plough and a team of oxen, as well as some timber land. The settlement was beginning to show signs of prosperity; few needed to borrow money, all were improving their situation, and the prospect was that they would gradually acquire reasonable wealth.

In the spring of 1878, the settlers celebrated the First Day of Summer as was customary in Iceland. In a speech, Stefán gave colourful descriptions of the moods of summer and winter and recalled memories of Iceland. On July 4 the settlers gathered again when Reverend Páll came from New Iceland to declare that Christian freedom was much more important than civil freedom. Stefán, on the other hand, praised civil liberty and the generous nature of the new foster-land in a poem to America.[18]

A few days later, he wrote a newsletter from the colony for the newspaper *Framfari*, published in New Iceland. He reported that farming was going well, that six Icelandic farmers each owned 160 acres of land, and that the settlement had a total population of 33 souls. They had over 30 head of cattle, five horses, four pigs, and well over 100 hens. There were only 25 sheep, so plans for large-scale sheep farming had obviously come to naught. Stefán and his father owned 160 acres of forested land, some of which was sandy and still mostly woodland, but with 12 cleared acres. They had four cows. The district was being settled mainly by Germans and Scandinavians, and he warned that Icelanders would either have to move to where there were more Icelanders or acculturate with Norwegians, Germans, and Americans.[19]

The young Icelandic bachelors in Wisconsin travelled around exchanging experiences by writing to each other in prose and verse. When Kristinn Kristinsson was working along the Wolf River, Stefán wrote him a verse asking whether the wolves had eaten him. On another occasion, Stefán was bed-ridden with a leg injury. He wrote a cheerful verse-letter to his sister, Sigurlaug, including an exaggerated self-portrait: his hat covers a bald head and underneath is a frowning, brown and dirty face. He has plenty of money and is chased every night by big, fat girls, but manages to escape them by limping into the woods.[20] It is evident from Stefán's poetry that he thought about women a great deal during his first years in Shawano. Among his poems is a translation (he claimed) from Greek about a mussel that was obviously a sexual metaphor, "Kvæði þýtt úr Grísku" (A Poem Translated from Greek). The speaker of the poem describes his lust for sex and is victorious in the end:

> *If I could fill up all of them,*
> *Like you, my dear mussel*
> *The pleasure would spread over thighs and flank*
> *I could then live happily.*
> *Drowsing sleep would come to me,*
> *The tool sleeps in the pants.*

At the end of the poem is an epilogue indicating that the poem is merely compensation for sexual frustration. As the speaker says, the tools are frozen because they don't get shelter under the skirts of the girls.[21]

Stefán often composed toasts to women and cheerful verses to girls. Some are about kissing, others more sexual in nature. Eventually, he began to focus his amorous glance on one of the Icelandic log cabins in Shawano County. The tone of his poetry changes and the sexual unruliness wanes, revealing gentler and milder thoughts as can be seen in this verse to an anonymous girl:

> *If you, girl, are bright and gentle,*
> *Then our minds are calm,*
> *In your sweet smile*
> *Is the joy of both of us.*[22]

It is as if he had spotted a companion for life, perhaps the girl he addresses in this little poem, "Um stúlku" (About a Girl):

> *You lean your dear head on the pillow*
> *As a flower bowing in the calm evening shadow*
> *And the locks spread over your white neck*
> *Like dusk on freshly fallen snow.*
> *Now beams fell from heaven to earth*
> *And I saw a gate open in the road of the clouds*
> *And a beautiful angel peeped through*
> *And stared at you in wonder, as I did.*[23]

Stefán's first cousin Helga Sigríður Jónsdóttir from Mjóidalur was now almost 17 years old. One day near the end of May in 1878, she tore up a tiny tree, roots and all. Stefán saw ambiguity in the fate of the tree and wrote the poem "Eftir tré" (In Memory of a Tiny Tree). It is at once a commemorative poem to the tree and a love poem to Helga. The tree has to wither. Death touches it on a spring day, and the singing bird will no longer sit on its branch, singing softly in the twilight. Nor will the tree be reflected in a cool brook at sunrise. The girl's tender hand is the cause of the tree's death, as she tears up its weak root. The poet identifies with the tree when the girl presses it to her warm bosom. The momentary tenderness of the girl towards the tree turns into its death agony "as when the sweet kiss disappeared/and a tender bosom/then you fell, dear tree/ in the bright spring." The death of the tree foreshadows the poet's life:

> *If the world tears me away*
> *From you, tender loving young girl,*
> *Whom I love now,*
> *I will turn pale, wither, fall and die*
> *And go like you.*
>
> *And perhaps nobody (like you)*
> *Will then have for me –*
> *When I, a pale corpse, fall*
> *To the earth –*
> *Tears of mixed love and sorrow*
> *Nor a commemorative poem.*[24]

On the surface, the poem states that if the world tears the poet from the girl, he will wither and die. His relationship with the tree, however, indicates ambiguity, another kind of a death: it loses its natural wildness by being tied to the girl. Stefán, therefore, must reject his unruliness. By doing so, his life must change course. Although he desires the girl, the final stanza indicates solitude, the solitude of the poet who can never rely on the understanding of others.

The courtship continued as Stefán, while cultivating the soil together with his father and Jón from Mjóidalur, continued writing poems to Helga. In the winter, he was away, missing the maiden's kisses since forests and mountains "prohibit a meeting with a maid." In 1877 he composed a long, beautiful love poem, "Til Helgu" (To Helga), in which the forested landscape and the weather carry the imagery.[25]

In the spring and summer of 1878, Stefán built a house with the help of Jón, Helga's father. In late August, they slaughtered a lamb, a calf, and perhaps a pig. They went to Shawano to buy provisions for a banquet for the approximately 30 souls in the settlement and presumably some neighbours of other nationalities. Reverend Páll Þorláksson then united Stefán and Helga in holy matrimony on August 24. The groom was 24 years old and the bride 19. As it was late in the summer, the heat was less intense, so it was comfortable to celebrate outdoors. This was

Reverend Páll's first marriage in the United States and he refused any payment. The fathers, Guðmundur and Jón – who were also brothers-in-law – acted as witnesses to the marriage.

The new couple moved into their recently finished house in November. Judging by Jón Jónsson's diaries, one could conclude that the marriage was a way out of Guðmundur and Stefán's debt to Jón. Guðmundur and Stefán paid the $8 cost of the wedding and on Jón's balance sheet for the year the debt was lowered by that amount. Jón also owed Helga some money that she had contributed to the household in the preceding years, and two years later Jón's balance sheet reveals that Guðmundur's debt passed to Helga, evidently as a dowry. The marriage had the flavour of the thriftiness of those from Mjóidalur, but it was hardly pure business.

Helga had inherited her father's prudence and drive. Stefán had enjoyed the wild bachelor life for a while and could now concentrate on new challenges in life. Perhaps Helga did not move in with Stefán until the new house was ready. Nine months later, on September 25, 1879, she gave birth to a son. Her father showed little emotion at the birth of his first grandchild. His September entry ended: "25th, the birth of a baby at Helga's." First and foremost a farmer, he wrote in the margin that day that a heifer had been taken to a bull.

Helga Sigríður Jónsdóttir, the daughter of Jón and Sigurbjörg of Mjóidalur, photographed in Milwaukee at age 16.

Jón, Helga's brother, was very fond of his little nephew and often came to Stefán and Helga's house. He was now almost 17 years old and called himself John Johnson. During the previous summer, he had earned $32. He spent some money on new clothes and a *carte-de-visite* photograph of himself – 12 prints for $2.50. He sent some of these to friends and relatives back in Iceland and gave one to Stefán and Helga.

By Jón's birthday, the little boy had not yet been baptized and was just called "Busi". He was grateful to his uncle for holding him when he was in a bad mood, so he "asks" his father to compose a poem on the occasion of his uncle's birthday. "My loving uncle," it says in the first line, and the first stanza ends: "I am not tall myself,/so this piece of paper will be small." Stefán's humour is softer than before and the last stanzas give a glimpse of Jón holding his little nephew when the baby's mother is too busy.[26] The little boy was eventually baptized Baldur, after a Norse god, on November 15, 1879. It is not known who baptized little Baldur, since by that time Páll Þorláksson had left Wisconsin for good.

A Synod Man or Radical? Exodus

In May of 1879 Páll Þorláksson, together with his parents, their family, and several others, had moved to an Icelandic settlement that was developing in Dakota Territory. Those who stayed behind were also considering moving. Reverend Páll had served as a pastor in New Iceland in 1877-1878, but he had lost out to Reverend Jón Bjarnason by popular vote. During the controversy leading up to this vote, Páll's close ties to the Norwegian Synod were an issue, as was the matter of his having solicited relief from the Synod on behalf of settlers in New Iceland, similar to support received through Reverend Homme during the first winter in Shawano. The Icelanders in Shawano wrote two letters to the Icelandic newspaper *Norðanfari* defending Reverend Páll and the Norwegian Synod. The style of the letters points to Stefán as author, and his name appears at the top of the signatory list. One letter defended

Jón Jónsson Jr. from Mjóidalur, the poet's cousin, friend, and brother-in-law.

the Synod's dogmatism, saying that the Synod could not be blamed for not allowing "human reason or the education of our times to challenge the truth of the Holy Scripture." The writers had learned from their catechism that the Scripture was inspired by God, and although they had learned more since, they would not regard it as dogmatic or intolerant to take the Scripture as a Word of God. One must accept the credo in order to be a Lutheran and the teachings of Christ to be called Christian. The ministers of the Norwegian Synod behaved well and were far from being arrogant or uneducated as had been stated in *Framfari*, and Reverend Páll was a "dutiful and true Christian, always wanting to effect positive change."[27] In a letter written a year later, Stefán mocked the attempts of *Framfari* to convince people that the Norwegian Synod refused to believe that the earth revolved around the sun by telling about a German minister who refused to accept the Copernican theory. It was a well-known method, Stefán wrote, to take words out of context and then identify them with the opponent.

These letters are important testimonials to Stefán's development. He had occasionally expressed doubt in religious matters, so his defence of such fundamentalist views might appear surprising. Stefán was personally very fond of Reverend Páll and naturally wanted to defend him. The religious dispute dealt primarily with the New Theology that made concessions in doctrine, but for Stefán it was a question of principle, Christian doctrine or not. He looked into the matter with an urgent need to find logic. For him it was not enough, as for most people, to quote the Word of God without further consideration. He had to reach the essence. Thus, he had sympathy with those who kept firmly to the principles of the doctrine and perhaps found the New Theology a kind of neither-nor. In these years, Stefán composed this verse:

> *In my youth I was like a child*
> *With the simple, childish religion*
> *By growing older I became doubtful*
> *And now I believe in nothing.*[28]

He invoked the name of God sparingly in his festive poems and psalms, while at the same time he was acquainting himself with the ideas of radical freethinkers who were gaining attention in the United States during these years. Among them was Robert Green Ingersoll, who held fierce public lectures against belief in God. Stefán followed the career of Ingersoll and he once wrote mockingly about a woman who had been fired from her job as a teacher "for telling the schoolboys that they could follow the example of Ingersoll in being fond of their mother and kind to women." He also read in a Norwegian paper about a minister who attacked Ingersoll. "He was there with Moses on his back, slopping in a pigpen, saying Ingersoll was hidden there somewhere. Then I stopped reading. I remembered that Moses did not like pigs and forbade the Jews to eat bacon, so I found it hardly appropriate to quote him there."[29]

Stefán did not compose much poetry during these years. He read what he found interesting in the literature of the New World and educated himself in the new liberalism by reading freethinker papers and journals. He also translated several American poems into Icelandic, such as Longfellow's "The Blacksmith". He was attracted to radical thought, but at this point his poems were still tempered with a certain sentimentality. He sent his cousins in Iceland a small handwritten volume containing some of his poetry. The second last poem, entitled "Áfram" (Onward), is a manifesto in which he urges his cousins to fight stupidity and prejudice. "Onward is the war cry of the new century of the world," he wrote, and one should obey this call. The poem is a challenge to the poor to break free of the fetters imposed by the powerful: "King and bishop shall soon be driven to escape/farmer and worker shall rule the countries," Stefán wrote, adding that nobody is higher than the Lord.[30]

Although he was exploring a variety of ideas, he swung between radicalism and sentimentality. In these years, he wrote the draft of a short story entitled "Drykkjumaðurinn" (The Drunkard), about a man who drank away all his possessions. Obviously Stefán had explored the shadowy streets of the cities of Wisconsin, but now he fully embraced his responsibility to his family. The drunkard's child dies because of his negligence and he is himself killed in a state of intoxication. "The light shone into his face, and the flush caused by the champagne and the half-burned cigar revealed what company he had kept that evening. It was dark in the street. The faint beam of the gas lamps could not break the darkness of the night. Theodore Northfield was on his way home, alone, or at least he thought so. 'Tomorrow, Theodore,' a voice resounded in his ears and he looked up. An angel, bright and angry-looking, stood before him. He hid his eyes before this ghastly vision. 'Tomorrow is the day that will bring to you all the misery and disgrace that you have for many years prepared for yourself. Tomorrow you will have to leave the home that to everyone else would have been so dear, precious, and sacred. And she, who trusted her happiness to you and never doubted your loyalty and nobility, you have seduced'."[31]

Stefán conjured up colourful images of life among the Icelanders in a verse-letter, "Alþýðlegt fréttabréf" (A Common Newsletter), written to a friend who had left for Dakota Territory in the summer of 1879. Altering names, he reports on marriageable girls, courtships, and break-ups – not only among the Icelanders, but among the Germans and Anglo-Saxons as well, an indication that there was considerable interaction among ethnic groups. Stefán also plays with names, anglicizing Icelandic names and transforming English names to Icelandic. Obviously, he observes, some of the girls fancied by the recipient of the letter will never be his. Two stanzas are a humorous description of a visit to the settlement:

> *There was a big festival here*
> *The entire district had a party –*
> *As a shipment arrived from Chicago,*
> *That however nobody received.*
> *Her name is Ida Todleson,*
> *Pure Icelandic, soft as eiderdown*
> *On the outside, white like innocence itself,*
> *An angel cast from cream and chalk!*
> *Once you knew this girl –*
> *I'm sure you will recognize her*
> *But then her name was Inga Þórðardóttir.*
>
> *But I guess Þórður's name is Todle now,*
> *That change of name is however a bit late,*
> *As that dignity reached him in the grave.*
> *This Ida was a jewel and a glory,*
> *A wonder that will never be explained:*
> *She had 'bow-catchers' in both her cheeks,*
> *– Wound with special pliers –*
> *With her hair 'banged' and a so-slender waist*
> *But like an armour, with rivets all around.*

Young men, of course, swarmed around such a visitor. Ida, or Inga, was Ingibjörg Þórðardóttir, daughter of the widow Guðrún Grímsdóttir, whose husband, Þórður Árnason, had died in Milwaukee the first year in America. Stefán mocks the change of name. Ida has enjoyed the sophisticated city life in Chicago. She is elegantly dressed in a hoop skirt to attract suitors and has her forelocks cut in the latest fashion. The poem was composed late in winter, when the soul "snows in and freezes." Stefán shudders at the thought of wading through the snow in the forests, but that is his destiny. The final stanza expresses doubt as to whether he, too, should go to Dakota.[32] There is also a sarcastic allusion to the dispute among the Icelandic congregations, with the faction following Reverend Páll Þorláksson accusing Reverend Jón Bjarnason's followers in New Iceland of having accepted a loan from the Canadian government, while that faction in turn accused Reverend Páll's followers of "begging" from the Norwegian Synod.

Stefán's turbulent mind was also facing the choice of leaving Shawano or staying. Obviously Páll Þorláksson's dream of an Icelandic colony there would never come true, and as Stefán had already pointed out, the Icelanders there would either have to leave or accept assimilation with the other nationalities. None of them wanted to go to New Iceland, but several had moved to an Icelandic settlement in Minnesota.

The last year by the Oconto River was lonely for those who remained. They tended their animals and felled trees, some for railway ties for a new line that was being built – an indication perhaps that the economy was recovering in the United States. Stefán soon reached a decision. On May 4, 1880, before seeding, he left for Dakota Territory by train, together with Hallgrímur Gíslason and Jón Jónsson Jr., to work and pave the way for the others who would follow.

In July, Guðmundur Stefánsson and Jón from Mjóidalur sold their land, Jón for $200, Guðmundur for $190. The value of each property had increased by more than $150 in six years. They then went into Shawano to register the sale of their land. As Stefán was away now, he could not take care of the paperwork. Guðmundur was not as fluent in English and obviously did not spell out the names for the clerks, who wrote down the names of those selling the land as "Goodman Stephenson" and his wife "Goodberg".

In mid-August, the women and children left Shawano for Dakota by train. Jón and Guðmundur purchased a team of oxen for $75 on August 23, and together with a few others – including the youngest in the group, the widow's son Hjörtur, who was now twelve years old – set off for Dakota on foot. They walked the entire distance, across prairies and through forests, fording rivers when there were no bridges and setting up tents at nightfall. Enduring rain, mud, and burning heat, they averaged between 15 and 20 miles each day, and one week after leaving Shawano they crossed the Mississippi River. They then walked across Minnesota, finally arriving in the new Icelandic settlement in Dakota in early October.[33]

Chapter 6

Gardar

Pioneers Again

The northeastern part of the Dakota Territory, especially the Red River Valley, had long been home to various aboriginal tribes, hunters, and fur traders. Beginning in 1870, land seekers, pushing ever westward, began settling up and down the valley. Hard on the pioneers' heels were the railways that gave the settlers access to eastern markets. Yet it had only been a few years since General Custer's famous defeat.[1]

The Icelandic settlement in Dakota was established in the spring of 1878 when a few of Reverend Páll Þorláksson's supporters left New Iceland and followed Páll south to the area along the Tongue River in Pembina County. Among those who left New Iceland was a brother of Jón Jónsson from Mjóidalur, Benedikt, who had adopted the surname *Bardal*. The pioneers erected log cabins and managed to plough and seed a couple of acres. During the first winter, they mainly lived on potatoes, bread, milk, and a little meat they purchased from the natives. The following spring brought 50 more settlers from New Iceland, as well as additional migrants from Shawano. These included Reverend Páll's parents and some of his siblings, who settled further south where two forested hills rose from the undulating prairies east of the Pembina Mountains. Originally called Vík, this was to become the nucleus of an Icelandic community later called Mountain. The hills gave shelter from the strong west winds and the new arrivals lived in tents until late fall.

It was not easy for the settlers, however, and in fact many found themselves in dire straits – having walked away from homesteads in New Iceland where they had already expended their initial resources and energies. Many had been unable to sell their improvements and there remained a nagging question about repayment of their share of the government loan,

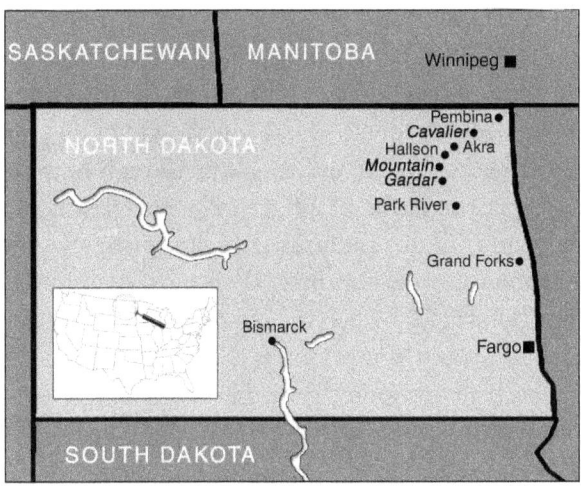

Until 1889 the state of North Dakota was part of Dakota Territory, which included Pembina County – the main site of Icelandic settlement. Among the earliest Icelandic communities in this area were Hallson, Akra, Vik (Mountain), and Gardar.

which they had accepted in the form of food, utensils, livestock, and seed. The new settlement nevertheless spread throughout the western part of Pembina County, as far south as the Park River district, a beautiful area with dense woods along the river. Beyond, the treeless yet fertile prairie stretched as far as the eye could see.

The following winter was extremely hard and the situation verged on famine. Páll Þorláksson, who by now was suffering from the advanced stages of tuberculosis, was in Minnesota seeking medical treatment. He stayed for a while with a Norwegian merchant, Harald Thorson of Northfield, with whom he struck a deal. By mortgaging all his belongings, Páll managed to get, in the form of a two-year loan from Thorson, 100 barrels of wheat and 40 head of cattle. These he had transported to Pembina County where he sold the grain and livestock to his countrymen for only slightly more than he paid, in order to cover the interest on the loan. Although this saved many of the Icelanders, some of them were suspicious as they were not accustomed to loans and interest payments. Páll, who earlier had been accused of poaching settlers from New Iceland for his Dakota settlement, was now slandered for this latest enterprise. Under the circumstances, however, this transaction could be regarded as one of the most remarkable achievements in the early history of the Icelandic settlement in Dakota.[2]

In the spring of 1880, Stefán and his cousin and brother-in-law, Jón Jónsson Jr., arrived at Park River and claimed land. While waiting for their families to arrive from Shawano, Stefán and Jón, along with Kristinn Kristinsson and Sveinn Björnsson, headed north to work at railway construction on a section of track that was to run between St. Vincent, in northwest Minnesota, and Winnipeg in Canada. The comrades got jobs unloading gravel from wagons and made a competition of trying to be the first to unload. Stefán was a tough worker, Sveinn recalled much later, and cheerful in the evening – as though he were fully rested. They boarded at the home of a Scot who lived just north of the Canadian border and thought themselves lucky to survive the chicory "coffee" and the bog water all summer. Their most memorable experience took place on Victoria Day when the red-bearded Scot drank all the whisky in honour of Queen Victoria. His daughters served the boarders. One of them was lean and bony, the other short and fat. The mates composed insulting verses about them, taking advantage of the fact that they did not understand Icelandic. Sveinn would make up the first two lines and Stefán would then complete each verse, commenting on their looks, their lack of morals, and their bodily fluids.[3]

In late summer the comrades quit their railway jobs and caught a riverboat up the Red River to Pembina County, where most of them found work with harvest crews. Stefán and Jón then went to Crookston, Minnesota, when the harvest was over, to meet their families, who were to arrive from Shawano by train. They then made their way to the town

A contemporary view of the poet's homestead, looking east from the wooded foot of the Pembina Escarpment.

of Pembina, where they stayed a few days before travelling the 30 miles west to Park River.[4]

The land in Pembina County had been surveyed the previous fall and the new settlement proved to be in Township 159 North in Range 56 west of the 5th meridian. Most of the western part of the township was settled by Icelanders, while many of the settlers in the east part were Irish or Norwegian. Stefán's homestead included 156 acres, comprising the south halves of the NE and NW quarters of Section 18, situated at the foot of an escarpment called the Pembina Mountains. The women and one year old Baldur took up residence in a provisional shelter nearby while Stefán began building a house near the west edge of his land – below a pretty wooded slope that faced the morning sun. Much of his land was flat and very arable, but it included an area densely wooded with oak and linden.[5]

Stefán's father, along with Jón from Mjóidalur and the others who had set off on foot from Shawano with the cattle, arrived on October 4, 1880. They all had sore feet and little Hjörtur Þórðarson, the son of widow Guðrún Grímsdóttir, had worn out his shoes, but there was no time to rest. Stefán's father-in-law, Jón, settled a little further south, while Jón's brothers, Benedikt Bardal and Gísli Dalmann, chose land to the east of Stefán's homestead. Kristinn Kristinsson also settled in the neighbourhood.[6]

The new arrivals immediately began helping Stefán build his house. The weather remained calm until the middle of the month, then got windy and rainy with cold and frost. Snow would soon follow and all the Icelandic pioneers in the district were building shelters for the winter – partial dugout houses on hillsides, sod huts, and log cabins. By now Stefán had some experience with building log houses, but he nevertheless found "chinking" between the logs tricky and the walls were not always very tight. During the first years, those in the northern part of the settlement where there was little timber built sod houses, which were warmer but leaked in the heavy summer rains. Each household had a root cellar where milk products and vegetables were stored.

By the first half of November, Stefán had almost completed the construction of his house. He then began to build stables and to help his father-in-law to build his house. On December 23, 1880, Gísli Dalmann hewed floorboards, and on the following day he worked on some beds. Stefán's unhewn log house was 4.8 by 5.4 metres. There was undoubtedly a window in one of the gables and another on the front facade. The beds of the two couples were in the corners, and between them, below the end window, was likely a table with a kerosene lamp. Other furniture would consist of a few chairs and worn wooden trunks from Iceland to sit on, and more beds along the walls. A wood stove was installed at the other gable end. Possibly some pictures were hung and a bookshelf was fastened to the wall above Stefán's bed, although most of the books he had acquired in Wisconsin had been destroyed in the move to Dakota.

During the first year in Dakota Territory the little house at the foot of the Pembina Mountains was crowded. Sigurlaug, Stefán's sister, probably worked away from home much of the time, but the household still included Stefán and Helga, little Baldur, and the old couple, Guðmundur and Guðbjörg. The widow Guðrún Grímsdóttir also stayed with them that first winter, with her two youngest sons, Árni and Hjörtur, 13 and 12 years of age. Her eldest son, Grímur, was staying elsewhere. Grímur and his mother had each claimed land and he had begun to build log houses on each claim. Guðrún kept one cow in Stefán's barn. Her son Hjörtur was an unusual child, rather withdrawn and introverted. When he was sent to tend the cows, people joked that the cows were tending him, absorbed as he was in studying old Norse runes and other mysteries. He did not bother much with the catechism, but Stefán later recalled how heartily the boy laughed while reading Benedikt Gröndal's satirical works. One day Hjörtur accidently broke one of the iron lids on Helga's stove. He was devastated, but Stefán was unconcerned about the lid and reassured him: "My boy, don't let this upset you. Maybe you can compensate Helga for the lid later."[7]

On Sunday, October 31, 1880, Páll Þorláksson held a service in Eiríkur Bergmann's spacious new house in the district – a sign of social activity in the settlement. In attendance were several who had been on the immigrant ship in 1873, among them Ólafur Ólafsson from Espihóll, an energetic and exceptionally intelligent farmer who lived two miles from Stefán, and Baldvin Helgason, who was so princely in appearance that some neighbours of the Icelanders imagined that he was an exiled brother of the King of Denmark. Many of those present took communion, but Stefán and Helga did not.

Two days later, some of the settlers in the Park River district set aside their tools long enough to go to Vík (Mountain) to elect county officials.

Land ownership in Pembina County circa 1888.

Ólafur Ólafsson was already involved in local politics and supported F. A. Wardwell, whom he had met in Pembina. Stefán went to vote at Ólafur's request. So too did Jónas Hallgrímsson, who had abbreviated his last name to *Hall*. Jónas, intelligent and self-educated, lived three miles south of Stefán and the two men walked home together. They discovered that they had much in common and from this meeting a lifelong friendship sprang up. Jónas stopped at Stefán's home overnight. Two days later he left Dakota to find work in Canada. His wife, Sigríður, was a hardy woman who stayed all winter in a dugout abode with two little boys and two cows.[8]

At the polling station, the settlers could sign a declaration of intention to become citizens of the United States, as Stefán's father had done at Green Bay in 1874. Such a declaration was a necessary condition to buying government land at a discount. Heads of families could buy an additional quarter section, known as a pre-emption, for agricultural purposes, but with the stipulation that they live on the land and cultivate it for three years. On July 13, 1882, Stefán paid $198.08 at a land office in Grand Forks for his 156.06 acres. His absolute ownership of the land was confirmed on October 15, 1884.[9]

Despite failing health, Reverend Páll Þorláksson did his best to help his countrymen get established in Dakota. On November 24, 1880, he called a meeting at Eiríkur Bergmann's house. Stefán was appointed secretary of the meeting, which was concerned with the establishment of a congregation in the Park River district. Páll read aloud the detailed constitution of a congregation he had served in New Iceland. His voice was weak, but full of conviction, and the constitution, although strict, was approved. This was the first Icelandic congregation in Pembina County and the attendees expressed the wish that Páll serve the congregation by performing a service every third Sunday. One of the farmers donated an acre of land for a churchyard and Eiríkur Bergmann and two others were elected as congregation representatives. Stefán was elected secretary. In all, 16 members contributed to a salary for Páll, each according to his ability. Eiríkur Bergmann, an aspiring leader of the community, paid the most, a handsome $8. Jón Jónsson paid $5, Stefán $4, and his father, Guðmundur, $1.

As the congregational members walked out into the November cold, Reverend Páll perused the minutes of the meeting and was surprised to note that Stefán had not signed the congregational by-laws. When he asked about this, Stefán gave two reasons: the text regarding the creed, and the lack of women's rights in congregational matters. "I have never seen some of the creeds and do not know what is in them, and I do not believe that the difference between men and women … is a command of God," Stefán said. Páll hesitated a little and then asked whether he could not add Stefán's name to the list with a reservation about these paragraphs. Stefán agreed to that and thus became a member of the congregation.[10]

At a gathering later that fall, Stefán read a new poem about the Pembina Mountains, sharing with his fellow settlers his hopes and dreams for their new community. Certainly the Pembina Mountains would be found lacking if compared to the mountains back in Iceland, but this was nevertheless a beautiful place, he asserted in the poem. He conceded, however, that he missed the ancient tales of supernatural beings, trolls, elves, and dwarfs, who lived in the mountains of Iceland. On the other hand, it was possible to forget all worldly worries while wandering in the Pembina Mountains and reading books in the lee of the mountains. Stefán's future vision for the settlement was bright:

> *The winter frost wraps the colourful*
> *Woods in eternal clothing,*
> *Of rime and winter snow,*
> *Cleaner than bright innocence;*
> *Waves in the sweet spring wind*
> *The summer dew,*
> *The mane of the fully ripe fields*
> *More beautiful than the brightest gold.*

The poem expresses the wish that the Pembina Mountains would become a Paradise safe from misfortune.[11]

Winter Journeys

Christmas was stormy and Stefán and his people celebrated the festive season on the dirt floor in Jón Jónsson's new, but still primitive, house. Early in the New Year of 1881, settlers in the Park River district gathered once again at the home of Eiríkur Bergmann, who was obviously consolidating himself as an entrepreneur and a leader of the settlement. A large man, brisk in conduct, he felt that it was urgent to have a post office. After the matter had been thoroughly discussed, those in attendance passed a resolution to ask postal authorities for permission to open a post office in Eiríkur Bergmann's home. A name for the post office was the next issue. Stefán suggested the name of *Garðar Svavarsson*, the first Norseman to discover Iceland. His name had not been very celebrated, Stefán said, and it was more attractive than an English name. A unique Icelandic name could thereby be preserved longer in

1928 Dakota Anniversary restoration of a pioneer log home typical of those built by the first Icelandic settlers in Dakota Territory.

local history, though it could easily be adapted into English. Eiríkur Bergmann suggested the name *Geysir*. A vote then decided that *Gardar* would be the new name.

A recommendation from a neighbouring post office had to accompany the petition, so a few days later Eiríkur and Stefán set off at dawn on a sleigh pulled by Eiríkur's oxen. They drove nearly 20 miles southeast to the post office at Sweden. Road conditions were difficult as there were no trails, and they alternately walked and drove all day. That night they stayed at Sweden, where postmaster McKenzie, a chummy sort of fellow, wrote a long letter of recommendation. Approval for Gardar Post Office was granted on March 15, 1881, on the condition that the petitioners maintain the postal service at their own expense for the first year. Now the Icelanders gathered to collect money to pay a postal carrier who would transport the mail 10 miles from Crystal to Gardar. He was to receive 50 cents per trip and Eiríkur Bergmann, as postmaster, would get 60% of the stamp revenue.

On March 7, 1881, Stefán went on another and longer winter journey, this time with his brother-in-law, Jón Jónsson Jr., and Hallgrímur Gíslason. Stefán and Hallgrímur had grain they wanted ground at the mill in Walhalla and Jón was going to buy some on the way. The trip was more than 30 miles as the crow flies, but the road wound through Cavalier, making the trip well over 50 miles each way. Hallgrímur had two oxen and a heavy sleigh and the brothers-in-law had four oxen and a lighter sleigh. The snow was more than half a metre deep, making the road difficult.

The first night was spent at Mountain, where Jón Jónsson's sister lived, and on the following night the companions stayed with an Icelander from whom Stefán and Hallgrímur bought more grain. They arrived in Cavalier just after noon the next day. The weather was warm and sunny, softening the snow. They then continued north across the prairie where the compacted snow on the road formed a high ridge, which was not very wide and made it difficult to keep the oxen on the road – especially those belonging to Stefán and Hallgrímur. When an ox slipped off the track, the entire yoke had to be driven half a circle to get both the animals and the sleigh back on top of the ridge. This caused many delays and the travellers struggled on all day and into the night.

The night sky was clear and the cold intensified. They stopped at St. Joseph, 10 miles from Walhalla, but found no shelter for the night. The men and oxen were all exhausted and the men's leather shoes were soaking wet after a thaw during the day. Hallgrímur's feet were ice cold and he lay down in a heap in the snow, complaining that he was about to die. Stefán and Jón pulled off his shoes, and Stefán thawed Hallgrímur's feet with his bare hands. With no place to stay, they had little choice but to sleep on the sleighs for the rest for the night. Needless to say, no one slept very much. They arrived in Walhalla around noon and had their grain ground. While they were at the mill, a farmer arrived from Cavalier. He stated with great contempt that Icelanders had damaged the road. Jón, not quite 20 years old, was slightly ashamed of his nationality.

The partners spent a night in Walhalla before returning to Cavalier, where they were allowed to sleep on the floor of Miller's store because a friend worked there. The next day, they struggled through a snowstorm as far the home of Jón Jónasson, known as 'Doctor Jón' even though he was only a self-educated homeopath. He treated Jón Jr., who was suffering from snowblindness.

Hallgrímur's oxen were exhausted by this time, so the next day another Jón Jónsson brought a fresh yoke of oxen to take Hallgrímur's sleigh to Mountain. The travellers continued to Sigurbjörn Hansson's house, where they had stayed the first night. There they rested a while, then drove the oxen to Hallgrímur's place – leaving the sleighs behind. Hallgrímur borrowed skis from Sigurbjörn, while Stefán and Jón waded through the deep snow, following the trail the oxen had made. By now they were totally exhausted and Jón sometimes sat down, wishing he did not have to stand up again. Stefán was silent and did not complain. When they returned home in the early hours of the morning, they had travelled for almost one week. Jón was half blind for a few days and his eyes remained sensitive for the rest of his life. Stefán caught a bad cold that left him feeling frail for an entire year.[12]

'Crossroots' on Stage

Where once there had been Indian tepees and buffalo, small log farmsteads occupied by Icelanders now dotted the countryside. Between 1878 and 1890, the population in what later became North Dakota increased from 16,000 to 191,000.[13] The Icelandic settlement reflected this boom, as the area teemed with people building houses, ploughing fields, sowing crops, and gathering the harvest.

In 1881, the poet Helga Steinvör Baldvinsdóttir, who had been on the same ship as Stefán in 1873 and was the daughter of the regal-looking Baldvin Helgason, arrived from Rosseau, Ontario, with her husband, Jakob Líndal. This couple settled three miles east of Stefán and Helga's homestead and became good friends. The women visited each other, had coffee, and compared notes on their experiences in the New World. Helga could tell stories from Shawano, Karólína Dalmann could do likewise from her Milwaukee experiences, and Helga Steinvör from Rosseau could tell how she had learned to make sugar and soap from an Irish woman, as well how to braid straw into broad-brimmed summer hats. These hats became popular both as protection from the summer heat and as Sunday 'best' hats. Stefán's mother learned this craft from Helga Steinvör and provided the family with hats for as long as she lived.

Now social activity began to bind the settlers and communities together. The pioneers lent books to one other, played cards, and gathered for discussions and readings. The men talked over beer or whisky and there were entertaining gatherings in Eiríkur Bergmann's big house, where the cheerful Karólína Dalmann provided concertina music for local dances. She, Stefán, Jakob Líndal, and Helga Steinvör all had strong poetic talent, and others, like Ólafur Ólafsson and Jónas Hall, were eloquent speakers. Poems were read and speeches were made about the bright future of the Icelandic colony. A new method emerged for distributing poetry. Pieces of paper with poetry written on them were fastened to trees along the road so a stroller on his way to a neighbour, for example, might find a poem about himself. Social life was gradually formalized as reading societies, progressive associations, and women's clubs were organized. The Fourth of July also became an annual event, and in the summer of 1880 this occasion was celebrated with a picnic on a nice grassy area called 'The Playing Fields' – formerly used by the native people for their gatherings and competitions.

During the next summer, Stefán's first in the settlement, a committee was elected to organize festivities in the Park River district. Stefán was called upon to write a play, and though he had no time for this, working as he did from dawn to dusk, he finally relented. In the evenings, after a day's work in the fields, he sat on the hillside west of his house and wrote as fast as he could, so the actors could start rehearsing their roles. He was awake the entire night before the celebration.

Dakota pioneers Jakob Líndal and Helga Steinvör Baldvinsdóttir with their first child. Helga, a gifted poet known as Undína, stopped composing poetry after a heart-breaking divorce.

The next day, dressed in their Sunday best, the family set off for the celebration on an ox-drawn wagon. Someone, however, had forgotten to water the oxen, and when they approached a stream along the way the creatures were so thirsty that they plunged into the stream, tipping the wagon over and getting the passengers all wet. Unperturbed, the family simply stopped at the next farm and dried their clothes before continuing.

This festival, held in a clearing in the woods, featured many speeches and poems. Stefán's three-act play, entitled *Heima og hér. Samræður í leikritsformi* (Home and Here. Discussions in Dramatic Form), was the first Icelandic play written and performed in the New World.[14] The first act, set in government official Balthasarsen's home in Iceland, introduces Balthasarsen's daughter; the housemaid, Gertrud, who is a distant relative; and the poet Halldór, who is engaged to the daughter. Halldór is depressed after losing all his belongings and having his poems rejected by an editor. The daughter breaks up with Halldór and becomes engaged to a liberal-intellectual named Teitur, who brags of having spoken to the King of America and expects to be elected to the Icelandic parliament. Gertrude, the intelligent housemaid, makes fun of the situation and encourages Halldór, whom she likes.

In the second act, Balthasarsen has lost his wife and office, and the braggart Teitur has just returned from parliament, boasting of his progressive issues, that in fact are quite trivial. 'Cowshed-Gunna', a simple minded and talkative housemaid, now rushes onto the scene, cursing while pushing the parish minister in a wheelbarrow. "I found him asleep on the dunghill," she said, "and I was so startled, although I'm not a fearful person, but there he lay, stone-dead, I thought. He must have fallen off his mare when he rode along the path by the dunghill." The pastor wakes up and gets his hands on some alcohol. He is also a Member of Parliament, a sarcastic representative of the old-fashioned government officials who are losing ground, and he detests Teitur's liberalism. Teitur is buried in debt, having borrowed money from some farmers. He asks his father-in-law, Balthasarsen, to lend him money and they quarrel. Teitur then calls the old man a stubborn slave and slaps him, but Gertrud comes and chases him away. Halldór enters the scene, now a successful Sheriff and a poet. He asks Gertrud to come with him to America. She agrees, on the condition that old Balthasarsen can go with them.

The last act takes place a few years later on a farm in America. Halldór has become a Member of the State Legislature due to the integrity and straightforwardness of the people. Old Balthasarsen finds it better to be a farmer in America than a government official in Iceland. Cowshed-Gunna is there too, and when she enters she had been lost – walking 10 to 20 miles instead of four – in order to avoid "crawling across dangerous elephants". She was supposed to take a "crossroot" straight west: "Well I brought the damn root! But I'm sure you can't find your way any better with a root! It's a superstition. I found nothing north of the woods except for a daisy and it had next to no roots at all, at least none pointing to the west. This one lay more or less to the southwest, so I picked it. To think this damned thing could point your way!" *Field* in English sounds like the Icelandic word *fíll*, which means elephant, and the word *crossroad* sounds like *krossrót*, which is not a genuine Icelandic word but could literally mean crossroot. This sort of humorous play on words was popular among Icelanders.

The braggart Teitur was also expected to immigrate to America and Halldór and Gertrud agree to give him a good reception. "You never know what will become of Teitur here in the West," Halldór says. "The free national spirit here is so keen that it may be able to make good men out of material that could not be used elsewhere in the world – and that is the main advantage of America."

The dramatic calibre of the play is debatable, but in this foray as a playwright Stefán managed to create an amusing interplay of comical characters (with the talented Karólína Dalmann as 'Cowshed-Gunna') while contrasting the old and the new, and comparing charlatan liberalism with genuine liberal views as he was coming to know them. Interestingly, he uses the female character Gertrud to bring forward liberal ideas – no doubt an indication of his support of women's rights.

After the play, there was more entertainment, coffee, and perhaps a little alcohol for the men. Stefán worked all the next day and the following night, as well as the day after, well into the evening. While mowing with Eiríkur Bergmann's horses, Polly and Dolly, he fell asleep and toppled off the mower.

Death, Birth, and Religion

Father and son Guðmundur and Stefán worked side by side in the fields that first summer of 1881. The land was much easier to work than the heavily forested land in Shawano. The plough easily sliced through the black, fertile soil. Through hard work, their fields quickly became as large as their former acreage in Shawano. They also improved their buildings, purchased livestock, and prepared a vegetable garden. In the fall, one of their countrymen brought the first Icelandic-owned threshing machine to the settlement, and Jón Jónsson from Mjóidalur duly recorded his harvest of three tons of wheat and a good quantity of oats. Stefán and Guðmundur must have reaped a similar amount.

Guðmundur was now over 60 years of age, worn out from work, and failing in strength. In November he fell ill with consumption that quickly progressed. He had been his own master for a few years at Kirkjuhóll, but had otherwise moved from farm to farm, labouring for others in order to support his family. In the New World, he had settled twice in order to find better opportunities for his family. Now he was at journey's end.

During the night of November 24, 1881, Stefán sat at his father's bedside in the faint lamplight until Guðmundur passed away at sunrise. His sunken eyes "prefigured to me the last calmness of death," Stefán wrote in the poem "Bréf til K.S." (A Letter to K.S.). Sorrow, not "the hardness of heart" nor calculated coldness, rendered him silent. "So, I walked away – my chest on fire."[15] Guðmundur was not buried for three weeks as the family decided to wait for Sigurlaug, who was not at home at the time. In the meantime, Helga gave birth to a boy on December 9th, four days before Guðmundur's burial. Normally, Reverend Páll would have officiated at the service, but he was in the advanced stages of tuberculosis and by December his health failed completely.

Despite being ill and unable to do much of his outdoor work most of this winter, likely due to jaundice following the extreme chill he had experienced on the trip to Walhalla, Stefán found himself involved in congregational matters. Reverend Páll was recommending his young cousin Hans B. Thorgrimsen, who was completing theological studies at the seminary in St. Louis, as his successor. Thorgrimsen was of the same strict theological stripe as Páll, a persuasion many of the settlers opposed although they liked Páll personally.

On January 2, 1882, the Park Congregation held a meeting. Reverend Páll was unable to attend, but a written address from him was read at the meeting. Stefán, Hallgrímur Gíslason, Ólafur Ólafsson, and cousins Eiríkur and Jón Bergmann formed a committee to reach a decision about what the

Ólafur Ólafsson, one of Stephan's best friends in Dakota, scouted for land in Alaska and moved to seven different locations in North America.

congregation should do. At the next meeting, Stefán announced their proposal: that in view of Reverend Páll's inability to carry out his work, he be allowed to retire in the hope this would give him the time and rest he needed to regain his health. The committee also conveyed the congregation's gratitude and respect to Reverend Páll, with the request that he conduct some ministerial services if his health permitted, but without any obligation. The attendees vowed to keep their faith and agreed to gather for Bible readings every second Sunday, as well as to hire a qualified person to instruct their children in Christianity.

The committee was interested in joining with other Icelandic congregations in the area to hire a minister from Iceland, and Stefán and Hallgrímur consulted with Páll. He acknowledged that hiring a minister from Iceland was a compromise and "… the only way out of the spiritual straits that he himself and Reverend Jón Bjarnason had brought to the religious lives of the Icelanders here [in America]." At the next congregational meeting, Stefán pledged $8, Eiríkur Bergmann $10, and Jón Jónsson $5 toward the salary, but the money was never collected as they were unable to find a candidate willing to take the position.

Now the settlers decided to re-write their outdated congregational laws themselves, and Stefán was elected to a committee to draft a new set of by-laws. While religion remained important to them, the congregational members wanted to be free from the strictures of Reverend Páll's conservative orthodoxy, and they had no intention of complying with his recommendation to hire his Norwegian Synod cousin Hans B. Thorgrimsen. Liberal winds were blowing through the colony. Páll's health deteriorated rapidly and he was unable to baptize Stefán's infant son. As a consequence, the child, named after his grandfather Guðmundur, was not baptized until February 10, 1882. Reverend Páll, just 32 years of age, died at his home on March 12th. The weather was so cold that he was not buried until April 2nd. The service was conducted by a Norwegian minister, Reverend Christian Flaten.[16]

Grant Us Equal Rights

"Greetings, farmer and housewife, farm workers, and dear children! Although you did not immediately recognize my voice when I came inside, it will not be concealed from you for long when I have pulled off my mittens, taken off my hat, and greeted you with a kiss and handshake in the Icelandic manner, that Eivindur of the Mountains is here! I hope my name will not offend you and that you will not imagine that the outlaw Eivindur has arrived in your neighbourhood – he who stole sheep from your great-grandfathers and great-grandmothers and is still alive in your folktales. That would, in any case, seem rather unlikely considering the fact that Eivindur is dead and buried long ago."[17]

Fjalla-Eivindur (Eyvindur of the Mountains), a handwritten paper put out by Stefán and some of his neighbours during the winter of 1882, bore the name of a semi-folkloristic though historical outlaw from about 1800, but it was also a symbolic reference to the Pembina Mountains. Others involved in this endeavour were Eiríkur Bergmann, Jakob Líndal, Sigurjón Sveinsson, and Kristinn Kristinsson, a member of Stefán's household at that time. Unlike the outlaw, the paper *Eivindur* cheerfully and bluntly refused to use the letter "y" in its name. *Eivindur* assured the people they would not have to worry about their livestock and claimed to know a great deal, for he had not been wandering in the mountains all his life, but also galloping between farms and towns, taking note of various things. He often stopped and asked people for news that would be either useful or entertaining. The 50 cent subscription fee was to defray the costs of the paper, the writing and other incidentals. The editor stated his intention of issuing the paper for three months, until spring chores called him away.

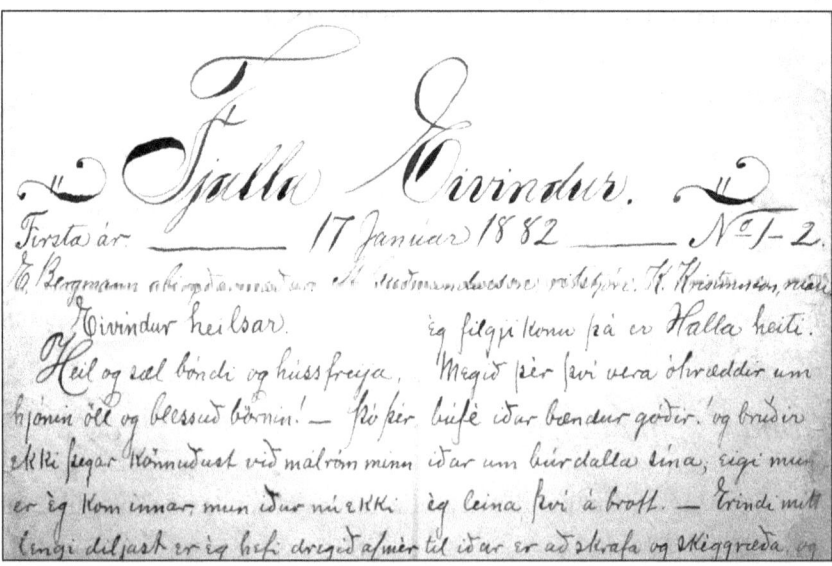

The first edition of the local newsletter *Fjalla Eivindur*, dated Jan. 17, 1882, with editor 'St. Guðmundarson'.

The first two issues came out on January 17, 1882. "The reasons for the paper were clear," wrote Stefán. "It stifled the spirit not to have a paper in Icelandic," he claimed. Since only a small minority of the Icelandic immigrants understood English, the address continued, Icelanders in America were in peril of falling behind in the developing culture of the world, "spiritually exposed on the cold ice of ignorance and stupidity, while their compatriots back in Iceland were advancing along the road of progress." *Eivindur* sought to entertain and help by bringing news, explaining various subjects, and supporting progress and liberal companionship. The content of the paper was diverse: news, essays on farming, and articles on social issues and the workings of American society. Stefán also contributed some of his poetry under the heading "The Editor's Wastebasket".

Eivindur also tackled some important issues facing the pioneers. In one article, Stefán compared the educational situations in the Old and the New Worlds. The settlers in the district must consider establishing a school for the children, he said. Education and advancement of the young were the foundations of bright hopes for young Icelanders in the West. "If we ignore this matter for long," Stefán stated, "with our usual indifference and insensitivity, we will soon have a good stock of urchins and delinquents – the natural product of both a lack of education and a deficient upbringing." He added that despite the freedom and progress achieved in the West, young people here were in a worse situation than their contemporaries in Iceland – itself "the tail of the world." "There are now among us many promising teenagers," Stefán wrote, "who are at the crossroads of youth and adulthood, who do not have the education necessary to get ahead in the West. Given the opportunity, they might be able to make up for some of the lost time. There can be no doubt that some of them would take advantage of proper schooling, but there must be no delay. The adult years approach quickly, drawing one away from studies and benumbing the thirst for education." Stefán now wrote from his own experience, and he also knew of a very special youth, Hjörtur Þórðarson, who had lived with the family the previous winter and needed the opportunity to study.

Local entrepreneur Eiríkur Bergmann wrote on railways in the first issue of *Eivindur*, while Ólafur Ólafsson from Espihóll contributed a variety of news items. The most controversial issue raised by Stefán was a discussion of women's rights. His poem "Húshjal" (Housechatting) is a woman's address to her grinning husband, in which she repeats his words that a "woman is the man's property" and that she should be his humble and obedient slave. She acknowledged that a man was Lord of the beasts, but then claimed that she was their Queen: "I then have the right to rule/and reign and govern with you," she declared. Everything that was good and noble elevated a man towards God, but it was just as important for a woman to evolve spiritually. Man and woman should go hand in hand, not walk separate paths. The woman ends her speech thus:

> You work on progress and freedom,
> And wonder at the slowness.
> Yet you banish from this work
> A good half of able-bodied humanity.
> Give us equal rights to work,
> And let us then see how it goes.

Following the poem, Stefán's sister, Sigurlaug, delivered an "Address to Women". She was now just over 20 years of age, and Kristinn Kristinsson might have been courting her, but she obviously held independent views. She urged the women of the district to accept the editor's offer of "participation in equal rights" by becoming contributors to the paper. "The boys have now placed us on the throne beside them, and although some are shocked to see us where males have ruled alone most of the time, women have been known ascend the throne before." Women, she said, were poor and ignorant, knowing little about fashion and jewellery, but they could share their knowledge of hygiene and cleanliness. That, Sigurlaug stated – in what was perhaps the first address on women's rights by an Icelandic woman – was their crowning achievement.

Sigurlaug Einara Guðmundardóttir, the poet's sister, better known as 'Lauga'.

A more powerful contribution came from Karólína Dalmann. She wrote a poem to welcome *Eivindur* and complemented Sigurlaug's article with a militant essay on women's rights, urging women to express themselves, to demand freedom, and to seek knowledge. Women, she declared, were not used to expressing themselves, being neither educated nor being taught how to conduct themselves in public. Instead, they were accustomed to milking cows and sheep, picking moss and knitting wool. Women blush at the thought of how little they know of the liberal arts, of which they have only the smallest notion. Ignorance and a lack of education had deprived them of the courage and strength to demand their rights. They were not so stupid, however, that that they did not know they were "free-born beings with full reason". Women accepted that a man was master of the house, but Karólína agreed with Stefán that women should rule the realm alongside men, enjoying freedom of speech and learning for themselves the wonders of science. "Women and girls! Now let it be seen that we are drawing closer to freedom and the rich wells of wealth and education, and let us celebrate, not secretly, but from the rooftops, so everybody can hear us say: Long live freedom!" Here was an Icelandic farm-woman in the New World, echoing the ideals of Margaret Fuller (1810-1850), a pioneer in the American women's rights movement. Fuller strove to open all paths to women, so they could realize their talents and potential just as men do.

An interesting flame ignited by the spark of Stefán's poem, this response in *Eivindur* may have been the first public discussion on women's rights in Icelandic. Icelanders in Dakota Territory, both men and women, were acquainting themselves with liberal ideas that had been developing in the United States.

Enjoy the House

Eivindur heralded new times. The editor was unable to do his outdoor chores because of illness, so he read and wrote. He read all the works of Shakespeare that winter and acquainted himself with the ideas of liberal American intellectuals, among them Ralph Waldo Emerson (1803-1882), who had died that spring. As the life of the old humanitarian philosopher was fading away in Massachusetts, his ideas developed in Stefán's mind. The poem "Lífshvöt" (Impulse of life), which appeared in *Eivindur*, reveals Emerson's influence. "Let us not sing with sorrow and tears/nostalgic poems of vanished youth," Stefán wrote. Youth is weak and unstable, if beautiful. It is praised too much in proportion to the other periods of a man's life, the poet claimed. The adult years are summertime, despite all the hard work, the sunburned forehead, and the sweat-streaked cheeks. One who struggles wholeheartedly to work well and to help will not long for his youth. The autumn of old age crowns a life spent in good works and honourable deeds, the poet said. Summer is more beautiful than youth, and "it does not matter/if you may become tired/compared to all the harvest/if your work is well done." This idea reminds one of Emerson's phrases: "The reward of a thing well done is to have done it."

Stefán's father had died before growing truly old, having worn himself out in the service of others. For him, work had been a Christian virtue, but above all an encumbrance. Stefán, on the other hand, looked to the future, defining work on his own terms. He wanted to avoid regretting the past; "short days and changing weather" were hindrances enough. One should take one's destiny into one's own hands, "above the flattery and backbiting of the mob/search out the truth by yourself."[18]

Eivindur faded out with various essays on farming and some rather trivial polemics, for instance on the entertainment value of Karólína Dalmann's accordion-playing when compared to the more fashionable fiddle. People loved to dance, and Kristinn Kristinsson, who was a great dancer, wrote mockingly about Karólína's accordion-playing. She had a strong temper and replied fiercely. Stefán made fun of the whole thing, but Karólína withdrew into silence.

Stefán's sister, Sigurlaug, known to friends and family as *Lauga*, was engaged to Kristinn, and in the spring of 1882 they married. A little earlier, Stefán's and Kristinn's friend Sveinn Björnsson had also married, and Stefán sent him a few verses outlining the advantages of being married. Obviously he thought that the two jackanapes had now reached the same safe haven as he had. "The falcons tangle their feet in the net/they are stuck and tame like a dove."[19]

Kristinn Kristinsson was a self-educated, hard-working man, and Lauga was an even match for him, intelligent, independent, and persevering. The brothers-in-law were good friends, although they did not always share the same opinions. When the young couple built a house, some thought Kristinn, who was nicknamed "Grandpa", was being a bit too ambitious. In Stefán's words:

> *"Grandpa" built a house so tall,*
> *That heaven was offended.*
> *It shadowed the sun in the south*
> *And blue darkness angered the region.*[20]

Stefán's essay on education in *Eivindur* was well received. In August 1882, the settlers in Park decided to levy a special tax to collect funds to pay for a teacher. Friðrik Bergmann was hired. Late in the fall, at a meeting at Eiríkur Bergmann's home, it was decided to borrow $1000, payable over 10 years, to build a schoolhouse despite the fact that some of the older men worried about taxes and debts. Eiríkur donated half an acre of land for the school. Sigurjón Sveinsson took on the construction for $739. Some people insinuated that the school board and Sigurjón made money on this initiative. Others thought the building proceeded too slowly. Despite the squabbling, the sounds of hammering soon resounded in the autumn stillness and the school was inaugurated at a gathering in the New Year of 1883. Stefán, who was on the school board, read a peculiar poem at the opening. It is unrhymed and oratorical in style. The poem, "Ræða" (Speech) connects the building of the schoolhouse with the unbridled, free, rhythm that was America, as it appears in Walt Whitman's poetry. The younger and more liberal in the audience listened carefully and understood, but others did not catch the significance of Stefán's choice of free verse.

> *Good evening! And be welcome to here,*
> *You old farmers, the best pillars of our settlement.*
> *Look, this is the house that you have built*
> *As a shelter for the youth.*
>   *And you found*
> *That it was a bad pauper, growing too slowly,*
> *Because it was often cold.*
>   *But your beards gave it a shelter,*
> *Until it rose high above your gray heads,*
> *As now, tonight.*
>   *Today*
> *It was rather cold and windy, but the frost became*
> *Hardest when the sun was setting.*
>   *Then*

> *Some were shivering with the cold, and shuddered at the thought*
> *Of going out into the dark of the night and the cold wind.*
> *Then you grinned in your frosted beards and said*
> *That you would not let the weather stop you on your way,*
> *And although you got a bit cold*
> *When looking over the schoolhouse – it did not harm,*
> *As the shivering would later disappear from your shoulders*
> *When struggling for ten years to pay the debt.*
> *But as you made the effort to come and see,*
> *You will easily win. It is so natural for you!*

Some of the women were startled when Stefán continued with an insistence on equal rights for the sexes. Both boys and girls were to attend the school, which was not always the case in those years, and the girls would sit on the west side of the schoolhouse while the boys would sit on the east side.

> *Good evening! And be also welcome,*
> *You housewives.*
> >*Although some schools are still locked*
> *To your daughters – this one is not closed!*
> *You remember that it is yours just as ours,*
> *And you have now received your half tonight.*
> *But take care that the west side of this house*
> *Will not become second to the other one that turns*
> *To the morning sun and is claimed by your husbands.*

This exhortation might have been all right if it had ended with the Word of God, some of the listeners may have thought, but there were no signs of conventional pieties. Stefán began mocking the worries of those who had been opposed to the debt the school had incurred.

> *Good evening! You were welcome long ago,*
> *You teenagers,*
> >*As the house was built for you,*
> *And the teacher has already greeted you here.*
> *Oh, learn to know the science, not his rod!*
> *You will gain from this house (I hope)*

More wealth and more promise in every way
Than did the school board, I myself and Sigurjón!

Good evening! And welcome to all
Enjoy the house well and for a long time, dear compatriots,
Because it is yours!
  The same counts for this evening
(oh, forget, if you have borrowed it!)
And all of you enjoy yourselves this only night,
As the rent will not rise at all
      If you laugh
  Sit in peace!
  I have no more to say,
And here are some people who want me to shut up.[21]

Whether or not Stefán's rhetoric was the reason, the school was well attended by both boys and girls.

Trade and Business

In the first issue of *Eivindur*, Stefán encouraged his countrymen to learn new farming techniques and keep detailed accounts of their farming. He suggested that they record what they did each day: when they ploughed and how deeply, how much they sowed, what kinds of soil produced the best and worst crops, how much seed cost and how much profit was realized from each type of grain. That way they would, little by little, learn from experience.

Stefán was evidently quite bullish about the potential of Dakota Territory. In issue 3-4 of *Eivindur*, he and Eiríkur Bergmann placed an advertisement asking those who planned "to buy agricultural equipment such as ploughs, harrows, seeders, mowers or reapers" to turn to them before purchasing elsewhere. They promised better deals than those to be found in the town of Pembina, resulting in savings of time, effort, and dollars. This was the most ambitious business venture of Stefán's career. There are no reports of sales, but he borrowed $400 that summer, in all likelihood mortgaging his land to buy machinery and horses. A boom was in the offing, with the railway expected to reach Gardar soon, and Eiríkur had plans to erect a sawmill.[22] He continued to expand his

An early advertisement for agricultural implements during the pioneer era.

business, going into partnership with his nephew Friðrik Bergmann to build a store under the name *Bergmann Bros*. The partnership dissolved a year later when Friðrik went to Norway to study theology, but Eiríkur continued on his own.

The Icelandic settlement was a small, rather socially closed world, yet it depended to a large extent on external powers such as railway magnates and grain merchants. Wheat, grown in the fertile Dakota soil, was the basis of their economy, which thus depended on railways and new technology. Minneapolis became the largest grain handling centre in America, with much of the grain coming from the Red River Valley where sky-high elevators rose one after another at railway sidings.[23] During the first years, the Icelandic settlers marketed their grain either in St. Vincent, nearly 60 miles from Gardar, or in Langdon, about 40 miles to the northwest in the Pembina Mountains. Stefán often went to Langdon, a day's journey, together with Jónas Hall, and the two comrades used the opportunity to discuss confidential matters.

In 1881, when a railway was constructed through St. Thomas, Glasston, and Hamilton, St. Thomas became the closest market town for Stefán and his neighbours. The settlers often set off with a load of grain in the evening, as it was cooler for the draught animals to pull the heavy loads during the night. They would then arrive at their destination in the morning, sell their grain, and return home that same day. The return journey in the daylight was safer, with less danger of running into robbers. Sometimes a number of farmers travelled to market together, and on their way home they would ride in one wagon, discussing events, singing old Icelandic folk songs, or chanting *rímur*. They often partook of some drink on such trips, and the liquor was sometimes of questionable quality.

One winter, Stefán and Jónas Hall made the trip to Park River. They left home with their respective teams of horses and oxen early in the morning and sold their wheat when they reached their destination in the evening. Having bought a bottle for the ride home, they had a sip two miles west of Park River, but when they stopped again two miles further down the road, the liquor was frozen. Repairs to the sleigh then delayed them and they did not get home until four o'clock in the morning, completely sober – with a full bottle of the strangely frozen alcohol.

The Icelandic settlement now spread over six townships, with the greatest concentration of Icelanders in three of them. Municipalities were established in 1882, with the Gardar, Eyford, and Mountain districts becoming the Municipality of Thingvalla. Among the Icelanders elected to office during those first years were Eiríkur Bergmann, Ólafur Ólafsson, Þorlákur Gunnar Jónsson, Jakob Líndal, Kristinn Kristinsson, Hallgrímur Gíslason, and Jónas Hall. Jónas, especially knowledgeable about the law, was appointed Justice of the Peace. Stefán avoided getting involved in local politics unless it was absolutely necessary.

Self-reliance

In the summer of 1882 Stefán hired 16 year old Snæbjörn Steingrímsson to take care of the cattle. In return, the boy's father wrote in a letter, Stefán and Helga agreed to teach their cowherd some English. "Farmer Stefán is a poet and an intelligent man in many ways," he added. [24] It was convenient for Stefán to have a helper as it allowed him more time for his interests. As he did not need much sleep, he often stayed awake until morning, reading and writing poetry. New ideas developed in Stefán's writing over the winter of 1882-1883, resulting in such interesting poems as "Frá æskudögum" (From Days of Youth) and "Bréf til K.S." (A Letter to K.S.), which was a verse-letter to the poet Kristinn Stefánsson.

"Frá æskudögum" (From Days of Youth) relates memories of a close boyhood friendship. The friend was of a higher social status, but Stefán was older and stronger. Sentimentally elevated in style, this poem describes youthful times together and the poignant moment of parting, when each boy had to go his own way. The friend is sad and tearful, his hands shaking and his cheeks burning, but Stefán responds differently. "I remained cheerful, smiled, and was in no way reserved,/I said goodbye to you smiling, my dear friend." In fact, however, he had found it necessary to muster all his inner strength to avoid showing his emotions, and he did not quite know how he had managed to produce a smile at the moment of departure. Then comes an insightful statement: "Now you shall be the slave of my will/you weak heart, I said, and suppressed the tears." The fate of the two boys had been different. Stefán's friend had lost his equilibrium and fallen into insobriety. Pained by this news, the poet wishes he could have supported his friend. This, he admits, is a foolish idea as he himself is frail and often at risk to the pitfalls of the world. Eventually, his friend manages to turn his life around and the poet recalls him warmly: "I can thank you for my self-reliance/you trusted me, taught me to dare."[25] Although the logic of the poem sometimes hangs by a thread, it is a poignant statement about the tolerance of human frailty.

It does not matter whether Stefán was actually writing about a real friend from his youth or was framing an idea about the struggle to control one's feelings. The boys are both good, each in his own way, but as Stefán cultivates his instincts of kindness, he also learns self-reliance by observing the weakness of his friend. This is possibly the first time the word for self-reliance appears in Icelandic – almost certainly due to the influence of Ralph Waldo Emerson's famous essay entitled "Self-Reliance".

Stefán wrote this poem in the first half of December 1882. In the following two weeks, he addressed the world in strong verses about death and noble life, about the poet who carries the sins of mankind on his shoulders, and about ideals that could light fires in ice-cold hearts. At Christmas he wrote a psalm and on New Year's, a poem. In the beginning of January 1883, he wrote a tearful romantic love poem, followed four days later by a satirical poem on a pompous government official in an entirely different style.[26]

On the evening of January 14, 1883, a blizzard hit while Stefán was feeding his cattle, that now numbered more than 10 head. Working by himself, he began to reflect on how he should answer a verse-letter from Kristinn Stefánsson, received a year earlier. At that time he had just left his father's deathbed and his feelings were in turmoil. Now, suddenly, lines of poetry whirled in his head like the blizzard outside, as he hurriedly watered the cattle and cleaned the barn. Before he went inside, however, he also chopped some firewood – murmuring the nascent lines as he worked.

Stefán had read many of Kristinn's poems and the man's hypersensitivity was beginning to irritate him. It was as if Stefán wanted to exorcise the emotional and sentimental style of poetry. In all likelihood he had seen periodicals from Iceland with new poetry such as Hannes Hafstein's "I love you, storm, that sweeps across the land,/ and evokes fluttering joy in the grove with strong leaves,/but defeats and breaks the gray and rotten branches,/and strengthens the birch trees while you blow." Hannes, a young poet who was among the pioneers of Realism in Icelandic literature, no doubt challenged Stefán's concepts of what poetry should be.

Kristinn Stefánsson (1856-1916) of Winnipeg, also a poet of note and an early target of Stephan G. Stephansson's critical pen.

In the evening, when all was quiet and everybody was asleep, he sat down and finished his verse-letter to Kristinn Stefánsson. After thanking him for his letter and friendship, he tells him about his father's death, then admits that the tears in Kristinn's verse-letter had left him unemotional at the time. "Yes, we have enough tears inside us,/ we do not have to borrow those of others," he wrote. Then, turning to his views on poetry, he states his preference for "poems as strong as a whirlwind" and concludes that he and Kristinn would now follow different paths. It does not matter, he adds, as many paths lead into the bright land of poetry, "across regions graced with flowers and birch trees,/across rough lava fields and deserts." Stefán then contrasts the two types of poetry:

> *Because the bright autumn rose, with rime on the brows,*
> *Fascinates you most, in a brisk breeze*
> *With ice cold tears of dew drops,*
> *And bows so pale, but does not fall down.*
> *I most adore the strong oak tree,*
> *That before was the pride of a green forest,*
> *but whom, in the play of wild weather,*
> *the winds felled and lightning struck.*
> *Your harp is made for a tearful, tender song;*
> *Mine resounds an entire song of raw strength.*

Stefán does not reject tenderness, but he wants to find his own tone that would be suited to reflecting life's struggles and challenging the world's injustices. This stance seems to reflect the philosophy of Danish critic Georg Brandes, a pioneer of Realism in Scandinavia, who called upon writers to debate contemporary problems. At the same time, Stefán is somewhat tolerant of Kristinn's writing, admitting that there can be different kinds of poetry, and at the end of the poem he describes his own situation: he is merely singing lullabies to himself and his own soul when the weather calms down and the sun shines on him, "If I catch some fragment of a beam,/I keep it. A larger soul than mine/shall, in better, sunny poems/let it shine again."[27]

It was almost morning, still cold and snowing, when Stefán signed the letter, blew out the lamp, and got some rest beside Helga. The next morning, when he pushed open the door of his "remote, low, and ugly hovel" and walked out into the frosty morning air to tend the animals, he was content. He had found a new direction for his poetry.

Congregational Fuss

Following the death of Páll Þorláksson, congregational matters changed – and so did Stefán's views. During the winter of 1882-1883, while he was redefining his poetic style, there was serious disagreement within the congregation. People did gather once in a while for Bible readings at first, but that soon came to an end, with power struggles simmering under the surface. Some parishioners wanted a minister from Iceland as soon as possible, before the fundamentalists nominated a minister linked to the Norwegian Synod. Others vacillated, wishing to have the matter settled, but also wanting a minister who did not cost too much and who preached in the traditional Icelandic way. A few, among them Stefán, questioned the church and its ministers and mocked the whole thing.

One afternoon in February, Baldvin Helgason called a congregational meeting in the schoolhouse. When the farmers arrived, however, there was a great fuss as the schoolhouse was locked. Friðrik Bergmann, who held conservative views on religious matters, was the schoolteacher who kept the key, and he refused to open the schoolhouse. The farmers gathered outside stamping their feet to keep warm. After arguing with Baldvin for some time and giving a variety of excuses, Friðrik eventually opened the schoolhouse.

The meeting began at 4:30 in the afternoon. Baldvin raised the issue of electing a spokesman to issue a formal call to a minister from Iceland. Friðrik Bergmann, using the classical procedural trick, declared the meeting illegal as it had not been properly advertised. Eventually, a committee of three men was elected to advertise another meeting in three weeks. When Stefán heard of these events, he wrote a short comical verse in which he mocked the opposing camps. As far as he could see, many souls would be lost and a priest and a flock would perish. In the end, he concludes that the key to heaven and hell, the souls of parishioners, their debates, as well as their money pouches, would be a minister.[28]

Rev. Friðrik Bergmann (1858-1918), educated at the Lutheran seminary in Decorah, Iowa, and later in Oslo and Philadelphia, served the Icelandic congregations in Pembina County following his ordination in 1886.

A crisis in church matters was building. In the original

dispute with Páll Þorláksson in New Iceland, Reverend Jón Bjarnason had maintained Icelandic independence against the institutional power of the Norwegian Synod. Now, liberal farmers opposed the conservatism of the Church as reflected in congregational meetings. Stefán attended the next meeting and was the only one to vote against a resolution that the congregation continue as the Park Congregation. In all likelihood he recognized that the conservatives were gaining the upper hand. A committee was then elected to redraft the congregational by-laws for the next meeting.

In March of 1883 the by-laws were passed and Friðrik Bergmann was elected to oversee a Sunday School and the Bible readings. It had been stated in Páll's by-laws that only men had the right to speak and vote at congregational meetings. Now, in article seven, there was a concession on women's rights: "Anyone who has joined the congregation, man or woman, and having reached 21 years of age ... is entitled to free speech and the right to vote at congregational meetings." Stefán did not sign the by-laws at this meeting, nor at the next one, but he did later join the congregation.[29] At the next meeting Eiríkur Bergmann got approval to raise money to hire a minister. Most of those who pledged contributions were Bergmann supporters and the split in the congregation became increasingly obvious.

As the never-ending quest for a minister continued, Reverend Hans B. Thorgrimsen served the Vík Congregation at Mountain and occasionally held services for the Park Congregation. He was informally asked to serve Park for

Baldvin Helgason, the talented father of poet Undína, was as unconventional in religion as he was in his life choices. Previously a settler in the Muskoka district of Ontario, he lived in Dakota Territory for several years before moving to Manitoba and eventually Oregon.

eight months, but he was both unwilling to serve as a mere substitute and unable to accept the congregational by-laws. He found an article on the creed intolerable and the concession on women's rights even worse. The congregation subsequently split that fall, after the majority rejected a motion from Sigfús Bergmann to alter the by-laws so that Reverend Hans could accept them. Now 11 men seceded, among them the three Bergmanns, Hallgrímur Gíslason, and Gísli Dalmann. Shortly thereafter they established the new congregation of Gardar.

Stefán likely did not concern himself much about the by-laws, but he did wish to support the liberalism of the Park Congregation. At the next meeting, held in Stefán and Helga's home, the by-laws were read aloud, as if to underline the rebellious spirit of the liberals. A number of people joined the congregation, among them several women. After this meeting, Stefán wrote a little morning hymn in which a "God of light" makes the mild morning sun shine on his personal progress. He counted on the protection of this God: "So, at the greatest peril of heart,/ Lord, who hast the greatest power,/I rest calmly in your hands."[30] At the congregation's annual meeting, held in the home of Kristinn and Sigurlaug Kristinsson on January 8, 1884, the by-laws were simplified – with no distinction made between men and women. Everyone, men and women, signed. Stefán's signature reads "Stephen G. Stephenson".

During the winter, Reverend Hans B. Thorgrimsen organized a meeting to establish an Icelandic Lutheran Synod. Reverend Jón Bjarnason, now minister of the Icelanders in Winnipeg, immediately took up this idea and supported it, and a general meeting was held at Mountain in the fall of 1884. The rebels of the Park Congregation were in favour of a Synod, but were satisfied holding meetings to read the scriptures and sing hymns – without a minister. Their resistance had borne fruit, as women's rights were discussed far and wide throughout the community.

In spite of the unrest, it was important to the settlers to have the sacraments of baptism, confirmation, marriage, and burial. Most were therefore in favour of a compromise that would expedite the hiring of a minister – Reverend Hans, for example. Debate between the liberals and conservatives over by-laws and congregational matters continued, however, as it was obvious that the conservatives would be better able to gain the upper hand in a Synod. Religious politics in the settlement were no longer on a friendly, personal level, as they had been between

Stefán and the late Páll Þorláksson. They had escalated to the beginnings of a complicated power struggle within the Icelandic community in North America.

Meaningful Nature

On Sunday, March 17, 1883, Jón Jónsson from Mjóidalur invited friends and neighbours to his large new home for a house-warming. Stefán addressed the party, talking about the settlement in a broader context than people were used to, and presenting ideas that might have seemed foreign to some. Despite the fact that Icelandic immigrants had chosen to move to the United States, and to Dakota Territory in specific, he criticized the American way of life – stressing the imbalance between nature and man, and presenting glimpses of the life and environment of the settlers.

Stefán acknowledged the importance of house and home to the pioneers, but he also expressed his love of the mountains and moors, wilderness and forests. He disliked the damage "done to the natural beauty of the forests and meadows. [Man's activities] have transformed the blossoming prairies into a landscape stripped of its grasses and deprived of fertility, and the green-leafed forests have been transformed into clear cuts, where piles of fresh-cut wood decay and rot. The songbirds are chased away by the bellowing of cows and the bleating of sheep, and the call of a cuckoo is seldom heard for the incessant grinding of the mills of avaricious King Fróði, whom American farmers worship in their constant pursuit of wealth."

Stefán nevertheless recognized that man's hand sometimes plants flowers with grace and taste, and he pointed out that this new house was skilfully built in that spirit so the clearing where it stood would become pretty again and the entire neighbourhood would be enhanced.

Then Stefán turned his attention to the Icelandic settlers. Some who had immigrated had become "American citizens and noble persons", while others had become lost to mankind – in particular those who "think of nothing but profit and the accumulation of wealth." That was not the case with the owners of this house, he stated. "Its construction had required many heavy swings of the axe to fell the timber and hew the walls. It had taken strength and skill to lift the huge logs and to join them at the corners." In the beginning, he said, the Icelanders had lived in humble huts because of their poverty and ignorance, but brighter times lay ahead. "This house or a similar one inhabited by Icelanders will someday produce an individual for whom Iceland is waiting – one who will "arouse from torpidity of habit" the ancient fame of the country and spread its reputation around the world, whether he be a poet or a wise man."[31]

Stefán's speech reveals an ambivalence towards the progress and economic boom Dakota was experiencing. He read much these years, constantly reconsidering his philosophy of life, and this critical view of progress combined with an idealization of nature was undoubtedly stimulated by Henry David Thoreau's inspired work *Walden*, on the creative partnership of man and nature. While he grudgingly took part in congregational disputes, Stefán began to express radical ideas and emotions in powerful verses.

In the spring of 1884, Stefán wrote a series of poems called "Voróður" (An Ode to Spring), in which nature's opposites – heat and cold, harshness and mildness – struggle. The first poem, "Hólmstefnan" (The Duel), describes a man's journey through a furious blizzard in the middle of winter. The traveller does not feel "the raging storm" that hurls "painfully frozen rockets of ice" at him. He neither blows on his hands nor rubs his nose, but walks straight north. His chest and forehead are hot and his soul is aflame: "O, do not fear that the breast will feel the biting cold,/as the heart is an erupting glacier within," he wrote. A similar conflict is described in the second poem, "Vetrarkvöld" (Winter Night). The poet, deep in thought, is sitting by a frosted window when he is startled by the sudden fury of a blizzard. The tension between the heat inside and the cold outside is a recurring theme. The poet finds his house "narrow and small", his life "humbly low", the soul turbulent, "an ocean of swelling laughter and tears." He wants "to fight the storm". It is as if the poet is bursting with a desire to fight, but the storm waylays him, and in the end he manages to control his rage, his mind and heart are calmed, and he thinks that now he can write his best poetry.[32]

The next poem, "Lækurinn" (The Brook), is another variation on this theme. In the beginning, the poet states that while the brooks that run east from the Pembina Mountains are usually calm, they swell during the spring thaw until their roar is capable of waking a poet from his sleep:

> *Tonight through sleep I heard the roar,*
> *Of a swelling small brook in a ravine in a steep forest*
> *That now is a big river, with a waterfall and pool.*
> *Before, it lulled me to sleep with its sweet purl.*
> *Now the roar of the current wakes me from sleep.*

The poet dresses hurriedly to go out and greet this friend and neighbour who usually passes quietly by his home. The brook is a symbol of fresh ideas, radical changes, and even political revolution. The poet says that he has watched as the brook struggles onwards "sweeping away barrages of rotten stems and branches" while the evening sun "unfolds flaming red flags in the west." The swift current of the brook cleans away the old, but it also carries with it the possibilities of life, causing seedlings to sprout in barren ground where they will grow into green and leafy trees. The poem ends by encouraging the brook to continue on its way. The red sun still hangs in the western sky, albeit a little lower. "My young mind follows you cheerfully,/as there is a similar pressure in my own heart."[33]

The fourth poem, entitled "Þrumuskúr" (Thundershower), describes a thunderstorm.[34]

The last poem is very different from the others in the series. Entitled "Fjólan" (The Violet), it is a commemorative poem about a flower struck down in a hailstorm. The violet was good and beautiful, but the poet had never kissed it, fearing that the heat from his kiss would burn the flower.[35] Although Stefán had rejected sentimentalism in his verse-letter to Kristinn Stefánsson, here he returns to the romantic tenderness that seems hard for him to avoid.

A Summer Night in Dakota

In the summer of 1883, Sigurjóna Sigurbjörnsdóttir, a first cousin to Helga, died at the age of 25. Stefán and she did not know each other well, but from her deathbed she had requested that he write a commemorative poem about her. He could not refuse such an unusual request.

In the poem, he pictures a black and cold grave "where the grass cannot grow on broken ground." He is surprised by her last wish. Why did she choose him to write her a lullaby "in a calm sleep in the middle of the night of death?" With his "soul in such turmoil" in its attempt to unite ice and fire in his poems, he is awestruck at her appearance – moribund, deathly pale, with sunken eyes – yet so calm, while his own mind is burning from unrest. At the end, the poet asks the earth not to let cypress (literally "crying wood" in Icelandic) grow on Sigurjóna's grave, but rather a big fir tree "that would extend green branches toward the changing weather." Here, Stefán reconciles life and death, a tension he had been wrestling with ever since his father's death. "Wer dem Tode ins Angesicht schauen kann? Der allein is ein freier Mann" [Only he who can face death is a free man – Schiller, *Wallenstein*], he jotted in German on a scrap of paper during these years.[36]

After an ethnically diverse Fourth of July celebration at Gardar in 1883, haying was followed by harvest. On August 28, 1883, after a long day of work, Stefán walked up the flowery slope behind his house and leaned for a while against an oak tree to enjoy the mild evening air. While light and shadow played in the last beams of sunlight, he composed the first version of a poem that has always been regarded one of his best. Originally entitled "Kvöldblíðan" (Evening Tenderness), this poem conjures up a serene image of the Dakota prairie, with farm work and nature intertwining. In this poem, Stefán seems to see himself and his work in a new light, one that is in harmony with nature and his surroundings. Some 17 years later, he completed this poem, renaming it "Við verkalok" (At Labour's End) and revising it slightly to make it flow more easily. Here are the first three stanzas of the final version:

> *When sunny slopes are swept with evening shadow*
> *In summer night*
> *And high up in the trees, the moon hangs*
> *Its half shield,*
> *When a crisp evening breeze again begins to cool*
> *My sweaty forehead,*
> *Then after a day's work, my tired life*
> *Welcomes the peace of night.*
>
> *Then in the distance, the sound of ringing bells is heard,*
> *Now slow, now quickly,*
> *And the evening poems of birds sound in my ears,*
> *So delicately moving;*
> *The breeze seems to sing half a line*

> *At its loudest whine*
> *And the laughter of children playing by the brook*
> *Floats gently to me.*
>
> *Fields wink like pale spots of moonshine,*
> *But more blue than the ground,*
> *And pale blue mist fills the low hollows*
> *By brook and bog,*
> *But low in the east, golden stars are shining,*
> *Through the trees;*
> *It is then that I sit outside by the wall of the house,*
> *In evening's calm.*

We can imagine the scene that might have inspired this poem: Helga, outside the house with new life stirring inside her, for she was now pregnant again, and Guðbjörg, knitting by the west side of the house, or perhaps the two of them picking berries in the woods on the hillside. Near the house is a large linden tree. Snæbjörn, the farm helper, is playing with the little boys, Baldur, almost four years old, and Guðmundur, nearly two. Next to the house is a vegetable garden with cabbage and potatoes. Beyond the barn are grazing cattle, mowed hayfields, and fields of swaying grain. The last two stanzas in the original version describe the poet's reaction to this beautiful scene, while also revealing the difficulties he experiences in expressing tender feelings:

> *Because my heart is full of rest and joy,*
> *My soul full of peace;*
> *Then I feel like eternal love and heavenly beauty*
> *Are a universal language,*
> *As if every thing in the world is saying my prayers*
> *And blessing me,*
> *At the heart of goodness itself, earth and heaven*
> *Are resting.*
>
> *And I feel like the moment just passing*
> *Is an eternal spring.*
> *From the love of my heart, if I should have to tell*

But I do not dare.
But often I feel like something at last is wetting
The hairs of my brow,
As if the first night dew was falling on them,
Or a few tears.

Night dew and tears symbolize Stefán's love of life. These stanzas are in contrast with the turbulent, challenging tone of his verse-letter to Kristinn Stefánsson and the series of poems "Voróður" (Ode to Spring), and they reveal that Stefán was still wrestling with expressions of tenderness. When he later revises the poem, the gradual evolution of his poetry becomes evident. He now wipes away the tears and inserts a new thought instead. Not only does he rename the poem, he also totally rewrites the last stanza. Now the poem transcends mere parochialism and evening calmness becomes a symbol of the poet's desire for reconciliation with the world.

But in the end when all the day is done
And all accounted for,
And whatever dues the world might estimate
That I have earned:
In such peace I'd choose to write
A calm and poignant poem,
And finally extend to the world a hand of conciliation
At sunset.[37]

In these lines of the final version of the poem, Stefán succeeds in giving his immediate surroundings and experiences universal meaning. The farmer's daily chores now take on new philosophical significance.

Chapter 7

Quest for Knowledge

Solomon's Temple Speech

The Gardar district was fully settled by the end of 1883, the peak year of the Dakota boom. Farming progressed more quickly at Gardar than in the other Icelandic settlements in Pembina County as many of the Gardar settlers had gained valuable experience, livestock, and a little money in Wisconsin and Minnesota. Horses were replacing oxen as draught animals, farmers were jointly purchasing farm equipment, and roads and bridges were being constructed. The population of the Gardar district reached 570, 50 of whom were farmers, and a village of the same name boasted a saloon, post office, Eiríkur Bergmann's store, and a steam-powered sawmill. Gísli Dalmann also had a blacksmith shop at Gardar and he was building "Hotel Thingvalla", which Karólína would manage.

Although only four years had passed since the area was homesteaded, some of the first settlers were well off, and it was tempting for some to take mortgages at interest rates as high as 10%. The boom, however, was slowing. It had been sparked by huge investments in railways, flourmills, and land.

Overall, not many of the settlers felt in a position to help those who came later. There had been little work the previous winter and some, like Steingrímur Grímsson, the father of Stefán's farm helper Snæbjörn, lived mainly on potatoes and milk. He wrote a letter home, complaining about most things except his son's situation and exploring the idea of settling elsewhere. There were many dangers, he claimed, including conflicts between the Norwegians and the English. "Men have been shot, and shots have also been fired at homes in an attempt to intimidate people. One hears of all kinds of mischief around us," he wrote.[1] Worst of all was the lack of a minister, a church, and religious services. Young adults nearly 20 years old had not been confirmed, people were buried in unconsecrated ground, and there was little indication that the parish would be able to afford a minister. There were also 50 newly-arrived settlers who had neither land nor livestock.

Stephan G. Stephansson in his prime during his Dakota years.

The established farmers, on the other hand, now owned more than 30 horses, 73 draught oxen, 138 cows, 184 calves and bullocks, 164 sheep, 47 pigs, and more than 500 fowl, and most of them also had a plough, harrows, and some machinery for sowing and harvesting. A few Icelandic farmers even owned a threshing machine in partnership with a Norwegian, and though there was still no railway, there were 31 wagons and 30 sleighs in the district. Over 1000 acres had been seeded to grain the previous summer and almost 500 acres of new breaking had been added. The largest fields were about 100 acres, whereas Stefán had about 30 acres under cultivation. Three sawmills were exploiting the nearby forests, including a beautiful old oak forest that, if it had not been so quickly destroyed, would have become many times more valuable a few years later. Lumber was frequently used before being properly dried and it consequently warped badly.

Of 270 Icelandic souls in the Gardar district, 200 belonged to the Park Congregation, and most of the rest to the Gardar Congregation, with its close ties to the Bergmanns. Stefán, together with most of his family and friends, belonged to the Park Congregation, and in the register he recorded his name as "Stephen G. Stephenson". He had used this or a similar anglicized form of his name on English documents since first arriving in America, and now this version appeared in a church

The poet was granted title to his homestead on Oct. 15, 1884, as 'Stephen G. Stephenson'. The document also includes the name of President Chester A. Arthur.

record. The original Icelandic spelling of his name, *Stefán*, seldom appeared again, and soon the poet adopted the spelling that has become best known – *Stephan G. Stephansson*.

After St. Thomas was connected to the railway in 1881-1882, hopes of getting an extension to Gardar were rekindled. Eiríkur Bergmann was keen on the idea, as railways connected farmers to markets and capital, enhancing business in railway towns and raising the price of land. Eiríkur called a meeting, urging the farmers to put money into the enterprise. Stephan, as was often the case, found himself in the minority, as he opposed the proposal.

Whether merely for enjoyment or as a form of social commentary, Stephan sometimes composed exaggerated satirical stories in verse form, and in March of 1884 he wrote "Musterisræða Salómons" (Solomon's Temple Speech), a long poem about Eiríkur's dream of a railway. In the Prologue, he expresses doubts that Solomon ever existed, but he then adds that recently some clay tablets had been found, inscribed with poetry indicating that Solomon was an eloquent speaker and quite familiar with formal procedure at meetings. Stephan then states that some Biblical texts ascribed to Solomon resemble Icelandic pornographic poetry, and he adds that some people regard these texts as a play, performed as a fundraiser for the building of Solomon's temple. Furthermore, he suggests, the famous sentence in Proverbs, that nothing is new under the sun, was a reference to the promiscuity of Solomon, who got "very tired of each woman and said this in an angry outburst because he found that there was nothing new about any of them."[2]

In the poem, Solomon's temple becomes a symbol of excess and avarice, and Solomon's speech is apparently a grotesque parody of Eiríkur's speech at a meeting, which evidently proceeded as follows – Stephan's exaggerations aside. First Eiríkur thoroughly discussed the unacceptability of not having a railway to Gardar. "I do not think we can over estimate the loss/as there is now so little traffic here," he began, citing the lack of business in town. Few goods are sold, and there is a constant shortage of supplies. The minister had even complained that it was almost impossible to read the Scripture, as the candle in the candlestick was half burned, only a "finger long wreck of a wax candle, gnawed by a mouse." There is hardly any iron or timber available, and not even a drop of alcohol in the saloon to fill the chalice.

Reverend Friðrik Bergmann and his first cousin Eiríkur Bergmann, with their respective wives, Guðrún and Ingibjörg, before 1890. Eiríkur was a community leader and a member of the state legislature by 1889. He and the poet held divergent views on most issues.

There is no point in "dying of paralysis", Eiríkur the entrepreneur states, pointing out that no lots in the town will sell. He proposes raising funds by performing his laudatory poem, and as soon as the money is there, people will get their temple in the form of a railway station – if they use it to bribe the railway kings. Those at the meeting promise both timber and money for the station:

> One donates a wisp of hay, another a stone,
> And donkey and buffalo bones are sold here!
> And the mob is used to shovel and dig.

> *It makes no difference for them to slave for a few days*
> *At building our temple here – by them,*
> *But I will pay them compliments!*

Eiríkur the entrepreneur adds that he is expecting a visit from an "extremely rich queen" living in Sheba, "with a black monkey-like body/ and I estimate she has already turned 30,/and she is coming to visit me." His reputation for "masculine beauty and royal wisdom" has driven her mad, and since she cannot walk such a long way it is necessary to construct a railway to Gardar:

> *Then she will soon come, riding on the railway cars –*
> *She stokes up the engine herself, – shaking her apron.*
> *She increases the flames and the speed – eager*
> *And praising the beauty and great wisdom of Solomon.*

Having thus heralded – as Solomon – the arrival of the Queen of Capitalism in Gardar, Eiríkur submits a motion that he hopes will be accepted, then sits down. The poem implies that no discussion or objections were to be entertained, "and denser than leaves in a clump of northern crowberries/the mob at the meeting put their hands up to the ceiling." Solomon grabs his hat and hurries to adjourn the meeting.

Stephan called the dream of a railway "self-interested blustering" and deemed that Eiríkur's promotion mixed his own private interests with public interest. The village was built on his land and a railway would raise the price of that land. He also foresaw a tightening of the monopolistic stranglehold of the large grain companies, supported by the railways.[3] Stephan took a firm stand against this development, doubting that it was progress and adhering to his ideal of protecting nature.

It is not known whether Eiríkur actually read "Musterisræða Salómons" (Solomon's Temple Speech) or whether Stephan shared it only with his closest friends. Such satirical poetry was common in those days and Eiríkur would likely have had little difficulty accepting it in jest.

A few years later, a railway was constructed through Milton, west of the Icelandic settlement, and in a newsletter Stephan mentioned the general disappointment that it did not come closer to Gardar.

A Conference in Winnipeg

Cultural life among the Icelanders in North America was lively despite the struggle to get established, and in Pembina County plays were performed in every district. Stephan wrote more plays during these years, most of which survive only as fragments. The one exception is a play in verse, regarding a folktale.

In the spring of 1884, Helga bore Stephan a third son, a little boy named Jón. Stephan's sister, Sigurlaug, and her husband already had two children, Stefán Kristinn Ólafur and Guðbjörg Lilja. Around this time Stephan got the final papers for his homestead, which he promptly mortgaged in order to have some investment capital. That fall he met Björn Halldórsson, a skilled carpenter recently arrived from Iceland, and on December 30th he hired Björn to build cabinets, a separate bedroom, a closet, and a cupboard, all of which made the home quite comfortable.

In February of 1885 Stephan chaired a meeting of the Park Congregation, at which the by-laws of the new Synod, established two weeks earlier, were approved. The liberals struggled with the fundamentalists, but neither faction gained the upper hand. Women's rights remained the main issue of contention. In May, Stephan and Jónas Hall were elected as delegates to the first conference of the Icelandic Lutheran Synod, to be held in Winnipeg under the leadership of Reverend Jón Bjarnason. After receiving $30-40 to cover their travelling costs, the two comrades set off for Winnipeg on a hot June day, with Stephan pledging to promote women's rights.

Winnipeg had become the largest city on the Canadian prairies and the centre of Icelandic cultural life in North America. The population, which included at least a thousand Icelanders, had grown from 8,000 to 20,000 over the past five years, and there were now broad avenues, warehouses, banks, a city hall, a courthouse, high schools, and telephone exchanges. Land speculation and house construction had flourished and then collapsed, and frivolity and morality struggled, as only two years had passed since the clergy had managed to have the brothels moved to the outskirts of the city.[4] Stories about stumbling, drunken Icelanders and girls fallen into prostitution circulated and god-fearing people campaigned against indecency.

An array of hotels and saloons along Main Street greeted Stephan and Jónas when they stepped off the train. After walking a short distance

Delegates at the 1885 conference of the Icelandic Lutheran Synod in Winnipeg. Stephan G. Stephansson, second from right in the back row, was among them.

south, they turned west on Jemima Street (now Elgin) and proceeded to number 137, the handsome building of the Icelandic Progressive Society, where 19 delegates from 12 Icelandic congregations in the West had gathered. There were also six delegates from congregations that had not yet formally joined the Synod, including old Þorlákur Gunnar Jónsson from Vík (Mountain) and the Bergmann cousins from Gardar.

This first conference of the Icelandic Lutheran Synod opened on Wednesday, June 24, 1885, with a service conducted by Reverend Jón, and it continued with psalms and prayers until Saturday. The Bergmanns from Gardar assumed a more prominent profile at the conference than Jónas and Stephan, though Stephan joined the fundraising committee and became Vice-Secretary after refusing to take on duties as Secretary. He felt that the person holding that post would have to live in Winnipeg, in order to be near President Jón Bjarnason. Stephan's interest was already waning, but he accepted the post as Vice-Secretary as he knew it would not entail much work. The issue of women's rights never came up, an overwhelming majority being opposed to this idea, "and it was impossible to deal with that mob," Stephan concluded.[5]

The partners from Gardar stayed in Winnipeg for a few days, during which Stephan addressed the Icelandic Progressive Society. While he acknowledged that the first steps of progress were being taken in Winnipeg, having just arrived from the panoramic Pembina Mountains he found the city flat and dominated by a rather narrow outlook – with too much "taste of flesh and blood" rather than a taste for spiritual nourishment. There was "more discussion about persons than issues" at the meetings, he observed, and progress was "sometimes more gilding than gold." "I am accustomed to the plain rural life," he added, "and perhaps I misunderstand city life. Maybe I merely fail to see the essence and seriousness that I think I would like to see under the external decoration."[6] There is no account of how the Icelanders in Winnipeg reacted to his speech.

When the Park and Gardar Congregations merged the following winter, Reverend Friðrik Bergmann became pastor to all the Icelandic congregations in Pembina County. Stephan and Friðrik were both on the by-law committee and reached agreement that the word "man" would denote both men and women – a by-law that Friðrik promised never to change. Stephan did not sign the by-laws although Friðrik pressed him. "Do you think it will be a pleasure for me to be a minister here at Gardar knowing that those whom I perhaps value most are not in my congregation?"[7]

Stephan did not change his mind and never did join the new parish. The Park Congregation had been a rebellious group that acknowledged women's rights and had insisted upon a minister from Iceland. When these disputes were at their peak, Stephan wrote a stanza that ended thus: "Do not tell me about pleasure in the upper realms,/Reverends in your crooked sermons./It is better to move slowly downward/there is more peace and grace down there."[8] Stephan sought a foothold closer to earth.

The Freethinkers

During these years, Stephan was clearly adopting the liberal and critical religious and social views prominent in American intellectual life at the time: support for women's rights, conservation of nature, and criticism of monopolies and capitalism. No doubt more concerned with these larger issues than with trivial congregational disputes, he acquainted himself with new scientific theories and read textbooks on natural history and languages. Stephan also received trial subscriptions to freethinking publications and he discussed new ideas with friends such as Jónas Hall, Jakob Líndal, and Ólafur Ólafsson. "You must have something to read, otherwise you become nothing but stomach and mouth," he said. More inclined towards common sense arguments than metaphysical ones, he demanded "from the freethinking papers scientific rigor that enhances understanding by bringing forward arguments that do not play upon people's prejudices and preconceptions." Stephan was familiar with a dozen such papers and all the contemporary debates taking place among American intellectuals.[9]

It takes time for a nation of pioneers to develop a distinctive voice in literature and philosophy. At first American culture was dominated by the Puritans, but changes occurred after 1820 with the rise of Unitarianism, which was a religious doctrine that took its name from its refusal to acknowledge the holy trinity of "Father, Son, and Holy Ghost". Instead, Unitarians regarded God as a unified being. They wanted to build religion on knowledge and reason.

Another threat to religious fundamentalism surfaced after 1830 in the works of Ralph Waldo Emerson, a theologian who was expelled from the church for preaching provocative sermons. Emerson sparked an increase in independent American thinking. His ideas, developed during the settlement phase of the United States, incorporated both the initiative of the young settler society and the philosophy of European thinkers. Instead of adhering to a uniform idea of God, as the fundamentalists did, Emerson adopted a more liberal position, maintaining human abilities independent of divine guidance. Under his influence, American poets and thinkers flourished, among them Walt Whitman, who embraced American nature and life in all its variety, and Henry David Thoreau, who wrote about man, nature, and civil disobedience. In Europe, the philosopher Friedrich Nietzsche was also influenced by Emerson, whose essay "Self-Reliance" was especially influential.[10]

Björn Pétursson, former member of parliament in Iceland and pioneer in New Iceland, had a checkered career. He became a strong advocate of Unitarianism among his countrymen in Winnipeg and Dakota Territory.

By the time Stephan began to acquaint himself with the intellectual life of the New World, the original frontier generation had more or less passed on. Now freethinkers were prominent. What united them was a critical attitude toward the church and a questioning of religion in the light of the new sciences. Some even preached atheism, the most radical of these being Robert Green Ingersoll (1833-1899), a self-educated lawyer and humanitarian inspired by Darwinism. He gave glowing speeches advocating faith in science, atheism, and Biblical criticism. Another outstanding freethinker was Felix Adler (1851-1933), a well-educated Jew who established an ethical society based upon the humanitarian principles of religion.

One of the freethinking papers Stephan read was *The Index*, published by the Free Religious Association, established in Boston in 1867. For a time, Stephan subscribed to this paper, binding two years into a large volume – much read and even scribbled upon by his children. Stephan made notations on essays dealing with such issues as morals, science, humanitarianism, Biblical content, possible scientific foundations of religion, and men's fear of women's rights. The aim of the Association was to find a new, scientific, and moral foundation for religion. The editors, W. J. Potter and B. F. Underwood, contributed articles to every issue, and a number of well-educated writers wrote whole series of essays on philosophy, science, the theory of knowledge, sociology, women's rights, literature, and religion. It was a rare issue that did not quote Emerson and other freethinkers – among them Kant, Hegel, Herbert Spencer, Darwin, and, quite prominently, Karl Marx. The paper rejected dogma, while acknowledging the humanitarian content of religion.

One of the articles that caught Stephan's eye and prompted him to make notations was by William Lloyd Garrison, Jr. (1838-1909), the son of famous abolitionist William Lloyd Garrison, Sr. (1805-1879). It was regarding the religious upbringing of children. Because of progress in the sciences, religion was dying, Garrison claimed. People denied instead of asking, he continued. Some 25 years earlier, fundamentalists had called upon God to "hook the jaw" of the disbeliever Theodore Parker, whose rejection of religion had become a doctrine. Now, thousands gathered to hear Ingersoll mock God. Garrison regretted the decline of the religious concept of elevating the spirit. Something was lost, he said, that was being replaced by empty materialism. He hesitated to take his children to Sunday school because of the formalities and credulity, but Ingersoll's lectures, according to Garrison, were no better. His eloquence was empty and artificial despite the fact that he rightly mocked creeds. One is left empty inside after such a lecture, contrary to the experience of listening to Parker or Emerson, he wrote.[11]

Judging from *The Index*, there was a growing impatience over how long it was taking to unite the liberal forces in religious matters. As often happens with radical dissidence, opinions were divided and religious views polarized between fundamentalism and atheism. Potter, in an article on liberal organizations, pointed to the pioneer work of Emerson and Parker. It was easy for "satellites" such as Ingersoll to attack the church and fundamentalism, but the real need was to organize a broad movement, he wrote.[12]

Stephan translated B. W. Ball's poem "Mountain Vale", which appeared in the January issue of *The Index*. Similar to poems Stephan had been writing lately, it dealt with the tension between strength and weakness, the wild and the cultivated.[13] Stephan also marked lines from a poem "Io Victis", by the sculptor and poet W. W. Story (1819-1895), quoted in an article on contemporary poetry in reference to Story's empathy for what the world sometimes calls failure. The poem recalls Walt Whitman's famous praise of the fallen in the 18th chapter of "Song of Myself". Whitman praised those who had fallen on the battlefield, whereas Story praised those who had succumbed to life's struggle.[14]

Stephan also underlined much of an article entitled "The Will and its Parasites", written by the Unitarian Minister Moncure D. Conway (1832-1907), a great abolitionist. Man's freedom and happiness depend on his successful self-actualization, Conway said. Religions suppress the natural will of man and reinforce control based on tradition and habit. Stephan underlined the question regarding the use of one's intellect. What was the purpose of humanity's will to seek truth if that truth was pre-determined, Conway asked. The goal of education, he wrote, should be to think for oneself, so as to arrive at one's own assessment of society.[15]

American thinkers had freed themselves from the strictures of religious dogma earlier in the century. Now, with their help, Stephan did the same. He was fascinated by single-minded freethinkers such as Ingersoll, as he needed such firm views in order to liberate himself from generally accepted ideas. This step toward atheism was difficult for a man such as him, however, having been brought up in a traditional religion that indoctrinated children with Balle's catechism before confirmation. Stephan's sense of spirituality involved caring deeply for other people and for the world, and that spirituality required a new channel.

Struggle, Culture, and Progress

On February 20, 1886, 100 people attended a party at Eiríkur Bergmann's home in Gardar. The occasion was the marriage of Jón Jónsson Jr. from Mjóidalur and Guðbjörg Guðmundsdóttir. Guests dined in three sittings, drinking a lot of punch that stimulated song and speeches, after which they went to the schoolhouse to dance and drink until morning. The bride was pregnant and three weeks later gave birth to a daughter, Emilía Sigurbjörg.

A few weeks after the wedding, Jón Sr. from Mjóidalur, now 50 years old, carefully calculated what he had paid his children and what their contributions in work had been to the household. The outstanding loan to Guðmundur, Stephan's father, was accounted to Helga, and Jón Sr. had also paid, on their behalf, a $15 debt to his sister Guðfinna. He had given Helga a sewing machine and a cow, each valued at $30. Jón Jr. had gone to school for a while, but worked mostly at home, so his father owed him in return. Jón bequeathed his son the land and household, but reserved for himself the income from any timber sold from the land. In return, Jón Jr. was to support his parents as long as they lived. Thus ended yet another chapter in the life of a thrifty man. He continued binding books and was a sales agent

Gardar pioneer Jón Jónsson, Jr. from Mjóidalur, the poet's brother-in-law, and his bride, Guðbjörg Guðmundsdóttir, around the time of their marriage in 1886. They lived out their lives at Gardar and had 13 children.

for *Sameiningin* (*Unity*), the Icelandic Synod's journal. His wife, Sigurbjörg, was now more than 60 years of age, suffering from a leg injury and hardly able to walk.

Two weeks after the wedding, Eiríkur Bergmann showed up unexpectedly on Stephan's doorstep. A plebiscite was underway to decide whether Thingvalla Municipality should be divided into two local government jurisdictions – Mountain and Gardar. Mountain had a larger population, and the farmers at Gardar, most of whom were better off, wanted the split because Mountain often flexed its greater voting power to swing elections. In order to split the municipality, however, a majority of votes was required.

People flocked to the polling station and as the day passed the Gardar men could see from the turnout that they would lose by two or three votes. Voting was to conclude at four o'clock in the afternoon and now Eiríkur had come to seek Stephan's counsel. After quickly formulating a plan, Stephan reached into his cupboard, grabbed a bottle of liquor, and accompanied Eiríkur back to Mountain. The plan was for Stephan to distract a few Mountain men who had not yet voted by offering them a drink and keeping them occupied in an out of the way spot until the voting was over.

The poet had no problem striking up a conversation with several men, but of course they did not want to leave the polling station until they had voted. Stephan convinced them that there would be no harm in sneaking away for a little drink, and since he himself had not yet voted, his persuasion worked. He took them as far away as he could, reciting verses, regaling them with stories, and giving each a drink from the bottle. Eventually, they heard a great shout from the polling station, a sign from Stephan's co-conspirators that the voting was over. The others were startled and asked Stephan what it meant. He answered that it was four o'clock and he had lost his chance to vote. His drinking companions hurried off, leaving Stephan laughing uproariously and calling after them that there was no point in rushing now. Mountain's community leaders were so furious at the stupidity of the drinkers that they swore at them and started a fight, which had to be broken up by the Gardar men. The outcome was that Thingvalla Municipality was split.[16]

Generally speaking, Stephan shrugged off municipal politics, despite the fact that he was prepared to get a few Mountain men drunk when necessary. He preferred to stick to his books, writing, poetry, and farming – and he was kept busy providing for his growing family. A fourth son, Jakob, was born June 8, 1886, and around that time Stephan built another addition to the house, this time with the help of his father-in-law. Perhaps that was the reason why he decided to fell a big tree growing near the front door, something he regretted doing after reflecting on the fact that the tree had been there for generations. This incident was the inspiration of a poem he called "Linditréð við húsdyrnar" (The Linden at the Door):

> *And there it had stood for a thousand years*
> *Enduring the weathers of the centuries,*
> *In front of the main door, so tall and beautiful,*
> *With its braided branches,*
> *The tree with the pretty leaves – as if the faithful goddess of trees*
> *Had selected her trustiest servant*
> *To stand on guard over the farm and household*
> *Committed to her protection.*

The old tree had stood there for generations. It had witnessed both joy and sorrow, and it had followed the progress of the little pioneer family, sheltering their house from sun and rain and watching over the little boys as they grew. The poet puts his everyday chores in the context of the eternal labour of nature: a hut, "a bungled work of fashion, low and ugly", is knocked together from poorly planed boards made from the tree. The poor building of the moment replaces an age-old tree. The little boys could no longer seek the shade of its leafy branches: "the sun shone burning hot around the house,/the children suffered in the heat."[17]

"The bungled work of fashion", however, was not that humble. The tree had remained long enough to witness the value of the property rise to more than $2000. The land was valued at $1600, improvements on the land were assessed at $230, and the buildings at $600. The tree had seen Stephan break more than 40 acres of land, and another 40 acres served as pastureland for 16 head of horned cattle and 20 sheep. Stephan also planned to break more land in the spring. There was a well with good water and the comfortable log house boasted a ceiling and a shingled roof. Near the house stood a granary measuring 14 feet by 14 feet and two barns, 26 feet by 30 feet and 14 feet by 16 feet respectively. Machinery and farm equipment including a wagon, a plough, a mower, harrows, and a rake – worth a total of $200. A road along the south side of the land provided good access, and the cultivated acreage already yielded 350 bushels of grain, 100 bushels of potatoes, and an abundance of vegetables. Helga worked both in the vegetable garden and in the field, as was usual for pioneer women.

In 1887 Stephan took out a $675 mortgage, although it was getting difficult to borrow money. The boom was now more or less over and debt was proving a heavy burden for many farmers. Stephan, however, was careful. He repaid an older loan and continued to make improvements, putting up fencing for the livestock and buying seed.[18]

Among the new arrivals in the settlement were Brynjólfur Brynjólfsson and his sons, the most prominent of whom were Skapti and Magnús. Together with Stephan's father, Brynjólfur had participated in the famous "ride north" in 1849. Formal debates were a popular form of entertainment and the schoolhouse resounded with lively discussions on a variety of subjects incuding politics, science, religion, the virtues of Iceland versus America, and the preservation of the Icelandic language. As always, there were two camps, the liberals and the conservatives. Patriarch Þorlákur Gunnar Jónsson and his sons from Mountain were the chief leaders among the conservatives. Gardar was the main bastion of the liberals, whose champions were Ólafur Ólafsson, Björn Halldórsson the carpenter, and the Brynjólfssons, most notably Skapti. The debaters researched *The Bible* for arguments and frequently

Dakota pioneer Brynjólfur Brynjólfsson, father of the prominent brothers Skapti and Magnús, who were loyal friends of the poet. Brynjólfur was among the Danish King's rebellious Icelandic subjects who "rode north" to the Governor's seat at Möðruvellir in protest in 1849.

consulted Stephan, who was very knowledgeable about the Scriptures. On one occasion, Jónas Hall came to consult and left with notations in his Bible pointing in all directions, resembling a ray with nine tails, as Stephan put it. Stephan evidently took little part in these debates as he was not a fluent speaker, though he occasionally gave talks in the manner of the poem on Solomon's temple.

During the winter of 1887, Stephan gave a lecture to the reading society at Mountain on the hero Andri of Gísli Konráðsson's *rímur*. He parodied the form of learned lectures on literature and gave descriptions of this giant-like hero. Andri's mother was a widow on a deserted island, and "her son Andri was brought up to the music of the resounding breakers from the roaring ocean... As a young boy, Andri is clearly influenced by this strong environment, and when he was happily romping he laughed so painfully loud that the palace trembled..." Andri was magnificent-looking, with a nose "broad and masculine, with flaring nostrils that were an indication of his passion and his powerful breathing when he was much moved."

Andri's intellectual abilities, however, were not in proportion to his physical prowess. His religious views were unclear, something like "the ideal of beauty" as the Danes would call it, Stephan said, poking fun at what he considered to be unclear and vague liberal religious views. He also made politically indelicate remarks by stating that Andri, simple minded as a troll, would never harm railway magnates or grain merchants. In Andri's time, everything in trade and politics was monopolized, so in Stephan's estimation Andri qualified as a monopolist. This satirical critique derived from Stephan's keen sense of literature and sharp powers of observation. Most of those present were thoroughly amused, but one man in the audience, who was not unintelligent, failed to realize that Stephan was joking and became very fond of Earl Andri.[19]

In March of 1887 Stephan wrote a poem entitled "Mér sýnist" (It seems to me), in which he states quite directly that it is sometimes unavoidable to draw the sword and wound the one who wounds. "I, who would prefer to sit silent, thinking,/or tell my children adventures, laughing," am forced to challenge a world "that laughs when tears run down the cheeks of the poor", when superstition and stupidity prevail. The heart shivers, then "it warms up, simmers, and boils over./ The froth is my poems. I have seen myself that/I was always provoked to write poems like this."[20]

Occasionally Stephan presented ideas like these to a larger audience, and when he spoke, he had a unique way of stressing his words, as if forcing them into the heads of the listeners. At the Fourth of July celebration held at Mountain in 1885, he delivered a speech in which he claimed that most people adored the wonders of the New World, praising its freedom and prosperity and comparing this to the misery and harsh climate back home. Icelanders had arrived too late to take part in America's War of Independence, he observed, but the struggle was not over, as not everyone enjoyed freedom. Much remained undone and Icelanders could still contribute their share.

In America there were 60 million people, he continued, his tone now heavier. Fewer than half of them enjoyed full human rights. There was democracy, but in fact a handful of business tycoons and railway kings ruled two or three million poor people who were willing to work, but were nonetheless unemployed at the worst time of the year. These citizens paid more than their share of the $100 million that was committed to be spent and would soon bankrupt the public purse. Another Jefferson was needed to write a new declaration of independence, and a new Lincoln to establish brotherhood. "Merciless wealth and suffering poverty have joined forces to fight for the power of suppression."

Stephan foresaw a hard class struggle and predicted that the new generation would be guided by humanitarian views and fairness. Now there was a chance for Icelanders to share in progress and liberty in America. "Then we can truly celebrate July the Fourth as a festival of freedom, not as its guests, but as its children." Icelanders will "never grow too big, nor too small, to contribute to America's progress."[21] A few listeners who were imbibing during the speech responded by blurting out "hear!" while others muttered curses about the impertinent poet who was against progress.

Daddy, I am Here!

Now Stephan did the chores with his growing boys at his side. Baldur, almost eight, could get the cows on his own and pick potatoes by now. Guðmundur was six, little Jón, with curly blond hair, was well over three, and Jakob was a year old. Sometimes Stephan took the older boys along to the fields or to tend the animals. He was a man of few words, but his affection was evident. He kept the boys working as much as possible, but he also enjoyed watching them discover the world as they chased rabbits or picked flowers.

In the fall of 1887, a diphtheria epidemic swept through the settlement and the boys caught it. They all recovered except little Jón. Helga and Stephan took turns at his bedside and sent for a doctor, but the child's illness grew continually worse until he died on October 27th. He was buried two days later.[22]

It was difficult for Stephan to accept little Jón's death and he wrote a number of memorial poems. On New Year's Eve of 1888, he reflected on the sorrows of the past year, that had exacted a few tears from him and inflicted a lifelong wound to his heart. He tried to be stoical, saying that the year had now passed with God's peace into the grave of past times, departing with the "sobbing of a blizzard, the tears of a frost storm." He sat by himself in the cold night, recalling the agony of his little boy's death. The father's sorrow and the boy's image remained alive, although snowdrifts now covered the grave:

> ... I still see the sheen of the clear, blue eyes,
> Still hear the voice of my little swan,
> Watch the head covered with pretty curls –
> It follows me, no matter how far I go.

Stephan wrote another poem on March 31, 1888, perhaps on the occasion of little Jón's birthday. The poem is tender and begins with a sweet recollection of the first summer flowers and the little boy running beside his father. No matter how precious this summer memory is, the moment of death haunts Stephan, who now walks on alone:

> On the slope toward autumn,
> The rimed leaves
> Froze to the path I walk –
> Your leg is now lifeless,
> Your mouth, ice-cold,
> Your little palms stiffened.
>
> I wander alone now,
> No-one picks for me

> *The flowers along the path –*
> *From a rose bush*
> *I hear a voice,*
> *A child's voice: "Daddy, I am here!"*

Stephan wrote a third poem about little Jón in October of 1895, exactly eight years after his death. In the father's mind, the boy's image is a gift of sunshine, but as before, the suffering of his final illness and the memory of the child's blond locks glistening with the "sweat of death" remain clear in his memory. Now, however, the boy's face assumes the calmness of death, turning his loss into a soothing memory. In the last lines of the poem, Stephan answers the accusation that he was concentrating on the grave without wanting to see heaven, making the loss so painful. His reply is another question: "Is it an irrecoverable loss, when all I have/are these flowers, these poems, these tears?"

Six years later Stephan wrote a poem on his own birthday, October 3rd. The poem is framed as a beautiful image of nature and Stephan is now reconciled with death, master of "the land of the evening shadows", but his grief remains, mixed with memories and devotion to the ground where the boy rests. The poem ends with a contemplation of the ordeal of heartache: life never unfolds as one wants, but this cannot be avoided. "Thus, it is unavoidable for one who does not run away from it,/that uncompensated grief is an ordeal of manhood." These four poems were later printed under the title "Kveðið eftir drenginn minn" (Poems After My Boy).[23] The cycle reveals Stephan's struggle with his emotions. As strong-willed as he was, he could not control his heart. Only with the passage of many years did he succeed in turning this painful experience into a sweet memory.

The Cultural Society and Reverend Jón

Björn Pétursson, former Member of Parliament in Iceland and the father of Stephan's friend Sveinn Björnsson, lived in Dakota Territory for a time and became acquainted with Unitarian theology – probably through Stephan. He subsequently got in touch with the Unitarian movement through the paper *Unity* in 1886 and became the first advocate of Unitarianism among the Icelanders in North America.[24] Occasionally an overnight guest at Stephan and Helga's home, Björn once discussed the "immortality of the individual" with Stephan, endlessly repeating the same arguments. As it turned out, he was deliberately testing Stephan's patience and he burst into laughter when Stephan eventually got so annoyed that he refused to discuss the subject further. Björn said that he had thought it was impossible to make Stephan angry.[25]

Over the years, Winnipeg had become the home of an increasing number of Icelanders in North America. They established newspapers, first *Leifur*, that lasted only a few years, then *Heimskringla* (1886) and finally *Lögberg* (1888). The latter two papers became a spiritual and worldly battlefield between various groups of Icelanders. *Lögberg* was liberal in politics but conservative in religious matters, while *Heimskringla* was conservative in politics but liberal in religion, as well as being a more literary paper. Frímann B. Arngrímsson, an eccentric idealist and co-founder of *Heimskringla*, once visited Stephan at Gardar. Stephan received him well, gave him coffee, and showed him the books he was reading. Afterwards, they walked outside and Stephan read Frímann a few poems. "These are just exercises," he said modestly. Frímann was fascinated by Stephan's works, but Stephan, still breaking in his literary Pegasus, did not yet want his poems published.[26]

Occasionally Stephan wrote newsletters for the papers and in the spring of 1888 he wrote one for *Lögberg*: The winter had been hard, but conditions of the settlers were good. The Icelandic settlers' houses were better than those of their Anglo-Saxon neighbours, Stephan wrote, and crops were good. Now the pioneers were considering building a church. There was a lively social life in the Icelandic communities and after prohibition had been implemented in Pembina County it had become almost impossible to distinguish between the abstainers and the drinkers. Icelandic plays were per-

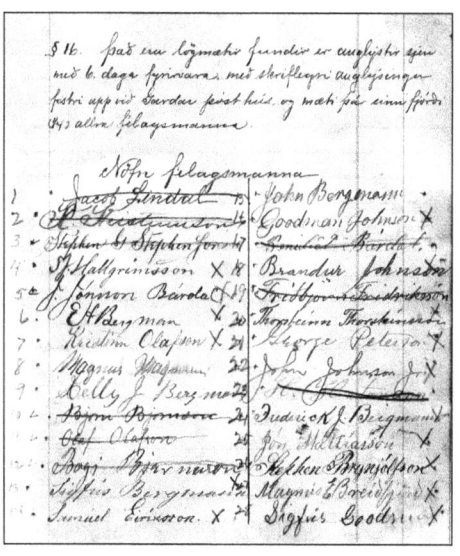

Among the cultural organizations at Gardar was the reading society **Gangleri**, *established in 1883. Stephan did not join until 1886.*

formed and Stephan praised the creative energies and thirst for culture evident amid such primitive circumstances. Those responsible for the performances had hardly ever attended decent theatre, but the results were surprisingly good. The municipal election was rather dull, Stephan reported, despite a variety of political views, and all the posts had been filled by Icelanders, including Stephan's brother-in-law, Jón. A variety of clubs and societies had been formed at Gardar, among them a reading society with nearly 100 volumes in Icelandic, English, and Danish. The older generation read the Icelandic books and Stephan thought that the teenagers, now fluent in English, should perhaps read a book occasionally, so their knowledge would not be less than that of their elders. There was little news of the Women's Society, but Stephan gave an update on the Farmers' Association founded in 1885. A co-operative, it operated a co-op store affiliated with the Dakota's Farmers' Association and was expected to prosper. The Farmers' Association was a strong movement that fought for free trade against growing efforts to monopolize the wheat trade. It was radical and had great social significance for the farmers who could read the Association's papers and attend its meetings.[27]

Stephan's newsletter closed with several lines about the latest club, a new Cultural Society that he promised to tell more about later. An astute political observer since his Wisconsin years, he had originally supported the Republicans because of President Lincoln's reputation from the civil war and the abolition cause. In Dakota, however, he became a Democrat because of their promise to lower protectionist tariffs.

Stephan examined social issues closely and developed a fascination with Felix Adler's ethical movement. Adler, a German Jew whose family immigrated to America in 1857, had studied on both sides of the Atlantic and had read the works of Emerson and Kant. In 1876 he established an ethical movement, the Society for Ethical Culture, among radical intellectuals. Clean living and intellectual development were the principal goals of the movement, and members were to donate all income exceeding their needs to the labour movement. Inspired by Adler's ideas, seven farmers at Gardar, Jónas Hall, Ólafur Ólafsson, Jakob Líndal, his brother Ásgeir, and the Brynjólfsson brothers, Skapti and Magnús, arranged to meet at Stephan's home on February 4, 1888. There they eagerly discussed the need to establish a society of liberal Icelanders who could accept neither the doctrines of the church nor the church's declaration that religion was the fortress of culture and progress. Anxious to collaborate in seeking the truth, the seven agreed to establish *Hið Íslenska Menningarfélag (The Icelandic Cultural Society)*. Stephan wrote the manifesto and he, Ólafur, and Jakob formulated some provisional by-laws. All seven signed the by-laws and Stephan's manifesto was recorded on the first page of the minute book under the heading "Humanity. Research. Freedom."

> *The aim of the Cultural Society is to support and disseminate culture and morality, that very morality and that very belief which is built upon experience, knowledge, and science. Instead of disagreement within the church, it aims to enhance humanity and brotherhood, rational and unhindered research instead of thoughtless confession, independent conviction instead of blind faith, and instead of stupidity and prejudice, spiritual freedom and progress that none can hinder.*[28]

Skapti Brynjólfsson was elected the first chairman, Stephan was the secretary, and Ólafur Ólafsson became the treasurer. Skapti was the spokesperson of the society, while Stephan was "the brain behind the curtain". Ólafur was somewhat older than the others, but among the wisest men Stephan had ever met. "He hardly agreed with anything except novelties, while they were novelties, and he was too reserved, as clever as he was. He trained his spiritual eye on the entire world and gained knowledge of everything by himself, including a working knowledge of English, French, German, Dutch, and the Scandinavian languages," Stephan wrote much later.[29]

Stephan sent the manifesto to *Lögberg*, along with a note on the new society, and the second meeting, held at the home of Brynjólfur Brynjólfsson on February 23, 1888, was attended by 22 new members. They did not include either of Stephan's brothers-in law, Jón or Kristinn. The members now formed groups in order to investigate various scholarly disciplines, such as natural history and the histories of religion, mythology, and poetry. These were the new fields of knowledge behind the liberal movement in religious matters, and each group was to prepare a lecture on a specific subject.

The first months of the society were lively. In April Ólafur lectured on spiritualism and Stephan delivered his new poem "Áraskipti" (Return of the Year). Reading slowly but clearly, he evoked powerful images of winter darkness, frost, snow, and dawn. One would have expected a conclusion with the New Year symbolizing change, but instead Stephan interrupted his reading, looked up, and asked, "But what is the New Year that shines now?" At this point the poem takes an unexpected turn: the year simply continues its age-old cycle. It is within each of us, Stephan continued, to find the strength to effect change on the external world. Grief and hardship can actually help us recognize the treasures of life. The joy of this discovery is pure, at the same time "healing and painful" as it "develops through laughter and tears," Stephan concluded, reading the last stanza even more slowly. Looking up from his poem with a peculiar glint in his eyes, this short, slight, and weatherworn pioneer with large calloused palms, clenched his jaws between words and emphasized the last stanza as if to drive its meaning into the consciousness of his companions. This might well have been the manifesto of the new society:

> *It is more brilliant, a more skilled hand,*
> *A stronger body, a more mature spirit;*
> *It is deeper thought and bolder speech;*
> *It is a more honourable look and a more sincere soul.*
> *It is the effort to see what is most right and most true*
> *And the conviction not to be swayed from it.*
> *It is a clearer consciousness about each virtue*
> *That is within us and how we nurture it.*[30]

Stephan continued to read about new values: that men should aim ever higher, without necessarily expecting to reach a preconceived destination. Then each new year would be a happy one.

The quest for knowledge had led Stephan far from those whose aim it was to control the thoughts of others, "who either want to tie men to old fashioned ideas or to erect tight barriers around the minds and opinions of men." Writing in Lögberg in 1888,[31] he declared that he was now a member of a society in which "each supports the other to become a little wiser and better, without dictating beforehand what to confess and what to refuse."

From the outset, the Cultural Society was troublesome to the Lutheran ministers. Shortly after its establishment, members Ólafur Ólafsson and the Brynjólfssons had publicly made profane references to the church and its publication, *Sameiningin*, and Reverend Friðrik Bergmann was not quick to forgive this affront. In the March issue of *Sameiningin*, an anonymous letter railed against the Society, and Reverend Jón Bjarnason, President of the Icelandic Synod and editor of *Sameiningin*, vouched for the truth of this letter, even though its writer apparently gave credence to rumours without having seen the Society's manifesto. The writer began by defending the Sunday Schools, which were now becoming targets of hostility. There were those who claimed that Sunday Schools were a cancerous sore on society, that beat the "intellectually lethal word of God and the Bible" into children. Then there was the so-called Cultural Society, the writer continued, whose members read Ingersoll, who advocated breaking the fetters of clerical doctrines and Biblical learning. These ideas had been circulated at debate meetings, but were now coming to public attention. The writer also claimed that someone at Gardar had accused *Sameiningin* of publishing lies about vice and corruption in America, to discourage Icelanders from settling there, and that *Lögberg* should have challenged this. This sort of thing was only a sample of the message of the Cultural Society, the writer stated.[32]

By referring to *Sameiningin* and *Lögberg* in this manner, the writer was evidently trying to gain the support of these papers in the battle against the Cultural Society. Obviously the strategy worked well with Reverend Jón Bjarnason, who wrote an editorial note following the letter. In it he stated that this was the first time in the history of the Icelanders that a society had been established against Christianity. He then mocked the members, saying that the unschooled farmers who had established the society "felt up to challenging the Christian church, the greatest empire in existence, and seem to be quite sure that they can defeat it. Boldness evidently increases when one gets to America," he concluded.[33]

In the next issue of *Sameiningin*, Jónas Hall replied on behalf of the Cultural Society, stating that it was neither a religious group nor a society of atheists, but rather an attempt by its members to acquire some knowledge "of their surroundings and the direction of the times." Reverend Jón responded to this article with accusations to the effect that the Society's members were now backing down from their anti-Christian stance and had only written the manifesto printed in *Lögberg* after news of the Society had appeared in *Sameiningin*. Elsewhere in the same issue, he asserted that the Society could not bear to see *Sameiningin* criticize the American way of life as they wanted to idealize everything and lure more people from Iceland. "What on earth are people in Iceland to think when such a society prospers here in America?"[34]

At a Cultural Society meeting on May 13, 1888, Reverend Jón's writings were read aloud. The members discussed what paper they should send a reply to. They all agreed that the rebuttal should be written by Stephan. Some thought that *Heimskringla* would be more favourable to them, but Stephan was in favour of sending the article to *Lögberg*. "I would rather that my most extreme challenge to religion appear in a catholic paper – where it is most needed," Stephan said, suggesting that it is most effective to confront an opponent directly. Skapti Brynjólfsson smiled and agreed. He never hesitated to speak up at meetings, even when he knew everybody was of a different opinion.[35] It was agreed that the article, to be sent to *Lögberg*, should be moderate and as non-provocative as possible.

Stephan's reply, printed in the June 20, 1888 issue of *Lögberg*, began ironically with a quote from *The Bible*, "But when King Herod heard this, he was frightened, and so was all Jerusalem." By comparing Reverend Jón Bjarnason to King Herod, he drew a parallel between the members of the Cultural Society and Christ. On the surface, Stephan was polite, but the article had a sharply sardonic tone. He suggested that his opponent's judgement had perhaps been clouded by distractions, as "such confusion and bluster were hardly typical of a reasonable person, as the editor of *Sameiningin* naturally is – unless he has fallen prey to the unbridled prejudice and importunity of unjust persons, which is apparently what has happened to the editor." The editor, having evidently relied on hearsay from those opposed to the Society, would hardly have vouched for the letter if he were better informed. He could hardly be of the apostolic opinion that it was "justifiable to bear false witness and lead people astray as long as one thinks that could benefit the glory of God or the church." He added that he was acquainted with the writer of the letter and knew that this individual had dreadful difficulties citing the opinions of his religious opponents accurately.

Stephan said he only wished to respond to three principal issues: that the Cultural Society was a society of disbelief, that the Society had called the opinions expressed in *Sameiningin* dangerous lies, and that the Society did not dare stand by its anti-Christian declaration. The Cultural Society was admittedly a society of disbelief, he said, if it is godlessness to incline toward beliefs and morality that are embraced by wise men as being conducive to human welfare, though they are not based on any credo. It was a society of disbelief, he continued, if it is persecution to hold that people can help each other to make everyday life and the world a better place regardless of Biblical teachings and the doctrines of clerics. The society was anti-Christian if it was unchristian to examine issues from more than one perspective rather than accepting the written word without reflection, and it was a society of disbelief if it was godlessness to want to free mankind from the fetters of prejudice.

Stephan also mocked the controversy stirred up over the situation in America. The Debating Society was much older than the Cultural Society, he pointed out, and it had been at a debate that someone had criticized the Icelandic newspaper *Lögberg* for not rebutting the vilification of America published in *Sameiningin*. This individual had later joined the Cultural Society. Stephan speculated that the first letter in *Sameiningin* had been calculated to incite the newspapers against the Society. This tactic had succeeded with regard to *Sameiningin*, Stephan said, but this periodical's attacks had nothing to do with the Society. He then suggested that in making such criticisms, *Sameiningin* was "close-cropping the pasture all around itself" – a farming metaphor alluding to a weak or tethered animal eating only the grass around itself. He thereby suggested that this was actually more of a reflection on *Sameiningin* than on the Society.

Finally, in response to the accusation that the Society did not dare maintain its anti-Christian stance, Stephan referred to those who had the courage of their convictions. He then alluded to Reverend Jón's salary. "And then one can contemplate who is risking more, a man who receives $1000 a year to perpetuate opinions that have long, long ago become accepted as tradition, or one who goes "straight against them" only to incur rudeness and contempt."[36]

Reverend Jón had the last word in this dispute. In the August 1, 1888 issue of *Lögberg*, he reiterated his opinion that by making science the foundation for free research, the Cultural Society was rejecting redemption and revelation, which were impossible to prove scientifically. Then he turned his attention to Stephan personally, recalling that Stefán Guðmundsson had been a delegate at the first Icelandic Lutheran Synod conference in 1885 and had approved its by-laws and creeds – then disappeared from the congregation in silence, only to return to the scene later, inspired by cultural spirit under the name Stephan G. Stephansson.

Jón had very firm religious convictions and he may have found that the end justified the suspect means. He often sought out the personal faults of his opponents or altered the issues slightly in order to strike a blow at others, and in this case he certainly did so. After that, Stephan often threw sarcastic verses at ministers on suitable occasions and he sometimes used the term "Reverend-Jónism" as a synonym for the dogmatism of the Synod.

Turning Point

Membership in the Cultural Society declined during the summer of 1888. In June, after discussing the publication of a newspaper, members bade a formal farewell to those about to leave for Canada – among them Ólafur Ólafsson. They encouraged their comrades to remain faithful to the ideals of the Society and as a parting gift presented them with a book entitled *Bible Myths*.

At the annual general meeting held on June 23, 1888, Jakob Líndal submitted his resignation in writing. He was Secretary of the Icelandic Lutheran Synod, and as the annual conference of the Synod was about to begin at Mountain, his reasons were obvious. Reverend Jón Bjarnason, of course, praised Jakob's 'reason'. The Society's misfortunes were compounded by the fact that the schoolhouse at Mountain, formerly used for meetings at a cost of five cents, was no longer available. Some Society members decided to attend a debate organized by the Synod, but it was agreed that they would not speak publicly unless challenged.

The atmosphere at Mountain virtually crackled with electricity on Sunday, June 27, 1888. After 6 o'clock in the evening, wagons began rolling into town and the church quickly filled. The subject of the debate was whether the church was for or against "free research". People whispered among themselves, wondering whether members of the Cultural Society would attend. Eventually they did and the meeting began. Various ministers took the position that the church allowed free research, but that the word of God was above all research. When they began directing comments at the Society, Björn Halldórsson, Björn Pétursson, and Skapti Brynjólfsson stood up in its defence and expressed new ideas based on the natural sciences. The Society and the belief or disbelief of its members nevertheless remained the focus of the discussion.

Jakob Líndal's resignation undoubtedly prompted subsequent discussion among Cultural Society members about participation in congregational matters. Most, in fact, were members of a congregation, with the exception of Stephan, who apparently took religious issues more seriously than the others. Freedom of opinion was a cornerstone of the Society, but the hostility of church leaders now created polarization among Society members and it became intolerable for someone liberal in thought and inclined to faith to be a member of the Society while also belonging to a congregation. For Stephan there were only two options: to submit to the word of God or reject it.

Around that time, Stephan delivered a lecture based on the question "Getur það orðið skylda vor að skilja við kirkjuna?" (Is it perhaps our duty to leave the Church?) The extant manuscript of this speech is incomplete and the contents are not accounted for in the Society's minutes, but it is obvious that Stephan was seriously troubled by this issue. Far too few of those who called themselves liberals, he stated, had thus far seriously contemplated resigning from their congregation – let alone reach a final decision. He confided that by articulating these thoughts, he was attempting to answer publicly that which he had long ago answered privately. Underlying differences of opinions among Society members were obviously behind this hesitation to act decisively, and in acknowledgement of this Stephan expressed the hope that whether or not his comrades agreed with him, the affinity of their views would enable them to accept his reflections as a tiny step in the direction the Society had charted: Humanity, Research, and Freedom.

He then offered some insight into the underlying reason for the disagreement. It was very common, he stated, for the word "belief" to be used in reference to "people's tenacious adherence to old ideas about one superior being and the relationship of that being to humankind." Every time the foundation of Christian beliefs was challenged by new knowledge, the pioneers of new ideas were called atheists. "Humans populate only the wildernesses in their own knowledge with supernatural gods," Stephan maintained, "while settled land is the domain of the natural." This metaphor echoes thoughts expressed in Felix Adler's works.[37]

To Stephan's way of thinking, faith was "man's relationship to everything there is, his understanding of the universe, his decisions, longings,

'Um Jafnrétti' (About Equality), an essay by Stephan G. Stephansson on the subject of equality and education for women.

and successes. These are the deepest questions of religion and the human spirit will never rest until it finds answers." The church, with all its promises, creeds, and confessions, claimed to have the answers, but ran into difficulties as soon as people's horizons widened. The old answers were no longer sufficient and disbelief in the church had now become so general that it could no longer be brushed aside. People's understanding of the nature of religion had broadened through increased knowledge of other faiths, but the Christian religion still maintained its infallibility – despite the obvious conflicts between revelations and miracles told of in *The Bible* and the laws of nature and reason.

The Church had begun to retreat, Stephan said, but it still presided over education, despite the fact that it had always limped behind progress and broadening horizons. The Church, for instance, had once defended slavery with sword or *Bible* in hand, though now that slavery had been abolished, it praised "God, who with its assistance had washed this stain from the shield of Christian people." Now the church was struggling against women's liberation. Looking a hundred years ahead, Stephan predicted sarcastically, "in the year 1988, the Church will bring her Lord a weekly thanksgiving address for having opened the eyes of the world to the simple truth that all people are persons."[38]

Stephan also accused the Church of failing to cultivate the potential within each person. "And let us then examine the methods the Church applies in the case of an individual who, she fears, is just about to loosen his "straightjacket". It was not the higher instincts of mankind, the nobility of man, honour, straightforwardness, or reason that it employed to restrain the soul. No, it was the baser instincts of the human spirit, the dregs at the bottom of the heart that it attempted to stir up – selfishness, frivolity, cowardice, and superstition – so rather than let down the Church, people betrayed themselves. Individuals were browbeaten into believing that their reputations were at stake and that their esteem and position in society would be ruined, that God would seek revenge, and that it was foolish to risk so much – even for one's true convictions. On the other hand, it was so very beautiful to join, to be content, and to please the majority, as people would otherwise be of no use – either to themselves or others." Prejudices rained down upon those who did not obey, or the facts were turned upside down with claims "that one was a Christian without knowing it."[39]

Nothing is known about the reactions to Stephan's talk. The end of the lecture is lost and it is impossible to know if he urged his fellows to follow his example and resign from the Church. In all likelihood he argued strongly for that. A fragment from near the end of the talk constitutes a beautiful continuation of the intellectual development of the boy who in Víðimýrarsel had wrestled with the catechism and the long poem "Njóla". Recalling his own difficulties at gaining knowledge, Stephan stated that those who were "convinced that the church was lost in so many ways" wished sincerely that their children could be brought up in the light of truth that for them had been but a faint glimmer almost beyond their reach. Experience had now taught them "what an obstacle prejudice was, and how high a price an individual had to pay in order to openly confess sincere convictions, because that meant going against public opinion." Stephan posed the question whether those with such convictions should flee the battlefield and abandon their obligation to the future and their children rather than confront prejudice. Should they not make this future goal a little more achievable for children than it had been for themselves?[40]

This lecture marks a milestone in Stephan's intellectual development. He had definitely embraced disbelief (atheism) and did not hesitate to admit it openly. Few of his contemporaries could go that far and some of them fought a lifelong struggle to liberalize the church. Stephan shared their quest for knowledge and liberal ideas, but he could not accept their religious views when their brand of liberalism only softened the Word of God. He had nothing at all in common with conservative church leaders. Having burned his bridges, Stephan would now have to walk new and unknown paths alone.

Work as Prayer

Perhaps Stephan's lecture to the Cultural Society became an issue of disagreement. In it, he had ventured beyond the point where his fellows could follow him, and much later he recalled that his opinions were often quite different from theirs. The Society's ideas, however, ran counter to dominating ideologies and obviously faced strong opposition, so the establishment of a newspaper was postponed.

In February of 1889, on the first anniversary of the Cultural Society, an open meeting was held. After Stephan had spoken on Robert Ingersoll, an intelligent farmer named Jónas Kortsson lectured on the Trinity and Church belief. A debate between church men and Cultural Society members ensued, lasting until after dark.

Stephan had studied Ingersoll's writings and had translated selections from his works on tolerance, ideals, death, and afterlife. In his talk, he stated that after reading Ingersoll for a week, he admired his eloquence, as well as his ability to communicate simply and effectively, making comprehensible the ideas that learned men expressed in very complicated and profound language. Stephan praised Ingersoll for championing dissidents such as Bruno, Spinoza, and Thomas Paine. He then discussed Ingersoll's repudiation of the notion of eternal torment and concluded that no-one knows anything about what happens after death: whether the "grave is only the end of this life, or the gate to another,

Early on in life Stephan adopted the philosophy that "work is its own reward" – and almost a form of prayer.

whether the evening here is not a morning somewhere else."[41] Later, he elevated this idea into a pretty little stanza.

Stephan was far from following Ingersoll in everything, but he was fascinated by this man's ability to render complicated ideas understandable to the public. He was also aware of the deeper ideas of more learned men such as Emerson, and in all likelihood it was while he was preparing this lecture that he wrote: "Work is a divine service. Work is the best prayer – cf. Emerson, he who works is praying."[42]

Stephan had earlier adopted the idea that the reward for work was to have done it. Now that he had rejected orthodox religion, it was important for him to find deeper meaning in his life and work. Emerson, having rejected the absolute validity of Holy scripture, had sought spirituality in human actions and the relationship of man to the environment and nature. Work, he maintained, united the material with the spiritual, the body with the soul. Physical work linked mind and action. Scholars and artists, for example, must live life no less than create. They cannot rid themselves of their humanity, and therefore physical work is also necessary for their welfare. There is virtue in the spade and the hoe, Emerson stated, for the learned as well as the unlearned.[43] Stephan adopted this idea and created the axiom that spiritual exercise was as necessary for the one doing physical work, as physical exercise was for one working in the spiritual realm.

There is prayer in human action, Emerson says in his essay "Self-Reliance", in which he praises independent thought. Self-serving prayers, he maintained, were theft deriving from a disengagement of the physical and the intellectual – the unity of which was the divine. When man becomes one with God, he does not pray. All his actions then become prayer. The prayer of the farmer who kneels in the field to rid it of weeds, and of the oarsman who kneels at the oar, these are true prayers that resonate everywhere in nature.[44] Emerson said that farm work was necessary to create balance. "Manual labour is the study of the external world" and at the same time an education received from God. Only he who has learned the secret of labour can learn the mysteries of nature.[45]

These peculiar ideas took root in Stephan's mind over the next years and decades. He rejected the idea of "a single highest being" and theological efforts to interpret the words of this being. This rejection, however, was far from an answer to the riddle of life. Emerson had wrestled with such classical philosophical questions as the meaning of life and the route to profound harmony with the ultimate laws of existence. Stephan took these questions with him when he went out to the barn and into the field, contemplating them there in his own way. Little by little, work became his religion.

Bergmannism and Church Gloom

Late in the fall of 1888, Stephan decided to move to Alberta in Canada. There were many reasons for his decision. Ólafur Ólafsson had migrated north to Alberta the previous spring and his letters convinced Stephan that the move would be good for him and his family. The future seemed limited at Gardar, where the land was fully settled – even a little over-crowded.

The situation at Gardar was constricted in more than one sense. The challenges of pioneer life during the first years had suited Stephan, as he attempted to put words to the great riddles of life. Now he referred to the atmosphere at Gardar as "Bergmannism and church gloom", implying that an attempt was being made to force all of society into the same mould.[46] Reverend Friðrik Bergmann was a proponent of this trend.

Stephan had sincerely tried to pioneer new ideas to counter stagnation and dogmatism in his community. It disappointed him that the Cultural Society had become a constant target of criticism and he found the silent majority too obedient to the spiritual authorities. The Synod's success at maintaining the upper hand was both depressing and intolerably moralistic. "And there is something else," Stephan wrote shortly after he left Dakota. "A society that you think is all wrong, which also thinks that you are all wrong, is hard to tolerate unless you have the time and means to be involved in constant battles..."[47]

Among his poetic outbursts around this time was "Hrútaatið" (The Ram Fight), a humorous comment on religious factionalism. In this satirical description of two congregational delegates quarrelling at a Synod conference, Stephan mocks Reverend Jón Bjarnason's flock by underlining words much used by Church leaders. "Reverend Snúður, have a look at/the spiritual feats of your rams!" the poem begins, setting the scene with two rams fighting and people gathering around to see which will win. "There is life and there is unity,/these beasts have opinions!" One of them is bruised and swollen, but only the vision of belief can see the wounds of the other. "The great flash of truth's light/ flames brightly around their short horns."[48]

While Reverend Friðrik Bergmann personified this hilarious spirituality of the Synod, his cousin Eiríkur Bergmann represented the spirit of capitalism. Farmers at Gardar were now bearing the brunt of the fickle whims of capitalism as an economic downturn set in. Many were on the verge of bankruptcy after having overextended themselves during the boom years. Stephan's situation, on the other hand, remained tolerable.

The weather during the winter of 1887-1888 was severe and crops were poor the following summer. Prices plummeted and many found themselves in dire straits. In Stephan's opinion, they were slaving for "the millionaires, the bankers, the railway kings, the loan sharks, all those who exploit their fellow humans."[49] Farmers were dependent upon the railway companies, who derived immense power from their wealth and their monopolies, and no less dependent upon the giant grain companies, that owned the grain elevators and mills – and collaborated closely with the railway companies. With this power behind them, grain buyers could suppress prices paid to farmers and even cheat on the weight.[50] Stephan disliked the overwhelming power these monopolies had over farmers. He also had doubts about single-crop, large-scale farming methods, instead favouring ecological mixed farming as a way of building up a prosperous small-scale farm economy little by little. Obviously some of his ideas were influenced by current socialist ideas. He had visions and expectations of another way of life and another kind of a society than the one developing in Dakota.

It seemed to Stephan that Eiríkur Bergmann, in addition to being among the conservatives in religious matters, had become a proponent of the treacherous union of interests between politicians and businessmen. He ridiculed Eiríkur's influence and is suspected of having penned a satirical poem lampooning Eiríkur's election to the Legislative Assembly of Dakota Territory in 1888. First of all, the poem recounts, Eiríkur had been elected as a delegate to a Synod conference, where "he became muddled until his head spun/as hypocrisy had already injured him." Then, almost elected county commissioner, he was struck by megalomania. Eventually he got all the way "up to the Dakota Assembly/ for dollars poured out of his pocket/and alcohol from a keg he carried around/to get the gullible mob dead drunk." Thus he succeeded in rising to the assembly of history, the poem states, with false conviction, foolishness, and hypocrisy.[51]

Conflict appears to have been dominant among the Icelanders in Dakota, where scornful verses flew back and forth between Gardar and Mountain, and poetry proved an effective weapon in a small society of people who were sensitive about their reputations. Ásgeir Líndal, for example, wrote a rebuttal to Reverend Jón Bjarnason's optimistic essay on life in America by noting that some Icelanders at Pembina had accepted welfare. He went on to mention the phenomenon of Dakota manure piles, suggesting that some farmers resorted to relocating their stables rather than moving the manure. This article inspired furious responses, including a lot of personal mud-slinging.

Stephan's short story "Dómarinn" (The Judge), written shortly before the Cultural Society was founded and dated January 11, 1888, was a sharp satire on life in a small pioneer village that dreamed of becoming a city. All kinds of businesses were established as people indulged in speculation, building stores and offices. All went bankrupt, however, except the liquor store, and Republicans and Democrats now struggled for power as the Icelanders learned the bad habits of the New World. The story depicts a Justice of the Peace, a judge "of the lowest rank", who was rather simple, but knew how to provoke his gullible countrymen into lawsuits so he could make money on their squabbling. Stephan's narrative describes a hilarious lawsuit and a dispute over women's rights. For a while it seemed that "ideas and convictions might pop up" among some of the townspeople, but the minister and better citizens of the community manage to suppress such things. Sometimes "these big issues of the world" stray into villages and lighten them up for a while, but then they fade away because the people are too narrow-minded to deal with such big concepts. In the end, the judge calculates his legal fees, but feels the sum is too small. "And the judge was right. He had not included the price of peace and unity that had been lost – things the surrounding district could ill afford to spare."⁵²

The sharp satire of this story betrays Stephan's growing bitterness and foreshadows his break with Dakota. It was as if this little society was growing too fast and people did not have time to develop intellectual and social maturity to match their material progress. Many Icelanders embraced the ways of the New World too readily, losing their bearings and adopting every novelty, opportunity, and attitude that came along – with mixed results. Some consequently became almost ridiculous in their addiction to material wealth and desperate in their newly-acquired religious fundamentalism. This story, which remained unpublished at that time, bears witness to an element of rootlessness and moral confusion among the immigrants.

There may well have been other reasons for Stephan's departure. As his radicalism grew, a widening split no doubt developed between him and his in-laws. None of the Mjóidalur people joined the Cultural Society, and both Jón Jr. and Sr. were Synod men. They were also more economically prosperous than Stephan, and if tension was developing between Stephan and his in-laws in religious matters, it would have been difficult for him to accept dependence on them in any way. In a poem written much later, Stephan made reference to unspecified difficulties at Gardar, and in a letter written after Stephan's death, Helga indicated that there were reasons for their move that she did not want to discuss. It is now impossible to be certain about the situation, but it may well have included a personal aspect.[53] As Helga was not a disbeliever, Stephan was on his own, spiritually speaking, and he may therefore have had difficulties justifying his views within the family.

Yet another reason cited for Stephan's departure from Dakota was excessive drinking in the settlement. Stephan, of course, was himself fond of drinking with friends on occasion, but some of his associates, such as Jakob Líndal, had serious drinking problems. Stephan recalled a trip Jónas Hall and he had once made in bad weather to see a play at Hallson, together with some others. One of the group managed to buy two bottles of bitters from an Icelandic merchant, but as it turned out the liquor was so diluted that they were all sober the day after.[54] If this is any indication of common practice among the men in the community, alcohol undoubtedly took a toll on family life, and it may well be that Stephan reached the conclusion that it would be better to get away from such company.

A Fence in a Churchyard

In December of 1888 Stephan and Helga's homestead at Gardar was sold to Helga's brother, Jón Jónsson Jr., and a neighbour, Hallgrímur Gíslason, for $1,200. The value of the estate had obviously declined since the assessment of 1887. The buyers assumed the 1887 mortgage, so Stephan had roughly $500 left over, plus the value of machinery and equipment

The contract of sale between 'Stephen G. Stephenson and Helga S. Stephenson' on the one hand, and 'John Johnson and Hallgrim Gislason' on the other, is dated Dec. 12, 1888. Stephan and Helga received $1200 for the homestead.

sold.[55] Among the others who left Gardar at that time were Stephan's sister, Sigurlaug, and her husband, Kristinn Kristinsson.

Large scale migration to Western Canada was now underway and Stephan was no doubt fascinated by the anarchy of such circumstances. In contrast to the stifling situation at Gardar, the challenges of starting over again in a new settlement must have been very appealing.

An experience from years before, Stephan's brief encounter with the ruins of a log cabin in Shawano County, had remained in the poet's memory all these years, and it now resurfaced in a poem he called "Píonerinn" (The Pioneer), completed in January of 1889. The poem begins with an image of the hut, where the lone pioneer lies on his death bed – the events of his life replaying in his mind. As a young man he had been an idealist who challenged oppression, but he had reaped only contempt from his contemporaries. Outlawed from his homeland, he had come to a new country with hopes of achieving his lifelong vision of progress and freedom. Here, however, history had simply repeated itself. He had scouted for land further and further west, travelling across entire states and through areas resembling scenes from Walt Whitman's poems "Starting from Paumanok" and "Song of Myself". The pioneer was always at the forefront of settlement, moving further into the wilderness as civilization followed. In the end, however, there was no one to dig his grave or bury him. The poem concludes that "the individual's ideal" must not be brought down from "the temple of high hopes" to the "dust and dirt of earth". Ideals must remain transcendent, above the dust, as was the case with this pioneer. Perhaps such a man has only two options: to disappear ahead and perish, or to allow the fetters of the masses to control progress.[56] The poem explores the idea of how far one should allow ideals to draw one away from society. Stephan chose to move far into a new wilderness to make his ideals come true.

On the occasion of the family's departure from Gardar, friends and relatives inscribed farewells to the couple in Helga's "autograph" book. Writing in English, Jakob Líndal predicted fame and greatness for his friend, "To Steve… And thy dominion by no sea is bounded/Thy work shall live in every age and clime/And men to whom thy name is never sounded/Will fill the power of a soul sublime." Jakob's wife, Helga Steinvör, added a warm farewell that reflected anxiety about her own fate:

> Farewell, and avoid a path of perils
> May luck guide your fate,
> Whatever mine will be.[57]

Helga Steinvör and Jakob Líndal divorced not long afterward as a result of Jakob's drinking and abusive conduct. She became a well-known poet, admired for her melancholy love poems. Their good wishes accompanied Stephan and Helga.

On April 9, 1889, Björn Halldórsson got an unusual carpentry job when Stephan asked him to construct a picket fence around the graves of his father and son. Beginning in a sleet storm on Palm Sunday, Björn continued in good weather over the next few days and primed the fence on Good Friday. On Easter Monday he painted it and helped Stephan prepare for the trip. On Wednesday, April 24th, they installed the fence in the churchyard.

After the weekend, some friends and members of the Cultural Society paid Stephan and Helga a visit to say goodbye. "Stephan is well-educated, a poet, and in general a man of integrity. There are many who will miss him," Björn wrote in his diary.[58]

Fencing the graves was a symbolic act that reflected Stephan's strong bonds with the soil. He then had to tear himself away from the earth consecrated to his father and son. Once a fence surrounded the hallowed soil in which the bones of Guðmundur and little Jón rested, they could leave. Perhaps Stephan wrote this little fragment of a poem while the fence was being built:

> *He stood there alone. By the doorpost*
> *In an open church door leaning,*
> *And with sad eyes peering in pain*
> *Around the churchyard, some graves*
> *Wrapped in grass, others low mounds.*
> *Like ruins not yet overgrown, remnants of a large building,*
> *Self-made, but ill-suited to both the game's beginning and end,*
> *Thus giving no indication of origin,*
> *Nor any guarantee of the future.*[59]

The large building symbolizes a world view. A magnificent idea was about to acquire wings in a poem that was never completed. Stephan, together with his wife, his mother, and the three boys, set off a few days later for the promised land – destined for new beginnings, but mindful of Fortune's impermanence.

Marker on the graves of the poet's father, who died at Gardar in 1881, and little Jón Stephansson, who died at age three in 1887.

Chapter 8

On the Banks of the Medicine River

Settlement in Alberta

Canada had just come into existence as an independent Dominion when Icelandic immigrants first settled in Ontario in 1873. After attempts at large-scale settlement in Ontario failed, the Icelanders moved en masse in 1875 to an unsettled area on Lake Winnipeg, north of the recently created province of Manitoba.

Efforts by the Dominion of Canada to attract immigrants to the Canadian Northwest resulted in a significant influx of settlers during the 1870s and 1880s, and the government moved aggressively to establish a framework that would accommodate massive settlement of the area. Until then, the Northwest had been the homeland of First Nations and Métis peoples whose cultures and livelihoods were now increasingly threatened by missionaries, fur traders, and settlers. With the signing of treaties, Native populations retained only reserves. In 1873 the North West Mounted Police (NWMP) were established to enforce control in the Northwest and quell increasing alcohol-based violence sparked by the activities of American whisky traders. They were also to protect the rights of the First Nations by ensuring that Treaties were respected.

Beginning in Manitoba, government surveyors now divided the pristine wilderness into townships six miles square, sub-dividing them into sections and quarter-sections. In 1882, as the Canadian Pacific Railway (CPR) was pushing its way across the Prairies to the Pacific, Alberta became a separate District within the North-West Territories, and in 1883 the CPR established a divisional point close to Fort Calgary, a NWMP post. Calgary was incorporated as a town in 1884 and the railway was completed through the Rocky Mountains in 1885. The lynch pin of Prime Minister John A. Macdonald's National Policy, the CPR would not only carry immigrants westward to take up homesteads, it would make possible the exchange of manufactured goods from Eastern Canada for grain and livestock produced on the Canadian Prairies. During the boom of the following decades, the settlement of Western Canada became one of the most rapid large-scale migrations in human history. A new nation was emerging in a huge country reaching from sea to sea.[1]

The first Icelander to settle in Alberta was Ólafur Guðmundsson (Goodman), who moved to Calgary in 1887. In the summer of 1888, Icelanders in Dakota Territory sponsored Sigurður Jósúa Björnsson to scout for land on the Prairies and reserve a desirable area for them. He did not find what he considered suitable land until on his way back through Calgary where he met Ólafur Goodman, who had already explored the Red Deer River area to the north. Accompanied by Ólafur's brother Sigfús, Sigurður Jósúa proceeded to this potential site and immediately reserved two townships for Icelandic settlement. Once the land was surveyed, homesteads would be inexpensive, only $10 for a quarter-section. Sigurður Jósúa then wrote to Jónas Hunford, reporting that he had found good prairie land interspersed with forested areas – suitable for mixed farming. Hunting and fishing were also good and the area enjoyed milder winters than those of Manitoba.

Shortly afterward, having sold their belongings at half price, a group of cash poor Icelanders set off from Dakota Territory. Among them were Jónas Hunford, Benedikt Ólafsson, and Ólafur Ólafsson of the Cultural Society, all of them friends of Stephan. Helga's uncles, brothers Benedikt Bardal and Gísli Dalmann, also made the move, and three other Icelanders joined the group in Winnipeg. They bought cattle and household equipment along the way, since they reasoned that these items would be more expensive in Alberta. On June 1, 1888, they arrived in Calgary, where they stayed for several weeks. Some of these migrants found work, while others bought horses, wagons, and harness for the 80 mile trip northward to the Red Deer River. Both horses and equipment proved bad and expensive.

The trip through the wilderness was difficult. It rained heavily and because the trails were so bad the men often had to unload the wagons and carry the women and children across the muddiest sections. The weather was cold and unsuitable for sleeping in tents with small children.

On the sixth day, the little group reached the Red Deer River. Always difficult to ford because of its steep banks and muddy bottom, it was now in flood. North of the river lay the Promised Land, looking like the desolate wilderness it was. There was only one house on the other side, belonging to a settler named Sage, and just two boats. Both were too small for the Icelanders' cargo, but some of the men used them to cross the river in order to meet with the settler.

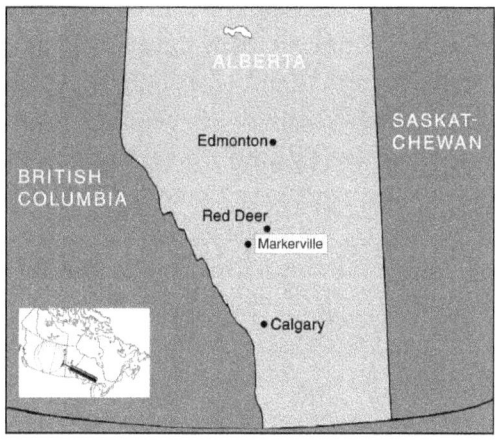

The first Icelandic settlers took up homesteads southwest of Red Deer, Alberta, starting in the years 1888 and 1899, around what became the village of Markerville.

Sage offered the Icelanders work floating logs to his sawmill, promising in return to help them fashion rafts to ferry their cargo across the river. The Icelanders fulfilled their part of the bargain, but no rafts were ever built. Fortunately, a few of the newcomers had brought lumber from Calgary, and Ólafur, Benedikt, and Gísli used some of it to build barges to ferry their families and goods across the river. The animals swam. That was on Tuesday, June 27, 1888, and Jónas Hunford suggested that day be designated the settlement's founding date.

Some of the men subsequently returned to Calgary for the winter, to earn some money working for Ólafur Goodman, who had established himself as a contractor. The winter was difficult for those who had pushed on to the new settlement. Supplies purchased in a store south of the settlement were expensive, and despite a mild winter and an early spring, many of the new families in the settlement were almost destitute by summer.

On the Train West

At the beginning of May 1889, Stephan Guðmundsson Stephansson, aged 35, left his homestead at Gardar together with his mother, nearly 60 years of age; his pregnant wife, almost 30 years old; and their three boys, Baldur, nine-and-a-half, Guðmundur, seven, and Jakob, not yet three. Joining them were Stephan's sister, Sigurlaug, her husband, Kristinn, and their three children, Stefán, Guðbjörg Lilja, and Hannes Frost. After loading their belongings on a wagon and buying a team of oxen and several cows, these migrants made their way north to Gretna, Manitoba, where they boarded a train to Winnipeg. From there they travelled by rail to Calgary.[2]

It was not the flatness of the prairies that captured Stephan's imagination during the train journey west, but rather the Native people who thronged to the stations as the train arrived at each stop. Their way of life had changed drastically over the preceding quarter-century. As late as the 1860s, many of the Plains people had traversed the prairies astride horses and provided for themselves by hunting bison and other wildlife. By 1870, whisky, illness, and tribal warfare were taking an increasingly heavy toll. Government officials began negotiations to establish these semi-nomadic people on reserves in preparation for settlement, but it is unlikely that the Natives truly understood the concept of private ownership, and treaties were written in a complicated and alien legal jargon. The last major treaty on the Canadian Prairies was signed in 1877, just as the last bison were being killed off. This was a severe blow for the traditional way of life of First Nations people.[3]

During the journey west, Stephan wrote the poem "Indíánarnir" (The Indians), in which empathy and irony counteract. The poem presents stark images of the Native peoples, while drawing parallels between their behaviour and those of the Icelanders in similar situations.

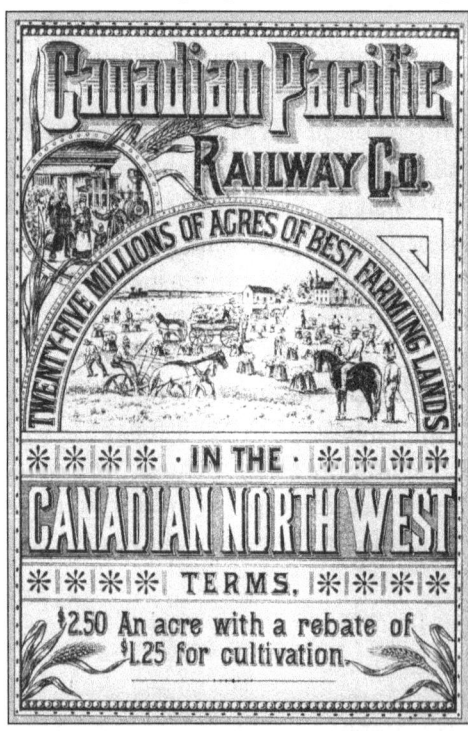

Canadian Pacific Railway advertisement for 25,000,000 acres of the "best farming lands in the Canadian Northwest".

When a group of Natives, who had been smoking and cooking on an open fire as they waited for the train, chaotically flocked to the station to meet the approaching locomotive, Stephan was reminded of how people in Iceland had flocked to the ports to stare at Flemish fishermen. The children on the train were frightened by these strange people, smelling like rotten fish but wearing colourful clothes, and in the poem Stephan recalls the smell of his godfather as he filled his large belly with alcohol and putrefied shark. Evidently Stephan found it painful to witness the humiliation of these once proud people, now reduced to holding forth polished buffalo horns for sale and bargaining with dirty fingers. They had sold their lands for liquor, he states in the poem, and their hunting grounds were now devoid of game. Their land was being burned to clear the woods and they were not allowed to wander freely, sad testimony to Christian charity, he observed. "Our Christian public education carries what remains of a nation/along the path to execution." The end of the poem expresses some Darwinian ideas. Caucasians might be somewhat further advanced in development, Stephan said, but he doubted their superiority. Instead he mused about the innocent youth of humankind on the prairies:

Stephan and Helga's three boys, Baldur, Guðmundur, and Jakob, photographed in Dakota shortly before the move to Alberta. This photo, inscribed 'addressa Tindastóll Alta. NWTerr. Canada' was sent by the poet to his uncle Stefán Hannesson in the United States.

> *But I feel, all the same, a battle of doubt,*
> *As I believe that what I long for is out there,*
> *Where the prairie stretches to the east*
> *With spring morning in their embrace –*

And thus forget so many things there,
While dreaming of the youth of humankind.[4]

This loss of innocence on the Prairies was also evident in the huge piles of bison bones at stations along the way. Deposited there by settlers who had collected them off the land to earn a little money, these bones were being sent back east to make fertilizer.

As the journey west continued, a new era revealed itself in ranches, herds of cattle, and cowboys. It was cloudy and snowing when the little group arrived at Calgary in early May. The fledgling city was developing as a meat processing centre for the surrounding ranches, and by 1889 it had 6000 inhabitants – a few of whom lived in large sandstone houses with electricity. Stephan sought out some countrymen to find accommodations for the group, while Helga and Sigurlaug immediately found work washing clothes for some of the city's wealthier people. Guðbjörg minded the children and tended the livestock while the parents were working.[5]

Stephan was favourably impressed with Calgary. There were many Americans, however, and conflict between Americans and Canadians was not infrequent. "There are no politics here. Prime Minister Sir John A. Macdonald and the CPR rule here like God Almighty, without anyone seeing them," Stephan commented in a letter to Jónas Hall. Calgary

Aboriginal people's lives and culture changed forever with the settlement of the West. Icelandic immigrants must have been fascinated to see native people wearing footgear almost identical to their own skinnskór.

The frontier town of Calgary around the time of Stephan and Helga's arrival there in 1889.

was booming, in particular the saloons and brothels, as was customary in frontier towns. Alcohol consumption was not excessive, Stephan observed, since hardly anyone, apart from the rich and the cowboys, could afford to drink. A shot of whisky was 25 cents while a glass of beer cost 10 cents, the same as in Dakota.[6]

Soon some old Dakota friends showed up to greet them. Ólafur Ólafsson from Espihóll, who had travelled widely, now seemed happy in Alberta. He "works like a bull, is as hardy as a horse, as cheerful as a snow bunting, and as content as a sheep," Stephan reported. The Mjóidalur brothers, Gísli Dalmann and Benedikt Bardal, also turned up. They were also quite content here and spoke negatively of Dakota while praising the new colony, although they found it somewhat isolated. A few Icelanders had found work at the Eau Claire Sawmill in Calgary, guiding logs down the river to the mill. They reported that people in the settlement were surviving on fish and potatoes and that livestock numbers there were still very limited. As Stephan did not want to leave his family behind, he decided to stay in Calgary temporarily and take a low-paying railway construction job north of town.

One fine day, as the weather was improving, Stephan lay down on a slope overlooking the Bow River. As the fog gradually lifted, the Rocky Mountains appeared, tremendous in the blue distance. A significant moment in Alberta's literary history now occurred. Muttering words and phrases, Stephan began crafting a poem worthy of this magnificent vision: "The dark clears up/and from the fog rise/the western rows of mountains." The rhythm of the poem "Klettafjöll" (The Rocky Mountains) is irregular, mirroring the profile of the mountains. "Magnificent, proud, and tall,/peaking high above the low grey hills,/with a helmet of fog/sweeping the tight/blowing veil from ice-pale faces." The poet's lines embrace the mountains, reflecting his feelings for this new place. Recalling Nordic myths he had learned as a boy, Stephan conjures up an image of the craftsman Völundur painting the blue mountains and white snow drifts. The poem ends with an allusion to Valhalla, where mountains are the dream world of ancient times. "Good night, my dear mountains," Stephan whispers at the end of the poem.[7]

The Call of the Wilderness

Stephan's sojourn in Calgary was not long. In early July he hitched his oxen to a heavy wagon and began his trek north – across prairies, over forested hills, and through dales of lush and beautiful land. Travelling 80 miles to the northeast, he then turned west at the hamlet of Poplar Grove and crossed the Red Deer River – now at low water. From there he continued across fertile prairie land until he stopped by the sandy, forested hills along the banks of the Medicine River. The landscape resembled Iceland more than the prairies of Dakota had, and the countryside appeared promising for raising sheep. There was also a good view of the Rocky Mountains to the west. "Hills, pastures, and large stretches of meadow alternate. The soil is fertile and grassy. Small poplar trees grow on the hills and evergreen trees called spruce clad the hillsides and hug the curving riverbanks – good timber for building houses and fences," Stephan wrote.[8]

There was no good timber near the site Stephan selected for his homestead, however, so he was obliged to go north along the Medicine River to cut logs and then float them downstream to the site he had chosen for his new home. He then used his oxen to haul the logs up the slope from the river and across a flat field to the top of a low hill, where he began the construction of a log house. Two settlers who had arrived the previous year helped him with the work. One of them, Jónas Hunford, became a lifelong friend. Stephan made a little verse about these two men working as hard as draught horses.[9]

Despite the hard work, Stephan could not refrain from teasing old enemies. The catalyst was an essay by Reverend Friðrik Bergmann in the May edition of *Sameiningin*, written in Jón Bjarnason's polemic style, about how Icelanders in America could best assist "...their old mother

The journey from Calgary to the settlement site on the Medicine River was made on wagons drawn by oxen.

Iceland". They were now living in the most technologically advanced society in the world, Bergmann wrote, while Icelanders were still mired in extreme backwardness. The only remedy, Reverend Bergmann maintained, was for those few Icelanders in America capable of wielding a pen to send cargos of bold ideas to Iceland, whose "...very survival now depends on sharp, merciless, thundering and lightning criticism of its spiritual wretchedness, coupled with a searing love of truth."[10]

In response, Stephan wrote a biting poetic parody of this essay, "Krítíkin okkar" (Our Criticism), and sent it to an old friend in Winnipeg, Unitarian minister Björn Pétursson. Björn in turn, sent it immediately to the Icelandic paper *Heimskringla*, and the editor, Eggert Jóhannsson, printed it. On Stephan's subscription copy of the paper Eggert wrote in pencil, "come again", together with his initials. In this poem Stephan mocks criticism as a method for saving Iceland, citing the futility of criticizing the frost, blizzards, and lack of grazing.[11] He also took every opportunity to ridicule Reverend Friðrik Bergmann and Reverend Jón Bjarnason.

At the end of July 1889, Stephan returned to Calgary to fetch his family and their belongings. An old neighbour from Skagafjörður, Jón Pétursson from Kolgröf, accompanied them. They travelled slowly, encountering only a few homes and expensive stopping houses along the way, until late one day they arrived on the banks of the Red Deer River. It was in flood, so they had to wait until next morning, when they consulted Sage, who lived across the river. He told them they could safely ford the river and offered to guide the oxen as they crossed.

The Medicine River was swollen with spring run-off when the family made their first crossing to reach the site of the homestead.

Stephan and Jón Pétursson each led an ox by the reins, while Helga, Guðbjörg, and the three boys sat atop of the loaded wagon. Many years later Stephan recalled "...struggling against the force of the river/with the oxen and wagon,/As he defended/all he owned, wife and children." As the strong current reached his armpits, Stephan found that he had been rather naive in leading an overloaded wagon into such a deep river, and when the current broke over his shoulders, "he felt his foot was like a feather/in deep water and no bottom." If the water had been any higher, they would have been in serious danger. Helga, "calm and smiling/in the seat between the children," watched her husband. They reached the bank on the other side safely and Helga later had no recollection of being afraid.[12]

The pioneer now proudly led his family to their new log home, where they unloaded their belongings: bed linen, clothing, cooking gear, a kerosene lamp, and Helga's sewing machine. There was also a trunk with a few books, as well as poems and prose in manuscript form. Among the books was *Vídalíns Postilla* (the old volume of sermons), *The Bible*, a bound volume of *The Index*, and a book of essays by Underwood, that Stephan's friends in the Cultural Society had given him on his departure from Dakota.

Stephan and Helga were expecting another child in the fall and there was much to do. On October 5, 1889, pregnant as she was, Helga went down to the river to get water. She returned carrying two buckets

The Stephansson home site, located on the banks of the Medicine River, consisted of wooded rolling sand hills interspersed with lowlands and sloughs. Almost unique in Central Alberta, this area was certainly not the most productive, but possibly the most attractive – which appealed to the poet.

full. The next day, in exceptionally fine weather, she gave birth to twin girls. Stephan's sister, Sigurlaug, was in Calgary, so Helga's aunt Sesselja Bardal undoubtedly helped deliver the two girls. The babies were like night and day. The older one, Stephaný Guðbjörg, was dark, while the younger, Jóný Sigurbjörg, was blonde. As they grew up, these girls were nicknamed Fanny and Jenny.[13]

Former Servants of the Devil

Following an age-old Icelandic custom, Stephan and his family named various landmarks on the homestead. North of the house were two hills, Fagrabrekka (Beautiful Slope) and Flagghóll (Flag Hill).[14] Stephan also continued his poetic musings and described in humorous verses the lifestyle of people living along the Red Deer River:

> *Cowboys live along it*
> *And their herds, in valleys and hollows,*
> *Spread. – And some are sheep*
> *And some are aggressive bulls.*
>
> *And former servants of the devil*
> *and men of God, but without office,*

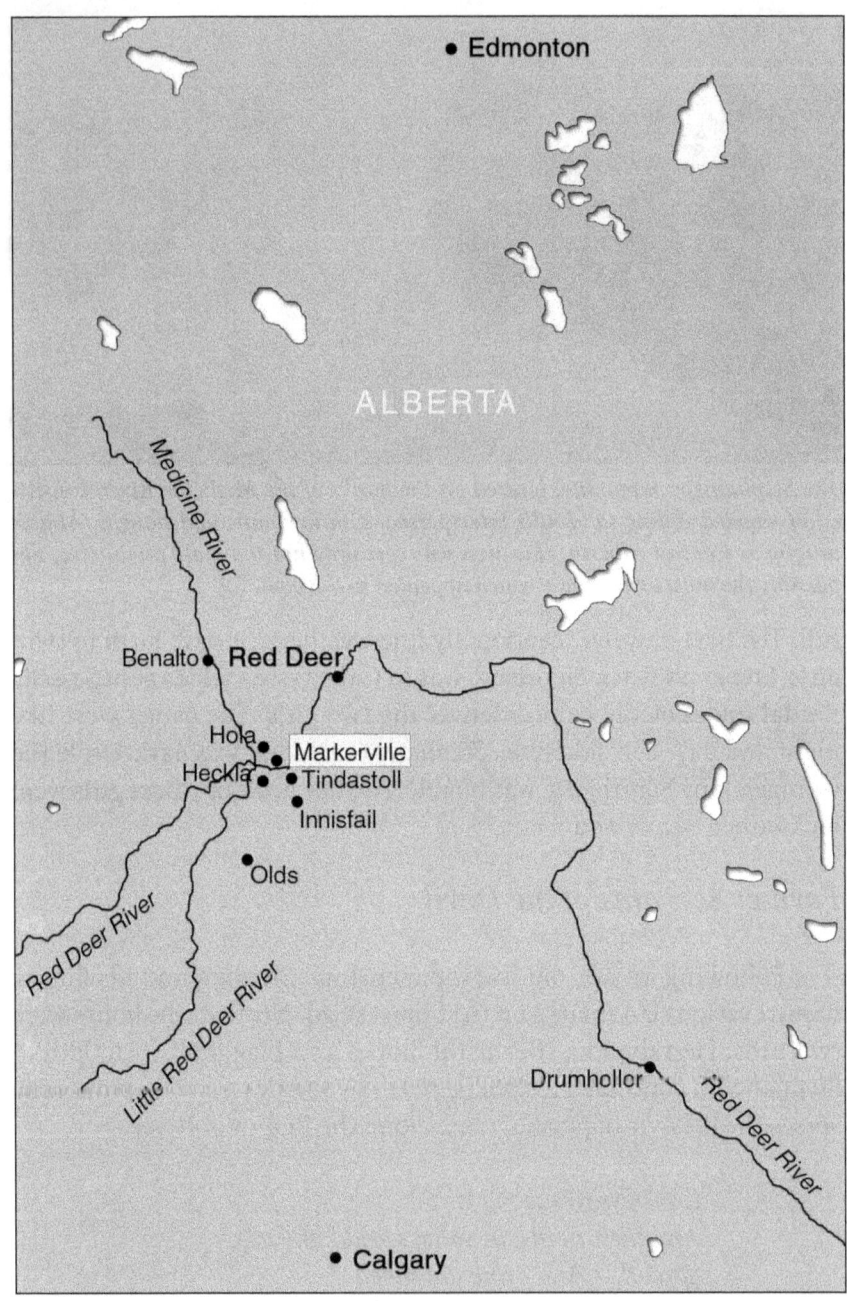

The Icelandic settlement in Alberta was originally called Tindastóll, which was the name of the first post office in the district. After the turn of the century, the post office was moved to the village of Markerville, named after the Provincial Dairy Commissioner, Marker. There were three schools in the district with Icelandic names: Heckla, Hola, and Tindastoll.

*are the closest neighbours,
by the river's thundering torrent.*[15]

Stephan's explanation of the latter stanza was that some cowboys living by the river had once been either priests or prisoners.[16]

The colourful life in this sparsely populated neighbourhood fascinated Stephan and he valued most those whose conduct stood out. He found Sage to be a gaudy character, an entrepreneur in his own way, and the smartest among the English settlers. It was rumoured that Sage had killed someone in the United States, though it was not quite clear how that had happened. Some of the Icelanders took a dislike to him, but Stephan acknowledged his role as the only wheeler-dealer in the area. He had successfully petitioned for a post office, which was given the name Cash City; he was lobbying to have a bridge built over the Red Deer River; and he wanted to establish both a cheese factory and a flourmill. "He is poor, just as we are, but offers to give half of his property to the rich if they will build something for the public welfare here," Stephan wrote in a letter in the fall of 1889. He continued with cheerful descriptions of this new society in the wilderness.

Another character of note was a man named Jackson, who lived on the south bank of the Red Deer River. Originally an American bounty hunter in search of Sage, Stephan claimed, Jackson had abandoned that mission and left Sage holding his head higher than ever. Sage now had a flock of 1,200 rented sheep, and Helga's uncles, Benedikt Bardal and Gísli Dalmann, together with another Icelander, also

In keeping with an old Icelandic custom, the poet named the landmarks on and around the homestead. One of these was Fagrabrekka (Fair Slope), in description of a beautiful hillside north of the building site.

took a few hundred sheep that fall. Their hay was so poor, however, that the sheep nearly starved and eventually Benedikt had to take care of all the sheep. The flock managed by Bendikt and Sage shared the same pasture and some claimed that Sage filched most of Benedikt's sheep in the process.

Then there was Dan Morrison, "a miller and a harmless person who does not believe in hell and asserts that priests make it all up. He can neither read nor write and claims to have been a thief back home in Scotland," Stephan wrote. He noted that there was no law enforcement in the area, but added that it was not really necessary since no one committed any serious crimes. There were admittedly some minor disputes, and Stephan included amusing reports of these in his letters.

Another man, James Brown, had arrived alone from Ontario before the Icelanders, with two heifers he had bought in Calgary for $75 each. "The heifers did not want to live with Brown and ran away," Stephan wrote. He got so bored living alone that he left the following spring to go back home. Brown got no further than Winnipeg, where he found everything so cold and miserable that he turned back. The following year, his parents and brothers joined him, so that by the time the Icelanders arrived he owned quite a herd of cattle.[17]

Stephan liked it so much in Alberta that he tried to convince his best friend, Jónas Hall, to move from Dakota. The insecurity and challenge of the new frontier had rekindled his spark of life, he wrote to Jónas, and despite poverty and primitive conditions in Alberta, he and Helga felt renewed energy and optimism. They were happy to have escaped the strife and broken hopes in Dakota. Stephan believed

Eggert Jóhannsson, 1884, editor of the Icelandic newspaper Heimskringla, *which commenced publication in Winnipeg in 1886.*

that grain could be grown in the new settlement and he was anxious to give it a try.[18]

More Icelandic homesteaders arrived in the settlement from Calgary as there was not much work in the city. Fishing was good in the Medicine River and Snake Lake (renamed Sylvan Lake) and the Icelanders bought both nets and boats. Stephan fished for eight days that fall, in stormy, cold weather, and the settlers also trapped wolves and foxes and found plenty of wild game for food.[19]

The first Christmas was celebrated with few luxuries. A cold winter wind blew around the few pioneer houses and there was "a hundred miles of snow and frost" between us, Stephan wrote in a verse-letter to a friend of his youth, Sigurður Jónsson from Víðimýri. Christmas comes to those who have humour, he claimed, and he tried to recapture the spirit of boyhood Christmases by means of poetry. On New Year's Eve of 1890, he admitted to wanting a little alcohol more than anything else.[20]

Stephan's "Krítík" (Critique) was the first of his poems to be published in *Heimskringla*. In the fall of 1889, however, he accepted editor Eggert Jóhannsson's invitation to "come again", this time sending a verse to encourage his friend Skapti Brynjólfsson, who was running for a seat in the Dakota Legislature. At Christmas, having decided that his apprenticeship as a poet was over, he submitted the poem "Klettafjöll" (The Rocky Mountains), which was published in the paper's January 23, 1890 issue. This poem earned him an enduring reputation as a poet as well as the title *Klettafjallaskáldið* – "The Rocky Mountain Poet".

The First Summer, 1890

In the spring of 1890, as the weather turned nice after mid-April, the tiny settlement came to life. Stephan read books and composed poetry, delighted by the new growth and happy with his daily bread. In good health and pleased with the increase in his livestock, he gently mocked those who complained about the occasional storm or frost, or lost heart over the vagaries of pioneer life. A cable ferry had been installed across the Red Deer River and a sawmill had begun operation near The Crossing. Regular postal service remained uncertain, however, and there were few other prospects for improvement until a railway was built.[21]

The rhythm of life in the settlement kept pace with the plodding of oxen and the gradual progress of hand tools. One spring day, Stephan and a neighbour set off to break an acreage west of Poplar Grove, south of the Red Deer River. With them were two 10 year old boys, one of them Stephan's son Baldur, who led the oxen. As the river was in flood, they had to make a detour all the way to the new ferry at The Crossing, and the job took them over a month.[22]

The number of livestock in the settlement increased gradually. In 1890, Icelandic homesteaders owned 8 oxen, 16 horses, almost 200 head of cattle, and a considerable number of sheep, pigs, and chickens. Some 25 acres were also under cultivation.

In spite of this, Ólafur Ólafsson from Espihóll became restless and left his homestead for an area further southeast. Stephan predicted that Ólafur would soon move to the West Coast if only someone would join him. Meanwhile, Stephan tried to persuade Jónas Hall to come from Dakota and take over Ólafur's abandoned homestead.[23]

It was peaceful in the settlement, Stephan reported, except for some minor friction between the brothers Benedikt Bardal and Gísli Dalmann, and Benedikt's feelings that everyone was against him. People in the district put on no airs and made no attempt to "cover their foolishness and conventionality with any icing of creed or Christian ornamentation,"

Benedikt Jónsson Bardal, a neighbour to the Stephansson family in the Alberta settlement and an uncle to Helga. One of the Mjóidalur brothers, he was a brother to Jón Jónsson Sr. at Gardar and Gísli Jónsson Dalmann.

Stephan wrote, but he added that two "frumps", Karólína Dalmann and Hólmfríður Goodman, were in a spiritual crisis because of the lack of a Lutheran minister in the area. Hólmfríður was related to Reverend Friðrik Bergmann, "so it would naturally be a disgrace to the family if she were to be lost eternally," he noted. The Goodmans were God-fearing people who had somehow landed outside the narrow path of virtue when Ólafur Goodman, Hólmfríður's brother-in-law, found himself about to rent a house in Calgary to prostitutes – until neighbours complained. He had then tried in vain to establish a Lutheran congregation in Calgary. These contrasting ambitions amused Stephan.[24]

By the autumn of 1890, small fields and gardens were evident throughout the settlement, but Stephan was not entirely content with his lot. The Icelandic settlers relied mainly on cattle, as experiments with grain growing had revealed that frost was a serious problem in the area. In mid-August, while Stephan was haying, frost damaged the potatoes, cabbages, and most of the grain. The acreage under cultivation was so little, however, that the overall loss was small. Sage had 15 acres of oats that survived undamaged, but at The Crossing a farmer named Gaetz lost all his wheat. His oats also suffered damage, but his black rye was not seriously affected. Stephan sent samples of grain to his friends in Dakota and reflected upon the area's potential for grain-growing.[25]

The railway pushed northward that summer, but uncertainty remained as to where it would cross the Red Deer River. Later in the summer it was rumoured that it would be at the Gaetz homestead, five miles east of The Crossing, where land for a townsite had already been bought by the railway company. Railway contractors Ross and McKenzie, however, wanted to buy a sawmill that had been set up in the vicinity of Stephan's homestead, and if they bought the mill and got a timber permit, the railway would likely cross the river there. Stephan did not much care, as he knew the railway would be somewhere within 20 miles, but he hoped that it would not be too close to his homestead as the neighbourhood would then become crowded and noisy.[26]

Many were disappointed in the summer of 1891 when the railway crossed the Red Deer River at The Crossing, where the town of Red Deer subsequently developed. The nearest railway station for the Icelanders was at Poplar Grove, later called Innisfail, south of the Red Deer River. The train came through once a week, but the Red Deer River remained a dangerous obstacle, particularly during spring thaw and autumn freeze-up. There was neither a bridge nor a ferry at Poplar Grove, despite petitions submitted to the government by both Stephan and Sage.

During the summer of 1890 Stephan speculated on the future of the settlement. Schools would soon be built, he said, as required by law, with the government paying three-quarters of the teacher's salary. The children in the settlement could easily fill two or three schoolhouses. The prices of many goods would drop, he predicted, but it would be a long time before the territory was fully settled as it would take years to exploit the forests and mines made accessible by the railways. The market for farm products would increase, since the soil was rich and the crops would be good.[27] In most of these things he proved correct.

Exploration to Edmonton

Stephan had not yet quite decided where he should settle permanently, and in the fall of 1890, having heard remarkable stories about crops in the vicinity of Edmonton, he and his brother-in-law Kristinn set off to scout for land in that area. Originally Fort Edmonton, established in 1795 by the Hudson's Bay Company, Edmonton was still just a village on the North Saskatchewan River, 160 miles north of the Icelandic settlement. It rained along the way and the roads were bad, but 20 miles out of Edmonton there was hardly any trace of the August frost. Nowhere had Stephan seen better gardens: two pound potatoes, huge tomatoes, and cornstalks as high as a man – with only slight frost damage on the leaves.

Stephan and Kristinn spent two nights with a Mr. McNabb, who had taken land 14 miles west of Edmonton nine years earlier. Now he had two quarter-sections of land, handsome log barns, more than 20 head of cattle, pigs, sheep, horses, and the usual collection of farm equip-

The Hudson's Bay fort at Edmonton on the North Saskatchewan River.

ment – and he owed only $75. Stephan examined the crops, measured the straw, collected some samples, and described the crops in letters to his friends in North Dakota. He claimed that cabbage and cauliflower heads grew as big as an armful and said they could knock him down or compose a libellous verses about him if they found he was lying. Kristinn and Stephan both reserved land provisionally. Stephan wanted to further examine a grassy slope, suitable for hay, that descended toward the river at the edge of a dense spruce forest. He read about geographical conditions, the landscape, and the elevation, seeking an explanation for the quality of the land, although it was hard to find decent books or knowledgeable men. He concluded that the later frosts were due to the fact that Edmonton was further from the Rockies than the Red Deer area and sheltered by more forest between the mountains and the settlement. Stephan foresaw that Edmonton would boom after the arrival of the railway. The trip to Edmonton lasted nearly two weeks and when Stephan returned home on September 11, 1890, there was a foot of snow in Calgary. Nevertheless, no one relocated to Edmonton at that time.[28]

Gísli and Karolína Dalmann with their boys, Jón, Páll, Valdimar, and Konráð, photographed in Winnipeg en route to Alberta in 1888.

Shortly after his return, Stephan received an odd verse-letter from Karólína Dalmann, who had been in the settlement for two years. She had heard that Stephan was considering moving north and asked him what the land was like. She also expressed concern about the community's social and spiritual life, and she evidently feared that Stephan's condemnations of Lutheran congregational work might interfere with a church being built in the settlement, so she would never be able to sing at church services. Karólína had difficulty understanding Stephan's ideas and she wished to keep to the traditional faith in which she had been raised. It disturbed her that she and Stephan did not see eye to eye. "You tear down all faith," she said. "It bothers me that you are like this/though I will never be your wife,/and we will never share a household." She then suggested that they could become good neighbours and friends even if they did not share a common belief. At the end of this missive she sent greetings to Stephan's mother, the "blessed children", "and your dear wife/whose company I would enjoy /if you and I were not at odds all the time."[29]

On his birthday, October 3, 1890, Stephan replied to Karólína in a beautiful verse letter. He did not respond on the subject of any personal matters she had raised, but depicted his view of life as reflecting his environment, his experience, and his worldly philosophy. A new outlook towards the land, life, and work was emerging in his mind. "I look around my settlement," he began, describing the prairie smiling gently to the sun. Everything is "so cheerful and light/and inviting in appearance" with green forests and meadows. He was most fascinated by the beauty of the wilderness, where evil weeds did not grow "from human sweat." He found the most joy in a place before it was ploughed, but nevertheless envisioned a prosperous district with fertile fields, grazing livestock, and beautiful horses. Most of all, however, he wanted to be among good people:

> *It is better to lack bread and milk*
> *And live among cows and oxen*
> *Than to linger among those people*
> *Who do not know how to think.*

Many people want only "to eat and gather wealth", Stephan observed, pointing out that he was looking for knowledge and fairness rather than slander and prejudice. He felt that the human spirit should be free and that each person should be at liberty to form an independent opinion, and he demanded that his opinions be respected in return. He asked Karólína whether she had not learned to respect the opinions of others. It was a mistake, he pointed out, to reject someone for not having the same religion. The poem ends with a summary of his ideals and his desire to "soften some of the ills of society, / to advocate the requisite matters."

> *Whenever the Goddess of death shall get me*
> *I will die happy because of this:*

Settlers commonly used oxen to break and till the land until they were able to afford horses, which were more expensive to acquire and feed. This gang of oxen belonged to Sören Hjaltalín.

> *I commend my work into the hands of the future,*
> *And the treasures of my hopes.*[30]

More Pioneers

This was Stephan's third time as a pioneer, so he was becoming quite experienced in such matters. He wrote a concise and lively description of the new settlement for an Icelandic immigrant paper, *Landneminn (The Settler)*, describing the fertile soil, the availability of water, and the good fishing. Breaking the land was easy since it did not need clearing, but there was enough timber available for buildings and firewood. The climate was milder than further to the east, despite severe cold in midwinter, and spring came in March or early April, making it possible to seed early – though there was a risk of frost in May. The weather could be quite hot and there was sometimes a lot of rain in June and July, with the risk of frost in August. Harvest began in August or September and autumns were long and mild. Usually it began to snow in November, with small accumulations until Christmas. The coldest and snowiest months were January through to March. The area was well suited to livestock, and while grain-growing was hardly profitable because of the sizeable investment required for machinery, many sorts of grain could be grown in good years.[31]

During the first years, drought and summer frost frequently ruined the crops, and in 1890 the few settlers who had ploughed small plots and seeded crops reaped only a meagre harvest. Most of them gave up, but not Stephan. He used the oxen he had brought from Dakota to plough, both for himself and others, and he was the first to successfully harvest a field crop, having been more patient and meticulous than others. It was not until the fourth fall that Stephan and Helga had a good crop of potatoes, however, having finally discovered that a potato garden should be on a hilltop instead of in a hollow where there was more risk of frost.[32]

During these early years, semi-nomadic Natives still pitched tepees here or there and stayed over the winter. Although their lives were marked by misfortune, they were reliable to deal with, and occasionally settlers who had to take work elsewhere relied on an Indian neighbour to keep an eye on the women and children, which they never failed to do.[33] Stephan often worked at railroad construction during the first winters, leaving Helga and Guðbjörg alone with the children. Helga was always in charge of milking the cows, but when Stephan was away she also had to feed and water them, as well as cut firewood and perform numerous other chores on the homestead.

Stephan still wanted his old friend Jónas Hall to come to Alberta and he encouraged him to try working at railway construction that winter, as there would be plenty of well-paid jobs on the new rail line to Edmonton. Jónas could also get a job in Calgary, he wrote, as Kristinn was there and had good connections. Besides, he continued, they could enjoy each other's company. Employment opportunities were irregular, however, and it was easy to spend most of one's income on booze, Stephan admitted.[34]

Stephan obviously missed Jónas Hall's company and conversations, as none of his neighbours in the Alberta settlement matched his old friend's intelligence or knowledge. Eventually Jónas accepted the invitation and visited Stephan for a month. While exploring the area, Stephan and Jónas camped at Snake Lake overnight, damming a brook and catching 200 pike. While discussing religion and poetry one night, they drank a seven year-old bottle of alcohol purchased at the Hudson's Bay store.[35] Jónas nevertheless did not move to Alberta.

The spring and summer of 1891 were cold, with frost every month. Although grain got a late start, it grew incredibly fast and Stephan was happy and content. He harvested good oats, and while some of the barley froze, the beans, cabbage, and turnips did well. Tireless in his grain growing experiments, he tried sowing oats, barley and wheat late in June. The hay crop was good, despite rain almost every day in August, and

Sigurlaug, the poet's sister, and her husband, Kristinn Kristinsson, around the time of their move from Dakota to Alberta.

the potatoes were ample, although Stephan's were frost-damaged. He also took time for other interests, among other things walking around the settlement for two days to sell copies of Jón Ólafsson's book of poetry.³⁶

Stephan's sister, Sigurlaug, and her husband, Kristinn Kristinsson, now prepared to move to the settlement, as employment in Calgary had become scarce. Kristinn purchased two mares, and Stephan caught the stagecoach to Calgary, stayed overnight with his sister, then left Calgary on Monday afternoon with this new team and some additional horses for neighbours in the settlement. Riding all the way back, Stephan led three horses by the reins, while two fillies followed. He camped out in the great outdoors, and during a thunderstorm he observed that the darkness was like a black veil, occasionally split by lightning that revealed the trees as gigantic shadows against the clouds sweeping across the sky. The storm made the horses so nervous that Stephan could not sleep. He continued his journey on Tuesday, arriving at Jóhann Björnsson's homestead late at night – wet, weatherworn, and exhausted. Jóhann's farm at the southern edge of the settlement was called Tindastóll, after a mountain in Skagafjörður – as was the new post office established there a year later. When Stephan eventually arrived home after this trip, he did some important chores and then sat down to write a poem he had composed along the way.³⁷

One sunny morning a few days later, Stephan walked to his neighbour's before breakfast and bought a piglet, which he carried home in a sack over his shoulder. He then began fashioning a muzzle for a calf that persisted in sucking the milk cows. The muzzle consisted of a metal point attached to an old water dipper, but it did not work very well. The poet then sat down to write a letter, but a short time later he was interrupted when someone rode into the yard. It was just one of the Bardal boys, however, and Stephan noted, "Of course he wanted to take up my time, but I just continued writing, answering the little man with nonsense." Thus Stephan's days passed with various chores and writing.[38]

The pioneer poet now had five acres of cultivated land, including an acre of garden. He owned two draught oxen, two cows, two bullocks, two sheep, and four hens. Most of the homesteads in the district were assessed at several hundred dollars and a majority of the settlers were debt free, with several acres of cultivated land, livestock, houses, and various farm implements. Some 140 Icelandic men, women, and children now lived in the settlement, on 32 homesteads, and Icelanders continued to move into the district, among them Sigurður from Víðimýri, a friend from Stephan's youth. Life was often colourful and in his letters Stephan sometimes recorded humorous stories about his neighbours. One such story involved two relatives who got into a fight over a mower. One ended up wielding a wrench as a weapon.[39]

Disbelief

The year 1891 was an intellectually turbulent one for Stephan. As indicated by several poems published in *Heimskringla* around that time, he was struggling on three different levels. Firstly, he began expressing his inner religious conflict as a form of creative disbelief; secondly, he further developed his own radical perspective under the influence of the Icelandic poet and editor Gestur Pálsson; and finally, in his poetry, he began coming to terms with his new home and surroundings.

Ever since Stephan had written the verse-letter to Kristinn Stefánsson eight years earlier, he had been reaching for various sparks of light along his path, hoping that these ideas would eventually catch fire and burn brightly. So they did in his great poem "Vantrúin" (Disbelief), composed early in 1891, in which Stephan personifies his disbelief as a woman.

> *She came as a spark of light into the cold darkness of a grave*
> *And the glowing light spread all over –*
> *And to me it seemed to glow through the ages,*
> *The world appeared to me as transparent meaning.*

Contrary to what might be expected, Stephan expressed his disbelief as a revelation rather than a renunciation. The female, Disbelief, illuminated the poet's environment so that his vision became "world-wide". He saw life in a new light. "And values changed," he said. What had always been highly-valued now proves of little worth, and gems lay hidden in the dirt and dark corners. He also discovered gems in his own mind, in the form of latent abilities that can flourish. As a conclusion, Disbelief "appeared briefly, in branches, as evening sparks glow,/but touched my wick and lighted a lamp."[40] As Stephan discovered his own inner values, a prolific creative force flared up.

Even so, creative poetry was not an easy task for a poet with the burden of farm chores. On one occasion Stephan had to leave a half-

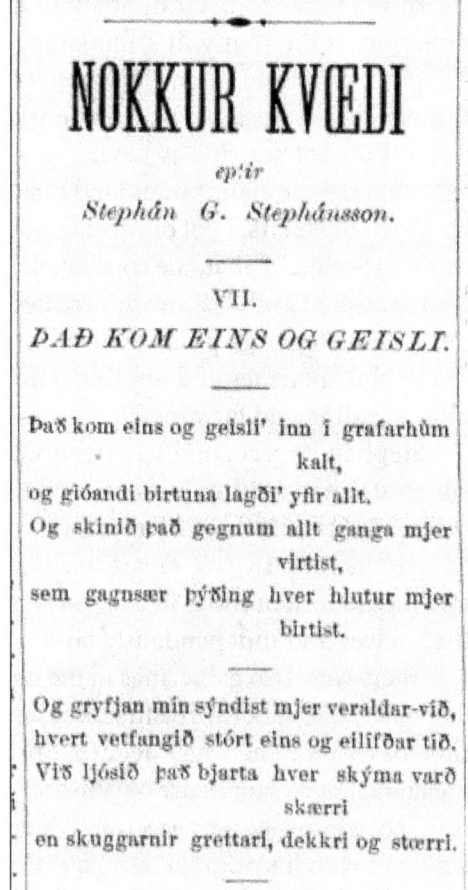

Stephan's poem "Vantrúin" (Disbelief), expressing misgivings about orthodox religion, first appeared under the title "Það Kom Eins og Geisli" (It Came Like a Ray of Light) in the March 4, 1891 issue of the Winnipeg newspaper Heimskringla.

finished letter to help neighbours fight a prairie fire, and after battling the fire all night and sleeping only a little, he went to work in the field until his plough broke. "Such is my farmer's life," he wrote in the letter to his old friend Sveinn Björnsson. "Up and down like this, highly variegated in colour, but I like this better than most other 'positions' I could possibly hold in life, simply because I feel I have a little more space around me." This small luxury helped him accept continually being pulled away from half-finished thoughts and poems.

In his letter to Sveinn, Stephan encourages his friend to seek a direction in life that will stimulate creative work. "This is how I see things. If my friend Sveinn Björnsson claims land in a very good place that effortlessly becomes worth hundreds of dollars, I think he deserves it, but I do not see this as having any great merit for Sveinn. On the other hand, if he claims poor land that after a few years becomes worth hundreds of dollars, I not only think he deserves it, I also regard it a great credit to Sveinn." "That," he concluded, "is the difference between Sveinn who is created and Sveinn who creates." This notion of self-creation is integral to Stephan's philosophy of farming: "I am trying to speak on the level of a farmer and am therefore putting everything in terms of homesteading and farming."[41]

Stephan appreciated the freedom he enjoyed in the settlement, which still had neither local council nor church, and thus no taxes or tithes. However, if the settlement was to ever live up to his vision, it had to take the initiative to "create itself", so to speak. Stephan was therefore pleased when those in the south part of the settlement organized themselves and independently built a schoolhouse in the fall of 1891.

There were two gatherings in the new schoolhouse early in 1892, and Stephan spoke at both. The first occasion was New Year's Eve, an annual time of renewal, he suggested, that brings to mind expectations both great and small. Hopes are optimistic "spring thoughts", possibly never fulfilled, but always in one's mind. Stephan never failed to surprise his audience with his original thoughts. Perhaps they did not realize at first where this was leading, as Stephan did not immediately equate spring with progress. "The progress of districts and nations depends least on climatic conditions," he continued, as it is precisely within oneself that good seasons lie. One must not let the foggy nights of the mind or a lack of sun cause us to lag behind. Stephan's point was that their small community must rely on its own abilities rather than on the government, and if people agree that the district would benefit from something, then they should take their hands out of their pockets and do it themselves. Although the government "shows support for schools" just as Christ cares for the church, neither comes down from heaven without self-reliance and effort. Stephan was therefore pleased that his fellow settlers had in the past year rejected putting all their faith in the government and had instead built their own schoolhouse, "in the realization that it did not require the power of almighty government to take that initiative."

Stephan invokes the concepts of good citizenship and cultivation in the settlement against slavish notions of adherence to government and politics. People should build up and nurture, "in return for which we reap the reward of becoming better and more useful men and the hope that the following generation will become more successful because of that." If he were to be identified as an Icelander, he said, he wanted to be remembered as a man "who had transformed a worthless tract of land into a prosperous farm" rather than one who had by sheer luck landed on some choice land and just managed to survive there. "It is not an achievement to have lived in Rome, but rather to have built it," he said.[42]

It was as if the ideas philosopher Emerson had once planted in Stephan's imagination were now maturing. The poem "Vantrúin" (Disbelief) was in fact an anthem to self-reliance – the confident belief in virtues within oneself. The emphasis on creative work that Stephan expressed in his letter to Sveinn Björnsson and applied to the independent initiative of the settlers is his own variation on Emerson's theme – that work's reward is work well done. Such a reward and self-reliance were in fact two sides of the same coin.

The second gathering at the new school was its inauguration on January 6, 1892, which according to Stephan was attended by all two-legged creatures in the settlement, except the hens and a few women who were either in bed or milking the cows – not to mention the odd farmer who stayed home to avoid the risk of having to make a donation. First, a school board was elected and a committee formed to raise what money was still needed. The committee decided to apply for a school grant. Godfearing souls suggested that apart from classes, only religious services – preferably for payment – should be allowed in the schoolhouse, although there was no minister. Stephan then stood up and presented a contrasting opinion, that all kinds of activities be allowed in the schoolhouse, free of charge. His advice won favour. The sum of $7 was raised on this occasion, toward the cost of seats, windows, and lumber for a ceiling. One of the farmers then recited a festive poem and Stephan gave an inauguration speech that several suggested be published in the papers – while various others requested written copies so they could read this speech to errant spouses who were not in attendance. Stephan thought this quaint. "How amazingly black and white is human life!" he mused. The night concluded with singing and dancing into the wee hours.

People hoped to be able to establish a private school in the new schoolhouse if they could not get a government grant, and Stephan and his neighbours considered building another schoolhouse upstream. If that could be accomplished in a year or so, it would then be possible to hire one good teacher who would teach alternately in the two schools, with the most promising students following.

When describing the weather around this time, Stephan lapsed spontaneously into traditional Icelandic alliteration and rhyme: the white winter cold, the grey clouds, loud cracks of frost resounding in every hill, and the lonely moon watching over the frozen earth.[43]

Gestur Pálsson's Bugle

Stephan had always been a radical, but after moving to Alberta new ideas consolidated in his mind and acquired poetic expression. He subscribed to *The Open Court*, a monthly established after *The Index* ceased, and he was also familiar with a dozen other liberal papers. He was in a fighting mood and wanted the freethinkers and Unitarians to organize themselves into freethinking societies, first locally and then in solidarity as a liberal progressive movement. It should be easy, he thought, to get young people to join, although humanity as a whole had advanced so little that only a few were likely to become true idealists.[44]

For Icelanders in North America, *Heimskringla* and *Lögberg* were the platforms for the struggle between progressive and conservative views, as well as for personal disputes and even outrageous slander. Around 1890, discussions in these papers were very lively. Writer Einar Hjörleifsson had been editor of *Lögberg* from its inception, and now Icelanders in Canada and the United States also attracted two of the best pens in Iceland, poet Jón Ólafsson and writer Gestur Pálsson.

Jón had first emigrated in the 1870s, then returned to Iceland, and had for some years been the most colourful editor in the history of Icelandic journalism. Now he came to Winnipeg as editor of *Lögberg*. Gestur, one of the pioneers of Realism in Iceland, had spent time in Copenhagen. He wrote original short stories in the style of Realism and held provocative public lectures on culture and literature in Iceland. Inspired by the Danish critic Georg Brandes, he demanded that writers bring real social issues to the fore. Brandes hailed free investigation and free thought and thus paralleled the message of North American freethinkers. In July of 1890, Gestur joined Eggert Jóhannsson as editor of *Heimskringla*, and he now repeated his lectures in Winnipeg, printing some of them in the paper. In Iceland it was claimed that Gestur had moved west to stem the flood of mediocre poetry flooding the pages of the Icelandic papers in Winnipeg.

Stephan was satisfied with the papers and thought the "spirit of spring" was blowing around the world. Jón Ólafsson and Gestur Pálsson were writing as radical reformers, in contrast to clergymen such as Friðrik Bergmann who wanted to imitate the sensationalists by invigorating church life. The speeches

Dapper and brilliant young Gestur Pálsson came from Iceland in 1890 to serve as editor of Heimskringla. *Tragically he lived only one year after arriving in Winnipeg.*

of "ministers who have no firm belief will not become religiously profound whether they throw away their manuscripts or keep them in their pocket," Stephan commented, adding that all good speeches, as with other good things, demand careful preparation.[45]

Gestur was new on the stage, fresher and more radical than Jón Ólafsson, and Stephan soon entered into a kind of an inner dialogue with him. He sent several poems to *Heimskringla* and contemplated Gestur's ideas, which he found to be very progressive. Jón, meanwhile, had become more content with the world as public opinion gradually caught up with him, so he was no longer a voice in the wilderness. The individual does not have the tireless resilience of time, Stephan observed, but he nevertheless considered Jón as constructive. "Gestur," he continued, "has told us that Icelandic, this beautiful-sounding language that seems created for great thoughts, has been cast off like some broken horn that nobody bothers to blow." "And what a startled reaction this statement elicited, just after the reform and cleansing the Icelandic language had undergone..."[46]

When Stephan's father-in-law sent him a summary of the lectures on Icelandic literature that Gestur held at Gardar, Stephan replied with an analysis of Gestur's views on Icelandic poetry. Stephan divided Icelandic poets into "heathen" and "Christian" poets, regardless of their confessed religion. The heathen poets, he said, were able to speak to God on their own terms, whereas the Christian poets spoke humbly. Stephan also praised the first Romantic poet in Iceland, Bjarni Thorarensen, for his extremely keen understanding of human life and his ability to portray a character's entire lifespan in four or five words, but he criticized him for failing to achieve a sense of tangible reality in his poems. Stephan disagreed with Gestur about the flaws in Grímur Thomsen's poetry and pointed out what fascinated him: "His poetry most often consists of picking up small grains of truth at our feet, so one is astonished by how much Grímur can find in such small and entirely common insignificance."[47] In his indirect dialogue with Gestur on Icelandic poetry, Stephan pointed out four criteria that served as his own poetic manifesto: human dignity in relation to God, precise character descriptions, a sense of tangible reality, and the significance of the insignificant.

Gestur's words about great thoughts and the Icelandic language's role in awakening individuals from lethargy were a revelation to Stephan, and they inspired him to express great thoughts in his own poetry. It was therefore natural that he should allude to these concepts in a poem entitled "Kveðja til Gests Pálssonar ritstjóra" (A Farewell to Editor Gestur Pálsson), composed on August 30, 1891, in response to news that Gestur was about to resign as editor of *Heimskringla* and move back to Iceland. The poem sends greetings across the ocean to herald the coming age, whose spirit found expression in the beautiful language that came from Gestur's heart. The poem then conveys the hope that Gestur's message will resound throughout Iceland like a trumpeting storm.[48]

On the very day he composed this poem, however, Stephan read in the paper that Gestur Pálsson was ill, so he deferred sending it. The next issue brought news of Gestur's death. He had succumbed to insobriety and opposition in Winnipeg, and over the following weeks fellow editors Einar Hjörleifsson and Jón Ólafsson argued in print which of them was more responsible for Gestur's death.

In response to this tragic news, Stephan composed an impassionate epitaph, "Við fréttina um lát Gests Pálssonar" (On the News of the Death of Gestur Pálsson). In it, he likens Gestur's death to the destruction of an avalanche in a beautiful valley and refers to Gestur as the child of sorrow and hardship. Although the path toward progress had now closed for a while, Gestur would soon become a bright star in the heaven of the arts, despite the opinions of hypocrites who held him in disdain for a lifestyle that did not fit their ideals of virtue. Stephan then raised a question about what now remained as the century drew to a close, while likening this young idealist to Christ on the cross:

> *You who fear, and do not find the warmth of heart*
> *– That the light of the world becomes, that cheers every human –*
> *That shines through the black shadows:*
> *From the cross, you are frightened by the piercing whine*
> *Of the poet, who carries the tormenting evils of the times*
> *On the conscience, in the mind, in the heart.*[49]

Gestur's lectures had swelled with passion, but they were also laden with pessimism derived from the situation in Iceland. With Georg Brandes as an intellectual backup, he had demanded renewal in both poetry and the national mind-set. While Gestur was editor of *Heimskringla*, Stephan had sent him several original poems, and in due course the inner dialogue he had thus established with Gestur would bear fruit.

Gestur had maintained that contemporary Icelandic poets did not have much to say and therefore lacked passion. They flirted with an idea or feeling, but did not go further than echoing other poets. In part he attributed this lack of passion to their nature, but he also cited their inability to devote themselves entirely to their poetry. They could not dedicate themselves, he said, while they were dealing with other things. Poetry demanded total commitment. To emphasize his point, Gestur used metaphors that resembled or perhaps reappeared in Stephan's poetry. The poetic nature, he maintained, was seldom able to withstand the pressures and distractions of day to day life, which takes "these morsels and melts them, boiling out of them a minister in a remote parish or baking them into an accountant in a store." If poetic nature was not altogether squelched, it became out of place, he said. Henrik Ibsen stated that it was a great sin to kill a beautiful thought, and Gestur found the sins of Iceland many. The fair thoughts that had perished, he observed, were more numerous than all the withered straws of Iceland's fields, because most poets did not have the opportunity to develop their talents. Instead, they had to "utilize their poetic nature to bake bread and churn butter in order to live."[50]

Gestur's description resonated with Stephan and may well have ignited his ambitions to transcend his circumstances and avoid merely echoing the poetry of others. By example he began to prove that poets could nurture their gift while conducting daily chores. "I steal from the night a short span,/sometimes to write," he said, at times sitting down to write despite "sixteen blisters on his behind" after a journey or hard work.[51] Although he sometimes found his poetic muse feeling neglected and frowning with displeasure, as when he sat down to pen a poem on the occasion of his birthday that year, he gradually developed a self-conscious image of the creative farmer – composing poetry while conducting his work, independent of all.

At a later date, Stephan added a stanza to the beginning of the unsent farewell poem to Gestur Pálsson. The result was the poem "Uppörvun" (Encouragement), which summarized Gestur's influence through his thought-provoking satire, his humanity, and his role as a wakening force through his language and poetry. The poem resembles a manifesto and begins with an allusion to the rebellious young men of the old sagas who burned down heathen temples:

Let, without fear, the temples of stupidity
Burn in the flames of mockery –
Praise mercy and heroic deeds,
While you can hold a pen.

Let the echo of your sounds open the doors for you,
Into the Icelandic huts,
And fight against the fact that the language that before was encouraging
Is a broken horn.

I understand that he is useful for the world
Who soothes and discourages –
But a more powerful force is in the hands of the poet,
Who arouses and instigates.[52]

This 1892 survey of Icelandic homesteaders in the Alberta settlement included statistics on such things as livestock and land improvements. "Stephan G. Stephansson" owned six cattle (two cows, two oxen, two yearlings), two sheep, and four chickens.

No Motherland – At Home

Stephan wrote prolifically throughout 1891, wrestling with more challenges than those raised by Gestur Pálsson. The April 15th issue of *Heimskringla* published two of his poems, each dealing independently with the themes of settlement and sense of place. "Útlegðin" (Outlawry) explores the emotional balance between loyalties to motherland and fosterland: "Somehow I now have,/no motherland," he wrote, while observing that the bonds of loyalty he feels for his native country are now even more tightly bound to his heart. His foster mother, Canada, though beautiful, does not yet entirely measure up as a true mother. There remains a tension between them, so the poet is never able to say that he is Canada's son. For him, the landscape is somehow lacking and the strange people who inhabit it do not share a "kinship in spirit". Although nature is pretty and gentle here, Stephan closes with the words that somehow he now has no motherland. Paradoxically he is an outlaw from both motherland and fosterland, though he has neither betrayed his motherland by leaving – an accusation levelled at many Icelandic emigrants – nor fully adapted to a new homeland.[53]

A different view appears in the other poem entitled "Landnámsmaðurinn" (The Settler). It refers to a half stanza well known in Iceland, attributed to the settler Önundur Tree-leg who was forced to immigrate to Iceland in the 10th century. He then composed a verse containing these lines: "My condition is harsh if I gain Cold-Back (a mountain)/ but lose fertile fields." Stephan's poem describes settling in a new country and depicts resounding images of a harsh and merciless landscape:

deadly glaciers, glacial rivers in dark gorges, rocky screes and mountain slopes, huge cliffs resembling giant mouths, vegetation hidden along rivers "and wherever he looked were frostbitten mountains/and fjord landscape weathered by storms and blizzards." The settler asks mother Iceland what he will get in exchange for his good fields. She replies with harsh changes of weather and thunders: "I offer you death if you sink in the ocean/but victory and luck if you float." If Önundur would not learn to trust himself, she would forbid him brotherhood and the company of fellow men:

> She taunted him: "Live in poverty and labour,
> In outlawry, that dispels your manhood,
> If you are afraid to cultivate a forest by the snowdrift
> And cover the frozen soil with grassroots."

The settler's answer is in fact a reply to the challenges of the settlement in the west:

> Then he said: "My lot and my honour is but one thing,
> To challenge you, Iceland, to a duel.
> And therefore I have vowed to fear nothing,
> Except the accusation: weakling that dares not!
>
> And therefore, I have to settle here.
> In your cold wind and hostility
> I believe, Iceland, that the mind and hand,
> Hardiness and courage will prevail."[34]

Late in the summer of 1892, Stephan wrote a poem that was published in *Heimskringla* under the title "Vestan úr landi" (From the Land in the West), but later acquired the name "Vestur í frumbýli" (On the Western Frontier). It appears as a response to "Útlegðin" (Outlawry), as Stephan now seems to feel at home in the new settlement after much travelling "to the huts of my youth,/by highland pastures and wide heaths." He finds it good to finally rest. His thoughts return to Dakota and Wisconsin when he says he has had enough wandering through sunburnt fields and dark forests, where life was dull and monotonous. "But here everything is so easy/and youthful-friendly,/and small homesteads are wrapped/in the peace of country life." Everything he had loved and composed about in his youth – scattered farms, fells and hills, springs, brooks, and shrubs – but had nevertheless torn himself away from when he emigrated, was now all here in what had become a new homeland:

> *And then I have reserved*
> *a little spot here,*
> *where in life's quiet evening,*
> *Icelandic bones will rest.*[55]

The bones of his father and son rested in the soil of Dakota, and now Stephan wanted to consummate his relationship with Canada by commending his bones to the soil of Alberta when the time came. Through his poetry, Stephan could now reconcile himself with his new fosterland and dispel the sense of outlawry he had felt.

Chapter 9

At the Turn of the Century

Departure of Friends

D ue to cold and frost, nothing grows here. Everything dries up, even the lakes and rivers, so the animals die from thirst. A railway will never come; a school will never be built; and there will be no market for our products."[1]

Such were the pessimistic predictions of some Icelandic homesteaders in the Red Deer region during the first years of settlement. Added to these temporal concerns were spiritual considerations expressed by people such as Karólína Dalmann and the Goodmans, who for Christmas of 1891 brought together a group of the devout for religious readings – without informing those known for their ungodly opinions. "There they bellowed their evening psalm," wrote Stephan sarcastically, though exclusion from this event no doubt hurt Helga and the children.[2]

The settlement had gained a reputation for lack of belief, and God-fearing people in other Icelandic settlements called it "the colony of runaways and the godless." The newspaper *Lögberg* reported that settlers there neither subscribed to the paper nor belonged to the Icelandic Synod, and one of Stephan's acquaintances wrote that his wife did not dare move to Alberta for fear of a lack of coffee and Christianity. Stephan replied in verse, saying that prospects were not too good: creeds drifted like cotton grass seed in an autumn storm; no inquiries were made about the Holy Ghost, and Christ was becoming a mortal. God remained the same riddle as before, and worst of all, Hell "had burned out its coals/ and Satan gone up in smoke." While store clerks struggled to choose between God and the Devil, Stephan offered a cup of coffee to anyone.[3]

The poet and his family on the front porch of their home.

There had been ups and downs in Stephan's dealings with Karólína Dalmann ever since she had acted in Stephan's little play at Gardar in 1881. She was fascinated by his intelligence and poetic talents, but a cup of coffee was not enough to relieve her of her religious concerns. She and her husband had begun to feel uncomfortable in the settlement and they now joined a group of Icelanders, including Ólafur Ólafsson from Espihóll, who had decided to move west to the Pacific Coast in the spring of 1892. Stephan attributed their decision to depart to a lack of perseverance and was so disappointed with them that he wanted to strike a Devil's bargain and get two hardy men for the six who were leaving. These six, he added, had done little to help develop the settlement either by way of cultivation or clearing of pasture land.[4]

In early June of 1892, Stephan rode to the Red Deer River to see the group off. Gísli Dalmann, Karólína's husband, had been in poor health and did not seem to be improving. After escorting the group across the river, Stephan said his farewells and stuck a note into Karólína's hand.[5] He then returned home, disappointed by the departure of his neighbours. Predictions of the settlement's failure had influenced some of them, while others had a record of never staying in the same place for long.

The settlement did gradually prosper and after the arrival of the railway, Red Deer and Innisfail grew quickly. Innisfail now had three stores, a guesthouse, blacksmith, meat market, hardware store, school, a pastor's house, and plans for a church, and lots in the village became valuable. Some people, such as Rich Gillingham, were even becoming wealthy. Whenever Stephan did business in Innisfail, he noticed that clerks would rush to serve Gillingham first, while the "common people" had to step back and wait. Stephan wrote a sarcastic stanza about people's reverence for the gold in Gillingham's purse.[6]

Local farmers now sold or bartered their butter, eggs, and potatoes for store goods in the villages. Prices were not bad: 13 to 15 pounds of butter for 100 pounds of flour, and four to five pounds of butter for 3 pounds of coffee or ten pounds of lump sugar.

By the summer of 1892, Alberta had become a popular destination for migrants from Nebraska and Washington State, and Calgary was experiencing a boom: "...millery, brewery, and tannery, but also debauchery and drinkery, though little fishery," Stephan wrote in a letter, alluding not too subtly to prostitution and booze.[7]

Stephan's disappointment at the exodus of his neighbours from the settlement was therefore understandable. The note he had slipped Karólína Dalmann was a poetic address in which he stated his determination not to leave the area. He saw the world as made up of both shadows and sunny spots, regardless of where one was, and while extending good wishes to those who persevered through difficulties and refused to be constricted by a straightjacket, he chose to stay where he was and continue building the community, which was no longer on the frontier. "The quest for Eden is but weary sprints/walking and merely wearing out shoes." He preferred stability, but at the same time expressed goodwill toward those who felt compelled to continue their search for the Promised Land. There was, however, a pessimistic jab in the final lines of the poem, wishing them a smooth path as they willingly followed "from place to place,/the deceptive light of shattered hopes" until the evening of their lives.[8]

The village of Red Deer in 1894.

Just as the group reached Calgary, Gísli Dalmann succumbed to his illness. "He was called away from the weariness and sufferings of this life," Karólína wrote in an announcement published in the June 28, 1892 issue of *Lögberg*. They had been married 19 years and had eight children, of whom four sons survived. The eldest son now continued west with the others in order to take care of the family's livestock.

Karólína, offended by Stephan's poem, took his criticism to heart. In her grief, she missed the warm wishes and saw only the teasing that she did not regard as friendly. "I was then like a shipwreck on desert sand. I hardly knew what to do, continue west or return east, but eventually I crept along west across the Rockies with the group, as if in a dream," she wrote decades later.[9] There she regained her composure and from her new home she wrote a furious verse-letter to Stephan that was printed in *Heimskringla* at the end of August, 1892. In her response, she declared Stephan's farewell mean-spirited and mocking. Unable to understand him or the intent of his poem, which angered her each time she read it, she wished he had sent his friends off with a more gentle farewell.

No doubt Karólína's public response pained Stephan – and Helga even more so, as she and Karólína had been close friends. Stephan wanted to avoid a public debate over private matters, however, so he remained silent. Instead, he wrote Gísli a poetic epitaph that was printed in *Heimskringla* in early January of 1893. The poem focuses on the travails of settlers as they wander across the wilderness in ox-wagons and put up their tents for the night. Unique among Stephan's poems for its gentle, melancholic tone, "Gísli Dalmann frá Mjóadal" (Gísli Dalmann from Mjóidalur) features an unusual stress at the end of each line, thereby creating a poetic tension underlining the pain of one who is always searching, but never finding peace:

> *And now he is lost from the caravan of life –*
> *He laid down for a rest at a destination,*
> *And the experience of life turned into wakefulness,*
> *And the effort of the day turned into suffering.*
> *The quiet night did not manage to calm the pain*
> *Nor the gentle sleep stop his moaning.*
>
> *Then, by his head, Death quietly lifted*
> *The door of the tent while nobody saw,*

> *And crept in disguise to his bed*
> *As the darkness and silence at midnight,*
> *And gave him the sleep that soothes all harm*
> *That brings final rest and soothes all pain.*
>
> *So now he is lost from the caravan of life –*
> *They set off in the morning, but he stayed behind,*
> *With light sunshine and flowers for a tombstone,*
> *And the funeral procession spread from a silent yard.*
> *His day's journey was a race over rocks and delay,*
> *And he finally found rest in a foreign grave.*
>
> *So all of us drop out of the caravan of life –*
> *And leave behind us neither path nor footstep –*
> *Perhaps visible in an ungrown, foreign field*
> *For a decade, our totally forgotten grave,*
> *As an empty camping place or broken down fireplace*
> *In burned coals, where the hearth of our life once stood.*[10]

Stephan's soothing epitaphs were often for those who had lost a child, but in this poem he expresses compassion for those unable to find rest. The last stanza conveys a melancholic image of the transience and insignificance of life.

Perhaps Stephan thought that Karólína had recovered sufficiently from her grief for the poem to help ease her pain, but instead she flared up again. The poem dedicated to her husband included neither the personal praise nor the Word of God she evidently felt appropriate. Judging by her response in *Lögberg*, she may have reacted hastily, without reading the poem carefully. In her reply, she recalled the long friendship and the family ties between the two couples and expressed dismay at the scornful remarks in the poem. She concluded that there was no tenderness left in Stephan's heart, confirmation of the common belief that unbelievers saw nothing but death and darkness.

A year earlier, on New Year's Day 1892, Stephan had composed a reply to such accusations, asking what use there was in pretending that darkness was brightness. "I think there is more joy in knowing that the darkness is black/it evokes my longing for light."[11] Although Karólína's accusations of meanness no doubt hurt him, he responded in *Lögberg* only because she ridiculed his opinion about religion and mentioned Christian poets. She imposed upon him religious beliefs, something he would not allow.

In his response, Stephan pointed out that Karólína knew quite well that he was an unbeliever in terms of the Church. Church leaders, he said, had repeatedly claimed that unbelievers saw only death and darkness in contrast to the life, light, and joy of God's grace felt among church-going people. Ideas of misery were easy to find among the Icelandic religious poets, but the main issue, he replied, was that opinions of life and death did not depend on Christian creeds. Death was ever-present and neither religious nor philosophical beliefs could entirely suppress that knowledge, so Christian faith with its ideas of an afterlife and eternal suffering could not be the cause of any pessimism among disbelievers.

Stephan also suggested that Karólína's references to blood and tears were somewhat of a pretense. It was of no use, he added, to complain while attacking an opponent. She should either fight without complaining, or not at all, and she should not attempt to act in a comedy with a sad look on her face. Stephan insisted that he was ready to defend his beliefs, but he was not going to argue with anyone, not even Karólína Dalmann, about whether or not he was an insensitive miscreant. Her opinions, he suggested, were so influenced by ministers who bewildered her that it was impossible to reason with her. He was not angry with Karólína, however, just surprised at the ardour of her reaction.[12]

Old and Irritated

The weather during the summer of 1892 was foul. Grass was slow to grow because of a dry spring and summer frost damaged the crops. Nevertheless, Stephan saw beauty even in destruction, as in a potato plant made white by hoarfrost, looking as if it had been sculpted out of cold marble.

In the fall of 1892, a prairie fire threatened the entire settlement. The settlers fought the fire for days, but one evening a southern windstorm threatened to spread it. Instead, pouring rain doused the fire. Later, when another prairie fire approached some distance north of Stephan's farm, he and his neighbours managed to defend their homesteads by ploughing a two-mile fireguard. They fought the fire day and night as it flared up again and again, until after a particularly hard-fought night a morning snowfall extinguished the last flames. A barn was burned and Rich Gillingham lost 60 tons of hay.[13]

Stephan sometimes found it hard to be tied to the farm and its daily chores when his mind wanted to rise above the proverbial dirt. Family responsibilities restricted his opportunities to read, think, and write. No doubt Helga found it hard to have a husband who had such a strong urge for knowledge and writing.

By October of 1892 Helga was pregnant again. Stephan's sister, Sigurlaug, and her husband had just arrived in the settlement and were living with them, and Stephan was helping build them a house just across the Medicine River. During this time he wrote a letter to his Dakota confidant Jónas Hall, who was a Justice of the Peace. Addressing Jónas as a "Justice in Unrest", he wrote a poem of appeal, describing the state of his domesticity:

> *I appeal, and ask whether I have not been*
> *Too severely punished for my small wiles*
> *When trying to scribble a letter in a heap of eight children*
> *Who fight and tumble and screech all around me.*
> *But four old ones shout with full strength of their voices*
> *About peace and revenge to teach these varmints some manners.*
> *In such a choir, many vocal chords burst,*
> *But the bass of the old is the worst.*[14]

At a Christmas housewarming in the new house, Stephan's brother-in-law, Kristinn, served alcoholic punch. Stephan got quite tight.[15]

On May 31, 1893, the population of Stephan and Helga's household increased by one with the birth of Gestur Cecil, who joined three brothers and twin sisters. This child was named for writer Gestur Pálsson and the attending midwife, Sesselja (Cecilia) Bardal. Later Stephan composed yet another verse about his household:

> *The boys teasing, beating –*
> *The girls crawling, squalling –*
> *The old lady complaining and nagging –*
> *The old man disciplining, silencing.*[16]

As the children grew both in size and number, Stephan reflected ever more on the conditions conducive to their development, and in a poem entitled "Við barn" (To a Child) he integrated these thoughts into his expanding view of life – a trinity of nature, vegetation, and work. In the first stanza, the weather becomes a metaphor for the mind of a child:

> *Child with temper woven from*
> *The gentle weather of the morning and the thundering rain,*
> *The weather where everything grows*
> *The entire world is so new for you.*

The changing weather in the child's moods evokes questions about how to nurture the development and vitality of a child. Rain and light are primary conditions for growth, a metaphor for mental development. Such diverse conditions cultivate the mind and stimulate curiosity. The next stanza offers another metaphor:

> *Although in the wall of your hopes and wisdom*
> *Many a gap exists,*
> *You have plenty of material*
> *To fix the wall immediately and make it good.*

The wall of hope and wisdom is likened to an unfinished stone wall with its many gaps waiting to be filled. The product and symbol of creative work, the wall parallels the previous image of the freshness of the changing weather.

The poem is in two parts. The first describes youth, the promising abilities of the child, its forthright curiosity, and the teasing of grumpy old men. It expresses the wish that a child's abilities be allowed to reach fulfillment. The second part echoes the same ideas with the same wording, but now the speaker wishes to cultivate these same traits in himself – industriousness, natural curiosity, and a playful attitude toward the superstitions of long bearded old men. In the end, he asks permission to borrow the child's heart and mind, "although my arm and leg stiffen":

> *On the wall of knowledge and needs*
> *You never get tired of filling in the gaps.*

> *To demand the highest reward*
> *For every task: to finish it.*
>
> *And with a calm and youthful state of mind,*
> *In the same way may kiss you good night,*
> *When the world for the last time,*
> *Puts its tired son to rest.*[17]

"The highest reward" – to be able to complete the task – echoes Emerson's concept of reward in work well done. When a grown man has adopted the child's inclinations to self-improvement, he can relax since he has then found a foothold in the constant struggle with the world.

Farm-work for children started at a young age and no doubt took a heavy toll on young and sensitive souls. Obviously Stephan felt he could learn something from the children although he, like other farmers, made them work. His poems often grew out of everyday events, although he removed anything that connected a poem to a certain time and place. Judging from the poem "Vikatelpan" (The Errand Girl), it seems that late one summer day he needed a horse from the pasture and sent an errand girl to fetch it quickly. She ran off, light of foot, but she was delayed and that irritated Stephan who began to prepare a rebuke upon her return. When she eventually returned, the farmer poet grabbed the horse's reins and threatened to thrash her for being so slow: "She startled and said to herself: /Oh, sunrise, you delayed me." The farmer, still angry, asks sarcastically how might that have happened? She then begins to describe a sunny morning on the farm:

> *"Now, like this," she replied,"when the sunshine is bright*
> *I see so many new things in the world:*
> *The night-dew is like silver and gold,*
> *The valleys and hollows are full of blue mist,*
> *While black mountains tower into the sky,*
> *Like tarred ships flying through the air.*
> *And the forest-tops are like rocks in the sea,*
> *And the brushwood over there is a hunting place*
> *With silken nets stretching from branch to branch,*
> *Glowing like silver, and so clean."*

Upon hearing this child poet's morning poem, Stephan realizes that this is his own mission: not to lose sight of beauty amidst the daily chores. His only reply is to brush a lock of hair from her forehead with his worn hand. Together, they are two poetic children.[18]

Between Calf and Afterbirth

Stephan was an exceptionally progressive, helpful, popular, and respected individual among his countrymen. According to friend and fellow settler Jónas Hunford, in an essay on the Alberta settlement, Stephan's neighbours sought his advice on most issues. "It takes time to get to know Stephan, but the longer you know him, the more you respect him, the more you like him, and the more you care about him." Jónas enjoyed visiting Stephan and Helga since their home was a cheerful place devoid of all hypocrisy and snobbery.[19]

Despite the poverty of the first years in Alberta, Stephan and Helga were happy and self-sufficient. "There was often fun in our little house," Helga said. "If the men in our neighbourhood wanted to have a good time, they came to us as our home was always open to them. We would then sing all through the night, every Icelandic song we knew."[20]

Stephan frequently contemplated poetry and culture despite his chores, which allowed him only sporadic moments of peace, and in the fall of 1892 he composed an essay on rhyme that was published in *Heimskringla*. It was one of very few articles not written for a special occasion. As he hurried to complete it, he wrote this little stanza:

> *The cows calve, and I put big bulls in their stalls*
> *I must – it is a shame, yet it is my duty –*
> *Write between calf and afterbirth.*[21]

In the essay, he reflects on whether the days of poets have passed and whether rhymed poetry has come to an end. There was an increasingly popular school of thought that rhyme was not a natural, uninhibited form of language, but rather a straightjacket that constricted content, distorted the language, and stifled poetic expression. Stephan's opinion, a concept not acknowledged in Iceland until decades later, was that poetry was more that just form provided by rhyme. Phrasing his idea beau-

Many settlers were very fond of the cow who provided for their families. Usually women did the milking, as most self-respecting Icelandic farmers had little experience in this art.

tifully, he stated: "Nothing in human thought changes shape as easily, so even if humans were to agree to think about nothing but price lists and write nothing but brand registers, poetry would still find a way to sneak in, even there, no less than into rocks and metals. It dresses according to the season and appears in rhyme while human memory is the only book to keep it, and when time and intellect break it up into tiny particles, it weaves itself into a poem like a wrapping so that it will not break down, and it remains possible to move it. When a group has gathered around, it takes its place on stage, dressed in the words and deeds of living persons, and at last, when it has some message to bring to the masses, into huts and palaces, where it is necessary to adjust to the habits of so many, it throws light over itself and dons the common cloak of narrative form. It is not likely, however, that rhyme will be abandoned for a long, long while yet as a guise of poetry."

Stephan pointed out that Walt Whitman had once rebelled against rhyme, the absence of which had temporarily spoiled the effect of his poetry, despite the attention gained by his revolutionary ideas. "The one who does not have the skill or time to let the small branches of his poetry unite with any whole usually loses the sense of a whole earlier if he spreads it in prose, except where the ties of rhyme become natural fetters." If rhyme is to be abandoned, it will make life easier for those who have difficulties with "kneading something into stanzas that never should have been put into words." Then again, it might become a problem for people to recognize actual poetry, Stephan suggested. It is as if this essay were a rehearsal for larger efforts. In writing about the subtle characteristics of poetry, he managed ever more skillfully to make the form serve his subject.[22]

Around this time, Stephan began composing a speech for his neighbours. While writing it, he occasionally rushed from his chores to his desk, a cup of coffee in hand, while he scribbled notes on the back of an envelope or a piece of paper. The cows allowed him to finish his speech and make a clean copy just in time for an event organized by the local reading society in mid-February of 1893. It took place in the schoolhouse at Tindastoll and was attended by most of the people in the settlement, who showed up to enjoy a play, singing, speeches, dancing, coffee, cakes, and punch. The punch was so diluted that Stephan thought he could have drunk it all himself without getting tight. It did not matter, however, as the gathering was enjoyable, casual, and free of "churchly atmosphere". Everyone contributed to the evening in his or her own way. Stephan's brother-in-law Kristinn Kristinsson and Jónas Hunford made fine speeches and Sesselja Bardal read a satirical story about a poet and his neighbours. Stephan was far from being offended. He found the story well written, even if the humour was a bit dull, and later that year he sent Sesselja a volume of Jón Ólafsson's poetry as a gift.[23]

Stephan's speech for this occasion was not everyday intellectual fare. He began by discussing education, stating that true education included more than what was learned in schools or books. The measure of how great a human being is, "the genius and nobility of man himself must be distinguished from what he has borrowed from schools and books." Education is the content, not the costume, of a man's maturity, he said. Learning is important nevertheless. "The schooled and widely read man is the well-equipped settler, with much knowledge and all the important tools at his disposal, while the unschooled and unread is Robinson Crusoe, a castaway, stranded by chance on a desert island with two empty hands and training in nothing."

Stephan then directed his comments at the reading of books and noted that most people read for diversion – pulp fiction or news about bank robberies and hangings. Such material does not educate, he claimed, and those who read too much of it may suffer from intellectual dullness "and loathe all labour of the mind." Many other people read to learn and know as much as possible, he said, but such reading presumes too much confidence in the written word. Stephan alluded to bookish men of all ages who learn everything like a child memorizing the multiplication table, but whose pedantry sits like a heavy rock atop other aspects of the intellect: intelligence, taste, acumen, and wit. Such men may know dates and long lists of names by heart, but they cannot see the beauty and nobility therein. These "bookshelves", as Stephan called all pedants, are common among Icelanders.

Jónas Jónsson Hunford, whose surname derived from his native region of Húnavatnssýsla, was one of Stephan and Helga's closest friends and neighbours. He and his wife, Margrét, raised a large family.

Some are "talking bibliographies of countless books and authors, who tend to chew on the opinions of remarkable men, knocking each other out with constant references to sources… If they can quote a phrase from a book or letter by Paul or Luther or Spencer or even Madam Blavatsky, they think they have found a good defense and fortress for their own words, though they are merely hiding behind the skeletons of the deceased."

A third group of readers consists of those who have used books to increase "their intellectual strength" that "grows from bookish wisdom, like grass from a spring rain." Such education is difficult to quantify, but it makes a man "more sensitive to everything that is good and beautiful, and connects him more closely and intimately to his species and to nature around him. It interprets the runes of previous centuries, explains the language of our times, and shows us the future in a clear vision. It prevents one's life from becoming a desert, separated from everything, like a rock that has rolled down to the level ground and lies there without moving and finally sinks into the ground. It lengthens the brief span of human life into the life span of the world, as the perceptions and feelings of the truly educated reach beyond the scope of one human life."

Stephan was in fact describing his own education, though he claimed to have read little himself. Poetry is important in every good book, he stated. "If there is no perceptive sensitivity toward the hearts and minds of strangers, no clear imagination to reveal that which is hidden, no perceptive eye penetrating like lightning into "the fog of dark ages" – and if these are not the characteristics of poetry, then I do not know what it is – then I cannot see how any book can be truly educational."

Stephan espoused broad-mindedness and mocked the narrow-mindedness of the clergy and church goers. So far as he could see, single-minded periodicals such as *Sameiningin*, published by the Icelandic Synod, did not educate readers who only memorized epithets about their opponents and their opinions, while remaining far from any real understanding of religious views. Such people reminded Stephan of the codfish he had witnessed in Iceland long ago – blind in one eye from endlessly circling the same shining iceberg. "The same has happened to the most avid readers of *Sameiningin*. They are blind in the eye that turns toward this periodical and its issues, but they swim around it all the same, as do all partisans in relation to their ultimate party publications."

Stephan advised the reading society to buy Byron and Dickens if they wished to buy English books. Icelandic books, however, were most important for young people, so they would learn what Icelandic is. Nevertheless, it would not harm Icelanders to understand both English and Icelandic and become familiar with the literature of both languages. It was also a matter of pride for Stephan to let other North Americans know that "we did not arrive without books..."[24] When Stephan's speech was printed in *Heimskringla*, editor and poet Jón Ólafsson noted it was the best essay ever printed in an Icelandic paper in North America – and among the best ever published in any Icelandic paper.

The School at Hola

Throughout the winter of 1893 the sound of axes rang in the woods as trees were felled and hauled down to the Medicine River. In the spring,

Of sturdy log construction, the Hola School stood for many years after it had outlived its role as a schoolhouse.

the logs were rafted down the river to a location near Stephan's house. He had proposed to his neighbours, although they were few, scattered, and poor, that they build a schoolhouse.

The school took shape over the summer, with Stephan doing much of the work and taking pains to plane the logs before dove-tailing them together at the corners. Construction proceeded well and at the beginning of August there was a great celebration near the site. People flocked to this event from all directions, walking, riding, or driving – all dressed in their Sunday best. It was Icelandic Day, by this time celebrated annually in many Icelandic settlements in North America.

Children wore their best and were not allowed to play in the grass. Little Gestur, still in swaddling clothes, was only two months old, but the twins, Fanny and Jenny, wore new dresses their mother had sewn. The boys wore straw hats made by their grandmother. Jakob (Kobbi or Jake as he was also known), seven and of dark complexion, with curly hair, was somewhat sullen over not being allowed to play with the other boys. Guðmundur and Baldur were big boys, almost 12 and 14 years of age, and perhaps a bit proud of their father, who was the master of ceremonies. They behaved rather seriously and did not allow themselves to be distracted by sports or other frivolities.

The program proceeded as Stephan and some of his neighbours made speeches, proposed toasts, and read poetry. Singing, instrumental music, and games followed. This occasion quickly grew in popularity and two years later more than 200 people attended the Icelandic Day held at Bardal's, which featured a procession of Icelandic boys who had been trained as cadets. Besides a new poem by Stephan and various speeches and songs, this celebration featured horse races and athletic contests.

By the fall of 1893, the schoolhouse at Hola was finished. It measured 8 by 5.5 meters and had a shingled roof. Stephan was elected to a committee charged with investigating the formalities of organizing an official school district.

On the evening of April 9, 1894, the schoolhouse was formally inaugurated with a gathering at which Stephan's old play from Dakota was performed. Later in the evening there was dancing and drinking, and when Stephan became a bit tipsy he recited his "Ástarvísur til Íslands" (Love Verses to Iceland), declaring his love for everything beautiful, whether mountains, a well-written manuscript, or a girl's eyes. Iceland was in his very nature, as was his love of the old land. "I loved you," he said in the end of the poem as his eyes glistened.[25]

On New Year's Eve of 1894, there was a holiday gathering in the schoolhouse at Hola. Gifts were hung on the tree and Stephan's sister, Sigurlaug, recited a poem in English. The school had not yet received official recognition from the authorities, but instruction nevertheless began with a young Icelander named Jón Guðmundsson as teacher. Paid for only three months, he taught the remaining four months for nothing. Some 30 children attended the new *Hólaskóli* (Hola School), among them Stephan and Helga's sons Baldur and Guðmundur, now 15 and 13 years of age. Sigurlaug and Kristinn's children were able to attend by crossing the frozen river, and children who lived further away often stayed overnight at Stephan and Helga's.

Although the new teacher was by and large unschooled, the children showed such improvement that this was regarded as one of the Hola School's most successful winters. Jón Guðmundsson's love of knowledge and the children's curiosity went hand in hand. Jón, young and single, was like a big brother or friend, just as Stephan's teacher Sigvaldi had been back in Iceland.

Stephan followed Jón's teaching closely and at the end of the school year he organized a social function for March 30, 1894. The evening began with the children reading aloud to show what they had learned. Jón then read a farewell poem to them, and two of Stephan's sons, Baldur and Guðmundur, replied with appropriate verses. A play was then performed and eventually Stephan read a poem that likened the children to the coming of spring. In the poem, the hills wear flapping shirts like the boys and the poplars swing their heads like the beautiful hair of the girls. Life at school is like a spring thaw "as youth finds it a poor performance,/if there is no jumping and loud talking,/just lying down as if locked in a trunk." Youthful hope is in the storm and as Stephan looks to the future he sees the "flighty and unruly" schoolchildren as "growing vegetation in the nation's field."[26]

Over the following years the school year was extended to eight months, and a more formally qualified teacher was hired in 1897.

Building a schoolhouse was evidently deemed more urgent than erecting a church, and the settlement remained without a minister or a church for a long time. The settlers knew they were on the road to progress, but they felt they could not afford another large commitment at that time. They relied on themselves, though most followed Christian customs, and ministers of other nationalities conducted baptisms and burials until July of 1898 when a young Icelandic minister from Manitoba, Runólfur Marteinsson, arrived in the settlement. He conducted four services that summer – none of which Stephan bothered to attend – then returned to the settlement in the winter of 1899-1900. A congregation was then established on January 21, 1900.

Settlement in Verse

Stephan often reflected upon "creative settlement" during his first years in Alberta, but his mind also ventured beyond the bounds of the settlement. Working like a skilled craftsman with pieces of wood, he spliced together the elements of poetry, the environment, and nature. On his many supply trips to Calgary by ox and wagon, he walked most of the way, sleeping outside overnight and observing nature around him, murmuring lines and verses and capturing nature in rhyme and rhythm. At that time, Canadian poets were beginning to free themselves from the constraints of English Romanticism and depict the magnificent Canadian landscape in simple imagery.[27] Stephan, whose images of nature were both original and powerful, was a ground-breaking pioneer in this movement.

Shortly after the death of Gestur Pálsson, Jón Ólafsson launched a paper called *Öldin*, that subsequently merged with *Heimskringla* in March of 1892. A year later, *Öldin* separated from *Heimskringla* and became an ambitious cultural magazine. A considerable number of Stephan's poems appeared in both publications, along with occasional verses about politics, life's wisdom, and Lutheran ministers. It was nature, however, that fascinated Stephan and became an inexhaustible source of inspiration for his poetry. "I... most preferably compose all my verses/to the notes of the moment and the weather of the day," he said.[28] Around 1893-94 he was evidently considering publishing a volume of poetry, as he produced a manuscript that seems to have been meant for publication.[29]

In his 1891 poem "Árferði í Alberta" (The Seasons in Alberta), Stephan makes light of the fact that summer weather could occur in winter and winter weather in summer. Young Alberta, he wrote, is unable to "discipline her temperament better than that,/nor congeal in the dullness of unchanging weather."[30] In "Minni Alberta" (Toast to Alberta), which may be one of the very first poems of its kind about the region, Stephan draws a panoramic picture of the Icelandic settlement, asking Alberta to foster the Icelanders in their exile from Iceland and to shelter them against those things he most disliked: "but spread wide your mountain arms /with frost and glacier walls/against the dominance of capitalism/ and the flames of religious extremism."[31]

Jón Ólafsson was among the first to recognize Stephan's talents and encourage him, and in January of 1894 Stephan wrote to thank Jón for his positive critiques. With this letter Stephan enclosed a series of short poems he called *Úti á víðavangi* (Out in the Wilderness), composed over a period of two or three years, but only recently polished into a clean copy. Shortly after the New Year he had injured himself, and being incapacitated for some time, he had taken the opportunity to work on these "favourite offspring". Doubtful that he would ever be able to make anything better of these poems, he asked Jón to either accept them or burn them – claiming that he would not be offended if they were rejected. Having gone so far as to invent occasional words, Stephan admitted to being bold in his use of the Icelandic language, since he knew nothing of grammar and did not adhere to any specific school of spelling.[32]

Jón immediately printed the poems in *Öldin* and praised them highly. Later he published them in a little book, printing 200 copies under the title *Úti á víðavangi* (Out in the Wilderness) and giving the entire print run to Stephan.

This publication was a milestone in Stephan's poetic career. He sent some of the copies to his friends as gifts and some of his supporters sold a few copies for him. *Úti á víðavangi* is also the first volume of poetry in the literary history of Alberta. Until then, there had been very little literary activity in Alberta, with the possible exception of First Nations oral traditions, travel accounts, missionary pamphlets, and some Native language dictionaries. Prose fiction began to appear in the last decade of the 19th century, but Alberta's first English book of poetry, a work on King Arthur by Lethbridge lawyer Charles P. Coynbeare, did not appear until 1902.[33] Alberta was therefore first pioneered in a literary sense by Stephan G. Stephansson, though Canadian literary histories are reticent to acknowledge a farmer who captured the wilderness in alliteration and rhyme while driving his oxen and wagon back and forth between Calgary and Red Deer.

Breaking new ground in these poems, Stephan endowed the Canadian landscape with the power of speech and reflected on its meaning. "Each headland speaks to me/and every neck has a tongue," he says in the poem "Léttara loft" (Lighter Air), but the language is inscrutable. "And the answers are sincere/that diversions allow me:/A strand of their being/as they are not book-learned."[34]

In this poetry Stephan recreates Icelandic poetic language, at the same time developing a new aspect of his own identity. His poem "Flóðið" (The Flood), composed on the way to Calgary, is an allegory, indepen-

The charismatic Jón Ólafsson 'ritstjóri' (editor) during his years as editor and entrepreneur in Winnipeg. A brother to Icelandic poet Páll Ólafsson and himself a poet of some note, Jón was among the first to recognize and acknowledge the exceptional calibre of Stephan's poetry.

Öldin, a periodical established in Winnipeg by Jón Ólafsson, began publishing poems by "Stephan G. Stephansson" in 1893.

dent of time and place, describing a threatening and devastating river in flood. The mother and fiancée of the speaker urge him not to flee the river, but he chooses to avoid the danger. It is not really flight, rather a "longing for rescue" that urges him onwards across deserts and mountains, all the way to the grave. "Thirst for continuation, not fear" drives him onwards. He is fated never to return to his old land, "that is doomed/I shall break every bridge behind/with enormous spiritual power." In destroying these bridges he becomes a flood himself, declaring war on stagnation. Stephan explained the poem as a description of the state of mind of a man who becomes convinced that accepted truth is an illusion.[35] In this original poem on nature, the turbulence in his own mind charts a new course.

Among Stephan's best known poems from these years is "Greniskógurinn" (The Spruce Forest), written as he was planting spruce saplings by his home. Spruce, the greenest of all conifers, grows "where all other trees/find it too low...", forever young and straight, high above the wilderness. It has evergreen needles above the ground and roots of hope under the surface. Many a man stands like a spruce tree in the winter storm, staring down into the decaying bogs that encircle his spirit. Thus, the forest becomes a symbol of one who stands alone, unsupported, against any unjust cause – and "Never bends but breaks/in the last big storm."[36]

The poem "Við vatnið" (By the Lake) seems to have been written when Stephan was fishing on Snake Lake. It contains the magnificent description of a storm on a lake, that serves a metaphor for the dangers of human life: the drops of water surge and boil, weak nerves are stretched "with the power of steel". "And life's duty and essence is to suffer/and feel the painful storms of one's times." It is the "spirit of time" that "crashes on the mind's ocean/until temples collapse and nations' anchors break/ listen to the cries and moans of many hearts/in the sounds of the breakers crashing through the darkness of time."[37] The poem echoes the exhortations of Georg Brandes and Gestur Pálsson to show compassion to those who struggle and suffer.

Shortly after the publication of *Úti á víðavangi*, Stephan wrote the poem "Áin" (The River), in which he likens human development to a river taking on various appearances on its way to the ocean. Its beginning is in a remote, barren valley, and its cradle is a gorge between glowering glacial cliffs. In its infancy the river learns to flow over mud and rocks, with ice as its toy. The poet finds little to admire in the river when it is in icy fetters, but its natural strength re-appears when it breaks free.

> *And at last, when you had freed yourself,*
> *You lay, as before,*
> *So clear and clean in a worn path*
> *Like a clear blue silken thread –*
> *Like a thought, so large and strong and free,*
> *That strengthens me and cheers,*
> *But struggles in the breach between language and rhyme*
> *And heaps up wrong alliteration.*[38]

Perhaps this is one of Stephan's most original images of his own struggle of fitting complicated thoughts into a verse form.

In "Sumarkveld í Alberta" (Summer Night in Alberta), Stephan gazes across his home district. Despite the twilight, the view is panoramic, including the mountain peaks far to the west and approaching night resembling the edge of an ocean in the east. The air is bright and the clouds are golden in the sunset. Then the bright summer nights of Iceland become part of the scene, reminding Stephan of his "…fjord back home, / when calm weather brought a fleet of ships / together in the sound between land and island." Despite strong ties to his homeland, Stephan nevertheless praises Alberta for giving him breathing space and shelter from the confusion of civilization.

To me this wilderness is a thousand times dearer,
Than crowded districts, though larger and richer,
Where space for life is so constricted in every way,
And a third of mankind is trampled underfoot.

I love you, western wilderness, land of life and help!
With your wide spaces, accommodating many hopes,
Without you there would be no reprieve from slavery
And western freedom would be a fairy tale and lie.[39]

One day in November of 1894, after a furious blizzard had deposited huge drifts of snow, Stephan hitched his horse Glæsir to a sleigh and took a long drive. By the time he had made his rounds and was ready to turn homeward, the cold and dark were intensifying, "the harness creaking and the runners squeaking/and the horse grey with hoarfrost," Stephan composed. In observing the snow, Stephan pondered how multi-skilful winter had redesigned the landscape. As it got darker still, the tracks disappeared, sound froze, and the moon rose, glittering in the snow like fiery eyes. Signs of human habitation transformed themselves and nature took on perilous aspects as winter bewildered Stephan's horse by creating a false path and changing the look of the houses. A wolf cub limped across the hard frozen snow – an image of misfortune. Either hunger or a bullet would end its life, Stephan mused, though the guilt over killing a wolf is increased by the fact that the body cannot be used

Alberta's beautiful foothills with the majestic Rocky Mountains in the distance.

for anything. He saw a parallel between the wolf and Grettir, the Icelandic saga outlaw, who was afraid of the dark since it constituted a sort of border between nature and the human world. The hungry howling of the wolf cut through the frozen night air and struck fear into both man and horse. Eventually, however, they reached their snow-covered homes.

As soon as Stephan had parked the sleigh and put Glæsir into the barn, he hurried into the house and asked Helga to make some coffee. Quickly finding a pencil and a piece of paper, the ice not yet melted from his moustache, with cold and stiff fingers he then began writing the first draft of the poem "Kveldið eftir bylinn" (The Night after the Blizzard), later renamed "Upprofið" (The Break).[40] The settlement in the Red Deer district was on the fringes between nature and the human world, and on that frontier Alberta's first poet was transforming natural forces into human poetry.

All Around

In the fall of 1894, J. M. Simpson ran for the legislature of the North-West Territories in Regina. There were two other candidates, but Stephan and some other Icelanders worked so hard for Simpson that he won "and all we Icelanders were turned into English citizens." The two losing candidates were so disappointed that they had both made plans to leave the area the following spring, Stephan wrote merrily in a jocose letter about his entry into Canadian politics.

Persons were eligible for naturalization after living in Canada for three years, and on October 20, 1894, Judge Rouleu of the Supreme Court of the North-West Territories confirmed that Stephan G. Stephangson [sic] was a British subject with all the rights and obligations of British subjects in Canada. Stephan continued his comical letter, parodying the gibberish of political propagandists. Simpson intended to make him a Justice of the Peace, but Stephan feared that Governor-General Mackintosh would not take the time needed to sign the nomination. Federal elections were approaching and Mackintosh, "that ... idiot, would refer everything south and I will never get this post because he belongs to the conspiracy of the regressive Ottawa government, but I would rather lean to basic Liberal principles and fight with Frank Oliver from Edmonton."[41]

Among Stephan's political opponents were his brother-in-law Kristinn Kristinsson, Jón from Kolgröf, and Sigfús Goodman. They supported "the Conservative Cochrane, a bloody villain and devilish bastard, to say nothing personal about the man. In fact, all these men were previously Liberals, but Kristinn was bought with a sack of flour, Kolgröf with a gallon of whisky, and Goodman with a ticket to Calgary."[42] After the election, Stephan expected to participate in establishing an Icelandic branch of the Liberal party. When he wrote this letter, the Liberals were gaining ground after a long period of Conservative government. Stephan supported the Liberals partly because they were against protective tariffs that had been used to promote industrialization in the eastern provinces. Because of these tariffs, farm machinery was more expensive for Canadian prairie farmers than it was for farmers south of the border.[43]

Stephan now had more than 30 head of cattle, several dozen sheep, and four horses. He dreamed of having a mixed farm, but so far his experiments in grain growing had not produced any significant results. His earnings were still rather scanty and in a letter to Jónas Hall he wrote that while he was not usually cold or hungry, he tended to be "rather short of money and alcohol." His health was good except for one disintegrating molar that gave him a toothache, "especially in a south-west wind, which is the direction of storms here." The tooth later fell out and Stephan eulogized it in verse.[44]

The Red Deer River was still a dangerous obstacle for those travelling from the Icelandic settlement to Innisfail, which was closer than Red Deer. The prosperity of the villages therefore by-passed the settlers for the most part, though Stephan and other farmers managed to barter some eggs and homemade butter. Gradually, however, they moved into the modern cash economy when they began selling milk from their Shorthorn cows[45] to a cheese factory established in 1894. Started with assistance from J. Powell, a man of Ontario-British background, the cheese factory soon ran into problems. Milk production was still on a small scale and transportation was difficult due to the lack of a bridge and proper roads. Milk wagons got stuck in the mud, cream cans sometimes floated away during river crossings, and milk often turned sour in the summer heat.

Helgi Jónasson, a local entrepreneur, then established a cheese factory and a little store, and in 1896 Jón Benediktsson established another store and a cheese factory that prospered. Helgi's and Jón's cheese became like currency, as they paid farmers either with cheese or store goods.

The farmers would then take their cheese to Red Deer to barter and it became a common sight to see Icelandic farmers go into Gaetz' store with a big cheese under each arm in order to buy a pair of overalls or some tobacco.⁴⁶

By spring of 1896, Stephan had ploughed and prepared 10 acres for seeding. He went to Innisfail and signed a promissory note for $9.36, which was double the value of the oat seed he purchased. If he repaid half of the note by April 1 of the following year, the remainder would be dropped. Stephan sowed 18 bushels of oats.⁴⁷

Markerville entrepreneur Jón Benediktsson, one of the first to establish a creamery and cheese plant.

Settlement in this part of Alberta was still so new that it was not until 1898 that Icelandic homesteaders could file formal entry for their lands. Stephan did so on February 10, registering his hayland in Section 22 in his own name and another quarter in his mother's name on July 25. In order to fulfill residency requirements on his own quarter, he built a 34 x 38 foot log house on this land and moved there for a year. Both he and his mother, who received her Canadian citizenship in 1900, obtained title to their homesteads two years later. By then, Stephan had cleared, cultivated, and fenced more land than anyone else in the Hola district.⁴⁸

In order to supplement his income, Stephan also took employment with survey crews from time to time, and during the summer of 1895 he worked on the survey of Townships 36, 37 and 38. The foreman of the crew was W. L. Woods and Stephan was on good terms with him. Usually the land was surveyed before being settled, but the Icelanders had arrived early and it turned out that some had settled on land owned by the railway company and others on homesteads where the property line dissected the barnyard between the house and the barn.⁴⁹

Stephan spent another summer on a survey team in northern Alberta, where he worked until winter. That experience produced the poem "Útivist" ("Outdoors" or "Away from Home"), that conjures up the winter experience of surveyors in the wilderness. They wake up and start work in the cold starlight as owls hoot in the trees and wolves howl in the forest. Snow covers the ground, freezing winds blow, and trees form a white arcade. Then it lightens in the east, the air turns grey, and shadows disappear. Trees snap in the cold, hoarfrost forms on the beards of the men, and the moon disappears amid the clouds over the mountains, "a bright day around each death-white mountain head/but night still in the slopes." It is as if silence creeps into the minds of the men until they stop by a row of beautiful spruce trees covered with snow, in Stephan's mind resembling confirmation girls in their white dresses. Then, minds brighten:

> *And perhaps frequently, despite everything,*
> *When we wade through the snow in silence,*
> *That in our souls the cold, black darkness is lightened up*
> *By a sunny smile from previous days.*
>
> *But all this little, our minds own,*
> *Of joy, beauty and wisdom,*
> *As the strength in the muscles it lies down in coma,*
> *Because of the labour and toil of the day.*[50]

A rough and ready survey crew on the Canadian frontier.

Stephan got along well on the survey crew as he was self-educated and skilled with horses. When he first arrived, he replaced a man who had just quit and so took over this man's horse and cart. The supervisor and many of the men were French-speaking Canadians. On the first day at work, when the equipment was supposed to be moved, Stephan hitched a bay mare named Nellie to the cart. He noticed that the Frenchmen laughed and commented among themselves. At noon he unharnessed Nellie, and when he harnessed her again he was ordered to the front of the line. The Frenchmen laughed again, but soon fell silent. On the following morning they laughed again, but less, and after that the laughter stopped. Stephan did not let the laughter bother him.

One of the crew kept a work journal, and when he quit, Stephan was asked to make the journal entries. He declined. His fellow worker insisted, however, pointing out that nobody else on the crew was capable of the task. Stephan found it unlikely that a dozen English-speaking men were less qualified, but that proved to be the case and he was obliged to take on this responsibility. His predecessor had graduated from a trade school, but had not done the job properly. There were no complaints over Stephan's entries, however, and he later blamed schools for the crew's lack of skills, stating that schools "are organized in a way that transforms too many children's heads into dugouts."

When Stephan left the survey crew, one of the Frenchmen asked him if he was not curious to know why they had laughed at him on the first day. Stephan then learned that the bay mare had been completely mulish with his predecessor and the only way to get her cooperation, it seemed, had been to unhitch her and ride her at a full gallop. The crew had therefore expected the mare to pull the same stunt with Stephan, but they had been disappointed. The next season, when the mare was given to another man, she behaved just as stubbornly as before. Stephan was ever grateful to Nellie for not having made a laughing stock of him.[51]

"The night is ... so long."

Although work was fundamental in Stephan's view of life, he sometimes found reason to complain about it. "Well, well, I think I am rather prospering at farming, although I do not feel too well," he wrote in a letter to Jónas Hall during Advent of 1897. "I am getting tired and my leisure hours get fewer and fewer. The good books I get hold of are last to be read and life is generally tasting more and more like water."[52]

Among the topics explored in Stephan's letters were religion, politics, and poetry, and when he was with a survey crew in 1896 he received a letter from a young poet and writer named Jóhann Magnús Bjarnason. Some of Jóhann Magnús' writings had been published in the papers and in letters Stephan had mocked him for his poor use of language, stating that he was the epitome of a class of unimaginative Icelandic common people. Stephan nevertheless wrote a friendly reply to this letter, explaining he was in the middle of nowhere and could not be found on any map. His second letter to Magnús, dated October of 1897, began with excuses and a description of how busy he was. It was Sunday and Stephan explained that since he had been very diligent at reading *The Bible* and sermons when he was a child, he could now spend some time writing letters on the Sabbath. He related his circumstances and described his poetic ambitions, stating that he felt ashamed of his lack of education and the flaws in his letters. He cited his struggle to make a living and praised Jóhann Magnús for his self-education. A sparse population and isolation were two reasons that young men in Iceland were drawn to books, but the hustle and bustle of the western world distracted them. Stephan mentioned his own literary endeavours, his inexhaustible efforts at self-education, and his support for a strong literary tradition. These, he stated, were the conditions for his poetry and the thoughts he was trying to develop. He followed closely what was going on in Iceland, read Icelandic papers and magazines, and commented on the most promising poets.[53]

The correspondence between Stephan and Jóhann Magnús became close and the letters were lengthy as Stephan had much to say. The relationship soon became like that of father and son. Stephan encouraged Jóhann Magnús to send his poems to the papers. He recognized the young poet's strengths and wanted him to overcome the naïve simplicity and sentimentality that sometimes coloured his literary judgment.

One quiet Christmas night, when Stephan found himself alone at home, he sat down to write to Jóhann Magnús. He was enjoying the peace and quiet he needed for contemplation and writing, but he was afraid it would not last as his brother-in-law Kristinn had insisted that he come over for a drink. Stephan had declined, but he felt certain that Kristinn would either come over in person or send for him. Stephan admitted to being a little eccentric, and now more than ever he wanted to "get away from bad company and become a recluse as much as possible," although he knew that he would be considered "anti-social and cranky, despite the fact that there is not a hint of crankiness about me, at least no more than an independent opinion in a congregational representative." He went on to discuss friendship and complained over being too busy, adding that while a minister had once predicted that he would have "some deficit on doomsday", he performed "an average amount of work every day and more in the evenings, preferably in midwinter as then I am least tired, because the night..."

Stephan then stopped mid-sentence. As he had not gone for a drink, it had come to him – in the person of Stephan's jug-toting brother-in-law Kristinn. Later, when his company had left, Stephan resumed the letter: "... is then so long. When others drowse and talk slower, I throw myself onto a chair or a bed, drink a cup of tea perhaps, and begin scribbling some stanzas with a pencil on a pad of paper." Stephan was tired of the interruptions, the overly-close quarters, and the sometimes tiresome people. His mind worked constantly and in this letter, ironically, he articulated his aesthetic principles. "If it is poetry to be able to put everyday thoughts into rhyme, then all of us here who write verses are poets, and if it demands skill to be able to put together flawless lines out of ordinary language, then we are all artists."[54]

Stephan explored ideas like these with Jón Ólafsson and Jóhann Magnús Bjarnason over the next years, sometimes dwelling on the hard work that was his lot, but more often discussing writers and airing his opinions on poetry. It was with Jóhann Magnús, however, that Stephan was most candid, and once he shared his opinion of the younger poet's work, at the same time complaining that people never gave him their honest opinions of his poetry. He admitted to being only a lukewarm realist. "Recording a photographic image of that which actually occurs and can be seen never constitutes a poetic work of art, I say. Life as it happens is hardly poetic, good Lord! I want to select only the most impressive chapters, one from here and one from there, and delete everything that has no meaning – even turn a whole year into one day if necessary. I am sometimes bored even by Tolstoy and Zola, as they do the opposite."[55]

Stephan then thanked Jóhann Magnús for his opinion of some poems that had recently appeared in *Dagskrá* and *Nýja Öldin*. "There is a bit of new nerve in them, though they are very stiff and tightly woven.

That is the problem, but perhaps they will endure for a while as they are composed from real life." Perhaps, he admitted, he should have burned all his poems at the outset. "If, by the way, the pathway to Hell is paved with good intentions, I would like to go there and see all the beginnings of various things I intended to do, but had torn out of my hands by life."

Despite the daily chores, poetry was tremendously important to Stephan. If an idea surfaced, he felt compelled to compose a poem, write it down, and send it for publication in a paper. Then he forgot about it. When he received a copy of the paper, he clipped out the poem and pasted it into a scrapbook, which he then put into a closet. These poems "are fragments of myself," he said, "what I want to be, and… whoever cannot understand and evaluate them correctly can neither understand nor judge me…"[56]

In 1898 Jóhann Magnús Bjarnason published a book of poetry and Stephan made an exception to his rule never to write reviews. He treated the work of his protégé gently, describing his poetry as on the "edge of day and night", plaintive, derived from the poetic climate of the New World. Jóhann Magnús was the poet of Icelandic immigrants, "a spokesman for the unhardened and the oppressed." Stephan deemed his work better than that created by English and Norwegian counterparts during their respective settlement eras. In these poems he heard a voice representing Icelandic immigrants in North America, and this, he stated, was important. Poets were a sort of touchstone, indicating the nature of the Icelandic immigrant experience. "Our land assessments will eventually get lost, our agricultural reports will be forgotten, even our churches will decay. What will en-

Teacher, poet, and author Jóhann Magnús Bjarnason in 1900, with a class at Fljótshlíð in the Geysir district of New Iceland.

dure, however, is the record Icelanders in America establish in nurturing the talents of Jóhann Magnús Bjarnason and tending the grave of the late Gestur Pálsson..."57

Around this same time, Stephan's own poetry was beginning to attract positive commentary in both North America and Iceland. Self-educated short story writer Þorgils Gjallandi, a farmer and one of the pioneers of Realism in Iceland, wrote a complimentary essay on Stephan's poetry in the periodical *Bjarki*. This was the first full-length essay on Stephan's poetry, but others followed – not all of them equally positive. A certain Jón Einarsson, for example, wrote an article for *Heimskringla* on Stephan's diction, criticizing him for using the word *vor* (spring) in a feminine context despite the fact that grammatically this word was neutral in gender. Jón's point was valid insofar as this "gender bending" did create a rather awkward line of poetry, but Stephan defended his usage in a short, sharp article, applying rather bold farmyard imagery to ridicule his critic. "Some scholars apply their judgment mainly to peek under the tails of individual words. No doubt this is a science, as such, but these men are seldom intellectually perceptive." He then cited other poets who had written about spring as a female entity, adding that it was sometimes necessary to break grammatical conventions in order to break new ground. "The greatest wealth of any language lies in comprehensive ideas rather than in mere grammatical introspection. Those who make a habit of producing long woolen threads of words with no content spoil the language, though their diction and syntax may be grammatically correct and stand perfectly upright like empty eggshells in a natural history museum." He who adds "even a single brilliant concept to his language" makes "a great contribution, even if in doing that he violates one of the grammatical commandments."58

Stephan found much contemporary poetry of that time tedious for its half-heartedness. In a work by Balzac, he found the soul described as "a huge passion that in the end deprives one of both heart and mind." "Balzac," Stephan observed, "is regarded as the most skillful of French writers, but some say he was a very minor poet. It is possible that this is art – one great advantage or disadvantage chiselled out of cold marble and given a human name. In my view, however, the greatest art is to portray life, with its frail minds and fickle hearts."59

While Stephan did not hesitate to go against the conventions of his time, neither did he shrink from giving advice to unborn generations.

Early in 1898 he sent this little verse to Icelandic poet Þorsteinn Erlingsson, who edited the periodical *Bjarki*:

> *I care least about*
> *Getting along with the present,*
> *But I would like to have my say*
> *In the century that is coming.*[60]

Historical Poems

In 1891 Stephan wrote two powerful poems presenting very decided interpretations of old Icelandic sagas and poems. One of them, "Grottasöngur" (The Song of Grotta), is a clear call to arms for the oppressed and exploited. "Rise against oppression, misery, and corruption/though it sets the age heaving like the ocean," he urged, advocating a stripping away of any deceptive gilding used to conceal the murky aspects of human life. It was time for the gods of stupidity, he stated, to topple from the thrones of convention.[61] The other poem was "Landnámsmaðurinn", discussed earlier.

Shortly after delivering his speech about book learning, in which he challenged people to stop idolizing the "greatness of ancient heroes", Stephan began exploring new themes in his poetry. Among his new works were original poems based on sagas he had read in manuscript form when he was still a boy at Víðimýrarsel. A series of these new poems appeared in the periodical *Öldin* in 1895 and later in various papers.

"Norna-Gestur", the first historical poem to appear in *Öldin*, can thus be viewed as a manifesto of sorts. It relates the story of a man who had lived for ages and fought alongside legendary heroes such as Siegfried. His destiny was to stay alive as long as a certain candle continued to burn, and now at the court of Ólafur Tryggvason, King of Norway, he regaled his audiences with stories of the heroes he had encountered during his long life. Stephan drew a parallel between Gestur and all poets, whose role is to interpret past ages and shed important light on the future.[62] Gestur created a connection between the past, present, and future, and Stephan sought that same kind of knowledge in the old stories – not to glorify the past, but rather to extract some wisdom that might help improve human existence in the future.

Grettissaga (The Saga of Grettir the Strong) was among Stephan's favourite sagas. Brought up within sight of the Isle of Drangey where the outlaw was killed, Stephan had written one of his first poems about Grettir at an early age. Now, in 1895, he wrote "Glámsaugun" (Glámur's Eyes), a remarkable interpretation of Grettir's life from a kind of an existential point of view. When Grettir returns to Iceland after three years' banishment in Norway, it is with notions of having improved himself greatly and achieved some measure of fame. Anxious to demonstrate his heroic status back in Iceland, he initially finds no worthy match in the relatively docile farmer society back home – until he encounters the monstrous ghost Glámur, whom he fights and eventually defeats. Before Glámur is driven away, however, he places a curse on Grettir, who is therefore destined to fear the dark and see Glámur's haunting eyes. Stephan interpreted the hauntings in this story as symbolic of the mindset of the times that preyed on Grettir's mind causing his anxiety. Stephan was one of the first to point out the ironic ambiguity expressed through Grettir's inner angst. The eyes of Glámur stared at Grettir just as "the ills of his age haunted him,/those evil spirits of his times" – and these eyes still stare "from the black night of history". To Stephan's way of thinking, every grown man in every age must wrestle with similar inner demons.[63]

The third poem in this heroic series is "Hervör á haugi Angantýs" (Hervör at Angantýr's Grave Mound), in which Stephan explores the issue of women's rights that he had first raised in Dakota a decade earlier. The poem is based on an ancient legend in which the heroine, Hervör, claims a family heirloom, the sword Tyrfingur, from the grave mound of her father, Angantýr. The spirit of Angantýr accepts his daughter's demands, but refuses to deliver the sword – which is cursed and destined to cause harm in the family. Hervör nonetheless claims the sword, stating that her father will not be able to keep it from her as victory makes heroes of men and gives them the power to rule the world. She wants to experience both. The reason is simple, a balance of terror: "in the shelter of a fatal sword/lie the truce and freedom of man."

Hervör finally acquires the sword, but with it come anxiety and doubt instead of the courage she had expected. She has received a son's freedom and rights in the shape of the sword, but when she realizes it, it is too late. The mound closes and "now she cannot return/the family heirloom to the dead." Ironically, having achieved her goal, Hervör loses her strength. The force that had driven her onward and then closed the mound was the vicious cycle of male power and violence. By the time she realizes this, however, there is no turning back.[64]

Stephan explored new paths in his historical poems and examined with discernment the tragic grief of not being able to break the vicious cycle of violence at the core of so many Icelandic sagas. He had a keen eye for such conflicts in the sagas as in the poem Elg-Fróði, half elk and half man, who was destined to kill when at the same time, warm emotions were within him. Stephan described this tragedy in poignant lines: "Behind the beast's black chest/bleeds a human heart."[65]

Stephan found material not only in the sagas, but in traditional legends and folk tales, and he often used this subject matter to explore aspects of the human condition. The poem "Jón hrak" (Jón the Outcast), for example, is based on a ghost story about an outcast who dies from exposure and haunts the grave diggers who have dug his grave in the churchyard along a north-south axis instead of an east-west axis. With this tale as his inspiration, Stephan creates a poem about a curious boy who strays from the normal path of life. Too lazy to memorize the word of God, but otherwise eager to learn, this youth gathers old lore that creates suspicions that he is dabbling black magic. From his own experiences in youth, Stephan empathized with Jón, who was not allowed to learn but reached the conclusion that the one who knew "the everyday hang of nature/could make work of life easier/and become more useful." Jón lived contrary to the conventions of his society, but succumbed because he was denied self-creation:

> *When everybody predicts misfortune for one,*
> *It comes true. There is no use in*
> *The brilliance or virtue of one man*
> *Against the prejudice of the many.*
> *In every mean prediction there is hidden*
> *A wish of a much worse misfortune –*
> *It is the promise of power to cause*
> *Harm to the less strong.*[66]

Stephan's fascination with individuals who went their own unique way is further demonstrated in his poem "Sigurður trölli" (Sigurd the Giant). A magnificent narrative, this poem is loosely based on Icelandic folktales about a man named Sigurður, who lived apart from other people and had the peculiar hobby of rescuing men who were about to perish from exposure on mountain trails. The poem weaves together powerful descriptions of Sigurður with images of the beautiful but harsh landscape where he gathers his sheep and rescues a traveller. Sigurður never attended church, but once passed by the parish church during a Christmas service, after which the minister visits him and feebly attempts to change his mind on Christian faith. The giant responds with gentle sarcasm, then accompanies the minister on his way home – along the way revealing the reason for his efforts to rescue travellers. He was, he explained, evening an old score with God, who through the forces of nature had deprived him of his parents. Sigurður's mother had perished in harsh weather on her way to church and his father had drowned. He wanted revenge, but he knew that his physical strength was no match for the forces of nature – except when he was able to rescue men from her deadly clutches. With every life Sigurður saves, however, his outlook on life brightens, and at the end of the poem he becomes reconciled with God:

> *But now, I owe nothing to the highest one!*
> *And from here on, I consider us reconciled.*
> *Although he took two lives from me,*
> *I managed to rescue eight from death.*[67]

While in Dakota, Stephan had become involved in skirmishes on the subject of the divinity, and although he had long ago rejected orthodox religion, his preoccupation with ideas about God and divine power persisted. In "Sigurður trölli" he promotes human dignity and rejects servility to God, subtly and ironically elevating his own concept of justice to a level above the creeds of the Christian church. By his own definition, this made him a heathen poet.

Stephan also wrote about Christ, but he was never able to accept the creeds of Christ's sacrificial death and atonement that he had first read about in his confirmation booklet. He found it unjust that one man should be crucified "...for the faults of his country/thus redeeming the sins of many."[68] He therefore sought his own interpretation of the life and work of Christ, which he articulated in the poem "Eloi lamma Sabakhtani!" ("My God, why hast thou forsaken me!") – echoing the words of Christ on the cross. Sent to *Heimskringla* as a Christmas poem in 1899, this poem deals with Christ's humanity, ideals, and frustrations. It also reveals Stephan's detailed knowledge of *The Bible*.

> *Such little news was his birth*
> *In the shepherd's crib,*
> *That nobody knows the day or year,*
> *And not one knows about his age.*

Stephan observed that Christ had received his education "in the poor people's school", where nobody was allowed to elevate himself above mediocrity. Those who achieved greatness were recognized only after death, whether prophets or poets. Christ's call was to "elevate the land and people/and cure the illnesses of his time." Cruelty, oppression, and inhumanity were the malignancies of those days, but Christ taught that "love of humans, warm and pure/was the only way to heaven." He defended the wayward and accused those who preached creeds. His words fascinated people, although most did not understand them. He could not comprehend why others did not recognize the truth that was so obvious to him. His words thus fell on the deaf ears of a public who instead wanted to hail him as king.

An ideal, Stephan stated, is not what comes to you in sermons or books. An ideal comes from within, "it is your soul," and it is rooted in the longing and contemplation of those who lived many centuries ago. This concept constitutes the foundation of Stephan's reflections over Christ's role:

> *Unable to ease the suffering of his brothers*
> *Became the bitterness of his death agony*
> *From such love and desire of the spirit,*
> *How small the results seemed to be!*
>
> *"My god, why did you forsake me?"*
> *Resounds from his grave all around you*
> *When you see the rage and superstition of the people*
> *Grouped together under his name.*

Idealists gather the beams of the spirit "into the focus of one soul," Stephan said, and Christ was one such idealist. His outcry on the cross, Stephan argued, was an expression of despair over having not been able to achieve something good. The effort of each idealist, however, was a tiny step in the right direction, even if it were a mere unexpressed hunch or an unwritten poem:

> *And the poet receives this lot,*
> *When the everyday life constricts,*
> *He who dies under busyness and delay*
> *And brings his best poems into the grave.*
>
> *And the farmer himself knows it well,*
> *Who wanted to cultivate the barren gravel plain,*
> *But dies so that he cannot see*
> *That the area begins to grow from his efforts.*[69]

In this way Stephan brought Christ down from the Cross and put him among the quiet reformers, such as the farmer and the poet. He thus placed Christ beside himself.

Work and Wakefulness

One night early in 1898 someone gave poisoned meat to Stephan's dog, Otur (Otter). He was fond of his big, beautiful, wise, glistening black dog who had killed a few coyotes in the surrounding forest. The dog died from this poison, having done nothing wrong, and in response Stephan wrote a commemorative poem – a lively description of Otur's heroic life and abilities. In this tribute, Stephan recalled the sharp wit and cheerfulness that shone from Otur's chestnut eyes, and he praised his dog's skills at attacking and defending bravely – getting the better of wolves in an honourable way. Otur's intelligence was such that he "understood both Icelandic and English/and could count a bit." He could also recognize both people and sheep, though he "had not attended school, but became, all the same / a truly educated dog."

Stephan had some notion as to who had done this mean-spirited deed and he alluded to this person in the poem without mentioning a name. It will turn out, Stephan predicted, that his name "will be known and/everybody will know the poem." When "hidden ghosts of wiles" wander around in the darkness of his mind, the "chestnut eyes of Otur" will haunt him. The poem ends with an expression of deep sorrow:

When I come home to the yard
Wet and weary from travelling,
I feel there are fewer friends
When poor Otur is away.[70]

Stephan was a great animal lover. "And should we not, my light hoofed Tóta and I/rouse our frail spirits to enjoy the evening calm," he asked in reference to his favourite mare in a poem describing the summer beauty of Alberta. The first horse Stephan acquired after arriving in the settlement, this mare was a small sorrel that in time grew very old. Her name, Tóta, was derived from an Icelandic ghost story about a girl who lingered after death because she wanted so much to play with the other children. Tóta was so kind that nobody feared her, but she was wall-eyed like all ghosts, and when another girl remarked on her ugly eyes, she walked away and was never seen again. "I know you are a beast!" Stephan continued, "but in spite of that you appreciate better than many/ the joys of summer after a winter in the barn." While riding Tóta to check his flock of sheep, he stopped to observe the neighbourhood from the top of a hill and watched as light smoke rising from the houses "turns into blue veils."[71] Stephan felt great freedom when out riding and checking on his sheep. Besides this small flock he had some 40 head of cattle in the barn down on the river flats. His pasture was on CPR land to the east of his homestead.

Over the summer of 1898 Stephan enlarged the family home. While this work was underway, his desk stood out in the yard with all his treasures, poems, and books, and in addition to interfering with Stephan's writing, this situation resulted in occasional rain damage. Stephan, however, did occasionally manage to sit down in the nearby schoolhouse to work on a poem.[72]

Jón Ólafsson, who had published Stephan's first book of poems, had since returned to Iceland to become editor of the monthly *Sunnanfari*. He wanted to publish another book of poetry by Stephan, but while Stephan was grateful, he was somewhat hesitant about another book. While in the process of composing a poem, he felt he was doing something original, but once a poem was printed it no longer seemed important. Stephan also felt he had not quite lived up to his own poetic talent. Nevertheless, in October of 1898, on the day before his 45th birthday, he mailed Jón a long poem entitled "Á ferð og flugi" (En Route), written as a sort

Canadian homestead regulations outlined the terms by which full ownership could be obtained. Qualifying improvements included buildings, livestock, fencing, breaking, and cultivation.

of travelogue in order to avoid straight narration. "I learned to speak as the sheep learned to bleat," Stephan noted by way of an excuse for any spelling errors, "that is, by inheritance and imitation."[73] He received no response from Jón, however, for several months.

Stephan and Helga's original log house, with its loft where the boys slept, remained at the centre of the new construction. A new kitchen was added to the east side, the north end of which was divided into a pantry and a little cubbyhole jokingly referred to as the "ram's shed". On the south side of the "big house" was an addition for the twin sisters, who were almost nine years old, and in the north end of the original building were two rooms where Stephan's mother had a table and bed and could sit at needlework.[74]

Among the ongoing issues that occupied Stephan's mind was the marketing of farm produce. Attempts at cheese making were not working out overly well, but the Territorial Department of Agriculture and the Federal Government joined forces with the farmers in building creameries, so Stephan and some 35 Icelandic shareholders now established a new company.

The only "foreigner" involved was Daniel Mörkeberg, who had left Denmark for the United States at the age of 20 and had settled in Alberta while en route to the Klondike. In Edmonton, Mörkeberg had met C. P. Marker, the government head of dairy products for the North West Territories, who hired him to establish creameries, first in Edmonton and then Leduc, in the spring 1899. Mörkeberg then joined the Icelanders, who raised $1,035 in capital stock. Competition from small cheese factories was deemed harmful, so the government purchased the cheese-making equipment owned by Helgi Jónasson and Jón Benediktsson, which was never used again. Butter production started on July 12, 1899, and on September 23 the company was registered as the Tindastoll Butter and Cheese Manufacturing Association. Both Stephan and Daniel Mörkeberg were on the board – Stephan as secretary and cashier. During the first year, the company produced 14,655 pounds of butter, and annual production soon reached 100,000 pounds. As a result, farmers in the settlement enjoyed considerably higher incomes than before.

Stephan and Helga now prospered. The older boys, handsome and good workers, acquired a few head of livestock themselves. Baldur was tall and blond, Guðmundur shorter and darker. Helga owned the chickens and had independent income from the eggs. She also milked the cows, while Stephan tended them when he was home and cut firewood in winter.

Interruptions to the daily routine were frequent. One day, for example, a neighbour came to visit just as Stephan was in the middle of a letter on the subject of poetry. When the guest had finished his coffee, he brought up his business with Stephan, requesting help with two letters in English. The first was about a ram that had drowned. The other had to do with the farmer's three cows and some accounting. Stephan was just about to finish the letter about the cows when the visitor mentioned another detail. He did not quite understand a legal paragraph and asked Stephan to translate it for him. Stephan's letter writing and poetry were often interrupted in this manner.[75]

Although the daily labour was tiring, Stephan found deep meaning in his work as a farmer and pioneer. He recognized the philosophical significance of cultivating the land as well as the humourous aspects of his work, and perhaps a few lines of Walt Whitman were in the back of his mind when he penned one of his best known quatrains, "Basl-hagmennið" (Jack of all trades), near the turn of the 20th century:

> *For years I was my own doctor,*
> *Lawyer, clergyman,*
> *Blacksmith, king, teacher,*
> *Cart, plough, horse.*[76]

Isolation made people self-reliant in many aspects of life. For Stephan, the wide-open spaces were also a guarantee against overcrowding. Homesteading had enabled him to settle new land, literally and intellectually – as well as poetically. His instinct was to pull away from common practice, in farming as well as in poetry, and this became an important aspect of his identity as a farmer. Perhaps this self-imposed 'exile' was derived to some extent from Stephan's disappointment over general public aloofness toward the social criticism of the idealists, which was at the core of his own work. He therefore kept himself at a comfortable distance from the mainstream, as critical as before, but no longer expecting swift reforms.

By the close of the 19th century, after spending much of his energy on the everyday chores of homesteading and farm life, Stephan became increasingly concerned with what he felt were the limitations of his poetry. His aching limbs told him that he was becoming physically worn out. "I can hardly write legibly these days," he wrote in the fall of 1898, a day before his 45th birthday. "The axe and fork have made me stiff at handling a pen. I have also pinched a nerve in my left shoulder and my fingers sometimes go numb."[77] Stephan's workday lasted from 6 in the morning until evening. Sometimes he wrote now and again during the day, and he would read well into the night. As he grew older, he suffered chronic insomnia, and sometimes he could not sleep at all, although he tried various sleep inducements, such as writing and reading until he grew tired. "When the 'swallows of insomnia' sit by my window, I have only one remedy – to work until I am completely exhausted and numb, which can take several days."[78*] Stephan was now middle-aged. Along with handling the difficult struggle to make a living, he had managed to develop his own view of life and express it in powerful poetry. His poems were more varied and numerous than

---

*"Swallows of insomnia" refers to a famous episode in *Egil Skallagrimsson's Saga*, chapter 60, when swallows kept Egill awake all night as he composed his famous poem "Head-Ransom".

the life's work of most other Icelandic poets. Nevertheless, his official career as a poet had just begun.

Evening

Perhaps Stephan sat down to rest in the stillness of the evening on his 46th birthday, October 3, 1899. The children were quiet, visitors had left, and Baldur and Guðmundur, now almost 20, were visiting neighbours. Helga, having made some tea and sat down to read a paper, dozed off. Guðbjörg, knitting in her room as usual, now made her way into the living room for some tea and stopped for a moment to observe her son. He had been reading, but was now perusing notes he had hurriedly jotted down over the last few days. Nothing broke the stillness except the rustling of papers. Stephan's weariness gradually passed, finding poetic expression in beautiful rhyme and alliteration in which nature became intertwined with the poet's toil and ideas:

> *In the dusk when I am all alone*
> *And have shed my working gear*
> *And Earth has pursued itself*
> *From sunshine into shadows,*
> *And all chatter falls silent*
> *And slumber mutes the barking of the dogs –*
>
> *And napping in the doorway, sit life's cares,*
> *Who all day long stand guard,*
> *And scare off all my light-winged poems,*
> *So they escape me without song,*
> *Like broken-winged thoughts that took flight*
> *Seeking to find heaven.*

Stephan had long felt the constrictions his daily cares imposed on his creativity, and sometimes he longed to forget reality and dream of the land of hope, earthly and without violence:

> *How glad I would be to forget and forgive all,*
> *If I could then freely choose*
> *To dream, in the stillness and darkness, of the land*

> *Where daylight has never shone,*
> *Where, from shipwrecks, eternal Hope washes up*
> *And the elusive desire of poets.*
>
> *That land has no great surplus*
> *And gains nothing in heaven,*
> *Where no man's success is the suffering of another,*
> *And power is not the highest goal,*
> *And victory is never anyone's pain,*
> *And fairness the highest commandment.*

Stephan knew all too well that this land did not exist in the real world, but it was not his care for life that kept him awake. Work just bound the wings of his creative thoughts. What kept him awake were thoughts of all those souls that had never realized their potential:

> *But then insomnia appears, hoary and pale*
> *And frightens away my rest and ease,*
> *And the lost souls besiege me,*
> *Cheated of their best potential,*
> *And these exposed infants of mankind then wail loudly -*
> *Mourning neglected abilities that died without care.*

These neglected abilities require the same attention a farmer devotes to his tasks – work that acquires the equivalence of religious faith. This is precisely the kind of work that becomes its own reward, but the poet also sees the opposite side of work: exploitation and violence, with idleness feeding off the labour of others:

> *And then I see the abyss of misery open up,*
> *Where labour is brought to its knees,*
> *While idle profit feeds on poverty*
> *Like decay in living trees,*
> *And the will and mind of the bewildered masses*
> *Is lead astray and controlled by the few.*
>
> *There, all business is equally dubious*
> *And the friendship of man is*
> *Like a loner who is lost in the night*

Among an army of outlaws,
And listens with closed eyes,
To warnings of the enemy's approach.

The business transactions of his fellow man, Stephan observed, could be less than forthright. He had witnessed the ability of people like Reverend Jón Bjarnason to manipulate the minds of the masses, thereby influencing society and impeding progress. Stephan, as if peering into the darkness in search of a little spark of light, nevertheless sought a glimpse of hope for human progress – hope derived from the same values that inspire a farmer's care and nurturing:

And the deceptive night of mankind, on a trackless earth,
Has become so terribly long, I find,
As if the glimmer of progress was just a lie
And the shadows as dark as before.
Because even in ancient times, the mind soared as high -
So what, then, has been gained?

Yes, culture has increased little by little,
Though each century carries it but a short distance -
It does not deepen, nor get higher, but stretches a little further
Like sunshine during longer days.
But the hand of the moment, short human life,
Still knows nothing of this difference.

But even into the solitude of the shepherd,
It sneaks as quietly as early morning sunshine
And brightens the minds, though subtly,
As the morning light goes so gently.
And I, who can compose for a bleak world
Such a poem in a wakeful night –

And with a calm mind step into that ultimate bed
From which I will never part:
So certain that in the world there remains
My every hope, with its light and warmth,
It lives, what is best in my own soul
That the sunshine still prevails![79]

It is now almost morning and the swallows of insomnia fall silent for a while as Stephan slumps in his chair and falls asleep. Outside, a new day begins. Soon, a new century will also begin – the age of violence – and Stephan will want to have a word about that.

Icelandic sculptor Ríkarður Jónsson's depiction of the farmer-poet Stephan G. Stephansson, composing poetry through wakeful nights on his homestead. The lettering is the opening line of one of the poet's best loved poems.

Part 2

Age of Violence

Chapter 10

Busy in a New Century

An Icelandic Prostitute in the New World

When Stephan heard nothing from Jón Ólafsson about the long poem he had written in the schoolhouse in the summer of 1898, he began to fear it was a failure. He then wrote Jón, saying he thought the poem was not that badly written, although he admitted the thread of the storyline was thin here and there. Jón, as it turned out, had resigned as editor of *Sunnanfari*, which had temporarily ceased publication, but he was nevertheless of the opinion that the poem should indeed reach the Icelandic readership. As Stephan's poetry was not widely known, some of the publishers Jón subsequently approached did not want to risk publishing it, although they realized what a gem the poem was, so Jón eventually published it himself, convinced that the future would acknowledge this unschooled farmer as one of the greatest Icelandic poets of the 19th century. Published as a book entitled *Á ferð og flugi*, this collection also contained a few shorter poems, including "Kveld" (Evening).[1]

The poem "Á ferð og flugi" (En Route) relates the story of Ragnheiður, an Icelandic girl who had gone sadly astray. Stephan could not accept that the individual was always to blame in such situations, so he described Ragnheiður's good nature and attempted to explain her misfortune through her having been torn "away from her ethnicity and inherited customs, christened and confirmed in a cursory manner into a community (the church) that most of all struggles to get people to confess and gather into a group."[2] Stephan wanted to enfold this tragedy in beautiful descriptions of nature and relate it without being lurid.

In this poem, Stephan reflects on his 25 years in America and draws upon personal experiences, including the train crash, his trip to a Synod conference, and hard labour in the wilderness. While on various journeys, the narrator of the poem catches occasional glimpses of Ragnheiður that form the framework of the poem. The storyline is set against a backdrop of life on the North American prairies in the final decades of the 19th century. On his first journey, the narrator is on his way to a Synod conference:

> *The locomotive carried us over plains and marshes*
> > *In a northerly direction.*
> *On the left, wading sluggishly along the outwash,*
> > *Was the slow, muddy river,*
> *That did not lift a foot in a waterfall nor rapids*
> > *As the speed, even of the stream, fades out,*
> *From wading for ages with the arms full*
> > *Of the blackest clay of the flatland.*[3]

The sparse population gravitates to the railway line in small villages with their stores, churches, and liquor outlets in the guise of drugstores.

> *The homesteads were scattered across the plains*
> > *Like skerries on a blank sea;*
> *And all the houses were so alike*
> > *And the shape of every farm,*
> *All the newly ploughed soil appeared so equally dark*
> > *And the blue-green flair of fields was the same.*
> *Every human spirit seemed to be doomed to think alike,*
> > *Every hand to be equally tame.*[4]

Stephan portrays the rootlessness of this new society by pointing out its lack of history and its focus on the present, "the customs and thoughts of today/dominate with unlimited power."[5] Progress does not allow memories to take root, unlike the situation in Iceland where history is ever-present through place-names, folklore, and the grassy graves of ancestors.

The narrator's destination is a mining town, but the description is based to some extent on Winnipeg at the time of the Icelandic Lutheran

Synod conference Stephan attended in 1885. The rows of houses look like palisades along canyon-like streets. The narrator feels that underground mining, where men emerge muddy and sweaty, docile like sheep, is unsuitable for his countrymen. Nor does he care for the garish nightlife in the town or the fact that a handful of men own most of the real estate. The townspeople, he feels, are like a flock of sheep, accepting lies and opinions promoted by political parties, "and I find the making of big profits similar to Viking raids/and all the bankruptcies like robberies."[6] Stephan was also disillusioned by a squabble at the Synod conference over Christ's identity.

In this town the narrator meets Ragnheiður, whose description is testament to the poet's empathy and understanding of human destiny. She is a frail character, defeated by her experiences:

> Like a spring morning's sunshine on a rimy hill
>   Was her hair, light blond and sleek,
> And stale air had set its bluish pallor
>   On the eyes of this child.
> It was as if that colour was not deep,
>   But shone, firm and transparent.
> Although appearance changed, one thought,
>   They would remain unchanged, easily recognizable and bright.
>
> And she looked like a planted lily to me,
>   With a loose and frail root,
> And so, if the wind should roll her in the mud,
>   She would toss about and become ugly.
> Although deep worries had not yet marked
>   This forehead, so white and broad,
> It seemed to me that something was withered
>   And razed from her smile and appearance,
> As if she had already reached old age –
>   Though she was barely eighteen;
> As her entire life was a struggle against the wind,
>   And her youth had begun there.
> Her body seemed grown up, pretty and sweet
>   And light of foot, slender and tall,

> But her temper and heart and mind had
> Hardly reached half-maturity.[7]

The poet explores Ragnheiður's childhood as a partial explanation of this sad situation. When she was 12 years of age, her father had been obliged to send her to work as a domestic in the town. He was an immigrant and had difficulty finding work. At first unable to relate to people who spoke a foreign tongue, Ragnheiður looks forward to returning home on weekends, though her wages are hardly enough for food and clothes for her three brothers. Forced to memorize a confirmation text, she begins to dislike books. Eventually she becomes fluent in English, and church events and dances are her main entertainments. When she visits her parents in the countryside, now a well-dressed cosmopolitan, she finds herself enjoying popularity at church fundraising events. More money is collected than usual and all the girls begin to imitate her. Ragnheiður, however, is no longer satisfied with rural isolation, and she returns to the town, where she has just arrived when the narrator encounters her. Town life has compromised her moral strength and left its mark on her natural beauty.

The narrator next meets Ragnheiður years later when he is returning home from working with a survey crew, just as Stephan had done in Alberta. It is midwinter and he travels with two Cree Indians, an Irishman, and a Frenchman. After a cold night under a clear sky, they shiver at the thought of walking all the way to the mining town of Golden. The Irishman cheers up the Icelander with the suggestion that he may find comfort "with a merry fellow countrywoman in Golden tonight/who is nice to travellers."[8] Golden is a typical gold rush town, with its mixture of sinners, drunks, women of questionable repute, God-fearing preachers, and speculators – symbolic of the 1897-1898 Klondike gold rush era. Gold seekers en route to the Klondike and prospectors hoping to find gold along the North Saskatchewan River had flooded into the town. Most of these dreams came to nothing, but while the boom lasted, every source of wealth became "the gold snare of the miser, tightened/around the fettered foot of the poor."[9] Now the peak of the gold rush was over, leaving rows of empty houses.

The narrator has to wait three days for a train, and on the last evening in Golden, while at a saloon, he meets the Irishman, loud and boisterous with his pockets full of money. Married to the Icelandic 'Sally', who has fallen into a sordid lifestyle that has made him easy money, O'Hara now has a change of heart. No longer willing to be associated with such a woman, he has thrown her out.

The next morning, as the narrator leaves on the train, he observes his dull-looking travel companions. In front of him sits an unfamiliar girl, evidently known to all the men and despised by the women because of her beauty – or her reputation.

> *To the slender limbs, beautifully fell*
>   *Every fold of the dark dress*
> *As a dusk blue evening shadow around a single aspen*
>   *With faded autumn leaves against the sun,*
> *Because youth has faded, a blue flush was visible*
>   *In a cup on the rose of the cheeks;*
> *On the soft, glowing hair was a brownish tinge*
>   *As if the gilding was worn off.*
> *From her attitude I could see that she knew herself,*
>   *And was hoping against the odds*
> *That she could regain what she had lost*
>   *By freely showing off what she still had.*
> *There was something in the face and words,*
>   *Towards everyone she flirted with,*
> *Not the youthful and careless rashness,*
>   *But the contrived, artificial, imitated.*[10]

This is the Icelandic Sally. When she begins to play with a five year-old girl, the flirting attitude of the courtesan disappears, and the narrator now observes how the characteristics of his fellow Icelanders follow them like a shadow, despite name changes. Suddenly the child's mother rushes in and snatches the little girl away from Sally, and when she looks up the narrator recognizes her eyes:

> *And only the clear, blue of the eyes,*
>   *Remained so firmly in my mind,*
> *That I could not without sorrow doubt what I saw:*
>   *Little Ragnheiður was there.*[11]

The narrator then moves to another car where he meets another countryman, this one a minister. They have known each other for years, but there has always been some hostility between them, like an armed truce. The narrator finds the pastor smugly self-important, evasive, and uninspired, yet learned in a superficial sense. He represents much of what Stephan despises most, and like Ragnheiður he has donned a mantle of affected mannerisms. (Some thought this pastor resembled Reverend Friðrik Bergmann, with whom Stephan had various dealings over the years, and Stephan did not always deny that Reverend Friðrik had fluttered through his mind while he was writing the poem.)

After falling asleep for a while, the narrator awakens with a start when there is a train crash that recalls the poet's experienced in August of 1873. In a moment, he catches a brief glimpse of Ragnheiður as she throws the child to safety, then stumbles to her own death when the passenger car is crushed. The child's mother appears, crying, "and the expression of self-righteousness had totally disappeared/when she found her child unharmed."[12]

The survivors are taken to the next town, where they remain overnight. Ragnheiður is to be buried there, but the Icelandic pastor hesitates to step forward to perform the service for fear that his good name may become tainted by her reputation – despite his wife's reminder that Ragnheiður's father had donated a large sum of money to the church after she had disappeared from home. The narrator gets the room next to theirs and through the thin wall overhears the pastor's wife ask about his own dubious reputation. The pastor answers her with innuendo, "to his mild judgment about all my nature,/were mischievous speculations slyly added;/in every excuse, an accusation was/added as poison into the chalice." The wife, however, expresses some doubt about her husband's judgment, having concluded that "humans become human without ordination/but the pastors are humans nevertheless." Her response pleases the narrator and he compares her with himself, both of them having learned skepticism that comes with age and experience. "I am as a snowy mountain on a remote peninsula,/you as a burned out volcanic crater."[13] She retains some charm, however, and he imagines amorous sparks between them.

Word spreads about the selfless heroism of Ragnheiður's final act. The child's affluent mother, who was also saved when Ragnheiður woke her, offers the pastor a goodly sum for taking care of the funeral. He relents, not least because Ragnheiður is now something of a heroine and he can deliver a good sermon. The minister's wife, unimpressed, begins a discussion with the narrator about Ragnheiður's heroic deed. She maintains that the spark of life has disappeared from Icelandic women and that Ragnheiður's life was worthless. Icelandic women have lost their integrity and become depraved, she continues, and life's experiences have ruined their moral strength. The narrator, on the contrary, says the girl had possessed many good qualities that circumstances had not allowed to flourish. She was like a piece of gold in the mud and her last deed was indeed heroic. At the end of the poem, the narrator visits Ragnheiður's grave, contemplating the tender compassion he feels for his fellow countrymen:

> *I feel brotherhood for foreign lands,*
> *Only lacking the sentimentality.*
> *But every piece of earth, where an Icelander is buried,*
> *Rouses feelings of kinship.*[14]

History, destiny, and the soil tie one to the motherland, but on Ragnheiður's gravestone stands nothing more than 'Sally O'Hara' – with the name 'Daisy' below, so people would know who had paid for it. The headstone symbolizes a sense of conflicting identity that many Icelandic immigrants were experiencing by the turn of the century.

On Par with Zola and Crane

Stephan was very pleased when *Á ferð og flugi* was published in Reykjavík at the beginning of 1900 – though the book received mixed reviews. His poem of this name touched on things that Icelanders in North America preferred not to acknowledge. Many among them idealized material success and saw themselves as heroic followers in the wake of their forefathers who had sailed to Vinland a millennium before. Ragnheiður's story, however, was neither pure fiction nor a single occurrence. Stephan knew of similar tragedies among his countrymen, and by employing new literary methods in this poem he was identifying a critical understanding of the immigrant experience.

Emilé Zola, among the most progressive writers in France in the second half of the 19th century, had written his novel *Nana* as an unflinching dissection of prostitution in French society. His portrayal of a prostitute as the heroine of the novel was a daring novelty in European literature at that time, and the book caused harsh reactions. Interested in the empirical methods of the natural sciences, Zola depicted the setting of this novel in great detail in order to establish the connection between environment and character.

Progressive writers in North America, equally daring in their subject matter, had also begun to depict the grittiness of human existence in the big cities, employing the same realistic methods. They wanted to force readers to face the dark underbelly of their society. Most famous was American writer Stephen Crane's 1893 novel *Maggie, a Girl of the Street*, about a gentle young girl mercilessly broken by her surroundings and driven into a life of prostitution.

Stephan followed new literary trends with considerable interest, not least the ideas of Realism and Naturalism. These schools of literary thought demanded that writers describe their times critically and realistically, showing how circumstances can mould the individual. Among the writers he most admired were Gestur Pálsson, Charles Dickens, George Eliot, Ivan Turgenev, and Emilé Zola – "when he is not pouring his spittoon in my face!"[15] Although Stephan learned from Naturalism, he was somewhat skeptical of the value of precise descriptions of an external reality. "It will never become a poetic work of art, I say, to take an exact photo of everything in sight," he wrote while composing the poem about Ragnheiður. "Life, as it passes, is not poetic, my goodness! I want to condense the most significant events, one from here, one from there, deleting everything insignificant that is just in the way, and turn a whole year into one day, if necessary."[16] He selected techniques at will, mixing Naturalism and Romanticism in order to portray the fate of Icelanders in North America and examine what it takes to break a human being. Stephan chose to tell Ragnheiður's tragic story with beautiful, melancholic imagery, in contrast to the naturalist dissection he found to be like a splash from Zola's spittoon. On the other hand, his subject was very much in the spirit of Naturalism.

Stephan's ground-breaking poem was such a novelty that Icelandic critics, hardly able to mention it aloud, seemed to avoid it. Predictably, the poem received harsh reviews in Iceland. Einar Hjörleifsson, a pioneer of Realism, had lived in Winnipeg for several years and was by now a strong spokesman for the New Theology as well as for spiritualism. In a review, he acknowledged Stephan's originality but criticized what he deemed a crude and unfair attack on the church and its clergy. Most of the heavy punches in the poem, he claimed, went amiss, and he went on at length

Icelandic poet and novelist Einar Hjörleifsson (Kvaran) (1859-1938) spent several years in Winnipeg as editor of Lögberg. *When he moved back to Iceland in 1895, it was with a comprehensive understanding of Icelandic society in North America.*

to praise the Icelandic clergy in the West. The principal question for the church, he stated, was precisely who Christ really was, and every truly educated man knew that – hinting at Stephan's lack of formal education. Despite these misdirected blows, Einar Hjörleifsson concluded that there was much gold among the mud in Stephan's poem. Another critic dismissed the poem as utter bad taste, padding, and incomprehensible insinuations. "Besides that, [Stephan] has begun to 'personify' everything between heaven and earth," he said.[17] The editor felt obliged to defend Stephan and point out his most brilliant poems, not included in the book.

In Winnipeg, Friðrik Bergmann printed a review of *Á ferð og flugi* in his periodical *Aldamót* – next to a glowing review of Reverend Jón Bjarnason's collection of sermons. Reverend Jón, who had fiercely attacked the Cultural Society in Dakota and had for a long time played a leading role in the Icelandic Synod, was Reverend Friðrik's comrade-in-arms. Though Reverend Friðrik praised Stephan's talent, he dubbed him a "folk-poet" and focussed on his dark pessimism, "a cold, cynical grin with pain hidden behind it" that made his poems bitter "in taste and hardly attractive." There was, however, "something majestic about this. There he sits in the "darkness", writing poetry between cows and calves." Friðrik concluded that Stephan was taking out his anger on the ministers because he had lost faith in humanity.[18]

Neither Einar Hjörleifsson nor Reverend Friðrik Bergmann could deny Stephan's genius, but they both felt compelled to discredit him. Pointing out his lack of education and his preoccupation with farm chores, they articulated an opinion that had been circulating for a long time: that Stephan was insensitive, hard to understand, and incredibly pessimistic. It was somewhat ironic, however, that a "folk-poet" – who had in such an original, innovative, and intentional manner digested the latest trends in world literature – should be accused of a lack of education.

The only positive review of this cutting-edge work of Stephan's was written by a woman. "It is as if an ever-cool and ever-fresh mountain breeze is embracing you when you read these poems," the militant and liberal Margrét J. Benedictson wrote in her journal *Freyja* – for

Margrét J. Benediktsson (Benedictson), publisher of the women's journal Freyja *and advocate for women's rights, with her husband, poet and publisher Sigfús Benediktsson, and their children.*

a time the only periodical in Canada dedicated to women's rights. "They breathe some deeply serious, cold flair, and have nothing in common with the spiritual dullness that thrives on the lowlands of cowardice." Margrét admired Stephan's daring in probing beneath the sophisticated gilding of society, which she felt explained his cynical attitude toward that society. She concluded by stating that Stephan was a spiritual giant.[19]

Stephan never indicated that he was offended by any of these reviews. On the contrary, he claimed to be very pleased with them as these criticisms of his work revealed many things. He also pointed out that the most enduring poetry expressed bold moral opinions and demonstrated skillful composition, not "rosy fringes that only support the shrivelled branches of outdated opinions." Later he also responded to the persistent accusations of pessimism. "Art is not just creating happy endings for stories. It is exactly because the stories of Gunnar and Grettir end as they do at Hlíðarendi and Drangey, that we have never been able to forget them."[20]

Icelandic Identity

While Stephan was a keen observer and critic of North American society, he saw life in Iceland in a different light. For him, his birthplace remained an ideal that was a crucial part of his evolving identity. Icelandic elements became a foundation for the critical stand he took on various issues, and two works written around the turn of the 20th century illustrate this Icelandic ballast.

Stephan had spent his formative years at the head of the Vatnsskarð Pass, with its extraordinary panoramic view, and this magnificent image never faded in his memory. Remarkably, however, this scene did not find poetic expression until 1899 when Stephan penned the poem "Skagafjörður" (Skagafjord), in which he personifies natural forces as ancient mythical powers. The gods and semi-gods Frosti, Ægir, Hlér, and Sól all participate in the fjord's formation over a long period of time. The cold Frosti chisels the rims of the mountains, breaks up the fjord's entry, and forms the rocks. The landscape is then further transformed by gentler methods when the sea god Ægir reaches in along the fjord with his blue arm to file and plane landmarks at the bottom of the fjord. Then the sun takes over:

> *She gently spreads her bosom of beams*
> *Over sands and moors,*
> *Busy letting the land grow,*
> *Combining day and night into one –*
> *Yet awake in the quiet spring night*
> *Warms pastures, hayfields, and bogs.*
> *With the help of the sun, spring repels night in the high north.*

After this genesis of natural forces, Stephan's memories play a part in describing human life and its struggles in Skagafjörður:

> *Did you read the mind of the teenager*
> *Who watched the flocks at night*
> *Up on the heaths and slopes of the fjord*
> *Or in a dell by a curve in the river?*
> *His hopes acquire the flight of wings –*
> *Spring does not abide any hindrances.*[21]

The basic idea of the poem is that both the creative power of nature and mythical forces are inherent in poetry. Stephan identifies with Skagafjörður, where both hardship and gentleness influenced his development, and in this poem he weaves together the themes of mythical creation, poetry, and the courage to face life. In death he wants to disappear into the embrace of the fjord with his poetic force, "younger, bigger, recreated." With these words he evokes a creative cycle of life in which the fjord lives within him and he lives in the fjord forever.

Stephan also sought inspiration from Iceland in a different way. In the spring of 1900 he wrote "Fráfall Guðmundar gamla students" (The Death of Old Guðmundur the Student), a short story about an eccentric man who challenges the generally accepted ideas of his time and withdraws to the margins of society. To some extent this character represents a strand of Stephan's identity. Bed-ridden and waiting for death, Guðmundur sends for his old friend and schoolmate Reverend Hákon, who on his way reviews Guðmundur's life. Most people bore grudges against him, but nobody actually knew of anything he had done wrong. As a student he had shown a sparkling intellect, but he had gradually distanced himself from his schoolmates and his skepticism about commonly accepted ideas had made him a recluse. His mates, though well-educated, were conventional thinkers who considered him arrogant. Guðmundur was ordained a minister despite his doubts about religious creeds, but he declined promotion to the status of dean. "He who is free himself, detests authority," he said. Soon he gave up life as a clergyman to become a farmer. The gentlefolk "accepted him as a shearling from an inferior sheep pen, his upbringing and habit having been placed for no reason at the manger among them, and he would thus have to be tolerated." Guðmundur, however, was highly regarded among the disadvantaged and "would almost have been able to gather tramps and troublemakers around him and turn them into decent people if, yes, if he would have managed to multiply his fish and bread by a miracle." Stephan likens Guðmundur to his namesake Guðmundur the Good, a medieval bishop who attracted a legion of tramps and unfortunates, and to Christ, who multiplied fishes and loaves.

Reverend Hákon expresses the hope that Guðmundur's attitude will change as he faces death. Guðmundur, however, maintains his old ideas and refuses to forgive his enemies as he feels this would be a betrayal of the truth. For him, eternal bliss in heaven holds little attraction. "And what on earth should I do there, where everybody is happy, where there is no cause to fight for, where there is none who needs a helping hand, and where there is no prejudice to deal with?" Guðmundur wants Hákon, rather than a liberal pastor, to take care of his funeral – as liberalism, "this indecisiveness that wants to flatter goodwill out of every old wives' tale, flirt with all modern protest, and mix it all together" – was the opposite of his straightforwardness. Liberalism, "a blend of superstition and rationalism", is subservient to power, and perhaps "a normal, momentous balance between the old that has lost its strength and the new that is immature."

Guðmundur wants none of this at his grave. He gives $200 to Hákon, asking him to hire a few poor friends to dig his grave. They would be too proud to accept money as a gift, so he wants to give them a chance to earn it. Two of these friends were Einar and Bergur. Einar lacks thriftiness but has a beautiful voice that nevertheless does not help him earn a living except when he is fed at parties for entertaining with his singing. Bergur is about to sell his cow so that his son can attend school. "The thirst for knowledge will be a misfortune for the boy if nothing is done about it. The school will probably choke all promise out of him, but his stomach will remain intact and thus he will be able to earn a living." At the end of the story, when Guðmundur has died, the New Year heralds a new day.[22]

It was the dawning of a new century for Stephan as well, and this age would have to be dealt with. Like Guðmundur, he was a dissident in a remote neighbourhood – opposed to various things and anxious about the world.

A Giant Oppressing a Little Dwarf

On September 4, 1900, in a letter to Jóhann Magnús Bjarnason, Stephan made a profound prediction. He found the imperialism of big nations ominous and foresaw that authoritarianism and oppression would ignite wars in the coming century. "I am a bit tired of the world," he said. "The age of ideals has passed ... and the age of violence has taken its place, and I have no use for such business. Small nations are being bullied into rejecting their nationality and everyone in the entire world is becoming a Russian or an Englishman or a German. That is like cutting the roots off world culture. All nations, including small ones, contribute their share to the world – precisely because they are different and can add what no other nation can. If the world is reduced to one or two nations, culture will stagnate. This will never happen, though," Stephan wrote, "because the human spirit will never allow itself to perish in this way. The current situation is a stupid and bloody attempt to make it happen, but it can only last for a while before it stops or splits in two."[23]

It was not without reason that Stephan predicted the coming age so bleakly. In preceding years newspapers had reported escalating alienation and war. Stephan followed the news closely and mastered new concepts and definitions of the world's power system. "The inner spirit of the time is the same all over, soldiery and aggression. They call it, I believe, 'imperialismus', and they see the sacrifice of human lives as the ultimate."[24] In another letter from that period, Stephan concluded that imperialism tended to sacrifice those individuals who did not accept current values. Many subjects of the British Empire, Canadians as well as others, believed they lived in an exemplary state and that it was the duty of each and every one to support its ideals. In their eyes, the superiority of the British justified the suppression of other nations.[25]

Skirmishes between the British and the Boers in South Africa erupted into full-scale war in October of 1899. The Boers, who had settled in South Africa in the 17th century, were of Dutch origin, industrious Calvinists who had suppressed the blacks with religion and military power, yet Stephan sympathized with them as settlers. The British had begun their conquest of South Africa at the beginning of the 19th century and soon incorporated the area into their economic and political empire, so by the middle of the century the Boers had moved further inland, establishing the republics of Transvaal and Orania. Following the discovery of gold and diamonds in Transvaal, the British attacked the Boers with their massive, superior strength. For the British, the war was an attempt to assert their economic and political dominance in that part of Africa. For the Boers, it was a struggle to maintain independence.

Despite propaganda and British self-glorification in the media, much of the world sympathized with the Boers, who were viewed as a handful of farmers defending themselves against a superpower. The Dominion of Canada, however, supported the British by sending a thousand volunteers to South Africa at the end of October, and thousands more joined them later in search of adventure.[26]

Stephan was furious at this injustice and wrote the poem "Transvaal", printed in *Heimskringla* in December of 1899 despite the editor's disagreement with its message. In this poem Stephan stands firmly alongside the Boers, frustrated at not being able to hinder the fratricide:

> *But, let us wait, I have words and a poem!*
> *And this time they shall become,*
> *Weighing heavily from the deepest state of mind,*
> *A brand on Cain's cheek,*
> *The complaint of Abel's death-blood,*
> *A ghost that shall shout an evil prediction*
> *To the English army from the dead Boers.*

"The unfortunates of England" think they can subjugate the countries of the world with their power, Stephan says, but they do not understand that "the sword cuts all ties of heart./Into your empire you can hardly cut/the minds of the people – turn away from that /as it has been tried to the last resort,/but there are sad ruins now." Stephan finds it cowardly of a giant to oppress a dwarf and believes Canada has been cajoled into participation. He states that he is willing to draw a sword, but only to defend his homeland. "So do not demand more – look around:/We are all brothers here,/but have each our own memories."[27] England deserves condemnation for such a major crime, Stephan says, in the name of those great men England has produced and everything that country has contributed to the world.

The main part of the poem is the story of a Boer father and son who attempt to defend themselves against the British, but fall against superior strength. The widow, who has lost her husband and son, is then addressed. She and her husband had not believed that God would allow the British to rob them of so little, but their misfortune did not excuse their behaviour towards the blacks, Stephan pointed out. In fact, the English were simply grabbing the plunder of the Boers and winning praise for their victory.

Stephan's demand that people be allowed to defend their freedom was in opposition to government policy and was not made without risk. *Lögberg* praised the British Empire during the war and reputedly wanted the poem translated into English with the possible aim of having Stephan and *Heimskringla* charged with high treason. This was the first time Stephan would be accused of treason. The only problem with this, he stated, was that nobody was able to translate the poem – though he was prepared to do that for them if they paid him decently![28] The war continued until 1902 when the Boers surrendered.

"Go make some coffee, Helga"

With his humanitarian view of life, Stephan concerned himself with every aspect of the world, but life at home was simple. His oldest son, the blond Baldur, was now 20 years old, a big, strong, calm horse-lover. Guðmundur was 18, shorter, brown-eyed, and of darker complexion. Jakob was 13, a taciturn youth with dark, curly hair. The twin girls were 10, similar in physiognomy but different in complexion. Fanny was dark and brown-eyed while Jenny was blond. Gestur was 6 years old, a blond-haired, playful boy. The youngest child, Rósa Siglaug, was born on July 24, 1900, delivered by Stephan's sister, Sigurlaug, who lived across the Medicine River with her husband, Kristinn, and their three children. Kristinn was always cheerful and on the move, while Sigurlaug, brown-eyed with black hair done in a style that never changed, was intelligent, calm, and stoic. Stephan and his sister were homebodies who seldom visited each other. It was sufficient for them to know that the other was nearby. Stephan's children, though, loved to visit their Auntie Lauga.[29]

Stephan and Helga's home was atop a low hill that afforded a panoramic view to the west. Beyond the forested hills, broken by small fields where settlers had planted their crops, stood the Rocky Mountains, while endless prairies stretched to the east.

Guðmundur, who had become a handy carpenter, helped his father make further additions to the house. The boys slept in the loft, while Guðbjörg, Stephan's mother, shared the two north rooms with the twins. Of fair complexion, with silver-grey hair, she was an unobtrusive and gentle woman who never fussed about the opinions of others, but stuck firmly to her own. Endowed with an exceptional memory, she read extensively and told the children endless stories, and in later years the twins often read aloud for her. Guðbjörg was very capable at all sorts of handwork such as carding, spinning, knitting, crocheting collars and edgings, and weaving hats from sedge and hemp. The family always kept some sheep for wool, which was washed in the river and dried on the banks.[30]

It was, no doubt, unusual in the history of Canada that an unschooled farmer should have a study in his home. Stephan's study, which gave him some privacy for reading and writing, featured a bookcase made by a neighbour and a desk and chair constructed by long-time friend Jón Strong. There was also an armchair in which the poet could lean far back and relax. On the walls were framed pictures of Stephan and Helga, as well as portraits of some major Icelandic poets. On the desk, besides inkwells and pens, were books of poetry in English and German. "I think Stephan could not live if he did not have something to read," Helga wrote to her mother.[31] The couple subscribed to a variety of papers and journals, including the *Family Herald*, *Heimskringla*, and the women's periodical *Freyja*. They also received papers from Iceland, sometimes by the bundle, and a few liberal North American journals.[32]

Stephan occasionally invited friends into his study to smoke a cigar or pipe and drink a little whisky or a pint of beer while discussing poetry and politics. He seldom left home except to visit neighbours. Early in the summer of 1900, he wrote to a friend about a party at which he and some friends had greatly enjoyed themselves reciting difficult stanzas and robustly chanting old rhymes. "Then I went to Eldon's, had still more to drink and ate some ham. Afterward I made my way home in the pouring rain and darkness and crawled into bed all wet – inside and outside – but woke up the next morning as fresh and shiny as a new coin. I can still manage that!"[33]

Stephan and Helga Stephansson's family about 1905: Gestur, Jakob, and Guðmundur standing left to right; Baldur, Fanny, and Jenny seated, with Rósa in front.

Little Rósa, the youngest of the children, was everybody's darling. In the fall after she turned one year old, she could already walk a little and speak a bit. She was "active and very cheerful, rather pretty with grey-blue eyes and brown curly hair," Helga wrote to her mother. While teething, Rósa fell ill and developed a high fever and an upset stomach. Stephan feared she might have meningitis and both he and Helga were very worried, but the closest doctor was in Red Deer. They sent to Innisfail for medicine, but that did not work, so when Rósa had been ill for more than a week Stephan wrote a description of her illness in English and sent one of the boys riding as fast as he could to the doctor in Red Deer, some 15 miles away. After reading the description, the doctor said in English, "Your father is an educated man." "Far from that," the boy said, "just an unschooled farmer." "In spite of that, he is," the doctor insisted. "I can tell from his letter. No one could have written it but an educated man. It was just as if I could see the child with my own eyes." The doctor prepared a medication and the boy rushed home. Soon Rósa began to recover.[34]

After her recovery, Rósa thrived. Even as a small child she was smart and industrious. One Ash Wednesday, having been given to understand that all people should carry ash on Ash Wednesday, she took some ash from the stove and put it into her father's shoes. Stephan was not pleased, and he put her on his knee and explained very seriously that people should not do such things. He was never playful, Rósa later recalled, although he was always gentle in manner and well-known for his even temper.

Stephan was short of stature, slim, and slightly stooped. Dark-haired, now graying, and with a reddish moustache, he had a rather rugged face and a high forehead. His eyes "were blue, sharp, and deep, and when he smiled it was if they twinkled," Rósa said. While tending the animals and haying or harvesting in the fields, he worked quietly, sometimes reciting lines of poetry half aloud to himself. In winter, Stephan often wrote letters in the morning, then did the chores and retired to his study after meals to write and compose. Sometimes he would rush in from chores in order to jot down some lines before he forgot them. In the evening, he sat at his desk, and when it was cold outside he built a fire in the stove in the middle of the room. Rósa sometimes sneaked in and curled up in a dark corner, listening to her father compose poems.

Helga always got up first in the morning and brought fresh coffee to everyone. She was small of stature and fair in complexion, more temperamental than her husband, agile and exceptionally industrious. She loved music and had a good singing voice, and she had a habit of humming while working. When she became frustrated, Stephan would comment, "Don't worry, it will all end one way or another." Helga still had the sewing machine her father had given her in Dakota, and she and her daughters sewed and knitted continuously. They also milked the cows and tended the garden.

"Go make some coffee, Helga. A friend has come," Rósa often heard her father call. Neighbours on their way to town would stop by for coffee when they collected the mail or when they delivered it on their way home. Occasionally the whole Stephansson family went somewhere for a visit and stayed overnight, and friends such as Jónas Hunford, Jón Strong, Sigurður from Víðimýri, or Stephan's brother-in-law Kristinn would come for an evening social visit. Sometimes they sang Icelandic songs until the wee hours of the morning, and while Stephan was not a great singer, when he was a bit tight he sometimes sang the English spiritual "In the Sweet By and By".[35]

Stephan liked the independence that farming allowed him. The poem "Eftirköst" (Aftermath), a kind of verse-letter, describes his circumstances and his view of life. In the beginning, he says he is a farmer who depends totally on the sun and rain, not the whims of humans. "The direction of the blowing wind/is never in accordance with the moods of men." He does not worry about offending anyone. Apart from that, the poem is mainly a comparison between self-education and formal education. His own education, Stephan admits, was negligible compared to the highest. He is, nevertheless, able to define the classical unity of academic learning, working skills, and moral knowledge that ideally go hand in hand:

> *Your strength and spirit are educated*
> *If you can offer,*
> *Keen understanding, a skilful hand,*
> *A true and kind heart.*

According to Stephan, the best educated is the "most and best he was and did/which was proper for a good man." Schools fill heads with facts but "care little about the heart and the hand", so education is often uneven.

For Stephan, striving for knowledge was the key. In his own situation:

> *I managed to grasp,*
> *The crumbs that fell to me,*
> *While the tired one slept,*
> *And the cheerful one played.*

A line about work, derived from Emerson's philosophy and formulated by Stephan more than a decade earlier, also found its way into this poem. Self-education is work, yielding its own reward, one that replaces outdated religious doctrines.

> *If you desire to nurse*
> *The welfare of people,*
> *Do not hesitate to set your hand to it,*
> *The strongest prayer is work.*

The poem, obviously auto-biographical, creates the image of an independent and self-educated farmer who acquires knowledge as he works the land. The conclusion of the poem makes a strong social comment, the main objective of Stephan's poetry since he was first influenced by Realism in 1883.

> *There is little help in the one*
> *Who lives to hesitate.*
> *I love to touch everything*
> *And make it come alive.*[36]

Colourful Culture

"The British and their descendants cannot tolerate herds of ignorant foreigners beating them in the political arena."[37] Something akin to this was a Conservative election slogan in Manitoba in 1899, though possibly distorted by the Liberals when it was published in the Liberal paper *Lögberg*. A Canadian identity was forming, but one that successive Canadian governments nurtured within the folds of the British Empire during a time of unbridled imperialism. The sun never set on the British Empire, giving Britain and its Dominions, such as Canada, the conviction that the Anglo-Saxon race, society, and culture were superior to

A settlement poster from 1900, authorized by Clifford Sifton, Minister of the Interior, who welcomed hardy pioneers from Eastern Europe.

others. On another level, maintaining strong ties to Britain was seen by the government as necessary to balance the growing influence and power of the United States.

In 1896, a change in government brought Wilfred Laurier's Liberals to power, and Clifford Sifton, Minister of the Interior, opened Canada's immigration doors to some traditionally "unpreferred" countries. An active campaign to attract immigrants from Europe and the United States coincided with a shortage of unsettled arable land south of the border, and over the following two decades nearly a million people of diverse ethnic origins – Eastern Europeans, Scandinavians, British, Germans, and Austrians – arrived to homestead in Canada. Many Canadians of British origin regarded those from Eastern Europe as a threat to British culture and demanded that immigrants of 'lower' ethnic origin assimilate into mainstream British culture. Some politicians even opposed extending citizenship to those who could not read English. Across Western Canada, provincial Departments of Education insisted that only English be taught and spoken in schools. Some Anglo-Saxon Protestants even believed that in this young country, a strong superior race would fulfill God's intentions on earth, and several churches established missions among immigrant bloc settlements to both 'Christianize' and Anglicize the newcomers, these two elements being seen as one and the same.[38]

The Icelanders were in a rather good position in relation to other immigrant groups. As Nordic people had always been viewed as "desirable" immigrants, Icelanders were designated a 'preferred' class of settlers. They were also among the first ethnic groups to settle in Western Canada, where they had ample time to adapt. Icelanders generally seemed to have accepted their place within the dominant culture, but Stephan was of a different opinion. Shortly before the turn of the 20th century, he objected to an opinion expressed by his friend Ásgeir Líndal, who averred that the Chinese in British Columbia were a plague flooding the province, taking jobs from the locals. Stephan found it absurd to exclude the Chinese, who came "here to work for little money". They were not bothering anyone, "except doing the worst jobs for the worst payment." That was hardly too good for them, Stephan thought, but added that Icelanders should be ranked higher than the Chinese.[39]

In 1899 the settlers in the Hola district celebrated Icelandic Day in a bower constructed by the Hola School, which stood on the hill near Stephan's house. As usual, speeches were delivered and poetry was recited. It was customary to propose a toast, in prose or verse, to Iceland, Canada, Alberta, and even Icelanders in North America. Stephan made a speech on Iceland and recited a new poem, "Kanada" (Canada), in which he describes – from an Icelandic point of view – the dreams of a utopia in the far West, "as there was a reserve for prosperity/and freedom and humanity, all that is best." The final stanza expresses a sincere hope for Canada:

> *And tired human hope turns its eyes*
> *From the east, to dream of you.*
> *You proved good to all, who love you dearly,*
> *Who belong to you in pleasure.*
> *May everything come true and take root in you,*
> *Which the unsettled human spirit dreams best!*[40]

On August 2, 1902, Stephan raised this idea once again while speaking from the platform on the hill. Half the Icelanders in the settlement came to this celebration, as did a number of Norwegian and English neighbours. A merchant set up a stand to sell refreshments and one of Stephan's friends discreetly dispensed pints of beer in the schoolhouse cloakroom.

The speeches were of varying quality, some humorous, others long-winded. Stephan gave the toast to Canada, in which he likened the settlers to the grass and the leaves that whither and fall to the ground, providing nourishment for a new generation and thus maintaining the cycle of life. When the settlers eventually disappear beneath the turf, he said, they have contributed their share to the education and progress of coming generations.

Then a unique moment in Canadian literary history occurred when Stephan concluded his toast with a poem to Canada. In this poem he praises his adopted land's tolerance and diversity, then cautions against the tendency of the times to press everyone into the same mould, whether by direct force, money, or urban industrialization. This, he warned, would halt the progress of culture. People should not "foster a narrow-minded spirit/regarding world affairs and government of the nation –/ that drawback of the world's progress,/that most certain foreboding of mankind growing old." It would not improve life on earth if the shepherd, the pasture, and the herds grew "as in a factory". Then comes a beautiful wish for Canada: "We choose to be fostered by you, young continent,/every free nationality and versatile tongue,/every true word and living poem that people sing."

Stephan criticized nationalistic rivalry, pointing out the futility of quarrelling over which nationality is best since fools are in the majority anyway. In the end, all nationalities are of the same origin in the distant past. He advocated rekindling this ancient kinship in Canada and discouraged what he regarded as boot-licking in the new land by backbiting one's land of origin. In this he was alluding to some of his compatriots in the West who sometimes sought to aggrandize themselves at the expense of Iceland.

> *So, Canada, warm up in your bosom,*
> *The cooled relationship and praise of the fosterland.*
> *Be the most free, be loyal to young ideals,*
> *Be the homeland of every nationality and tongue!*
> *And though an intruding flatterer praises you too much,*
> *Thereby dishonouring his native land, do not believe him,*
> *For if he were tested, he would sell your honour for money,*
> *His horizon is a quick profit –*
> *The disposition that runs in the blood of assassins.*[41]

People of every origin contribute to the world's culture, Stephan said, and it is pointless to imagine that one nation is superior to others. It is precisely the differences between nations that are valuable as such, and those who are disloyal to their origins cannot be loyal to a new land. The poem concludes on this theme by referring to the fabled golden tablets found in the grass after Ragnarök, the world's end as recounted in Norse mythology. There, the tablets are symbols of rebirth, having withstood both fire and war. By analogy, Icelandic cultural memories are golden tablets symbolizing rebirth in the New World – a valuable contribution to the new Canadian nation.

Here, remarkably, was an Icelandic pioneer in a young country with few literary traditions of its own, speaking to a few compatriots and others who barely understood the language in which he spoke – openly challenging the presumed superiority of British culture and the current rise of nationalism. In his poem he depicts visions of the progress of mankind and an ideal of Canadian culture that resembles the multicultural policy officially adopted by the nation some 70 years later. The message was apparently well received by the audience. "This was a magnificent poem that 'Miss Canada' could well be proud of," Jóhann Björnsson of Tindastoll wrote excitedly in a newsletter to *Lögberg*.[42]

Modernity Arrives

The Icelanders in the settlement along the Medicine River were not isolated from the great influx of immigrants during the first decade of the new century. People of other origins – particularly Scandinavians and Americans – now settled in the neighbourhood. Icelanders, however, because they had homesteaded earlier, were in the lead in many respects and managed to maintain their ethnicity and solidarity. Rapid development on the western prairies went hand in hand with the rise of urban centres in the eastern provinces. Grain production increased, in part due to larger markets both in cities and abroad, and the prairies, in turn, became a market for industrial production from eastern centers. Capital now flowed into the country, largely from Britain, as there were ample opportunities for profitable investments.

Tindastoll Post Office, established in Jóhann Björnsson's home nine years earlier, was now moved to one of the stores on the banks of Medicine River five kilometres south of Stephan's farm, near the creamery. On December 5, 1901, Stephan carefully composed a petition to the provincial government, asking for bridge across the Medicine River. The 30 local farmers who signed it regularly put themselves in danger every time they crossed at the ford and they also incurred significant additional costs to ferry their cream across the river. These area residents volunteered to fell timber for the bridge and transport it to the ford by the creamery. The petition, written in excellent English, resulted in a bridge being built in March of 1902, before the ice melted from the river, and a second bridge was built across the Red Deer River between the settlement and Innisfail. In 1906 the rough road to Innisfail was raised, graveled, and ditched, making it a good wagon road. The settlement was becoming less isolated and more modernized in every way.

Jóhann Björnsson, Tindastoll postmaster, and his third wife, Sigurást Daðadóttir.

Stephan had been among the prime movers behind the initial establishment of the creamery and in 1902 he was active in having a larger creamery built. In 1903 a hardware store was established nearby, lots were surveyed, and the new village was given the name Markerville, in the honour of C. P. Marker, dairy commissioner for the North-West Territories. A blacksmith shop, a boarding house, a butcher shop, and a poolroom were also built, but it was the creamery that was the centre of the village. Prices of store goods dropped and cash from cream sales bolstered farm income in the area, including Stephan and Helga's. Milk was separated on the farms and the cream was then transported to town in containers, some with false bottoms containing ice. Every Monday, when farmers received their cream cheques, Markerville came to life. People of different nationalities met and exchanged news and gossip, picked up their mail, and did some shopping. In 1907 the community library was moved from Tindastoll to the Benediktson store in Markerville.

Farmers in the area also sold considerable quantities of pork and beef. In order to establish ownership of livestock, cattle were branded, and Stephan's brand was C6X. After the setbacks of frost during the first

The village of Markerville on the Medicine River

years, Stephan eventually succeeded in growing potatoes as well, and the acreage under cultivation increased. He was also the first to harvest a significant amount of grain, after years of experimenting on a small-scale, and like most farmers he kept draught horses and equipment for harvesting, as well as mowers and rakes. The few threshing machines in the district moved from farm to farm during the harvest.[43]

Despite increasing prosperity, Stephan and Helga's financial situation was always difficult, and it saddened them not to be able to offer their children more opportunities. The boys were not able to complete their formal education – though it is not known whether they were inclined to continue – and Baldur purchased his own land after the turn of the century. When Stephan turned 50, he wanted to reduce his chores so he could dedicate more time to reading and writing, but his circumstances did not permit this. There was usually a debt with the two merchants in Markerville, Johnson and Benediktson, and in 1902 the latter refused Stephan further credit because of an outstanding balance of $178.50 at the end of the year. In November of 1902 Stephan purchased some nails, mustard, rubber boots, painkiller, and an axe handle at Johnson's store, increasing his debt there to $37.10.[44]

Despite financial pressures, Stephan took on various community responsibilities. He served as treasurer of the Creamery Association and also conducted the local census. To do this he had to travel throughout the neighbourhood in all kinds of weather, for days at a time, and this took time from his chores and poetry as well as his other literary activities. He was paid for this work, however.

In 1904 the Hola School was rebuilt closer to Medicine River, just across from the home of Stephan's sister and her husband, Kristinn Kristinsson. As Markerville prospered, a school was also built there. Stephan served on the Hola School Board and he and Helga frequently boarded teachers at their home. Stephan's opinion of schools was ambiguous. While he admitted the necessity for formal education, he maintained that the initiative inherent in self-education was also necessary, and he believed that schools often had the effect of reducing "the spiritual independence of the people". Acquiring knowledge was important, although learning was "usually very slow, and for intelligent youngsters the waste of time in schools was almost unconscionable." In 1905 he wrote the poem "Barnaskólinn" (The Children's School), which suggested that the curious minds of children fared badly when subjected to pedantic facts and theories instead of an acknowledgment that "all life is in fact motion". "Do they do a disservice/.../exposing the intelligence of a child/to the glacier of creeds," he asks in the poem.[45] When little Rósa went to school for the first time, she was very shy and did not know a word of English. Stephan took her by the hand and led her down the path along the river to the new schoolhouse and commended her to the teacher. Then, she felt safe. The Stephansson children generally sought out their father when anything difficult came up in their studies.[46]

In 1905 Stephan and Helga's two oldest sons, Baldur and Guðmundur, were both married. On January 5, Guðmundur married Regina Strong in Innisfail, and in the evening there was a big celebration at the Stephansson home. Regina was the daughter of Stephan's talented friend and neighbour Jón Strong, the carpenter who had made some of the furniture in his study. Baldur married his cousin Sigurlína Bardal, the daughter of Helga's uncle Benedikt Bardal from Mjóidalur. Both young couples lived with Stephan and Helga for part of the first year, and Baldur later built a house nearby, from where he continued farming with Stephan.

Various organizations characteristic of North American society appeared in Markerville during those early years. Stephan was not interested in the International Order of Good Templars (IOGT), a temperance movement, but he did purchase a life insurance policy from an insurance society. In 1903 a community hall was built by the 'Fensala' Young People's Society, and the Johnson family formed a dance orchestra shortly after the turn of the century. Stephan and Helga's sons Guðmundur and Jakob later joined the Markerville Brass Band, established in 1907, and began attending weekly rehearsals in the schoolhouse.⁴⁷

The Alberta settlement's reputation for lack of religious belief was not entirely unfounded. Only 30 souls belonged to the congregation that hired a pastor for a month and then began collecting funds to hire a full-time minister. People outside the congregation also contributed, however, and in 1902 Reverend Pétur Hjálmsson arrived. At first he served the congregation on a part time basis, but in 1905 he was hired full time, and in 1907 a church was built in Markerville.

Reverend Pétur Hjálmsson (1863-1950) of Markerville and his wife, Jónína Jónsdóttir.

Reverend Pétur was then dismissed in 1909, ostensibly due to a lack of funds – though some said the real reason was the vanity of the parish leaders. Stephan, amused by these developments, commented that he and Reverend Pétur were the only disbelievers around, each in his own way. Reverend Pétur took up farming, doing some pastoral work in his spare time, and he remained in the settlement for the rest of his life. He was a straightforward, hot-tempered, fair, and dutiful man, but not a great theologian.

One possible explanation for Reverend Pétur's dismissal was a mounting disagreement in the Icelandic Synod between fundamentalists and the New Theologians. Stephan followed the dispute with interest, pleased that some of the radicalism of the Cultural Society in Dakota remained intact. Wherever some of its old influence survived, the fundamentalism of Reverend Jón Bjarnason seemed to give way.⁴⁸

Heather from Home and Belief in... Life

During the first years of the new century, Stephan's reputation grew both in Iceland and among Icelanders in North America. One Icelander wrote in *Lögberg* that he was "a fruit tree that had never been nurtured, although many enjoyed the fruits," adding that it had to be admitted that the fruits were meaty, if not always sweet. Guðmundur Friðjónsson, a rural poet in Iceland, wrote that Stephan was the greatest poetic craftsman in the Icelandic language and suggested that the Icelandic parliament offer him and his family a financial incentive to return home – and a salary as a resident poet in Iceland. "His kin is too good and precious to end up in the ocean of nations."[49]

Stephan, however, remained in the ocean of nations of the New World, faithful to his identity as a farmer. When asked by Jóhann Magnús Bjarnason to hurry a publisher in printing his first novel, he declined. "I guess this is a gentleman who would not care if a cowherd from Alberta is geeing him up," he wrote, surmising that the publisher was "trying to get rather good books, and that always brings a small blessing, next to having written a good book oneself."[50] Jóhann Magnús also encouraged Stephan to have this publisher produce a book of his own poems, suggesting that they would sell better than those of any other poet.

Stephan was gaining admirers everywhere. In the fall of 1902, a young man who was looking for lost sheep in Mjóidalur, the valley where Stephan had spent his last years in Iceland, picked a sprig of heather that he took home and sent to Stephan. "Dear friend," he wrote on December 2, "This little twig of heather enclosed is from Mjóidalur. It is meant to convey my heartfelt gratitude for your poems in *Öldin*, *Heimskringla*, and other publications. The valley of Mjóidalur is now abandoned, but the river still sings, 'To own the entire valley,/as the shepherd at home/ who herded sheep in summer.' Your friend, Sigurður Baldvinsson."[51]

This was the first letter Stephan received from an admirer and through the following months the heather nested in his mind while he cut firewood, tended cows, fed the pigs, and worked at the harvest. Stephan's reply to Sigurður, penned on his 50th birthday, October 3, 1903, later acquired the title "Lyng frá auðum æskustöðvum" (Heather from the Deserted Home of Youth). It begins with a winter image of the poet's home in Alberta, where life is in the fetters of sleep during the long night, "the multi-voiced brook .../lay frozen, tongue-tied," and the mind is bedridden so poems freeze on the lips. Then the sprig of heather arrives with "a sigh of life from the far north", "from a heath where sand and snow blew/with memories of youth, my playground, my first poems". Evocative of youthful hopes and longings, the heather draws the poet's mind back to Mjóidalur where silence and emptiness now prevail. Stephan thinks fondly of the sprig of heather growing back in Iceland, resisting the life-threatening sands of erosion. Rhyme and alliteration will not revive dying vegetation, but the rocks resound with their eternal message: those who are at work now cannot break the curse of destruction; their minds are set on profit. "But the time will come when everyone will evaluate his life and work/in relation to the needs of ages, not annual profits."[52] The last stanza describes a future vision of the worker cultivating the desert that is his inheritance. The progress of the homeland is his legacy and the hope of immortality is hidden in the growth.

The sprig of heather is symbolic of human actions that are tiny when measured against eternity, but carry hope for the future, just as when a single worker cultivates the land and makes deserts habitable. In this poem Stephan is developing the idea that a life's work is best measured against the yardstick of the future. Growth and the work of the settler and farmer are symbols of progress that can only be comprehended in the light of the ages.

Although Stephan had rejected God early on, he nevertheless spent his entire life wrestling with Him and searching for a substitute. It was easy to renounce God when this action was primarily a rejection of dogmatic Synods or pastors. It was more difficult to dismiss man's age-old quest to understand existence, life, and death. Stephan was faced with finding new answers to questions that Christianity had ostensibly answered about both earthly and eternal life.

This struggle is obvious in many of Stephan's commemorative poems, which are devoid of any mention of God. Many regarded this a serious flaw. Instead, he depicted those lasting values he believed could soothe the grief of survivors.

In 1901 Stephan composed the final lines of a poem to his son Jón, who had died in Dakota in 1887. He claimed that he had long ago become reconciled with death, the lord of the "land of evening shadows". He then echoes a concept from his poem on the prostitute Ragnheiður, expressing devotion to the ground in which the bones of Icelanders lie buried. The poem includes the same refrain as the poem on the twig of heather: hope of immortality lives in growth itself – an idea fully developed by 1904. In the first years of settlement, Stephan had praised the wilderness in its pristine state, capturing nature with his poetic language and embracing the vitality of the virgin land. Now, in a second settlement, work, cultivation, and the nurturing of culture transformed Canada into the motherland of those who were raised there.

Sigurbjörn Jóhannsson, a poor but outspoken poet in Iceland and later in the Argyle Settlement in Manitoba, was well known on both sides of the ocean. He emigrated at age 50 in 1889, with a wife and two young children, a four-year-old son who died soon after arrival in Canada and a daughter, Jakobína, who later became a well-known poet. After settling in Argyle, he was called upon to recite a poem at almost every celebration in the area. An admirer of Stephan and especially of "Á ferð og flugi", Sigurbjörn saw his own collection of poetry published in 1902. In the summer of 1903, however, he fell ill and died.

Stephan's poem in memory of Sigurbjörn is to some extent a self-

Sigurbjörn Jóhannsson, pioneer and poet in the Argyle Settlement of Manitoba and father of poet Jakobína Johnson, later of Seattle.

portrait, in that both lived under similar conditions. In this tribute, Stephan likens poetry to a farmer's cultivation of virgin land. Verses help people get through adversities, he states, warming and stimulating in cold and weariness. The poem is "a harvest of blessings/in a home that did not own much," Stephan wrote. The power of poetry is integrated with tools and labour. "And did your song not create joy in toil/urging your soft scythe onward?" The metaphorical union of poetry and work deepens in reference to the indigent farmer's pursuit of knowledge. Like Stephan, Sigurbjörn spent wakeful nights composing poetry, grasping fragments of knowledge with great determination under adverse circumstances. He also expressed opposition to various widely accepted beliefs and certain authority, but he was at his best as a pioneer taming virgin land with the rhythm of poems that embraced life and work. The strings of the poet's harp reach from Iceland to the West where poets settle the land in their own way, their poems merging with labour and the soil:

> *And you carved alliteration onto the field and oak*
> *With the complexion of people and earth*
> *And you composed dedications for gatherings and games*
> *And you sang at the burial of the settler.*[53]

Around this time, Stephan also composed a poem of consolation to his friend Jón Strong entitled "Í rökkrinu" (In the Dusk), in memory of Jón's wife, Helga Davíðsdóttir. "In the dusk, I invite myself to sit by you/ and sing for you, if you will listen," he wrote, conceding that he knows it is of little help for one mourning through long, wakeful nights. No words touch the innermost strings and the bitterest sorrow finds no expression, but, Stephan continues, she is not dead who is "integrated/in the lives of surviving friends." The graves of beloved friends and family evoke grateful memories of their work. Little by little, a worldly idea of eternity emerges, the work is delivered to the future:

> *From the little tree, the only child of the wilderness,*
> *Grew a fully wooded mountain slope in the spring –*
> *In the same way the hope-grown effort of man is maintained,*
> *It was not taken to the grave.*
> *His single trail becomes a beaten track,*
> *Although the ages fill his footsteps with snow.*[54]

The home of neighbours Jón and Helga Strong, whose daughter Regína became the wife of Guðmundur Stephansson.

The "hope-inspired effort of man" that survives the grave parallels the hope of immortality hidden in the growth in Stephan's poem about the sprig of heather. By regarding work in the context of eternity, Stephan gives it religious value. Work, the strongest form of prayer, acquires new significance in the context of the land and poetry. Life's labour is consummated in sowing and reaping the harvest. These two factors, work and permanence, replace the Mosaic Law and redemption that Stephan had learned about in Bishop Balle's catechism long before. Creative work is the good that man should pursue; its fruit is a better future. Such an idea could only occur in the poet's mind through contemplation and dialogue about religion. Stephan's conclusion contrasts with the anxiety over the lack of a foothold in modern life that was emerging in literature and philosophy at that time.

A few years later, Stephan wrote to a friend that he had faith in life and humans, but thought less about God and Heaven. "Life is eternal. As far as can be seen, it existed and will continue to exist. It matters in every way that it will fare well. What an individual has in common with others will survive, although he dies." Stephan did not want the "erroneous scales of theology" to be the only measure of human value.[55]

When Stephan's mother-in-law died on April 16, 1904, he wrote the memorial poem "Sigurbjörg Stefánsdóttir". Composed in the same spirit as "Í rökkrinu", this poem recalls the journey of the family "from east to west in settling the world/with our cradles and graves." Although that journey was difficult, it is a consolation when their kin began to make their mark on the land. The scythe and rake are not consigned to the grave though gaps appear in the family ranks. The land has been settled for the next generation and on that land the work of the settlers continues.[56]

A similar – though more political idea – appears in "Landnámskonan" (The Settler Woman), written by Stephan late in 1904. In this poem, which is a tribute to Margrét Björnsdóttir, the wife of Jóhann Björnsson of Tindastoll, Stephan depicts various people and images of nature in the settlement. Together, the settlers cultivate both the land and the community with their labour. Nobody listens to the poet who "walks in an autumn night reciting his poems/at unknown, humble graves," Stephan says. Then he raises his voice. "But you should know, world, that here are those/who kept you to the homeland when you needed it most/while the big heroes of history slept." The achievements of "great men" often damage people and nations, Stephan says, but each man's life is a benefit "if he leaves behind in the open land/a needed piece of work, a beautiful thought." He is not writing poetry for fame, he adds, only to ask the future whether the energies of the people "who turned the wasteland to a motherland/the empty house to a home" were spent in vain.[57]

God and Heaven remain absent from Stephan's commemorative poems written in 1903-1904. Instead of happiness in Heaven, a concept of worldly eternity is expressed. By cultivating the soil, the settlers prepare the land for new life on earth, and poets intertwine verse and land. This consolation serves the same purpose as Heaven and a life of virtue in traditional Lutheran poems. Stephan had long contemplated this idea, which had matured in the face of nature's destructive forces, the erosion of the Mjóidalur Valley, and the passing of the older generation of settlers.

Far Traveller

By 1904 Stephan had lived in the Markerville settlement for some 15 years. His circumstances were changing and the influx of settlers heralded an economic boom on the prairies. Stephan worked hard at farming, writing poetry, rebuking the world's authorities, praising nature, and forging universal ideas that he substituted for old religious ones. He also wrote on Canadian life, striving for harmony with his adopted home. Nevertheless, Iceland remained the focal point in his mind.

On Icelandic Day in Alberta in 1904, Stephan was the master of ceremonies, and in a short but powerfully-worded opening speech he recalled his youth while expressing hopes for the future. Though this speech was short, it was among his most remarkable, as he concluded with two poems – the first of which was destined to become his best-known poem. Recalling folktales of trolls who call to each other across oceans and lands, Stephan suggests that the ancestors had "spun these stories out of their wishes for a telephone line and express-news." He then refers to Iceland as the Lady of the Mountains (a national symbol) and Canada the Lady of Snow. At present, he points out, it takes almost a month for the two to exchange greetings, but once the radiogram is up and running, they will be able to communicate back and forth in a moment. The Lady of Snow then addresses the Lady of the Mountains, a little high-toned due to her young age. She states that Icelanders in North America are much more prosperous than those in the old country and claims to have made them rich, "great intellectuals and great politicians." The Lady of the Mountains thanks her for the news, but reminds her that she had herself nurtured and educated these children in their youth. They are her contribution to the world and Canada has received capable, fully mature people to exploit her natural resources. Although they cannot boast much education, the "Icelandic lack of education" is perhaps not much worse than the product of Canadian public schools.

Then Stephan read what was to become his best-known poem, "Úr Íslendingadags ræðu" (From a Speech on the Icelandic Day), composed in an exotic metre. "Though you were to travel far,/and traverse every land,/your mind and heart would still bear/ your homeland's mould." Waterfalls and mountain slopes grace the future lands of the well-travelled and broad-minded man. The Icelander brings these dreamlands with him; they are a part of his being and he gives from the wealth of this land within, setting an Icelandic mark on every place he visits. The qualities of this dreamland, however, are paradoxical, perhaps ironic, as they include both "cliffs grown with flowers,/every glacier cap warm."[58]

"Langförull" (Far Traveller), as Stephan later called this poem, is only a part of his speech. Next he turns his attention to the fosterland that lies before the audience and reads another poem with no particular title, not as deeply significant, but in a pure Icelandic metre. In it he describes the broad western view of the mountains, the mild weather, the forests and hayfields. This is the land, with its beautifully green, sunny fields, on which Icelanders are to set their mark.[59] Stephan then returns to the idea expressed in his address to Canada composed two years earlier. The work and culture of the Icelandic settlers are golden tablets in the Canadian grass, signifying rebirth and eternal life in a new world.

At the end of this mentally turbulent year, these core ideas re-appear in simple, lyrical lines in the poem "Fósturlandið" (The Fosterland), in which Stephan applies to himself his concept of eternity, the merging of poetry, work, and the soil.

> *The land, my work is dedicated to,*
> *The cradle of my children!*
> *I have inscribed, in a song and a line,*
> *My poem in your grass –*
> *Later, over my head,*
> *You will compose your grass!*

The poem is a tribute to the fosterland. He repeats the first two lines at the end, changing only one word, stretching the poem further into the future of their descendants:

> *The land, my work is dedicated to,*
> *The cradle of my descendants!*[60]

Chapter 11

An Act of Friendship

Animals Small and Large

One day, after leading little Rósa by the hand around the farmyard to inspect her "farm animals" – ankle and leg bones representing real animals – Stephan took his little daughter into his study, set his pipe aside, moved some papers out of the way, and sat her on his knee. While she fiddled with his stubbly whiskers, he composed a poetic report on her "farm", a rhyming-letter from Rósa to her sisters, who were staying at their brother Baldur's house. The letter related good grazing for the ankle and leg bones, who were growing fat under Rósa's care, but it was going less well with the dolls, who were naughty and always fighting.[1]

Such imaginary animals of bone traditionally prepared children for more demanding work later in life. As mixed farming required the participation of all, every family member owned his or her livestock and even the children helped with chores. The youngest were sometimes given the job of placing poison bate in gopher holes, but Stephan was an animal lover and even when eliminating magpies he could only destroy their nests. He fed the snow buntings in winter and often tolerated the encroachment of the neighbours' livestock. He also found it hard to kill animals, even chickens, so Helga had to do that.[2]

The family always kept some horses, and Stephan was especially fond of Tóta, the mare he rode while composing "Sumarkvöld í Alberta" (Summer Night in Alberta). When she died, he wrote the poem "Útigöngubikkjan" (The Nag in the Wild) in her memory, saying that he no longer felt as free to travel. In this poem he describes Tóta's preference for graz-

Stephan G. Stephansson in his fifth decade.

ing in the open rather than eating hay from a manger, and the gleam in her eye inherited from wild broncos. Perhaps he recognized something of himself in her character, as something wild within him yearned to escape the crowd and all modern amenities, longing instead to engage with the raw elements. Tóta was a good saddle horse, but the most obvious parallel between the two of them was their common desire "to live and enjoy/the home-made arts" rather than dreaming of fame.[3]

In the spring of 1904 Stephan wrote a verse-letter to his friend Sigurður from Víðimýri, asking him to do something he could not do for himself. "Could you come, dear friend/to castrate my calves?" Some men were rough with their knives, but Stephan believed Sigurður could do the job without causing unnecessary pain. The letter turned into a description of snow thawing in the mountain valleys.[4]

Stephan empathized with wild animals no less than domestic ones. In the fall of 1903 he wanted to save two ducklings that he found on the river ice after the other birds had flown south. "Yesterday one of them got out. I could not find him anywhere. Stupidity will kill him," he wrote in a letter.[5]

Three years later, the poet predicted a hard winter, and he was right. The winter of 1906-07 was one of the harshest in recorded history – so cold that men could barely do their chores and cut firewood. Farmers and ranchers alike ran short of hay by mid-winter and cattle froze to death by the hundreds. There were rumours that some herds of over a thousand head were lost, but Stephan did not lose any livestock.[6]

By the end of this winter, Stephan felt he had no endurance left for hard work, and in a letter he admitted that he was now doing hardly any work. "I sit indoors and starve myself to keep my health, but I hope to crawl out of my lair in the spring, a bit skinny and ragged, and as eager as the bears." Stephan's health was so poor around this time that it occurred to him that this might be the end. He pondered his worldly circumstances, realizing that each man can only make a small contribution to the future. His farm was large enough and he had managed thus far through hard work, but he was far from wealthy and he worried about arranging his estate in such a way that his children would enjoy better conditions than he had at their age. Had he been alone, his situation would not have worried him, as he was accustomed to an austere lifestyle and could always manage. He hoped to be in a better position next year,[7] however, and he had some reasons to be hopeful.

Eggert and Rögnvaldur: Ideas of Publication

After the publication of *Á ferð og flugi*, people either supported Stephan or turned against him. Some idolized his genius, although they did not necessarily agree with everything he wrote, while others faulted him in every possible way – not least for his obtuse language and poetic form. There was a growing school of thought that Stephan was primarily a poet of extreme ideas and complicated imagery, and there was some truth in that, especially as there was almost no tradition for philosophical idiom in Icelandic poetry.

Eggert Jóhannsson, a great admirer, had published Stephan's first "serious" poem in *Heimskringla*. Among the pioneers of Icelandic journalism in North America, Eggert was a self-educated intellectual who had edited *Heimskringla* until 1897, when he began working at the Manitoba Land Titles office. This was a demanding but poorly paid job, so it was necessary for him to supplement his income by editing and writing. Very straightforward in both his admiration and criticism of Stephan's work, he found "Transvaal" a magnificent poem despite the fact that he disagreed with the stance Stephan had taken.

The poet's friend and advocate Eggert Jóhannsson and his wife, Elín.

Eggert regarded Stephan as the spokesman of the North American Icelandic outlook that was so different from the Copenhagen-dominated ideas prevalent in intellectual life back in Iceland. Stephan was the only Icelander in the West whom intellectuals in both Iceland and Copenhagen respected. "Those who know more than the majority *cannot* avoid acknowledging it, while those who know less but are more boastful do not dare to avoid it."[8] Eggert therefore asked Stephan to write an article in defense of Jóhann Magnús Bjarnason following the appearance of a negative review by a Copenhagen intellectual. Stephan replied that he never wrote reviews, with the exception of an article he had written about Jóhann Magnús' book of verse in 1898, but he wrote Jóhann Magnús directly to tell him that he was much more popular than he himself and had fewer enemies. Stephan pointed out that few in the West wanted his books of poetry. From 200 copies of *Á ferð og flugi*, he had earned only $5 and 25 copies, most of which he had given away. Papers and publishers lived by authors' unpaid work, he concluded.[9]

Stephan's own situation with regard to creative work was difficult. While he seldom had the opportunity to perfect his poems as he would have liked, poetry was the art best suited for a farmer as he could compose and recite while doing his chores. Originally he had intended to write stories, but his time to write was scarce and fragmented. "Narrative vibrancy" quickly faded and new stories pushed older ones aside before they were written down. Gradually, Stephan had accepted this.[10]

Stephan continued to make new friends. In the spring of 1904 he received a letter from a young man named Rögnvaldur Pétursson, with an awkward apology for imposing on such a famous man – and a request that he write an introductory poem for a new Unitarian periodical named *Heimir*. Rögnvaldur, born in Iceland in 1877, had grown up in North Dakota and studied theology at Harvard. He was now pastor of the Icelandic Unitarian congregation in Winnipeg.

Stephan cheerfully responded that he celebrated every new publication attempting to broaden the public's outlook, whether he agreed with it or not. The most important thing, he felt, was that publications stimulated people's minds while remaining sincere and free from rigid rhetoric. He would contribute a poem to *Heimir*, he said, but he did not have any suitable ones at the moment and could not compose upon request, so he would have to find his own approach to the subject. Apart from that, he was "busy with farm chores" and losing his stamina for work.[11]

The answer nevertheless pleased Rögnvaldur, who replied that he would welcome a poem whenever it was ready. Stephan then sent him "Landnámskonan" (The Settler Woman) in the autumn of 1904, apologizing for the fact that it was a commemorative poem and hardly revolutionary. Everything in it, however, challenged generally accepted views, he pointed out, adding that he preferred that his revolutionary poems be published in the "most acrid reactionary papers" rather than liberal papers, as the healthy have no need of a doctor.[12] Rögnvaldur Pétursson soon became one of Stephan's closest friends and remained so for the rest of his life.

Shortly after this friendly correspondence, one of Stephan's other friendships dissolved. Early in 1906 he sent a poem to *Heimskringla*, but editor Baldvin L. Baldvinsson printed only parts of it, making negative insinuations about of the unprinted stanzas. Stephan was enraged. Baldvin had for a long time sent him the paper free of charge, and as editor he had accused the Liberal Party that Stephan supported "of theft, betrayal, and lies 52 times in one year," Stephan wrote in *Lögberg*. It was Baldvin's despicable method that offended Stephan, who for years had sent poems to Baldvin and other editors, usually upon request, not caring in the least whether they were returned. He understood that editors had to strike a balance in the content of their papers between honesty and profit, and he did not want his poems to compromise the popularity of the papers. As far as he was concerned, Baldvin could have done anything, but to cut up his poem and make insinuations about what was omitted was unforgivable. Stephan had trusted that editors would not do such a thing. He did not mind if *Heimskringla* was nothing but reactionary rubbish, but he no longer wanted to rely on the integrity of Baldvin as editor.[13] After this incident, Stephan began dealing with Reverend Stefán Björnsson, editor of *Lögberg*, who was a distant relative. Even though they disagreed on religious matters, Stephan found the minister direct and honest in his dealings with writers.

Baldvin L. Baldvinsson, immigration agent and editor of Heimskringla*, was elected to Manitoba's Legislature as a Conservative MLA.*

Around Christmas of 1905, Eggert Jóhannsson suggested the possibility of raising funds to publish Stephan's poems. Stephan wrote back immediately, stating that he was far from able to fund any publication. The worst thing about the lack of money, he wrote, was not being able to show more support for people or causes he cared about. His poverty, he admitted, was self-inflicted. "If I had applied the little intelligence I have to earning some money, as much as the laws allow, I imagine that I could be equal to the average apathetic miser."[14] Now that he was being offered the support he had wanted to give others, he found it hard to accept. Eggert's letter forced him to think seriously about things he had previously brushed aside. Obviously he found it difficult to accept assistance, but apart from that he was rather dissatisfied with much of his poetry as he had not been able to fine tune his work.

Stephan believed that poets should stand in the vanguard against vice, which was in part why he infuriated some people. This stance also gained him friends, however, and that meant much to him. He therefore wanted to accept this friendly gesture of support, recognizing that it would be loutish of him to turn down such an unselfish offer. He could accept a voluntary contribution without any middlemen, but not that which is "cadged out with cake gatherings, box socials, and such kind of trickery; I detest it." He could accept payment for what he had written, but not for poetry still to be composed. Although Stephan doubted his own popularity and found it problematic not to be able to publish his own work, he liked Eggert's idea. He also knew that without being a member of any political party it would be almost impossible to leverage support for publication.[15]

Stephan's response was not sufficiently straightforward, so Eggert repeated the question. Concerned that his enemies might make use of his answer, Stephan replied in confidence that he could not refuse Eggert's offer because he was among the freethinkers whom public leaders had always slandered. "Every public tribute to such men is a defeat for anti-liberalism." If this offer was a spontaneous tribute to him as a freethinker and a dissident, he could justify accepting it. He could not refuse it due to his eccentric determination to be independent of everyone.

Many had encouraged Stephan to publish his poetry in the past, but he had never had time to prepare his poems for print – nor could he think of his friends working for him unpaid. He told Eggert that he would "need a whole year, with nothing else demanded of me. Life has loaded me with all the work I can handle, and my neighbours bring all their correspondence and social affairs, which I cannot refuse. Now I lack the strength to work and must spare myself. I am still tied to a rather large farm and my family, and other challenges often arise. Of course I could have spent my few leisure hours compiling what I have already done instead of writing something new, but that has never been my inclination. I have to grow still older for that."

This explains why Stephan had not published his own work. He was exceptionally prolific and it would take a year just to edit his poems – something nobody had the means to sponsor. He would therefore wait. "Sometime, when I grow old – and I intend to become old – I will get my finances to a point where I can live for about a year like those who "neither sow nor harvest", and then I will go through my rubbish heap of poetry and polish it as I would like it to be when I depart this life of mine."

Stephan had now defined what he needed: money and a year's time to rework his poems.[16]

Reconciliation with Reverend Friðrik

"Far be it from me to endorse Guðmundur Friðjónsson's absurd opinion that Stephan G. Stephansson is our greatest poet," wrote Reverend Friðrik Bergmann in 1902. "That would make life tedious and signal the end of Icelandic poetry."[17] Stephan and Friðrik had known each other ever since they studied together at Halldórsstaðir in Iceland in 1873, and they had even worked together in a lumber camp in Wisconsin. Their paths had diverged, however, when Friðrik, as a pastor in Dakota, had joined Reverend Jón Bjarnason and the Icelandic Synod, a move that Stephan strongly opposed. He had subsequently attacked Reverend Friðrik in a satirical poem.

Reverend Friðrik Bergmann now lived in Winnipeg and was more liberal, while Reverend Jón Bjarnason had become ever more rigid in religious matters. In 1906 Friðrik relayed to Stephan an offer from Ólafur Thorgeirsson, an Icelandic printer in Winnipeg, to publish his poems. He also echoed Guðmundur Friðjónsson's proposal from 1902 that Icelanders raise money to invite Stephan to Iceland. Stephan suspected that Friðrik was attempting "with dexterity to dispatch every issue he did not like."[18] Reverend Friðrik then wrote Stephan directly in the summer of 1906, saying that he hoped Stephan "did not want to avoid the pastor" and requesting a poem for his new periodical, *Breiðablik*. Stephan replied in a friendly manner, saying that he could distinguish between class and individual, and adding that he believed Friðrik was a practical person rather than an obedient partisan, and thus able to edit a broad-minded paper. Since Reverend Friðrik was now regarded a disbeliever by the most stringent members of the Lutheran Synod, Stephan rather wanted to give him a hand,[19] and the two now became allies – a great surprise for those who believed Friðrik was the pastor in "Á ferð og flugi". Reverend Friðrik had found himself increasingly at odds with Reverend Jón and the Synod's orthodox beliefs, and perhaps he now aligned himself more with freethinkers for the same reason that Stephan had rejected his religion in Dakota – Reverend Jón Bjarnason's dictatorship. It was therefore natural for Stephan to support Reverend Friðrik Bergmann in this struggle.

Eggert Jóhannsson, on the other hand, disapproved of Stephan's new friendship with Reverend Friðrik, whom freethinkers regarded with suspicion. They considered Reverend Friðrik as polite and peaceful on the surface, but capable of falseness to achieve his ends if necessary. It would be easy "to bridle and lead when everyone had learned that it is shameful to cast a stone and disrespectful to speak up." Eggert suspected that Reverend Friðrik was befriending Stephan because the poet had become so respected that he found advantage in a friendship.[20]

Rev Friðrik Bergmann, pastor in North Dakota for 15 years, moved to Winnipeg in 1902.

In the spring of 1907 Stephan wrote a long essay in *Baldur*, a newspaper published at Gimli, Manitoba. In this article he defended *Vafurlogar*, Reverend Friðrik's collection of essays on disputed religious issues. He also squared up his former dealings with Reverend Friðrik, acknowledging Friðrik's unfavorable review of *Á ferð og flugi* and some other incidences of disagreement between them. Reverend Friðrik, grateful, said Stephan understood his beliefs better that any other critic. He admitted, however, that he did not agree with everything that Stephan wrote and he disputed Stephan's claim that his negative review of *Á ferð og flugi* had been written to please Einar Hjörleifsson.[21]

Oddly enough, Einar Hjörleifsson travelled to Alberta and met Stephan the following autumn. Stephan received him graciously despite Einar's having been rather opposed to him over the years. Impressed by Stephan's exceptional personal affection and intelligence, Einar concluded that it was a shame that such a great Icelandic poet had to dig in the mud at the foot of the Rocky Mountains. He reported that Stephan's neighbours were fond of him and that some of them knew much of his poetry by heart. He also stated that while Stephan had kept his personal circumstances private, it was evident that he would like to visit Iceland, though it might prove difficult for him to return.

"I Will Sort Out My Heap of Rubbish"

Late in the summer of 1906, in a letter to Eggert Jóhannsson, Stephan outlined the circumstances under which he could foresee the publication of his poetry. "If I live long enough to be able to set aside all worldly worries for something like a half or a whole year, I would be able to sort out my heap of rubbish. I cannot do it any faster, as much as I would like to." He then suggested that if publishers could offer him $20 a month for a year, so that he could prepare his poems for printing, he would be able to manage. "That is to say, I would sell my life's work in return for one year's support."

Stephan clearly felt it was unlikely that this would happen,[22] but Eggert Jóhannsson immediately began organizing the fund raising. First he contacted Skafti and Magnús Brynjólfsson, Stephan's old friends from the Dakota Cultural Society, for their help in raising some money to relieve Stephan of his chores long enough to prepare every poem he wanted to publish, as well as pay the costs of publication. They calculated the cost for 2500 or 3000 copies of a 400-page book at about $1500, and if pledges for this amount could be secured, the plan called for the formation of a supervisory committee consisting of two men from Dakota and two from Winnipeg. Those who put up money for the project would be repaid, with interest, as soon as the book began to sell, and Stephan alone would enjoy any profit after the advance was paid off.

Eggert then asked Stephan if he would be prepared to deliver his manuscript in monthly installments sent in the same sequence as the poems were to appear in print. That way the printer could begin setting the type sooner. If Stephan needed time to think this over, Eggert suggested that the most important information for the committee was the number of manuscript pages Stephan anticipated.

At this point Stephan revealed to Eggert that Reverend Friðrik Bergmann had made an offer on behalf of publisher Ólafur Thorgeirsson, but that he had rejected it because he preferred to avoid entanglements with the church. Eggert was relieved on behalf of the freethinkers, as they were the critical voice of Icelandic society, though they did not have as much money. The Synod only professed to have a monopoly on the truth, Eggert continued. They had the money, the manpower, and an entire hierarchy behind them, but it would have been intolerable to have the pillars of the Lutheran Synod publish Stephan's poetry and then receive credit for taking the initiative. They would then be able to claim that Stephan's allies had been too feeble to publish his poems.

In mid-September Stephan suggested that a $500 debenture or insurance policy be set up so backers would not risk anything if he passed away. The backers of the debenture would then own publishing rights, and whether the poems were published right away or not, they would have the manuscripts as collateral. Stephan preferred that his poems be printed in Iceland, in a series of small booklets, as they would sell better there and would be less expensive in that format. *Á ferð og flugi*, for example, had sold out long ago in Iceland, but was still available in Bardal's bookstore in Winnipeg.[23] Eggert, however, was more ambitious. He felt that two large hard cover volumes would be much better than a number of small booklets that would inevitably be printed on various kinds of paper, rendering the final product mottled and unattractive when bound together.

The unselfish motive of Eggert and his associates was merely to see Stephan's poetry printed in appropriate form, and in order to make this happen many of them undertook a large amount of work for which they received no recompense. An exceptional enterprise and a great gesture of integrity,

Stephan's loyal friend and supporter Magnús Brynjólfsson was instrumental in backing the publication of the first volumes of Andvökur.

this initiative was headed by Skafti Brynjólfsson of Winnipeg, who together with Stephan had been a leader of the Cultural Society in Dakota. He managed the business affairs and oversaw fundraising, while Eggert took on editorial arrangements with Stephan. Magnús Brynjólfsson, Skafti's brother, raised money in Dakota. The committee regarded it unwise to accept large contributions, but $15 was set as a minimum and no maximum was set on donations. No interest would be paid. The organizers estimated that one third of the cost would be sufficient to launch the project, even though they did not know the exact length of the manuscript or the final cost of printing. It was decided that the committee would purchase Stephan's manuscript for $500, which was the amount he needed to hire a farmhand so he could work exclusively on his manuscript. He would retain the rights to the poems in later editions, however, and would receive any profit from the publication after costs were paid. Magnús Brynjólfsson, an attorney, drafted the contract, and among those who joined the committee were Jónas Hall, Stephan's brother-in-law Jón Jónsson, Gardar entrepreneur Eiríkur Bergmann, and Hannes Marinó Hannesson, a grandson of Stephan's uncle Hannes.

The project proceeded and by December of 1906 Stephan counted over 11,000 edited lines of poetry ready for publication, not including "Á ferð og flugi", a few polemic verses, and some new poems. The committee decided to include the year each poem was composed. Stephan, for his part, requested some dictionaries as he acknowledged his limitations when it came to standardized spellings and that he often strained the flexibility of the language.

In January of 1907 Stephan received his first payment. Leafing through his poems and contemplating their wider context within his own experience and philosophies, he sorted and selected "everything that somehow touches upon the history of our way of thinking, reflects the age we live in, or shows my methods of composing and thinking". He wanted to omit doggerel and satirical personal verses.

By the end of January, Stephan had finished organizing the contents of the proposed volumes. He found poetry books arranged chronologically tedious, so he divided his poems into seven thematic groups: "From Without Foundation" (single stanzas, humour and proverbial poems), "Into the Open Air" (the seasons), "In Memory of Land and People" (patriotic and occasional poems), "Seeing at Home" (on currents of ideas), "Out in the Open" (descriptions of nature), "From Tales and Stories" (from the old sagas), and "Dreaming of Events" (historical poems on contemporary events, imagined or true).[24]

In March Stephan signed the contract and accepted the remainder of the money. Now his only worry was whether he could actually fulfill his obligations in such a way that the publishers would avoid financial loss. Over the next several months he worked on his poems, trimming and reviewing them from an external standpoint, as if they were by someone else. Working in isolation was difficult. He lacked dictionaries and he wished he had access to other poets with whom he could discuss single words and lines. He also found it difficult to decide which poems to select and which to reject. Some poems must be included, as they were important documents from the past even if they might not be particularly good work. He was well aware that many thought his vocabulary and syntax were terse, but sometimes that was intentional. "There are two approaches to an artful form, to weave the words together as lightly and softly as threads of silk, or to chisel them together, strong and majestic like basalt pillars." He had tried both ways in his poems, he said. Some stanzas, however, were rather like heaps of rocks, bearing the marks of his attempts to put complicated thoughts into words and phrases, but unpolished for lack of time.[25]

When Stephan delivered his manuscript late in the summer of 1907, it was clear that the poems would fill two volumes. He dedicated the first volume to The Cultural Society and the second to those "who had a kind word for my poems".[26] Eggert Jóhannsson, Rögnvaldur Pétursson, Skafti Brynjólfsson, and Kristján Stefánsson scrutinized the manuscript carefully as they found it incredible that Stephan had achieved so much in such a

Skafti Brynjólfsson of Winnipeg, another key supporter of the poet and the publication of the anthology Andvökur.

short time. There had to be some faults. They noticed that Stephan had left out certain poems and sometimes they felt Stephan's refinements were to the worse. Stephan replied to these comments in letters, explaining his changes, expressing some views on poetry, and revealing which poems were his favourites.

The publishers sometimes remarked that they found his phrasing unclear. Stephan conceded the point, explaining that sometimes when he tried to clarify wording, the thought tended to slip away. The publishers also wanted him to include some of his polemic poems, but Stephan replied that if they wanted to write an overview of his life, they could include such poems there. Shortly after the New Year of 1908, he wrote his last letter on the subject, saying that he would now make no further changes. He would love to spend time debating the finer points so that he could prove his point (for he felt that he was right in every instance), but he pointed out that it was futile trying to resolve these issues via the mail.[27]

A new problem arose when the text was almost finalized. The publishers wanted good photographs of Skagafjörður and the Rocky Mountains, but all attempts to procure suitable photos failed. They then asked Stephan to describe the mountains in such a way that an Icelandic artist in Winnipeg could paint a picture. Stephan wrote a long description of the Rockies, with their peaks, glaciers, passes, weather, and variations of colours, and he also described his birthplace in Iceland.[28] The artist made paintings based on Stephan's descriptions, but Skafti declared them a total failure and said they would only spoil the book.

A Reading in Winnipeg

On a Thursday evening, November 5, 1908, Stephan G. Stephansson found himself sitting on the stage of the new Good Templar Hall located on the corner of Sergeant Avenue and McGee Street in Winnipeg. The hall seated several hundred people, but it was far from full. There was obvious anticipation in the faces of the majority of people who shared radical views – Freethinkers, Unitarians, and even socialists. Those few members of the Lutheran Synod who were in attendance kept a low profile, hoping nobody would recognize them. The atmosphere was charged.

Skafti Brynjólfsson, Master of Ceremonies, welcomed the guests and introduced the poet sitting on the stage beside him. It was as though Skafti's well-known vigour had been diminished and some even sensed that he was excusing "...the guest as if he were introducing something that required an excuse," suffragette Margrét Benedictson wrote in her journal *Freyja*.[29] When Stephan rose to his feet, small of stature, he seemed unaffected by the situation – though nobody could tell what he was really thinking. His hair was not yet grey, but he seemed worn out by hard work. This was the first time he had left his home district to present his poetry publicly.

The publication of Stephan's anthologies had proceeded rather slowly that year, but by the end of summer plans were in place for this first promotional tour. Winter darkness had been rather hard on Stephan in previous years, and an offhand allusion to his "Christmas courage" in one of his letters hinted at midwinter depression. Stephan therefore welcomed the opportunity to go on a trip, for his own "profit, knowledge and enjoyment, to every remote Icelandic settlement that is likely to receive me well, though I know nothing about these settlements, the people there, or their way of thinking." He anticipated a good reception from the publishing group and Reverend Friðrik Bergmann, but predicted hostility from the Lutheran Synod.[30]

A few members of the publishing committee had met secretly in order to select a varied group of Stephan's acquaintances from the Icelandic congregations. There was still strong antagonism in the Synod between the supporters of Reverend Friðrik and Reverend Jón Bjarnason, and Stephan's supporters wanted to steer him clear of this dispute. They felt there was a better chance of good attendance if a broad committee organized the reading. Hoping all would go well, they decided to hold the event in the Good Templar Hall, even though the rent was high.[31]

Stephan had arrived in Winnipeg on Tuesday, November 3, 1908. The city was now much larger than when Stephan had attended the Lutheran Synod convention back in 1885, and its population now stood at 150,000, having nearly tripled in the last decade. People migrating to the prairies often stopped over in Winnipeg, with many settling there permanently, and the city had emerged as a serious threat to Minneapolis as the largest grain-handling centre on the continent. The streets echoed with the sounds of rumbling horse-drawn wagons, carriages, and throngs of people who crowded the boulevards of the city centre.

Portage Avenue in bustling downtown Winnipeg.

Numerous stately houses were being built and Icelandic carpenters were among the contractors and real estate developers. Residential development was expanding to the north, south, and west of the city center, especially along the two rivers, the Red and the Assiniboine. The newest Icelandic quarter was in the rapidly growing "West End" of the city, along Sargent Avenue. Stephan was hosted by Eggert Jóhannsson and his wife at 689 Agnes Street.[32]

Everything seemed to be in order until the evening of the reading, when some of those who had promised to provide entertainment failed to show and others withdrew from the organizing committee. Sigríður Hall, a talented singer and the daughter-in-law of Stephan's best friend, Jónas Hall, had promised to perform, but at the last minute she backed out, claiming she had bronchitis. Earlier that same day, however, she had sung in the First Lutheran Church, of which Reverend Jón Bjarnason was pastor. By chance Stephan had been there and heard her. He did not want to make a fuss over this, but his friends were offended as they had gone to some lengths to arrange the programme. When Sigríður's father-in-law heard about this, he wanted to reprimand Sigríður. His son, composer Steingrímur K. Hall, was neutral in religious matters, but Sigríður "strongly believed in Reverend Jón and feared Friðrik and the Unitarians." Evidently she had thought there was no danger in singing at this event, however, until someone changed her mind," Jónas wrote to Stephan.[33] Probably that was also the case in other similar instances, as influential Synod members tried to spoil the gathering.

Stephan did not let these machinations upset him. Once on stage, he read in a strong, clear voice. There was something majestic about his reading, and his vigour gained momentum as he proceeded. He spoke slowly, enunciating clearly, so the audience found him easy to understand despite his reputation for obscurity, and it was as if he gained in stature with every poem he read.

First Stephan read a series of poems called "Frumbýlingurinn" (The Pioneer), (later entitled "Flutningurinn í nýja húsið"/"Moving into the New House"), a tableaux of fragmented stories from his pioneering past. The pioneers in the poem, he pointed out, could be of any nationality, but the audience was in no doubt that he was referring to the Icelandic experience. After the reading, Skafti called on two men from the audience to respond, one of whom was Reverend Friðrik Bergmann. The other was Wilhelm H. Paulson, an old friend who gave a short lecture on Stephan's poetry. After the programme, Stephan mingled with members of the audience, who thanked him and found him very cordial and unassuming in manner.[34]

Stephan spent some days in Winnipeg, hosted by Eggert Jóhannsson and his wife, Elín Hjörleifsdóttir, whose little daughters, Erna and Lillie, were attracted to this warm old chap. The girls even accompanied him to the theatre. Stephan also spent some time with Reverend Friðrik Bergmann and some of the editorial committee, among them Rögnvaldur Pétursson, whom he now met for the first time. Another person whose acquaintance Stephan made on this occasion was Baldur Sveinsson, the young co-editor of *Lögberg* and the son of people Stephan and Helga had known in Iceland. Stephan and Baldur became good friends who would correspond as long as both lived.

Poets Meet

Before the turn of the 20th century, aspiring poet and author Jóhann Magnús Bjarnason had become Stephan's spiritual protégé. He now lived at Marshland, Manitoba, and Stephan intended to stay with him on his tour through the Icelandic settlements. On the day of Stephan's arrival at Marshland, Jóhann Magnús waited with anticipation, thinking about the man he admired so much and speculating how he would look in person. He had only seen a photo of Stephan in *Öldin* and tried to enlarge it in his mind. He contemplated Stephan's first poems, powerful and original, and the letters from Stephan that he kept as mementos. He also thought about the short stories called "Ar" ("Specks of Dust in a Sunbeam"), that had appeared in *Heimskringla*. He felt they testified to such a peculiar genius that if Stephan had written prose, his work would find a place in world literature. Finally he wondered whether Stephan would have become such a great poet if he had become a hard-working urban intellectual rather than a pioneer on the land.

Various poems ran through Jóhann Magnús' mind, including Stephan's vivid descriptions of the Alberta landscape – mountains, valleys, lakes, rivers, and forests, not just as elements of the landscape but as living things. It did not matter whether Stephan was tall or short, handsome or homely, gentle or taciturn. He was majestic and noble in spirit and among the greatest poets of his nation. With these thoughts, Jóhann Magnús gradually dozed off, and when he awoke it was to the sound of a vehicle approaching the house. Outside someone spoke in a low voice and then drove away, then someone tapped lightly on the window. Jóhann Magnús knew who it was, but called out all the same, "Who's there?" "The boys!" replied someone in a cheerful and gentle tone. Jóhann Magnús invited them in.

"And now I had seen Stephan G. Stephansson," he wrote much later, recalling this event and adding that he had not been disappointed either by Stephan's appearance or demeanor. "He was like a cheerful youth, very jolly and [...] rather small of stature. Though he was definitely not handsome (in a conventional sense), he was so obliging, friendly, and charming that I immediately became very fond of him." They conversed long into the night and Jóhann Magnús enjoyed listening to Stephan. "I found his voice pleasant and he spoke clearly, choosing his words carefully. His eyes glittered with passion when he spoke of something dear to him." The following evening, Stephan gave a reading in the community hall, "so well and plainly that I heard every single word," Jóhann Magnús noted, adding that he felt he understood the poems that much better because Stephan read them in person.[35]

Stephan's next destination was the Argyle Settlement in Southern Manitoba, a large and prosperous Icelandic district where Stephan struck up a friendship with an affluent farmer named Árni Sveinsson. Stephan, however, found the Argyle people a bit materialistic and too closely affiliated with the Synod. He concluded that the peaceful life there was an indication of spiritual lethargy, something he and Árni discussed in later correspondence.

From Argyle, Stephan traveled north to the Shoal Lake Settlement east of Lake Manitoba. At that time this district was the home of young Icelandic poet Guttormur J. Guttormsson, who had wanted to meet Stephan for some time and had therefore organized a reading in the local community hall. The event was not much of a success, however, as the visit only served to magnify internal tensions in the community. Guttormur was unhappy, feeling that he could have done more for the travellers, and he felt certain that it must have been an ordeal for Stephan to meet such "crawling savages". Stephan made light of the situation and shouldered some of the responsibility, pointing out that he had not learned the art of establishing peace on earth and adding that the one who said that he came to do so was in for trouble! Guttormur was also concerned that Stephan's health would not withstand the itinerary in such cold.[36]

Guttormur J. Guttormsson, New Iceland poet-farmer of Víðivellir near Riverton.

Guttormur was by then one of the two most promising poets among the Icelanders in North America, and people wondered who would become Stephan's most worthy heir. Guttormur found this speculation shocking as he believed that Stephan's Icelandic equal would be born only once in a thousand years. He also felt it was difficult to get established as a poet in Stephan's shadow and he once wrote to Stephan, "We 'versemakers' have no reason at all to like you. Our poems would be regarded as just fine if you had never written anything. Yes, you have destroyed all our best poems. What a man! We would have been regarded as great poets and Reverend Friðrik would have kissed us, but instead he is now filled with 'holy wrath' when he reads our confounded "rubbish in the papers'."[37] Stephan liked Guttormur and his frankness, and he subsequently shared good advice with him in their correspondence.

Back in Dakota

After his visit to the Shoal Lake Settlement, Stephan gave readings in New Iceland on Lake Winnipeg. He then spent a few more days in Winnipeg before going south to Duluth, Minnesota. En route, the train passed the town of Superior, Wisconsin, and Stephan peered eastward over snowy hills towards Shawano where he had once lived. In Duluth he stayed with Kristján Jónsson, alias Chris Johnson, who managed the Forest Hill Cemetery, the biggest graveyard in Duluth. Chris was quite wealthy and even owned some land in the Alberta settlement, that Stephan later tried to sell for him. After the reading in Duluth, Stephan travelled over night to Gardar, North Dakota, where he had lived for almost a decade. It was a cheerful reunion with friends and family whom he had not seen for nearly 20 years, including Stephan's best friend, Jónas Hall, and his brother-in-law Jón Jónsson Jr., with his wife and their flock of children. Stephan's father-in-law, Jón from Mjóidalur, had by this time been bedridden for eight years and he died six months later. Stephan also met Káinn, the humorous Dakota poet, farmhand, and gravedigger, and they became good friends.

Stephan remained at Gardar for a month, during which he wrote the poem "Á gömlum slóðum" ("On Old Paths"), based on memories that came to him from every hill, hollow, overgrown path, and ruin. Here were the footprints of his young soul, he wrote, and images of his father and son who were buried there flooded back. "But when, by coincidence, my poem passes by/the graves surviving here,/I feel it almost like a temptation,/the longing to lie down here and fall silent."[38]

In the New Year, a farewell party was held at the home of Jón Jónsson – quite a contrast to the tense event in Winnipeg. The festivities lasted until morning with song, poetry, and impromptu speeches. Most of the guests were fonder of the man than the poet, *Heimskringla*'s reporter pointed out, as Stephan was among old friends rather than admirers. On his departure, his friends at Gardar gave him a gold ring

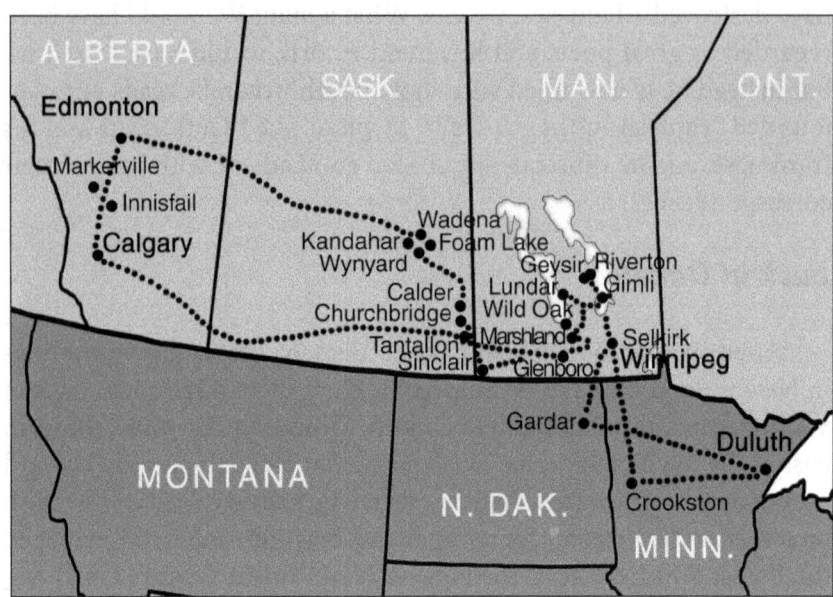

Stephan G. Stephansson's speaking tour of the Western Canadian and American Icelandic communities in the winter of 1908.

which they called *Draupnir*, after the mythological ring of that name in a poem Stephan had read.

On January 6, 1909, Stephan returned to Winnipeg in such cold that the wood stove in the passenger car froze. He then set off homeward shortly afterward, giving readings in various places in Manitoba and Saskatchewan, including Churchbridge where he read at three events and stayed with Magnús Hinriksson, who hosted a lively party for the occasion. Like Stephan, Magnús was a self-educated and liberal farmer known for his integrity, and Stephan encouraged him to take a trip to the Pacific Coast and stop in Alberta. "I could not treat you half as well as you have received me, but as we are both farmers that would not be a problem," Stephan wrote, adding that he too would like to see the ocean again.[39]

Stephan was also well received in Wynyard, Saskatchewan, where one of his poems was sung to a new tune. In Foam Lake he looked around for the familiar face of Jón Jónsson from Mýri in Bárðardalur, who like many other single men had been turned away from the emigrant ship at Akureyri in 1873. Now, 30 years later and a widower with many children, Jón had emigrated after all and homesteaded near Foam Lake. Jón, however, was not present to greet Stephan as the ride he had been promised had not materialized. He subsequently wrote Stephan an explanatory letter and the two corresponded for the rest of their lives.

After being snow-bound in Wadena, Saskatchewan, for two days, Stephan arrived in Edmonton on Friday, February 5, 1909. He reached Red Deer that evening and arrived home with the full bottle of whisky from Eggert and a corkscrew in his pocket. When he wrote Eggert a week later, he had only the corkscrew.

Stephan's neighbours claimed that he looked years younger after the trip and Helga was grateful to Eggert's wife for taking such good care of him. For years afterward, Stephan always included greetings to Eggert's daughters in his letters, and as they recognized his handwriting they always got excited when there was a letter from Mr. Stephansson. Erna lost a favorite brooch the year after Stephan's visit, and when Stephan heard this he sent her a new one, telling her that the east wind had informed him of her misfortune and that a rainbow had found a new brooch for her. The girl wrote back in English, excusing the east wind's indiscretion and saying that the rainbow had just brought the brooch bought with money stolen from Stephan, something it should not have done. Nevertheless, she was so happy and excited about the gift that she had no appetite for dinner the evening she received it.[40]

Admission to one of Stephan's readings was usually $.25. He was paid any profit after expenses had been cleared, and in total he earned $120 on his trip. Fully one half of that amount was earned during the latter part of the journey.

Back in Alberta, Stephan's neighbours welcomed him home, and Reverend Pétur Hjálmsson and a few others presented him with a couch on the occasion of his successful tour. Stephan gave a well-attended reading in Markerville. At the end of February his friends in Winnipeg sent him a $50 cheque and a black buffalo drinking horn, 12 inches long, with a stanza from an Eddaic poem engraved on a silver plate. The success of Stephan's tour reflected the deep friendship of those who admired his poetry, as well as the indifference and resistance of his opponents. In a letter to Eggert, Stephan revealed that he would like to travel more, not on a planned schedule, but "just as the head is inclined."[41]

Gestur

While Stephan was away on his travels, his sons Jakob and Gestur did the chores at home. The boys were as different as day and night, yet

Gestur, the poet's son.

very close. Jakob was now more than 20 years old, a hard worker but rather uneven in temper and slow to reply. Gestur was nearly 16, an exceptionally kind-hearted boy. Guðmundur, Stephan and Helga's second oldest son, and his wife, Regina, and their two children were leaving their farm to move to Markerville where "Mundi" was going into business with Jón Benediktsson. This amused Stephan who wrote to Jónas Hall, "Who would have believed that we would turn out to be fathers of merchants?"[42] Stephan and Helga's twin daughters were still at home. Fanny looked increasingly like Stephan's aunt Guðný, while Jenny resembled Stephan's mother's people. Little Rósa was eight, blonde and precocious.

While Stephan was on his reading tour, the publication committee was growing impatient over the printing that Jón Ólafsson was to oversee in Iceland. Skafti Brynjólfsson and his wife Gróa had gone to Iceland with the manuscript just before Christmas and Skafti had struck a deal with a printer, as well as retaining poet Þorsteinn Erlingsson to do the proofreading. Skafti remained in Iceland for some months, supervising the production. Typesetting began in early May and Skafti decided on two volumes. Any additional poems that might come later would have to fill a third volume. One poem excluded was "Á ferð og flugi".

In the end, 2000 copies of the anthology were printed, 1000 for the Icelandic market and 1000 for North America. Each volume was twenty quires, or 320 pages. There was not paper for more and Skafti feared the books would be too expensive for the general public if they were larger.

While Skafti managed the project in Iceland, Stephan was busy back home, trying to hire a teacher for the Hola School. Eventually he learned that Eggert Jóhannsson's 20 year old son, Laurenz, needed a job and it was decided that he would teach at Hola. Laurenz arrived in early June, shortly after Stephan had received the first proofs. The young man was a little nervous as this was the first time he had been away from home, but he settled in comfortably at Stephan and Helga's and soon became good friends with Jakob and Gestur.

On the evening of July 16, 1909, a huge black cloud darkened the sky and brought a thunderstorm, with a cloud burst and hail the size of hens' eggs. Gestur and Jakob, who were working in the field, ran for shelter in an old barn as it began to rain and Laurenz joined them there with some schoolchildren. When the worst of the thunderstorm seemed to have passed, Gestur left the shelter and headed toward the house. Just as he was crossing the barbed wire fence, however, a bolt of lightning struck with a great crack of thunder. Gestur turned black and fell down dead, with a black scar on his chin.[43]

Fréttabréf.

(Frá fréttaritara Hkr.).

MARKERVILLE.

20. júli 1909.

Voðalegt slys varð hér siðastastliðinn föstudag (16. þ.m.), að þrumuelding sló til bana unglingspilt Gest Stephansson, Stephanssonar skálds, 16 ára gamlan. — Piltur þessi var hinn mannvænlegasti, vel mentaður og siðprúður, og góður og ástrækinn sonur og bróðir.

Jarðarförin fór fram í gærdag (19.), í grafreit þeim á landi bónda C. Christinnssonar, sem mun ákveðinn legstaður ættfólksins í framtiðinni. Flestallir Íslendingar í þessari bygð fylgdu Gesti sál. til grafar, og sýndu innilega og verðuga hluttöku í þessu sorgartilfelli.

Heimskringla reported Gestur's death by lightning strike at age 16 on July 16, 1909, and added that the funeral was attended by virtually all of the Icelanders who lived in the settlement.

On the following day, Stephan sent a terse message to Eggert Jóhannsson. "My dear Eggert. Last night, lightning struck my youngest son, Gestur, killing him near the house. Everyone else is fine. I will try to fulfill my duties to the living again as soon as I can."[44] This was the second time Stephan and Helga had lost a son. Little Jón had died in the fall of 1887 and it had taken Stephan a long time to deal with that grief. Stephan had considered telephoning Rögnvaldur Pétursson immediately after the accident, but in the summer heat Gestur had to be buried immediately and there was no time to wait for Rögnvaldur to arrive from Winnipeg. Stephan and Helga's neighbour Jón Strong made the coffin.

On the other side of the Medicine River, a graveyard had been marked out on the homestead of Stephan's sister, Sigurlaug, and her husband,

Kristinn Kristinsson. Stephan hitched a horse to a wagon and the funeral procession of family and neighbours crossed the river. Words on a garland on the coffin expressed Stephan's disbelief and Helga's faith: "Whatever occurs to your mind,/our hearts will follow you."[45] Pastor Pétur Hjálmsson spoke so well at the funeral that even Stephan approved.

Gestur was buried beside Kristinn and Sigurlaug's son who had died in 1905. Stephan spoke at the gravesite. "We are sincerely grateful to family and friends for their concern and to him who will remain here for being with us as a son. He was a good son and a good brother to his siblings. I never witnessed him deliberately betray his integrity. A longer life could have made him a bigger man, but never better. I do not worry about him. A good man can nowhere fare badly and every part of him that could feel pain and suffering is now in this coffin and will never feel pain again. He has enriched my memories, and although it is painful to lose him like this, the void would be greater still if I had never had him or the pleasure of his presence. My thanks and blessings go with you, my child, as long as I live."[46]

Rögnvaldur sent warm condolences, for which Stephan later thanked him in a letter dated July 27th. "Yes, my dear Rögnvaldur, I am sure nothing has come from nothing, and nothing will turn into nothing. I, and everything I love, are within our existence, and existence will be our mother forever, whatever the changes, and although I lose something, I live while I can for that which remains. I enclose a new poem only so that you, who care about me, will understand how I am doing. I cannot describe it otherwise."[47]

This poem is dated July 16, 1909, and if that is correct, Stephan wrote it on the night following Gestur's death. It is unlikely, however, that he finished it then. Entitled "Gestur", it can be ranked with the best poems of that kind in the Icelandic language, alongside the elegies Egill Skallagrímsson and Hallgrímur Pétursson composed for children they lost. The poem communicates the same thought as Stephan's note to Eggert, his address by the grave, and his letter to Rögnvaldur.

> *The law that destroys life,*
> *Did not keep me up with long fear of expectation,*
> *But sent lightning from heaven*
> *Into the heart of him I loved.*
> *And there is relief in this knowledge of no suffering*
> *Over this parting – as I had to lose.*

Yes, it softened the grief to know
That what hit you like this, my boy,
Was not a knowing power, intending to harm,
Nor make us used to the good and then attack with accidents!
Because the deeds of cruelty – whatever they teach!
Burn every heart most of all.

And it is easier to accept what has happened
When fear and punishment are absent.
The good had no grudge against you,
And it would never have beaten you.
And it could never have hit so hard,
All the hearts who miss you and mourn.

And evil will never affect the good
In eternity! whatever life and death bode,
It now has no power to reach you –
And the lightning that hit you
Was innocent – it was not in ambush for your life –
As you were in its way by coincidence.

These first stanzas, a sort of contemplation on man's relation to life and death, suggest that good which remains immune to evil is independent of religious doctrines. The lightning strike was a physical coincidence, not the act of an evil power. Stephan seems certain about the circumstances of his earthly existence and thus musters the strength to withstand this terrible blow. He also manages to mitigate his grief through the plaintive means of poetry.

So I wrap you into the plaintiveness of a poem,
Deceased, into tearful, yet happy lines. –
In the ranks of the angels of happiness and goodness
My Gestur will be – and nowhere else!
I bid you farewell without fear, then the wounds heal.
Afterwards, a blessing, thanks and the tears.

At the end of the poem, Stephan acknowledges Gestur's help in enabling him to prepare his poems for printing. His memory was thus interwoven with the poems. They are, however, mere ephemera, whereas

Stephan's memory of Gestur was sacred.

> *I bid you farewell without fear. But I feel,*
> *Towards all those who grieve your death,*
> *That I want to carry more than my part*
> *Of their grief: being without you now. –*
> *For the rest of my life, I bear the mark,*
> *You are with me, in my poems and my works.*
>
> *Nothing of your love will be obliterated,*
> *It is and remains for me in the treasure trove of time.*
> *Although the whole of a future, based on you, has changed,*
> *I carry a wealth from our life together, my boy!*
> *And when I am carried out of the land of poetry,*
> *Life will defend him, with its hands of preservation.*
>
> *O, child of my heart, your helpful hand*
> *Lightened my burden in my old days,*
> *That my hand, worn out, would be freed*
> *To preserve many a forgotten line from oblivion.*
> *That property of both of us, I would gladly give,*
> *If I could, and dared to lengthen your life.*
>
> *And still it shall be a pleasure to write poems and greet you!*
> *And my evening sun shall still set,*
> *When my world in the end sets for me*
> *In the west, by your grassy grave. –*
> *So the path to my coffin,*
> *And my last poem, is consecrated by your memory.*[48]

Some critics found the poem cold and insensitive. This was far from the case, however. Stephan was struggling to control and channel his grief, as Egill Skallagrímsson had done through poetry and Hallgrímur Pétursson by religious faith. By means of the stand he had taken in life, Stephan managed to confront death and deal straightforwardly with the earthly reality he faced, converting shock into a grateful memory rather than retreating. He avoided the lamentation of traditional elegies, instead addressing death as a neutral phenomenon, swift and without cruelty or painful foreboding.

Conscious of the fact that his young house guest might feel uncomfortable in the home during this time of sorrow, Stephan asked Laurenz if he would rather stay with Sigurlaug and Kristinn. Laurenz, however, declined the offer and remained with the family, trying to do what he could ease the burden. The shock for Jakob was terrible as he loved Gestur more than anyone else, and Laurenz tried to comfort him as best he could. Helga's reaction during these events is unknown. Possibly Stephan's stoicism eased her grief somewhat, but it took her a long time to recover. From that day forth she found thunderstorms unbearable, as every lightning strike startled her.[49]

A Great Event in the History of Poetry

Late in the summer of 1909 the first two volumes of *Andvökur* were printed and the publishers began the marketing. At the same time, they were making plans for a third volume. It would be a bit smaller than the first two, 240 pages in length, with much of it being long poems such as "Á ferð og flugi" and a poem Stephan had read on his tour. "Gestur", the poet's tribute to his son, would be the last poem in volume III.

In all, the three volumes would total 884 pages, handsomely bound, and priced at $3.50 for the set. The first copies arrived in Winnipeg in September and Stephan's supporters immediately undertook sales. Eggert Jóhannsson composed a flyer for sales agents in the Icelandic settlements, pointing out that the poet had written more poetry than most other Icelandic poets without ever getting paid, so should enjoy the profit if there was one. Sales agents were offered a $.50 commission per set, but if they were willing to sell the volumes without commission, the committee would ensure that the poet was made aware of their contribution. Sales agents could only sell the volumes as a set, though they could arrange individualized terms for payment.

Sales were brisk in some areas, but not where the Synod held sway. Grímur Grímsson, Stephan's friend, sold some 50 copies in the poet's neighborhood, and Stephan knew of only four homes where the books were not purchased because of his religious views. Even in the "orthodoxden" of Argyle, Stephan's wealthy friend Árni Sveinsson was an effective salesperson, as was Chris Johnson in Duluth. Magnús Hinriksson also had good luck in the Churchbridge area, although the local pastor preached against the books three Sundays in a row.

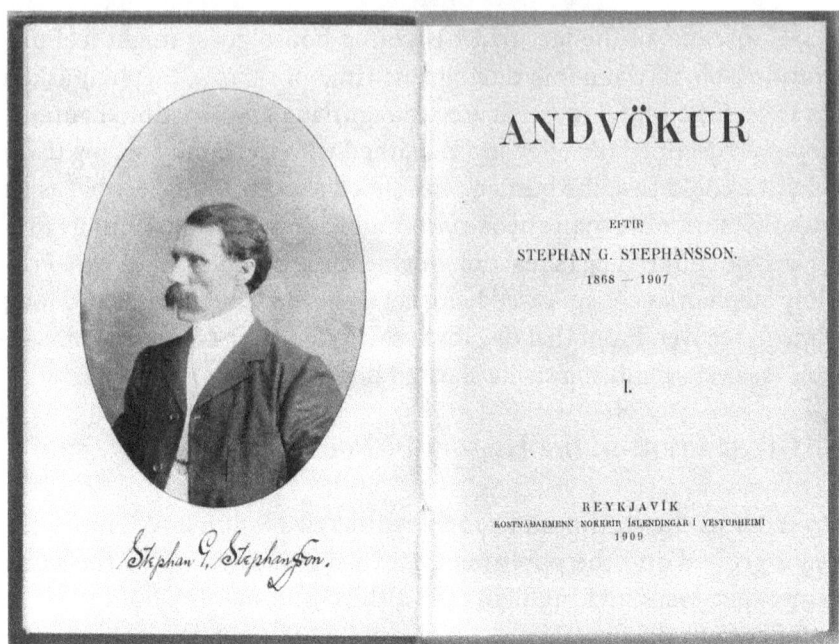

The publication of volumes I-III of Andvökur *in 1909 was a milestone in the literary career of Stephan G. Stephansson.*

Sales then declined for a while as the printing of the third volume was delayed until May. When these books arrived at Eggert Jóhannsson's home in Winnipeg on June 21, 1910, the family helped carry the boxes down to the basement. "I can guarantee that no private house in Winnipeg kept such excellent goods in the basement as this house did," Eggert wrote. His girls proudly "ran on the wings of the winds up and down with packages of books and were disappointed that there were not more books in the boxes." They were proud to carry "Mr. Stephansson's books" and were astonished that he had written them all by himself.[50]

Critics were unanimous in their excitement. "It seldom happens 'that whales are beached in Trékyllisvík' and this is quite a beaching in our literary history, this anthology of poetry by this Icelander in the West," the great Nestor of Icelandic poets, Reverend Matthías Jochumsson, wrote. His fascination was obvious, yet his enthusiasm was tempered with a hint of reservation. He acknowledged that Stephan was a great poet, a luminary, "but he is obscure, stiff and proud. As a master of verse-making, he is indeed a major poet, but not one of the heart." Old Matthías vacillated back and forth, fascinated by Stephan's intellectual power and resolve against dogmatism, but critical of his lack of lyrical and religious sentiment. "He has never written doggerel. Stephan G. Stephansson is a poet of nature, a poet of human life, a poet of social commentary, a poet of contemplations, a poet of humour, civilization and freedom. He is usually callous, especially in wit and humour." Matthías found "Úti á víðavangi" the best part of the volumes and wrote to a friend. "There he is at home, in his entirety. That is his huge, divine contribution, to get to Alberta, become an outlaw, poet, and pioneer with his genius." Matthías concluded that there was nobody who could challenge Stephan's freedom.

Matthías ended his review of *Andvökur* with an inspired sermon. "Stephan G. Stephansson: Get up, if your spirit is still young, and walk west to the great mountain that towers over the entire continent and do not stop until you stand on the peak of Nebo! There you will see how God's holy sun gilds the East and reaches all the way west to the waves of the Pacific. See for yourself that this is the land of the living and not 'the tired, lost, and dead'! Sing there, strong Stephan, your swan song, and you will do more than fulfill the mental categories of Kant; you will become a poet of both the head and the heart, and you will die not 'into the mountain', but to a life in another and higher place where no Rocky Mountains will limit the broad view to the ocean of eternity."

Matthías could not discern Stephan's emotional essence and therefore spoke of the "mental categories" of the rationalist philosopher Immanuel Kant. Stephan could easily fulfill these categories, but would have to transcend them in order to achieve the

Reverend Matthías Jochumsson, one of Iceland's principal poets, penned the words to Iceland's national anthem. In 1893 he had visited Chicago, Winnipeg, and the Dakota Settlement as a guest of Icelanders in Canada and the United States.

spirituality he lacked, Matthías claimed. "And fare well, poet and sage, whom the valleys of Skagafjörður sent as the greatest spirit west across the ocean, where the New World fostered you, nurturing and strengthening your spirit – girding you for the rest of your life with the magic belt of the mightiest influence as the first national poet of Icelanders in the West."[51]

Not entirely content with this dramatic and inspired review, Stephan suggested that old Matthías was just a little cranky. Before *Andvökur* was published, Matthías had in fact stated that Stephan was just average in the art of poetry, lacking faith and "emotional fire" despite his originality. Stephan, on the other hand, found Matthías' outpouring of emotion a bit excessive and lacking in balance, which was ironically the exact opposite of what Matthías thought of him. The good pastor was so emotional, Stephan pointed out, that in his writings "everything becomes praise, prayer, and 'preaching', exactly when he most wants to give one a warm welcome. The good old man can never forget that he himself is the greatest. I am not saying this out of spite," Stephan wrote.[52]

Nobody denied that Stephan was a major poet. Most reviews, in fact, praised his original, intelligent, and profound ideas and the extraordinary wealth of his diction and imagery. They found fault, however, with occasional metrical faults and clumsy sentences. Reverend Friðrik Bergmann wrote in *Heimskringla* that he doubted Stephan's equal could be found among the self-educated of other nations, while the newspaper *Fjallkonan* claimed that Stephan over-emphasized his difference from others and poked at intellectuals for no reason. Icelandic poet Þorsteinn Erlingsson stated that Stephan had mastered the very rare art of "distilling solid arguments, yet giving them wing as sound carried on the lightest feather." Baldur Sveinsson pointed out that Stephan's faith was unclear, perhaps rightly so in a certain sense, although Stephan did not want to admit that himself. Baldur challenged Reverend Matthías' claim that Stephan's poetry lacked feeling and suggested that the emotion was just under the surface, quoting Stephan's own reference to poets: "A deep fire is/hidden in a thin layer of ash."[53]

Stephan was now in his late 50's and after this great publication project undertaken by his friends and admirers, his poetic reputation seemed indisputable. The alleged high treason cited by his opponents after the Boer War seemed long forgotten, as were accusations of his hatred for pastors.

The Mirages Disappear Faster

Proceeds from the sale of *Andvökur* soon covered the direct costs and more, and Stephan now faced an interesting dilemma. He wanted those who had put up the money for the project to divide the profits among themselves. If more money came in later, then he had a wallet. Leaders of the publication committee, however, wanted Stephan to receive the profits, and he did not want to insult his benefactors by refusing to accept what they intended for him. They felt it important that he should be able to retire from heavy farmwork, not least for the benefit of the Icelandic nation, and they hoped the profits from *Andvökur* would make this possible. If Stephan could escape the burden of farmwork, they felt he would be able to write his best poems over the next few years. That would be the best return for those who had invested in this project.

Stephan had no such expectations. He regarded his poetry as an avocation, regardless of the amount of time he put into it, and it was hard for him to assign a monetary value to this creative work. He did not want to owe anyone anything, and the many men who had backed the project had to be repaid. This was even more important to Stephan when he heard that some of his opponents had been tricked into supporting the project – men who did not even want to have *Andvökur* under their roof. He therefore wanted all shareholders, especially those who opposed his opinions, to get their share first. Stephan, however, could not control what the publishers did with the money and early in April of 1911 they sent him $500. He was grateful, but he felt that the money belonged to someone else and wanted to return it. He relented, however. The money came in handy as he was far from wealthy.[54]

Late in 1911 the publication committee decided to sell individual volumes of *Andvökur* rather than only the set, and the remaining inventory was turned over to booksellers. Gradually the informal publication committee dissolved once those who had put up the money had been repaid. Some had expected huge sales. In the end *Andvökur* sold somewhat less than expected – though better than most Icelandic books in North America.

Andvökur generated a considerable sum of money for Stephan. During the winter of 1913-1914 he received another $80, having by then received a total of $1080, and in the years that followed he occasionally received additional sums. The most significant result of the publication of *And-*

Hjörtur (Chester) Thórðarson, the little boy who had lost his father in Wisconsin and had stayed a winter with Stephan and Helga in Dakota, was now a wealthy inventor and electrical industrialist in Chicago.

vökur, however, was that most of Stephan's poems were now much more accessible than otherwise would have been the case, and Stephan found this gratifying. Deeply touched by the support and good will shown, he wrote an address of gratitude that appeared in the February 1, 1912 issue of *Lögberg*. In it he praised the integrity and concern of the committee, while speculating that the cultural circumstances of Icelanders in North America were sufficiently promising that perhaps they would "someday produce a real artist."[55]

At the end of 1911 Stephan received a *deluxe* edition of *Andvökur*, specially bound and embossed with his gilded signature, and signed by members of the publication committee. Stephan ordered five such sets for friends, four for fellow poets in Iceland – Jón Ólafsson, Þorsteinn Erlingsson, Guðmundur Friðjónsson, and Þorgils Gjallandi – all of whom had played a part in gaining him recognition as a poet and the last two of whom were self-educated farmers like himself. The fifth set was for Chicago millionaire Chester Thordarson (Hjörtur Þórðarson), who as an introverted but brilliant youth had spent a winter in Stephan's home in Dakota Territory. Now an electrical engineer, inventor, and industrial magnate, he had often sent gifts of books to his old benefactors, Stephan and Helga, in acknowledgement of their friendship and care. An avid book collector, Hjörtur now owned some of the rarest books in the world.

He knew several of Stephan's poems by heart, and upon receiving the special edition of *Andvökur* he told Stephan that these volumes meant more to him than any others in his possession. "And Hjörtur is no sweet talker," Stephan added proudly.⁵⁶

The successful publication of *Andvökur* was a Herculean task on the part of Stephan's liberal-minded countrymen in North America, and it constituted a significant blow to the regressive mindset of the Synod. Both religion and Icelandic culture were already on the wane in North America, however, and when *Andvökur* was published, "Athugull" (The Observant One) from Alberta wrote an article in *Heimskringla* entitled "Íslenskan hálfdauð og lúterskan kriplingur" (Icelandic Half Dead and Lutheranism a cripple). "Athugull" claimed that the Icelandic language was no longer being taught to Icelandic children in North America, as it was considered an impediment to their progress. Religion, too, was on the retreat and skepticism was becoming widespread. "The Alberta settlement has an exemplary person whom youngsters regard with admiration and respect," he added, "whom they see as a true leader in both local and civic affairs. They consider his conduct and religious opinions examples to follow. Although he has done nothing to hinder the progress of Lutheranism here in the Alberta settlement, his silence, actions, and poetry have influenced the somewhat unique religious views of the younger generation more than anything else."⁵⁷

Andvökur I-III, published in Iceland in 1909, were bound in handsome burgundy covers embossed with gold.

The greatest honour for the successful publication of *Andvökur* must fall to the quiet intellectual Eggert Jóhannsson, who initiated the project and was, together with Rögnvaldur Pétursson and Skafti Brynjólfsson, the life and soul of the entire endeavour. Increasingly confident as the

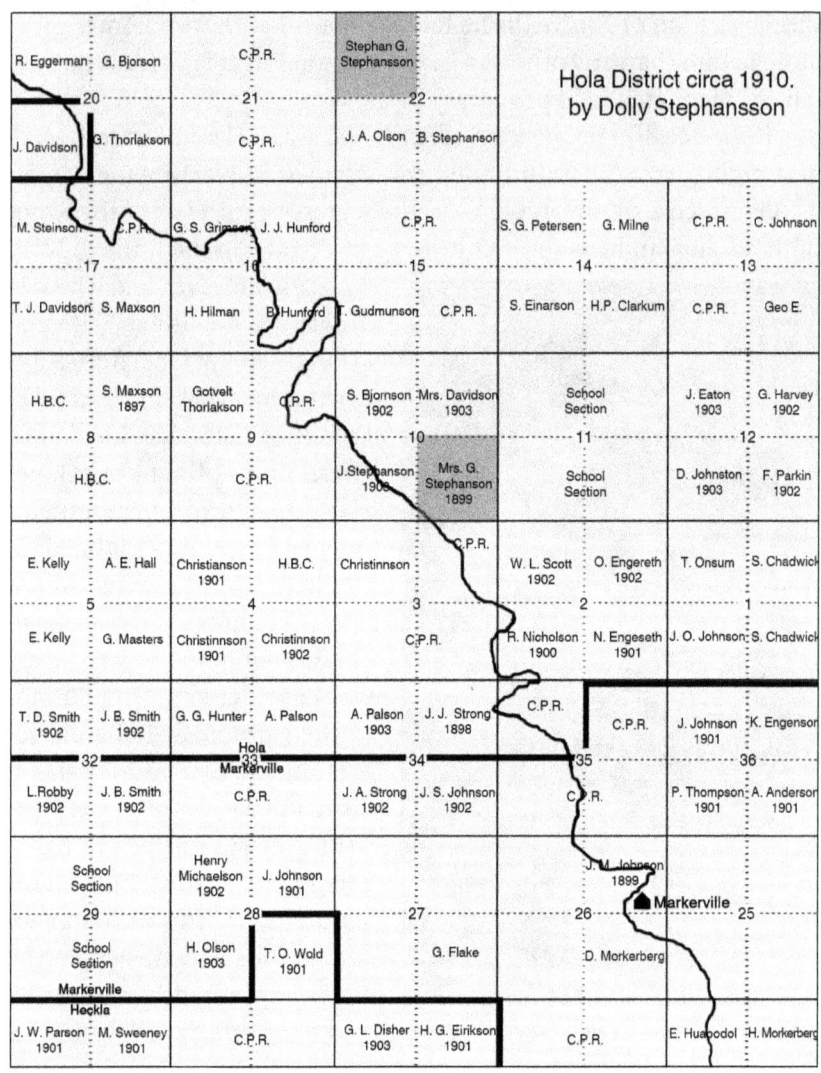

Land ownership in the Markerville District circa 1910. Each "homesteader" could claim a quarter section, improve it, and then get title. The Stephansson homesite, with its rolling land and tree-covered hills on the river, was claimed by Stephan's mother, Mrs. G. Stephansson. Stephan claimed a quarter section of hay land north of the homesite for feed for the livestock.

C.P.R.–Canadian Pacific Railway land grants
H.B.C.–Hudson Bay Company land grants

project progressed, Eggert subsequently sought to relieve Stephan of his burdens so that, as he explained in his letters, the poet's increased experience would result in more beautiful form and smoother metres, although his ideals could hardly grow stronger with age.

The poet, not unlike a naughty child pretending to obey but stubbornly persisting, claimed to have cut back on his chores to spare his health, while maintaining that work was, nevertheless, a blessing no less than a burden. "I will retire soon. That will happen automatically, I realize. Just recently, for example, I was chopping down a tree.

> *In old times I had the most timber*
> *felled out in the forest.*
> *My pile is the smallest now,*
> *but more strain all the same.*

I honestly love work, but I do not believe in "ploughing one day and then being abed for a week," as Sophie said of her man Tolstoy. "Now I want to withdraw as much as possible from winter work and lapse into total laziness when I turn 60, in about two years."[58]

The publication of *Andvökur* was a turning point in Stephan's life. His energy was declining and this was reflected in his poetic output. He was tired, but reluctant to admit that his work was a burden. He said while his poetic form had improved, other aspects of his poetry had become weaker. He now had less passion for his avocation "and it is now harder for me to keep poetic concepts in my memory unprocessed until I have time to write them down. The mirages that come to me now disappear faster." Hard work, he suggested, was less of a burden than it was an excuse for less poetic craftsmanship. "If I have become somewhat absent-minded and long for something, it is only one thing: Rest."[59]

Chapter 12

Poetry Against Satan

Mother and World

After the publication of *Andvökur*, life became less hectic for Stephan, but he and Helga now had a new burden to shoulder. Stephan's mother, though over 80 years old, had always been healthy, but now her health began to fail. Following a flu epidemic during the winter of 1910-1911, most people recovered by Christmas, but Guðbjörg remained in bed. Dr. Parsons was consulted, but to no avail. Stephan and his sister, Sigurlaug, both tended their mother in turn, but in the end most of this task fell to Helga.

Rögnvaldur Pétursson and Eggert Jóhannsson had planned to visit Stephan in January. Eggert was keen to meet Guðbjörg, having heard about her from his son in the summer of 1909, but on the morning of January 18, 1911, she passed away. Though Stephan acknowledged in a letter to Baldur Sveinsson that "this sort of thing is nothing but the ordinary distress of living people," he was naturally grief stricken. Guðbjörg was buried on January 22, the day after Rögnvaldur and Eggert arrived.

"My mother and I had been in the same home ever since I was born, except for about three years," Stephan wrote to Baldur.[1] Always quiet and calm, Guðbjörg had often eased Stephan's pain from the time of his humiliating boyhood reading test with his father. The full impact of Guðbjörg's presence in Stephan's life, however, was most obvious in his memorial poem, which was more sincere and personal than most of his other poems. In it, he intertwined the events of their respective lives with the changes in the weather the day Guðbjörg died. She was a child of sunshine, he wrote, and the moment of her death came just as the sun broke through a snowstorm. Guðbjörg's kindly countenance merges with daylight in the poem, and the brightness of her face elevates her above common sorrows. "Forgive me, if more heavily than before/the head of your almost 60-year-old boy/is now bowed, on this cold dawn," he wrote, recalling the years of his youth with her and the subtle encouragement she had given a restless boy. She had guided his hand the first time he grasped a quill pen, and ever since then he had felt the caress of her loving hand whenever he needed encouragement.

> *You would also caress on the head,*
> *The sad greetings, when others emphasized*
> *The cold calmness of my poems.*[2]

Stephan was growing old, yet he remained young in spirit. "It is a pleasure for me to receive letters from some, but I am getting lazier to read than I used to be, even excellent books," he wrote to his friend Baldur Sveinsson in March of 1911. "Sometimes I think it is like reading half forgotten prayers from my youth. You recognize and remember various thoughts that you have met in their own homes, even though you have never before seen the book that housed them. I suspect that this is the beginning of becoming 'old and lazy'. It is more disturbing, however, not to receive any news of our times, people's circumstances, or world issues, be they those we like or dislike."[3]

Guðbjörg Hannesdóttir Stephansson, the poet's mother.

Stephan had been interested in foreign affairs since was a young boy. As a child he had read the poem "Njóla" (Dark Fog), about the design of the world, and after reading newspaper accounts of the Poles' struggle for freedom in the 1860s, he had written a poem about these events. By the turn of the 20th century he was writing about events that placed world order and human rights at risk. His poems "Transvaal" (The Transvaal) and "Filipseyjar" (The Philippines) raise the spectre of warfare, while "Heimskautafararnir" (The Polar Explorers), about a failed expedition to the North Pole, conveys both the heroic mood and sorrows of a dying explorer. Although the explorer's search ends in death, the "dubious trails" of the world are reduced in number as a result of the light cast by his explorations "on a route trodden by his lost ancestors/to the unfound Pole – the pole of truth". In 1899 Stephan had written the poem "Rennes" about the Dreyfus Affair in Rennes, France, in the 1890s, and "Pétursborg" (St. Petersburg) is about unarmed workers shot dead on their way to petition the tsar. In 1908 Stephan completed the long poem "Aftaka óeirðamannsins" (The Execution of the Rebel), inspired by a painting by the Russian painter Vasily Vereshchagin (1842-1904), known for his critical, realist paintings of war. In Stephan's mind this picture represented the arrogant abuse of power versus the dignity of an oppressed hero who refused to expose his comrades even to save his own life.

The poem "Bræðrabýti" (The Brothers' Share), written in 1906, reveals Stephan's progressive ideas on the preservation of nature. In this poem, two brothers inherit a poor piece of land that had been exploited for generations. Their handling of their respective shares of this inheritance differs. One greedily smashes the rocks in search of gold inside the mountain, while the other wants to heal the over-grazed land by encouraging growth on the barren land and letting heather spread up to the mountainsides. Although they are brothers, the two are opponents in political matters, and the poet asks which represents progress. When both eventually die, the greedy brother's body lies in Fleecing Gully, where his "weathered skeleton" gleams in the shadows in the moonlight. In contrast, flowers grow on the grave of the brother who had "been the first to plant that forest/and tie the sandstorm with ropes of greensward". The gold seeker irrevocably destroyed the land, while new life flourished in the footsteps of his brother. Stephan's thoughts are summarized in the lines "To think not in years but in ages,/not to demand the entire wage each evening/as thus human life is most prolonged," and the poem concludes:

It is not the world
Of an over-praised present day,
But an improved and happier future,
That the visionary sees.[4]

There is a distinctive harmony in Stephan's ideas. The North American Freethinkers had helped him shed the shackles of religious dogma and forge his own critical beliefs, and he was fascinated by Socialism and Marx's ideas. After 1890 his views became very radical and revolutionary, and though he relented somewhat later, he remained a critical thinker throughout his life.

In the spring of 1910, Stephan wrote "Markvörðurinn" (The Forester), a poem about an idealist who always sets the highest possible personal goal, but is impatient and even arrogant toward those who do not share his high ideals. Rögnvaldur Pétursson thought this poem belittled the efforts of the liberals, but Stephan explained, "No, I composed "Markvörðurinn" after much reading, even the speeches of the 'Marxists' (the craziest Socialists) who would revile the reform efforts of others." He also hinted at the "relentless focus on the individual, i.e. the 'individualismus', strongly depicted by Spencer and Ibsen, as logically representative of the worst in spiritual and worldly enchainment". Thus critical of two of the main currents of 20th century totalitarianism, communism and fascism, Stephan claimed to favour attempts at reform, fumbling attempts though they might be, and added that he had in fact often defended the liberals. He did not agree with them in everything, he admitted, but their views were better than those of many others. In the end, however, he was bound by neither politics nor theology, was neither a Marxist nor a Democrat, neither a Lutheran nor a Unitarian. "I want to understand where the currents flow and would never scold a child's hand in its fumbling attempts at progress, though I see how short it reaches."[5]

Stephan's understanding of Marxist economics was influenced by his world-view as a farmer. To him it mattered most to be working and keeping in good physical shape, and he supported the struggle against inequality, both economic and class. He also adhered to the Marxist view that labour was the basis of the value of things. "In conclusion, I should receive as much for a barrel of potatoes as you for a barrel of gold if the effort of both of us is the same. Any other economic valuation,

I think, becomes a labyrinth out of which no-one can find an escape. Those who address our needs for mental and physical sustenance are the only useful men."⁶

A socialist and a free trader, Stephan voted Liberal for lack of other alternatives. He disliked the Conservatives and found tariff protection stupid, "as free trade and communication between nations is, to my way of thinking, a precursor to the 'brotherhood' that everybody talks about nowadays." At this point, the Liberals had been in power for several years under the leadership of Prime Minister Wilfrid Laurier, who before the election of 1911 announced a new reciprocal trade policy with the United States. If implemented, this deal would abolish protective tariffs that had maintained high prices for farm machinery, causing difficulties for prairie farmers, but supporting manufacturers in Eastern Canada. Free trade in natural resources and agricultural products, favourable to farmers, had been established with the United States. The Conservatives, however, predicted the gradually annexation of Canada by the Americans through such free trade. This strategy was successful and the Liberals lost the 1911 election to the Conservatives, whose leader, Robert Borden, became the new Prime Minister. Protective tariffs therefore remained in effect.⁷

Politics were a never-ending topic of debate and concern. Icelandic-Canadian artist Charles Thorson had his own style of political commentary.

Stephan followed these matters closely and he became increasingly anxious over the changes he observed in world affairs: increasing armament in Europe, widespread ethnic oppression, and growing international conflict. He expressed his anxiety in "Ræfladans" (Dance of the Wretches), a poem printed in *Lögberg* in the spring of 1911. Different in style and rhythm from most of Stephan's poems, it evokes discomfort through its form rather than a rational analysis of ideas. Ragged wretches dance madly, shaking their fetters. "Let us dance on the spears/let us dance fast so we can enjoy our fetters."[8] Stephan's anxiety increased as inflation increased and the threat of war loomed ever larger. The British regarded the German economic boom with increasing unease and it appeared that the poet's prediction of an age of violence would come true.

A Rainy Summer

It was difficult for Stephan to stand by and witness Helga's grief after the tragic death of their son Gestur, and in an effort to find a diversion for her he suggested that she travel. Finally she acquiesced and on July 10th Stephan and Jakob drove her to Innisfail, where Jenny, who was working there as a housemaid, accompanied her to the train station. On the way back they stopped at Mundi's store in Markerville, where a call was made to make sure that Helga had in fact caught the train. They stayed in Markerville for a while, as Fanny and Rosa were at a choral rehearsal until 11 o'clock that evening, and when they arrived home around midnight Stephan went out to feed the bull and the pigs before going to bed.[9]

Helga first travelled to Winnipeg where Eggert Jóhannsson met her at the train station. There she also met Baldur Sveinsson and explored the city with her old friend Karólína Dalmann, who had once had such a fierce dispute with Stephan. Helga bought a dress for Rósa, then visited the office of *Heimskringla* and had coffee with Baldvin L. Baldvinsson, with whom Stephan had wrangled so harshly some years before.

From Winnipeg, Helga went to visit her North Dakota relatives, whom she had not seen in 22 years. Both her parents were now deceased, her mother in 1904 and her father in 1909, but her brother, Jón Jónsson Jr., now John Johnson, was still living at Gardar.

Stephan and Helga's daughter Fanny had a good singing voice and Stephan wanted her go to music school. Around this time, an Icelandic composer named Sigurður Helgason lived in the neighbourhood and gave her some lessons. The Sunday after Helga left, the family all went to Markerville, Fanny to sing and Stephan to listen to music that Sigurður had composed to one of his poems. He found the composer "doing well in changing the tones in accordance with the content of the poem, which is not easy to do, although it does not jump particularly high or low in tones, nor tremble in merged tones."[10]

A few days later, near midnight, Stephan sat down in his small office and opened a letter addressed to him in an unknown handwriting. It turned out to be from an old neighbour and distant relative, Andrés Gíslason, who lived in the Icelandic settlement on Lake Manitoba and had lost his only son, a promising boy, in a shooting accident. Andrés was blind and his wife wrote for him, saying that despite bad luck he remained reasonably well. Stephan was contemplative over this letter, and admiring Andrés' stoicism, he decided to respond with a few lines to comfort him. He then began leafing through *Buch der Lieder* by the German poet Heinrich Heine (1797-1856), a recent gift from Reverend Pétur Hjálmsson. In the morning Stephan wrote Andrés, mentioning that almost everyone liked his memorial poems. Andrés, who had hinted at such a poem in his letter, replied immediately with some personal details about his son. His wife added some words of her own, saying that she had cried over Stephan's epitaph for his mother as its sentiment was so similar to her own bright hopes when her son was little.[11]

It now rained continually, and Jakob went to Innisfail in pouring rain on Saturday, July 22, to have some teeth pulled. The following day was clear and they all drove to Baldur's house where the men had a good time until they had to return home for the evening milking. Monday, dry and sunny, was Rósa's birthday. Baldur gave her a wristwatch and Jakob gave her a dollar. Jakob then went to mow Flag Hill with their new mower while Stephan weeded the vegetable garden.[12]

As July wore on, Stephan decided to cancel his trip to Wynyard, Saskatchewan, where he was to read poems on Icelandic Day. Rain had delayed the haying and Helga was still in Dakota. Stephan sent her more money so she could stay longer. The weather remained poor in Alberta. Heavy thunderstorms persisted, but between the showers Stephan tried to stack the hay they had mowed on the riverbank. High winds scattered the hay and he repeatedly had to re-stack it. On the other hand, the potato crop flourished and the family had new potatoes to eat. Icelandic Day at Markerville was now approaching. Stephan was tired and had little interest in going, but people insisted that there would be no festival if he were not there.[13]

It poured the night before the celebrations, but in the morning Stephan went to the celebration with the girls as he had promised to help. The roads were so bad after the rain that festivities did not start until after 3 o'clock in the afternoon. Even then the brass band from Innisfail was late because of the roads. Some of Stephan's friends delivered speeches, including Oldham, the town attorney in Innisfail, who spoke in English. Stephan said a few words but was in a bad mood. "The speeches were poor," he later wrote to Helga. "The singing did not fit with anything that August the Second means, just some songs spouted into the air, although perhaps sung a little better than usual. It turned out fine, however, as people were pleased with everything (except the late start). All public festivities are becoming stupid affairs aimed at entertaining people. That is the law." A large number of the attendees at the Icelandic Day festivities were of English descent and some of the revelers, such as the baseball team from Raven, made a racket "using

Fanny and Jenny, Stephan and Helga's twin daughters.

some kind of a contraption as a noisemaker at every throw of the ball. There was also screaming and whining, especially by the girls." Despite all this, Stephan found it almost amusing to observe the young people entertaining themselves.[14]

Around seven o'clock in the evening, the girls and Stephan left the celebration and drove out to Kristinn and Sigurlaug's house. Stephan walked home from there, but the girls planned to return to Markerville later in the evening. Stephan asked them to leave Rósa, who was only 11 years old, with Sigurlaug, as she had no business with this 'bloody crowd' in Markerville at night. The old man's meddling may have irritated the girls but Rósa obeyed her father and stayed overnight with her aunt.

After the chores Stephan wrote a letter to Helga, concluding with a lyrical description of the beauty of nature. "Outside, the night is calm, clear, yet cool and damp, with stars shining in the vault of the heavens and black lace clouds suspended between heaven and earth, except in the North where it is perfectly clear and there are signs of the Northern Lights. The faint light of the new moon has now faded. The riverbank and Flag Hill are covered with wet haystacks. I have not yet been able to stack all the hay because of the rain, but I can always see something beautiful in nature, no matter what is going on. Otherwise I would have gone insane long ago."[15]

Rain continued during the days that followed, making it impossible to stack the hay and leaving most of the meadows soaked with water. There was nothing to do but "get as wet inside" as well, so some friends gathered at Kristinn's with a supply of beer. Stephan could not avoid joining them and drank until morning when he went home and slept until midday. He awoke, fit as a fiddle, and after chores he visited Kristinn, who had a hangover and complained that his family was angry with him.[16]

Everyone in the district was depressed by the wet weather. Stephan began cutting around the house with his scythe, between the trees and everywhere that the new mower could not reach. His young friends envied his skill with the scythe. The grain grew well. The heads were tight and well filled, rather coarse and beginning to bend over. The fields were so wet, however, that harvesting the grain seemed questionable, and it might have to be cut for fodder. The wet weather continued into September.

Helga returned with an excellent desk chair as a gift for Stephan. It seemed to him that she had benefited from the trip, "as everybody does who travels far enough from home. It loosens up the deadlocks in your mind, for a while at least." The autumn weather continued to be poor. The hay crop was meager and although much of the grain was harvested, a good deal of it was damaged. There was plenty of straw and enough fodder for the animals, however. By the end of October the fields remained unploughed and some grain was still unthreshed. Frost set in and it began to snow. Potatoes froze in the ground and farmers threshed into the winter. The yield, though, was better than expected.[17]

Fanny never did take singing lessons. Stephan asked Jónas Hall about the cost and quality of training in Winnipeg that fall, and Jónas checked out the possibilities of getting her a job as a housemaid with some people who were involved in music and might not mind giving her some singing lessons. There were, however, many hindrances, so Fanny did not go that winter. Stephan also got some negative feedback about the singing lessons in Winnipeg. They were "in the distorted 'French style' that is supposed to be scientific but is really just stupidity." To "bellow with a trembling voice" was something Stephan did not care for, as he said in a letter to Jónas Hall.[18]

Reunion with the Ocean

Eggert Jóhannsson's trip to the Pacific during the winter of 1911 had improved his health. During the rainy summer that followed, hardly able to stand the office where he worked, he considered moving to Alberta or Vancouver. When he shared these thoughts, Stephan suggested that Eggert was such a good employee that rather than moving he should try to find a better job, perhaps in administration. Nevertheless, Eggert moved to Vancouver in August of 1912, which may have caused Stephan to reconsider his own options. Perhaps old Matthías Jochumsson's challenge stuck in his mind: to cross the great mountains and observe the waves of the Pacific. The outside world had finally found the Icelandic settlement in Alberta, so there were few new challenges there. Eggert, happy in his new surroundings, sent Stephan *Rhymes of a Rolling Stone* by a promising poet, Robert Service (1874–1958). Perhaps it was not a masterpiece, he commented, but at least it included "Western Characters".

Stephan read the book with great pleasure and perhaps Robert Service's images of human life and globetrotting inspired him somewhat. "You could hardly have selected a book more to my liking, as my mindset was at that time," he said. "You are damaged by office work and I

Stephan G. Stephansson's speaking tour to the West Coast in 1911.

am worn out by dung heaps, my dear Eggert." Then, in confidence, he added, "I am thinking of quitting farming this year and moving away from here, preferably west to the Pacific if I can get some work that is suitable for an old, unskilled, and austere man. I neither can (nor want to) sell my land now, however, as it is all I own. There is much to consider, but the main reason is that my patience and perseverance with the work is beginning to fail."[19] Stephan had for some years pondered retiring when he reached the age of 60.

The Icelanders in Vancouver asked Stephan for a poem for their Icelandic club and Eggert now took things a step further by suggesting that they invite Stephan to present the poem in person. Jóhann Magnús Bjarnason, who had also moved to the Pacific Coast, supported the idea. Stephan accepted the invitation with gratitude and set off on the journey at the beginning of February 1913.

Stephan's impressions of the Rocky Mountains on the way west were such that 20 storey buildings in Vancouver appeared ridiculously small in comparison. The poet was also thrilled to see the ocean again, after almost 40 years, and it now seemed to him like "a picture from a half-forgotten dream" with its vast emptiness stretching westwards. He remembered his youthful pleasure in watching the ocean. "It is also just as if every thought/ascends from the ocean pure and washed."[20]

Some 350 Icelanders from the Vancouver area attended the banquet in Stephan's honour. An uninhibited atmosphere prevailed and there was a great clattering of forks and knives as guests ate the best imitation of Icelandic specialties ever served in North America. Reverend Hjörtur Leó, who two years earlier had preached against Stephan's books at Wynyard, and Eggert Jóhannsson made introductory speeches, after which Stephan took the podium. His talk was a blend of prose and poetry on themes that included distances, personal impressions of the magnificent Rockies, and the old sagas. Stephan's audience whispered among themselves, commenting on what a great poet he was, and a radical namesake of his put forth the belief that Stephan had yet to attain his greatest achievements. His seatmate added that the *Andvökur* anthology was just morning alpenglow, prefiguring what was yet to come.[21]

Two days later Stephan continued west to Victoria, where he stayed with Arngrímur Jónsson, a brother to Thomas H. Johnson of Winnipeg, who later became a cabinet minister in the Manitoba Government and will reappear in this story. Some of Stephan's old friends from the Dakota years were also living in Victoria, among them Ásgeir Líndal, who gave him a tour of the parks, museums, and the Legislative Building. They then drove to the top of Mount Douglas where Stephan looked out over the great ocean – just as the old poet Matthías had urged him to do.

Stephan read some poems at a gathering in Victoria a few days later. After the reading, Ásgeir Líndal addressed the poet and announced that a few friends had gathered a little sum of money in the hope that this might become the beginning of a greater award for Stephan and other poets. Ásgeir also expressed the hope that Stephan might later travel to Iceland by means of such a grant. Stephan then received an ebony walking stick, after which he expressed his thanks, almost in tears. On his last day in Victoria he visited the City Theatre

Aspiring poet J. Ásgeir Líndal of Victoria, a brother to Jakob Líndal and a former neighbour from Dakota.

to attend an address by William "Big Bill" D. Haywood, leader of the Western Federation of Miners and the most radical labour unionist in North America.

From Victoria, Stephan travelled south to Seattle where he met Kristján Gíslason, the son of Dakota pioneer Hallgrímur Gíslason. Kristján had been just nine years old when his parents homesteaded near Gardar in 1880. Stephan also met his old friend Sveinn Björnsson, who had worked with him on the railroad during the summer of 1880 and had corresponded with Stephan for years. Stephan's most memorable visit in Seattle, however, was with the young mother of several children. Small of stature, with beautiful eyes, she resembled a child herself, while all around her were children, books of poetry, and coffeepots. She presented Stephan with some flowers. "I could hardly believe how summery and cheerful her life was, any more than I could understand how she could go out to her garden and pick flowers in the middle of winter."[22] This was Jakobína Johnson, the daughter of poet Sigurbjörn Jóhannsson about whom Stephan had written a beautiful eulogy. Now 30 years old, Jakobína had inherited her father's poetic talent in abundance and was just about to have her first poems published.

In Blaine, Washington, Stephan stayed with Magnús Jónsson "from Fjall", whom he had known during his youth in Skagafjörður, and when in Crescent, British Columbia, he stayed with Sigurður Christopherson, who had visited him in Alberta when little Rósa was ill. Sigurður's daughter presented him with a book of poetry by Pauline Johnson (1861-1913), who was of Native descent and who, by chance, died in Vancouver while Stephan was there.

Stephan remained in Vancouver until March 8th, and on the last evening he attended another Icelandic gathering. There he read a new poem dedicated

Poet Jakobína Johnson of Seattle.

to his friend and benefactor Eggert Jóhannsson, thanking him for his cordiality to the muse of poetry. The poem describes Eggert's service to truth and art, neither of which found favour with the rich and powerful. Eggert, Stephan maintained, had never lost his dignity. The final stanza is about a man who retreats from the noise of the world into the quiet shadows of autumn as the light shines on the last footsteps of a humble man of genius.[23]

Not long afterward, an article by Ásgeir Líndal appeared in *Heimskringla*, describing Stephan's visit to the Coast and proposing a poet's salary for Stephan. In response, Lárus Guðmundsson, well-known for articles that scolded poets who did not address God in every second line, mocked the idea rather churlishly by saying that many poets deserved such a salary more than Stephan.

Stephan was overwhelmed by the friendship and kindness he had been shown during his travels. It was the traditional Icelandic hospitality that he had thought was on the wane among Icelanders in the New World. He had also received enough money to cover all his travel costs. Now Stephan foresaw that he, together with his friend Jónas Hall and his brother-in-law Jón Johnson, would "move to the Pacific Coast, not to make money, but spend their last years in a beautiful place, in mild weather, to depart from the world in the most comfortable manner – when due to old age one's body has become overly sensitive to the weather and cannot stand the cold anymore."[24]

Stephan retained his fond notions of the West Coast and a couple of years later, in the spring of 1913, he wrote to a friend to ask about the possibility of finding a decent job there, should he move west. He acknowledged it was foolish to think he could continue to manage hard manual labour as the young men did. His family discussed the matter and even considered whether the twin sisters should go ahead first, to explore and see if they liked the West Coast. Baldur's wife was ill that summer, however, so the twins had to help and never did go west. The dream of moving west then faded into the background when Helga bluntly refused to go. Stephan's sister, Sigurlaug, and her husband, Kristinn, however, did move to Smith's Island off the coast of British Columbia, where they remained for two years.[25]

Stephan did not sleep at all during the long train trip back from the West Coast. In Calgary he bought a $.50 bottle of whisky to drink on the last leg of his journey, during which he read Pauline Johnson's poems.

He arrived home tired and without sleep, carrying flowers from Jakobína and an assortment of other gifts. Once home, he could scarcely finish all the chores that awaited him, as his energy and stamina had declined, and after the day's work he lay in bed for a time – sore from weariness throughout his entire body and unable to read or write.

Soon after returning home, Stephan composed a long poem he called "Ferðaföggur" (Travelling Gear), in which he presents powerful images of the mountains, the ocean, the city, and the coast. It also reflects on the sad fate of the Native peoples and alludes to Pauline Johnson, also known as 'Tekahionwake', who had travelled across Canada, the United States, and England, reciting poems while dressed in deerskin clothing. It was as if her poetry introduced a strain of melancholic sadness into Stephan's cultural vision, replacing the disdain in the poem he had written about Indians on the way from Dakota to Alberta years earlier. On his way through the mountains, Stephan had passed through wretched Native villages, looking "as if the spirit of the mountain was buried there." It was, he said, like "the winter sunset of a begging nation,/set before summer arrived to the land."

> *Habitation and the ocean carry the only records,*
> *Distorted names given away by an extinct tongue,*
> *To its places, spelled by wrong mouths.*
> *I hear refrains from the realm of death:*
> *"Our culture rose highest in the truth,*
> *That we know how to die like men."*
>
> *Lost and hidden in a forgotten past*
> *Are the people who hunted and struggled here,*
> *From the darkness of the world of death*
> *Deep in the spruce wood, low as a weak toll of a bell,*
> *A quivering sound: "Te-ka-hi-on-wa-ke!"*
> *While the fir tree grows and the valley can dream.*

Stephan sometimes felt that Icelanders were looked down upon because of their nationality, and near the end of the poem he set out his ideas of humanity and equality by stating that he could never remember "which is the greatest nation".

I do not adore the struggle of the great nations
To make the biggest wheeling and dealing, nor the shame and toil
Of the rich countries to exploit the subservient.
The most important and best is the nation
I think, which most nobly and best
Does to the world from the smallest means.

He felt it was hypocrisy to pretend to see and understand the whole world. "Cosmopolitanism is the whitewash of disgust/cosmopolitan patriotism is too big for everyone."[26] As in many other issues, Stephan was far ahead of his time with his ideas of the value and rights of small nations and ethnic groups.

As Stephan grew old and tired, the settlement continued to move with the times. Automobiles were becoming a familiar sight and Jakob bought a car so he could drive the family to and from town. In 1911 a steel bridge had been built across Medicine River, between the homes of Stephan and his sister, Sigurlaug. Huge telephone poles, soon to be planted into the ground, lay along the road. This modern form of communication would entirely change how the Icelanders in the Markerville area exchanged news and ideas.

It might seem strange that Stephan, in spite of his weariness, now produced as much poetry as before. In fact his output increased after the publication of *Andvökur*. Yet he was always full of doubt when wrestling with his poetic muse, feeling that his poetry was never as good as he wished. When he turned 60 in 1913, he reflected upon his lot in a poem entitled "Afmælisgjöfin" (The Birthday Present). The speaker of the poem, lying awake in his bed near morning, recognizes the footfall of his muse and grabs his harp to play, but the strings are stiff and every sound is like a stuttering tongue. The muse announces that she has come to bid farewell, forever. The poet believes this to be an omen of death since he cannot foresee life without poetry. Although his production had been meager, he argues, he had tried his best to fulfil his obligations to her.

She replied: "I sought you out,
But you often ran away from me, to the hayfield or the woods!
And I do not want to be a partner with
A frail mind or a weakling.
You dedicated your daytime strength to toil,
But only snowstorms, nights, and weariness to me."

The Hola Bridge, constructed across the Medicine River near the Stephansson homestead in 1911.

The poet replies that he had silently carried her with him everywhere he went. If he did not always obey her, it was not to belittle her, but rather because he had other duties – including having to provide for his family. She replies coldly that he has betrayed virtue. "As the god of your art owns your entire mind/duty turns into heresy." Darkness faces the poet when the muse turns her back on him in such a haughty manner. "But a golden bracelet remained, made of sunbeams/glowing at my bedside." The morning sun had begun to shine over the white, frost-covered ground, and the golden bracelet is a symbol for the poet:

> *That it were the kind spirits of those*
> *Who loved my verses.*[27]

Lost Context of Culture

"You, unaware, become nationalistic as you grow older," Stephan wrote in his first letter to farmer Jón Jónsson from Sleðbrjótur, a former parliamentary member in Iceland who had immigrated to Canada and became Stephan's friend.[28] Although Stephan had reconciled himself with the new country long ago in his poetry, Iceland remained on his mind. The relationship of Icelanders in North America to Iceland was complicated. Many had left the country with the compound burden of poverty, frustration with the situation in Iceland, and accusations of treason from those who remained. Such a burden brought mixed feelings: bitter contempt, regret, and ambition to prove to themselves and others that their emigration was neither misguided nor treasonous. People believed in a better future in the West, even though many endured unbearable hardships, especially during their first years, and some tended to exaggerate both the benefits of the New World and the misery of Iceland. Eager to share with their compatriots at home all the glory of their progress in the West, they often sent money home to Iceland to support the modernization of the old country. A group of Icelanders from North America, for instance, sent one of the first automobiles to Iceland in 1913. Arrogance, however, was seldom far behind and some even boasted that they could easily buy Iceland if they wished.

Stephan took a different stance. While fully aware of the superiority of the western world in terms of material resources, progress, and various aspects of culture, he recognized the values Icelanders had brought with them from home – the thirst for education, for example, that he found diminished rather quickly in the West. As time passed, papers such as *Lögberg* published glowing stories of the progress of Icelanders in Canada and the United States. Stephan had mocked this tendency in 1899 with a poem, "Um Íslendingadags ræður" (About Speeches on the Icelandic Day).

> *Western World Folly wearing a tailcoat*
> *Bragging of his own achievements,*
> *Strolling to the rostrum,*
> *At a cocky Icelandic Festival*
> *Feels that if he were silent,*
> *No one would praise him,*
> *"Your own hand is the most loyal"*
> *He thinks and starts boasting,*
> *Says that poor Iceland is lacking,*
> *And God and men are against him.*
> *No one wants a grumbling nag,*
> *To take away the laughter from people.*
> *The bragging will be the worse for him,*
> *If he is allowed to celebrate undisturbed,*
> *His folly day of stupidity.*[29]

This poem implies that many bragging speeches at the Icelandic Festival were mere self-praise. Later, Stephan revealed that he had composed the poem in reaction to a speech delivered by the well-known polar explorer Vilhjálmur Stefánsson. "That is a dead case now and since he was a youth then, I would prefer to spare Villi, so the poem will be put in a 'store of generalities'."[30] Stephan is specific about only one misguided characteristic of festival speeches, namely the tendency to build an identity upon the wretched misery of their Icelandic homeland.

Stephan subscribed to various Icelandic papers and journals and followed rather impatiently his homeland's progress and struggle for independence. As efforts intensified shortly after the turn of the 20th century, he followed still more closely, advocating free trade and the investment of more capital. Over the following decade, Stephan and many of his friends at Markerville tended to support the most radical demands in the independence movement and he sometimes sent poems to the Icelandic papers, which were strongly hostile toward Danish rule. "I worry so much about Icelandic affairs," he confided to Baldur Sveinsson, and in another letter to Baldur he explained that he found both the political leaders in Iceland and the business and cultural climate there so heavily influenced by Danish rule that radical changes were necessary. This, he felt, would only happen with a new generation.[31]

After a fierce struggle in 1912, the independence movement slowed somewhat as Icelanders began to concentrate on developing their economy. One priority was to establish an Icelandic steamship company, a project that united political elements as they all agreed that control of transportation was important for their future independence. The Icelandic papers in Canada published many articles about this initiative, which Stephan supported with a poem, and in September of 1913 Icelanders in North America established a committee to sell shares in Eimskipafélag Íslands, a new Icelandic steamship company. The Icelandic government promised 100,000 *krónur*; the sale of shares in Iceland was expected to raise 400,000 *krónur*; and Icelanders in Canada and the United States set themselves a goal of raising 200,000 *krónur*. Stephan alone collected 4500 *krónur* in the Markerville area. He personally bought shares worth 250 *krónur*, as did Reverend Pétur Hjálmsson, and two of Stephan's sons bought shares worth 50 and 100 *krónur*. Eventually, Icelanders in North America succeeded in reaching their target of 200,000 *krónur*.

Eimskipafélag Íslands (The Steamship Company of Iceland), vital to economic progress in Iceland, was finally established in 1914 with the support of many Icelandic shareholders in Canada and the United States. Pictured is the founding Board of Directors. The company's flagships were the Gullfoss *and* Goðafoss, *named for Icelandic waterfalls.*

Owning ships and controlling domestic enterprise were the keys to Icelandic independence, and Stephan observed Icelandic culture in similar terms. His distance from the old country and his encounters with different cultural currents enabled him to discern the outlines and distinctive features of Icelandic literature with greater clarity, and from this vantage point he expressed his hopes that a more original and independent modern literature would soon appear in Iceland. "Icelandic stories and plays are but an echo of the external world. Only the poetry is partly original," he said in a letter to his friend Rögnvaldur Pétursson. Literature must be "home born and raised. This imported manure will never become anything but glorified cowshed dung, Danish or English, Norwegian or German." It would be nice, he added, if "here in the West we could contribute a hint of inspiration at how to transform the domestic literary heritage."[32]

The hint Stephan had in mind is apparent in a 1907 memorial poem on Benedikt Ólafsson, one of the first pioneers in the Alberta settlement:

During your upbringing, the hut dweller was not taught,
Nor was the nation forced into schools,
But stories and poetry were a self-acquired education,
That taught you intellect and language by song.[33]

In this epitaph, Stephan weaves together elements of Icelandic nature, language, and poetic form with Benedikt's person to create an image of Iceland. Words, songs, and nature had been at the core of both Stephan's and Benedikt's lives, in both Iceland and in the West, and storytelling and poetry were the basis of their autodidactic education.

It soon became evident that Stephan was reflecting on *rímur*, a branch of Icelandic folk literature that had suffered a serious setback when Romantic poet Jónas Hallgrímsson had attacked the genre in a famous review on a book of *rímur* in 1837. His criticism was based on the standards of new Romantic aesthetics.

In the fall of 1913 Stephan found himself unable to work for several days due to a minor injury, and this became an opportunity for him to complete a poem entitled "Kolbeinslag" (Kolbeinn's Song), loosely modelled on the traditional form of *rímur*.[34] This narrative is based on a semi-historical figure, a peasant-poet named Kolbeinn, who composed *rímur*, psalms, and other poetry. Intellectuals had held him in disdain, but according to legend he had once outwitted Satan himself in verse-making. "Kolbeinslag" is in fact a monumental story that Stephan turns into a parable on the significance of poetry for Icelandic culture. Ever since his childhood, Stephan had been fascinated by folktales of Kolbeinn, and not merely with the supernatural aspect, but also with the power of poetry. While the official literary history of Iceland glorified the psalm poet Hallgrímur Pétursson, Stephan preferred to honour the memory of this peasant poet – as the nation owed a debt of gratitude to such poets for maintaining its language and various cultural elements.

Rímur were composed in endless variations of a basic quatrain and "Kolbeinslag" is a free adaptation of that form. Stephan altered and augmented the known tales of Kolbeinn, rendering Satan not only a predator seeking Kolbeinn's soul, but "the chief of this world" bent on distorting the culture of those who were reasonably cultivated. His strategy was to degrade their language, and in Iceland the main obstacles to his plans were self-educated peasant poets – one of whom was Kolbeinn. The poem is pure fiction, but Stephan maintained that it was a description of those who at that time upheld the poetic traditions.

In the original folktale, Kolbeinn wins a competition with Satan and saves his soul with an awkwardly wrought rhyme. In Stephan's poem, however, Kolbeinn and Satan compete by composing powerful verses on the fate of Iceland. The end of the poem is derived from a tale about Kolbeinn's burial on a riverbank, which had stopped the river from eroding more of the land. By adding to and changing the content of the story, Stephan makes the poem a universal ode to traditional poetic culture and its importance down through the centuries. At the same time, the poem deals with the relationship between poetry and power, material values and culture. Satan, as chief of the world, personifies the materialism that Stephan believed was spoiling the Icelandic language and culture.

In October of 1913, Rögnvaldur Pétursson wrote Stephan to request a poem for publication in *Heimskringla*. A new company had purchased the paper and hired Rögnvaldur as editor. The political stance of the paper remained unchanged, but Rögnvaldur had ambitions with regard to the paper's literary policies and suggested to Stephan that the paper would again be a venue for liberal minds. Stephan wished Rögnvaldur well, but at that time he did not have a new poem since he had just sent some to other papers. His poetry, he wrote, depended upon the whims of chance and he feared the Greeks might be correct in their belief that people were unable to do anything of importance after age 60. "The Birthday Present" was a kind of receipt to those who liked his poetry.[35] Stephan, however, later sent Rögnvaldur "Kolbeinslag", which was not printed until April of 1914 – and then anonymously with a few explanations by the author. Rögnvaldur thought that few would understand the storyline without explanation, as most Icelanders in North America were rather uninformed about the old tales. The poem was then published in a separate booklet later that year.

Kolbeinn, the Poet of the Rocky Mountains

"Kolbeinslag" appeared in six segments, each with its own introduction. In the first part, Satan is introduced as the chief of this world. A conniver, he is variously black or white or brown in appearance, and he is allied with the Church, aiming at de-civilizing mankind everywhere:

> *The easiest way to turn people into a mob*
> *Is to damage their language.*
> *From lack of thought, the regression is fast*
> *To apes, brothers of man.*

Satan's ultimate goal is to corrupt the Icelandic language, but first he must deal with poets – especially the self-educated ones. The lore of their poems is the core of the Icelandic nationality.

Kolbeinn, foremost among these self-educated poets, is introduced in the second chapter, and in his description of Kolbeinn, Stephan uses images from the trailblazing of lumberjacks, thus deliberately mixing "western" reality with the Icelandic one. The idea is that poets, just like pioneers who venture into the unknown lands, must blaze a trail for others to follow. Kolbeinn's labour and poetry interlace with aspects of his image. His inner strength contrasts with his appearance, which is not unlike Stephan's. Kolbeinn, however, lives in his hut "alive and dead" and is immortal, having composed poetry "for 300 years".

> *Yet there was not much heroic about Kolbeinn:*
> *His cheeks weatherworn and wizened,*
> *And he was not big of stature,*
> *And his image dark of complexion and small.*
>
> *His knees and back bent*
> *And his big palms were wrinkled*
> *He looked like a plant from a meadow, that by coincidence*
> *Was thrown into the barren desert to wither or survive.*
>
> *When his mood warmed up, he was in good shape,*
> *Bright and daring in appearance*
> *And brightened up like the crooked scrubs,*
> *When the buds open in the spring.*
>
> *And his shed was called a lair or a booth,*
> *And the farmstead all scree and bogs.*
> *For his door, he had no lock at all*
> *Nor for his religion.*

But his poems were flung across the heaths
And to the anglers on the sea.
And he was often the help for the one who was afraid of the dark
And the pride of the district at banquets.

The absence of a lock on Kolbeinn's door symbolizes liberal religious ideas, and his image at banquets recalls Scottish peasant and national poet Robert Burns, of whom Stephan was very fond. Invited on a trip with noblemen, Burns found that he was nevertheless assigned to dine with the common people, though after the meal he was expected to entertain the dignitaries. Refusing to be a poetic jester, he delivers a bitter impromptu poem on paper instead. Stephan later translated this poem into Icelandic.

The third segment of "Kolbeinslag" describes the meeting between Kolbeinn and Satan. Kolbeinn is fishing that day and everything goes wrong. The fish nibble at the hooks, but always tear themselves free, and it occurs to Kolbeinn that the bottom of the sea might be haunted. That evening, Kolbeinn's lead sheep falls over a cliff and dies, and while herding the remaining sheep into the fold that evening Kolbeinn sees a fleeting shadow. "Who the hell is here?" he shouts. Then Satan steps forward, stating that he has some business with Kolbeinn. When Kolbeinn invites Satan home, his wife receives them coldly. The family is starving and Kolbeinn has returned empty handed. It was an old and well-known accusation that those with a passion for poetry were often poor providers. Kolbeinn's wife, however, hospitably serves the guest the last food in the hut. Satan greedily drinks all the milk and leaves the remnants of an old fish for Kolbeinn.

'Kolbeinslag: Gamanríma' (The Lay of Kolbeinn: A Humourous Ballad) appeared in print in the April 9, 1914 issue of the Winnipeg newspaper **Heimskringla**.

Satan then raises his business with Kolbeinn, challenging him to a poetic duel on Draugasker (Ghost Skerry). Kolbeinn accepts the challenge, but stipulates time limits for the contest, which would begin when it "gets coal dark around the Western Star" and would end "when the declining moon opens/its deadly eye above Þverfellshyrna Peak." Satan states that during the first half of the night he will compose the first halves of the stanzas which Kolbeinn must then complete. During the latter half of the night Kolbeinn would compose the first halves and Satan the second. Kolbeinn agrees on the condition that they should switch at the turn of the tide.

Ghost Skerry, the setting for this encounter between Kolbeinn and the dark powers, is a magnificent scene of northern lights and winter darkness. As Kolbeinn rows out to the island, which was half way to the fishing bank, his physical exertion and poetry intertwine:

Have you ever looked around in the lands,
That the poets visit in their imagination?
With a poem in mind and an oar in the hand,
In resistance, sitting on the thwart.

Kolbeinn stepped on board the boat from where the route opened
From the land out of the bay towards the isle.
There was a line in the cruising when the prow thrust forward,
And alliteration in pulling the oars.

Because Kolbeinn's nature was superior,
He managed to do what only few were able to do,
To eat up the crumbs on the path of life
And not let the struggle reduce him.

The term 'superior' may relate to Nietzsche's idea of the 'übermensch'/ superman or Kipling's similar ideas. Stephan said, "I also believe in the 'superman' but not in the way Kipling does. Mine are those who elevate others up to their own level despite any differences in talent. That is the special talent of the 'superman'."[36]

While rowing out to Ghost Skerry, Kolbeinn composes poems on heroic deeds, thus building up his creative momentum. The island is a ghastly place, looking like "an escape vessel for lost souls" with apparitions of the dead clinging to the keel. Satan then sneaks up to Kolbeinn's ear and the contest begins, with Satan composing the first halves and Kolbeinn the 'bottoms'. Each first half is Satan's curse on a certain aspect of culture that Kolbeinn then reverses with his second half. These are the first two:

> *Satan:*
> *The poetic forms we intend to*
> *Undermine by our small strength.*
>
> *Kolbeinn:*
> *Good forces master the form*
> *Let us play with delicate strands.*
>
> *Satan:*
> *Let us scrounge from the foremost peoples*
> *The most famous figures of speech.*
>
> *Kolbeinn:*
> *Let us reign above the wretches, relying*
> *On our own poetic traditions.*

Satan focuses on empty minds, lack of courage, exaggerated rhetoric, degraded language, and superficiality, while Kolbeinn parries in each verse by turning the theme to courageous deeds, constructive energy, creative language, and sincere thoughts:

> *Satan:*
> *At the first verse, you stumbled, but you alliterate*
> *All the others, as a rock on a firm ground.*
>
> *Kolbeinn:*
> *I grow stronger at the metric rhythm.*

During the second half of the night, it is Satan's turn to compose the 'bottoms' (second halves) of the verses. Kolbeinn describes daybreak and beauty, freedom and truth, while Satan turns everything into darkness, spite, oppression, and lies. Normally the composer of the first lines had an advantage, as he could start a verse that was difficult or impossible to finish, but now Kolbeinn realizes that as long as Satan has the last word, he will always have the upper hand. The final meaning of the verses, after all, is what counts, and every positive beginning made by Kolbeinn is being turned into a curse he is unable to break. Kolbeinn therefore has to find another way to defeat Satan before daybreak. The regenerating powers of culture now come to Kolbeinn's rescue as he invents a new metre, "as the devil and oppression are most alike/in having difficulty dealing with innovation."

The final stage of the contest now begins. Darkness, furious waves, and flickering moonlight create an eerie atmosphere as Kolbeinn challenges Satan with the new metre. Satan, in despair, now protests that this metre is nowhere to be found among established poetic forms, so Kolbeinn composes the 'bottom' himself. Satan's weakness is to be tied to everything known. A slave to convention, he is at a disadvantage when it comes to the creative power of poetry. With a subtle verse Kolbeinn then orders Satan to plunge into the ocean. This scene, reflecting Stephan's skill with traditional poetic forms, ends with Kolbeinn's conclusion:

> *So meanly man is made,*
> *And abuses his power:*
> *That more slavish than the slaves*
> *The slave master finally becomes.*[37]

The last segment of the poem, set in modern times, depicts the grassy riverbank of Kolbeinn's deserted farmstead. Kolbeinn's burial place has resisted erosion as if by magic, just like the enchanted spot in Jónas Hallgrímsson's poem "Gunnarshólmi" (Gunnar's Islet), which is a symbol of the Icelandic people's perseverance through centuries of perils. Stephan's poem is thus a subtle parallel and response to Jónas' literary dismissal of *rímur* in 1837.

Stephan did not sign his name to "Kolbeinslag" when it was first printed, "in order to allow people to ponder the identity of the idiot who composed it."[38] However, he did encode his name into the last three stanzas, as the initial letters in the last lines form the words "Stebbi frá Seli" – the nickname by which he had been known when he was a boy at Víðimýrarsel. These stanzas foreshadow the future with an image of cheerful young travellers camping on Kolbeinn's farmstead, but they do not provide an answer to the question of future destruction. Meanwhile, Stephan's hidden signature identifies the poet both with Kolbeinn and the future – at the same time establishing a connection with his youth at Víðimýrarsel. Stephan thereby renews poetic tradition, just as Kolbeinn had done, and praises self-made poets by presenting their heritage to the future. "Kolbeinslag" is Stephan's self-portrait – that of both a dissident poet maintaining the vitality of a culture and a cosmopolitan citizen of the world in the guise of a farmer – intellectually competing with the "chieftains of this world".

The Good Shepherd

In February of 1914 Stephan received a letter from an Icelandic woman in British Columbia who addressed him as "Honoured friend" and then quoted a letter from her sister in Iceland. "I want so much to have an epitaph in memory of my boy composed by your passionate Poet of the Rocky Mountains. In fact my son's favourite poems were those of Stephan G. and I sometimes noticed him slipping them into his pocket as he went out to tend the sheep." Three years earlier, while rounding up his flocks, this young man had tried to rescue a sheep from a swollen brook full of ice floes. The strong current had overpowered him and his body was found after a day's search. An intelligent and promising young man of about 20, he had been the future hope of his parents. The letter writer acknowledged that asking for such a poem was a major request and that it was not possible to pay a fair price.[39]

Stephan, however, could not refuse such a request, and out of it came "Móðurmuni" (Mother's Desire). Icelandic nature, a mother's love, and the young man tending his flocks are at the core of this poem about a good man who dies young while doing noble work. The consolation offered by the poem is similar to that found by Stephan when he lost his son Gestur. Composed in the words of the mother, the poem also echoes Stephan's relationship with his own mother. It begins with a playful brook tumbling down the hillside, singing like a young boy, then darkens as the brook claims the life of the young man. The mother grieves deeply, recalling her dreams for his future in a motherland "beautiful but harsh". The boy's death, however, is portrayed as noble because he "died protecting and rescuing", and the heroic circumstances of his departure make it easier to accept his death – yet another variation on Stephan's theme that humans live on in their work and accomplishments.

A few months after Stephan wrote this epitaph, Reverend Jón Bjarnason, the shepherd of the majority of Icelanders in the Lutheran congregations of the Icelandic Synod, died. Jón had been popular among those who believed in him and he cared for the disadvantaged, but he was rather harsh against those who disagreed with him. A God-fearing woman once eagerly claimed in *Lögberg* that every time something went wrong in her life, she went straight to Jón and received consolation. Kristján Geiteyingur, a well-known storyteller among the Icelanders, composed a verse as the words of the woman:

> *When distress becomes dire*
> *And damage threatens,*
> *I stick the pin of religion*
> *In Reverend Jón's prick.*[40]

It had been many years since Stephan had sparred with Reverend Jón over what the pastor called the atheism of the Cultural Society in Dakota. Stephan, however, had occasionally responded to Reverend Jón's moralizing with a poisonous missive in verse. Now some people expressed the hope that Stephan might write a poem to mark Reverend Jón's death on June 3, 1914, but as Stephan knew only one side of his old opponent, he was not inclined to do so. "I did not know him as he was at home, which no doubt was the sunny side of knowing him," Stephan wrote to a friend. He did not doubt that Reverend Jón was a man of great talent or that many Icelanders in North America owed him their gratitude, he explained, but he felt that the pastor was also to blame for some misfortunes. He had dedicated his talents to maintaining "with somewhat uneven results, a direction in religious matters that has no future." There was much that was "good and unique in Reverend Jón's sermons, but those glimpses of light are completely concealed from the future by layers of a fossilized system of creeds that few are able to penetrate." Although Reverend Jón's writing style was delightful, it was seldom that of a genius, and while he was no doubt a patriotic democrat and a man of integrity, "his talents reached behind themselves."[41]

Stephan did not believe in Christian forgiveness and found it unnecessary to disregard a man's faults just because he was deceased. Four

Despite Stephan's religious antipathy and influence in the community, Markerville had its own Lutheran Congregation, served for many years by Reverend Peter Hjalmsson, seen here with his confirmation class c 1915. From left to right: Helga and Lillian Benedictson, Regina Olson, Louis Sveinson and Sigurdur Vilberg Benediktson, who in 1928 married Stephan and Helga's daughter Rosa.

years later, he expressed his views on Reverend Jón in stronger terms. "The main tenet of the mass is the fear of being called something other than Lutheran, and Reverend Jón kindled that notion more than anyone else. I will never forgive him for being the man of insinuations he was. ... In this way he bullied people from exercising critical thought, leading people to suspect that anyone who did not believe as he did, was bound to be unfaithful in everything. Thus he diminished the spiritual strength of our community and that of his own congregation most of all, while promoting something else – religious arrogance."[42] Such was Stephan's conclusion in 1918 when he had for several years observed political leaders rallying people around a cause he detested.

Chapter 13

The War Years

Blood Sacrifice

Stephan eventually went to Wynyard, Saskatchewan, for the Icelandic Celebration held there on August 3, 1914. Helga went with him and they visited with friends for a week. Stephan's speech at the celebration was about citizenship and the honour of contributing one's best to one's country, no matter which nation fed and fostered him. At the same time he advocated strengthening bonds of brotherhood between the nations of the world.[1]

Just a day before, the Germans had attacked Russia and France, and a day later, on August 4th, the British declared war on Germany. The First World War had begun.

The world had been on tenterhooks in anticipation of this war as the European superpowers, in response to one crisis after another, had formed alliances and proceeded with an ever-escalating armaments race. War seemed inevitable, with only a spark needed to ignite the tinder, and that spark came with the assassination of the Austrian Archduke Franz Ferdinand in Sarajevo on June 28, 1914. By August 3 Austria-Hungary and Germany had declared war on Russia and France, then Belgium the day after, which in turn prompted Great Britain to declare war on Germany.

Canada entered this war as part of the British Empire. Initially there was no conscription, so voluntary enlistment relied upon a combination of patriotism, militant nationalism, and propaganda to inspire thousands of Canada's young men to sign up. Some 20,000 Canadian soldiers were sent overseas almost immediately and 10,000 more soon afterward. At first the war was swaddled in heroic glory, as nobody at that time could imagine how long and violent it would become. As trenches were being dug along the battlefront in Europe, a battlefront was also taking shape in national life back in Canada.

Some Icelanders, many of them Canadian born, responded swiftly to the call to arms and enlisted. A few of them had participated in earlier Canadian wars such as the North-West Uprising in 1885 and the Boer War, to which Stephan had objected so strongly. By now, 42 years had passed since the first Icelander had settled in Canada and immigration from Iceland was in decline. While many immigrant groups were subjected to racist behaviour at the hands of an Anglo-Saxon majority in Canada, Icelanders had gained a large degree of acceptance – though some remained somewhat ambivalent in their loyalties, wanting to maintain their ethnic identity while at the same time conforming to the Canadian way of life. Many prominent Icelanders in Winnipeg, mainly prosperous businessmen, felt that their countrymen had a duty to prove themselves to their new country.

A recruitment poster from the 'Great War' asking young Canadian men to become "One of Kitchener's Own" – in reference to Lord Kitchener, British Secretary of State for War.

It was important for immigrants to demonstrate their loyalty to Canada and the Crown. It was as if it was not enough to offer one's strength, cultivate the soil, and raise a family, as Stephan emphasised in his poems. Now Canadian patriotism, inseparable from loyalty to the British Empire, demanded bloodstained assimilation that resembled a ritualistic sacrifice, as described in an essay written after the war by Reverend Björn B. Jónsson of Winnipeg. This essay examined the motivations of young Icelandic Canadian men who had enlisted: ambition, noble idealism, and conscientiousness. The glorious gain, he wrote, was full acceptance as Canadians. "History teaches that a homeland is seldom dear to its people until they have watered it with their blood. Now it has happened that Icelandic blood has been shed for this new homeland, and we do not love it with mere grandiloquence, but with our blood – blood as hot as that which has poured from the hearts of soldiers who died for us. The atrocities of war, the wounds and the tears, have bought us sincere patriotic feeling for this country. We have now withstood the trials of war alongside soldiers of other nationalities in this country, we have mixed our blood with theirs, we have sworn a common oath of brotherhood with them, and we pledge our honour that this oath will never be broken."[2]

For the most part, the Icelandic papers in Winnipeg supported the participation of Icelandic Canadians in the war. They were, however, caught in the dilemma of either pleasing their readership, many of whom disliked the war, or catering to the political parties that subsidized the papers, both of which supported the war effort. Reverend Rögnvaldur Pétursson, editor of *Heimskringla*, was personally opposed to the war and gave it neutral coverage. Probably due to the publisher's dissatisfaction with this standpoint, he resigned in October and another Unitarian minister, Reverend Magnús J. Skaftason, took over. Eager to praise Canada and the British Empire, Reverend Skaftason proved a fiery supporter of the war.

Cocky Icelandic Canadian recruits at Gimli, Manitoba.

Sigurður Júlíus Jóhannesson, Winnipeg poet, physician, and radical humanist, had edited *Lögberg* since early 1914. He turned briskly against the war, stating that newspaper accounts were pure fiction since the news was being censored. He refused to print many columns on the war and wrote his own critical articles. Within a month he was dismissed and he narrowly avoided prosecution for high treason. His final postscript in the September 3rd issue claimed that his enemies had translated his articles into English and showed them to Canadian authorities. No charges were laid, however, and a pro-war editor took over.[3] Stephan responded to this incident with a little stanza in *Lögberg*, suggesting that Sigurður had been the victim of slander. He wanted to defend the right of men to take an independent social stance and demanded loyalty to the truth that now slept "fettered at the guillotine/under a soldier's sword".[4]

Pacifist editor and poet Dr. Sigurður Júlíus Jóhannesson, affectionately known as 'Siggi Júl', with his wife, Halldóra (Fjeldsted).

Lögberg now began to print news of the war and encourage Icelandic Canadians to enlist in the army. Icelandic leaders in Winnipeg regarded it their patriotic duty to the British Empire to encourage Icelandic participation in the war, and eventually some 1300 Icelandic Canadians enlisted for military service. It was claimed that this was a high percentage per capita compared with enlistment from other ethnic groups, but this was an exaggeration. A patriotic fund was established to support the families of soldiers, but donations were meager. As the war progressed, Icelandic women in Winnipeg established a chapter of the IODE (Imperial Order of the Daughters of the Empire) in support of Icelandic soldiers, to whom they wrote and sent parcels. Funds were also raised for the Red Cross.[5]

At Markerville, as elsewhere, money was raised for the patriotic fund. In November, a choir conducted by Innisfail pharmacist William

Geary performed, and Geary subsequently took the choir from village to village, each of which competed to raise the most money. The community of Markerville raised the sum of $82 and the Women's Institute donated $10 to the Red Cross.

The Spirit of Regression

In the early spring of 1914 Stephan became anxious. "Despite all my sinfulness, or maybe because of it, it so happens that I care most about my own species – humanity." For some days he found himself unable to tend to his farm work and during that time he wrote the poem "Assverus" (Ahasuerus), based on the tale of a wandering Jew called Ahasuerus, who denied Christ and was therefore doomed to eternal wandering. Stephan regarded the treaties between the superpowers as based upon a balance of mutual threat, whereby each military power felt insufficiently armed to defeat the other. He considered "that the world was resting on falseness and the peace on embers." From these thoughts, he composed "Assverus".[6]

The poem, which is without rhyme, expresses disruption and panic. Stephan extended the image of the Wandering Jew to all evil persons in history. Heroes and priests had the same frame of mind, independent of religion. "The holy cross and the Arabic crescent moon/I hang on poles above corpses and slaves." His protagonist wanders the world, blessing murder weapons, strengthening people's folly, and sharpening their killing skills.

> *I wander through all taught history*
> *Under the pseudonym of defiled virtue:*
> *If freedom manages to triumph,*
> *I find out and give it evil advice,*
> *Then bring around slander about licence and frolic*
> *All the way between sense and stupidity.*

"Look, I am the spirit of regression," declares Ahasuerus, whose soul is damaged "after warfare against freedom."[7]

Stephan could not accept that war was an issue that could be accurately viewed as black or white, but it was difficult to oppose the rhetoric of religious leaders who spoke of blood sacrifice and revenge as key concepts. In his letters, Stephan ironically analyzed and explained the causes of the war in the manner of contemporary radical intellectuals such as the American socialists with whom he was familiar. Despite the fact that war had broken out suddenly, it had been predictable, he claimed, due to systemic exploitation by which men and nations preyed upon the labour of others. Now the force of arms would decide "who shall eat or be eaten". Capitalists and kings fight over this. Britain has "eaten almost all that is edible of the world and Mad Wilhelm awaits his turn," Stephan wrote, referring to the German Kaiser. The ruling classes celebrated the war since it reduced the threat of proletarian revolution. "I hope all the superpowers lose enough blood. Then they might become a bit wiser. Improvements generally follow in the wake of revolutions."[8]

Stephan held forth the opinion that so-called nations were really nothing more than heads of state and capitalist interests, thereby indicating that nationality was a product of the 19th century. The only difference between the two major antagonists of the war, according to Stephan, was that the British already controlled a larger share of the market while the Germans were struggling to create areas of growth for their capitalists. Later research partially confirms Stephan's view that Germany's heavy industry did take advantage of its close ties with the state in order to initiate a war – which in turn would make Germany a world power on par with Britain.[9]

Some suggested that Stephan showed a pro-German bias, but his mockery of "Mad Wilhelm" does not support that claim. In fact he disliked all extremes and he was shocked by the persecution of Germans in Canada. "Apart from all the other stupidity going on, we Canadians are going mad for fear of the Germans," he wrote. "Even here in Alberta, in my district, they drag old farmers to court martial. Indeed some have been gibbering stupidly about German military efficiency, but that is almost understandable as their nation is abused so disgracefully by the others, especially in the newspapers."[10]

Shortly after the beginning of the war, Stephan's anti-war poetry began appearing in the Icelandic newspapers, first *Heimskringla*, then *Lögberg*. In the poem "Ögranir" (Provocations), printed in the September 17, 1914 issue of *Heimskringla*, he expressed outright anger:

> *When every thug and loudmouth*
> *Stirred up the stupidity to a tumult,*

> *Yet ready to spare himself and his kin,*
> *Not going to go himself!*
> *Egged most the common man*
> *To sacrifice his life for the fosterland,*
> *Certain to profit*
> *Some honour and wealth from his blood,*
> *By the shallow shouts of false bravado*
> *By the title of popularity:*
> *Then it demanded the greatest guts,*
> *To dare not to participate.*[11]

That it was in fact courageous to withstand the dominant mob mentality was Stephan's firm standpoint throughout the war.

The poem "Hleiðra"*, printed in the November 19, 1914 issue of *Heimskringla*, is based on the legend of a great battle in which two noble heroes defy evil powers. The Viking Böðvar is a man of peace who fights defensively by merely parrying the weapons of his enemies, "blunting the edges of malignity". His companion, Hjalti, fights aggressively. In the battle, Hjalti eggs Böðvar on and thus spoils Böðvar's ability to blunt the weapons of evil. Böðvar, now forced to fight, proclaims that Hjalti is no different than the enemies. His soliloquy ends thus: "The most powerful Viking hand/breaks weapons and pacifies the land."[12] In this poem, based on an ancient Viking legend, Stephan presents his concept of the pacifist ideal.

News from the Battlefield

Following the death of Skafti B. Brynjólfsson – Stephan's former comrade in the Dakota Cultural Society and his benefactor through the publication of *Andvökur* – Stephan wrote a memorial poem focusing on Skafti's leadership and ability to stand alone against the crowd. When the poem was printed in *Lögberg*, Reverend Magnús J. Skaftason, editor of *Heimskringla*, impulsively wrote to Stephan claiming that he was doing so on behalf of Skafti's widow and accusing Stephan of sending the poem to a paper that had always showed Skafti contempt. Stephan, he stated, should have let the widow decide where the poem was to be published, and he added that she considered this decision a poor reward for everything Skafti had done for Stephan.

---

* "Lejre", a place name in Denmark

Stephan responded with a long, sharp letter to Reverend Magnús, stating that Skafti had never rebuked him for publishing in *Lögberg* and that it was too much to expect that he should be party to petty factionalism in Winnipeg. Skafti had been righteous and free of prejudice, Stephan pointed out, and Reverend Magnús would never have dared write such a letter if Skafti were still alive. With regard to all that Skafti and his brother had done for Stephan in connection with the publication of *Andvökur*, he pointed out that those who had implemented the project had done so on their own initiative, despite his own attempts to discourage them. "I understand people a bit and suspected that this could later lead energetic persons like you, Magnús, ... to claim the right to reproach me if I, willingly or unwillingly, stepped upon one or another toe... That has now happened, but I know that the Brynjólfsson brothers themselves would never have resorted to such a tactic..."

Stephan went on to explain his poem, pointing out that Skafti's contemporaries in the Cultural Society had never fully appreciated his exceptional abilities or been able to find him a task befitting his talents. With regard to the "cardinal sin" of having published the poem in an "enemy paper", Stephan echoed his earlier words to the Cultural Society during the feud with Reverend Jón Bjarnason, stating that he much preferred to publish his atheist works in a Catholic paper. Skafti had smiled at this response as he had understood the argument.[13]

In February of 1915, Skafti's widow, Gróa, wrote Stephan to apologize for having been the cause of this outburst from Reverend Magnús. She understood and appreciated Stephan's poem and asked him for a handwritten copy. Skafti had collected all the poems about his brother Magnús at the time of his death a few years earlier, including a poem by Stephan, and

Reverend Magnús Skaptason (1850-1932), the popular but controversial Unitarian minister and editor.

now Gróa wanted to collect the poems about Skafti. Stephan responded warmly and sent the poem, but by now he had seriously provoked the Icelandic factions in Winnipeg, which had changed allegiances due to the war. Former opponents now united in support of the war, and since Stephan had revealed anti-war opinions, many undoubtedly wanted him silenced.

While this went on, *Lögberg* and *Heimskringla* brought news of the war to the homes of Icelandic families in Canada and the United States. In November of 1914, for example, *Lögberg* reported on the misfortunes of Canadian troops before they reached the battlefield. They had encountered rain and illness on the Salisbury Plains in England, and their boots were so bad that they fell apart in the mud. Corrupt politicians were to blame for that, while the British government obtained 75,000 pairs of watertight boots. Early in the spring of 1915, the first Canadian troops – including numerous soldiers of Icelandic parentage – were sent to the battlefront, and before long they were among the victims of disease, hunger, and human sacrifice.

A short, sharp attack was expected to break the German line of defense, but that did not happen and a deadlock settled in over the trenches. The Icelandic newspapers described vividly the terrible misery among the Germans and the heroic nobility of the Allies. Reports became increasingly sombre as time passed, but there were also regular accounts of the outstanding achievements of Icelandic soldiers, such as master marksman Jóhann V. Austmann, whose letters to his father were printed in *Heimskringla*. Articles took a more sinister turn with news of the first Icelandic casualties at the end of April of 1915.

Censorship took immediate effect in Canada, but Stephan evidently received newspapers from the United States with more impartial reports of the war. Figures for the numbers of casualties varied widely and Stephan did not trust the official bulletins. By the summer of 1915 he estimated that between 9,000 and 10,000 Canadians had lost their lives, a much higher number than that appearing in *Lögberg* in the fall.[14] The papers also printed letters from soldiers who had been taken prisoner by the Germans, yet who remained in good condition. Their letters, though censored, contradicted stories of German cruelty. Most of the prisoners requested food and in response *Heimskringla* printed their postal addresses with appeals for a direct public response. When Jóhann Austmann was taken prisoner, his letters included requests for books, as he was studying French and wanted to learn German.

While hatred of the Germans increased in Canada, occasional news of friendly interaction at the battlefront also appeared. In the beginning of 1915, *Lögberg* printed an account entitled "Cease-fire in Secret", about the amicability soldiers showed each other when they could, especially at Christmas, even though there was no official armistice during the Christmas holiday. In many places along the front there was only a short distance between enemy trenches and sometimes jokes were exchanged across the line.

An Icelandic Canadian recruit to the 'Great War' photographed in Winnipeg with the women in his life. His mother's look is one of protective defiance.

Food was cooked in underground kitchens and carried to the trenches through tunnels. The couriers who delivered food sometimes took a shortcut above ground as there was mutual agreement between the opposing sides that couriers would not be shot. It was also mutually agreed that soldiers could come up from their trenches in the morning, stretch a bit and get some fresh air, though they had to be unarmed. As soon as they returned to their trenches, however, shooting would resume.

Lögberg also printed an account from German and British lines some distance from the main battlefield. Six days had passed without shooting and the opposing soldiers had begun exchanging words and small packages. Two days later, the Germans raised a white flag and came unarmed out of their trenches. Enemy soldiers began talking to each other and some decided to share trenches until they received further orders. They dined, smoked, and even kept each other company overnight. They also exchanged newspapers, however, and when they read the accounts of each other's deeds and misdeeds, the friendly dealings dissolved in fistfights and the mutual visits came to an end.

Obviously this account impressed Stephan since it inspired him to compose a long poem that he started in February of 1915. A young Icelandic minister, who later became Bishop of Iceland, had served in Markerville during the summer of 1914 and once stayed overnight with Stephan and Helga. Stephan liked him, found him intelligent and kind, and discovered that this young man liked his poems. After this minister's return to Iceland, the two corresponded, and in the spring of 1915 Stephan sent him the long poem he had finally finished. It was entitled "Vopnahlé" (Cease-fire) and as Stephan may well have feared censorship in Canada, he asked his friend to have this poem published in Iceland. Favorably impressed, the young minister took it to Guðmundur Finnbogason, editor of *Skírnir*, which was the journal of the Icelandic Literary Society. Guðmundur gladly accepted the poem for the summer issue of this prominent journal and paid well for it.

Guðmundur subsequently thanked Stephan for his submission, saying that he admired his poetry and often quoted him in speeches and essays. Stephan replied that he was surprised to receive payment, as he was content simply to have his poems published. He also acknowledged that editors of Canadian newspapers and journals would have been reluctant to publish the poem, "no wonder, as opposed as it is to their needs these days, and so critical of the war god they praise."[15]

Cease-fire

"Vopnahlé", a long narrative poem running 28 pages, is about two enemy soldiers, one young and the other elderly. Set during a brief cease-fire, the poem begins with their conversation, which first conjures up the horrors of war and then gradually reveals its causes and implications, analyzing the societies and mindsets behind the war. The old soldier is experienced and sarcastic, while the younger man is just beginning to develop a more mature perspective of things. Humanism is the basic theme running through the entire poem and is revealed through both the conversation and appearance of the two men.[16]

The poetic form is pentameter without rhyme. The stanzas are uneven in length and the lines are sometimes half-length, interfering with any mechanical rhythm. The beginning of the poem depicts a horrible scene:

The gunfire had ceased for a while,
The fierce attacks and defence shortly halted.
The pile of corpses had reduced the chances
Of both sides continuing the slaughter,
The lines of battle could not get near each other,
The heap between had blocked their arms.
This human flow of maggots,
Rotten, breaking quicksand of corpses
Black with putrefaction, some places moving.

An agreement had been made for a few hours,
A cease fire, as the corpse-heaps were to be removed.

After that the battle was to begin
Again, on a cleaned trail to hell.

Every pawn sat on his square meanwhile
As the chess game of slaughter waited.
The calling distance was the width of the battlefield
Between the frontline killers.

Then "father and son" – as the two soldiers often address one another – make their respective appearances. The younger man, the son, stands up from behind a tattered bush where he had crawled into a freezing pool of blood and mud during the long, cold autumn night:

It was still sweet for his strong youth,
To rise up into sunshine and peace.

On the other side, an elderly man clad in wet and bloody clothes rises from a festering grave between the corpses of his youngest son and his best friend. Glad to be able to sit up awhile, he greets the young man – who could be his son's killer – as "a companion in the distress of deadly perils and hateful chance". In contrast to the powers behind the war, the compassion shown by the two men in the middle of all the horror is the core of the poem.

The old soldier greets the young man in his own language and the young soldier replies in a friendly fashion to "my enemy a short while ago,/now a father". It is not without pain, however, that the older man addresses the young soldier as his son:

> *"I should call you a son,*
> *As you address me as father.*
> *Yet I feel I cannot call another*
> *A son than him, who lies here*
> *A corpse beside me, in our common grave.*
> *But that does not mean enmity*
> *Between us."*

The "son" praises the older soldier for how well he "defends his fatherland's honour", but the father objects. He does not own a "foot of the fatherland!/I have not grasped arms for that," he says, as his family has lived as landless tenants for generations. Centuries ago, the land owned by his forefathers had been seized and given to a nobleman as his inheritance. Now, he said, the squire sits at home unharmed while the old man and his son lay down their lives on the battlefield. He then asks the young soldier whether he is defending his father's house. That is far from the case, however, as the boy is a "city-dweller/just goods on the market for those lords/who decide the working hours and wages."

The nationality of these two soldiers is unclear and Stephan analyzes the powers behind the war without regard to nationality or political rhetoric. The young man regards the old soldier's country as too militant, but the "father" claims that in his country people had spoken only of peace – though to little effect. The rich, who exploit the common people, had at first found global peace to their advantage, but they now considered war more profitable. He asks the young soldier whether it is the same in his country. The young man then tells of the leading pacifist in his country, who had always demanded freedom and peace for the poor and the workers but had received nothing but scorn and hatred from the leaders. When he had protested against nationalist saber rattling, it was those he had sought to protect – "we, who jumped up and raised our fists/shouting: you should shut up!"

The "son" asks the old soldier whether a lack of religious faith is to blame for this. The old soldier's response reflects the religious views expressed by Reverend Björn B. Jónsson, cited above. Christianity and heathendom had gone hand in hand during the crusades, he points out, with the clergy calling for sharp, blood-covered weapons and applauding the call to arms. He then describes the priest of his parish:

Took up the Bible from the shelf,
proving that anyone who did not now fight,
for the cause of God and good manners,
could not have understood Christianity,
being blinded by heathen frame of mind.

The "son", having witnessed the same in his homeland, asks whether the "father" is fighting in the hope that traditional religion will be restored. The old soldier replies that he does not believe in a 2000 year-old Word of God. In school he had been taught manslaughter according to the law, and if he had refused to serve in the army he would have been court martialed and shot.

I have children and wanted to venture to live
for them. War is open death,
but sometimes you can get away alive,
while court martial is always final. I chose the war.

He then asks the young soldier whether he had voluntarily joined the army in a country free from conscription. The "son's" reply is similar. External forces had influenced him to join the army: economic crisis, labour strikes, unemployment, inflation, and – if he had stayed at home – the contempt of his fellow citizens.

The conversation then turns to the delicate issue of who was responsible for starting the war. The "son" blames the monarch of the opposing nation, while the "father" has a wider perspective on the situation. Like many people, after long contemplation he had begun to suspect that there was something wrong with the "increased slavery" he was witnessing in society. The establishment then began to "tremble with fear, those who are/the same in all countries and derive support/from each other." Power and class structures are the same in all countries, he pointed out, and political leaders everywhere look after the same interests, in order to maintain power. These leaders had started the war so that the common people would forget their dissatisfaction at home. The old soldier then calls it "patriotic arrogance" for those in power to seek to mould the entire world in the manner of their own nation. Their "war mongering" is a threat to the diversity of culture. "World culture is created by all nations/based on the ways of life in every country," he says.

The young soldier recognizes the pattern, but points out that his own country's leaders have another way of putting it: "to protect freedom". He then relates how some aristocrats had visited the battlefront during a cease-fire and asked the soldiers what they wanted most. The soldiers had hesitated, since they did not wish to offend the nobles, but a military doctor had spoken up:

> *You can, he said, get yourself a shovel.*
> *As you want to help us a little bit,*
> *And please clear away some of this*
> *Rotting flesh. We can't keep up,*
> *We are tired. How quickly they then*
> *Bade us farewell and left. I never again*
> *Heard of this bunch coming to the front.*

The young man then speaks of the hardiness of his fellow soldiers against superior strength, in contrast to those who know that victory is theirs due to superior numbers. The word *victory*, however, provokes a bitter reply from the "father", who rips the illusion of *victory* to pieces and points out the vicious cycle of violence.

> *Victory! my friend, I do not care about victory!*
> *The victory of states turns to defeat soon after.*
> *A defeated nation that is allowed to live,*
> *Lives for revenge, as the power*
> *Always falls due to its own victories*
> *In the end. The cost of victory is revenge.*

These words strike a chord with the young soldier. He had doubted the logic of war when he had witnessed its destruction, but he had suppressed the thought since he knew that it was high treason to disobey. The conversation between the two soldiers now kindles new ideas, mutual understanding, and recognition that dialogue should prevent war in civilized society. The young man then expresses the hope that this world horror is in reality the death agony of war, after which peace will reign.

The old soldier, however, cannot share this optimism while neither of them enjoys real freedom. He says that individual rights are weak against martial law and prejudice, and that no-one is allowed to be impartial. The best and bravest of the new generation are also being sacrificed, so the future will be in the hands of those who are cowardly and self-serving.

With regard to his side, the young soldier states that society at its best has been forced to defend itself, since the enemy had seldom followed the path of invention and progress. Regression and crisis would therefore follow in the wake of the enemy's assumption of world power. The old soldier does not deny this and concedes that his country has been embroiled in a religious war for 30 years. He points out, however, that a new "religion" is now asserting itself in the world, a system of shallow technocracy, factory slavery, and world economic competition. Those nations who practice it have built their economic wealth on the weak – their colonies – and they are therefore not really fighting for freedom, but for empire.

The poet during a speaking engagement around the time of the war.

The idea that colonial exploitation was an economic premise of the war was new at that time. Perhaps Stephan had heard this theory from W. E. B. DuBois, a black leader who had lectured on that topic in Alberta and other locations during the fall of 1914.[17] Stephan recognized that technological progress was already bringing destruction, although this was long before the age of weapons of mass destruction and the nuclear arms race. It is as if Stephan foresaw the upcoming deadlock of trench warfare:

> *Perhaps the end of man*
> *Is death by his own means?*
> *They immediately turn tricks against dodges,*

> *Until they can neither move forward nor backward,*
> *Their hopes of victory are torn down,*
> *Will they have to rescue themselves from the burden*
> *Of their monstrous knowledge, made to destroy?*

The young soldier then tells of a war machine his comrades had tried to protect, but which the enemy had managed to destroy. Such machines, he says, are a far cry from the ancient heroes people used to admire. The old soldier adds that warfare is a cold, detached game of chess, calculated to use men as bait in hope that the enemy will make a fatal move. "We are a captive herd, whom the leaders/have driven into the fold, under the knife." Now bravery and battle skills have given way to ignominious slaughter and fatal disease.

The "son" then recounts an unusual story of bravery. A young man who had refused to join the army was accused of cowardice, even though he had the courage of his convictions to "stick to the peace". Not far from where this young pacifist lived, an enemy regiment had laid siege to a town. The young soldier's troop had then recruited him as a guide, but the young pacifist had led them on a wild goose chase until the officer demanded that he immediately take them within enemy range:

> *The young man looked at the gun and smiled:*
> *I cannot obey your order, Sir.*
> *Now you will never reach your enemy,*
> *I have led you astray,*
> *To spare a few lives, temporarily*
> *For mine in return and now you can fire!*
> *Dozens of rifles immediately resounded,*
> *Leaving a bloody corpse.*

The young soldier asks whether this pacifist's conduct, similar to the neutrality of small nations, does not evoke some hope for the future. This, in turn, prompts a long speech by the father. "Neutral! My boy, who is neutral?" He goes on to claim that people will continue this war as long as they can afford it, and then they will borrow funds from other nations. The global economic system maintains the war, therefore nobody can be truly neutral. He expresses the wish that some nations might avoid sacrificing their best blood in this catastrophe, so they might keep their young men and maintain some hope for the future.

This madness rages on as never before, however, and it requires a great deal of optimism to have any hope, he concludes. Even if some nations want to sit by and remain neutral, the warring nations will force them to participate in some way, as they want to drag everyone with them into the worst Hell. "In the realm of Hell there has never/been any room for a smallest bit of humanity," the old man says, and little hope exists in this terrible catastrophe in which pacifists are oppressed. Mutual compassion, however, on the part of all those who lose their beloved in the war, might eventually lead to international reconciliation.

With that, the removal of the dead from between the opposing trenches is over and the battle must resume. As the young soldier takes some food from his haversack, the old soldier turns away, but "son" now offers "father" a bite to eat, saying that he had lost his appetite when he had learned that the old soldier had been kept in the trenches for four consecutive days while younger soldiers were being rotated in shifts so they could eat something during the battle. The old soldier thanks the young man and with that the conversation between them ends just before the battle resumes:

> *"Many thanks for the kindness!*
> *That it still exists among common people,*
> *Our masses, here in this hostility,*
> *Is the only hope. But the kindness to me*
> *Matters little, as there is not much time left.*
>
> *I could not bear, young man, to watch you eat,*
> *Unsure that a hungry wolf's empty stomach*
> *Could resist such a challenge.*
> *I was determined not to harm you,*
> *And therefore wanted to turn away from you.*
>
> ❦
>
> *"It is now time to resume the game,*
> *Our trumpets fiercely signal an attack!"*
>
> ❦
>
> *"Our drums are beating for defence!"*
>
> ❦
>
> *"Beware my weapon, father!"*
>
> ❦
>
> *"Welcome to my grave, son!"*[18]

The poem is a description of the merciless rules of society, economic systems, and their appetite for war. The only ray of hope, weaker than in most of Stephan's other works, is found in the spontaneous solidarity kindled by a conversation between enemy soldiers, the admiration of pacifism, and empathy among those who lose their beloved in the war. Compassion transcends the horror of the battlefield and defeats basic impulses like hunger.

Life in Markerville

Lögberg carried half-hearted and somewhat inaccurate news of the publication of "Vopnahlé" and noted that its subject matter was quite crude. Neither the poem nor its actual content, however, was printed in North America during the war since it was deemed unacceptable by leaders of the Icelandic community in Winnipeg, who were definitely not eager to promote this kind of Icelandic poetry. Had the poem been in English, it would likely have been banned.

Despite the shadow of war, life in Markerville continued as usual – sometimes with occasions for celebration. In early August of 1915, Stephan's brother-in-law Jón Jónsson (Johnson) came from North Dakota to visit, and Stephan and Helga hosted a party for some 30 friends and relatives the evening before he left. In his address to the guest of honour, Stephan pointed out that Jón had been a State congressman and a worthy opponent for the Conservatives. He also praised Jón's solid self-education. Having been raised the Icelandic way in America, he had acquired some knowledge of literature and a good grasp of contemporary trends, Stephan said. The 'school of life' in the forests of Wisconsin and on the prairies of Dakota

> Vopnahlé.
>
> Formáli:
> »Kvöddu í mig klökkva
> Karl, með ljóði þínu!
> Hreyfðu ei höfði mínu,
> Hlíðu þessum nökkva«.
>
> Eftirmáli:
> Taki ei vit á tilfinningu
> Taumhaldið, kann enginn segja
> Hvernig hennar brautir beygja
> Byljir á tíðar straum-hvirfingu.
> Hún hefir verið voði, í höndum
> Vanhyggju, í öllum löndum.
>
> * * *
>
> Skothríðin um stundar-bil var stytt upp,
> Stöðvað snöggvast áhlaups-geys og viðnám.
> Hræ-valurinn hafði hvorutveggjum
> Hindrað tök, að láta brytja niður,
> Fylkingarnar hvergi í færi komist,
> Kösin milli borið skildi á vopnin.
> Ófær var sú manna maðka-veita:
> Morkið, hrannað kviksyndi at náum.
> Yldu-svörtum, sumstaðar á iði.
> Samist hafði því um fárra tíma
> Vopnahlé, því valinn átti að ryðja.

Stephan's pacifist poem "Vopnahlé" was provocative material during the 'Great War' and was first published in Iceland.

had stood him in good stead, he added. Singing and dancing followed, and Stephan's twin daughters managed to get both Jón and their uncle Kristinn onto the dance floor, though neither old timer had danced for some 20 years.[19]

Hail damaged Stephan's crops that fall, and unsettled weather, alternating between rain, snow, and freezing temperatures, spoiled the hay. The economy, however, boomed during the war years as the demand for agricultural produce increased and prices rose, and Stephan often had as much as $100 in the bank.

Rósa Stephansson, the youngest daughter of Stephan and Helga.

The war, on the other hand, was also used to justify more intervention in people's lives. Prohibition became law in 1915 and went into effect during the summer of 1916. The government also resorted to promoting extreme patriotism in its drive to recruit more soldiers and solicit funds for the war.[20] "This 'pleading patriotism' for the war is out of control," Stephan wrote in a letter late in 1915. "Attempts to rally support are made by begging, dancing, playing, singing, etc., preferably every week." On New Year's Eve of 1916, Jakob and the twins went to a Christmas fundraising dance for the patriotic fund.[21]

The new year, 1916, arrived on a cold Saturday. Rósa, now 15 years old, began keeping a diary in English, referring to her siblings in the English manner – Jake, Fan, and Jen – and documenting the daily life of the family, including both work and entertainment. She and her siblings played cards at the homes of neighbours and went to church, although Rósa echoed her father's religious views in references to the pastor's nonsense. Two young men, Árni Bardal and Sigurður Kristjánsson, often came to visit the Stephanssons, obviously courting the twins.[22]

Along with the usual daily chores, there were frequent trips to Markerville for the mail and shopping. Stephan also served as electoral officer during the municipal elections that always took place in the New Year. Rósa enjoyed novels such as Tolstoy's *Anna Karenina*, while her father read Tolstoy's essays, a Christmas gift from his old friend Eggert Jóhannsson. The telephone had arrived, so Helga could now call Baldur to hear how her grandchildren were doing. She and Jenny often went to help when Baldur's children were ill, and the men helped each other with chores and caring for the livestock.

It was a cold January. During an epidemic that winter the sisters fell ill and a neighbourhood child died. Rósa read novels eagerly, sometimes aloud for her mother. Helga's little black calf died, despite efforts to save it, and the cow Urt was "getting burðarleg" (likely to calve soon), Rósa wrote in her diary, mixing the two languages. By February the weather was getting warmer and on Valentine's Day Rósa received 10 cards. Not allowed to go to a masquerade dance four days later, she pledged her determination to go wherever she liked when she grew older. Leap year's day, February 29th, was bitterly cold again, but that did not prevent Baldur, Jakob, and their friend Sigurður from attending a socialist meeting in Markerville.

Stephan withdrew increasingly from family life and retreated to his study where he received visits from his sons and neighbours. He preferred to observe his grandchildren from an appropriate distance and they in return found him rather unapproachable. Helga gave them cookies and told them stories about the pioneer years in Wisconsin and Dakota. Life became ever-more anglicized, which Stephan rather disliked, though his own language usage also included English phrases.[23]

Occasionally, the monotony of this rural society was broken by some unexpected event. In 1916, for example, young Prince Erik of Denmark, grandson of King Christian IX, stayed for a time at the home of Daniel Mörkeberg, the Danish manager of the creamery at Markerville. Erik was a reserved boy who had no interest in war and preferred to do chores with the other teenagers. Court life, he declared, was "no damn good". Stephan felt insincere when he met the boy and quipped, "Glad to meet you, Prince Erik."[24]

Rósa had long since graduated from playing with the animal bone livestock she had owned as a child. Those toys were now overgrown with grass, and one day as Stephan walked by and noticed them, a little poem came to mind.

Grief steers my verses
My little girl
When I see abandoned
The toys of your childhood.
May you never outgrow
Building palaces to live in,
From small belongings.
That would be a change:
Certainly harmful for you,
*And the world would lose a poet.*²⁵

A Good Guest

Dr. Guðmundur Finnbogason, editor of the Icelandic journal *Skírnir*, had been an infant in his cradle when Stephan and his parents – on their way to take passage to North America – had ridden by his childhood home in July of 1873. Now Director of the National Library and among the most influential intellectuals in Iceland, he was invited to Canada in the spring of 1916. Stephan knew that Guðmundur planned to visit Markerville, and on Saturday, May 20th, his son Mundi received a telegram asking if Stephan would be able to meet Guðmundur on Monday, at the railway station in Innisfail. Mundi and Stephan conferred over the telephone on Sunday and decided to borrow a car. Having just sat down in his study after talking to Mundi, Stephan was surprised when "the door to my den opened and there stood a handsome man with dark eyebrows, swarthy cheeks, and black eyes, whom I recognized immediately from photographs as Dr. Guðmundur Finnbogason. I greeted him by that name, although he did not expect me to recognize him at first sight." There had been a change of plans and Guðmundur had arrived in Edmonton the day before. After giving his talk, he and his party had taken the train to Red Deer and hired a car from there.²⁶

The guests stayed at Stephan's for two nights. Guðmundur delivered a well-attended talk in Markerville the day after he arrived and Stephan liked the speaker's articulation. He sensed no hollow pontification, which was fairly typical of elaborate rhetoricians, and he was impressed by Guðmundur's knowledge of Icelandic poetry. "Just as an Icelandic oarsman chants a pretty sailing verse to make the rowing easier, Guðmundur lightened his talk with Icelandic poems, resting his mind as he recited them." Stephan took an immediate liking to Guðmundur and they conversed at length. "We covered many topics ranging from Icelandic *skyr* to the concept of existence as a spiral or a circle," Stephan said.[27] No doubt what was discussed was whether existence is closed in an eternal circle or whether progress makes the eternal cycle a spiral.

In the evening, more visitors arrived at Markerville. Among them was Hannes Marinó Hannesson, a lawyer from Winnipeg, Stephan's cousin and one of the publishers of *Andvökur*. He was there, however, on a very different errand. As a high-ranking military officer and commander of the Scandinavian Division of the Canadian military forces, he was a key person in supporting Icelandic participation in the war. Stephan said only that Marinó was a nice man and that he trusted him to handle this "evil" issue well. "Whatever local people's thoughts and interests may be with regard to this war, some undoubtedly wished he had stayed a bit longer, but he only stayed here overnight."[28]

On Tuesday morning, Mundi and Stephan drove their guests to Innisfail by horse and wagon. Marinó Hannesson returned a few days later with Thomas H. Johnson, recently appointed to the cabinet of the provincial government of Manitoba and the first Icelander to attain such high office. Stephan, however, quickly grew tired of these recruiting agents and called them military beggars who were supposed to work everyone into a frenzy of support for the army. "What bloody idiots these government people are," he wrote, "not to take the old men first, such as you and me, in order to spare the nation's seed..." Others admired the eloquence and elegance of the visitors. There was only one flaw with the recruitment

Stephan's influential friend Guðmundur Finnbogason, head of the National Library of Iceland.

meeting held at Markerville. Not one man enlisted, perhaps due to Stephan's influence.[29]

On one occasion Stephan asked Marinó whether his understanding of Canadian naturalization laws was correct – that naturalization applied only in Canada, while outside its borders a man was a citizen of the country in which he originated. Hannes smiled and conceded the point.[30] This clause was never mentioned during recruitment efforts and therefore many Icelandic born soldiers who joined the Canadian military were in fact Danish citizens.

More Icelandic recruiting agents made the rounds throughout the summer with similar results – only one young man joining the brass band of the Scandinavian Division. Stephan, who thoroughly disliked these recruitment efforts, commented that it was bad enough that the government was rounding up young men, but worse still that cliques in Winnipeg were now competing with each other in "appearing as patriots and leaders."[31]

Despite the war, the world was quickly becoming "smaller" due to a global economic boom that had lasted since the turn of the century. As trade and the flow of money increased, new consumer goods even found their way into the homes of the settlers. Mundi's store in Markerville, for example, offered an ever-increasing variety of goods for sale, while people also ordered goods from the catalogues of urban department stores such as Eaton's. Stephan received a good price for his grain in the fall of 1916 and purchased a new reading lamp.

In October, while loading firewood on a sleigh, Stephan injured himself. The load was fairly high and Stephan stumbled, falling on a log and breaking a rib. Though the break eventually healed itself, it hampered Stephan's ability to work. I have "two or three lumps on my side," Stephan commented, "but I guess my wings will conceal them when I have turned into a real angel."[32] Stephan invariably clenched his pipe between his teeth as he set to work, "although the fire always dies."[33] In his study, he enjoyed sitting in conversation with guests and sometimes having a drink with them. "Prohibition makes no difference to me," he wrote to his friend Grímur Grímsson the summer of 1916. "I am as short of booze as always, as others always drink it from me."[34]

The civilized self-concept of the Western World was now rapidly collapsing with the "Great War". The belief in progress and liberalism that Stephan had adopted over the last third of a century, in order to emancipate himself from traditional creeds, was now giving way to mysticism and a tendency for introspection. Stephan regarded faith without reason as senseless, but he did not interfere with the beliefs of others as long as people did not relinquish their rationality. As he grew older, his most sincere wish was that empathy would prevail among liberal people. Once, in a letter to Rögnvaldur Pétursson, he fell into philosophical musings on this matter. "Those who cannot leave God alone for this (I, for instance) should not bother about whether He is inherent in all things or an offspring of all things, as long as He is not a mean person, as that would be to take one's God from below oneself and that cannot lead to good luck. [...] I was interrupted just now, in the middle of all this theology, to disentangle some barbed wire. No wonder everything I am concerned with ends up in a mess!"[35]

The poets of Stephan's generation were beginning to die, but new poets were making an appearance. Late in 1916 Stephan received a letter from Jóhannes P. Pálsson, a young physician and aspiring writer living at Wynyard, Saskatchewan. It always pleased him when young people showed interest in his ideas and poems. "It is as if hope begins to grow within oneself that one has not been writing in vain. This happens especially when you grow old and the chill begins to seek inwards."[36]

Stephan was treading on thin ice when he mocked government censorship, but he found it curious to "live in a country where the government determines what you are allowed to read, speak, and write – only with regard to international affairs."[37] He found it difficult to persevere in his creativity with the war on his mind. "Just as wild boars gather fat in the summer," he concluded, "in order to survive the winter when all the nuts are under snow, I have not used up everything I had gathered before all culture and poetic imagination froze due to the war."[38] He survived solely on the will to live.

As the war dragged on and propaganda no longer inspired aspiring heroes to enlist, the government broadened age-eligibility for military service and moved toward universal conscription. "Perhaps I will write my next letter from a military camp," Stephan wrote to Jónas Hall. "All Canadian men between 18 and 65 are supposed to register with a postcard that they receive by mail and which I answered in my own way. When recruitment gets harder still, conscription will come, but I am not worried for myself."[39]

Conscription was proclaimed in August 1917, but by then Stephan was far away.

Chapter 14

The Land of Summer

"Dear Poet"

"Now you must heed the call of our youth and come to Iceland," Guðmundur Finnbogason wrote to Stephan in January of 1917, inviting him to visit Iceland. A calligraphed letter followed. "Dear poet! It has often been mentioned among people here… what a great pleasure it would be for us, your compatriots, if we might just once see you here at home in your motherland. Naturally you have many friends here who love and admire your poetry and they would like nothing more than to be able to show you some token of the respect and gratitude the Icelandic nation feels."

Stephan was invited to stay in Iceland for an entire summer, travelling around the country as he pleased. "We hope that such a journey would be of some pleasure for you, if the Icelandic summer greets you as you deserve." All expenses from Stephan's doorstep and home again were to be paid, and if he should accept this offer, Stephan was to respond as soon as possible with a telegram reading: "Dr. Finnbogason Reykjavík Yes Stephansson."[1]

The invitation took Stephan aback. Such a trip had been mentioned as early as Guðmundur Friðjónsson's suggestion from 1902 and Stephan had often dreamed of visiting Iceland, but he had never allowed himself to consider it seriously. He could not afford such a trip himself and he did not want others to pay for him. People in Iceland, however, longed to see him, and both their assumed debt to him and the straightforward plan made it impossible for him to decline the invitation. He telegrammed his acceptance on February 8, 1917.

The idea of inviting Stephan G. Stephansson to visit Iceland had been presented in *Skinfaxi*, a paper published by the Icelandic Youth Organization, and preparations had begun in the fall of 1916. A committee had been organized, including Guðmundur Finnbogason, Ágúst H. Bjarnason, and poet Theódóra Thoroddsen, and the hope was that Stephan could make the journey aboard *Gullfoss*, the flagship of the new Icelandic Steamship Company, which would sail from New York to Iceland in May of 1917. A few days after sending his acceptance telegram, Stephan wrote to Guðmundur saying that he would plan to sail on *Gullfoss*, but that he feared the ship might be intercepted en route to Iceland as the Americans had just entered the war. With regard to possible military service, Stephan was still eligible for conscription, as the age limit had just been raised to 65.

The poet in 1917.

Back in Iceland, a letter soliciting funds for the planned visit was written in December of 1916, making the case that Stephan G. Stephansson's contribution to Icelandic literature could not be ignored. His compatriots in North America had shown him their gratitude and it was now the Icelandic nation's turn. The Icelandic Youth Organization distributed the letter far and wide, and to help raise funds a booklet containing a selection of poems from *Andvökur* was printed and sold. Many fundraising events were also held and the drive was a success. Large landowners donated as much as 10 Icelandic *krónur*, children contributed from their savings, and a farmer from east of Reykjavík, Páll Guðmundsson of Hjálmsstaðir, together with his entire household, donated as much as the population of the entire municipality. Two leading Icelandic poets, Ólöf "from Hlaðir" and Hulda, both donated and collected money. In Reykjavík, one wealthy woman donated 100 *krónur*, while several members of parliament, merchants, and professors donated between 5 and 25 *krónur* each. Interestingly, it seems that doctors, lawyers, and government officials were reluctant to donate.

Stephan wrote to his friends about the invitation, commenting that it was an "exceptionally nice and kind-hearted"[2] offer and adding that while he looked forward to making the journey, he feared that he might disappoint his friends in Iceland. He felt unworthy of the invitation and uneasy at the thought of jumping straight from the cow barn into a crowd of dignitaries, academics, and students. It was absurd to do such a thing, but it was better than to refuse the invitation. Thus he broke his own creed "never to mingle with dignitaries, although I do not fear nor dislike doing so."[3]

For Stephan, there was no time to waste. First he had to resolve his legal status as his naturalization papers were inadequate as travel documents. An inquiry to the Ministry of Home Affairs was disappointing. As there was no certificate of citizenship from before 1902, Stephan was informed that it was impossible for the government to issue him a passport.[4] Meanwhile it was even questionable to assume that Stephan could get to Iceland, as the war was now at its high point. The United States had recently joined the fray and the Germans, in a desperate attempt to starve Britain into surrender, had resorted to submarine warfare. All Allied ships that crossed the Atlantic had to travel in convoys.

There were other reasons to be somewhat anxious about the journey. Stephan had entered into a rather harsh polemic with Guðmundur Friðjónsson, one of his farmer-poet colleagues in Iceland, over the politics of Iceland's independence. Having followed Iceland's national affairs closely, Stephan was impatient for her independence and insisted that Iceland's political leaders inform the nation about what was going on. In a letter to a new correspondent, Jón Jónsson of Sleðbrjótur, he wrote, "These are matters of concern for every person in the country – and nobody has any prerogative to conceal them. This stupid secrecy, which is a worldwide habit and a curse of governments, undermines the tenets of democracy more than anything else." "Silence about national problems," he claimed, was among the underlying causes of the war, along with the wheeling and dealing of those in power. "All planning and negotiations between nations are public matters and should be made public immediately through publication in legal and ministerial gazettes.

Then there would be less of the speculation, corruption, duplicity, and concealment that debases nations."5

During the war years the issue of a separate flag for Iceland came to the fore, and the debate around a new flag gave Stephan occasion to present the concept of Iceland as a peace-making nation. It irritated him to see the Icelanders try to emulate big nations. "It is so petty nationalistic to consider only what you see next to you, while being unable to understand either the advantages or the disadvantages." Stephan felt that flags should be diverse and that it was good for a small nation to have an unusual flag that people would notice. The current Icelandic flag was similar to many other flags. "Other [nations] have… taken the sun, the moon, and the stars … but Iceland has the "northern lights" that nobody has yet claimed. There was also the "peacebow" (rainbow), that would be appropriate anywhere that rain falls and the sun shines. It had not yet been adopted by any nation and would be a worthy symbol of a people who always cross the oceans in peace."6

There was much for Stephan to do before he left home. He had been making arrangements to invite William Irvine, a radical political leader in Alberta, to speak on Icelandic Day, and this task he now assigned to his son Mundi and a friend, Grímur Grímsson. He also had to host a party, as on Sunday, May 6, 1917 – the day before he departed – his daughter Fanny married her cousin Árni Bardal, the brother of Baldur's wife, Lina.7

Across a Continent and an Ocean

On the day of his departure for Iceland, Stephan still had to resolve his lack of travel documents, so while passing through Innisfail he stopped at the bank to obtain the manager's testimonial that he was a person well-known and should be allowed back into Canada. This might not have been adequate, so when Stephan arrived in Winnipeg on May 10, 1917, he visited Ólafur S. Thorgeirsson, Consul General of Denmark, who also penned an attestation for him.8

Stephan stopped over in Winnipeg for a few days, awaiting news of the whereabouts of the ship *Gullfoss*. A farewell party held in the finest hall of the city on May 19th was attended by a who's who of prominent Icelanders – including pastors and others who had criticized Stephan for his outspoken poetry. Cabinet Minister Thomas H. Johnson ad-

Icelandic poet Guðmundur Friðjónsson publicly praised Stephan and even suggested inviting the poet and his family to move to Iceland, but in 1912 he and Stephan became embroiled in a bitter personal exchange.

dressed the party and Reverend Friðrik Bergmann proposed a toast to Stephan – with water as prohibition was in effect. Stephan then took the train to New York where a $5 room had been booked for him at the Hotel Astor, but he found it too extravagant and stayed instead in a first class berth aboard the *Gullfoss*. There he enjoyed good food and cigars, as well as the company of an Icelandic guide hired by the invitation fund. The two explored Broadway and Fifth Avenue and listened to the preaching of Billy Sunday, an American evangelist. Stephan found his message remarkably stupid. He "got as close to heaven as anyone gets in New York – the top tower of the Woolworth skyscraper." One rainy evening Stephan also went to Coney Island, "where all the cheerfulness of New York gathers and goes mad, and all the 'humbug' of the world frolics and seduces in fairy halls of electric lights."[9]

On May 30th *Gullfoss* sailed from New York, bound for Halifax. It arrived there just before noon on a cold and foggy June 3rd, but because of the war nobody was allowed to go ashore, though inspectors came on board to examine passports and luggage, looking for forbidden reading material. This concerned Stephan as his bag contained a poetry manuscript that was unlikely to please officials of the British Empire if they knew the contents. No remarks were made about the manuscripts, however, or about some copies of Heimskringla or a box of Stephan's booklet *Kolbeinslag*, which was assumed to be patriotic poetry. *Gullfoss* got underway again the following day.¹⁰

The May 17, 1917 issue of Heimskringla *carried news of Stephan's arrival in Winnipeg on his way to New York to catch the* Gullfoss.

Stephan enjoyed the trip across the Atlantic. Officials on board invited him to their quarters, showed him all around the ship, and offered him "everything from beer to champagne, but do not imagine we are drunk all the time," he wrote to Helga, assuring her that the captain was a careful abstainer. The steersman gave him a copy of the journal *Iðunn* with an essay about him by Ágúst H. Bjarnason, and when Stephan later read an article about himself in an Icelandic newspaper he began to fear that he would be too well received in Reykjavík.¹¹

As *Gullfoss* cut through the waves of the North Atlantic, sailing ever further northward, the days became longer. Stephan had trouble sleeping as the ship approached Iceland and when he came up on deck on the bright morning of June 16ᵗʰ he beheld Iceland for the first time in 44 years. To the north was the glacier Snæfellsjökull, imbued by the sun with such beautiful colours that Stephan felt that he had never seen anything like it. His fondest dream was coming true and as the ship approached land he quietly murmured a new poem, one in which Iceland's white mother's hand receives the poet in the morning dawn. "The return would not be so urgent/had not it been as the poems of youth/in the mouth of the east-wind was my impulse," Stephan observed in the poem "Af skipsfjöl" (From on Board Ship). It was with his youth and childhood dreams in mind that he was returning to his motherland, and the "new world" now lay behind him under yesterday's sun. He only wanted to rediscover the poetic rhythm of the waterfalls and the silence of the mountains, and to lie in his mother's lap in the sun and rain through the long summer nights. He wanted to "touch the origins of the strings,/that connected me to life and the wide world." At the same time he realized that he must be realistic about his expectations:

> *Blessed land of dreams and people*
> *Of my poems – however you are!*[12]

The Town of Reykjavík

Gullfoss sailed into Reykjavík Harbour in a cold northwesterly wind. The poet stood alone on the deck, his coat buttoned up to his neck and his hands deep in his pockets, watching the shore with a gleam in his eyes. In an interview with a journalist who came aboard the ship, the poet expressed his joy at having arrived, but also some doubts about his ability to manage the long riding tour as he was now 63 years old. The journalist mentioned that many Icelanders knew Stephan's poems. "Well then, they also know me," Stephan replied. "I am just like my poems, although a bit worse." He also relayed a number of greetings from Icelanders in North America.

Reykjavík's waterfront about the time of Stephan's visit to Iceland.

The invitation committee also came on board when the ship docked, and they now clustered around the short farmer from the Rocky Mountains. A crowd on the wharf shouted "hurrahs" at the prompting of parliamentarian Benedikt Sveinsson, who was a brother to Baldur Sveinsson whom Stephan had met in Winnipeg. Baldur, more reserved in manner, was also there to greet the poet. The committee then escorted Stephan to Vonarstræti 12, the home of poet Theódóra Thoroddsen, who had offered to host Stephan in her home to save on hotel bills as the committee was still a bit short of cash, because some of the wealthiest people in Reykjavík did not want to donate to the fund. Aspiring artist Ásgeir Bjarnþórsson, who was painting Theódóra's house, wrote in his memoirs that he was astonished when he first laid eyes on Stephan. He had expected a tall, magnificent figure of a man rather than "… a skinny, little farmer, unusually worn out and tired looking. In such a humble body resided this elevated spirit, this genius of words and thought, who spoke with authority and knowledge about the world and life." He doubted that "such a great thinker and poetic genius, in the figure of an uneducated, toiling farmer" could be found anywhere else in the world."[13]

Reykjavík had grown steadily with urban migration from Iceland's countryside and the city now boasted a population of some 15,000 inhabitants. A serious lack of housing had resulted and Reykjavík now had many street urchins, some of whom were both ragged and naughty. Horses were gradually getting accustomed to the increasing number of cars and the ever-escalating speed of traffic.

Austurstræti in downtown Reykjavík about the time of Stephan's visit to Iceland.

The day after Stephan's arrival was June 17th, Iceland's national holiday, and festivities at the sports arena focused mainly on the speech Stephan gave. A banquet followed that evening, with some of the city's dignitaries and well over 100 guests filling the house to enjoy a dinner of salmon and stirred butter, veal with vegetables, biscuits, cheese, skyr with cream, and coffee. Guðmundur Finnbogason delivered the main speech, in which he stated that Stephan was a pioneer of Icelandic language and thought, an independent spiritual leader, a "follower of only what he perceived as most true and fair. All paths are single paths in the beginning, all leaders are loners, but where a good man leads, despite everyone's disfavour, others will follow."[14] Stephan thanked everyone, apologizing for the fact that he gave speeches seldom and badly. The prairies and forests of the west where he had lived for the past half century, he pointed out, were the "domain of silence, different from your land with the sound of the sea in every fjord, the drone of a river in every valley, and the purl of a brook on every mountain slope." What prompted him to speak now, he explained, was that a bad speech was less of a shame than accepting everything that had been done for him, past and present, in utter silence. He felt as if he were in the middle of a fairy tale and was most grateful. Although he had forgotten his good manners in the backwoods where he lived, he now wanted to finish his speech with the poem "Af skipsfjöl" (From on Board Ship), which he had composed on the morning of his arrival in Iceland. "After all, it is because of my poetic prattle that I am here."[15]

Over the next few days Stephan found himself immersed in Reykavík society. The guest of honour on Women's Day on June 19th, he delivered a speech and a poetic toast to women, praising them for nurturing those virtues neglected by men. Poet Ingibjörg Benediktsdóttir acknowledged Stephan's longtime support for women's rights. His tributes to women, she stated, were free of sentimentality, and any woman would be better off receiving two or three lines from Stephan rather than a long poem of conventional praise.

During his stay in Reykjavík, Stephan took long walks with some of Iceland's most prominent intellectuals and attended an endless round of receptions and parties. He even went on a sightseeing tour to Þingvellir, the sacred site of Iceland's ancient parliament, and together with Ágúst H. Bjarnason and Guðmundur Finnbogason he drank some "medicinal spirits" from silver drams, despite prohibition. Stephan was well provided with food and tobacco, and Theódóra Thoroddsen took care of his clothes.

Around the Country

At the end of June, with an extensive trip planned through rural Iceland, the invitation committee invested in rain gear, boots, and a riding whip for Stephan. The journey around the country then began early on the morning of July 4th aboard the coastal steamer *Botnía*, which sailed along the southern coast all the way to Reyðarfjörður in the East Fjords. Having studied a map of Iceland, Stephan now scrutinized the coastline, jotting comments in a notebook trimmed to fit into his pocket. His last glimpse of the glacier Vatnajökull had been in 1873. Now, his travelling companions worried that fog might conceal the beauty of the glaciers.

The various dignitaries on board included deans and doctors, rich men and politicians. Lárus H. Bjarnason, a member of parliament and a brother to Ágúst H. Bjarnason, was to accompany Stephan all the way to Akureyri. The two men became good friends during the journey, and while Stephan found Lárus "formidable in appearance and cold in words", he discovered that Lárus was kindness itself if his haughty manner were ignored. Stephan addressed him informally from the beginning, though Lárus used the honorific form all the way east. Lárus enjoyed seeing how well Stephan was received and commented, "I have noticed one thing, Stephan. You are unspoiled by all these ceremonies and you don't let all the attention go to your head."[16]

On this journey to Reyðarfjörður, Stephan wrote a long poem entitled "Með ströndum fram" (Along the Coast). Upon arrival on the morning of July 6th,[17] he and his companions set off on horseback through the fjords and valleys of the East for nine days, visiting schools and farms. A highlight for Stephan was Skriðuklaustur, where according to legend Jón hrak (Jón the Outcast) – the character from his poem of that title – was said to be buried.

On July 15th the poet and his entourage ventured northwest across the vast wasteland Möðrudalsöræfi, where Stephan began composing a poem based on folklore and inspired by the freedom of nature in the wide, open spaces. The group then took a ferry across the glacial river Jökulsá, while four men waited on the west side to accompany them through the geothermal pass known as Námaskarð and down to Lake Mývatn.

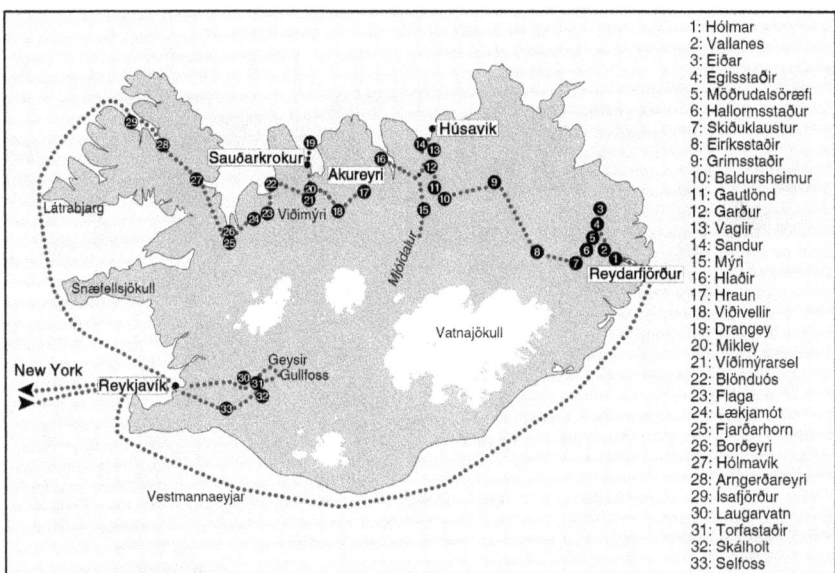

Stephan G. Stephansson's speaking tour in Iceland in the summer of 1917.

Stephan's reputation had been established early in this region of Northern Iceland that was renowned for its progressive cultural and political outlook, and as he and his companions descended from the pass, Stephan was astounded to encounter a crowd of people singing and celebrating as they rode to meet him. "There, on the rocky path ... where harsh lava and human habitation merge, people came riding in a long procession, evidently on their way to some gathering."[18] Stephan first thought they must be riding to town, but then recalled that any towns were by the sea, not inland. When these people in the procession dismounted from their horses and waited for him, he realized that this was in fact a display of Icelandic hospitality. Although it was a good dry day in the middle of the haying, people had left the hayfields to come and meet him. In the West, such frivolity would have met with scorn, but here Stephan encountered that unspoiled joy of life that enabled people to transcend their worldly worries. The group sang the anthem of the Icelandic countryside by local poet Sigurður Jónsson of Arnarvatn, who met them by the river. Stephan felt this poem was a wonderful expression of the essence of country people.

The people of the Lake Mývatn district organized a gathering for Stephan and escorted him from farm to farm, showing him their agricultural operations. He stayed first at the farm Baldursheimur, with Þórólfur Sigurðsson, then with the family at Gautlönd. He liked the

Icelandic farm folk gather to welcome a visitor from abroad.

people on these farms and was fascinated by their ideals and desire for progress. He was especially cheered by the broadmindedness he found in the political and economic journal *Réttur*, edited by Þórólfur Sigurðsson, and in the conversations about philosophy and literature he had with the residents of Gautlönd.

Wherever Stephan went on this trip, he was greeted with flags, speeches, and song. At Ytra-Fjall in the valley of Aðaldalur he had a lively discussion with farmer-poet Indriði Þorkelsson, an intelligent man who spoke beautiful Icelandic. He was just as industrious as Stephan in both farming and poetry, and no less knowledgeable about community affairs. The sun was shining this Friday, July 20th, and Indriði had been mowing hay with his sons. He stopped cutting unusually early, however, went inside, washed his hands, and put on a clean jacket. His young son Indriði knew that Stephan was coming and that his father was going to meet the poet. The boy had read many of Stephan's poems and had listened to his father and cousins discuss them thoroughly. His father had also composed a tune to Stephan's "Vögguvísur" (Lullaby), that his mother had often sung to him.

The only telephone in the neighbourhood was at Ytra-Fjall and the operator informed Indriði that Stephan might even stop there for a visit. Young Indriði asked his father if he could go along with him to meet Stephan. He feared his father would not find it respectable that they should share a horse, but to his surprise his father agreed with a smile. After a short wait, father and son spotted two men approaching, and young Indriði immediately recognized Þórólfur of Baldursheimur, who sat tall and straight in the saddle. The other man was shorter and stooped. "I do not think I need to introduce you," Þórólfur said cheerfully after all had exchanged greetings, "but this is Indriði, and everybody knows Stephan." Stephan and the elder Indriði shook hands warmly. Stephan then noticed that Indriði was hiding someone behind his back. The boy stretched out his hand and what followed was an unforgettable moment. "The handshake was comfortable, his hand was not large, but a little weary ... It was impossible to recognize Stephan from his picture in *Andvökur*... which showed him with a shock of thick black hair, a moustache, and an impressive expression. Here was a weary, swarthy, balding man, not unlike some of my neighbours. Of course the photograph had been taken a long time ago." The conversation between the two farmers was somewhat disappointing to the boy. "They chatted about the grass growth on the hayfields they had seen along the way, and the condition of pastures, and the heaths Stephan had been travelling across during the last few days".[19]

At Ytra Fjall Stephan met a nephew of Rögnvaldur Pétursson's wife, and a lively discussion ensued. They talked far into the night and Stephan refused an offer to rest, as such company was too precious to miss. When it came to the next stage of the journey, Stephan insisted that he must see Sigurður of Garður, the man who many years before had sent him the sprig of heather from Mjóidalur that had inspired the poem "Lyng frá auðum æskustöðvum" (Heather from the Deserted Home of Youth).

It was the dead of night when Stephan left Ytra Fjall and the twilight ride along a new road across a lava field was memorable. "From amidst the rough lava, leafy branches were sticking up wherever they had found shelter and moisture. It was as if this road through the countryside had decided, when time passes, to become a boulevard in a city," Stephan wrote.[20] As the group approached the village of Húsavík at 6 o'clock in the morning, the poet Hulda, together with her husband and a few dignitaries, rode out to meet them. That evening, a gathering was held in Stephan's honour.

While at Húsavík, Stephan rode to Sandur to meet Guðmundur Friðjónsson, the poet with whom he had exchanged acrimonious words a few years earlier. Guðmundur was mowing hay when he heard that

Stephan was coming and he hurried so much that he did not bother to wash the grass stains off his hands. They sat in the living room discussing poetry and other matters long into the night, like old friends, though this was the first time they had met. The dispute was totally forgotten.

The Homecoming

On the following day, while on his way to the valley of Bárðardalur, Stephan met his old admirer Sigurður of Garður, and at 3 o'clock in the morning of July 23rd he arrived at Eyjardalsá, a farm he had last seen 44 years before while en route to the port of Akureyri. His cousins Stefán and Guðni were among the very few men Stephan kissed on this journey, in accordance with old Icelandic custom, and at Eyjardalsá memories flooded back to him as never before. A grand circle was now complete as Eyjardalsá had been Stephan's last stop when he left Bárðardalur on the way to America in 1873. He had found and created a new homeland in the West, for himself and his descendants, but now he had returned to the old homeland.

Stephan also visited the churchyard at Ljósavatn, where he found the grave of his Aunt Guðný. It was she who had prompted the local playwright Tómas Jónasson to compose the farewell poem that had been recited as the emigrants took leave of the valley and set off on their voyage. It had expressed warm wishes for success and prosperity, while

The entrance to Bárðardalur, looking southwest across the river Skjálfandafljót, just upstream from the waterfall Goðafoss.

acknowledging that fate was separating kinsfolk and creating a gap in the ranks of Icelanders. Now, by way of response, Stephan composed "Heimkoman" (The Homecoming) at Guðný's grave. More personal than most of his poems, it recalls the moment of parting that had slumbered all those years in Stephan's photographic memory.

At the beginning of the poem, a "district queen" bids a skinny youth farewell. Taciturn but warm, she states that it is very hard to see him leave the country. The boy promises to bring home the fruit of his aspirations, and "that will be a bigger boy/Aunt, than the one who is leaving you -/ otherwise I will never return." Ten years later, the emigrant receives a message that she is still waiting for him, but he excuses himself by stating that he had grown less than even his smallest hopes. The last part of the poem returns to the moment of composition:

An old wanderer stands at a grassy grave
Of hers, a lifetime later,
At the grave of his times.

You who rest there, would not have recognized him any more
Still a half homebred,
A half-foreign changeling.

He asks forgiveness for not having kept his promise. He had been too stubborn to return, defeated, even with the knowledge that he would have been well received. The speaker then elevates the meaning of the poem. The determination to work well, an inherited value that had prevented a disgraceful return, was exactly what this little valley had contributed to the world. A beautiful ideal for the future is revealed, and the homeland's loss expressed in the original farewell poem acquires a new meaning.

There everyone should work, who is sent from home
Gain new friends, new foes,
New problems on both sides.

His kinfolk remain alone, with gaps in their ranks.
Thus the little districts of mountain and valley
Foster the settlement of the entire Earth.

Until pioneering, square by square, has created
Throughout earth, one and beautiful,
A global community of all nations.

Guðný's heartfelt farewell and the good wishes of others, Stephan now realizes, had been "the most precious gold on his path,/luck that did not fail to come true."[21] This expresses Stephan's humanism in a nutshell: to offer the world the best of one's own heritage. His journey home to Iceland now confirmed that he had preserved the places of his youth within himself, wherever he went. Now he could only go home, as the world was his home.

Early the next morning Stephan rode with his cousins Stefán and Guðni, along with their children and a few others, up the valley in the direction of Mjóidalur. They stopped at a few farms along the way, including Mýri. Stephan had dreaded the thought of visiting the farms where he had lived as a young man, as he knew they were now deserted and in ruin. When they arrived at the farm Mjóidalur, memories of the house that had been Stephan's last home in Iceland rushed back, and after finding the corner where his bed had been, he sat there for a while. He then walked alone down the old hayfield to the riverbank where he had limped, seriously ill, as a teenager. His companions left him to his thoughts.

The weather had been unpleasant during the day, but as they rode back toward Mýri that evening, the sky cleared. "Suddenly it became bright and warm," Stephan wrote. "This was how Mjóidalur bade me farewell. I had never understood it as well as then, as it lay before me there in the summer evening sun. Eroding even when I lived there, it was the last outpost of greenery all the way south to the wasteland sands. The 'islands' of turf remaining on the gravel slopes, I remembered, had been small. …. Now, however, one could see new grass taking root between the old turf islands: destruction in order to help growth!"[22]

As they rode down the valley and along the glacial river after leaving Mýri around midnight, everyone was tired and silent. Stephan, ever observant, contemplated the scene in his own way. "In my mind I was admiring how beautiful it would be when the land was ploughed and levelled, green and productive, when Bárðardalur has changed to the Meadow Valley or Field Valley. … On the slopes were the beginnings of new woods where none had been when I was young. I imagined what the eye would behold when looking down from the woods, over the great fields along the entire river."[23]

Poets Meet in Akureyri

Iceland's national poet Reverend Matthías Jochumsson lived in the town of Akureyri. In correspondence from both him and Stephan to their respective friends, there is an obvious tension between these two great poets, evidently rooted in their extreme differences. Each, however, admitted the genius of the other, though Stephan criticized Matthías' wavering mind and his tendency to allow sentimentality to overwhelm ideas, while in a review of *Andvökur*, Matthías suggested exactly the opposite of Stephan.

Asked whether he would write a poem on the occasion of Stephan's arrival, Matthías exclaimed, "No, I don't think so. He can compose himself, the damned chap." He added that Stephan did not think much of his poetry. He also brought up the subject of some satirical verses he thought were about him, but when it was pointed out that these contained a direct reference to another poet, Matthías burst out in laughter, "Oh, this is damned good! I could almost sign this in agreement."[24]

Reverend Matthías did agree to deliver the main speech at the banquet in Stephan's honour at Hotel Akureyri, which was attended by about 100 guests. In this speech he claimed that Stephan had gone to the West to fight giants. Then he addressed Stephan directly, "Was it not daring of you to take on the entire world?" Stephan, he pointed out, had been an iconoclast in the eyes of the public, with no more regard for "the almighty dollar [...] than for a forged cent." He regarded " … the most prominent Russians and Rockefellers like 90 year old paupers shivering in their night-chairs, hundreds of miles behind the times." Stephan's nature poems, he claimed, were best regarded in the same way as paintings by the great masters.[25]

Following many speeches and poems, read and sung, Stephan stood to express his thanks. He also read two poems. The banquet lasted until 2 o'clock in the morning, which was well before Stephan's usual bedtime, so he invited the poets to his room. A very promising young poet, Davíð Stefánsson, only 20 years old, joined them, having read a poem at the banquet. A young doctor on the invitation committee misused his position to procure some alcohol from the drugstore, despite prohibition, and they all poured a few drops into their glasses. Matthías was most cheerful and the centre of attention. Old sedition was forgotten and the poets spoke about everything but poetry. At one point, Matthías confided in Stephan that he did not expect to live much longer, and though

Downtown Akureyri (circa 1935) had changed when the poet revisited there in 1917 from his brief visit while awaiting the Queen *in 1873.*

he would have preferred to remain in this world, where life had treated him well, he did not regard himself as worthy of a better world. Stephan was astonished, as this notion was so similar to his own view.[26]

Before leaving Akureyri, Stephan went to say goodbye to Matthías. With him was young Davíð Stefánsson, who described the parting of these two great poets in a narrative written decades later. "Matthías was rather stout and jolly in appearance, while Stephan was thin and weary. Matthías was lively and glib. Stephan was slow and reserved. Now the two of them sat together, each in his corner of the parlour at Sigurhæðir. As they looked into each other's eyes – for the last time – I sensed that these two old heroes were enjoying each other's company. Although their poems were very different in form and style, the two poets shared similar ideals and dreams of good fortune for the future of mankind. While Stephan's poems were weather-worn and Matthías' poetry was gloriously bright, both poets had achieved a level of genius that is only possible when a great spirit and a tender heart join forces."

Eventually, Stephan rose from his seat, as did Matthías. For a few moments they stood opposite each other, silent and short of words. For some reason the two poets found it difficult to talk and their conversation was mundane, deprived of inspiration. "If spiritual beings from other worlds can approach Earth, then I am convinced that at this moment Matthías' living-room was full of invisible white souls. There they were, two chieftains of spirit from different continents, but nonetheless both sons of the same nation and Icelandic to the core. Both had performed great deeds. Both enjoyed the love and reverence of the Icelandic people. Here, Icelandic poetic culture, the nation's high-culture of the ages, had its best representatives, and God only knows when such men would greet and bid farewell again. A great moment was unfolding, one of the most remarkable events in the common history of Icelanders, both at home and abroad."

Stephan now reached out his heavily veined and weary hand, slightly trembling. Matthías unfolded his arms, lunged at Stephan, embracing and kissing him with tears in his eyes. "Stephan did not shed any tears. It was as if his face were chiselled from rock, rough and hard, with only the eyes gleaming ... I knew then, as now, however, that this parting was much more difficult and painful for Stephan than for Matthías. It was as if Stephan was bidding farewell to all of Iceland and the Icelandic nation on this side of the ocean for the last time, with this one kiss. Now he was starting on his way home, to the west."

The two poets walked out of Sigurhæðir together and Matthías accompanied Stephan around the corner of the house. "It's a pity we did not become acquainted earlier. We could have become friends," Matthías said. "Now my time is coming to an end," he added. Stephan replied that he hoped this was not the case. "I will put it in writing so you will believe it," Matthías replied. "I would refuse to accept it," Stephan said, and they both smiled. As Stephan walked away, Matthías called out, "May all God's angels and all good beings bless you." Stephan stopped a moment and looked back. "I shall myself tether the ghosts *Þorgeirsboli* and *Húsavíkurskotta*,"* Matthías added, "so they will not harm you." Stephan walked away in silence. Davíð sensed that Matthías wanted to defend Stephan from the evil of society and the ignorance with which they had both struggled.

When Davíð met with Matthías the following day, the old poet talked a great deal about Stephan, but stuck to his old position. He stated that Stephan composed more with his brain than his heart. "But Stebbi is damned good, and he is likely a major poet, the dear old chap."[27]

---

*Þorgeirsboli and Húsavíkurskotta, two famous ghosts in Icelandic folk-belief.

Places of Youth

Stephan was getting travel weary and declined visits to the farms where his father's people had lived in the valley south of Akureyri. He wanted, however, to meet the poet Ólöf "of Hlaðir", who had contributed so generously to the fund for his visit, and when he and his companions set off west for Skagafjörður on July 31st, he insisted on stopping at her farm north of Akureyri.

Jónas Jónsson, a farmer at Vaglir in Skagafjörður, was a big man, expressive and vigorous in appearance, gentle-natured yet hot-tempered. He had a great passion for poetry and had been a dedicated admirer of Stephan from the age of 13, when he had first read some of Stephan's poems in *Heimskringla*. In 1900 he had acquired Stephan's *Á ferð og flugi*, which he had devoured, reading the title poem aloud over and over until he had memorized it. Jónas was unable to afford *Andvökur* and had been unsuccessful in convincing the local reading society to purchase it, as Reverend Björn Jónsson of Miklibær, a great admirer of Matthías Jochumsson, was opposed to the idea.

Jónas had waited eagerly for Stephan's arrival in Skagafjörður and when he received word that the poet had come on the sunny morning of August 2nd, he left his hay mower, washed his hands, and hurried to Víðivellir where Stephan greeted him. Like many others, Jónas' found that his expectations had exceeded reality. The description of the poet Kolbeinn in Stephan's great poem "Kolbeinslag" had captured his imagination, " ... but he was not of great stature." When they had spoken for a while, however, he recognized the "same wise and great man revealed in his poetry." Stephan spoke slowly, sometimes as if searching for words, "and then his face twitched, almost as if in pain. Once the words he was seeking were found, however, and the sentence completed, then his face – chiselled and illuminated – brightened so delightfully that one warmed right to the heartstrings. I have never seen such a magical glow in the expression of anyone else," Jónas said.[28]

Jónas and Stephan later rode north through Skagafjörður, stopping at Miklibær where Reverend Björn Jónsson lived. The pastor was curious about the poet's political opinions, but Stephan stated that no party had been able to attract him. "Though there is no reason to hide the fact that I have, for a long time, had a keen eye for socialism." The pastor asked whether Stephan did not exercise his right to vote, as there were only two political parties in Canada. "When there are only two options," Stephan replied, "and neither of them is good, you choose the lesser evil."²⁹

On their way to the ferry that provided transportation across the glacial river dividing Skagafjörður, Jónas and Stephan came to Mikley, where Stephan's boyhood friend Daníel Árnason lived. Daníel had become somewhat of an eccentric recluse, renowned for being hot-tempered, even aggressive when drunk. His appearance had also become strange, as described by a local writer, "short of stature ... with a full beard so overwhelming that practically the entire face was one shag of a beard. The nose was rather short, with dark blue tip. He always had a hat on his head, pulled so far forward that his eyes were hardly visible, with the result that all that could be seen of his face was the beard-shag with a dark blue nose protruding from it like a basalt-rock on a forested hill." Nor was Daníel much for washing, though he was very thrifty about clothing and always had them mended when necessary. Still he had decent Sunday-best clothes and good boots.

When Stephan rode into the farmyard, Daníel was outside, his hat covering his eyes as usual. "How are you doing, my dear Daníel?" said Stephan, walking straight up to him. "I hardly expect you to know me." Daníel did not recognize his visitor and was rather disgruntled. "Do you not remember Stebbi from Sel?" Stephan asked. With that Daníel brightened up. "Stebbi from Sel? Yes, sure I remember him, that bloody joker. Are you Stebbi from Sel?" Daníel broke into a grin from under the brim of his hat. "Well, hell, you don't look any better than I do, although you have been living in the luxury of the West all these years while I have had to crawl along in the cold and snow here in Iceland." "You are right, Daníel," Stephan smiled, "and once again the old proverb proves true, that there is something good about everyone. Your frankness will be your redemption on the great day of judgement."³⁰

There was to be a farewell banquet for Stephan at the village of Sauðárkrókur on Sunday, August 12, and Jónas was to write a poem. Jónas said he would come, with or without a poem. Before they parted, Jónas told Stephan that once in a dream he had travelled all the way to America to see him. When he knocked at the poet's door, he explained his errand. In the dream, Stephan dropped his head for a moment, then looked up into Jónas' eyes and recited this verse:

> *For most people, it is a difficult trip*
> *By the breakers of life.*

You have travelled a long way,
To check out a petty matter.

Stephan smiled and wrote down the verse. "I won't presume to claim this verse as mine if another book of my poetry is ever printed," he commented. "Yet this one could be by me."[31]

Stephan and his entourage spent the night at Geldingaholt, where late that evening Stephan wrote a letter to Helga, updating her on his travels and reporting good health, though sometimes he felt a bit dazed from staying up so late. He also mentioned that he was continually overwhelmed by the reception he received wherever he went. As he wrote this letter, a well-attended Icelandic Celebration was drawing to a close back in Markerville. Reverend Pétur Hjálmsson had delivered a speech, as had a few others, and socialist leader Bill Irvine, invited by Stephan, had given an excellent address. Helga had by then received the poem "Minni kvenna" (Toast for Women) presented by Stephan in Reykjavík on June 19th. She loved it and had wanted to read it at the celebration, but was too shy, so Reverend Pétur had read it for her.

On August 4th a feast in Stephan's honour, attended by 50 local people, was held at Víðimýri. The next day he attended a service in the very church where he had been confirmed 50 years earlier, and afterward he recounted the famous long service and told stories about Reverend Hannes. Stephan then toured the district, visiting old neighbours and playmates, and memories of youth came flooding back when he visited the ruins of Víðimýrarsel and Kirkjuhóll. Among the spots he found was the hillock where he had erected a cairn over his father's dead horse. "There were still a few stones, but silent about whether or not they were mine."[32] In solitary silence he stared down into the gully just north of the ruins and surveyed the broad panorama of mountains, ridges, and the fjord, with the isle of Drangey to the north. As he inspected the vegetation covering the grassy ruins, memories of his childhood came to life in the poem "Berjamór" (Berry Moor), dated August 4, 1917. In this cheerful poem about old pathways, children's games, and berry-picking, elements of familiarity and alienation form a delicate balance. The poet finds old paths, recalls the games and contests of his youth, and addresses contemporary children, pretending to recognize them as the descendants of his old playmates – boys with whom he had wrestled and shepherd girls who had won his heart. "Although you are far from being/prettier than your mother,/I shall help you pick berries/without blushing cheeks!" Still, he is unsure whether the birds or the children know him:

> *There, the ringed plover earlier*
> *Sang and flew across gravel plains and turf,*
> *Thinking she had carefully confused us*
> *And her nest was in security.*
> *There, on the hill, a raven sat*
> *Looking for berries.*
> *Will the neat plover be able to*
> *Entice the guest away from her nest?*
> *Will the children picking berries*
> *Run away from an old man?*
> *And, wearing a hat and English shoes,*
> *Will I be recognizable to the raven?*[33]

Historic Sites

After revisiting the places of his youth, Stephan and his entourage rode north to the old bishopric of Hólar, stopping at many farms along the way and greeting people who had come out of their homes to witness this historic visit. The people of Skagafjörður eagerly offered Stephan good horses to ride, and this pleased him. "If I had never emigrated to America," he remarked after a brisk sprint on horseback at the flying gait, "I might have composed less poetry, but I would have composed more verses about horses."[34] He composed a poem in which he praised the agility and sureness of Icelandic horses, their friendly company and noble gait.

Stephan spent the day at Hólar, where the weather was cold, windy, and foggy, and while there he climbed the steep mountainside to a terrace named for Bishop Guðmundur the Good, who in the tumultuous 13th century had gained a reputation for consecrating wells and cliffs – and for attracting a retinue of beggars and tramps. As Stephan reached the terrace, the clouds dissipated and the sun bathed the entire valley in light. Stephan suggested that Bishop Guðmundur must have caused this change in the weather and he later composed the poem "Gvendarbrunnar" (Guðmundur's Wells). "The entire neighbourhood covered in stench and blood!/ – And this vision turns into a poem," he begins, as if the changing weather had inspired a bloody vision of ancient feuds. The poem then expresses Stephan's esteem for Bishop Guðmundur, who rose up against the mighty chieftains and "[g]ave shelter in his Paradise/ to the mob and rogues."[35]

During Stephan's subsequent stay at Sauðárkrókur, a group of men escorted him out to the island of Drangey in the only motorboat from the village – using the last available petroleum, which was scarce because of the war. A stiff northeasterly wind made raincoats indispensable and the steep climb up the scree on the island called for sturdy boots. The climbers then hiked along a narrow ledge, up another steep slope, then skirted a cliff with a sheer drop to the sea until they arrived at the so-called "altar", a rock where visitors to the island traditionally stopped and prayed. Now this ritual was deemed unnecessary. After the final ascent, made with the aid of a heavy chain installed to give climbers a secure handhold, the group explored the top of the island and enjoyed a picnic by the ruins of a hut regarded as the site occupied by the saga outlaw Grettir during his last years of exile. Reverend Hálfdan Guðjónsson, having brought *The Saga of Grettir* and a few books of poetry along, read some poems about Grettir, then handed *Andvökur* to Stephan and asked him to read "Illugadrápa" (The Lay of Illugi), about Grettir's younger brother who had tried to defend Grettir when he was deathly ill and under attack. Stephan read the poem slowly and with emphasis, after which the audience was more convinced than ever of the excellence of this poem. The group then rested in the grass in silence, reflecting on Grettir's fate and pondering his swim to Reykir for fire. Finally Stephan broke the silence with a verse:

> *They say that many a magnificent sailing*
> *Could be seen from Drangey Island –*
> *Yet Grettir's head stands highest*
> *Above the sea in the Reykir Strait.*[36]

A Feast in Sauðárkrókur

Sunday, August 12th, brought fine weather to Skagafjörður, and towards evening the whole district seemed to be on the move. Men from far and wide arrived at Sauðárkrókur on their best horses to attend a feast in honour of their poet in the largest hall in the village. Jónas of

Vaglir had composed a poem of 12 stanzas while wielding his scythe over the last few days, and after hurriedly jotting it down and riding to Sauðárkrókur, he took a seat by the door, the hall being almost full. Stephan G. Stephansson, the guest of honour, was at the head table, seated under the Icelandic flag and flanked on both sides by members of the invitation committee. The meal was followed by speeches and poetry readings, some of questionable quality, and Jónas of Vaglir whispered to his seatmate an impromptu verse about people baptizing the good poet with "clay" – the symbol for bad poetry. When challenged by this seatmate to recite his own poem, Jónas stood up tall and impressive, and after addressing the guest somewhat haltingly at first, he gained his composure and delivered his new poem in a strong and resonant voice. The poem echoed Stephan's own vocabulary and thought, reflecting his influence on Jónas, and some regarded this as the best poem recited for Stephan on his entire journey.

> *Hail to you, Viking, from the west,*
> *Welcome back to the fjord.*
> *Accept my verses – of little artfulness,*
> *From under the winter snow, a sprig of heather,*
> *That grew by the ridge in the wilderness.*[37]

Jónas expressed his gratitude to Stephan for clearing the sky when darkness and hopelessness had haunted him, rescuing him from Icelandic narrow-mindedness. "May I keep the note?" Stephan asked everyone who read him a poem. Jónas, however, declined to give Stephan his rough original copy of the poem, but later sent him a clean copy that Stephan submitted for publication in a Reykjavík paper. He subsequently apologized to Jónas for not asking his permission to have the poem published, but he felt that the poem was simply too good not to be printed.

The last speaker of the evening was Reverend Hálfdan Guðjónsson, who claimed that he had "for a long time wanted to reach this old chap sitting there at the head table," who had often shown disdain for pastors. "I had a little chick that I loved dearly. I had hoped it would someday be able to fly far and wide and carry the reputation of its owner, but on becoming acquainted with Stephan G. I realized that my chick would never be able to fly – so I nurtured it less and less until it languished and died ... This magnificent chap who is our guest today killed the rhymester in me." Reverend Hálfdan had a good command of the Icelandic

Early view of the village of Sauðárkrókur, non-existent during the poet's boyhood in Skagafjörður – now the region's principal town.

language. "Then this chap comes on the scene, this self-educated common man who snags me with his sharp poetic claw, puts me on his knee, and begins teaching me Icelandic. At first I found that hard to accept."[38]

At the close of this event Stephan delivered a thank you speech, stating that he was short of words to express his feelings and so found silence his best shelter. He read two poems, however, the first being "Við landfestar" (By the Moorings), dated that same day. The struggle between youthfulness and old age, a recurrent theme in Stephan's poems from his stay in Skagafjörður, is at its deepest in this poem, which he read slowly and with such genuine emotion that the audience was moved. The poem begins with a depiction of the district with its snow-capped mountains and islands in the fjord. Addressing his native district as a once "abducted child" who still finds the fjord's "arms the best and most spacious", he expresses the fear that he will find his fjord deprived of joy in old age, friends gone and the party over. "Was it my own longing to go abroad," the poet asks, "returning after a fool's errand, to kneel in the sand?" After this personal introduction, the poet turns to the history of the district and asks whether valley and bay have recovered from Danish oppression. He then states that despite the area's tragic history, there is no reason to complain, though he himself becomes emotional over the past and is more stooped than he used to be. The mountains still entice him to climb their slopes, he states, the church and croft remain, and faithful friends wait.

> *But where are the children on the farm?*
> *Did youth turn into a mad changeling there?*

> *Does the green sward now conceal*
> *All our courtship, my old district?*

Why is the church emptier than before, he continues, and where are the confirmation classes?

> *Who comes to the green homefield hollow*
> *And challenges a contestant from the group?*
> *Where is the shepherd on the slope,*
> *Who unbidden exchanges his horse for mine?*
> *Who digs up old poems for the children*
> *And offers to teach me? Though in secret. –*
> *Who lends me a poem or story?*
> *Who now lends, or gives me, his candle?*

Stephan became quite emotional while describing this world that would never return, but he then articulated his words even more sharply when he started the next verse. At the end, he softened his tone again as he acknowledged the old values of generosity and hospitality, still evident in Skagafjörður, as was mutual helpfulness.

> *If there existed such a regenerating power,*
> *That could lift the burden of my years,*
> *And make me young again*
> *And grant my wish, I would choose to be with you!*[39]

It was a sacred moment and no one applauded when he finished the poem. Some members of the audience had strained to hear every word and were obviously quite emotional. Stephan remained standing as he regained his composure. He then suggested that it is always best to part with a smile and good cheer, and to lift the crowd's spirits he read the poem "Berjamór" (Berry Moor). Afterward Jónas of Vaglir and all his friends agreed that they had indeed "seen and heard a great man."[40]

Eventually Stephan had to leave his beloved fjord, and on his departure the people of Skagafjörður presented him with an ornate inkstand, with two inkwells and a paperknife made from the jawbone of a whale. Several men accompanied him as he rode out of Sauðárkrókur and at one point he turned his horse and spoke:

On his departure from Skagafjörður, the poet was presented with a unique ink stand and whalebone paper knife on behalf of the people of his native region.

> *Although we part for now,*
> *We can take comfort:*
> *That in future all our wishes*
> *Will eventually merge.*[41]

Building Palaces

Stephan's final night in Skagafjörður was spent at Víðimýri. The next day, while riding west toward the heath, he and his guide swung off their horses by Arnarstapi, a little hill near the ruins of Stephan's boyhood home Víðimýrarsel. Stephan stood there for a long while, taking in the whole district. The two then rode to the nearby ruins of Víðimýrarsel, where Stephan remained on his own for a while before they rode slowly westward over the Vatnsskarð Pass.

Following an overnight stop at Blönduós, Stephan continued west through Húnavatnssýsla, then north through the region of Strandasýsla, stopping at various farms along the way. On August 24th he arrived at Ísafjörður, where he stayed with his good friend Baldur Sveinsson, who had written to Stephan in the spring and described his two daughters, Ragnheiður, nicknamed Rænka, and Kristjana, who had subsequently died on April 14th. "It has been by far my greatest comfort to read your poems," Baldur had written, "especially the one that begins, 'In the dusk, I invite myself to sit by you'."

"As always, Baldur is like the best of brothers to me," Stephan wrote to Helga.[42] He and Baldur chatted and enjoyed comfortable silence together. They also walked down to the pier to have a look at the activity there, including women gutting and cutting herring in the cold northern wind. Baldur's surviving daughter, Rænka, was a bright child who began speaking unusually early and learned some "raven verses" before she was two years old. Stephan enjoyed chatting with her and she grew very fond of this warm old chap, even to the point of accepting his help as she built her palaces of wooden blocks.

It was now autumn and the Icelandic weather was becoming unpredictable, so Stephan decided to make a direct journey to Reykjavík by motorboat. As he was about to leave Baldur's home in the early morning of September 6th, he paused for a moment, then tip-toed to where little Rænka lay sleeping and kissed her on the forehead.

Homeward Bound

Stephan remained in Reykjavík only two days before leaving for the districts east of Reykjavík with his friend Guðmundur Finnbogason. Páll Guðmundsson of Hjálmsstaðir, a farmer who had donated most generously to the invitation fund, was their guide to Geysir and the waterfall Gullfoss. Like many others, Páll was initially unimpressed with Stephan's appearance. "He looked like an overburdened and weathered labourer. He was small of stature and skinny, though agile, and his face looked as if it had been chiselled by experience and the perseverance of ages. His neck appeared gaunt and his skin hard. The eyes were sharp and bright, however, and he shook my hand tightly and smiled. His eyes were observant and it was as if he was looking for something in my expression. Perhaps he wondered about our kinship or found me a kindred spirit. Since then I have often reflected on just how little connection there is between intelligence and physical attributes. In his poems, I had encountered a man of spiritual greatness. Now there stood beside me a worn-out labourer, bearing the expression of perils and hardship, though his inner vision was such that it could encompass the entire world."

Páll and Stephan formed an immediate bond. The night passed in discussion about farming and Páll admired the fact that Stephan was a keen farmer. "He had flown on the wings of poetic vision, but without forgetting the soil – as often happens with poetically inclined minds. Instead he was bound to the soil." Despite Stephan's radical opinions, Páll found tolerance his most apparent strength.⁴³

During a feast held for Stephan at Geysir, Guðmundur Finnbogason delivered a speech which he began by quoting from the middle of the poem "Greniskógurinn" (The Spruce Forest) – claiming, with a twinkle in his eye, that he couldn't remember the beginning. Interpreting this as a challenge, Páll of Hjálmsstaðir recited the first stanza and the beginning of the next, at which point Stephan leaned to him and whispered, "You have not purchased my *Andvökur* just because I'm around." In some homes he had noticed that *Andvökur* had hardly been touched. Stephan composed a poem for Páll based on the idea that he resembled the landscape in which he lived. Páll, however, could never bring himself to read his own poem written for Stephan.⁴⁴

Stephan returned to Reykjavík on September 15, 1917, and stayed with Theodóra Thoroddsen until the end of the month. During this time he fine-tuned the poems he had composed on his journey. He had managed to forget the war while travelling, but now he handed the manuscript he had brought with him to Guðmundur Finnbogason, saying that it could

The poet's mature profile by Icelandic sculptor Ríkarður Jónsson looks toward his birthplace at Kirkjuhóll. The monument commemorating Stephan G. Stephansson, which stands on the hill Arnarstapi, was dedicated in 1953, the centennial year of the poet's birth.

be printed once the war was over. One evening he discussed spiritualism with Ágúst H. Bjarnason. They were both sceptics. All the same, Stephan wrote on a piece of paper what he would say if he were ever to appear at a séance after he died. He sealed it and mailed it to Ágúst with instructions that he and his descendants not open it until someone could claim to have connected with Stephan from the beyond. The letter, now in the care of Ágúst's descendants, is in a safety deposit box in a bank in Reykjavík – still unopened.

This was Stephan's longest stay in a city and there was much to see. He went to movies and concerts, strolled along the streets, and spent much time at the National Library reading old books and manuscripts. Stephan also met with Indriði Einarsson, the boy from his youth who had ridden away to Reykjavík to attend school, leaving Stephan feeling isolated and hopeless on the hillside near Víðimýrarsel. Now Indriði was a respected economist and a prominent playwright. The past was dear to them both, and among other things they recalled the handwritten papers they had composed in boyhood and stories of the "rebels" of Skagafjörður who had "ridden north".

While at Akureyri Stephan had been impressed by the young poet Davíð Stefánsson, but he was concerned that Davíð " ... did not have the

On July 19, 1953, some 35 years after the poet's visit to his birthplace and 100 years after his birth, this monument on Arnarstapi was dedicated to the life and work of Stephan G. Stephansson.

physical stamina to continue with his schooling." Davíð had contracted tuberculosis and "was frail, rather skinny and pale, but a handsome lad, slightly darker than blond." Stephan had also heard that Davíð had problems at home. "He is neither suited as a manual labourer due to his frail health, nor as a scholar due to his inclination for poetry. His mother is said to be an intelligent woman who is inclined to learning, but she has been unable to obtain any education due to her workload and worries. His father is no great spirit." One day Davíð's father, a farmer and member of parliament, visited Stephan. Concerned about his son, he asked Stephan, "What do you think of him as a poet?" Stephan's reply was that Davíð was one of the most promising young poets in the country. "What most astonishes me about him is that nowhere does one find the usual faults that amateurs have in their poems." His father was also worried about the boy's lack of achievement at school. "That is normal, yet a tricky matter. You must not press him too much due to his health," Stephan cautioned. "Look, even those who are healthy and are doing well often encounter something in the school system that they dislike, but have to swallow against their will. Davíð must not do so, even if he could, due to his health." Farmer Stefán agreed happily and Stephan hoped that he would realize that there is more than one way to get ahead in life.[45]

Stephan spent his final days in Reykjavík at a hotel, waiting for the *Gullfoss*. Few remembered his 64th birthday except Baldur Sveinsson, who sent him a telegram in the form of a witty poetic pun about birthdays. Baldur had noticed the recurrent theme of youth in the poems Stephan had composed on his journey and also that Stephan seemed younger during this trip. Stephan replied

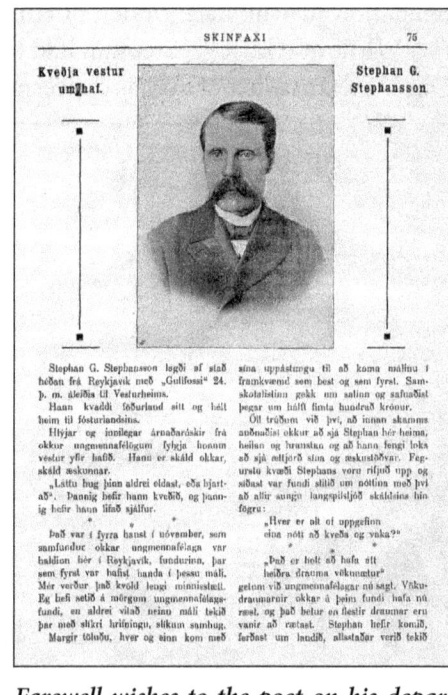

Farewell wishes to the poet on his departure for home on September 24th were published in the Icelandic paper **Skinfaxi**.

immediately with a stanza about cold weather and warm thoughts from Ísafjörður and sent greetings to Maren and little Rænka. "It's a pity that nobody remembered your birthday except Maren and I," Baldur noted, "and Rænka! She often talks about you and brings us such joy. Our other little daughter would have been one year old if she had lived." Thus he ended his letter.[46]

Perhaps Stephan had grown tired of the parties and idleness, so he walked to the district of Reykjavík known as Skuggahverfi (Shadow Quarter), where farmers brought their lambs to the slaughterhouse. Páll Guðmundsson of Hjálmsstaðir stayed in Reykjavík for a week and visited Stephan every evening. Stephan always invited Páll to come again and as soon as Páll had taken a seat he would fetch a little bottle and two glasses. The two would then sit sipping and chatting about everything under the sun. These were unforgettable evenings for Páll and he listened carefully to every word that came from Stephan's mouth. "It is quite remarkable," he wrote, "that the aura around great spirits when seen from the distance often disappears on closer personal encounter – unless this energy is genuine. The aura around Stephan G. is real."[47]

On October 11th the *Gullfoss* docked at Reykjavík. A farewell banquet was held for Stephan and the gifts he received were put on display in Ársæll Árnason's bookstore window for a few days. These included an Icelandic table-penant, writing utensils, a walking stick, two paintings of the Icelandic landscape, a portrait and bust of the poet, and a set of *Andvökur* bound in shark skin. The Icelandic parliament decided to donate 5000 *krónur* as an honorary gift to Stephan.

The day before his departure from Iceland, Stephan visited a government office to obtain a written statement to reduce the risk of being detained abroad in these perilous times. Signed by the Minister of Justice, the statement declared that Stephan had been a guest of the Icelandic nation, that parliament had honoured him, and that he was an honorary member of the Icelandic Literary Society. The Ministry recommended that he not be hindered on his return to Canada.

On the evening of Wednesday, October 24th, a number of people escorted Stephan to Reykjavík Harbour and gathered on the dock to say goodbye. In Stephan's notebook was a long list of small favours he had promised to do for people when he returned to Canada, such as finding lost relatives and even procuring seeds from various northern trees. He left behind a manuscript for a book of poetry, having evidently intended to compose his way around the country and reward the Icelandic people with his poems. The book, which contains some 40 poems of varying lengths, is a collection of images from the places he visited and reflections on the themes of oppression and freedom, youth and age. Folkloristic beings, culture, nature, and horses represent those who do not accept the oppression of toil, greed, and materialism.

Among the poems was "Óskasteinninn" (The Wish Stone) based on a folktale of a wish stone on the top of a mountain. The poem is about a young man who climbs a mountain and finds the stone. As soon as he grabs it, he feels flaming hopes and the thirst for victory flow through his body. Wanting to test the stone, he asks for a ship to sail around the world, but there was no ship in the fjord. Then, he wishes for a forest on the sand, but the barren scree remains. Lastly, he asks for good shoes, but receives none. He throws away the stone, saying it is useless and causes only evil. The poem is Stephan's address to contemporary Icelandic youth with whom he had more in common than with the older generation. In fact, he was fascinated by the young people and felt that the future of the country lay in their ideals. He indicates that the impatience of the young is exactly the power necessary to move things forward. The poem ends with a description of the boy when he is much older:

> *He stood by a new age and youth*
> *In the last steps, at later times,*
> *And the ship was ready for him on the fjord.*
> *In the distance, he saw the bushes in a slope.*
> *Every shepherd could put on flying shoes,*
> *Although the mountains were steep and the spring nights cool.*
> *And the frustrations of the youngster were compensated for.*
> *First now he understood how the wishes came true.*
> *They succeed at last, as a clear prayer for everyone,*
> *Although they fail for the one who climbs in the mountains.*
> *In his open palm he saw the glowing wishing stone,*
> *He always had carried in his hand.*[48]

The poems were published before the end of that year.

During Stephan's stay in Iceland, he had become better acquainted with the country's people, problems, poetry, economics, and politics, and he was able to observe the nation in the context of North-American capitalism. Iceland was a land of physical challenges, but it had great wealth in its people, especially in its women, to whom the country owed everything. Stephan found Iceland's progress great. "I doubt that so few common people anywhere else in the world have contributed a larger share to various progressive enterprises."[49] He also foresaw a struggle between workers and farmers on the one hand and "merchants and the wealth-mongers" on the other, which would prove well founded in many ways. He acknowledged the fact that there were also wastrels in Iceland, rich "farm-speculators and waterfall philanderers", all kinds of people who did not risk a cent of their own money, yet profited on commissions and investments. The idea of harnessing Iceland's waterpower was a dream worthy of much bigger countries, but it would require heavy industry. If successful, this development would only mean profits for an individual rather than prosperity for the country's people. Iceland's waterfalls, he concluded, should be owned by the state, and although he found it acceptable to harness them to "rest over-weary hands", he doubted whether development would be that simple. He also pointed out that Iceland had no raw materials for heavy industry.[50]

Stephan favoured slow and steady progress that was rooted in the rural areas and he expressed astonishment at how many people derived their livelihoods from small Icelandic farms, while he and other farmers in the West struggled to survive on much larger farms. He had reservations about urban life and favoured a flourishing rural economy. Also still skeptical about the influences of schools on body and soul, he suggested an educational system based on the Danish Grundtvig model. "Let everyone, both teachers and students, work toward a balance between body and soul, with farming and practical work at every school."[51] Such work would also pay the costs of the school.

"The year I felt good/remains the longest in my memory," Stephan said about his journey to Iceland.[52] As time passed, Icelandic rural culture became a utopian symbol that was expressed most clearly in his sharp social criticism in the essay "Jökulgöngur" (Glacial Hiking).

Chapter 15

The Memorial

Volatile Atmosphere

Stephan caught sight of North America again on the morning of October 31, 1917. He wanted Helga to meet him in Winnipeg, as he could afford the travel expenses, but for some reason she did not. He first travelled to Gardar, North Dakota, for a week's visit, then attended a banquet held in his honour in Winnipeg on November 28th. By December 1st, after a short stop in Wynyard, he was back home on the farm at Markerville.

Two of Stephan's trunks contained gifts he had received in Iceland, including the national costume for Helga, a gift from the women of Iceland. The dress fit Helga well, Stephan wrote to Theodóra Thoroddsen. Apparently he planned to have a photograph taken of Helga in the outfit, but since it was an hour's trip to the nearest photographer's studio, he left that for summer. Whether Helga ever had this portrait taken is unknown, but if so the photograph has not survived.

Stephan was rather unwell after his return home. "I probably caught a chill on my bald head," he said, conceding in letters to friends that he had needed all his strength to "revel through the whole thing."[1] At a party organized by his neighbours, Stephan recounted details of the trip and read some of his poems. Among the numerous errands he now had to take care of was obtaining seedlings for the tree nursery at Akureyri, though his attempts seem to have failed.

On the day of his return from Iceland, Stephan deposited $1820.53 in his bank account at Markerville, and by the end of 1917, with all his debts paid off, his account stood at $1221.24 – the most savings he had ever had. With some of that sum he purchased more land, in order to improve prospects for his family, but this belief in the land and the future turned out to be a heavy burden as it took him a long time to finish paying for it. Stephan also had a furnace installed in a new basement under the house, which made the wood heater in his study unnecessary. This made his work place more spacious and comfortable, yet he missed the old wood stove. "We have been flaming together in the winter cold for such a long time," he quipped.[2]

By New Year's of 1918, Stephan had recovered from his journey to Iceland and regained much of his spiritual vigour. It was his impression that Icelanders in North America did not have the same joy of life as their counterparts in the homeland, and to him they seemed querulous and reluctant to invest in their own spiritual well being, although they spent fortunes on ostentation.

Another reality also awaited him at home in the volatile wartime atmosphere in Canada. Tensions mounted as the "Great War" continued with increasingly intense fundraising and recruitment. By 1916, voluntary recruitment was beginning to flag, reflecting the growing unpopularity of the Conservatives under Sir Robert Borden, and contrary to former promises, Prime Minister Borden now felt the need to implement conscription. Signed on August 28, 1917, conscription legislation came into effect the following day, making military registration compulsory and imposing severe penalties for failure to comply. There were exemptions for farmers, as they were needed at home to produce food for the war effort, but any expression of resistance to the law was forbidden.

The aging Liberal leader, Sir Wilfred Laurier, refused to accept conscription and demanded a national refer-

Stephan G. Stephansson following his visit to Iceland, with Dakota friends Jónas Hall (seated) and Kristján Níels (K.N.) Júlíus.

endum. His party split over this contentious issue, however, and Prime Minister Borden now recognized an opportunity to form an alliance with those Liberals who accepted conscription. He therefore called a federal election for December 17, 1917, and when his alliance won the election, a new government was formed under his leadership. Stephan was fond of Laurier and said he had lost with dignity, but in reality he had not expected any great changes if Laurier had won. What he felt mattered most, however, was for a government to respect democracy and for the electorate to overthrow any government that manipulated electoral laws in order to remain in power.[3]

Sigurður Júlíus Jóhannesson, who was editor of *Lögberg* again, had supported Laurier's campaign. Fired after the election, he established a new paper in the beginning of 1918 and named it *Voröld* (Age of Spring), a title taken from Stephan's poem "Langförull". *Voröld* was sponsored by socialists and farmers, many of whom were from Wynyard, Saskatchewan, and it was a relatively radical publication. Declaring liberal and independent views and going as far as possible in resisting the war effort, *Voröld* called for solidarity among workers, farmers, and soldiers, and went so far as to support the Bolshevik revolution in Russia. Although Sigurður Júlíus was somewhat haphazard in his editing, Stephan supported the paper by donating $20 and sending poems and articles. Icelandic opponents of *Voröld* reported the paper to the authorities, who scrutinized it for evidence of high treason – without success.[4]

The poet with pen in hand, around the time of his visit to Iceland in 1917.

Stephan's political stance grew steadily more radical during these years. He joined the Non-Partisan League, a semi-socialist, populist agrarian party challenging the two-party stranglehold that existed in Canadian politics. Stephan and his friend Grímur Grímsson were in direct contact with League leader William Irvine, who had spoken at the last Icelandic Day in Markerville, and Stephan subscribed to the party organ, *The Western Independent*, edited by Irvine. Stephan liked Irvine. "I think he will sacrifice himself before his time, always reading, always thinking, always writing, always debating at the podium, and mostly about difficult and unpopular issues – more freedom of religion, a better society."

At a party convention in Innisfail, Stephan met Mrs. Louise McKinney, who had won a seat in Alberta's provincial legislature in 1917 – the first woman elected to a legislature in the British Empire. She impressed him as articulate and energetic, but not quite a match for her Icelandic counterpart Bríet Bjarnhéðinsdóttir. Stephan shook her hand after the meeting and said in a letter to a friend that he hoped for a kiss the next time he met her.[5]

Stephan now began to follow the events of the Russian revolution with some expectation. In the poem "Bolsheviki" (The Bolshevist), written in February of 1918, he asks whether the peasant's son had come to claim power to free the oppressed.

Is he bent by the evil of the world,
Bloody, rising and growing taller,
Making our masses stronger, bigger?
Witness of truth, yet distorted by lies!
A light that hundred years ago,
The French extinguished in their own wounds?
The morning red of the weak?
The peace messenger of those oppressed.[6]

The Battle at Yankee Bluff

In the spring of 1918, the Germans launched a major offensive in Europe and Canada's exemption of farmers' sons from conscription was repealed. A son of Stephan's friend Jón from Sleðbrjótur was called up, and as encouragement Stephan expressed the hope that this "revolt of all devils" would soon end and the highnesses of the world would roll over.[7] The first conscripts from Markerville were now sent overseas to England, and in a letter to Rögnvaldur Pétursson Stephan noted, "teenagers are now being taken captive."⁸ Asked whether he would not want to travel to the battlefield after the war, the poet replied:

> *Even if offered the fare,*
> *It would disgust me to go there,*
> *Where the world's greatest stupidity*
> *Was fought for the greatest evil.*⁹

With regard to himself and his sons, Stephan had a strategy in the event that he or his sons were ever called up. As soon as they were outside the borders of Canada, according to the letter of their naturalization papers they were no longer citizens of the British Empire, but of Denmark.

Stephan objected to the "patriotic babble" of the politicians as he felt that the stupidity behind the war rested in self-complacency.¹⁰ Once again he began to compose pacifist poetry and in April he sent *Voröld* a translation of Robert Service's poem "The Stretcher-Bearer". At the beginning of May, he submitted a verse in which he mocks the boastful declarations of the Americans about their role in the war:

> *The United States threatened,*
> *That their storm would be "rough".*
> *Yet almost no soldier fell*
> *In the battle at "Yankee-Bluff".*¹¹*

Stephan wrote the words "Yankee Bluff" in English as a pun – *bluff* meaning both *hill* and *deception*. The verse hit sensitive nerves south of the border and in late May Stephan received a letter in English from Sveinbjörn Johnson, a lawyer in Grand Forks, North Dakota. Sveinbjörn stated that he felt compelled to challenge Stephan's verse in order to counteract its negative influence and he demanded that Stephan apologize to both Canada and the United States.¹² Unapologetic, Stephan vigorously defended his views, mocking Sveinbjörn's over-reaction as a "tempest in a teapot" and characterizing his letter as an encyclopaedia of American participation in the war. He then explained his verse and ridiculed his critic by elaborating on the pun. As the battle on the Western front had taken place in a hilly area, he had allowed himself to dub

---

*Stephan's own translation of this verse: "*Our storm* voiced the States –/"In its rage will be rough."/Yet nearly no man fell dead/In the battle at "Yankee Bluff".

the place Yankee Bluff, but since the Americans had in fact filled an eight-mile gap on wide-open terrain, he could just as well have named the verse Yankee Plain or Yankee Flat – though this could also have been interpreted as mockery. Stephan was quick to state that he was pleased there had been few casualties among the Americans so far. They were lucky compared to the Canadians. As he spoke only for himself, he concluded, he did not owe anyone an apology. "I do not know you, Mr. Johnson, personally or in any other way. If I had received a letter such as yours from some strange watchdog of obscure war interests, I would not have bothered to answer, but as a token of respect to your good name, as you sign the letter, and as you are an educated gentleman, I make the effort to reply".[13]

Sveinbjörn Johnson, North Dakota Attorney General and Justice of the Supreme Court, disapproved of Stephan's opinions.

Stephan asked his friend Rögnvaldur Pétursson to forward his response to Sveinbjörn Johnson. Rögnvaldur was furious with Sveinbjörn and found it "incredible how far the impudence of fools can go." He forwarded Stephan's letter as requested.[14]

Stephan's opponents saw this verse as an opportunity to have him charged with treason. That this did not happen was probably due to Rögnvaldur Pétursson's influence. "His keen, bright eyes," Rögnvaldur later wrote, "cast a more beautiful light than the brightest and most beautiful heavenly stars that shone coldly and without compassion over the blood-stained corpses. Nobody has ever undergone a greater trial of conviction than he did then, but he weathered that trial and thus earned the greatest gift to our nation." As far as Stephan was concerned, "they can throw me in jail if they want. I have fewer years left than have passed, so there is no reason to betray my convictions now."[15]

The End of War

In November of 1918 a guest arrived at Stephan and Helga's home. Jóhannes Stefánsson, better known by the surname Birkiland, had been in North America since 1909, wandering among Icelanders and others, writing poetry in English and Icelandic. Now he was writing a novel entitled *Love and Pride* under the pseudonym Emil V. Sommerleaf. Stephan pitied this aspiring writer and offered him the use of his study for a few days.

Birkiland was a peculiar person, intelligent in many ways, but somewhat paranoid due to the abuse he had endured in his youth, as is evident in his autobiography *Harmsaga ævi minnar (The Tragedy of my Life)*. He felt persecuted in most places, but he was comfortable at Stephan's home. One evening, however, one of Stephan's sons, who had been drinking, came for a visit. "He said to his father that he should kick me out into the cold because I was a tramp and a wretch. 'He is out in the cold,' replied the greatest poet among Icelanders in North America."[16]

Stephan empathized with those individuals who could not follow the beaten track, as can be seen in his poem "Jón the Outcast". Recognizing Birkiland's talent under his weak appearance, he observed, "What misery it is to be born with the many whims of genius if you never have the good fortune to create a masterpiece as geniuses do." Birkiland had various talents, he pointed out, "but all of them are undeveloped and he is without a focus unless directed onto the right track by some chance." Birkiland's novel was published in 1920, but it was not well received and he continued his wanderings until 1925 when he returned to Iceland.[17]

On November 11, 1918, while Birkiland sat writing in Stephan's study, the "Great War" came to an end. Stephan was pleased that the Icelandic soldiers from Markerville had not yet reached the battlefield, as the armistice was signed three days before they were to be sent to France. The son of Jón from Sleðbrjótur also returned home unharmed, but the loss to the Icelandic community was nevertheless great. Of the approximately 1300 soldiers of Icelandic descent who had gone to war from Canada and the United States, at least 144 had lost their lives.

Stephan stubbornly opposed exalting anything to do with the war and he received returned soldiers in a manner different than most people. In the poem "Fjallkonan til hermannanna, sem heim koma" (The Maid of the Mountains Addresses the Soldiers who Return Home), he states it would be sad to receive them with brothers' blood on their swords. The war was fratricide and the greatest achievement was either to stop it or refuse to take part in it. This was also his message in an address to local soldiers a year after they returned. "I still remember," Stephan said, "how sad I felt the day after you boys were called up, although I did not talk about it or have any family members in that group." It was no disgrace that they escaped battle, he claimed, and he was relieved to have them home. He refused to flatter them, however, saying that domestic problems were just as important as the war, and he concluded that the greatest honour to the fallen would be to prevent this catastrophe from ever being repeated. For him, the end of war augured spring, his favourite season, and he hoped for better times ahead. Most improvements in society began among the common people rather than with authorities, he pointed out, and "all spring growth begins on the flat fields rather than in the mountains." "But boys, welcome back to your parents' homes, back to our district, back to Canada, and back to the country of spring renewal."[18]

Personal memorial or glorification of war? This young Icelandic Canadian volunteer enlisted in January of 1916 and died on the battlefields of France on August 16, 1918, at 24 years of age.

The spirit of spring, however, soon faded from Stephan's mind. Those who had supported the war, now inspired by new Canadian nationalism, believed that evil had been expelled from the world, but cruelty and fanaticism were still present in society. Labour protests such as the Winnipeg General Strike in May of 1919 brought class differences into sharp relief, and labour unrest was also evident in Alberta, particularly among coal miners. This was the 'Red Spring' of 1919 and the most radical socialists were persecuted.

New fault lines were now forming between ethnic groups and creating divisions between urban and rural society.[19]

During the cold spring of 1919 people became increasingly anxious as a highly contagious and deadly disease called Spanish influenza appeared in Alberta. Stephan regarded the epidemic as a consequence of the war that he could never forgive. Gatherings were banned as the death toll mounted, and at the end of November two youngsters in the Icelandic settlement fell victim to this plague.

Collapsed Palaces

When Stephan received news that the flu epidemic had reached Iceland, his thoughts turned to his friends there. Due to censorship, he had corresponded very little after his return home, but in January of 1918 Baldur Sveinsson had written him a letter – in English due to the censorship. He reported polar ice in the fjord and joked that young Rænka believed that Stephan could chase it away by means of poetry. Stephan was glad to hear from Baldur, but he admitted to feeling uneasy about having accepted the invitation to visit Iceland, realizing the economic burden it had caused when there were so many hardships to deal with. It pleased him that Rænka thought he could handle the ice. "What a wonder is youth," he said, including a little verse asking spring to bring her sun and southern breezes.[20]

On January 9, 1919, another letter from Baldur arrived. Somehow anxious about it, Stephan did not immediately open it. Eventually, however, he went into his study and closed the door. "My dearest friend," it began. "It becomes dark indeed when our little darlings are extinguished, as you have described, and so it is now for my wife and me as we sit alone and grieve our good little darling. We have lost our little Rænka, who died on the 17th of last month after having been confined to bed by influenza for over a week. Somehow I have not been able to bring myself to write you until now." At the funeral, the pastor had quoted from a poem by Stephan, which had pleased Baldur, and it was some consolation that she had met Stephan and had not forgotten him. "I often had to build a house for Stephan G. when she was playing," Baldur wrote, "and I have never experienced a more special moment than when you said goodbye to little Rænka asleep by kissing her on the forehead."[21]

The Memorial

Ragnheiður Baldursdóttir (little Rænka), July 5, 1915 – November 17, 1918

As Stephan read Baldur's letter, the little girl's image returned to him. He worked even more quietly over the following days. The frozen firewood split easily in the January frost and flew faster than usual from the chopping block. The poet wrestled with unexpressive words, unable to compose as poignantly as he wanted, but he nevertheless soon completed a poem. In his letter to Baldur, he revealed a glimpse of his own feelings. "Dear, faithful friend," he began, describing the strange anxiety he had felt when the letter had arrived. He understood the emptiness and grief that came with losing a child, he said, and to deal with these feelings he had worked until exhausted in body and soul, "but each person has his own way of coping." He enclosed a few stanzas "with the same tune as our lullabies." Still he was not satisfied. He did not find the verse as sincere and gentle as Baldur was himself. "But why am I doing this?" he asked. Despite everything, he explained, to express some benevolent vulnerability was the only way to create a little warmth in such a barren place.[22]

The poem is tight in form, underlining the sorrow, and the images are strong and fragile at the same time. The child is a symbol of youth and eternity, while the image of the aging poet is transient:

> I.
> We built palaces
> For each other, but separate.
> Yours was roofed for me,
> Mine was meant for you.

The building that your
Child's hand built,
Has not moved –
Mine has collapsed.

II.
The heavenly hall of a child's mind
Was your palace,
The glowing gold of a poetic world
Was flaming there.

Yours was made of
Eternal youth. –
My building was
Made of transience.

I prepared for you
A long life of happiness,
The eternal sheds:
Royalty and fame.

III.
Over ages and eternities,
Distant continents,
Over breakers and blue sky
The child's hand reaches.

In grief and in happiness,
Your hand is with me. –
At your funeral and tombstone
My hand is lame.

IV.
You will always be safe
From hardships:
Eternal, unchanged,
Always a wonderful child.

Farewell – swan-white
Sleeping in bed,
A forehead sealed
With loving kisses.[23]

The death of little Rænka was a personal finale to the tragedy the war represented for Stephan. His palaces had collapsed, but latent hope remained in the unspoiled palace of youth. The western world had to be rebuilt from the ruins of war – a war that everyone had lost.

Two Major Issues

Two important issues now faced the Icelandic community in North America. Shortly before the end of the war it had been suggested that a memorial be raised in remembrance of soldiers of Icelandic descent who had lost their lives. Around the same time, the founding of an Icelandic patriotic society had been proposed. A meeting to discuss the patriotic society was called in Winnipeg for January 7, 1919, and a meeting on the memorial concept was set for January 14th.

Several pillars of Winnipeg's Icelandic community participated in both committees. The memorial committee included such men as Lieutenant Walter Lindal (later Judge Lindal) and Stephan's cousin Marinó Hannesson, while the patriotic committee included Rögnvaldur Pétursson, Sigurður Júlíus Jóhannesson (editor of *Voröld*), and some Conservatives. Dr. Brandur J. Brandson and cabinet minister Thomas H. Johnson were on both committees. Addresses from both groups were printed on the front page of the February 13th issue of *Lögberg*.

"An Address to Icelanders in North America", issued by the patriotic committee, showed no evidence of an inferiority complex in the Icelandic community. Arguably tinged with aspects of racism, this article referred to Icelandic nationality and culture in North America as a dynamic treasure that should be preserved for the future. The Icelandic language, it maintained, should be taught to descendants of the Icelandic settlers, and "Nordic thought, Nordic personality, Nordic understanding of the demands and purpose of human life [is] in our judgment ... superior to that of some other nations." As there were many ethnic groups in Canada, Icelandic patriots wanted to cultivate their heritage so that it would contribute to the whole of Canadian society. They proposed supporting intellectuals and writers through publications and lectures; supporting the study of Icelandic at North American universities; sponsoring awards in Nordic studies; and not least, enhancing relations between Icelanders in North America and Iceland.[24]

The vision of the memorial committee was no less pompous. It advocated honoring the memory of those "who had lost their lives while serving the noble and just cause for which the Allies had fought victoriously." Not only the fallen heroes were to be commemorated. Icelandic immigrants had participated in building Canada, and by going to war their descendants had offered their lives to ensure the freedom necessary to improve the culture and prosperity of the nation.[25]

Opinions were divided on both issues. Some felt that Icelandic patriotism undermined loyalty to Canada and the United States and others thought that the time for Icelandic ethnicity had come to an end. In a letter to Rögnvaldur Pétursson, one member of the community pointed out that in a few decades most of the immigrant generation would be dead, and their descendants, born and raised in North America, were not Icelanders as they were shaped by Anglo-Saxon culture. English was the language of the future, and the writer felt that it was wrong to maintain the Icelandic language as this would only serve to set Icelandic people apart as foreigners and generate suspicion. The more languages, the more "suspicion, partisan politics, and isolation."[26] Indeed, some Anglo-Saxons in Canada, especially after the war, openly discriminated against people of other ethnic origins, and this made the patriotic issue even more delicate.

Lampinn (The Lamp), Icelandic sculptor Einar Jónsson's concept for a monument to Icelandic-Canadian soldiers who had served in the "Great War".

In Winnipeg, the Jón Sigurðsson Chapter of the IODE (Imperial Order of the Daughters of the Empire) pledged $500 toward a memorial if agreement could be reached. When Icelandic sculptor Einar Jónsson's concept of a 12 meter high memorial was unveiled, however, nearly a third of the 150 people in attendance expressed outright opposition or skepticism, underlining the fact the Icelandic community was far from unanimous about participation in the war. Many earnest articles were published, especially in *Lögberg*, in favour of the memorial, but others suggested a more meaningful option be found to honour the fallen. The most powerful voice against the concept of a memorial came from the foothills of the Rocky Mountains.

Multiculturalism – Bread and Stones

For Stephan, the war memorial was both a symbol of fossilized thought and a glorification of the war he detested so much. On the other hand, he supported the patriotic movement and hesitated to criticize the memorial until he was certain he would not also harm the patriotic cause. On February 18, 1919, however, he wrote to *Voröld* to point out that the memorial committee was obviously in a great hurry, thinking that a memorial was the best way to help the soldiers who were lucky enough to return "alive, indeed, yet lame mentally and physically." He felt that money collected should be used instead for the urgent needs of those who had returned disabled. He did not doubt that Einar Jónson could design a magnificent memorial, but that was not the issue. What was important, he felt, was the welfare of the living – the returned soldiers and their families. The soldiers had been promised all kinds of benefits before they went to war and the Icelandic community should demand that these promises be kept. Stephan praised *Voröld* for offering to assist soldiers in claiming their rights and added that those who had been seduced into the army with nationalistic fanfare should have the right to jobs and other benefits. As matters stood, only those veterans who suffered from obvious infirmity could claim a pension and Stephan found that although soldiers had perhaps not sacrificed more for their country than those who toiled at home, all promises to the soldiers must be kept. Fairness does not increase "if two injustices are added up."

He also supported an idea from Emile Walters, a painter of Icelandic descent, to establish an Icelandic art museum where a modest memorial could be erected. That was a good idea, he thought, especially with the dissolution of the times in mind. "Great and expensive memorials erected over militant kings and military fame tend to collapse before their time, when urban mobs with a brown conscience go berserk in city squares." The general public, he maintained, hardly notices outdoor memorials in the cities. "In a museum, however, they are seen by those who appreciate them." Stephan feared that the memorial would be so expensive that there would be nothing left for the artist except praise and flattery. He then shot a poisonous arrow at affluent Icelanders in Winnipeg. "Nobody should be denied the washing of a stain from his neck cloth, by whatever manner he can think of," he said, referring to a legend of Oliver Cromwell, "a strong and tyrannical man who had a bloodstain on his neck cloth that never disappeared despite many washings."[27]

On March 3, 1919, Markerville Icelanders held a meeting on the matter of a patriotic society. After reading the address of the Winnipeg committee, Stephan delivered a remarkable lecture on ethnicity, language, and culture, very different from the racist address he had just read. He outlined current schools of thought against the preservation of ethnicity and refuted them with his own original ideas. That "Canada will never become a complete nation unless one single language is spoken in the country" was a common opinion. Stephan objected to this and pointed out that patriotism rested no less on another fundamental, "that the country is home to oneself and everything that one holds dear." A number of countries where more than one language was spoken could be cited. Another misconception Stephan raised was that it would be too hard for children to learn two languages. Children, he said, could easily learn two or more languages. He found another argument even more specious: that teaching the Icelandic language would inhibit the learning of English and isolate children. On this subject, the poet spoke in no uncertain terms. "He who is the most isolated is the one who is acquainted with but one home, has read only one book, and knows only one language. Normally a man is somewhat more sophisticated if he has visited two districts, has read two volumes of human history, and can speak for himself in two languages. … A nation unwilling to accommodate more than one language isolates itself and flirts with two extremes: the arrogance that one's own nation is the whole world, or the wretchedness that imagines everything poor and wretched about itself." The best way to understand one's own language and nationality is to be able to compare it with others. Stephan also claimed that those children in the settlement doing poorly in English at school were from Icelandic homes where only poor English was spoken.[28]

Toward the end of the meeting, the Markerville Icelanders approved the proposal in the patriotic address and registered a $12 pledge once a society was established. Eventually they discussed the memorial as well. Reverend Pétur Hjálmsson supported it while Stephan outlined his arguments against it, and although Reverend Pétur was a hot-tempered man they were able to discuss the matter in a friendly manner. In the end, only a few were in favour of the memorial.

A few days later, Stephan sent Rögnvaldur Péturssyn a poem he had composed while forking manure in the barn, saying that he hoped it would not smell too badly. The poem, a greeting to the patriotic cause, was read at the inaugural meeting of the *Þjóðræknisfélag Íslendinga í Vesturheimi* (Icelandic National League of North America), held in Winnipeg from March 25 to 27, 1919. Rögnvaldur was elected president of the new society and entrusted with editing its annual journal, *Tímarit*. Stephan's poem, "Gamla landið" (The Old Country), was printed in the first issue. At the second annual meeting, Rögnvaldur supported Stephan's nomination as an honorary member.

While the Icelandic National League was established without much controversy, dispute over the memorial escalated in the Icelandic papers in Winnipeg. A lively exchange developed between Stephan on the one

The Þjóðræknisfélag Íslendinga í Vesturheimi *(Icelandic National League) was successfully established in 1919, shortly after the end of the 'Great War'. In addition to promoting Icelandic culture and ties with Iceland, it pledged to promote good citizenship among the descendants of Icelandic immigrants.*

hand and *Lögberg*'s editor Jón J. Bíldfell and Árni Sveinsson, a prosperous farmer in the Argyle Settlement, on the other. Stephan replied to Jón Bíldfell's attack on his views with a sarcastic article printed in *Voröld*. Entitled "Villuvörður" (Misleading Cairns), the article alluded to confusing cairns or markers randomly erected away from established mountain trails. He included mention of a conversation he had once heard about a well-known memorial in Winnipeg. Only the most knowledgeable of the public knew that it was actually a memorial to those who had died in the Riel Rebellion. When looking at the memorial, most people thought it was for Riel, not those who had fought against him, and the names of the soldiers were thus completely forgotten. "Contemporary history is always a bit cross-eyed," Stephan said. "Its oblique glance often wanders as time goes by. In a quarter of a century, he speculated, a Winnipeg memorial to Icelandic soldiers would most likely remind the forgetful public of Kaiser Wilhelm."[29]

Árni Sveinsson's personal attacks on Stephan hurt the most. Árni had been effective in selling *Andvökur* and he had corresponded with Stephan for a time, but he did not recognize the humanitarian focus of Stephan's views. Instead he attacked Stephan personally in a manner that was hurtful, accusing him of being malicious, uncaring about the soldiers, and too stingy to donate any money to charity. In addition he reminded Stephan that members of the Icelandic community had funded the publication of his poetry.

Árni's insinuation that Stephan was a burden on the community hurt more than the usual accusations that his poetry was abstruse, and Stephan replied to this attack in *Voröld*. Explaining that there was a tendency to aggrandize those who had died in order to justify the war, he noted that government and church had "proselytized to the people that this apocalyptic flame had been lit for a more beautiful heaven and a more prosperous earth in the future," and those sacrificed became holy. A memorial, however, was not the answer, Stephan maintained, and he disagreed that his article had been disrespectful towards the soldiers. At the same time he mockingly conceded to some of the things of which Árni accused him. Big farmers like Árni Sveinsson could easily overlook the smaller contributions of others, he pointed out, alluding to the biblical story of the poor widow who gave her last coin – a story that Árni may "have heard about". In this way he implied that Árni's arrogance was mixed with religious hypocrisy.[30]

Not everyone disagreed with Stephan. From Washington State in the Pacific Northwest, Magnús Jónsson "from Fjall", whom Stephan had known during his youth in Skagafjörður and had met again on his trip to the Pacific in 1913, wrote a supportive letter. Now nearly blind, Magnús expressed astonishment at the attacks on Stephan. "Their purpose can only be to gain some prominence among the most ignorant people in order to secure a little power and attention. Only petty souls boast of respect for ignorance. … Árni has now received a brilliant lesson, but he likely does not have the sense to recognize it."[31] More writers also came to Stephan's defence, accusing Árni of encouraging others to send their sons to the war while he ensured that his own sons did not go.

Árni replied vigorously to Stephan's letter in the April 17th issue of *Lögberg*, but Stephan did not bother with a rebuttal. Instead he delivered his heaviest blow in the May 13th issue of *Voröld*, in an article entitled "Brauð og steinn" ("Bread and Stone"). In it he focused on the national economy after the war – the heavy debt, the increased taxes, and the high interest rates – then reiterated what he considered to be the essence of the issue – the immediate needs of returned soldiers. This matter needed to be properly addressed, he maintained. Veterans should receive fair pay and the public would have to bear with them after four years of hardship. Despite promises of "restoration" made to the soldiers in Alberta, nothing much had happened and their families complained daily in the papers. Stephan also quoted a Provincial Government report stating that half the able-bodied returned soldiers were now unemployed. Many of them, he pointed out, had seemed lively and clear-headed when they had first returned home, so doctors denied them compensation. These soldiers often experienced emotional and psychological problems, however, with the result that nothing worked out for them. Stephan insisted that the government accept the demands of soldiers without hesitation. Although "nobody wants a memorial except the Winnipeg committee," he felt that it was acceptable to collect funds in support of the returned soldiers, and he was actually surprised by the silence around the subject of war injuries that had to be dealt with. He concluded his "Bread and Stones" article with a brilliant reference to *The Bible*. "It may be that some of our own glory can be preserved in a pyramid that will not erode in the desert of the ages, but it is misguided humanity to take bread from the mouths of the living in order to give a stone to the dead."[32]

It is difficult to know whether the memorial issue faded from public attention because of the impact of Stephan's objections or due to a general lack of interest. Many individuals raised objections, pointing out other ways of honouring the soldiers, and in the end a memorial book edited by Rögnvaldur Pétursson was published, including photos and short biographies of most Canadian and American soldiers of Icelandic descent – hardly a lesser memorial than a 12 meter sculpture.

Perhaps not surprisingly, Stephan was not invited to the Icelandic Celebration in Winnipeg during the summer of 1920, but his countrymen in Saskatchewan welcomed him to the celebration in Wynyard. During Stephan and Helga's two week visit there, Stephan met with Rögnvaldur Pétursson on the subject of having an additional volume of *Andvökur* published. Stephan felt this volume should include the poems he had left in Iceland, though he had not heard anything about that manuscript and he did not have a copy of those poems. Aware that their content might evoke a harsh reaction and reduce the sales of a new book, however, he preferred to wait.

Chapter 16

Trail of War

Malingering and Glacier Walks

In addition to the Spanish flu epidemic and labour unrest, western farmers in Canada faced difficult times after the war. Grain prices fell and prospects for farming became bleak. Parts of the prairie and parkland experienced severe drought and Stephan was glad for the slough land he had bought despite negative prophecies by his neighbours. Now it was good hayland for his 30 head of cattle and the horses he and Jakob owned. Despite these challenges, Stephan and Jakob broke more land for cultivation. The autumn of 1919 was harsh and the weather remained so for most of the winter, with heavy snow and little grazing. Stephan tended the cattle in the barn and cut firewood, which was hard work as he was rather sickly.

There were now fewer people in the Stephansson home. Rósa, at 19 years of age, was attending Olds Agricultural College. Stephan expressed reservations as to whether she should have the educational opportunities he and Helga had not been able to give the other children, but Helga eventually made that decision. Only Jenny and Jakob were left at home. Jakob was quiet and industrious, often on the run here and there. If he had too much to drink, he sometimes raised his voice and pounded his fist on the table. Jenny, almost 30 years of age and cheerful, liked contemporary Canadian entertainment. Helga worked constantly, milking the cows and doing housework, sewing and knitting, always thinking of the well-being of her children and grandchildren. Home life was very peaceful and if Stephan was not doing chores he was reading or writing, distancing himself from the outside world.

Stephan's sister, Sigurlaug, and her husband moved again, this time to Prince Rupert, British Columbia, after having turned the farm over to their married daughter, Guðbjörg. Guðbjörg's health was frail, so her husband tended the home and children, baked bread and washed the floors. Sigurlaug wrote to Rósa about the severe cold at the West Coast and complained about the unruly "Swedish hags" there. She also described the rough life of fishermen "who come loaded with fish from the Bering Strait. It is hard to comprehend how those wretches survive the cold out there because only some of them have woolen clothes. Many of them brew a little drop and it seems as if everybody knows how to do that nowadays. The police go on raids most nights and earn a lot of money by catching those who trade in booze, opium, morphine, and cocaine. Most of them are Chinese who make all kinds of mixtures that the whites smoke, whatever it costs – even their lives. Mankind is still just a half-wit, I think," she wrote. "Well, my dear," she concluded, "I know this school is good for you. I know you have to get away from the doorstep a little."[1]

Jenny wrote to Rósa variously in Icelandic or in English, sometimes combining the two languages. She wrote about Kate, Rósa's cow, who prematurely delivered a stillborn calf in December of 1919. "All of a sudden she began to "búast til", made a little bag [...] she is feeling perfectly allright, *hildir og allt kom í einu* so I think it will not affect her any, she may give a little milk."[2] ("búast til" means prepare for birth by producing milk, and "hildir og allt kom í einu" means "the placenta and suddenly everything all comes at once").

Stephan wrote a poem for Jenny to enclose with her letter to Rósa. "He thinks it is so nice," she said in English. Rósa wrote to her father in Icelandic. "You cannot imagine how much I enjoyed the verses. They pleased me so and I will keep them as my best souvenir." In reference to her studies, she remarked, "I find "chemistry" – is it "efnafræði" in Icelandic? – the most difficult." She liked college, however, and attained good marks.[3]

The letters to Rósa convey a sense of daily life on the farm. Jenny reported on calving and sent news of the piglet, Louis, who was growing fast and would fetch up to $50. Mamie the ewe had quit bleating but the ram, Vargur, remained just as nasty as ever, sometimes crossing the river to pester the neighbours. Kate the milk cow yielded more than expected, yet the cheque from the creamery was smaller than usual. The hens, on the other hand, had stopped laying, so they were finding their way to the dinner table one by one. A calf disappeared in the slough near the farm and the prettiest Hereford heifer went out on the ice one night and died because the boys did not count the cattle when they stabled them. Occasionally a lynx killed a sheep if the flock was not looked after. "My, I was so angry when it was killed," Helga wrote when one of Rósa's lambs was attacked, adding that the sheep were being "allowed to stray all over." "By all means burn this nonsense," Jenny wrote on the margin of one of her letters to Rosa.[4] Almost 30, she evidently thought she was being too childish.

Stephan now caught a virus and his health deteriorated further. He could not work for two days and was rather feeble all winter. His daughters thought he worked far too much. Stephan considered selling some land to family members, but late in February of 1920 he hired a man to do some clearing. The man's name was Brandur and he was so talkative that even the taciturn Jakob engaged in conversation with him. After the two had brought some logs home on a sleigh one evening, they talked so much that Jenny could barely concentrate on writing to Rósa. "Don't scold me if this letter is in bits as Brandur & them talk so much that I can only listen but not think. *Brandur skrapp nú út fyrir dyr og situr svo hér beint á móti mér og er að hneppa að sér buxnaklaufinni*" (Brandur just popped out for a moment and now sits here right in front of me buttoning up his fly).[5]

The hard winter lasted until April, with several blizzards. There was a shortage of hay and reports of livestock losses came from other districts. Hay and fodder were expensive, but Stephan was able to avoid buying any. In the spring of 1920, the river flooded "and made Reverend Pétur's cows homeless," Stephan noted.[6] The flooded schoolhouse had to be closed for a week. That summer, during an illness of some days, Stephan composed the poem "Kör" (Bedridden). He disliked sitting by while others were working, but now he had to face the fact that he was unable to be of service during the haying season.

Still preoccupied with memories of his trip to Iceland in 1917, Stephan wrote a sharp criticism of western capitalism in an essay entitled "Jökulgöngur" (Glacier Walks), printed in the May 20, 1920 issue of *Voröld*. "Here in the West, my reputation for "Jökulgöngur" swings from being the darkest of darks that I, the King of Darkness himself, have ever imposed upon sensible people, to being one of the best essays published in a Western Icelandic paper in North America," Stephan wrote to his friend Þórólfur Sigurðsson in Iceland.[7] "Jökulgöngur" is about the potential for an individual to transcend his external conditions by means of culture. In the essay, Stephan contrasts the cynical capitalism of the West with certain distinctive features of Icelandic culture. He begins by describing a local fair attended by a large number of well-dressed people who amused themselves by listening to bands and looking at "amazingly fat pigs and oxen of noble descent." Stephan found such affairs trivial and noted that the owner of most of the prize animals had neglected to develop his own mental abilities and had even begun to resemble his own livestock.

Stephan then described how certain photographers had experimented with composing an average human face by superimposing numerous images one on top of another. Society and circumstances do the same to people, he claimed, recalling a boyhood friend with whom he had emigrated. The two had not seen each other for 40 years, until Stephan visited the prosperous settlement where his friend had become a rich farmer. He was now old and worn out, however, and as his children had moved to the city his only pleasure was his wealth. He had been "a fair man, artistically inclined by nature and well disposed, but all of his youth had left him long ago and he no longer had any interests outside the fences surrounding his own lands, except perhaps winning a prize for the most prosperous farming operation at the local fair." As materially poor as Stephan was by comparison, he would not have changed places with his former friend, as "this last image of my old playmate was a like the superimposed artificial composition of a photographer, in effect the product of this society…".

In contrast to this sad description, Stephan then recounted how the people of the Lake Mývatn district had received him during his visit, setting aside their scythes and rakes in the middle of the haying season in order to welcome a visitor. That is the way to transcend daily toil and enrich one's life. While in the Mývatn district he had gained a wider perspective of poetry of the ages, which inspired comparisons of such diverse poets as Shakespeare and a local rhymester, Illugi Helgason. They had a subject in common, as Illugi had composed a poem based on the legend of Hamlet. Both had realized it was a good story, but their conditions were completely different. "The Icelandic verse-maker was not as healthy as the English genius." He was mentally ill, but had managed

Memories of his travels in Iceland lived on in the poet's mind. Impressed by the joy of life he found there, he thought back to the busy haymakers at Lake Mývatn who had laid aside their scythes and rakes to welcome him and celebrate his poetry.

to rid himself of half of his affliction by means of poetry. Poetry was an escape for Illugi, as it was for the Icelandic nation. Stephan then quotes from a stanza by 17th century poet Páll Bjarnason, "I feel like the bird/ that flies against the storm." Perhaps even Shakespeare, he suggested, might not have been able to express as subtly the historical essence of the Icelandic people, who "for more than a thousand years had flown singing and reciting against the storm."

Stephan then contrasts the culture of rural Iceland with that of increasing urbanization, alienation, and economic hegemony. He admires the mindset of Iceland's rural population, mentions the journal *Réttur* ("réttur" means both "rights" and "court"), edited by the farmer Þórólfur Sigurðsson of Baldursheimur, and recalls his conversations with the intellectual siblings at Gautlönd. They "had spent wakeful nights raising personal questions about issues usually discussed by those regarded as scholars and prophets among more populous nations." Yet their interest in culture in no way hindered their progressive attitude toward farming, such as their interest in sheep breeding.

Stephan's memories of the Icelandic culture that had moulded him during his youth were his spiritual retreat in a tormented world. As he grew older, he developed a growing aversion toward over-crowded and industrialized urban society, and he felt that city workers, who lived under harsh conditions, had been literally cut down during the war. Everywhere, cities encroach on rural communities "until they end up like the industrial nations, paupers of the world... Proletarians are sacrificed in wars so that cities can last a bit longer on what is left, the crumbs, to accommodate those who are strongest. The sons and daughters of the countryside move to the industrialized cities and most of their descendants gradually sink into the morass as time goes by." Stephan hoped that Icelandic people in North America could avoid this fate and "sing themselves into unity with the land". In Canada "there are still no songs in the mouths of common people to give wing to the thoughts that elevate them above the ordinary clay, no resonance that is not hoarse with the fat sound of administration and profit."[8]

A similar aversion to urbanization characterized Icelandic political debate over the following decades, but in North America Stephan's essay received mixed reviews among his countrymen since it challenged the premise on which many in the Icelandic community based their success.

A Late Flare-up

There had been little response to the pacifist poems Stephan had written at the beginning of the "Great War", as they had not received much attention in the patriotic upsurge at that time. After the war, however, the public's mood was more sensitive, as illustrated by the dispute over an Icelandic war memorial. Cold reality lay ahead: crisis, crippled soldiers, collapsed palaces. Public debate became intense when there was no more glory to be had and warmongers grew petulant in their attempts to justify what had happened. The repression of opinions became more blatant and censorship remained in effect.

Stephan kept his opponents busy during this time, writing sharply critical pacifist poems that were printed in *Voröld* and *Heimskringla*. He received no news, however, of the manuscript he had left in Iceland – until September of 1920 when an Icelandic bookseller in Winnipeg wrote him to say that he had just received his new book from Iceland. The title was *Vígslóði* (*Trail of War*) and the volume contained all of the pacifist poetry Stephan had written up to the time of his journey to Iceland.

In the preface of *Vígslóði*, Guðmundur Finnbogason stated that these poems revealed "what waves this monstrous tumult of the world had provoked in Stephan's soul, and he probably presumed that people would read them with better understanding when the war was over."⁹ *Heimskringla* reprinted a favourable review from an Icelandic paper – in the name of freedom of speech and because Stephan was "our king of poetry". The editor nevertheless found it safer to declare it a bad book and in no time the Icelandic papers in Winnipeg were full of articles on *Vígslóði*, condemning Stephan more than ever. *Voröld* was going bankrupt, but the last issue, printed at the beginning of 1921, had a long, approving essay on *Vígslóði*. After that, the battle was fought only on the pages of *Lögberg* and *Heimskringla*, and their respective stances on the book were in accordance with their political and religious partisanship. Stephan, certain that many regretted having encouraged their compatriots to join the army, maintained that supporters of recruitment now wanted to plaster over their guilt with the memorial. He was defiant, saying that he wanted to draw the warmongers out into the daylight so that they would reveal themselves. He expressed disappointment with many of his countrymen, however, as he felt they had "grown uncultivated and spiritually superficial here in this country ... They alone are in charge of the papers now. They may be richer than others – richest in dictatorship and bluster."[10]

J. J. Bíldfell, editor of *Lögberg*, attacked Stephan with the most derogatory terms he could find in his vocabulary, concluding his review by stating that Stephan had not only spoiled plans for the memorial, but had also "raised a memorial, the mark of Cain, the mark of fratricide, over the graves and memories of those Icelanders who had died in Europe in the last war."[11]

Stephan replied to Bíldfell in a long article, "Gáði seint að reiðast" ("Late at Flaring Up,"), printed in the November 24th issue of *Heimskringla*.

Stephan's anthology of anti-war poems Vígslóði (Trail of War) was discussed in the newspaper Voröld.

Many of the poems in *Vígslóði*, he pointed out, had appeared in both *Lögberg* and *Heimskringla* during the first year of the war, and he utilized this fact to mock *Lögberg*'s hypocrisy. Most of his article was a re-iteration of his established views, but he also addressed the opinion sometimes expressed in North America that Icelanders back home rather favoured the Germans. Stephan refuted this charge and added that Icelanders had been surprised by the participation of their North American kinsmen in the war. He said that he had sensed among the Icelanders a calm, caring

Stephan's stand against the war and a monument made him unpopular with many, among them Jón Bíldfell of Winnipeg, editor of Lögberg.

concern for their "lost siblings". For Stephan, Iceland had become a symbol of humanism, and he felt that the position of those "at home" proved that "patriotic care and love of humanity were one and the same." Icelanders in North America, however, had torn this apart.

Stephan's philosophical ideal was patriotic caring in the context of a remarkable internationalism. "Devotion to parents and fatherland," he claimed, "has evolved to a point where the true cosmopolitan wishes of all humans – including his own people – to enjoy everything that was good, does not claim for his race any worldly authority... and regrets the participation of all nations in any evil... caused by others, foreign or local, world wars or civil wars."

Stephan also defended some of his words and sentences that had been found offensive, such as "Cain's mark" and the statement that soldiers had come back as "lesser men". He had personally heard a man say,

"I am less of a man now than before I went to the war." The world had lost 10,000,000 young men in their prime. "Countries now hardly have enough shelter for all their lame, blind, and castrated." Hardly anyone could regard "the homecoming ... without sorrow."[12]

Stephan could not betray his ideals. "I had to write *Vígslóði*," he later said,[13] "in spite of my friends or how my relationship with them might be affected. The war was totally contrary to his view of life and he felt compelled to confront it. His opponents often overlooked, deliberately or otherwise, the main point in his arguments and the flawless humanism of his poems. On the other hand, it is easy to understand those who had lost sons in the war. Heroic glory was their consolation and clearly many condemned Stephan after swallowing the undigested misunderstanding of people like Jón Bíldfell. Others, though they supported the Allied war effort, understood Stephan's point, admired his poems despite their content, and refrained from commenting. One of these was Stephan's friend Eggert Jóhannsson, who had two sons who went to war but returned alive.

The controversy continued as many in the Icelandic community in North America attacked Stephan with articles in the papers. One of these took his anger a step further. Thomas H. Johnson, a leading member of the memorial committee and now Attorney General of Manitoba, took *Vígslóði* to police authorities, demanding that they confiscate the imprint. The RCMP, finding it strange that an elderly farmer in Alberta, writing in Icelandic, would be that dangerous, accordingly did nothing.[14]

Many assisted in the sale of *Vígslóði*, which quickly sold out in North America. Stephan received many letters of support, even from strangers, and one of them contained a newspaper clipping about soldiers who had returned from the war in poor condition. Rögnvaldur supported Stephan and facilitated the publication of his articles in *Heimskringla*. To thank this loyal friend and supporter, Stephan asked that his publisher in Iceland use the royalties from *Vígslóði* to pay for the registration of Rögnvaldur as a lifelong member of the Icelandic Historical Society.

Back at Markerville, most people supported Stephan, as described in a letter written by Jónas Hunford. "Here around me, only Stephan increases spiritual light and expands broad-mindedness. Whenever I leave his company, it is brighter around me than when I arrived." He conceded, however, that Stephan's categorical views were too dogmatic for him to be seen as a good leader, and he acknowledged that Stephan was provocative to the point of disturbing the peace. Jónas feared that the terseness and pessimism of *Vígslóði* would cause an uproar, although he did not doubt its wisdom.[15] Another neighbour, Jóhann Björnsson, agreed with Bíldfell's review, and the settlement's biggest Icelandic farmer, Jón Sveinsson, in fact did not like the book, though he supported Stephan in a letter to Rögnvaldur Petursson, stating that the mothers of all young men in the settlement were grateful to him for "having discouraged them from going to war until conscription forced them to do otherwise, and that was no doubt the reason why they were all unharmed."[16]

In one of the articles, Stephan was accused of preventing Icelandic men from enlisting. Although Reverend Pétur Hjálmsson disagreed with Stephan over the memorial issue, he protested this accusation in *Lögberg*, saying that it would be possible to get young men to testify on Stephan's behalf. In the March 17, 1921 issue of *Lögberg*, however, a returned soldier wrote that it had been necessary to stop the Germans and asked whether those who had joined the army should have neglected their civic duties. He found *Vígslóði* a bitter libel and accused Stephan of violating his own principles. Would he not defend his own home and belongings if bandits attacked him? There was no question that it had been necessary for the Allies to win this war. Suspicious that this soldier was related to an old friend of his, Stephan later heard that the young man had written only a small part of the letter himself.

Markerville Picnic 1921 – "Times change and people change with them..." The poet (back left) appears almost lost among the younger generation.

In his longest article of defense, Stephan refuted the accusation that he had a pro-German bias. He explained that the causes of the war were in fact greed, capitalism, and imperialism rather than being the fault of any one man or nation. He did not boast of being Icelandic or British and refused to rely on an empire. "It is almost a pleasure for me to know that I have no support except humanity among alien nations, and we can be grateful that it [i.e. humanity] can still be trusted nowadays... I feel privileged that no-one in other countries will regard the little nation with which I have been most connected as a threat."[17] Stephan later re-iterated this in a letter. "We are just what I like most: creatures-of-all nations."[18]

"The Old Man Sleeps"

Family and farm affairs continued to dominate the lives of Stephan and Helga. Baldur now had a prosperous farm, and Mundi, a merchant in Markerville, enjoyed some wealth "mostly due to speculation unrelated to his store," Stephan said, noting that business was otherwise poor because of the downturn in the economy. Jakob owned a considerable amount of land and livestock. Fanny and her husband, Árni Bardal, lived a few miles west of the home farm. They were rather poor. Jenny suffered from intestinal gastritis. Rósa returned to college in Olds in October of 1921 and Stephan and Helga occasionally sent her money so she could concentrate on her schooling rather than having to work part time. "Maybe your clothes are not fancy enough for all those fine gatherings. Are the girls not elegant?" Helga asked. She encouraged Rósa to take piano lessons if she could find an instrument on which to practice.[19]

Stephan's copies of *Vígslóði* arrived in the autumn just as harvest was beginning. While Jón Bíldfell and his companions swelled with indignation, Stephan stooked grain and helped with the threshing. Although the harvest was similar to that of the previous year and the number of livestock remained the same, prices for farm produce had dropped after the war and the market for horses had now collapsed. Helga was astonished at how the dollars disappeared. In a letter to Rósa, she recounted details of the cost of living, "I bought meat for over $2, apples for $.60, a comb for $.24, two milk jugs for over $2, pictures of the girls for $3, paid $1.25 for medicine, bought gloves for Jakob for $2. … I paid your father $6 and Hannes $3 for meat and I gave $10 to Jenny. I have just over a dollar left. This is how the money slips away."[20]

When the winter of 1921 arrived, Stephan began to sleep in longer in the mornings. He tended about 30 head of cattle, but did not feed them in the morning as he said his *corpus* was getting worn out. "The old man now sleeps until noon, nice, is it not?" Helga wrote in a letter to Rósa. She was still spry and hardworking and the comment was not without some sarcasm.

The kitchen was now remodeled and Jenny painted it. Helga knitted and Jenny sewed for both themselves and the neighbours. The evenings were quiet, as Helga sat at the kitchen table writing to Rósa while Stephan sat in his study reading abusive articles about himself, writing and composing poetry. Helga found the days tedious and longed for more company. "Your father is in his study, Jenny is taking a nap, Jakob is across the river, and I am alone scribbling this in the kitchen, so I have enough privacy." Even the weather reflected her ennui. "The weather is tiresome and everything is miserable."[21]

"Jenny is ill as usual, the old illness and the other thing too, I think," Helga wrote to Rósa.[22] Two years had now passed since Jenny's appendix operation and in March of 1921 she had to have her gallbladder removed. For this operation she travelled to the Mayo Clinic in Rochester, Minnesota, accompanied by her cousins Hannes Frost and Guðbjörg, who also needed operations. The cost for this trip was about $1000 and Jenny tried to minimize this by taking temporary work while her cousins recovered. The three returned from Rochester at the end of May. Jenny and Hannes regained their health fairly well, but Guðbjörg's health deteriorated further.

Early in December of 1920, the family received a visit from an unusual Icelander who had many names, "*Vésteinn Styrkár Steinn Dofri* and some others," Stephan wrote to Grímur Grímsson, adding that this man was "knowledgeable, intelligent, and just a decent creature like us." Steinn Dofri was a migrant worker, a lay scholar, a versifier, a keen genealogist, and an avid Bolshevik. He was "rather edgy in his verses and writing style," Stephan said, and therefore not popular.[23]

Dofri had decided to visit because Stephan had given a common opponent a rough ride in the dispute over *Vígslóði*. Stephan received this guest well and invited him to stay. They talked and examined books well into the night and Dofri developed an immediate admiration for Stephan's integrity, kindness, and broad-mindedness. He travelled throughout the settlement but stayed mostly with Stephan because "there I feel best. He understands me better than all the others around here."[24]

Steinn Dofri had been in North America for 17 years and had accumulated 12 trunks of books and manuscripts that he kept here and there. Stephan feared that some of this material could be lost during his wanderings. Dofri stored six trunks with Jónas Hunford, who had recently suffered injuries in a dispute with his shepherd dog, and he remained in the settlement until summer. Stephan encouraged his friends to commission this folk scholar to compile genealogies for them.

Steinn Dofri, a guest in Stephan and Helga's home, was an eccentric but renowned genealogist who loved cats.

Stephan liked Dofri's work. "I appreciate his diligence and his varied knowledge, but I do not know about the scholarly value of it all." He felt that if Dofri's writings were to get lost in his wanderings, however, this would be on par with the loss of works by masters of the old scribal culture of previous centuries. Dofri must return to Iceland, he stated, where experts can look into his work. "The world should learn two things," Stephan said, "to reward all its faithful servants before their time here is up, and no less importantly, to stash as widely as possible the troublesome talent where the assets can be enjoyed, while faults will be least noticed..."[25] At Stephan's request, Guðmundur Finnbogason tried to help this unique individual return to Iceland, but with no results. Dofri remained in the West for 17 more years.

Building on Ruins

In the fall of 1921, Stephan composed "Á rústum hruninna halla" (On the Ruins of Collapsed Palaces), a poem about a man who meets an old girlfriend of 50 years before. She is able to accept the loss of her husband and an older son in war, but is disappointed with her younger son, whom she loved the most. He had refused "to obey/the legal duty of conscription/choosing rather to be driven from home/as a coward to prison." From prison he had returned home as a frail changeling who fell happily into his mother's arms. From her he had received the strength to endure "the provocations, ordeals and taunts."

Yet I am victorious, Mother!
In that no innocent widow
Mourns the loss of a son,
Caused by me.

The fatherland is just as dear to me
As to those who went and fell. –
Would I have been a truer son, Mother,
If I had betrayed the dearest in you?

When the grandchildren become
The most noble men of each country,
Their great grandmothers
Receive the highest reward of virtue.

The mother is now relieved as she realizes that her son's refusal to join the army was testimony to the best she had given him and that this would be passed on to his descendants. She stops believing in the "false consolation" of war and begins doubting those who had sacrificed themselves to an unjust cause, and she gains insight into the future. The endurance of those who dare to refuse becomes "a service in the realm of truth." This prophecy consoles her when she looks to the future. "Over our seductions and losses/a beacon shall be lit on every shore."

She could whisper to me this premonition:
God and Man's Paradises
Are unfulfilled truths,
Pointing towards his future.

The narrator thanks her for this evening song that has given him the strength to stay awake, although all the candles had burned out before dawn.

Its wounds will follow a wanderer
Through the dark across lands of seduction,

As on the chest, brought from home,
The holy relic of a pilgrim.[26]

There are religious overtones in this story of the suffering and resurrection of a man who refused to go to war. The son thus becomes a parallel to Christ, and the passion is the imprisonment of a living man rather than crucifixion and death. God and Paradise are unfulfilled dreams, the woman's harp "an echoing cathedral" resounding with the "holy relic of a pilgrim". In this poem Stephan sanctifies the refusal of military service and transforms conscientious objection into a vision for the future. The poem expresses the essence of his stance against war. Only refusal in the name of pure humanity, a mother's love, can break the vicious cycle of violence that Stephan had described so memorably in the poem of Hervör on her father's burial mound and had reiterated in *Vopnahlé*.

When "Á rústum hruninna halla" was printed in *Tímarit*, the journal of the Icelandic National League, the attacks on Stephan flared up yet again. Jónas Hunford shook his head at Stephan's continuous provocations. "It is useless to persist in telling the truth to a public that does not have the vision to understand it."[27] Stephan sent a few verses in reply but took a long time to write his full response in an essay, "Þakkargerð" ("Thanksgiving"), that was printed in *Heimskringla* in February of 1923. In it, Stephan refutes the main objections to the poem and refers to a book just published in England about conscientious objectors. He discusses the vision of the future expressed at the end of that book and concludes with a quote from Lord Buckmaster's words, "We face the growing discontent of a disillusioned people."

The essay would be Stephan's last contribution to public debate of any kind and he now expressed his gratitude to his opponents for their companionship. "I was always rather skeptical about how much light I was able to cast, so these satellites have pleased me. They have orbited around me according to the law of gravity, some for half a lifetime, having become so consistent that I need never fear they will fade into eternity while I am alive. I have had many an evening's entertainment from them, even those planets seen only once. Yet I know that I will never follow their paths."[28] Stephan asserted that he had only warm regards for those who had scolded him. "I feel goodwill towards all men, though I heartily detest the currents with which some allow themselves to be carried."[29]

An Aging Revolutionary Poet

"I myself am everything evil: a member of the United Farmers of Alberta, a Non-Partisan, a Socialist, a Bolshevik, and a dishonest individual," Stephan had written to fellow poet Guttormur J. Guttormsson in April of 1919.[30] For a while he had favoured slow social progress, but after the war he was forced to abandon the idea of "a long, yet slow progression of successful changes in human society." Mankind was in dire straits, he said in a letter to a friend, as all sense had disappeared from an unjust and half-collapsed social order. Capitalism had thrown itself over a cliff during the war, and the slaving of workers did not earn them enough for food and taxes.[31]

Stephan's vision of the overthrow of this state of affairs without resorting to arms seems to have been shaped by two influential socialists, Henry Wise Wood and William Irvine. In Alberta, radical politics and various socialist and co-operative ideas had found a voice in the popular United Farmers of Alberta under Wise Wood's leadership, and in 1919 the UFA had merged with the Non-Partisans led by William Irvine. Wood and Irvine were not revolutionaries, but they did sharply criticize the two-party system, political intrigues, and corruption, and both organizations called upon farmers and industrial labourers to work together for mutual benefit. Irvine was elected to Ottawa in 1921 as one of two representatives of the Labour Party – the first Socialists to sit in Canada's Parliament.[32]

Grímur Grímsson was Stephan's brother-in-arms in Alberta and the two exchanged radical reading material. By 1920 Stephan claimed that he was reading few books, but many papers in which he tried "to plunge his hand into the eddy, wherever I can, to find out the direction of the currents – and get a grasp of various issues that approach the truth. What the press has to say nowadays, I know well from a long acquaintance with partisan papers that have always lied, but never more dangerously than after the war broke out."[33] Stephan had more regard for the 'red' papers that Grímur shared with him.

Stephan's radicalism was farmer-oriented. In his judgment, farmers were fettered by the "self-infliction of property rights". We should stop "grabbing up more land than we can work with our own two hands," he said, adding that farmers have nothing in common with the rich and should instead unite with the workers. This "must happen soon for our world to be more prosperous and to prevent the black death of all of our so-called culture."³⁴ Ironically, this was written at a time when Stephan had just purchased more land, and increasingly he found the marks of slavery on his own body. He was now tired and unable to achieve much, although his thirst for reading and his rebelliousness were unchanged.

Stephan now leaned ever more towards the Bolshevism in Russia. In his estimation it was the fairest and "the only way out of the inferno in which humankind finds itself." The only question in Stephan's mind was whether the revolution would take over by good means or bad. He had reached the same conclusion as the Marxists, that only those who performed the work should set the rules. He wanted to "make wealth undesirable" by putting the means of production into the hands of the workers. All jobs should be done for the well-being of everyone and "not as a means for individuals to amass wealth." The Bolsheviks were making this a reality. Stephan had read their "agricultural and workers law" and he saw no oppression there, nor anything else wrong with these basic principles. He advocated denying himself and others ownership of everything in favour of a commonwealth.³⁵

Long time friend and neighbour Grímur Grímsson was Stephan's "comrade in arms" on social issues.

Long fascinated with the example set by Christ, Stephan had written one of his best poems on the life of this religious leader – with whom he now linked Karl Marx. Though he had identified the malignancies of his society, Christ had not suggested any remedies "other than the ideal of the individual. Centuries later another Jew, Karl Marx, occupied himself with figuring out a body and shape for this 'Son of God', and since then socialists (detested underdogs), workers, and common people have been trying to push this in the right direction. The spiritual and secular realms, however, have both renounced Christ and Karl Marx."[36]

Stephan's philosophy on social matters reaches maturity in his poem "Martius" (March), published early in 1922. The form of this poem is strange and eccentric, "as is usual with me," although it does resemble some folk songs. The poem is a polyphonic tribute to spring and revolution, written partly without rhyme and with irregular rhythms. In it, Stephan braids together ideas that are both familiar and unexpected. The introduction predicts the death agony of winter. Then, cheerful sunny days with their quivers full of warm sunbeams pass by the poet's window. The poet calls upon the forces of spring - the sun and golden morning clouds - to take control. Battle resounds and the red spirit of spring has a renewing effect on poetry. Stephan makes spring a militant symbol of revolution, but there is also a reference from the poem on little Rænka:

Nor although the secret thread of poems
Is homeward bound, there
Where youth and old age
Know its beginning and end. -
Both build palaces
From small children's toys.

In the second part of the poem, spring is addressed in a recurrent refrain, "spring with vitality and mud." Mud is an unavoidable aspect of spring that carries light and life. The grey icy arms of winter hold small seeds in captivity, but blood bursts from under the nails of the seeds when winter's imprisoning clutches loosen their fetters. The tribute and encouragement to a redemptive life-giver have a religious connotation:

Spring, spring –
Spring with vitality and mud!
Morning calls
Sound clearly
Your thaw, at lava and birch,
The herald in the desert!

Wake the song of swans
The long and sunny days. –
The grasses, then growing in the field
On lowland and highest peaks,
Even the mosses,
Pale and frozen,
Are all a part of the procession of the Lord.
Christians, men of the cross
The settlers of light and life,
Crusaders,
Flocked to conquer the cradles,
More hopeful than the graves.

The scene then shifts from spring to humanity. "Similar happens to earth and man!" Rotting, withered grass delays God in healing the frozen vegetation. Here, God is a metaphor for powers of freedom and progress, a revolutionary God igniting the minds of people that will eventually melt the fetters of winter. "His heritage is the young and small – not shrivelled high and lo – /his favourite child, the common people."

The poem reveals familiar images of Stephan's poetry. He channels his life's work into a revolutionary vision. The struggle between wild nature and the cultivated calls for redemption, one in which people, not Christ, release the world:

People, do not wait for the saviour,
Release yourself! Spare what is yours. –
Often it were the fetters of the leaders
That tied you the hardest.
History most often attributes to the single one
Your achievements, shattered mass!

At the end of the poem, universal ideals of humanity are held forth as a holy scripture. Summer's hopes walk by the poet's window and toward the land of a bright future.

Carried the most holy scriptures
Of the world of ideals
Where all the nations had

By each its prophet
The witness of the coming of spring:
Verse and chapter.
Began singing the songs of the sun
The common heirs of earth,
Every nationality recognised
Its own tongue.[37]

The reference to the "tongues" of the nations is complex. Some 20 years earlier, Stephan had expressed the wish that Canada should become the homeland of every nation and tongue, but this could also be an allusion to Whitsun, when the disciples of Christ, struck by the Holy Spirit, suddenly "spoke in tongues". That event marks the annunciation of the Evangel. In 1922 it was still possible to believe in the gospel of enlightened commoners who would be able to throw off the fetters of oppression and envision the world as a common inheritance, though every nation retained its own tongue. Enlightenment was at the core of Stephan's ideals. Now he had composed poems relating to three main events of Christianity: the birth of Christ, the Passion, and Christ's ascension to the right hand of God. In each poem, he treated the subject matter in his own unique way. "Martius" is the Whitsun psalm of Stephan's secular, earthly belief.

On February 3, 1922, Stephan ended a letter to Rögnvaldur Pétursson with this verse:

Frozen snow covers the world.
The road is dark.
I'm the child of light –
Still expecting day![38]

Soon the poet's own road would become darker. In this same letter to Rögnvaldur, Stephan now inquired about Dr. Whaley in Winnipeg and whether he could cure more with his eccentricities than ordinary doctors did in the countryside.

Chapter 17

Failing Strength

Years of Crisis

Now 69 years of age and concerned by his failing health, Stephan wrote to his trusted friend Rögnvaldur Pétursson in the fall of 1922 to inquire about Dr. Whaley, a gastro-intestinal specialist who advertised his services in *Heimskringla*. The old poet had long suffered from constipation, "a family curse, self-inflicted, too much cold, bad accommodations, and years of hardships." Now, likely suffering from piles, he had been to a doctor twice.[1]

Jenny's health, on the other hand, had improved, and during the summer of 1922 she had married Sigurður Kristjánsson. The young couple lived four miles north of the Stephansson farm, so there were now just four persons left in the old home – Stephan, Helga, Jakob, and Rósa. Stephan's niece Guðbjörg was now seriously ill as well, and a chiropractor who called on her sometimes stopped to work on Stephan's back, so he could continue to work. Stephan's health improved somewhat, but not significantly. Crops were decent, but prices slumped and livestock was now practically given away. Economic woes were widespread.

As winter wore on, Stephan's health deteriorated further and doctors now disagreed whether it was intestinal swelling or a kidney ailment. Still, the old timer was able to tend the cattle and chop wood, and in a letter written around that time he quipped about his mouth still being big and healthy.[2]

The eccentric folk-scholar Steinn Dofri was in the Markerville area off and on during these years, and over the hot, dry summer of 1922 he had helped Jakob during haying season. He found Jakob demanding.

In 1922 Jenny Stephansson married Sigurður Kristjánsson.

This itinerant labourer and genealogist had a keen eye for the girls in the settlement, including Rósa Stephansson, but he found educated girls too proud. While employed by Reverend Pétur Hjálmsson, whom he flattered as a great man, Dofri once commented that Jakob and Helga Stephansson were too stingy to let him to stay, and that Stephan had no say in the home except when celebrities visited. Dofri was a rather quarrelsome individual who was inclined to speak ill of people, so Reverend Pétur took him aside and advised him to mind his wagging tongue.

The crisis was not limited to the Canadian economy during these years. Serious drought in Southern Alberta drove many farmers to abandon their lands, and the whims of the markets were more elusive than pioneering and subsistence farming. This situation tended to make the farmers in Alberta ever more radical, and in the provincial election of 1922 the United Farmers of Alberta, led by Henry Wise Wood, was elected. They would remain in power for more than a decade and Stephan was optimistic about Woods' brand of socialism, though he felt that opening the party to all classes of society would be ill-advised.[3]

Stephan experienced the same conditions as other farmers in the area. Perhaps his health problems stemmed in part from his worship of labour, as work was both a pleasure and a burden to him. Ongoing payments on the land he had bought during the war chained him even more tightly to his duties.

A widespread generational shift was now occurring among North Americans of Icelandic descent. The pioneers, motivated by a thirst for knowledge and their interest in culture, had grown old. Many had died. Occasionally these old timers decided to support cultural issues by raising funds for artists or poets, but that was becoming ever more difficult. If they wanted to spend some money "on something other than profit or entertainment," they had to do it behind the backs of their children and even their wives. This was the reverse of the situation as it used to be in Iceland, Stephan noted. "Our grandmothers and great-grandmothers had often hidden a lump of butter or a bowl of gruel under their aprons so that their husbands would not notice when they gave it to the poor!"[4]

Stephan still played a role in bringing guests to Alberta, however, and in March of 1923 an Icelandic singer named Eggert Stefánsson performed in the church at Markerville. His singing kindled memories of Iceland and Stephan imagined that the songs were expressions of something he had experienced or thought himself. "Such a childish notion of the art of singing is, of course, amateurish compared to the artistic conception of those who are 'inspired', but it is the only explanation for those of us who have such 'thick' hearing as I do," he wrote in a review on the concert for *Heimskringla*. After Eggert's first Italian song, Stephan felt the dollar admission he had paid was fully justified, as the singer's voice was so "sweet and pure". The next song, also Italian, was "a resounding song of joy" that inspired memories of the waterfall Gígjarfoss near Víðimýrarsel. "When I was a teenager, I sometimes lay on the trembling bedrock until I felt as if I was one of the streams in the cascading water – sweeping, laughing, bounding carelessly down through the canyon." During a song by Sveinbjörn Sveinbjörnsson, Stephan found himself imagining another river near Víðimýrarsel, and his mind then strayed to Mjóidalur and the rolling river of Grjótá. Nothing, however, was so awe inspiring as Eggert's voice, especially when he sang Stephan's poem "Langförull", the tune for which had been composed by Icelandic composer Sigvaldi Kaldalóns. Others had also put this poem to music, but the version by Kaldalóns became the best known by far. Stephan sometimes felt a bit shy or awkward about his poems after he had written them, but this time he felt "some warmth from the embers with which the poem had once been forged."

As he was leaving this event, Stephan heard someone comment that one would have to pay $4 or $5 for such a performance in the big cities, and on the way home he contemplated the potential of Icelandic culture. "...Then I thought about the singer who sets off on a journey in order to give his scattered compatriots a taste of the higher art of singing better than they had ever dreamed of, and to demonstrate to other nations that Iceland also has a song and a voice. Everything is such an effort for this performer: the time and weather conditions, small vehicles, difficult circumstances, and an unprepared public with their insensitive ears. Everywhere he is a loner, except when he encounters the hospitality of compatriots who have not yet forgotten what it is like to be a stranger in a strange land."[5]

During his travels in Iceland, Stephan had met Ágúst H. Bjarnason and his wife, Sigríður, who now visited Markerville in July of 1923. Escorted by Rögnvaldur Pétursson, this Icelandic couple were met at the train station in Innisfail by Stephan, who in Ágúst's opinion had not aged during the six years since they had met in Iceland. He found Stephan as taciturn as ever and as agile in his movements as he walked with the aid of the silver cane he had been given in Iceland.

Ágúst was to deliver a lecture in the church at Markerville one evening, but when they arrived the church appeared to be locked and there were few only a people. The guests therefore waited with Stephan and his family by Mundi's store. Finally, growing impatient, Stephan went over, yanked the church door open, and found a big lamp that he lit and carried into the dark building. "Ever since," Ágúst later wrote in his travelogue, "I always visualize Stephan as a kind of torch bearer who wades through the darkness of night, lighting the way for others, even into the church itself."

After the lecture, they drove in the darkness to Stephan and Helga's farm. Finding no matches, they had to grope their way through the back door and into the kitchen, then into the parlour, where Ágúst noticed a piano illuminated by a beam of a light from the kitchen. They returned to the kitchen where Helga put a cloth on the table and soon the entire kitchen warmed with hospitality. Ágúst thought Helga a pretty woman, but the children resembled Stephan – who was never regarded as good looking.

After enjoying supper, the hosts and their company talked until midnight when the guests were ushered to bed on the upper floor. Ágúst lay awake awhile, pondering where he was, far from the metropols of world culture, on the great Canadian prairie where people earned a living by the sweat of their brows – in the humble home of a hard working man who had such a great message for the world "and who has always thought more about ideals than his stomach, although he has always

The Markerville Band – Stephan and Helga's sons were among the band members.

cultivated the soil with his bare hands, as shown by the marks of weariness on his body. He is a man who has neither lost his nationality nor his language, but has received from both such great spiritual gifts that he has grown and evolved and now elevates the language and culture like bright stars to the heaven of ideals for the Icelandic nation... and what a remarkable man, so aggressive and hard-hitting on the one hand that he spares nothing when the occasion demands, while on the other hand so humble and sensitive that he cannot bear to see anything weak that he does not cherish or defend. He is so infinitely faithful to those ideals he believes will move mankind towards prosperity and progress that he is willing to sacrifice everything, himself and all that he loves." Ágúst felt that Stephan should not respond to his opponents with sharp verses in the papers as he did, "because noble men should not exchange words with those who interpret everything in the worst way." To do so, however, only demonstrated Stephan's humanity, "with weaknesses and strengths like the rest of us, in fact." Ágúst regarded Stephan as the "only spiritually great man" to rise to prominence thus far among the Icelandic people in North America.

When Ágúst got up in the morning, Stephan was already doing his chores. After breakfast, he led his guest to the top of a hill to show him the Rocky Mountains in the distance, his fields closer at hand, and a grove of trees he had planted and dubbed 'New Wood'. To Ágúst, these trees "symbolized the new roots and life of new generations in a new land." He found the Stephansson farm "prosperous looking in midsummer, although farming barely paid and inflation was about to smother any prosperity." As they walked back to the farmhouse they encountered a flock of chickens in the yard and Stephan stopped to pet the dog and the cat. They then went into Stephan's study where the poet kept his treasured gifts from Iceland, under glass. Ágúst noted the abundance of books, while among the periodicals were *Outlook* and some other American journals. Stephan then pulled a large bundle out of the bookcase, seven handwritten books of poetry, all written over the last few years in anticipation of another publication. While Ágúst leafed through the manuscripts, he noticed Stephan's adjoining bedroom behind a curtain, "bare and spartan as a monk's cell, but with a kind of sanctity about it." In his mind, Ágúst thought of it as the "cell of insomnia".[6]

Later Stephan and Ágúst strolled across the river to visit Sigurlaug and Kristinn, who had returned from British Columbia. They then visited the graveyard where Stephan intended to find his final rest in a plot beside his son Gestur and his mother, Guðbjörg. Although Stephan's mind often drifted to the old country, he could not think of leaving this place where he was surrounded by youth – whether it was his 'New Wood' or his children and grandchildren.

Birthday Publication

Stephan's supporters were not unlike disciples who felt a calling to spread his word and nurture his poetry, and three years had now passed

An early photo of the Markerville Church, still unpainted in 1910.

since a new volume of *Andvökur* had been suggested. By now, however, the post-war economic crisis was at its peak and these friends were worse off financially than before. On the other hand, they had the advantage of experience gained from the publication of the first three volumes in 1909-1910, and Rögnvaldur Pétursson now had easier access to funds. Still, the viability of another publication was not self-evident, as some volumes of the first publication remained unsold, and in the spring of 1920 Jónas Hall had written to Rögnvaldur with his thoughts on how they could sell the rest of the first printing so that Stephan would benefit. Jónas speculated that it might be possible to sell the books in Iceland if not in North America. "Stephan's future is in Iceland; [there is] no future [for him] here. People understand him there, not here. There he will be relevant in a 100 years... while here he will be forgotten."[7]

Rögnvaldur's intention was to publish the new volume of *Andvökur* on the occasion of Stephan's 70th birthday, and in the fall of 1922 – with the fury over "Á rústum hruninna halla" (On the Ruins of Collapsed Palaces) at its peak – preparations began. Over the summer Rögnvaldur spoke to men in Wynyard, Arborg, and Winnipeg, and Stephan was asked to estimate the total length of a new publication that would include the three small volumes *Kolbeinslag*, *Heimleiðis*, and *Vígslóði*. The new committee also had to know what Stephan needed in order to be able to prepare the manuscript for print, when he could have the material ready, and whether these volumes should be published as a continuation of the previous series of three volumes. The plan was to print the books in Winnipeg once a contract with Stephan had been drawn up and the funds had been raised.

Stephan replied quickly, saying that his "rubbish" was in good order. His poems, including *Kolbeinslag* but not *Heimleiðis* and *Vígslóði*, added up to 864 pages, which he estimated would reduce to some 760 printed pages. He wanted everything included. For the sake of poetry, it was indeed right to include only his best work, but including all his poems would help readers understand his way of thinking, the spirit of times, and the cultural context. A future readership might also find something of value in what was presently considered of little worth. Stephan also preferred to keep the title *Andvökur*, continue numbering the volumes, and retain the original appearance. As for his needs, Stephan noted, "I would prefer to do this for nothing if I could, but I will have to free myself up from the cow barn next winter as I am untrained and slow at this kind of editing." To a friend at Wynyard, he confided, "It is easier for me to fork cow manure than to prepare a book for print, although I will not confess to everyone that I am unable to do both."[8] Nevertheless, he expected to deliver his manuscript before the 'First Day of Summer' in the spring of 1923.[9]

By April Stephan was almost finished the editing and most arrangements had been made. His supporters at Wynyard agreed to raise one third of the $1,500 expenses and take care of sales in the area. Rögnvaldur ordered paper for a July printing and suggested that Stephan travel to Winnipeg for a month to check over the proofs and do some visiting. By May the manuscript was ready.

It had been difficult for Stephan to scrutinize the manuscripts as he knew the material by heart, but at the same time he was proud of his achievement in the name of self-education. In early July, he sent off the manuscript and went to Red Deer to have a photograph taken for the forthcoming publication.

Not all was well, however. Problems had arisen among the sponsors, with disagreement over concerns about the financial outcome of the enterprise and a hostile reaction from Stephan's opponents. When Jakob Normann suggested that the committee appeal to the public for funds by advertising in the Icelandic newspapers in Winnipeg, Stephan disagreed, feeling that this would only create an opportunity for criticism from antagonists. He could already hear their complaint that he was being lionized at the expense of other poets who were more popular. "They would take advantage of any vulnerability revealed," and Stephan declared that he would rather stop the project than have his friends "break

The poet's desk and chair on display at the University of Manitoba's Icelandic Collection. The gifts Stephan received on his departure from Skagafjörður in 1917 are also displayed.

themselves into pieces" for his sake. One option for lowering costs would be to print only 1000 copies.[10] In the end, Jakob Norman and his companions at Wynyard managed to scare up most of the funds promised, despite their failure at securing a bank loan. "The bank managers around here just shake their heads and say that it is not their job to lend money to publish Icelandic books. If we were planning to raise English pigs or sheep, things would have been different," Jakob wrote to Rögnvaldur.[11]

Stephan's health remained reasonably good for most of 1923 while he was working on his poems, but by the beginning of August he was "so sleet-like" that he could hardly stand upright. When harvest time came, however, he tried to help stook the grain, perhaps mainly to be able to boast of still being useful in his 70th year.[12]

Stephan's 70th birthday came and went in both glory and silence, reflecting the contrasting attitudes towards the poet in East and West. On his birthday, *Heimskringla* printed a congratulatory poem written by Stephan on the occasion of Rögnvaldur and Hólmfríður Pétursson's silver wedding anniversary – without so much as mentioning his birthday. A week later, however, his new photograph was printed with a short but positive article. In the West, only Grímur Grímsson, Jónas Hall, and Jakobína Johnson sent him congratulatory telegrams, while in Iceland news of his 70th birthday was received very differently. When the Prime Minister of Iceland and Baldur Sveinsson sent telegrams, Stephan sent them on to *Heimskringla* – perhaps to show that people in Iceland were more loyal than those in the West. Baldur also published a long biographical essay based on notes from Stephan, and all the papers in Iceland mentioned his birthday. The Student Society even gathered in his honour and the front page of the paper *Dagur* carried a poem by Hulda, whom Stephan had met in 1917, one of the finest poems ever composed about the poet. After conjuring up beautiful images of the places of Stephan's youth, the poem states that he had never betrayed anything inherited from his motherland. The paper went on to state that Stephan had few detractors in Iceland and that he had sown seeds that would be more appreciated as the nation's educational and cultural awareness increased.

Eggert Jóhannsson had not corresponded with Stephan for some time. He disagreed with Stephan's anti-war stance, but he was shocked by the reactionary responses his poems had elicited and wanted to calm the waters. He felt that a new publication of Stephan's poems would be

Heimskringla announced Stephan G. Stephansson's 70th birthday, including a few words of advance publicity on the forthcoming volumes of Andvökur.

like pouring gasoline on the fire of fanaticism, but still supportive of Stephan he suggested to Rögnvaldur that instead of using the funds to publish more volumes of poetry, the money could be given to Stephan as a birthday present "in order to delight, on his 70th birthday, the man who has done more for the benefit and fame of Icelanders in North America than perhaps anyone else, but has received less reward and gratitude than anyone I can mention." The more donors this fund could attract, the more Stephan's opponents would be isolated.[13] No such fundraising was undertaken, however.

On the evening of his birthday, Stephan received an Icelandic delicacy, aged shark, from his friend Jakob Normann, and a bottle of whisky from his brother-in-law, Kristinn, so a little Icelandic celebration was held. Stephan gave all his friends a taste of the shark.

The crop of 1923 was good, but prices for most products remained low, except for pork, "as the traders of the world love most what resembles them," Stephan commented, noting that he had never been busier or "had more difficulties holding myself upright with a book or a pen, either because of weariness or illness".[14]

While there was disagreement over Stephan's contribution to the world, he continued to follow current events. Farmers in Alberta joined forces and established a wheat pool in opposition to the grain merchants they felt were cheating them. Stephan and Jakob sold their entire crop to the new pool, of which they were both members. The market price was just over $.60 a bushel and their share was $.39. The rest went to various middlemen, but there was hope of a bonus if sales were good. "This method of selling is still in its infancy and everyone is opposed to it, the grain merchants, the elevator companies, and even the banks – although not much is said above a whisper," Stephan said. He hoped that solidarity among farmers would strengthen the pool so it could become an effective alternative to its opponents. The pool only bought wheat, but Stephan and Jakob also sold a wagonload of oats, seven oxen, two heifers, and 19 six month old pigs. "Taxes on the land are high, but my return is such that I have not yet been hung for debt."[15] With some of the oats and barley still unsold, Stephan's income was about $1,200, though only $500 was left after taxes and the hired help had been paid. Helga, in the meantime, sold cream, eggs, and turkeys.[16] Even so, their income was obviously that low that Stephan was obliged to continue working.

It was a substantial farm. Stephan owned nearly 500 acres, of which 100 acres were under cultivation. The rest of the land was divided into pastures, hayfields, and forestland. Stephan still owed $1000 on the land he had bought from Chris Johnson and his payments covered little more than the annual interest. Jakob owned an additional 200 acres, of which 50-60 acres were under cultivation. Besides 50 head of cattle and 20 pigs, there were 20 horses, of which Stephan owned two. Helga and Rósa owned 20 sheep as well as 100 chickens and turkeys. In Iceland this would have been considered a better than average farm, yet Stephan found that farmers in Iceland seemed relatively better off.

Early in December of 1923, two additional volumes of *Andvökur* rolled off the presses in Winnipeg.

Helga Stephansson.

Andvökur I-V was now the largest anthology of poetry by an Icelandic poet, a fitting memorial to both a hard-working farmer's compelling urge to express himself and to the unselfish support of his loyal friends. Rögnvaldur Pétursson sent Stephan 50 copies. On looking through the new volumes, Stephan promptly found 20 typographical errors, but he blamed himself as he had received the proofs at harvest time when he was busy.

All indications were that sales of volumes IV and V would be slow. Stephan's supporters realized that hostility towards the poet would impact sales, and even many older people who loved Stephan's work were reluctant to buy – certain that once they passed away, none of their children would ever open the books again. Lutherans tended to receive *Andvökur* salesmen badly, and both Guttormur J. Guttormsson and Dr. Jóhannes P. Pálsson were frustrated by the poor response the books received. People they had considered certain customers were either away or could not afford the books. In North Dakota, Jónas Hall, old and busy, regretted that he was unable to help much. He recognized that Stephan was not "popular, as nobody is a prophet in his own land. People pretend not to understand him, or probably partly they do not try to, and some

Andvökur IV *and* V *were published in Winnipeg in 1923, featuring the aging poet's portrait in* Volume IV.

certainly because he is not enough of a churchgoer. If he had written some Bible poems with a Synod flair, it would have helped." Jónas felt it was virtual blasphemy to offer the books at a mere $6.00. He managed to sell a few copies, but the overall sales were poor.[17]

Stephan did not have time to go around the neighborhood selling books before Christmas and postponed his marketing efforts until the New Year. On January 3, 1924, while he was putting the sheep into the barn, a ram attacked him from behind. Stephan fell, breaking his left forearm, and he spent the next six days in the hospital at Innisfail, where he was well cared for "by doctors and nursing nymphs". He enjoyed himself there, joking with the nurses who said he was their favourite.[18] The break healed badly, but Stephan was unconcerned as he did not expect to use the arm much from now on. He returned home on January 9th.

Surprisingly little was written about *Andvökur* in Iceland. Stephan sent copies to his friends who were among the leading intellectuals in the country, but perhaps they thought they were too close to Stephan to write reviews, and it was in North America that the new volumes were reviewed. *Heimskringla*'s editor Stefán Einarsson wrote a glowing review, stating that despite Stephan's age and career of hard work, his poetry still evoked "the rush of strong wings, with hawk's eyes as sharp and clairvoyant as before when he surveys the world from the heights of poetic flight." He felt it unjust that Stephan had to continue toiling at his age, something that would not happen to a great poet of 70 if he lived in another nation. "I know that the Icelandic nation is poor and small in population...but is it always too small to do anything else than take?"[19] *Lögberg* printed a positive review as well, by the young poet Einar Páll Jónsson, who didn't seem to be aware of the paper's history with Stephan. He claimed that Stephan's poetry was neither hard to understand or less relevant because of the poet's age.

Female Trolls Wrestling

Lárus Guðmundsson quickly brought *Lögberg* back on track when he wrote in March of 1924 that he had never read any books as painstakingly as *Andvökur*, not even *The Viking Heart* by his own daughter. "Only great poets and highly educated professors can wade through that flow of words and elaborate thoughts," he criticized, then going on about *Vígslóði* and the war memorial issue and picking out some words

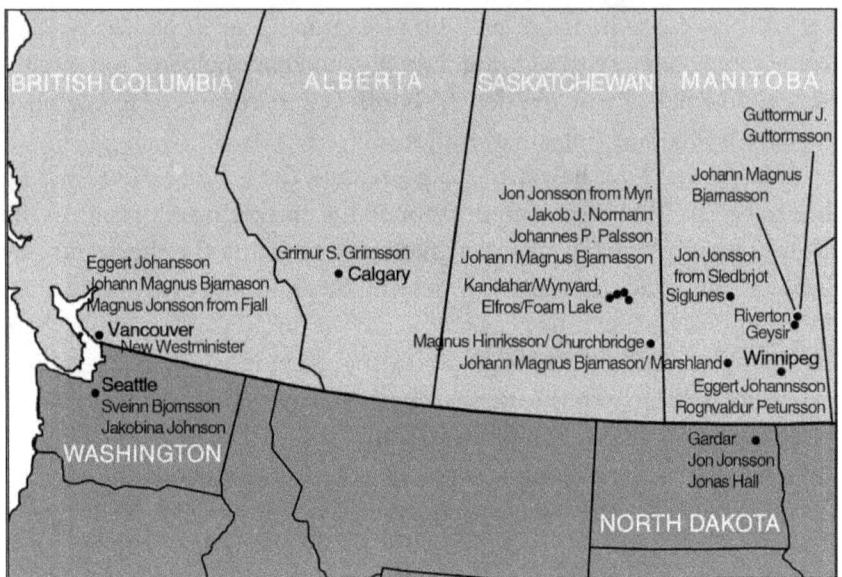

Stephan G. Stephansson's principal correspondents in Canada and the United States.

he found strange in Stephan's poems. He alluded to the slow sales and suggested how frustrating it must be for a great poet not to have gained favour with the highest and most infallible judge – the public, "the most precious treasure, more valuable than all the supreme court judgements of the learned geniuses."[20]

Lárus' daughter was Laura Goodman Salverson, a young writer who was making a name for herself in Canadian letters. In the fall of 1923, her first novel was published under the title *The Viking Heart*. It holds a prominent place in Canadian literary history as the first novel to describe the immigrant experience from a non-English pioneer's point of view. The Icelandic community in North America was proud of her and she received favourable reviews in *Lögberg* and various English language papers.[21]

Stephan was in no way taken with Salverson's success. "I felt I could recognize the original sin of the daughter that I had noticed in the writings of the father," he wrote before the novel was released. When he saw a review in *Lögberg*, describing what kind of novel it was, he leafed through the book and quickly came to the conclusion that Salverson belonged to *Lögberg*'s fundamentalist flock, which in his estimation chewed on the husk while spitting out the kernel – the spirit. Fundamentalism killed all esprit and ideals.[22]

There were also allegations that Salverson had acted incorrectly in marketing her book. Jóhannes P. Pálsson, for example, sent Stephan a clipping by Mrs. Winifred Reeve, a novelist of Chinese descent who sometimes wrote under the pseudonym *Onoto Watanna*. She was president of the Canadian Authors' Association branch in Calgary, where she and Salverson were prominent in literary circles. In a letter sent to the literary journal *Canadian Bookman*, Reeve accused an unnamed author who had just published her first book of buying favourable reviews, claiming that the author had confided in her that she had hired a special 'critic' for 15% of her royalties. This critic had edited her book, promoted it to publishers, and then written a number of reviews. The last point, in Reeves' opinion, was inexcusable, though it could likely be explained by the author's inexperience.[23]

Shortly afterwards, Stephan was surprised to receive a letter from Mrs. Reeve, the purpose of which was threefold. Firstly, she asked for his honest opinion of *The Viking Heart*. Salverson had told her that the work had "the unqualified approval of Icelandic literary people who hailed it as 'a great work of art'. It seemed to [her] that if this was the case, then there [was] something wrong with the literary taste of the modern Icelander." Though she did not want to "disparage the work. Technically, it can hardly be called a novel, being rather an incoherent record of people who came to

Lárus Guðmundsson, a contributor of articles to the Icelandic newspapers and the father of author Laura Goodman Salverson.

Winnipeg, but the first few chapters are fine and the graphic description of Icelanders fleeing from the volcano seems to me probably the best thing in the book." The description of the volcanic eruption was in fact inaccurate and was therefore criticized by many Icelanders.

Mrs. Reeve then questioned Salverson's claim that all the characters in her book were "authentic and representative of the Icelanders" and then sniped at Salverson's "being the niece of the Governor of Iceland and of noble birth…" She also claimed that the author was about to publish a very bad book of poetry. This extremely personal attack on the author is curious since Salverson was regarded as Mrs. Reeve's protégé.[24]

Stephan was amused by the letter. If the picture he was getting of Salverson was anywhere near the truth, the daughter did indeed take after her father in simplistic self-esteem. Stephan replied to Mrs. Reeve with exaggerated modesty. "I have never considered myself to be a literary critic of any sort – least of all of novels. [I] have never reviewed the works of others, but have let the literary world pass by unchallenged, while I went my own way." He explained that if his doubt of the literary merit of this book became known, his opinions would be regarded as jealousy. "As you probably know, I have been charged with doing some little writing myself. To that I must plead guilty. I have never done it from pride or ambition, but only to save for myself some little atom of my own soul in my struggle for physical life." He also acknowledged the bad blood between himself and Salverson's father, who has "been after my 'literary scalp' in the papers for a quarter of a century or more… He has not done me any harm, but I have had some fun with him and rather like the old fellow for keeping my name so continually before the public. I have no grudge against him or his. All the same, in case of an openly made opinion of mine, that *The Viking Heart* was not all 'a work of art', the cry would be made at once, that I was, from revenge, heaping the sins of the father on the head of the child."

In Stephan's opinion, *The Viking Heart* was "mediocrity, not to be compared to the better works in the same field done by writers in Iceland." He found Salverson's perspective of the pioneer years too narrow, her story too localized, and her unconscious tendency to glorify a certain spiritual direction among Icelanders as too provincial. He qualified his comments, however, by adding that a closer reading might unearth "the most beautiful sapling of a young birch tree, or a pool of clearest water in some nook or crannie in the vastitude of a lava field."

He also recognized that Salverson would have needed to create something twice as good to be considered a writer of only average talent. She was handicapped from "the start by choosing, for the mainsprings of her novel, people, thoughts, and things hardly understood by an English reading public and hampered still further by the fact that she belongs to a class that has been named 'hyphenated Americans', but … I know my people and some day some of them will carry their colours further up over the flatness of our common Canadian literature." By way of conclusion, Stephan stated that he had not seen any evidence of the strong expression and deep thought that characterized the best Nordic authors. Possibly she was related to "a former Governor of Iceland, I do not know her family tree. In Iceland we have not had any nobility in the English sense of that word. With us, the rule has been "noble is who nobly does", and in that meaning almost every Icelander can claim kinship to some nobleman."

The second reason for Mrs. Reeve's letter to Stephan was to invite him to join the Canadian Authors Association, on the recommendation of Jóhannes P. Pálsson. Stephan thanked her, but he felt that his membership would lead nowhere for him or for the Association. "I am a 'workman' not a 'literary man' and likely well up to the 'end of my tether' being seventy years old."

Stephan's letter to Mrs. Reeve is one of very few extant letters in English written by the poet. In a postscript, Mrs. Reeve wondered if Stephan had anything in English, including his own books, to contribute to a literary column in a paper she edited. "I would most gladly accept your kind offer to review some of my own 'literary accidents' if they were in English, but this is just what prevents it – I have used my mother tongue, the Icelandic language. All the same, thank you very much," Stephan replied.[25]

Over the next months, Stephan joked about this "wrestling of the female trolls". In his eyes, *The Viking Heart* was typical of the regression among a younger generation who had lost connection with their language and their past. It didn't make any sense to discount the artistic demands to those who wrote in English. In a letter to poet Jakobína Johnson of Seattle, Stephan recounted the outcome of the dispute. Mrs. Reeve had been obliged to apologize to Salverson.[26] He respected Jakobína Johnson's poetry, written in Icelandic in the conventional form. Laura Goodman Salverson, on the other hand, represented a new generation of Canadians of Icelandic descent, who were naturally drifting away from their roots. Writing in English, she had adapted her Icelandic subject matter to Canadian literary tastes with uneven results, and she had obviously tried to adopt the latest marketing techniques, though the older generation would have considered these tactics questionable at best. She was, though, undeniably a pioneer in Canadian literature. What Stephan undoubtedly disliked most about her writing was her glorification of blood-sacrifice in the war, which figures prominently toward the end of the novel.

Tidal Changes

When Stefán Einarsson became editor of *Heimskringla* in 1919, the paper became for a time a liberal organ supporting the Progressive Party that was making ripples in Canadian politics around that time and was affiliated with the United Farmers of Alberta. Sigfús Halldórs, a sincere admirer of Stephan, became editor of *Heimskringla* in 1924, and while Sigurður Nordal had claimed that Stephan was the greatest poet in the colonies of the British Empire, Sigfús took this praise a step further by declaring Stephan to be the greatest poet in the entire Empire. It is, however, unclear to what extent these two men were actually familiar with the literature of the Empire.

During the 1920's, several of Stephan's closest friends and neighbors died, among them Jón Jónsson from Sleðbrjótur, a self-educated Icelandic farmer on Lake Manitoba who had corresponded with Stephan for a decade. In his memory Stephan composed a poem containing this stanza:

And that is Iceland's greatest praise,
in mindful visions and writings,
to have these bright eyes
in the faces of common people,
who can look out, from the low farmer's seat
over the entire world
from rural neighborhoods and despite obstacles
to see where the ocean's currents flow.[27]

Jónas Hunford, one of Stephan and Helga's longtime neighbours, lost his wife, Margrét, in March of 1924. Though a devout Lutheran, Jónas asked Stephan to speak at Margrét's graveside, and while reluctant to infringe on Reverend Pétur Hjálmsson's role, Stephan could not refuse. On March 19th, with family members and neighbors gathered in the Tindastoll Cemetery, he took his place between Jónas and Pétur, two old friends who did not always agree with him, but had never turned against him. He began by addressing both men at the same time. "It is by request rather than on my initiative that I say a few words here today. This is something I could not decline and I am speaking with the kind permission of the individual who usually officiates at these occasions and has the task of consoling those who find themselves in the same footsteps as we are now." He then stepped to the side of the mourners and spoke the words of consolation, something of which he was very capable. "I will not presume to express the feelings of those standing closest to this grave. They have the strength to express themselves... Least of all will I attempt to read the mind of the one who will leave here on his own, as he will be accompanied by the longest and brightest memories. I know, however, that a recurrent theme in these memories will be along these lines.

The poet with an old friend

A long day has passed,
The last afternoon sheds light
On the waiting!
The evening dusk comes closer
So that this head can lean to
The hope of rest and peace of night."

Stephan spoke on behalf of the many neighbors who so often had accepted a cup of coffee in Margrét's kitchen. "I know this is true for all of us in one respect," he said, then recited a verse suggesting that Margrét had hardly known how much they all loved her. It was Margrét's Icelandic luck "to make herself welcome in most places -/without knowing until the end" that everybody she knew had good memories of her. Therein lies happiness on the Day of Judgement.[28]

Stephan did few farm chores during the winter of 1923-24. Instead he read a great deal, and friends sent him their new writings before the ink was dry. Sigurður Nordal sent him a new Icelandic literary anthology that included an introductory essay about the continuity of Icelandic literature. This pleased Stephan as it supported his belief that Icelandic literature had not fallen asleep after the era of the medieval sagas and poetry. "That claim always put me in a bad mood, a kind of a perplexed anger, as I felt that I lacked evidence and knowledge to exorcise this ghost."[29] Stephan had in fact presented the essence of this argument some 10 years earlier in his long poem "Kolbeinslag". Stephan's poem "Jón hrak" (Jón the Outcast) was in Nordal's anthology and this recognition of the common man pleased the poet. "I hope that 'Hrak' finds his way to university too! That would be an amusing fate for him!"[30]

Stephan became increasingly aware of the turbulent changes in culture and society signalled by an ever greater shift from rural to urban living and more rationalized ways of life. By absorbing the ideas of American freethinkers and melding these with the perspective of down-to-earth farmers with a thirst for knowledge, Stephan and his friends had developed strongly critical liberal views during the last decades of the 19th century. Now, as the 20th century marched ahead, the value of their traditional literary culture became ever more clear to them. Jón from Sleðbrjótur, Magnús the blind, Jónas Hall, and other widely read men with whom Stephan had corresponded, represented a culture in retreat. Their roots became dearer to them as they grew older, and though they were somewhat nostalgic in their outlook, they retained an unfailing ability to understand and analyze their society and had no reason to feel inferior when comparing their own self-education with that provided by schools in North America. Jónas Hall, for example, told Stephan that he had written to a woman of Danish descent who was teaching at Gordon College in Baltimore because she had written a book on the Vikings that he wanted to buy. When she sent the book, she asked how he had learned to write such excellent English. He replied by saying that while he had never attended school, neither in Canada nor the United States, he had learned Danish when he was 10 years old, with the help of an Icelandic textbook in Danish that an uncle had given him. The knowledge he had gained in Danish had enabled him to struggle through a Danish textbook in English. "It is my opinion," Jónas wrote to Stephan, "that far too much material is put into the hands of youngsters… Schools of higher learning accept dimwits who can never become anything other than dimwits, just because their families are wealthy and the fashion of the times dictates."[31]

The culture of Icelanders in North America was in decline, Stephan believed, and he worried about the lack of young people with a talent to write, for instance, pioneer history. "After all our boasting about the North American education system and our level of learning here, none of our intellectuals in the West seems up to writing an essay with any literary qualities or of decent length in the language of our origin. Our schools produce 'dead souls', so at present we must look to Iceland," he said, referring to the fact that the Icelandic papers in Winnipeg had to hire editors from Iceland.[32]

Icelanders in Iceland and North America disputed educational matters fiercely. "Sometimes we hear Icelanders in North America boast of their children's schooling," Sigurður Nordal wrote, "while deriding the self-education of Icelandic folk scholars, but as long as their schools produce no Stephan G. Stephansson, and as long as they fail to hold him in high regard, they should think twice about this."[33] Nordal's comment on the low regard the North American Icelandic community had for Stephan's poetry was provocative and this statement ignited ongoing disputes in the papers.

Many Icelandic Canadian and American intellectuals had become successful due to their background in self-education. The dispute, however, encompassed not only deep-reaching changes in society, but also two contrasting philosophical mindsets – one that looked critically at society, ideologies, and institutions of power, and the other that endorsed a society that lionized external symbols of culture and relied on a silent majority for support. Resilience had been a prominent aspect of the old literary culture. Now, hostile toward the inevitable changes, this conservative traditional culture began to stagnate. Stephan recognized this and realized that to some extent he had to be cautious of his own defensiveness. He acknowledged, for example, in connection with his own dislike of jazz and other novelties, that "Indeed, I know that all human arts must rejuvenate themselves in order to avoid dying of old age, and there is nothing to do about it when men like me tend to find the first steps odd. The problem, as I see it, is that young people's tastes change so fast that fashions now wither away before they can grow and mature, leaving no enduring footsteps in the sands of time..."[34]

In the spring of 1925, just when Stephan had his mind set on going to North Dakota with Helga to attend Jónas and Sigríður Hall's golden wedding anniversary, his health problems flared up again. Furthermore, his chores and a lack of money made the trip unrealistic, so Stephan had to content himself with donating to a present and sending a poem. The party for his old friend was the biggest in the history of the Icelandic settlement in Dakota.

Exaggerated News of Death

"I dreamed I was in the home of Stephan G. Stephansson at Markerville late in the day and there was a faint light inside," Steinn Dofri wrote in his diary on Tuesday, November 24, 1924, while he was employed in Manitoba.[35] "No one was there except Stephan's daughter Rósa, as everyone else was at church or in the barn. Rósa asked if I wanted to follow her to the church (barn?) and we went out and across the road to Stephan's granary. It was so dark that nothing was visible. Rósa then walked to a high pole or a big tower on which there was a large, blue, ringing pendulum. She struck it as if it was a ball and it flew high up. It seemed that this was a bell in a church tower and the church was south of the hill by the school. Then Rósa asked me to do as she had done, but as I was unable to hit the ball well, I gave up... I seem to remember hearing the sound of a bell when she struck the ball and I suspect this may forebode changes in the weather. It may also be that Stephan is fated to die soon, unless he is already dead, or possibly Rósa is married to a man who obeys her easily, as the ball did."

Stephan's health had indeed deteriorated during the summer of 1924, leaving him bedridden and in pain, but by the end of August he was feeling somewhat better. In a letter to Baldur Sveinsson, he reported that rumours of his pending death were circulating. "In no way do I want those who care for me to believe these exaggerated reports. I plan to come home [to Iceland] for the celebrations in 1930 and see your children, my dear Baldur." Stephan let on as if he was well, but privately he acknowledged that his final day might be approaching. Others, it seems, were even more certain. Lárus Guðmundsson heard of his failing health, probably from Rögnvaldur Pétursson, who likely hoped to dissuade Lárus from attacking Stephan in the papers. Instead, Lárus apparently exaggerated what he had heard and reported that Stephan was virtually moribund.

When Stephan had consulted with Dr. Wagner of Innisfail three or four years earlier, the diagnosis had been piles. Medication had helped but had not cured this condition and Stephan joked about his affliction with Dr. Wagner, who was a rather dry character. Stephan, on the other hand, was humorous and forthright and they got along well. When Dr. Wagner asked if he was very ill, Stephan made light of his problems and joked that he only wanted to be tuned up a bit before harvest. Now Dr. Wagner took some X-rays, which showed no abnormalities, so Stephan suggested that he could find the problem if he used his finger. When Dr. Wagner finally located the problem area, he concluded that the malady was a common condition, and when asked if it was cancer he replied that it was an enlarged vein, incurable except by an operation he considered too risky for such an old man. "Well, I'm a pretty tough guy," Stephan quipped. Dr. Wagner replied that three of his patients had been found to have the same symptoms, and one of them, younger than Stephan, had died after an operation in Calgary. He then showed Stephan pictures of the condition, which prompted questions from Stephan about potential enlargement and blockage. Perhaps and perhaps not, the doctor replied, prescribing some medication to be taken three times a day, the effects of which Stephan was to monitor carefully.[36]

Jóhannes P. Pálsson, a medical doctor and writer, was among Stephan's best friends, and Stephan now wrote him a thorough description of his condition in the hope of getting alternative advice and help. He subsequently tried a variety of remedies, including flaxseed that proved useless and glycerin suppositories that reduced the pain of bowel movements. He often suffered from flatulence as well and joked about selling gas to warring nations for great profit. This condition, he suspected, ran in the family to some extent, though it was partly a consequence of uneven diet and possibly even illnesses from his years in Dakota when he had suffered from jaundice. Now he could scarcely bear sitting on a mower or a horse.

Stephan's natural inclination was to figure things out scientifically and he now sought out reading material on his condition, although he could not access proper medical books. He stayed up each evening until 10, limiting his work to carrying wood to the stove, writing letters, and reading books. His preferred diet included brown bread, raw eggs, a little fruit, and a bit of fish if any was to be had, and he liked to drink chocolate at mealtimes. He took paraffin oil with his food and before bedtime he warmed the bed and drank hot water. He often felt uncomfortable during the first half of the night, but a little better by morning. Sometimes his health took a turn for the worse, particularly if the weather changed.[37]

By autumn, Stephan had recovered sufficiently to do a little work. Around the same time, his benefactor Hjörtur (Chester) Thordarson of Chicago donated $1,200 to the latest publication of *Andvökur*. Rögnvaldur Pétursson insisted that half of this go Stephan and Hjörtur agreed, so long as just the three of them knew these details. Rögnvaldur sent him the $600, which was of great help, and Stephan noted that it was fortunate "that such unpalatable food as poetry sometimes seems to turn into real food."[38]

After a visit of a few weeks, Stephan's longtime friend Grímur Grímsson reported that Stephan's health had deteriorated further. He found Stephan occasionally rather absent-minded and uninterested in any topic other than his journey to Iceland. "That, he talked about with vitality and interest."[39]

The Eyes of Pleasure

Despite failing health, Stephan followed contemporary currents in poetry and philosophy, read about Nietzsche and Freud, called the Italian fascists "the most narrow minded nationalists" and the expressionists "gling gling glo's".[40] He discussed politics and culture with the younger generation of intellectuals in Iceland and found people there well supplied with reading material compared to what he had access to when he was young.

Stephan contemplated the function and content of poetry, fully aware that he could never fully catch up with the whims of the times. During the summer of 1924, while he was ill, he read T. S. Eliot's "The Waste Land", of which he was quite critical. "My understanding went away embarrassed, but not astonished as it had previously had a sniff of 'symbolism', 'impressionism', 'futurism', 'cubism', 'dadaism', and all kinds of poetic 'colic'. Most of it gives me no pleasure and is quite senseless, but it does not shock me. Some of it has long been an ingredient in good, old poetry, well suited. Now, it has been turned into an inedible monotonous diet, but it may eventually turn into decent food, and of course poetry may never be allowed to stagnate." The old poet composed a satirical verse about "The Waste Land", saying he had lost his eyesight in a sandstorm in a new desert.[41]

T.S. Eliot's "The Waste Land" begins with the "Burial of the Dead". When Stephan read the poem, disabled by his illness, he was also occupied with a memorial poem on André Courmont, the French Consul in Reykjavík. Stephan had met this sympathetic and intelligent man in Reykjavík in 1917 and they had got along very well, though they did not agree on everything. Courmont had first arrived in Iceland in 1911 to teach French at the new University of Iceland. In 1913 he had returned home to join the French army and he had been seriously wounded in the war. He had then returned to Iceland as the French Consul in 1917 and had served there until the time of his death in 1923. He had never fully recovered, mentally or physically, from the impact of the war, and Iceland and Icelandic culture had become his passion. He had become so fascinated with Stephan's poetry that he had wanted to write a doctoral thesis on it. "The little I learned about him won my affection and admiration," Stephan wrote in a letter. Courmont might have disapproved of *Vígslóði*, he noted, because he was "a passionate patriot and pacifist in his own, whole-hearted way. ... I feel more in debt to Courmont than to most others, after such a short encounter in this field."[42]

Whereas the flow of imagery in "The Waste Land" is an epitaph to a world destroyed by the First World War, Stephan's poem attempts to endow the world with endurance and permanence. Like "The Waste Land", it begins laboriously, without rhyme and irregular in rhythm, stanza length, and alliteration. Written as a dialogue like that in "Vopnahlé", it unfolds in twelve chapters of uneven length. The first chapter is only three lines:

You greeted me left-handed, foreigner!
More domestic in most things than I!
You a guest, while I was at home.

Running throughout the poem is the paradox of origin and dwelling place in which the guest has become more at home than the poet who is visiting the land of his youth. The poem is about how two men meet in spirit. Courmont is likened to the Norse god Týr, who sacrificed his hand to the jaws of the wolf in order to rescue his people's world. Stephan understood the sacrificial mindset that could prompt such willingness, but he felt that the offering had changed nothing since the war had turned against everything that was worth offering oneself for.

In the poem, the farmer and the Consul discuss nationality. Stephan admires the Frenchman's

André Courmont, Cambridge-educated grammarian and instructor in French at the University of Iceland, was France's Ambassador to Iceland 1917-1923.

love of Iceland while Courmont says, "Iceland has nothing to thank me for/I thank it for everything." The poet blushes at the thought that he might have been tempted to say that he had left his country with nothing, owing it nothing, while he had in fact received everything from it, "every talent, sense, and characteristic." Courmont says that France is more than just Paris. The country lies in the shadow of the city, but in the rural areas there is a "more gentle intelligence". "Town children from Iceland's valleys/can recognize that," he says. That human compassion has no borders is the essence of the poem, depicted in many variations. Courmont has always suspected that all nations had men "similar in spirit, related at heart," although distances between many countries are vast. The poet then addresses Courmont.

> *With you, there seemed to be no fjord*
> *Separating the ports of the courtier and the shepherd,*
> *Between the ports of the university and the croft.*

At the time of their parting, Courmont says, "Farewell from Iceland, Stefán./Perhaps we will never meet/again in this world. But we shall/meet again elsewhere!" He repeats this, without any discussion of spiritual eternity, but Stephan does not interpret the words in the conventional way. For him the land of the future is "far out in the world of eternity/an island of beauty with harbors of pleasure/farthest out in the distance of the most broadminded hopes." There, Courmont's friends will accept his invitation. Stephan feels he will be welcome there, although he hardly dares count himself among Courmont's friends. In the spirit of common goodwill, he is ready to sail with Courmont across unknown oceans.

At this point in the poem, Stephan begins an ode to life that brings growth to the wastelands and brightens "an inch of dark soil". He wants to nurture those who have been marginalized, those whose human potential has not been realized. This idea echoes the themes of earlier poems such as "Kveld" and "Jón hrak".

I often felt worst about the discarded plants,
That grew to no useful purpose,
And is hindered from trying again –
And the more so, if it is perhaps
Our fault, our ignorance,
Not to know how to utilize the weeds,
Or allow ourselves to discover their virtues. –

Like T. S. Eliot, Stephan alludes to ancient scriptures, claiming that they teach, "He who has seen the true God,/is less equipped/to live his life./Thus he becomes most content." In other words, a man acquainted with divinity will not get any further in life, and has thus no reason to consider earthly well-being. Stephan, on the other hand, advocated a focus on temporal life as he doubted the existence of an afterlife:

Prospects for a continuation are heavy with doubt
As to whether we can ever hope for certainty of this. –
Life is self-realization. The self-realization of us all
An effort, and sometimes demanding of our strength.
The strength to mature may wither,
Then only pain and feeling remain.

Progress is the true happiness of life.
Life without it, worse than worthless.

One must not run away from life, as wrestling with it helps mankind mature. Life is an eternal quest for the land of progress. This quest "for a more beautiful life and a more perfect maturity" unites two unlike men of different nationalities who meet only briefly, yet manage to connect through a common ideal of a better life on earth. Stephan understands the words of Courmont, "we shall meet again elsewhere," in an earthly manner:

Long after our days here, we will
See the pride of Iceland with your sweet
Rural eyes – with mine the beauty of France,
That I longed to see, but never did behold –
Belief and ideal, meadows and orchards
To see, and see with our eyes of pleasure –
Eyes of similar origin!

The poem concludes with a half-rhymed quatrain, whispering its essence:

Never will he become lost
The being who took shape here,
From an echo of a higher world,
From a wish for a happier earth.[43]

The Custodian and the Heap

When Rögnvaldur Pétursson had visited Markerville in 1923, Stephan had asked him "to become the custodian of my insolvent spiritual estate, all that I have written in my life, verse and prose, printed and unprinted." The following year, as his health worsened, Stephan requested that Rögnvaldur find a lawyer to draw up his will. He wanted the Icelandic National League to have publication rights to all of his writings so that no reactionaries could gain control of his legacy, and he hoped that some of his work might be published in the future for a little profit. He admitted to being "a little fond of his rubbish" and hoped there might be something useful in it. "Here, nobody would take care of it," he said, entrusting it to Rögnvaldur.⁴⁴

Rögnvaldur quickly hired a lawyer and arranged for an addendum to the actual will, as Stephan did not want to attach his intellectual property to a regular will. He had penned many wills for his neighbors and knew that the inheritance tax would be hundreds of dollars even for a small homestead. Unconvinced that he owed the provincial treasury that much, he decided to transfer his material wealth to his family while he was still alive. Helga would get the homestead, that was debt-free, and the land he had bought from Chris Johnson, on which he still owed money, would be sold to his sons if they were interested. During the winter, Stephan also composed an "intellectual will" in the finest "government style" in both English and Icelandic. Writing in a blue book dated March 4, 1926, he designated Rögnvaldur executor of his estate. Excluded from his papers were a few autobiographical fragments already in the possession of Baldur Sveinsson. Stephan, Helga, and their children signed the will, which was then mailed to Rögnvaldur.⁴⁵

Rögnvaldur Pétursson, the poet's friend, supporter, and executor of his estate.

The weather was harsh that winter and in mid December Stephan stopped doing outdoor chores. For a long time he had enjoyed the reputation (among those who never knew him) for "never bothering about anything except books". Now it was time to make that a reality. The family hired a farmhand to tend the cattle while Stephan worked on his papers, gathering what had "been written about him, blurb and objurgation."⁴⁶

The spring of 1925 came extremely late. Stephan spared himself, staying indoors and stoking the furnace, cranking the cream separator, and assisting with the laundry. His brother-in-law, Kristinn, had foolishly gone traipsing around the settlement selling insurance and had caught a cold. His health deteriorated seriously and he suffered from high blood pressure.

By summer, Stephan was well enough to help with haying and the harvest. Rögnvaldur and Dr. Jóhannes P. Pálsson wanted him to seek treatment in Winnipeg and offered to provide him with an escort and the train fare, but Stephan was reluctant to go since he was feeling a little better and was even capable of doing some work. He knew that his "working days" were at an end and did not want to be a burden on his friends. At the same time, he did not want to reject such a generous offer entirely if his health depended on it.[47]

Stephan could ill afford the medical help he needed. He was not far from his father's situation at the end, worn out and poor, yet he was richer in property. He also had friends who would do anything for him and who pressed him to take care of himself. Jakob J. Normann even considered moving to Markerville to be closer to Stephan. Contemplating the concern of his friends, Stephan was reassured that "despite all evil, men do care for each other. That is… the spark that will eventually warm up all human life!"[48]

During the fall and early winter of 1925-26, Stephan was able to tend 20 head of cattle and a few pigs. Nevertheless, his health declined and

Sigurlaug Kristinsson (Christinnson), the poet's sister, in the cemetery on her homestead along the Medicine River.

his hearing worsened. By December, no longer able do any chores, he stayed indoors and took care of the fire. In the New Year of 1926, his brother-in-law became seriously ill, making it difficult for Stephan's sister, Sigurlaug. In the past it had been sufficient for Stephan and his sister simply to know that the other was close at hand. Now Stephan visited Sigurlaug more often, as he knew that she liked to have him near. He could not think of going to Winnipeg for treatment while this situation persisted. When Kristinn died on February 11, 1926, he made arrangements for the funeral.

Memorials

Once the war hysteria had passed, *Lögberg* largely ignored Stephan in favour of lionizing Icelandic poet Einar Benediktsson. These two poetic giants were later often compared to each other, although they were unlike in appearance, financial situation, and background (Einar being a prominent lawyer and entrepreneur), because both included magnificent imagery and provocative ideas in their poetry. *Lögberg* finally got its long-awaited revenge on Stephan on August 6, 1925, when it published Einar's magnificent tribute to an Icelandic soldier who had met a heroic death during the war. Praising God and one's duty to the fatherland, the poem seems to be a rejoinder to Stephan's pacifist poetry, even mentioning Cain in direct contradiction to Stephan's interpretation of that story. In the next issue of *Lögberg*, someone under the pseudonym *Grímur* praised this poem highly, stating that one would have to read Einar's poem again and again to acquire its full meaning. This comment was somewhat ironic in light of the common criticism that Stephan's poetry was so terse and hard to understand that only a few bothered to go through the exercise of reading it. *Grímur* concluded that Einar Benediktsson was the greatest Icelandic poet and that he had now created an appropriate memorial to the Icelandic soldiers.

Around that time, Icelandic scholar Sigurður Nordal asked Jónas Hall to record some memories of Stephan that could be used in a lecture. Though too busy to undertake this, Jónas quoted Nordal's comments about Stephan in a letter to Rögnvaldur Pétursson. "Those living a century or more from now will verify," he stated, "that as remarkable as Stephan's poems are, his biography – the epic struggle of this great man of literature under the circumstances of a pioneer and a single worker –

is even more remarkable." Jónas, who had made a similar observation, noted, "Sigurður goes further and I can follow him."⁴⁹

Stephan had indeed encountered his share of struggles throughout his lifetime and two of the most colourful Icelandic heroes of the medieval sagas were fixed in his mind – the outlaw Grettir the Strong and the poet Egill Skallagrímsson. Stephan's poem "Erfðir" (Inheritance) focuses on Grettir's parting with his mother and on her consolation that her sons had led heroic, albeit short lives, and since 1921 Stephan had pondered a certain interpretation of the character Egill. In a poem assigned to Egill, a metaphor relates to "bringing together the morning works of a *málþjónn*", i.e. a *language servant* according to the usual interpretation. The word *mál*, however, not only means *language*, but also the time of day when animals are tended, morning and evening. Stephan preferred to interpret the phrase as meaning "between chores", evidence that Egill was in fact a farmer with chores, no less than a warrior. "It is a point of pride with me to think that Egill tended livestock just as I do," Stephan commented, recalling that his opponents had mocked his farm chores during the dispute about *Vígslóði*.⁵⁰

Stephan also disagreed with the common interpretation of Egill's character as being avaricious. Grief-stricken over the death of his brother Þórólfur, who had fallen in battle, Egill quickly recovered when the King presented him with a golden bracelet in compensation, and he subsequently took possession of two chests of silver the King sent his father as compensation. Egill also had a long struggle with Norwegian royalty over his wife's inheritance. Stephan, however, claimed that Egill had acted out of pride rather than avarice. "Egill overcame his grief because of the honour shown by the King's payment of compensation for his brother – and he goes through the perils of claiming his wife's inheritance so that nobody could say that his wife was of low birth [...]. That he got angry when others wore his most beautiful garments, while he carried them best himself, was merely evidence of his pride, as was his humiliation at finding himself a frail old man, underfoot in the kitchen, his poetry and story forgotten... and hence his infamous determination to use his money to establish some lasting claim to fame."⁵¹ Through this interpretation, Stephan is also alluding to his own pride. Possibly he wanted to prove that Einar Benediktsson was not the only one capable of composing powerful poetry, and it is perhaps no coincidence that Einar had already written a poem on Egill that has been interpreted as a reflection of his self-image.

While Stephan was ill during the fall and winter of 1925-26, he wrote an unusual poem about Egill that had a peculiar visual structure. Set up in two vertical columns, the phrases of this poem were to be matched horizontally – the gap between the two columns indicating a pause in each line to make the reading easier. The poem is in the spirit of Stephan's unique interpretation of Egill's character, drawing a stormy picture of Egill and echoing his thoughts and pride. Obviously Stephan identified with this ancient saga character – a magnificent poet who stands alone against the world. The poem begins by intertwining Egill's chores with his poetry.

An Icelandic blizzard   Banned the chores
Neither scythe nor oars   Could be used against it
The storm roared,   Breaking on sandy shores.

Having done the chores   Carved in alliteration
The painful sorrow   Of the last commemorative poem,
Directing his anger   At the world of the gods
For executing the innocent –   Egill walked to his shed.

The art of poetry was Egill's most valued asset. Opening his chest, he surveyed the treasures he had received for his poetry – from the duck eggs that had been a gift from his grandfather, to the compensation the king had granted him for the loss of his brother. His ambition fulfilled, farmer stood equal to king. He then took up the long-trained robe a friend at court had given him, a royal garment he had once worn at the Althing. The poem compares the majesty of the farmer with that of the king:

One was, when ready   In a grey wolfskin cloak
In bad weather   Doing outdoor chores
He walked the farmer's domain Early in the morning.

Egill was glad, to be able to   Attend an assembly
Most chieftainly – but at home   Most yeomanly,
Knew how to bear garments   Of both farm and court.

All the same, Egill's reputation as a poet invariably gave way to his reputation for greed. His quest for worldly wealth became a more lasting legacy than his magnificent poems. Egill, however, had in fact been motivated by the ambitions of the poet-farmer rather than by the treasures he had amassed in reward for his poetry, which explains why he decided to incite a demonstration of human greed by scattering silver coins at a general assembly:

> Robberies and injuries   Should rise from the metal of slander
> Greed would keep up   The saga of Egill.[52]

Stephan and Egill had much in common, most importantly their shared estimation of the high value of artfully composed poetry. While Stephan spent his life doing humble chores, he was also fully competent in the intellectual realm where he could match wits with anyone. His formidable intellectual strength was no less than Egill's and he was therefore able to challenge authority throughout his life.

Soon to reach the 'end of his tether', Stephan now sought to square away the past through a number of new poems. He was now preoccupied with the themes of life and death and the earth-bound philosophy he had developed. The concept expressed in his poem "Lengst lífsvon" (The Longest Hope of Life) is that a love of life remains longest with those "who have the strength in their hearts/to become younger with every grief."[53] He nurtured a pragmatic stoicism about death, and in a poem to Icelandic friend and former hostess Theódóra Thoroddsen he combined the images of morning red and sunset into one:

> Will not the game's end be most beautiful
> In life, for those who before anyone expects,
> Get to disappear into the morning red,
> While no shadow clouds the desires of youth;
> Moons wither into the world of sun.[54]

Stephan now gave careful consideration to his own demise. In a letter to his friend Baldur Sveinsson, with whom he had always been exceptionally forthright, he asked a favour. "As things stand, I sometimes contemplate making a little nest for myself on the riverbank here [...]. When the time comes, you never know but what someone might come along and slam a pole and a pile of rock on top of my remains," he half-joked, a little worried that his funeral might become too formal and expensive. He wanted to prevent that by dictating the details himself. "My mind is set on an Icelandic cairn. I have enough river rock, and concrete is cheap and strong. I have trouble imagining what shape this heap should have, however, so that it will look good. I built all kinds of cairns back in Iceland, although I'm not too proud of their designs, and now I've half forgotten how I did it." He therefore asked Baldur to contact Icelandic sculptor Einar Jónsson with a request that he design a cairn "without making it too huge." The inscription was to read:

   Hér var (Here was)
    Stefán G.
     grafinn (buried).[55]

The cairn erected in 1936 to mark the grave of Stephan G. Stephansson in the 'Christinnson-Stephansson Cemetery'.

Chapter 18

Moments of Farewell

Croaking at a Window

On May 20, 1926, a frail and aged Stephan G. Stephansson set off for Winnipeg by train, accompanied by longtime friend Dr. Jóhannes P. Pálsson. The poet's health had deteriorated to the point that he slept very little and now felt obliged to accept the offer of treatment in Winnipeg, though he commented, "I don't think this is urgent. My 'corpse' is not worth much anyway."[1] This left him between a rock and a hard place. Very independent by nature, he had been determined to manage on his own, but at the same time he didn't want to offend his benefactors and he now found justification for the trip by reminding himself that he actually had other business in Winnipeg.

Once in the city, Stephan stayed with his friends Mr. and Mrs. Rögnvaldur Pétursson while going to daily medical appointments with Dr. Baldur Olson, who did not charge for his time. Dr. Olson's examination and x-rays showed that Stephan was suffering from high blood pressure, chronic nephritis, and chronic constipation. Treatment began immediately. Stephan received medications at a cost of $8.50 and visits from a nurse twice a week, to rinse his intestines and administer a white liquid that eased his chronic pain. He also had a root canal inflammation, so he decided to have his teeth pulled, two teeth every other day, at a total cost of $25. He did not accept the offer of a set of dentures at a cost of $45, however, saying he would wait until he got home. He then had his ears cleaned free of charge by an Icelandic doctor, but he declined a costly hearing aid. Nothing acutely fatal afflicted him and there was no indication of cancer related to the intestinal inflammation. The nephritis was incurable, but it was possible to control both it and his high blood pressure. The doctor concluded that fatigue was the old poet's worst problem. Stephan joked that he never expected it would be possible to make a new man out of him, but he was curious to see if he could be made a better man!

More concerned with the thought of Helga wearing herself out, Stephan thought she ought to get hired help in the house. They would find the money somehow and he didn't want her concerning herself about that. Helga reported visiting with her sister-in-law Sigurlaug and discussing moving into an Old Folk's Home. Stephan wrote back quickly, stating that surely they were not that desperate, as nobody would go to such a place voluntarily.

The monument in Stephansson Park at Markerville, erected in 1950 by the Historic Sites and Monuments Board of Canada.

On June 11th, just after Stephan had returned to the Péturssons' home from an appointment with the dentist, the phone rang. It was his cousin and brother-in-law Jón Jónsson, who together with Jónas Hall had come to Winnipeg from North Dakota just to see him. A few minutes later, they knocked at the door. After chatting with these old friends a while, Stephan accompanied them to the home of one of Jón's daughters, where they had coffee. Stephan subsequently wrote to his daughter Rósa and invited her to come to Winnipeg so she could accompany him to North Dakota and visit her cousins.

During the few days that Jón and Jónas stayed in Winnipeg, Stephan spent hours chatting with them about the old days in Dakota. Jón "resembled himself", as the old adage went, while Jónas had become old and frail. The three friends enjoyed exchanging pioneer tales and Stephan urged Jónas to commit his reminiscences to paper.

On the day of Jón and Jónas' departure from Winnipeg, Stephan joined Rögnvaldur in accompanying a young Icelander to the train station, where he was to begin his journey back to Iceland. "Give my regards to Iceland," Stephan said passionately as the young man stepped up into the passenger car. It was as if the old man's soul accompanied these words, and tears welled up in the young man's eyes as he said "goodbye to the poetic giant of the Icelandic nation."[2]

Although over-exertion was unhealthy for Stephan, he kept himself busy. News of his stay in Winnipeg had leaked out and *Heimskringla* reported his every move, though *Lögberg* remained cool. One Sunday he spoke at the Unitarian church. The good company, he claimed, had tempted him to engage with the community, as he still very much enjoyed being among people who tolerated his renunciations rather than expecting confessions. His speech on this occasion described his vision of the "future land" along the same lines as his poem on Courmont.

Stephan gave other speeches as well, and he enjoyed himself at various parties in Winnipeg. He also strolled around the city, bidding goodbye to the world, cheerful in appearance, mournful within. People he didn't know sent him presents in gratitude for his poems and he visited the office of *Lögberg* to chat with two of his old opponents in matters of war and religion. As it turned out, they were delighted to shake hands with him. *Lögberg* editor Jón Bíldfell had to step out briefly, but he invited Stephan to wait. The old poet did not bother to do so.

Stephan spent one evening at Dr. Ólafur Björnsson's home, where together with two other doctors and Rögnvaldur he took part in a lively conversation well lubricated by Scotch whisky. Quite tipsy by the time he and Rögnvaldur left, Stephan toppled into a bush on his behind. Dr. Björnsson turned to his daughter who was on the doorstep and commented, "Now remember, my daughter, that tonight you have seen a great poet."[3]

Another party at yet another doctor's house the next evening lasted until 4 o'clock in the morning, with talented young people singing Icelandic songs. At 11 o'clock the following morning, a sleepy poet scratched a short letter to his Helga, not mentioning the parties of the past evenings. Later that day he made the trip from Winnipeg to Gimli to attend a Unitarian Synod convention. On the last day of this event, Rögnvaldur pointed out that it had been 40 years since their guest of honour had attended his last synod convention, the 1885 Winnipeg convention of the

Icelandic Lutheran Synod, as a delegate for the Park Congregation in Dakota. On that occasion he had stood up for women's rights and ever since then he had been a spokesman for spiritual and religious freedom.

Stephan had agreed to go to Gimli so that he could meet his friend and fellow poet Guttormur J. Guttormsson, who lived at Icelandic River in New Iceland. Guttormur, who was inclined to be temperamental and sarcastic, had looked forward to spending some time with his spiritual mentor, as he had never had an opportunity to enjoy Stephan's presence except in the company of others. He quickly got into an argument with Rögnvaldur while riding with Stephan in the car. Perhaps it irritated him that his only opportunity to meet Stephan was in connection with the Unitarian convention, which he knew the old poet had been obliged to endure just to please his benefactor. Although Guttormur was a dissenter, Rögnvaldur thought he should take a stand in support of the Unitarians against the Lutheran Synod. Guttormur pronounced all church activities humbug and declared that the church had committed suicide during the war years and now existed only as a ghost of its former self. The battle between Unitarians and Lutherans, he declared, was "not to free

Poet and humorist Guttormur J. Guttormsson of Víðivellir near Riverton regales three local children with stories and poems.

Stephan G. Stephansson (left) during his visit to Dakota in 1926, with his brother-in-law Jón Jónsson on the front step of the Jónsson home near Gardar.

slaves, oh no, but rather to steal slaves from each other and have them erect temples, support pastoral offices, and maintain the pyramid of folly."[4]

Guttormur and Rögnvaldur eventually made peace, but Stephan was amused by Guttormur's boyish frankness and he later wrote a long letter explaining his own stance. He regarded it his duty, he said, to take sides with the most liberal view in every dispute, even though this view was not necessarily the best argument. The big problem, as Stephan saw it, was that all spiritual movements ended up as institutions, dictatorial and narrow-minded. He expressed concern about what would become "of our children in the religious folly here, after one is dead? There is no denying it – they are even worse prepared and more ignorant in these matters [than their parents] – so they are vulnerable to such outrageously stupid religious groups as 'Holyrollers', 'Adventists', and all kinds of spiritual clowns... The only defense is to acquaint them with the most liberal party there is."[5]

Stephan's friends and relatives wanted him to visit North Dakota, and though he was tired of parties and invitations the old poet felt this was his last chance. His daughter Rósa then joined him in Winnipeg and accompanied him south to Gardar where he spent two days visiting with Jónas Hall and looking over his friend's old documents. Father and daughter then visited the Jón Jónsson family at Gardar, where Stephan had an opportunity to read the old diaries of his father-in-law, Jón Jónsson from Mjóidalur. In all, they stayed a week at Gardar, and at the farewell party on July 24th, Stephan gave a speech about the kindness that made the world a good place. He ended with a verse on the theme of bedtime and sunset. A week after Stephan returned to Winnipeg, Jónas Hall wrote to a friend, "Stephan G. came here and left a week ago, probably for the last time. He never belonged here in the West – in a spiritual sense. Iceland is his future land."[6]

Back in Manitoba, Stephan was a guest of honour without any obligation at the August 2nd Icelandic Celebration in Winnipeg. A few days later, he travelled to Selkirk to dine with Magnús J. Skaptason and his cousin Marinó Hannesson, both prominent supporters of the

Rósa Stephansson accompanied her father to North Dakota in 1926 and posed by the tree on his homestead near Gardar.

war effort and the war memorial. Stephan was reluctant to go because of his health, but he said that he had long since gotten out of the habit of avoiding people, especially relatives and friends, regardless of their religious and political opinions.

Stephan's final farewell speech in Winnipeg was delivered under somewhat ironic conditions. At the Icelandic National League farewell banquet, he was hailed by friends and foes alike. Reverend Jónas A. Sigurðsson, president of the League, was a Synod and *Lögberg* man who had sometimes criticized Stephan, but now praised him as the most unique poet in Icelandic literature in the last several centuries. Jón J. Bíldfell, a bitter opponent of Stephan on anti-war issues, now declared that Stephan had cast light on both the West and the homeland and expressed the wish that this would long continue. The last speaker, editor Sigfús Halldórs of *Heimskringla*, spoke about the poet's profound vision and declared him the greatest of all poets - although an enigma to some due to his mastery of words. Sigfús declared Stephan an inspiration, as despite his lack of any formal education he was "the most widely travelled of Icelandic poets." He then presented Stephan with an ornately written scroll and $125 as "a token of gratitude from friends."[7]

Stephan, weary but cheerful in appearance, then delivered a speech entitled "At the end of the reading hour" – which was to be his last public address. "God pays for the raven, as the saying goes," he quipped while thanking the previous speakers for their kindness, adding that it pleased him that those in attendance had forgiven him his satirical verses. He expressed doubt, however, that it would be to the advantage of Icelandic poetry if all strong language was scratched out. In the end, he quoted a poem about a raven by Davíð Stefánsson, his favourite young Icelandic poet. "Do not deride the songs / though they come from black chests." He added that he had often been warned against "croaking at the window" of pastors and editors and even greater men, and his bold replies had sometimes caused even him concern. Some pastors and editors, however, had actually proven better to him than most others. This, he felt, had been demonstrated by those "who have addressed me tonight," obviously not wishing to "deride the songs coming from a black chest." At the end of my errand here, I have one burning wish for us all, that in the future you will not be blamed for showing me benevolence and friendship."[8]

The banquet finished early and approximately 150 people shook Stephan's hand as they left. There were more invitations to parties, but Stephan found "the evenings had too long tails" and he wanted to go home.[9] Rósa, who was in Winnipeg, rejoined him at a farewell party at the home of the Péturssons on August 9th, then accompanied him back to Markerville with a stopover of a few days in the main Icelandic settlement in Saskatchewan.

Stephan was so tired when he arrived home that he had to rest for a week. His memories from Winnipeg cheered him up, however, especially those of the young musicians and intellectuals, and the friendship he had been shown would last him into the land of the future. After writing a number of letters about the trip, he joined in the harvest work and "survived. I felt I was quite tough."[10]

Swan Song

Despite his doctoring in Winnipeg, Stephan's health did not improve significantly after the trip. The socializing and travelling had taken their toll, and by the autumn his health was no better than it had been. In an unfinished poem, he now confronted death:

– And do you think I dare not be silent
Who always dared to write?
Do you think I fear dying
When I never feared living?
Do you think I dread the darkness...[11]

On the evening of December 16, 1926, as Stephan was preparing for bed, he was overwhelmed with such weakness that he had to be supported to bed. After examining him, Dr. Wagner stated that the old man had suffered a stroke. He advised moving Stephan to the hospital, but to no avail. Helga wrote Rögnvaldur Pétursson, commending her husband to the God he did not believe in and ending her letter thus, "He is no worse, and in fact we think he is a bit better. I thought you would want to know about his situation. You and others there have been so exceptionally

Helga with Stephan after his stroke.

kind to him. I hope the Creator allows him to recover, as he has been fairly well lately. Forgive this scribbling and these unworthy lines. I am in a hurry. We try to tend him as much as possible."[12]

Helga and Rósa took care of Stephan as best they could over the next days, with occasional visits from Dr. Wagner. Stephan remained conscious and spoke fluently, but he could not use his hands very much. He could still read, but not write, so Rósa wrote for him, and as soon as he was able to correspond in this way he adopted his usual stance and made fun of his situation. Four days after his stroke, he had Rósa write Baldur Sveinsson a short description of his situation, at the end of which he showed his black humour. "Of course I expect a letter from you, when you know for sure where to send it."[13]

This is the tone found in most of Stephan's letters. Armed with stoicism and humour, he concealed the trepidation he must certainly have felt. Over time he began to recover, and on New Year's Eve, after eating some soup, he asked for a pencil and paper. Once again he managed to write, although now his handwriting was greatly changed:

The writing speaks for itself,
This is now my hand.
To decipher it is a tiresome joke,
Whether written by a horn or a cloven hoof.[14]

Over the next few weeks, Stephan sent the Christmas and New Year's greetings he had been unable to write sooner. He also followed up on various matters he felt were of importance, such as his advice to Jónas Hall to work on his memoirs, letters, and papers. Nothing should be lost "of what was bequeathed to us Icelanders and that will, in the fullness of time, bear a fairer fruit than all the cow prices we may leave our heirs."[15]

In mid-January of 1927, Stephan achieved another victory. He managed a few steps along his bedside. He then asked Helga for paper and pencil, with which he scribbled his first letter to Rögnvaldur in five weeks – an incredibly long missive, considering his condition. The letter was not about himself, but about his wish to see all the Icelandic books belonging to the various reading societies in North America donated to Iceland, where they could perhaps be used in schools.

Helga found her husband's scrambling a bit too much and wrote Rögnvaldur a long description of Stephan's condition. He was recovering without pain, but he limped and showed occasional absent-mindedness. "Of course his memory has failed a bit, but that began some time ago, naturally, as happens with old age." She refused to take Stephan to a hospital as she and Rósa could easily nurse him. "We keep everything around him as clean as possible and make sure he has hot water bottles for his feet and cold packs for his head when necessary. We also turn him twice a day, and now his mind is a little clearer," she wrote.[16] She was skeptical of sending him to the hospital in Innisfail, as recommended by Dr. Wagner, as she felt Stephan should not travel until the weather got warmer. She suspected that not enough had been done in Winnipeg about his high blood pressure, but found it a blessing that he had plenty to read.

With practice, Stephan gradually improved his writing and in late January, contrary to Helga and Rósa's instructions, he began to take halting steps around his bed once a day. He wanted to decide for himself, while Helga insisted that he stay in bed while it remained cold.

A month after his stroke, Stephan began writing poetry again. His mind drifted back to Iceland and in fulfillment of an old promise he sent Baldur Sveinsson a sweet and melancholic poem using simple imagery to express his feelings upon leaving Iceland in 1917. In another verse, sent to the Icelandic poet Hulda, he said it was a pleasure to hear the singing of Icelandic swans in her poems.

Stephan now managed to toddle to the kitchen and back twice a day with the women struggling to keep him upright, like "a sheep dying of hunger."[17] Early in February he wrote to Jónas Hall, once again on the theme of Icelandic self-education, urging Jónas to

Magnús Jónsson 'from Fjall', known in his latter years as 'Magnús the Blind', used a wire grid to guide his handwriting.

preserve his writings. He even asked Rögnvaldur Pétursson to encourage Jónas and assist him in working on his papers and reminiscences. Nothing would happen, he claimed, unless someone rescued the old chap from his chores.

Now Stephan improved enough to sneak into the kitchen and peek into the pots. He wrote an ever increasing number of letters and survived a bout of flu that was going around the neighbourhood. News of his illness, of course, spread across Iceland and North America, and Magnús the Blind now wrote Stephan a letter of encouragement from Blaine, Washington, telling him that he had bequeathed to "the world a great cultural treasure."[18]

Icelandic composer Björgvin Guðmundsson, at one time of Leslie, Saskatchewan.

In the race with death and in fulfillment of another promise, Stephan now began adding to this treasure. When he and Rósa had stopped over in Saskatchewan on their way home from Winnipeg, he had met a young composer named Björgvin Guðmundsson, who had asked him to write the lyrics for a cantata he was composing. By this time several other composers had created music to Stephan's poems, but Björgvin Guðmundsson was the only one to ask for lyrics to an entire cantata. Challenged by the task of writing lyrics to music, Stephan had consented, even though this was an unfamiliar field for him, and now, despite his condition, he rolled up his sleeves and began piecing together the phrases. In mid-March he sent his creation to Björgvin, who replied that the poem lived up to his expectations of Stephan as a poet. "From a musical point of view, I think it is even better than I expected," he added.[19]

"My paw can still manage pen and ink," Stephan wrote to Björgvin in a letter explaining the poem. The lay is in 17 chapters and nearly 40 stanzas in length, irregular in rhyme and line length, and composed in a loose conversational style with narrative segments in between. Entitled "Þiðranda-kviða" (The Lay of Þiðrandi), these lyrics were based on a semi-pagan and semi-Christian legend that had fascinated Stephan ever since his youth.[20] In this 14th century tale, dark nymphs representing pagan beliefs succeed in killing Þiðrandi, the promising young son of an Icelandic chieftain, because the white nymphs, representing Christianity, arrive too late. A seer named Þórhallur had predicted this outcome. In the poem, Stephan's descriptions of the events and setting build with a "horrible abundance of weather" and "suctions of death" that glide through the air in a snowy wind that stains the windows with blood. There is a knock at the door and Þiðrandi walks out, alone. Nobody knew what had happened until morning.

The moon smirked at the blizzard's assaults,
Dawn broke over drifts of snow,
Feeble light illuminated inside the house.
Dusk was relenting.

Þórhallur was the only one,
Lightly dozing,
Able to break the fetters of sleep. –
Yet somehow wearied:
By omens of unknown mishaps,
Wide awake, but unable to smile,
Looked around the sleeping hall,
Seeking among the benches;
It was unavoidable to conclude:
Þiðrandi's bed was empty.

Þiðrandi is carried in, mortally wounded, and before death claims him he sees the nymphs of light, "beams of morning sun and youth!" arriving from the south. Þórhallur's interpretation of this event was that a dying belief had succeeded in committing one last evil deed – the killing a promising youth. "The fey fetches/of ancient customs/added Þiðrandi to their heap of corpses." Old gods, though vanquished, had conspired to take Þiðrandi with them to their heaven. Þórhallur smiles and explains how old customs give way to new beliefs – a parallel to Stephan's vision of the future:

> *I see through times, forests, and hills.*
> *Driven from the land*
> *Every evil spirit,*
> *Every noxious witch of night,*
> *Malicious nymphs, when deadly battles*
> *Of dark ages excited cold masks;*
> *Noble, young, daring perils*
> *Þiðrandi is reborn.*

The swan song of a farmer-poet, this poem is also an address to Iceland and the entire world. It describes not the victory of one custom over another, but rather the vitality of eternal resurrection that always comes after times of peril.

> *Although the fetches of past ages*
> *Killed many descendants of Iceland*
> *During the cold night of witches*
> *- Shortages and cruel climate killed many -*
> *But never buried the entire race.*
> *Always when day broke*
> *Summer-warm with the sun's flame:*
> *The nine nymphs of light and life*
> *Radiated up from the nation's meadow,*
> *Happy, good.*
> *They will keep that same custom*
> *In the sunny times of ages to come.*[21]

The Final Hand of Conciliation

Toward the spring of 1927 Stephan recovered a little. He wrote still more verses, some of which were friendly, optimistic addresses to friends, others satirical pokes at himself and his inability to work. In April he made his way to the barnyard, "swaying from side to side." He continued his efforts to rescue Jónas Hall from his chores so that he could devote himself to more useful tasks, escaping with all his things "so far from the shore that you neither hear cows bellowing nor see a smokeless chimney for about two weeks." All his encouragement was in vain, however, as Jónas Hall's papers do not seem to have been preserved.²²

Stephan's old friend Grímur Grímsson now came to stay with him in May. They chatted about radicalism and politics, which Stephan found encouraging:

I would be glad to – you should know –
Still be able to keep on harrying,
To gain one more good friend,
*And a good cause to defend.*²³

During the summer months, however, Stephan's recovery came to a halt and he became hard to manage. "He dresses most days, strolls outside a little and sits in the sun on the veranda when it shines... but his nerves are bad and he is often quite restless. He sleeps rather well most nights, but he occasionally has difficulty falling asleep and uses all sorts of medicine. I guess that helps somewhat," Helga wrote to Dr. Jóhannes P. Pálsson. She noticed that Stephan now had all kinds of strange ideas in his head.²⁴

No longer able to pursue his interests, Stephan now wondered aloud whether this chalice might be taken away from him. He became quarrelsome with Helga and Rósa and tried to find out if there was any hope for recovery. If not, he felt it was incumbent on a doctor to administer some medication that would end his life.

The last letter Stephan managed to write by himself, dated July 1, 1927, was to Grímur Grímsson. He had not written anything for a

Helga Stephansson on the homestead.

long time, yet "somehow feeling so 'exhausted' and 'the odd man out', I'm doing this out of pride." He felt his arm stiffening[25] and after that Rósa wrote for him. Still feisty, he continued his attacks on ignorance and creeds, but with only the two old pioneers in the last days of their lives, homelife was somewhat spiritless. Siggi from Víðimýri, Stephan's boyhood playmate, stayed for two weeks in July, but he was even weaker than Stephan and their conversations revolved around their illnesses. Stephan continued his feeble walks about the yard and made fun of himself. His last preserved verse was composed on July 29, 1927.

Weariness of old age haunts me
And dissipation.
I have weak legs,
A frail weakling.[26]

Despite his declining circumstances, Stephan's urge to help others remained evident. Thorstína Jackson, an Icelandic writer from North Dakota, was to give an illustrated talk about Iceland in Markerville, and though he could not attend, Stephan asked others to make sure that she was well received. On August 7th, the day after giving her talk, Thorstína paid Stephan a visit and showed him the pictures. Overjoyed, Stephan kissed her and exclaimed that her visit was the most pleasant time he had enjoyed in years. When she left, he walked with her down to the gate, and when she last saw him he was still waiving a white handkerchief.

Another old friend, Jakob Normann from Wynyard, had been planning to visit Stephan for some time. Suddenly, on August 8th, he awoke with a sense of urgency that he had to see Stephan immediately, and he arrived at the Stephansson farm late on August 9th. Edwin, Mundi Stephansson's son, was visiting his grandparents at the time, and he ambled along with the two old men, who chatted away without paying much attention to him. "Speak Icelandic to the boy," Stephan instructed Helga when they entered the house.[27]

Helga, Rósa, and Jakob did the evening chores while Stephan and his guest continued their visit in the poet's study. Suddenly uncomfortable and weak, Stephan declared he could not sit and insisted on walking outside. Just as he got to the study doorway, however, he turned and collapsed into a chair. Stephan's guest called for help, but by the time the young people came in from the stable Stephan could barely speak. His son Jakob carried him to his bed.

Virtually unconscious, Stephan was now watched closely by Helga and Rósa. Though his bright eyes were now veiled by unseeing eyelids, he at first made some feeble attempts to move his right hand a little – perhaps "extending to the world a hand of conciliation at sunset." Then he lay motionless.

As soon as Dr. Wagner had been notified, calls were made to the other Stephansson children – Jenny, Fanny, Baldur, and Mundi. Stephan had suffered another stroke and the doctor held little hope for recovery.

After Dr. Wagner had left, Helga, the children, and Stephan's sister watched over the dying poet. Now nobody could tell what thoughts about the world were flickering through his restless mind. Upstairs, young Edwin found it impossible to sleep for his grandfather's heavy breathing – until 12 minutes past midnight on August 10th. Then the breathing stopped and the curious eyes that had first opened in the humble turf hut on the farm of Kirkjuhóll, nearly 74 years earlier, had closed for the last time.

Notes

References throughout this work are made to all sources relating to Stephan G. Stephansson and his family. The edition of poetry referred to in the notes is, unless otherwise indicated, *Andvökur* I-IV, ed. by Þorkell Jóhannesson, Reykjavík 1953-58, which includes extensive notes on the publication of each poem in vol. IV. Most of Stephan's prose writing is published in the four-volume edition of letters and essays, *Bréf og ritgerðir* I-IV, ed. by Þorkell Jóhannesson, Reykjavík 1938-48. A variety of unpublished material is preserved in a few manuscript collections (see Bibliography below) and a selection of letters to Stephan is published in *Bréf til Stephans G. Stephanssonar* I-III, ed. by Finnbogi Guðmundsson, Reykjavík 1971-1975.

The only other references to sources in Icelandic are to direct quotations. It was regarded pointless to include extensive references to such sources that are inaccessible to an English speaking readership. Those sources in Icelandic not referred to in the notes below are generally referred to at the beginning of the notes for each chapter, apart from works on history and literary history. These sources are cited thoroughly in the two-volume Icelandic biography by the present author: *Landneminn mikli*, Reykjavík 2002 and *Andvökuskáld*, Reykjavík 2003.

Stephan G. Stephansson's poetry, as well as his autobiographical fragments, is translated by the author, but references are also made to existing translations of both his prose and poems: *Selected Translations*, edited by Jane Ross; Kristjana Gunnars' *Selected Prose & Poetry*; and Gunnars' translations in Finnbogi Guðmundsson's collection of essays, *Stephan G. Stephansson in Retrospect*. Some of the poetry quoted will also be found in a forthcoming anthology by Moorea Gray, and additional translations by Bernard Scudder are accessible on the website http://www.stephangstephansson.com/. It should be kept in mind that while these translations are of uneven quality, multiple translations of a given poem can result in a broader understanding. A number of translations of the same poem, accompanied by this biography, might then begin to resemble what Kristjana Gunnars calls "thick translations", which are "simply the production of a hypertext along with the translated text", this hypertext being annotations and glosses. ("Translating the Subaltern." Canadian Ethnic Studies 29.3 (1997): 80).

Preface
1. Sigurður Guðmundsson, *Á sal*. Reykjavik, 1948; 251
2. Sigurður Nordal; "Stephan G. Stephansson" in Stephan G Stephansson; *Andvökur. Úrval*, Reykjavik 1938; LXX

Chapter 1

Icelandic sources: Church records, weather diaries, annals, biographical accounts, accounts of folk traditions, farm assessments, memoirs, parish farming reports, 19th century descriptions of counties and parishes, local tales, genealogies, a variety of historical research. Many of Stephan's childhood and teenage poems, as well as poetry from his first years in America, are preserved in *Skrifbók Guðna Jónssonar á Eyjardalsá* (see Bibliography).

1. Rosa Benediktson, "My Parents", in Joanne White: *Stephan's Daughter*, 22-23.
2. ÞÍ E 243. Hermann Jónasson. Essay on Stephan G. Stephansson (manuscript).
3. ÞÍ E 243. Hermann Jónasson. Essay on Stephan G. Stephansson (manuscript).
4. Stefán Jónsson. *Ritsafn* III: 199. See also *Selected Prose & Poetry*: 17-18.
5. *Andvökur* I: 111.
6. *Bréf og ritgerðir* IV: 90. *Selected Prose & Poetry*: 28.
7. *Andvökur* II: 269.
8. *Bréf og ritgerðir* IV: 89. *Selected Prose & Poetry*: 26.
9. *Bréf og ritgerðir* IV: 83. *Selected Prose & Poetry*: 19.
10. Jón Jónsson from Mýri. "Minningar": 44 (a typed manuscript owned by Heimir Pálsson).
11. Stephan G. Stephansson. *Bréf og ritgerðir* IV: 89-90. *Selected Prose & Poetry*: 27.
12. Stephan G. Stephansson. *Bréf og ritgerðir* IV: 89. *Selected Prose & Poetry*: 26-27.
13. Stephan G. Stephansson. *Bréf og ritgerðir* IV: 90-91. *Selected Prose & Poetry*: 28.

Chapter 2

Icelandic sources: Church records, diaries, annals, biographical accounts, memoirs, 19th century descriptions of counties and parishes, local tales, a variety of historical research. Details of the "long service" are based on three different handwritten accounts.

1. *Andvökur* I: 258-259.
2. Stephan G. Stephansson. *Bréf og ritgerðir* IV: 91-92. *Selected Prose & Poetry*: 29-30.
3. Stephan G. Stephansson. "Eftir jól" (After Christmas) *Andvökur* I: 258-259.
4. *Skrifbók Guðna Jónssonar á Eyjardalsá*.
5. *Skrifbók Guðna Jónssonar á Eyjardalsá*.
6. *Skrifbók Guðna Jónssonar á Eyjardalsá*.
7. Stephan G. Stephansson. "Um Andra jarl" (On Earl Andri). *Bréf og ritgerðir* IV: 141-146.
8. Stephan G. Stephansson. *Bréf og ritgerðir* IV: 91. *Selected Prose & Poetry*: 28.
9. N.E. Balle. *Lærdómskver í evangelisk-kristilegum Trúarbrögðum handa unglingum*: 21, 34, 72, 121, 152.
10. Stephan G. Stephansson. *Barnaskólinn (The Children's School) Andvökur* I: 47.
11. Stephan G. Stephansson. "Benedikt Ólafsson frá Eiðsstöðum" (Benedikt Ólafsson of Eiðsstaðir) *Andvökur* I: 182.
12. Konrad Maurer. *Íslandsferð 1858*: 261.
13. Stephan G. Stephansson. *Bréf og ritgerðir* IV: 83-90. *Selected Prose & Poetry*: 20.
14. Stephan G. Stephansson. "Úr barns-minni" (From a Childhood Memory) *Andvökur* I: 300.

15. Ólafur Sigurðsson. "Stephan G. Stephansson. Nokkrar minningar..." *Heima er bezt* 11, 7 (1961): 224.
16. Lbs 5080 4to. Stephan G. Stephansson to Indriði Einarsson, March 21, 1922.
17. *Bréf og ritgerðir* IV: 93. *Selected Prose & Poetry*: 31-32.
18. Björn Gunnlaugsson. *Njóla eða hugmynd um alheimsáformið*. 3. edition. Reykjavík 1884 (Njóla means fog)
19. Björn Gunnlaugsson. *Njóla eða hugmynd um alheimsáformið*: 1.
20. Jón Þorkelsson Vídalín. *Vídalínspostilla*: 27.
21. *Bréf og ritgerðir* IV: 93. *Selected Prose & Poetry*: 26.
22. Stephan G. Stephansson. *Andvökur* IV: 368 (An older version of the poem "Útivist" (Being Outdoors), *Andvökur* I: 339-340).
23. *Skrifbók Guðna Jónssonar á Eyjardalsá.*
24. *Skrifbók Guðna Jónssonar á Eyjardalsá.*
25. "Sumarkoman 1869" (The coming of summer 1869). *Skrifbók Guðna Jónssonar á Eyjardalsá.*
26. *Skrifbók Guðna Jónssonar á Eyjardalsá.*
27. *Bréf og ritgerðir* IV: 92. *Selected Prose & Poetry*: 30.
28. *Bréf og ritgerðir* IV: 92. *Selected Prose & Poetry*: 30.
29. ÞÍ E 243. Hermann Jónasson. Essay on Stephan G. Stephansson (manuscript)
30. *Bréf og ritgerðir* IV: 92. *Selected Prose & Poetry*: 30. ÞÍ E 243. Hermann Jónasson. Essay on Stephan G. Stephansson (manuscript)

Chapter 3

Icelandic sources: Church and parish records, 19th century descriptions of counties and parishes, local histories, correspondence of Icelandic emigrants, the diaries of Jón Jónsson and Tómas Jónasson and a variety of other personal documents, local tales and lore, genealogies, unpublished memoirs of Jón Jónsson from Mýri, Icelandic newspapers, educational literature for young men, accounts of self-educated Icelanders.

1. Lbs 4258 8vo. The diary of Jón Jónsson from Mjóidalur.
2. *Skrifbók Guðna Jónssonar á Eyjardalsá.*
3. *Bréf og ritgerðir* "Af blöðum Konráðs Vilhjálmssonar". *Árbók Þingeyinga* 1964: 87-91; *Bréf og ritgerðir* To Jónas Hall, December 17. 1890.
4. *Skrifbók Guðna Jónssonar á Eyjardalsá.*
5. *Skrifbók Guðna Jónssonar á Eyjardalsá.*
6. *Bréf og ritgerðir* IV: 85. *Selected Prose & Poetry*: 21-22.
7. *Bréf og ritgerðir* IV: 84. *Selected Prose & Poetry*: 22.
8. *Skrifbók Guðna Jónssonar á Eyjardalsá.*
9. *Skrifbók Guðna Jónssonar á Eyjardalsá.*
10. Sveinbjörn Hallgrímsson. *Lítið Ungsmannsgaman*: 62; *Skrifbók Guðna*
11. Lbs 2954a 4to.
12. *Bréf og ritgerðir* IV: 92-93. *Selected Prose &Poetry*: 30-31.
13. *Skrifbók Guðna Jónssonar á Eyjardalsá.*
14. *Skrifbók Guðna Jónssonar á Eyjardalsá.*
15. "Úr skólasögunni" (From the School-History). *Bréf og ritgerðir* IV: 101-102.

16. "Sigríður Jónsdóttir". *Skrifbók Guðna Jónssonar á Eyjardalsá*. Finnbogi Guðmundsson. "Tvö gömul erfiljóð Stephans G. Stephanssonar" *Árbók Landsbókasafns Íslands*: 104-111.
17. "Sigríður Jónsdóttir". *Skrifbók Guðna Jónssonar á Eyjardalsá*. Finnbogi Guðmundsson. "Tvö gömul erfiljóð Stephans G. Stephanssonar" *Árbók Landsbókasafns Íslands*: 104-111.
18. *Skrifbók Guðna Jónssonar á Eyjardalsá*.
19. *Skrifbók Guðna Jónssonar á Eyjardalsá*.
20. On the first Icelandic emigration to North America, see: George J. Houser, *Pioneer Icelandic Pastor*, pp. 5-36 and Jonas Thor, *Icelanders in North America*: 7-42.
21. Lbs 4258 8vo. The diary of Jón Jónsson from Mjóidalur.
22. *Skrifbók Guðna Jónssonar á Eyjardalsá*.
23. "Úr skólasögunni" (From the School-History). *Bréf og ritgerðir* IV: 101. The present chapter is based on this account, pp. 98-105.
24. *Skrifbók Guðna Jónssonar á Eyjardalsá*.
25. "Heimkoman" (The Homecoming). *Andvökur* III. 292.
26. *Skrifbók Guðna Jónssonar á Eyjardalsá*. See: http://servefir.ruv.is/vesturfarar/e/FyrTomas.html.
27. "Ferðasaga frá Íslandi til Ameríku árið 1873" (Travelogue from Iceland to America 1873). *Bréf og ritgerðir* IV: 111-134. This and the following chapters are based on this travelogue as well as Stefán's Notebook (Lbs 3870 4to), and Guðmundur Stefánsson's travelogue which is translated into English: http://servefir.ruv.is/vesturfarar/e/FyrGudmund.html.
28. Lbs 5080 4to. Letter from Stephan G. Stephansson to Indriði Einarsson, January 5, 1922.
29. *Bréf og ritgerðir* IV: 112.
30. http://servefir.ruv.is/vesturfarar/e/FyrGudmund.html.
31. *Bréf og ritgerðir* IV: 113-114.
32. *Andvökur* IV: 108-109.

Chapter 4

Icelandic sources: Jón Jónsson's diaries, Hjörtur Þórðarson's (Chester Thordarson's) biography, Icelandic newspapers, letters and writings of Rev. Jón Bjarnason, correspondence of Icelandic emigrants, *Vesturfaraskrá* (register of Icelandic emigrants).
1. Undína [Helga Steinvör Baldvinsdóttir]. "Á burtsigling frá Íslandi 1873". *Kvæði*: 5-6.
2. Lbs 3870 4to. Vasabók (Notebook).
3. "Ferðasaga frá Íslandi til Ameríku árið 1873". *Bréf og ritgerðir* IV: 115.
4. http://servefir.ruv.is/vesturfarar/e/FyrGudmund.html.
5. http://servefir.ruv.is/vesturfarar/e/FyrGudmund.html.
6. "Ferðasaga frá Íslandi til Ameríku árið 1873". *Bréf og ritgerðir* IV: 112.
7. http://servefir.ruv.is/vesturfarar/e/FyrGudmund.html.
8. "Ferðasaga frá Íslandi til Ameríku árið 1873". *Bréf og ritgerðir* IV: 120.

9. http://servefir.ruv.is/vesturfarar/e/FyrGudmund.html.
10. http://servefir.ruv.is/vesturfarar/e/FyrGudmund.html.
11. "Ferðasaga frá Íslandi til Ameríku árið 1873". *Bréf og ritgerðir* IV: 122.
12. "Ferðasaga frá Íslandi til Ameríku árið 1873". *Bréf og ritgerðir* IV: 124.
13. "Ferðasaga frá Íslandi til Ameríku árið 1873". *Bréf og ritgerðir* IV; 125. *Andvökur* IV: 111.
14. "Ferðasaga frá Íslandi til Ameríku árið 1873". *Bréf og ritgerðir* IV: 126.
15. "Ferðasaga frá Íslandi til Ameríku árið 1873". *Bréf og ritgerðir* IV: 127.
16. *Andvökur* IV: 109-110.
17. Lbs 3870 4to. Vasabók.
18. George J. Houser. *Pioneer Icelandic Pastor*: 30-31.
19. Lbs 3870 4to. Vasabók.
20. Lbs 3870 4to. Vasabók. On this trip, see also George J. Houser. *Pioneer Icelandic Pastor*: 31-36.
21. "Ferðasaga frá Íslandi til Ameríku árið 1873". *Bréf og ritgerðir* IV: 129.
22. "Ferðasaga frá Íslandi til Ameríku árið 1873". *Bréf og ritgerðir* IV: 131.
23. http://servefir.ruv.is/vesturfarar/e/FyrGudmund.html.
24. http://servefir.ruv.is/vesturfarar/e/FyrGudmund.html.
25. "Ferðasaga frá Íslandi til Ameríku árið 1873". *Bréf og ritgerðir* IV: 133.
26. Lbs 3870 4to. Vasabók.
27. Vernon Louis Parrington. *Main Currents in American Thought* II; Van Wyck Brooks. *America's Coming of Age*; Warren I. Susman. *Culture and History*: 7-26.
28. Walt Whitman. *Leaves of Grass. The First (1855) Edition*: 5, 24.
29. Walt Whitman. *Leaves of Grass. (The Deathbed Edition)*: 29-41.
30. Walt Whitman. *Leaves of Grass. (The Deathbed Edition)*: 42.
31. http://servefir.ruv.is/vesturfarar/e/FyrGudmund.html.
32. http://servefir.ruv.is/vesturfarar/e/FyrGudmund.html.
33. http://servefir.ruv.is/vesturfarar/e/FyrGudmund.html.
34. *Skrifbók Guðna Jónssonar á Eyjardalsá*.
35. *Skrifbók Guðna Jónssonar á Eyjardalsá*.
36. *Skrifbók Guðna Jónssonar á Eyjardalsá*.
37. *Andvökur* IV, 112-120. *Skrifbók Guðna Jónssonar á Eyjardalsá*.
38. *Andvökur* IV, 121.
39. *Skrifbók Guðna Jónssonar á Eyjardalsá*.
40. *Skrifbók Guðna Jónssonar á Eyjardalsá*.
41. *Skrifbók Guðna Jónssonar á Eyjardalsá*.
42. *Bréf og ritgerðir* IV: 82-83. *Selected Prose & Poetry*: 18-19.
43. *Skrifbók Guðna Jónssonar á Eyjardalsá*.
44. *Bréf og ritgerðir* IV: 93. *Selected Prose &Poetry*: 31-32.
45. These books are preserved in Stephan's collection in the Icelandic collection at the Elizabeth Dafoe Library at the University of Manitoba.

Chapter 5

Icelandic sources: Jón Jónsson's diaries, Icelandic newspapers, a variety of Icelandic works on the Icelandic emigrants, Hjörtur Þórðarson's (Chester

Thordarson's) biography, correspondence of Icelandic emigrants.
1. *Norðanfari* April 19, 1873. On the Shawano settlement, see George J. Houser: *Pioneer Icelandic Pastor*: 75-98.
2. Ila Hill Moede. *Grandma's Footprints*: 11-14, 43-56.
3. "Abstract of title to Lot 1 Section 25 Towhship 28 Range 17. A xerox copy in the possession of Douglas Yanke. Jane McCracken. *Stephan G. Stephansson: The Poet of the Rocky Mountains*: 21.
4. *Andvökur* I: 561.
5. Naturalization Records, Area Research Center, University of Wisconsin - Green Bay.
6. *Skrifbók Guðna Jónssonar á Eyjardalsá*.
7. Wisconsin State Historical Society: MAD 4/19/D5-E5. Rasmus B. Anderson Papers. Páll Þorláksson to R. B. Anderson October 9 and November 20, 1874, January 15, 1875.
8. *Skrifbók Guðna Jónssonar á Eyjardalsá*.
9. George J. Houser. Pioneer Icelandic Pastor: 92, 98.
10. *Skrifbók Guðna Jónssonar á Eyjardalsá*.
11. *Bréf og ritgerðir* IV: 95-96. *Selected Prose & Poetry*: 33-34.
12. *Skrifbók Guðna Jónssonar á Eyjardalsá*.
13. *Bréf og ritgerðir* IV: 96. *Selected Prose & Poetry*: 34.
14. *Andvökur* I, 480-487, IV: 404-412.
15. *Bréf og ritgerðir* IV: 96. *Selected Prose & Poetry*: 34-35.
16. *Skrifbók Guðna Jónssonar á Eyjardalsá*.
17. *Andvökur* I 561-566. This story is based on the poem *Kurlý* (*Curly*), and Stephan's notes in *Andvökur* IV, 429-430).
18. *Andvökur* IV, 126-127. *Framfari*, October 5, 1878.
19. *Framfari*, October 5, 1878.
20. "Úr bréfi til systur" (From a letter to sister), *Skrifbók Guðna Jónssonar á Eyjardalsá*.
21. *Skrifbók Guðna Jónssonar á Eyjardalsá*.
22. *Skrifbók Guðna Jónssonar á Eyjardalsá*.
23. *Skrifbók Guðna Jónssonar á Eyjardalsá*.
24. *Andvökur* IV, 122-123.
25. *Andvökur* IV, 124-126.
26. *Andvökur* IV, 128.
27. *Norðanfari*, September 14, 1878. See also George J. Houser. *Pioneer Icelandic Pastor*: 85-160.
28. *Skrifbók Guðna Jónssonar á Eyjardalsá*.
29. Lbs 2954a 4to. (From a lecture on Ingersoll).
30. *Skrifbók Guðna Jónssonar á Eyjardalsá*.
31. Lbs 2954a 4to.
32. *Andvökur* I, 192-195.
33. Neil M. Clark. "The Flare of the Northern Lights..." *The American Magazine*, December 1926.

Chapter 6

Icelandic sources: Various accounts of the Icelandic pioneer history and memoirs in *Almanak Ólafs S. Thorgeirssonar* and Icelandic papers in North-America, Jón Jónsson's diaries, correspondence, minutes from congregational meetings.

1. Elwyn B. Robinson. *History of North Dakota*, 1-72.
2. Elwyn B. Robinson. *History of North Dakota*, 109-132; Georg J. Houser. *Icelandic Pioneer Pastor*: 161-194.
3. *Bréf og ritgerðir* I: 315. To Sveinn Björnsson, March 18, 1913.
4. Rosa Benediktson. "From Wisconsin to North Dakota to Alberta", in Joanne White: *Stephan's Daughter*: 11.
5. Rosa Benediktson. "From Wisconsin to North Dakota to Alberta", in Joanne White: *Stephan's Daughter*: 11. Lbs 2953 4to. Stefán's loan application to Dakota Investment Company í Grand Forks, 28. sept. 1887 (draft).
6. Magnus Olafson. "Gardar Township." Heritage 89. Pembina County North Dakota: 41.Pembina Courthouse, Plat Book of Grand Forks, Walsh & Pembina Co's NORTH DAKOTA 1893:17.
7. Rosa Benediktson. "My Parents", in Joanne White: *Stephan's Daughter*: 25.
8. Papers on Jónas and Sigríður Hall, owned by Magnus Olafson, author's xerox copy.
9. Pembina Courthouse. Preemption papers, 4188; Jane McCracken. *Stephan G. Stephansson: The Poet of the Rocky Mountains*: 41.
10. *Bréf og ritgerðir* IV: 87. *Selected Prose & Poetry*: 23-24.
11. *Andvökur* IV: 129-131, 507.
12. Jón Jónsson. "Mylluferð". *Bréf og ritgerðir* IV: 108-110.
13. Elwyn B. Robinson. *History of North Dakota*: 134.
14. Lbs 440 4to.
15. *Andvökur* IV, 169-170.
16. George J. Houser. *Pioneer Icelandic Pastor*: 185-190.
17. Lbs 525 fol. *Fjalla Eivindur*. A few issues of the paper are preserved. This chapter is based on those.
18. Lbs 525 fol. *Fjalla-Eivindur* 3-4: 23. *Andvökur* I: 196-198; Ralph Waldo Emerson. *Essays and Lectures*: 608
19. Lbs 2952 4to. Letter from Sveinn Björnsson to Rögnvaldur Pétursson, March 19, 1928.
20. Lbs 2952 4to. Letter from Sveinn Björnsson to Rögnvaldur Pétursson, March 19, 1928.
21. *Andvökur* IV, 134-135.
22. Lbs 525 fol. *Fjalla-Eivindur* 3-4; Lbs 518 fol. A clipping from a newspaper in English, containing a newsletter by Stefán.
23. Elwyn B. Robinson. *History of North Dakota*: 133-140.
24. *Bréf Vestur-íslendinga* I: 400. Steingrímur Grímsson to Jón Steingrímsson, December 26, 1882.
25. *Andvökur* IV: 148-152.
26. *Andvökur* IV: 158, 164, 169.

27. *Andvökur* IV, 169-173. Paula Vermeyden has pointed out that this poem marks a turning point in Stefán's poetry.
28. *Andvökur* IV: 189-190.
29. Lbs. 3060 4to. Documents of the Park-congregation.
30. *Andvökur* IV, 202.
31. "Ræða haldin í húsi J. Bardals nýbyggðu" (A speech delivered in J. Bardal's new house) *Bréf og ritgerðir* IV: 138-139. A part of it translated by Kristjana Gunnars in *Stephan G. Stephansson in retrospect*, pp. 17-18.
32. Strigabók (Book of Canvas) Lbs 2954a 4to.
33. Strigabók (Book of Canvas) Lbs 2954a 4to. Published as an independent poem in *Andvökur* I: 346-349.
34. Strigabók (Book of Canvas) Lbs 2954a 4to, *Andvökur* IV: 192-193. Rewritten in the poem *Skruggubylur* (*Thunderstorm*), *Andvökur* I: 75-76.
35. Strigabók (Book of Canvas) Lbs 2954a 4to, *Andvökur* IV: 194.
36. *Andvökur* I:86-87; Lbs 2953 4to.
37. *Andvökur* I: 303-304, IV: 356-357. Translated as "At Close of Day" by Jakobína Johnson in *Selected translations from Andvökur* pp. 30-31 (and http://www.stephangstephansson.com/at-close-of-day.html), and as "At Labor's end" by Kristjana Gunnars in *Selected Prose and Poetry*, pp. 47-49.

Chapter 7

Icelandic sources: Various pioneer diaries and correspondence, *Almanak Ólafs S. Thorgeirssonar* and Icelandic papers in North-America, collections of handwritten poetry.
1. *Bréf Vestur-Íslendinga* I: 402-404. Steingrímur Grímsson to Jón Steingrímsson, May 13, 1883.
2. "Musterisræða Salómons". Lbs 2953 4to. The following account is based on this source.
3. See Melwyn B. Robinson. *History of North Dakota*: 135-206.
4. See James H. Gray. *Booze*: 1-21; and *Red Light on the Prairies* 29-65.
5. *Bréf og ritgerðir* IV, 87. *Selected Prose & Poetry*: 24.
6. "Að skilnaði. Ræða haldin í Winnipeg, líkl. 1886" (A farewell speech, delivered in Winnipeg, probably 1886). *Bréf og ritgerðir* IV, 140-141.
7. *Bréf og ritgerðir* IV, 87-88. *Selected Prose & Poetry*: 25.
8. Lbs. 2952 4to. Letter from Sveinn Björnsson to Rögnvaldur Pétursson, March 19, 1928.
9. *Bréf og ritgerðir* I: 9-11. To Sveinn Björnsson, May 28, 1890.
10. Vernon Louis Parrington: *Main Currents in American Thought* III: 12.
11. *The Index*, April 30, 1885: 522-523. Stephan's bound copy is preserved in the Icelandic Collection of the Elizabeth Dafoe Library at the University of Manitoba.
12. *The Index* March 18, 1886: 446.
13. *The Index* January 7, 1886: 330.
14. *The Index* August 13, 1885: Walt Whitman. *Leaves of Grass*: 43.
15. *The Index* July 15, 1886.

16. *Bréf og ritgerðir* III: 236-7. To Jónas Hall August 30, 1925.
17. *Andvökur* IV: 357-359. A younger version, entitled *Helgispell* (*Sacrilege*) is printed in *Andvökur* I: 305-307.
18. Lbs 2953 4to. Draft of Stephan's loan application to Dakota Investment Company í Grand Forks, 28. sept. 1887. Pembina Courthouse. Mortgage records, Book 31: 593-596.
19. "Um Andra jarl" (On Earl Andri) *Bréf og ritgerðir* IV: 141-146.
20. *Andvökur* IV: 223-24.
21. "Fyrir minni Bandaríkjanna" (A toast to the United States) *Bréf og ritgerðir* IV: 146-149.
22. Rosa Benediktson. "From Wisconsin to North Dakota to Alberta", in Joanne White: *Stephan's Daughter*: 12.
23. *Andvökur* I: 92-94; IV: 320-321. Translated as "To My Lost Son" by Paul Sigurdson in *Selected translations from Andvökur*, pp. 36-39.
24. V. Emil Gudmundson: *The Unitarian Connection. Beginnings of Icelandic Unitarianism in North America, 1885-1900*: 32.
25. *Bréf og ritgerðir* II: 69-70. To Jón Jónsson from Sleðbrjótur, April 21, 1915.
26. *Bréf til Stephans G. Stephanssonar* II: 26. From Frímann B. Arngrímsson July 28, 1899.
27. "Frá Garðar. Fréttabréf" (From Gardar. A Newsletter) *Bréf og ritgerðir* IV:150-151. See also Elwyn B. Robinson. *History of North Dakota*: 203-206.
28. Fundargerðabók Hins íslenska menningarfélags (The Minutes of the Icelandic Cultural Society), Icelandic Collection, Elizabeth Dafoe Libraries: 14.
29. *Bréf og ritgerðir* III: 243-244. To Sigurður Guðmundsson, September 17, 1925.
30. *Andvökur* IV: 212-219.
31. "Hið íslenska menningarfélag. Mannúð. Rannsókn. Frelsi" (The Icelandic Cultural Society. Humanity. Research. Freedom) *Bréf og ritgerðir* IV: 152.
32. Jane McCracken. *Stephan G. Stephansson* 1982: 68; *Sameiningin* 3/1, March 1988: 12-13.
33. *Sameiningin* 3/1, March 1988: 13-14.
34. *Sameiningin* 3/2, April 1988: 31-32.
35. *Bréf og ritgerðir* II: 61. To Magnús J. Skaftason, February 5, 1915.
36. "Menningarfélagið og Sameiningin" (The Cultural Society and Sameiningin") *Bréf og ritgerðir* IV: 260-263.
37. Lbs 2954a 4to; Felix Adler. *Creed and Deed*: 48.
38. Lbs 2954a 4to.
39. Lbs 2954a 4to.
40. Lbs 2954a 4to.
41. Lbs 2954a 4to.
42. Lbs 2953 4to.
43. Ralph Waldo Emerson. "The American Scholar". *Essays and Lectures*, 53-71, especially pp. 59-63.
44. Ralph Waldo Emerson. "Self-reliance". *Essays and Lectures*, 257-282, especially pp. 275-276.

45. Ralph Waldo Emerson. "Man the Reformer". *Essays and Lectures*, 140.
46. *Bréf og ritgerðir* I: 50. To Jónas Hall, March 4, 1893.
47. *Bréf og ritgerðir* I: 15. To Jónas Hall, August 24, 1890.
48. Lbs 2953 4to.
49. *Bréf og ritgerðir* I: 15. To Jónas Hall, August 24, 1890.
50. Elwyn B. Robinson. *History of North Dakota*: 197-206. *Bréf og ritgerðir* I: 15. To Jónas Hall, August 24, 1890.
51. Lbs 2181 8vo. Poetry collected by Sigmundur Long: 52-53. Lbs 2953 4to.
52. *Bréf og ritgerðir* IV: 11-40. The story was first published in *Bréf og ritgerðir*. Quotations from pages 38 and 40.
53. Lbs 556 fol. Letter from Helga Stephansson to Rögnvaldur Pétursson January 5, 1931.
54. *Bréf og ritgerðir* I: 50. To Jónas Hall, March 4, 1893.
55. Pembina Courthouse. A contract of sale of the homestead.
56. *Andvökur* IV: 404.
57. Papers of Rosa Benediktson, Red Deer and District Archives, Acc. No. 003-106.
58. Lbs 3148 8vo. Björn Halldórsson's diary, April 9-29 1889.
59. Lbs 2953 4to.

Chapter 8

Icelandic sources: Various pioneer diaries and correspondence, *Almanak Ólafs S. Thorgeirssonar* and Icelandic papers in North-America.
1. Gerald Friesen. *The Canadian Prairies*: 162-186. *The Illustrated History of Canada*: vii, 347-359.
2. Rosa Benediktson. "Speech for an Anniversary of Gudbjorg Hannesdottir", in Joanne White: *Stephan's Daughter*: 20. Papers of Rosa Benediktson, Red Deer and District Archives, Acc. No. 003-106. Letter from Helga Stephansson to Sigurbjörg Stefánsdóttir October 27, 1901.
3. *Andvökur* IV: 414; Gerald Friesen. *The Canadian Prairies*: 130-160.
4. *Andvökur* I: 488-494.
5. Rosa Benediktson. "My Parents", in Joanne White: *Stephan's Daughter*: 20.
6. *Bréf og ritgerðir* I: 1-2. To Jónas Hall June 17, 1889. James H. Gray. *Booze*. James H. Gray. *Red Light on the Prairies*: 140-174.
7. *Andvökur* I: 307-310; IV: 361. The last two lines where the poet bids goodnight are omitted in *Andvökur*.
8. "Albertanýlendan. Eftir bréfi þaðan í marz 1891" (The Alberta settlement. A letter from there in March 1891). *Bréf og ritgerðir* IV: 153.
9. Rosa Benediktson. "Speech for an Anniversary of Gudbjorg Hannesdottir", in Joanne White: *Stephan's Daughter*: 9. Lbs 2953 4to. *Andvökur* III: 458.
10. Friðrik Bergmann. "Skyldur vorar við Ísland". *Sameiningin*, May 1888, pp. 33-40.
11. *Andvökur* IV: 341-342; *Andvökur* I: 199-200; *Heimskringla* 22/8 1889.
12. Lbs 556 fol. Letter from Helga Stephansson to Rögnvaldur Pétursson January 5 1931; *Andvökur* I:149-50. Rosa Benediktson. "My Parents", in Joanne White: *Stephan's Daughter*: 21-22. Interview with Edwin Stephenson October 22, 2000.

13. Rosa Benediktson. "My Parents", in Joanne White: *Stephan's Daughter*: 22.
14. Rosa Benediktson. "My Parents", in Joanne White: *Stephan's Daughter*: 21-23.
15. *Bréf og ritgerðir* I: 3. To Jónas Hall September 22, 1889. Translated as "From a New Neighbourhood" by Helgi Hornford in *Selected translations from Andvökur*, p. 14, and as "My New Neighbourhood" by Watson Kirkconnell, http://www.stephangstephansson.com/my-new-neighbourhood.html
16. A manuscript with poems, p. 13, Lbs. 2953 4to.
17. *Bréf og ritgerðir* I: 3-5. To Jónas Hall September 22, 1889.
18. *Bréf og ritgerðir* I: 6-7. To Jónas Hall, December 4, 1889.
19. *Bréf og ritgerðir* I: 6-7. To Jónas Hall, December 4, 1889.
20. *Andvökur* I: 257. A poetry manuscript, p. 13, Lbs 2953 4to.
21. *Bréf og ritgerðir* I: 8. To Sveinn Björnsson, May 28, 1890.
22. Lbs 556 fol. Helga Stephansson to Rögnvaldur Pétursson January 5, 1931.
23. *Bréf og ritgerðir* I: 11, 14. To Sveinn Björnsson July 30, 1890, and Jónas Hall August 24, 1890.
24. Papers of Rosa Benediktson, Red Deer and District Archives, Acc. No. 003-106. Letter from Stephan to Jón Jónsson Jr., August 12, 1890. *Bréf og ritgerðir* I: 14-15. To Jónas Hall August 24, 1890.
25. Papers of Rosa Benediktson, Red Deer and District Archives, Acc. No. 003-106. Letter from Stephan to Jón Jónsson Jr., August 12, 1890; *Bréf og ritgerðir* I: 12-13, 16. To Jónas Hall August 24, and October 8, 1890.
26. Papers of Rosa Benediktson, Red Deer and District Archives, Acc. No. 003-106. Letter from Stephan to Jón Jónsson Jr., August 12, 1890; *Bréf og ritgerðir* I: 13. To Jónas Hall August 24, 1890.
27. *Bréf og ritgerðir* I: 13. To Jónas Hall August 24, 1890.
28. *Bréf og ritgerðir* I: 16-20. To Jónas Hall October 8, 1890.
29. Lbs 2952 4to. Verse letter from Karólína Dalmann, no date.
30. *Bréf og ritgerðir* II: 5-8. Verse to Karólína Dalmann, wrongly dated October 3 1893. The right year is 1890.
31. "Albertanýlendan. Eftir bréfi þaðan í marz 1891. *Bréf og ritgerðir* IV: 153-5. Translated by Bjorgvin Sigurdson in *Selected translations from Andvökur*, pp. 10-13.
32. Lbs 556 fol. Letter from Helga Stephansson to Rögnvaldur Pétursson January 5, 1931.
33. *Sod Shacks and Wagon Tracks*: 232.
34. *Bréf og ritgerðir* I: 23-24. To Jónas Hall December 17, 1890.
35. *Bréf og ritgerðir* I: 30, 37. To Jónas Hall June 17 and November 25, 1891.
36. *Bréf og ritgerðir* I: 33-35, 36-38. To Jónas Hall, August 24 and November 25, 1890.
37. *Bréf og ritgerðir* I: 33-35, 36-38. To Jónas Hall, August 24 and November 25, 1890.
38. *Bréf og ritgerðir* I: 34. To Jónas Hall, August 24, 1890.
39. Lbs 2452 4to. Farming report from 1891. *Bréf og ritgerðir* I: 34-35. To Jónas Hall, August 24, 1890.
40. *Andvökur* I: 19-20. Translated as "Searching" by Helgi Hornford in *Selected translations from Andvökur*, p. 48. Finnbogi Guðmundsson has emphasised the importance of the year 1891 for Stephan's development by publishing separately

everything he wrote that year.
41. *Bréf og ritgerðir* I: 28. To Sveinn Björnsson April 13, 1891.
42. "Á gamlárskveld 1891" (On New Years Eve 1891). *Bréf og ritgerðir* IV: 155-158. Partly translated by Kristjana Gunnars in *Stephan G. Stephansson in retrospect*, pp. 28-29.
43. *Bréf og ritgerðir* I: 41-2. To Jónas Hall, January 8, 1892.
44. *Bréf og ritgerðir* I: 9. To Sveinn Björnsson May 20, 1890.
45. *Bréf og ritgerðir* I: 26. To Sveinn Björnsson January 9, 1891.
46. *Bréf og ritgerðir* I: 28-29. To Sveinn Björnsson April 13, 1891.
47. *Bréf og ritgerðir* IV: 39-40. Stephan to Jón Jónsson Sr., no date, 1891
48. *Andvökur* IV: 249.
49. *Andvökur* IV: 250-251.
50. Gestur Pálsson. "Nýi skáldskapurinn" *Ritsafn* 395-397.
51. A poetry manuscript, p. 66, 69, Lbs 2953 4to.
52. *Andvökur* I: 17-18. Translated by Kristjana Gunnars in *Stephan G. Stephansson in retrospect*, p. 100.
53. *Andvökur* I: 101-102. Translated as "The Exile" by Paul Sigurdson in *Selected translations from Andvökur*, p. 6, and by Kristjana Gunnars in *Selected Prose and Poetry*, pp. 75-77.
54. *Andvökur* I: 388-390.
55. *Andvökur* I: 103-4. Translated as "West to the Settlement" by Kristjana Gunnars in *Stephan G. Stephansson in retrospect*, pp. 58-59.

Chapter 9

Icelandic sources: *Almanak Ólafs S. Thorgeirssonar* and Icelandic papers in Iceland and North-America.
1. Jónas Hunford. *Almanak* 1912: 70.
2. *Andvökur* III: 465-466. A poetry manuscript, p. 32-3, Lbs. 2953 4to.
3. *Andvökur* III: 461-2.
4. A poetry manuscript, p. 85, Lbs 2953 4to. See also *Andvökur* III: 344.
5. A poetry manuscript, p. 83, Lbs 2953 4to.
6. *Andvökur* III: 463.
7. *Bréf og ritgerðir* I: 42, 47. Letters to Jónas Hall, January 8 and October 23, 1892.
8. *Andvökur* I: 255-256. This story of Karólína Dalmann's dramatic departure is thoroughly accounted for by Finnbogi Guðmundsson, ""They left in the morning and he stayed behind." A western drama." Stephan G. Stephansson in Retrospect: 56-72, where there are translations of verses and newspaper articles. The poem is translated on pp. 62-63. Also translated as "At Parting", by Helgi Hornford in *Selected translations from Andvökur*, p. 16-17.
9. *Lögberg* April 13, 1922.
10. *Andvökur* I, 105. Translated by Kristjana Gunnars in *Stephan G. Stephansson in Retrospect*, p. 56.
11. *Andvökur* I: 256-257. A poetry manuscript, p. 80-81, where the poem is dated, Lbs 2953 4to. Translated as "Pessimism" by Kristjana Gunnars in *Stephan G. Stephansson in Retrospect*, p. 66.
12. *Lögberg*, March 11, 1893. *Bréf og ritgerðir* IV: 266-269. *Bréf og ritgerðir* I: 51.

To Jónas Hall, March 4, 1893.
13. *Bréf og ritgerðir* I: 46-7. To Jónas Hall October 23, 1892.
14. *Bréf og ritgerðir* I: 44. To Jónas Hall October 23, 1892.
15. *Bréf og ritgerðir* I: 49. To Jónas Hall October 23, 1892.
16. *Andvökur* I: 23; IV: 302.
17. *Andvökur* I: 111-113.
18. *Andvökur* I: 507-508. Translated as "Little Helper" by Sigurdur Wopnford in *Selected translations from Andvökur*, pp. 25-26.
19. Jónas Hunford. *Almanak* 1911: 62-3; 1913: 77.
20. Lbs 556 fol. Letter from Helga Stephansson to Rögnvaldur Pétursson January 5, 1931.
21. A poetry manuscript, p. 82, Lbs 2953 4to.
22. "Um rím" (On Rhyme). *Bréf og ritgerðir* IV: 163-165.
23. *Bréf og ritgerðir* I: 42, 51. To Jónas Hall January 8, 1892 and March 4, 1893.
24. "Um bóklestur" (On the Reading of Books) *Bréf og ritgerðir* IV: 167-175.
25. *Andvökur* I: 116-117.
26. *Andvökur* IV: 280-82/513. Jane McCracken *Stephan G. Stephansson*: 100.
27. J. M. Bumsted. *The Peoples of Canada*: 131-132.
28. *Andvökur* I: 330.
29. A poetry manuscript, Lbs 2953 4to.
30. *Andvökur* I: 61. Translated as "Seasons in Alberta" by Kristjana Gunnars in *Selected Prose and Poetry*, p. 61, and as "The Climate in Alberta" by Bernard Scudder in http://www.stephangstephansson.com/poetry.html.
31. *Andvökur* I: 106-107. Translated as "Toast to Alberta" by Watson Kirckonnell in *Selected translations from Andvökur*, p. 2.
32. *Bréf og ritgerðir* I: 54-55. To Jón Ólafsson January 14, 1894.
33. George Melnyk, *The Literary History of Alberta*, 67.
34. *Andvökur* I: 313.
35. *Andvökur* I: 310-313; *Bréf og ritgerðir* I: 55. To Jón Ólafsson January 14, 1894.
36. *Andvökur* I: 317-319. Translated as "The Spruce Forest" by Watson Kirckonnell in http://www.stephangstephansson.com/the-spruce-forest.html and Kristjana Gunnars in *Selected Prose and Poetry*, p. 55-59.
37. *Andvökur* I: 323-324.
38. *Andvökur* I: 368. Translated as "The River" by Paul Sigurdson in *Selected translations from Andvökur*, p. 22-24.
39. *Andvökur* I: 330-332.
40. *Andvökur* I: 333-336.
41. *Bréf og ritgerðir* I: 58. To Jónas Hall March 23, 1895; Naturalization documents, Edwin Stephenson's papers.
42. *Bréf og ritgerðir* I: 58. To Jónas Hall March 23, 1895.
43. *The Illustrated History of Canada*: 334-374.
44. *Bréf og ritgerðir* I: 57-8. To Jónas Hall March 23, 1895; *Andvökur* IV: 269-270.
45. Jane McCracken: *Stephan G. Stephansson*: 100.
46. *Calgary Herald* cf. McCracken, *Stephan G. Stephansson* 101-102.
47. Receipt for oat seed. Edwin Stephenson's Papers.
48. Jane McCracken: *Stephan G. Stephansson*, 93-96. Naturalization documents,

Edwin Stephenson's Papers.
49. Jane Ross, personal communication. *Heimskringla July* 26, 1895.
50. *Andvökur* I: 339-340; IV: 368.
51. *Bréf og ritgerðir* IV: 97-8. *Selected Prose & Poetry*: 37.
52. *Bréf og ritgerðir* I: 63. To Jónas Hall December 21, 1897.
53. *Bréf og ritgerðir* I: 60-61. To Jóhann Magnús Bjarnason October 24, 1897. See also: Finnbogi Guðmundsson, "On Stephan G. Stephansson and Jóhann Magnús Bjarnason's Friendship and Correspondence", in *Stephan G. Stephansson in Retrospect*, pp. 36-55.
54. *Bréf og ritgerðir* I: 67-68. To Jóhann Magnús Bjarnason December 24, 1897.
55. *Bréf og ritgerðir* I: 72-73. To Jóhann Magnús Bjarnason July 20, 1898.
56. *Bréf og ritgerðir* I: 72-73. To Jóhann Magnús Bjarnason, July 20, 1898.
57. "Um ljóðmæli eftir Jóhann Magnús Bjarnason" (On the poetry of Jóhann Magnús Bjarnason) *Bréf og ritgerðir* IV: 178-187.
58. "Skrifað upp Jóni Einarssyni til minnis" (Written in order to remind Jón Einarsson) *Bréf og ritgerðir* IV: 270-271. *Heimskringla,* August 17, 1899.
59. *Bréf og ritgerðir* I: 102. To Jóhann Magnús Bjarnason, May 27, 1900.
60. *Andvökur* III: 337.
61. *Andvökur* I: 386-387. Two stanzas are translated as "Grottasong" by Kristjana Gunnars in *Stephan G. Stephansson in Retrospect*, p. 100-101.
62. *Andvökur* I: 390-392. Translated by Bernard Scudder in http://www.stephangstephansson.com/poetry.html.
63. *Andvökur* I: 398-401.
64. *Andvökur* I: 412-419.
65. *Andvökur* I: 419-423.
66. *Andvökur* I: 430-434.
67. *Andvökur* I: 509-522.
68. *Andvökur* I: 207.
69. *Andvökur* I: 434-439; IV: 391-392. Translated as "Eloi Lamma Sabakhthani" by Paul Sigurdson in *Selected Translations from Andvökur*, p. 70-73.
70. *Andvökur* I: 131-132; IV: 331-332.
71. *Andvökur* I: 330-332.
72. *Bréf og ritgerðir* I: 71-2. To Jóhann Magnús Bjarnason July 29, 1898.
73. *Bréf og ritgerðir* I, 75-79. To Jón Ólafsson, October 2, 1898.
74. Rosa Benediktson. "My Old Home", in Joanne White: *Stephan's Daughter*: 127-129.
75. *Bréf og ritgerðir* I: 63. To Jóhann Magnús Bjarnason October 24, 1897.
76. *Andvökur* I: 30. Translated as "Jack of All Trades" by Sigurdur Wopnford in *Selected Translations from Andvökur*, p. 14.
77. *Bréf og ritgerðir* I: 77. To Jón Ólafsson October 2, 1898.
78. *Bréf og ritgerðir* I: 71-2. To Jóhann Magnús Bjarnason July 20, 1898.
79. *Andvökur* I: 210-213. Translated as "Evening" by Jakobína Johnson in *Selected Translations from Andvökur*, p. 62-64.

Chapter 10

Icelandic sources: *Almanak Ólafs S. Thorgeirssonar*, Icelandic journals and papers in Iceland and North-America.
1. Stephan G. Stephansson. *Á ferð og flugi*. Reykjavík 1900.
2. *Bréf og ritgerðir* I, 105-106. To Jóhann Magnús Bjarnason, September 4, 1900.
3. *Andvökur* II, 13. Chapters 1 and 12 are translated as "En Route" and "On the Train" by Watson Kirkconnell in *Selected translations from Andvökur*, pp. 8-10.
4. *Andvökur* II, 14.
5. *Andvökur* II, 14.
6. *Andvökur* II, 17.
7. *Andvökur* II, 18-19.
8. *Andvökur* II, 26.
9. *Andvökur* II, 28.
10. *Andvökur* II, 36.
11. *Andvökur* II, 37.
12. *Andvökur* II, 43.
13. *Andvökur* II, 50.
14. *Andvökur* II, 54.
15. *Bréf og ritgerðir* I, 82. To Jóhann Magnús Bjarnason January 4, 1899.
16. *Bréf og ritgerðir* I, 73. To Jóhann Magnús Bjarnason July 20, 1898.
17. *Þjóðólfur* February 2, 1900.
18. *Aldamót* 10 (1900), 137-157.
19. *Freyja* 3 (1900), 2.-3. hefti: 38-39.
20. *Bréf og ritgerðir* I: 101. To Jóhann Magnús Bjarnason, May 27, 1900. "Í veðrinu út af "Vafurlogum"" (In the fuss over Vafurlogar), *Bréf og ritgerðir* IV: 280.
21. *Andvökur* I, 134-140. Excerpt from the poem is translated by Bernard Scudder in http://www.stephangstephansson.com/poetry.html.
22. Stephan G. Stephansson. "Fráfall Guðmundar gamla stúdents". *Bréf og ritgerðir* IV, 56-67. The story is translated by Árný Hjaltadóttir as "The Death of Old Guðmundur the Student" in *Western Icelandic Short Stories*, pp. 91-102.
23. *Bréf og ritgerðir* I, 104. To Jóhann Magnús Bjarnason September 4, 1900. This paragraph is translated by Kristjana Gunnars in *Stephan G. Stephansson in Retrospect*, p. 104.
24. *Bréf og ritgerðir* I, 90. To Jón Ólafsson, October 11, 1899.
25. J. M. Bumsted, *The Peoples of Canada*, 151-156.
26. J. M. Bumsted, *The Peoples of Canada*, 151-156. *The Illustrated History of Canada*, 372-373.
27. *Andvökur* I, 536-546.
28. *Bréf og ritgerðir* I, 98-99. To Jón Ólafsson, February 10, 1900.
29. Papers of Rosa Benediktson, Red Deer and District Archives, Acc. No. 003-106. Letter from Helga Stephansson to Sigurbjörg Stefánsdóttir October 27, 1901. Rosa Benediktson. "My Parents", in Joanne White: *Stephan's Daughter*: 22.
30. Rosa Benediktson. "My Parents", in Joanne White: *Stephan's Daughter*: 22-23.
31. Papers of Rosa Benediktson, Red Deer and District Archives, Acc. No. 003-106. Letter from Helga Stephansson to Sigurbjörg Stefánsdóttir October 27, 1901.
32. Páll Jóhannesson, "Heimsókn til Stephans G." *Heimskringla* 5. apríl 1905.
33. Letter from Stephan to Jón Kjærnested May 25, 1900. *Skírnir* 166. vol. (Spring

1992).
34. Papers of Rosa Benediktson, Red Deer and District Archives, Acc. No. 003-106. Bréf frá Helgu til Sigurbjargar Stefánsdóttur 27. október 1901. Lbs 4349 4to, undated letter from Stephan (1925) to Jóhannes P. Pálsson.
35. Rosa Benediktson. "My Parents", in Joanne White: *Stephan's Daughter*: 25-26.
36. *Andvökur* I, 223-228.
37. *Lögberg*, November 23, December 7, 1899.
38. Peter Waite. "Between Three Oceans: Challenges of a Continental Destiny 1840-1900". *The Illustrated History of Canada*: 369-374. J. M. Bumsted. *The Peoples of Canada*, 157-162. W. H. New. *A History of Canadian Literature*, 81; *Literary History of Canada* I, 205-221.
39. Ramsay Cook, "The Triumphs and Trials of Materialism". *The Illustrated History of Canada*, 383-393. Lbs 5007 4to. Letter from Jóhannes Ásgeir Líndal to Stephan, June 6, 1896.
40. *Andvökur* I, 142-143. Translated as "Canada" by Thorvaldur Johnson in *Selected translations from Andvökur*, p. 1, and by Kristjana Gunnars in *Selected Prose and Poetry*, p. 71.
41. *Andvökur* I, 147-9.
42. *Lögberg*, August 21, 1902.
43. Jane McCracken, *Stephan G. Stephansson: The Poet of the Rocky Mountains* 72-89. Carl Morkeberg, *Markerville Story*: 207-209. *Alberta Horse and Cattle Brands*, 204.
44. Papers of Rosa Benediktson, Red Deer and District Archives, Acc. No. 003-106. Letter from Helga Stephansson to Sigurbjörg Stefánsdóttir October 27, 1901. Jane McCracken, *Stephan G. Stephansson: The Poet of the Rocky Mountains*, 75-81.
45. *Andvökur* I: 47.
46. Rosa Benediktson, "My Parents", in Joanne White: *Stephan's Daughter*, 24-25.
47. Jane McCracken, *Stephan G. Stephansson: The Poet of the Rocky Mountains*: 79. Interview with Edwin Stephenson, October 22, 2000.
48. *Bréf og ritgerðir* I, 183, 190, 223. To Rögnvaldur Péturssonar February 19 and March 28, 1909 and to Jónas Hall January 26, 1910.
49. *Lögberg* November 21, 1901. *Heimskringla* August 10, 1899. *Sunnanfari* X (1902) 3-4, 19-23, 26-31.
50. *Bréf og ritgerðir* I, 113. To Jóhann Magnús Bjarnason April 13, 1902.
51. Lbs. 5007 4to. Letter from Sigurður Baldvinsson to Stephan, December 2, 1902.
52. *Andvökur* I, 264-265.Three stanzas are translated as "Heather from Deserted Scenes of Childhood" by Kristjana Gunnars in *Stephan G. Stephansson in Retrospect*, p. 97.
53. *Andvökur* I, 156-158.
54. *Andvökur* I, 262-263.
55. *Bréf og ritgerðir* I, 220. To Baldur Sveinsson January 8, 1910.
56. *Andvökur* I, 159-160.
57. *Andvökur* I, 161-164.
58. *Andvökur* I, 158-159. Translated by Bernard Scudder
59. "Ávarp á Íslendingadag 2. ágúst 1904" (An Address on the Icelandic Day, 2

August 1904) *Bréf og ritgerðir* IV, 188-190. Both poems and the address translated by Bjorgvin Sigurdson in *Selected translations from Andvökur*, pp. 3-5. It is also translated as "From an Íslendingadagur Address" by Kristjana Gunnars in *Selected Prose and Poetry*, p. 53, and by Bernard Scudder in http://www.stephangstephansson.com/poetry.html as "From The Icelanders' Day Address". 60. *Andvökur* I, 164-165.

Chapter 11

Excerpts from some of the letters quoted in this chapter are translated by Kristjana Gunnars in Finnbogi Guðmundsson's essay, "Stephan G. Stephansson's Conception of Himself as a Poet" in *Stephan G. Stephansson in Retrospect*, pp. 98-117. In this and the remaining chapters, the main Icelandic sources are *Almanak Ólafs S. Thorgeirssonar*, Icelandic journals and papers in Iceland and North-America.
1. Papers of Rosa Benediktson, Red Deer and District Archives, Acc. No. 003-106.
2. Jane McCracken, *Stephan G. Stephansson: The Poet of the Rocky Mountains*, 91.
3. *Andvökur* II, 103-105.
4. *Bréf og ritgerðir* I, 120. To Sigurður Jónsson from Víðimýri April 5, 1905.
5. *Bréf og ritgerðir* I, 118-119. To Vilhelm Pálsson November 24, 1903.
6. Carl Morkeberg, *Markerville Story*: 30-32. Jane McCracken, *Stephan G. Stephansson: The Poet of the Rocky Mountains*, 75, 89.
7. *Bréf og ritgerðir* I, 151-152. To Jón Ólafsson, March 8, 1907.
8. *Bréf til Stephans G. Stephanssonar* I, 26-27. From Eggert Jóhannsson December 12, 1904.
9. *Bréf og ritgerðir* I, 123-125. To Jóhann Magnús Bjarnason December 30, 1904.
10. *Bréf og ritgerðir* I, 122-123. To Eggert Jóhannsson December 23, 1904.
11. *Bréf og ritgerðir* I, 344-345. To Rögnvaldur Pétursson May 29, 1904.
12. *Bréf og ritgerðir* I, 345-346. To Rögnvaldur Pétursson October 16, 1904.
13. "Kveðja" (A Farewell). *Bréf og ritgerðir* IV, 273-4.
14. *Bréf og ritgerðir* I, 125-129. To Eggert Jóhannsson January 6, 1906.
15. *Bréf og ritgerðir* I, 128. To Eggert Jóhannsson January 6, 1906.
16. *Bréf og ritgerðir* I, 133-134. To Eggert Jóhannsson April 11, 1906.
17. *Bréf Vestur Íslendinga* II, 506. From Friðrik Bergmann to Einar Hjörleifsson July 16, 1902.
18. *Bréf og ritgerðir* I, 132-135. To Eggert Jóhannsson April 13 and September 16, 1906.
19. *Bréf og ritgerðir* I, 135. To Eggert Jóhannsson July 23, 1906.
20. *Bréf til Stephans G. Stephanssonar* I: 35-36. From Eggert Jóhannsson April 2, 1907.
21. "Í veðrinu út af "Vafurlogum" (In the Storm Caused by Vafurlogar), *Bréf og ritgerðir* IV: 275-301.
22. *Bréf og ritgerðir* I, 137. To Eggert Jóhannsson, probably July 23, 1906. In *Bréf og ritgerðir* this epilogue is wrongly put after a letter from September 16.
23. *Bréf og ritgerðir* I, 136-138. To Eggert Jóhannsson September 16, 1906.
24. *Bréf og ritgerðir* I, 154-155, 148-149. To Eggert Jóhannsson April 1 and January 25, 1907.
25. *Bréf og ritgerðir* I, 160-162. To Eggert Jóhannsson December 12, 1907.

26. *Andvökur* I-II (the 1909 edition).
27. *Bréf og ritgerðir* I, 164-168. To Eggert Jóhannsson December 12 and 14, 1907 and January 19, 1908.
28. *Bréf og ritgerðir* I, 168-171. To Eggert Jóhannsson January 19, 1908.
29. *Freyja* XI, 4 (November 1908), 94-95.
30. *Bréf og ritgerðir* I, 177. To Eggert Jóhannsson August 12, 1908.
31. *Bréf og ritgerðir* I, 356-357. Rögnvaldur Pétursson's account in the endnotes is the main source about this trip.
32. G. Friesen, *The Canadian* Prairies: 513. Eric Jonasson, "An Historic Tour of "Icelandic Winnipeg"". *The Icelandic Canadian* L, nr. 4 (1992): 244-262.
33. *Bréf og ritgerðir* I, 191. To Jónas Hall April 11, 1909. *Bréf til Stephans G. Stephanssonar* II. From Jónas Hall April 18, 1909.
34. *Lögberg* November 12, 1908. *Freyja* XI, 4 (November 1908), 94-95.
35. Jóhann Magnús Bjarnason. "Endurminning um Stephan G. Stephansson." *Tímarit Þjóðræknisfélags Íslendinga* IX, 46-49.
36. *Bréf til Stephans G. Stephanssonar* III, 95. From Guttormur J. Guttormsson November 1, 1908. *Bréf og ritgerðir* I, 198-199. To Guttormur J. Guttormsson June 16, 1909.
37. *Bréf til Stephans G. Stephanssonar* III, 96. From Guttormur J. Guttormsson May 19, 1909.
38. *Andvökur* II, 176-177, IV, 439.
39. *Bréf og ritgerðir* I, 194. To Magnús Hinriksson May 12, 1909.
40. Lbs 5007. Undated letter from Erna Jóhannsson: *Bréf til Stephans G. Stephanssonar* I, 87. From Eggert Jóhannsson October 7, 1910.
41. *Bréf og ritgerðir* I, 182. To Eggert Jóhannsson February 17, 1909.
42. *Bréf og ritgerðir* I, 191. To Jónas Hall on Easter 1909.
43. *The Province*, Innisfail, 22. júlí 1909. Interview with Edwin Stephenson, October 22, 2000.
44. *Bréf og ritgerðir* I, 200. To Eggert Jóhannsson July 17, 1909.
45. *Bréf og ritgerðir* IV, 136. *Bréf og ritgerðir* I: 201-202. To Rögnvaldur Pétursson July 27, 1909. Jane McCracken, *Stephan G. Stephansson. The Poet of the Rocky Mountains*, 95.
46. Bréf og ritgerðir IV, 136. Translated by Bjorgvin Sigurdson in *Selected translations from Andvökur*, p. 34.
47. *Bréf og ritgerðir* I, 201-202. To Rögnvaldur Pétursson, July 27, 1909.
48. *Andvökur* II, 251-3. Translated by Paul Sigurdson in *Selected translations from Andvökur*, p. 34-36.
49. *Bréf og ritgerðir* I, 202-203. To Eggert Jóhannsson July 30, 1909. Interview with Edwin Stephenson, October 22, 2000.
50. *Bréf til Stephans G. Stephanssonar* I, 81-82. From Eggert Jóhannsson June 21, 1910.
51. *Norðri* January 7 1910; *Bréf Matthíasar Jochumssonar*, 651. To Guðmundur Hannesson, Christmas 1909.
52. *Bréf og ritgerðir* I, 230. To Eggert Jóhannsson March 13, 1910.
53. *Fjallkonan* October 30 and November 15, 1909. *Ísafold* January 15, 1910.

Þjóðólfur November 26 and December 3, 1909. Þjóðviljinn June 27, 1910. Heimskringla September 16, 1909. Lögberg October 14 and 28 and December 3, 1909. Andvökur I, 22.
54. Bréf og ritgerðir I, 260. To Eggerts Jóhannsson March 21, 1911. Bréf og ritgerðir I, 262. To Eggert Jóhannsson April 2, 1911. Bréf og ritgerðir I, 361. Endnotes by Rögnvaldur Pétursson.
55. Bréf til Stephans G. Stephanssonar I, 91-2 and 94. From Eggert Jóhannsson March 15 and April 9, 1911. Bréf og ritgerðir II, 98. To Rögnvaldur Pétursson May 10, 1916. Bréf og ritgerðir IV, 196.
56. Bréf og ritgerðir I, 268 og 288. To Eggert Jóhannsson June 25, 1911 and February 2, 1912.
57. Heimskringla October 28, 1909.
58. Bréf og ritgerðir I, 265-266. To Eggert Jóhannsson May 11, 1911.
59. Bréf og ritgerðir I, 260-261. To Eggert Jóhannsson March 21, 1911.

Chapter 12

1. Bréf og ritgerðir I, 251. To Baldur Sveinsson February 8, 1911.
2. The poem "Guðbjörg Hannesdóttir". Andvökur II, 267-270.
3. Bréf og ritgerðir I, 256. To Baldur Sveinsson, March 9, 1911.
4. Andvökur I, 576-581. Translated by Paul Sigurdson in Selected translations from Andvökur, p. 50-54.
5. Bréf og ritgerðir I, 232-233. To Rögnvaldur Pétursson April 28, 1910.
6. Bréf og ritgerðir I, 330. To Jón Jónsson from Sleðbrjótur August 11, 1913.
7. Bréf og ritgerðir I, 275. To Baldur Sveinsson October 7, 1911. Ramsay Cook. "The Triumphs and Trials of Materialism 1900-1945" The Illustrated History of Canada, 375-406.
8. Andvökur III, 121-122.
9. Bréf og ritgerðir III, 6. To Helga Stephansson July 11, 1911.
10. Bréf og ritgerðir III, 6. To Helga Stephansson July 19, 1911.
11. Bréf og ritgerðir III, 6. To Helga Stephansson July 19, 1911.
12. Bréf og ritgerðir III, 8-9. To Helga Stephansson July 24, 1911.
13. Bréf og ritgerðir III, 9-10. To Helga Stephansson July 30, 1911.
14. Bréf og ritgerðir III, 10-11. To Helga Stephansson August 2, 1911.
15. Bréf og ritgerðir III, 10-11. To Helga Stephansson August 2, 1911.
16. Bréf og ritgerðir III, 11-12. To Helga Stephansson August 6, 1911.
17. Bréf og ritgerðir III, 11-12. Lbs. 4585 4to. Letter from Stephan to Jón Jónsson October 30, 1911. Jane McCracken. Stephan G. Stephansson, The Poet of the Rocky Mountains, 92.
18. Bréf og ritgerðir II, 19-20. To Jónas Hall, November 1, 1911 and January 1, 1912.
19. Bréf og ritgerðir I, 310. To Eggert Jóhannsson January 5, 1913.
20. Andvökur II, 414, 418.
21. "Kveldúlfsminni". Bréf og ritgerðir IV, 196-197. Lbs 5007 4to. Letter from Stefán Guðmundsson to Stephan, February 26, 1924.
22. Bréf og ritgerðir II, 162, 169. To Jakobína Johnson June 1918 and Rögnvaldur Pétursson October 15, 1918.

23. *Andvökur* II, 293-295.
24. *Bréf og ritgerðir* I, 319-320. To Jónas Hall March 24, 1913.
25. *The Province* December 11, 1913. Jane McCracken, *The Poet of the Rocky Mountains*, 138.
26. *Andvökur* II, 408-423. This stanza on "cosmopolitanism" is translated by Skuli Johnson in *Stephan G. Stephansson in Retrospect*, p. 28.
27. *Andvökur* II, 427-430. Translated as "The Birthday Gift" by Paul Sigurdson in *Stephan G. Stephansson in Retrospect*, pp. 59-61.
28. *Bréf og ritgerðir* I, 323. To Jón Jónsson from Sleðbrjótur April 27, 1913.
29. *Andvökur* I, 26.
30. *Bréf og ritgerðir* I, 61. To Eggert Jóhannsson December 14, 1907.
31. *Bréf og ritgerðir* I, 228-229, 272. To Baldur Sveinsson March 6, 1910 and July 7, 1911.
32. *Bréf og ritgerðir* I, 336-337. To Rögnvaldur Pétursson, October 31, 1913.
33. *Andvökur* I, 182.
34. On this poem, see Haraldur Bessason 1967. "Where the Limitations of Language and Geography Cease to Exist." *The Icelandic Canadian* 25,4, 47-53, 72-76.
35. *Bréf og ritgerðir* I, 342-343. To Rögnvaldur Pétursson December 19, 1913.
36. *Bréf og ritgerðir* I, 292. To Aðalsteinn Kristjánsson February 7, 1912.
37. *Andvökur* III, 73-98.
38. *Bréf og ritgerðir* I, 343. To Rögnvaldur Pétursson December 19, 1913.
39. Lbs 5007 4to. Letter to Stephan from Rosa Ericson February 18, 1914.
40. Lbs. 552 fol. A letter from "S. J. A." to Rögnvaldur Pétursson July 1, 1922.
41. *Bréf og ritgerðir* II, 41-42. To Jón Jónsson from Sleðbrjótur June 7, 1914.
42. *Bréf og ritgerðir* II, 168. To Rögnvaldur Pétursson October 15, 1918.

Chapter 13

1. "Íslendingadagserindi" (Address on the Day of Icelanders). *Bréf og ritgerðir* IV: 199-202.
2. Vigfús Geirdal. "Foreigners They Will Be No Longer in This Country": 61-64. Björn B. Jónsson. "Vestur-Íslendingar og stríðið". *Minningarbók íslenskra hermanna 1914-1918*: 45.
3. Vigfús Geirdal: "Foreigners They Will Be no Longer in this Country: 22-30.
4. *Andvökur* III: 131.
5. Vigfús Geirdal. "Foreigners They Will Be No Longer in This Country":37-43.
6. "Gáði seint að reiðast" (Too late getting angry). *Bréf og ritgerðir* IV: 348-349.
7. *Andvökur* III: 125.
8. *Bréf og ritgerðir* II: 47. To Jón Jónsson from Sleðbrjótur September 6, 1914.
9. Eric Hobsbawm. *The Age of Empire*: 302-327.
10. *Bréf og ritgerðir* II:55-56. To Jón Jónsson from Sleðbrjótur December 11, 1914.
11. *Andvökur* III: 131.
12. *Andvökur* III: 125-131.
13. *Bréf og ritgerðir* II: 58-63. To Magnús J. Skaftason February 5, 1915.
14. *Bréf og ritgerðir* II: 72. To Jónas Hall June 1, 1915.

15. *Bréf og ritgerðir* II: 82. To Guðmundur Finnbogason August 6, 1915.
16. On Stephan's political analysis, see Vigfús Geirdal. "Foreigners They Will Be No Longer in This Country": 73-78.
17. DuBois published in the spring 1915 the essay "The African Roots of War" in the journal *Atlantic Monthly*. See Vigfús Geirdal. "Foreigners They Will Be No Longer in This Country": 77-78.
18. *Andvökur* III: 132-159. Translated as "Battle Pause" by Paul Sigurdson in *Selected translations from Andvökur*, p. 82-105 and as "Ceasefire" by by Kristjana Gunnars in *Selected Prose and Poetry*, pp. 87-151.
19. "Gestkoma" (A visit). *Bréf og ritgerðir* IV: 202-205.
20. J. M. Bumstead. *The Peoples of Canada* Toronto 1992: 169-70.
21. Lbs 4585 4to. A letter from Stephan to Jón Jónsson December 7, 1915.
22. Rosa Benediktson, "My Diary", in Joanne White: *Stephan's Daughter*, 33-47. What follows in this chapter is based on Rosa's diary, unless otherwise indicated.
23. Interview with Edwin Stephenson. *Bréf og ritgerðir* I: 167 and II: 41. To Eggert Jóhannsson January 19, 1908 and Jón Jónsson from Sleðbrjótur, June 7, 1914.
24. *Bréf og ritgerðir* II: 103. To Jónas Hall May 29, 1916.
25. "Fyrir minni lúðraflokksins" (A toast for the brass band). *Bréf og ritgerðir* IV: 190-192. The address is wrongly dated 1906, it should be 1916.
26. *Bréf og ritgerðir* II: 101-103. To Jónas Hall May 29, 1916.
27. *Bréf og ritgerðir* II: 102. To Jónas Hall May 29, 1916.
28. "Aðkomumenn" (Visitors) *Bréf og ritgerðir* IV: 207-213.
29. *Bréf og ritgerðir* II: 101-3. To Jónas Hall May 29, 1916. *Bréf og ritgerðir* II: 105. To Jón Jónsson from Sleðbrjótur June 4, 1916. *The Province* June 8, 1916.
30. *Bréf og ritgerðir* II: 222. To Jón Jónsson from Sleðbrjótur June 2, 1920.
31. Lbs 4585 4to. Letter to Jón Jónsson July 23 and November 17, 1916.
32. *Bréf og ritgerðir* II: 114. To Rögnvaldur Pétursson December 8, 1916.
33. *Bréf og ritgerðir* II: 100. To Jón Jónsson May 11, 1916.
34. *Bréf og ritgerðir* II: 106. To Grímur Grímsson July 9, 1916.
35. *Bréf og ritgerðir* II: 108. Til Rögnvalds Péturssonar July 12, 1916.
36. *Bréf og ritgerðir* II: 114-115. To Jóhannes P. Pálsson January 1, 1917.
37. *Bréf og ritgerðir* II: 110. To Guðmundur Finnbogason November 15, 1916.
38. *Bréf og ritgerðir* II: 190. To Guttormur J. Guttormsson April 5, 1919.
39. J. M. Bumstead. *The Peoples of Canada*: 170; *Bréf og ritgerðir* II: 118. To Jónas Hall January 24 1917.

Chapter 14

Many of the texts and poems related to this journey to Iceland are translated in Finnbogi Guðmundsson's essay, "Stephan G. Stephansson's Trip to Iceland in 1917" in *Stephan G. Stephansson in Retrospect*, pp. 73-89. Various documents concerning Stephan's visit are kept in the National Archives of Iceland, ÞÍ E 154.

1. Almanak Ólafs Þorgeirssonar 1918 24-25.
2. *Bréf og ritgerðir* II: 122. To Jón Jónsson from Sleðbrjótur February 25, 1917.
3. *Bréf og ritgerðir* II: 124-5. To Jónas Hall February 22, 1917.
4. Edwin Stephenson's papers.

5. *Bréf og ritgerðir* II: 73-74. To Jón Jónsson from Sleðbrjótur June 20, 1915.
6. *Bréf og ritgerðir* II: 75-82. To Jón Jónsson from Sleðbrjótur July 14, 1915.
7. *Bréf og ritgerðir* II: 125-126, 129-131. To Grímur Grímsson March 18 and Jón Jónsson from Sleðbrjótur April 19, 1917.
8. Edwin Stephenson's papers.
9. *Bréf og ritgerðir* III: 19. To Helga Stephansson May 28, 1917. Lbs. 2952 4to. Stephan's letter to an unknown recipient May 30, 1917.
10. *Bréf og ritgerðir* III: 20-21 og II: 233-234. To Helga Stephansson June 4, 1917 and Jakob J. Normann January 7, 1921.
11. *Bréf og ritgerðir* III: 21-23. To Helgu Stephansson June 15, 1917.
12. *Andvökur* III: 278-279. Translated as "From on Board" by by Kristjana Gunnars in *Stephan G. Stephansson in Retrospect*, pp. 77-78.
13. *Af lífi og sál,* Andrés Kristjánsson ræðir við Ásgeir Bjarnþórsson: 175.
14. *Almanak Ólafs Þorgeirssonar* 1918: 27-31.
15. Stephan G. Stephansson, "Ræða flutt í Reykjavík 17. júní 1917" (A speech) *Almanak Hins íslenska þjóðvinafélags* 1981: 172-175.
16. *Bréf og ritgerðir* II: 174. To Jón Jónsson fom Sleðbrjótur November 28, 1918.
17. Two stanzas translated as "Along the Coastline" by Kristjana Gunnars in *Stephan G. Stephansson in Retrospect*, p. 80.
18. "Jökulgöngur". *Bréf og ritgerðir* IV: 226-227.
19. Indriði Indriðason, "Endurminning frá sumrinu 1917" *Andvari* (1975): 116-21.
20. Unpublished letter to Hermann Guðnason of Hvarf, September 12, 1925, owned by Jón Hermannson.
21. *Andvökur* III: 291-294. The five last stanzas translated as "The Homecoming" by Kristjana Gunnars in *Stephan G. Stephansson in Retrospect*, pp. 83-84.
22. "Úrlausn" *Bréf og ritgerðir* IV: 103.
23. Undated (1924) unpublished letter to Hermann Guðnason of Hvarf, owned by Jón Hermannsson.
24. *Bréf og ritgerðir* II: 147-148. To Jón Jónsson from Sleðbrjótur April 28 1918.
25. Davíð Stefánsson. *Mælt mál* 31.
26. *Bréf og ritgerðir* III: 215-216. To Sigfús Halldórs from Hafnir, May 10, 1925.
27. Davíð Stefánsson, *Mælt mál*: 32-34.
28. Jónas Jónasson, "Minningaslitur um Stephan G." *Hofdala Jónas* 333-337.
29. Jónas Jónasson, "Minningaslitur um Stephan G." *Hofdala Jónas* 337-338.
30. Jónas Jónasson, "Minningaslitur um Stephan G." *Hofdala Jónas* 338.
31. Jónas Jónasson, "Minningaslitur um Stephan G." *Hofdala Jónas* 334-335.
32. "Úrlausn," *Bréf og ritgerðir* IV: 90, *Selected Prose & Poetry*, 27.
33. *Andvökur* III: 301-302.
34. Stefán Vagnsson. *Úr fórum Stefáns Vagnssonar á Hjaltastöðum*: 119.
35. *Andvökur* III: 313-316.
36. *Andvökur* III: 302. Translated by Kristjana Gunnars in Stephan G. Stephansson in Retrospect, p. 85.
37. Jónas Jónasson, *Hofdala Jónas*: 408.
38. Jónas Jónasson, *Hofdala Jónas*: 339-340.
39. *Andvökur* III: 302-305. The last three stanzas translated as "By the Moorings"

by Kristjana Gunnars in *Stephan G. Stephansson in Retrospect*, p. 85-86.
40. Jónas Jónasson, *Hofdala Jónas*: 341.
41. *Andvökur* III: 308.
42. *Bréf til Stephans G. Stephanssonar* III: 142-5. From Baldur Sveinsson February 19, and April 29, 1917. *Bréf og ritgerðir* III: 26. To Helga Stephansson August 26, 1917.
43. Vilhjálmur S. Vilhjálmsson, *Tak hnakk þinn og hest*: 181-184.
44. Vilhjálmur S. Vilhjálmsson, *Tak hnakk þinn og hest*: 184.
45. *Bréf og ritgerðir* II: 177-178. To Jón Jónsson from Sleðbrjótur November 28, 1918.
46. *Bréf til Stephans G. Stephanssonar* III: 145. From Baldur Sveinsson October 10, 1917.
47. Vilhjálmur S. Vilhjálmsson, *Tak hnakk þinn og hest*: 185.
48. *Andvökur* III: 306-307.
49. *Bréf og ritgerðir* II: 134. To Jón Jónsson from Sleðbrjótur December 14, 1917.
50. *Bréf og ritgerðir* II: 146. To Jón Jónsson from Sleðbrjótur April 28, 1918.
51. Undated (1924) unpublished letter to Hermann Guðnason of Hvarf, owned by Jón Hermannsson.
52. *Andvökur* III: 319.

Chapter 15

1. *Bréf og ritgerðir* II: 138. To Jónas Hall January 11, 1918.
2. Edwin Stephenson's papers, Stephan's bankbooks. Lbs. 4585 4to. Letter to Jón Jónsson July 12, 1918.
3. Ramsay Cook. "The Triumphs and Trials of Materialism". *The Illustrated History of Canada*: 415-17. *Bréf og ritgerðir* II: 138. To Grímur Grímsson January 11, 1918.
4. Vigfús Geirdal, "Foreigners They will be no Longer in this Country," 93-99.
5. *Bréf og ritgerðir* II: 169-170. To Rögnvaldur Pétursson October 15, 1918.
6. *Andvökur* II: 479.
7. *Bréf og ritgerðir* II: 144-145. To Jón Jónsson from Sleðbrjótur April 28, 1918.
8. *Bréf og ritgerðir* II: 161. To Rögnvaldur Pétursson May 24, 1918.
9. *Andvökur* III: 180. Translated as "Question and Answer" by Hallberg Hallmundsson in *Selected translations from Andvökur*, p. 78.
10. *Bréf og ritgerðir* II: 161. To Rögnvaldur Pétursson May 24, 1918.
11. *Andvökur* III: 176. Lbs 2952 4to, Stephan's draft of a letter to Sveinbjorn Johnson.
12. *Bréf og ritgerðir* II: 278. Lbs 2952 4to. Letter to Stephan from Sveinbjorn Johnson, May 23, 1918.
13. Lbs 2952 4to. Stephan's draft of a letter to Sveinbjörn Johnson.
14. Lbs 5007 4to. Letter from Rögnvaldur Pétursson June 9, 1918; *Bréf og ritgerðir* II: 278. Notes.
15. Rögnvaldur Pétursson, *Fögur er foldin*. Reykjavík 1950: 366-367.
16. Jóhannes Birkiland, *Harmsaga æfi minnar* III, Reykjavík 1946: 42.
17. *Bréf og ritgerðir* II: 178. To Jón Jónsson from Sleðbrjótur November 28, 1918.
18. "Góðar heimtur úr helju". *Bréf og ritgerðir* IV: 217-221.
19. David Jones. *Feasting on Misfortune*: 179-186.
20. *Bréf og ritgerðir* II: 152-153. To Baldur Sveinsson May 5, 1918.

21. *Bréf til Stephans G. Stephanssonar* III: 146-147. From Baldur Sveinsson December 15, 1918.
22. *Bréf og ritgerðir* II: 180-181. To Baldur Sveinsson January 13, 1919.
23. *Andvökur* II: 337-339. Translated as "Little Ranka" by Thorvaldur Johnson in *Selected translations from Andvökur*, p. 39-40.
24. *Lögberg* February 13, 1919.
25. *Lögberg* February 13, 1919.
26. Lbs 553 fol. Letter from S. O. Eiriksson to Rögnvaldur Pétursson June 10, 1919.
27. "Minnisvarðamálefni" (On the memorial issue). *Bréf og ritgerðir* IV: 306-311.
28. Lbs. 2954a 4to. Stephan's lecture-notes.
29. "Villuvörður" (Misleading cairns), *Bréf og ritgerðir* IV: 315-316.
30. "Árni Sveinsson til sanns vegar færður" (Árni Sveinsson corrected) *Bréf og ritgerðir* IV: 316-322.
31. Lbs 5007 4to. Letter to Stephan from Magnús Jónsson from Fjall April 9, 1919.
32. "Brauð og steinn" (Bread and stone), *Bréf og ritgerðir* IV: 327-332.

Chapter 16

1. Papers of Rosa Benediktson, Red Deer and District Archives, Acc. No. 003-106. Letter from Sigurlaug Christinnson January 27, 1920.
2. Papers of Rosa Benediktson, Red Deer and District Archives, Acc. No. 003-106. Letter from Jóný Stephansson to Rósa Stephansson November 23, 1919.
3. Lbs 5007 4to. Undated letter from Rósa Stephansson/Benediktson to Stephan.
4. Papers of Rosa Benediktson, Red Deer and District Archives, Acc. No. 003-106. Letters from Jóný Stephansson to Rósa Stephansson February 14 and March 2, 1920 and undated letters from Helga Stephansson to Rósa.
5. Papers of Rosa Benediktson, Red Deer and District Archives, Acc. No. 003-106. Letter from Jóný Stephansson to Rósa Stephansson March 2, 1920.
6. *Bréf og ritgerðir* II: 219. To Sigurður Jónsson May 16, 1920.
7. Sigurður Þórólfsson's private archive. Letter from Stephan to Þórólfur Sigurðsson.
8. Jökulgöngur. *Bréf og ritgerðir* IV: 224-231.
9. Stephan G. Stephansson. *Vígslóði*. Preface by Guðmundur Finnbogason.
10. *Bréf og ritgerðir* II: 237-238. To Ásgeir Ingimundarson January 19, 1921.
11. *Lögberg* October 21, 1920.
12. "Gáði seint að reiðast". *Bréf og ritgerðir* IV: 347-359.
13. *Bréf og ritgerðir* III: 207. To Rögnvaldur Pétursson April 4, 1925.
14. Kealey og Whitaker (ed.). *R.C.M.P. Security Bulletins. The Early Years 1919-1929*: 267.
15. Lbs 549 fol. Letters from Jónas Hunford to Rögnvaldur Pétursson October 15, 1918 and November 4, 1920.
16. Lbs 549 fol. Letter from Jón Sveinsson to Rögnvaldur Pétursson December 18, 1920.
17. "Nikulásarmessa" *Bréf og ritgerðir* IV: 367.
18. *Bréf og ritgerðir* II: 222. To Jón Jónsson from Sleðbrjótur May 16, 1920.
19. Papers of Rosa Benediktson, Red Deer and District Archives, Acc. No. 003-

106. Undated letter from Helga Stephansson to Rósa Stephansson.
20. Papers of Rosa Benediktson, Red Deer and District Archives, Acc. No. 003-106. Undated letter from Helga Stephansson to Rósa Stephansson.
21. Papers of Rosa Benediktson, Red Deer and District Archives, Acc. No. 003-106. Undated letter from Helga Stephansson to Rósa Stephansson.
22. Papers of Rosa Benediktson, Red Deer and District Archives, Acc. No. 003-106. Undated letter from Helga Stephansson to Rósa Stephansson.
23. *Bréf og ritgerðir* II: 233, 239. To Grímur S. Grímsson December 30, 1920 and January 22, 1921.
24. Lbs without number. Steinn Dofri's diaries.
25. *Bréf og ritgerðir* II: 255. To Rögnvaldur Pétursson May 17, 1921.
26. *Andvökur* III: 198-208.
27. Lbs 549 fol. Letter from Jónas Hunford to Rögnvaldur Pétursson December 14, 1922.
28. "Þakkargerð" (Thanks). *Bréf og ritgerðir* IV: 374-379.
29. Jóhannes P. Pálsson 1927."Stephan G. Stephansson. (nokkur orð um skáldið og manninn)". *Tímarit Þjóðræknisfélags Íslendinga*: 1927: 39.
30. *Bréf og ritgerðir* II: 191. To Guttormur J. Guttormsson April 5, 1919.
31. *Bréf og ritgerðir* II: 199-200. To Jón Jónsson from Sleðbrjótur September 6, 1919.
32. Anthony Mardiros. *William Irvine. The Life of a Prairie Radical*: 53-109.
33. *Bréf og ritgerðir* II: 212-213. To Jón Jónsson from Sleðbrjótur March 14, 1920.
34. *Bréf og ritgerðir* II: 199-200. To Jón Jónsson from Sleðbrjótur September 6, 1919.
35. *Bréf og ritgerðir* II: 212-213. To Jón Jónsson from Sleðbrjótur March 14, 1920.
36. *Bréf og ritgerðir* II: 252. To Jón Jónsson from Sleðbrjótur May 5, 1921.
37. *Andvökur* II: 511-518.
38. *Andvökur* II: 511. *Bréf og ritgerðir* III: 38. To Rögnvaldur Pétursson February 3, 1922.

Chapter 17

1. *Bréf og ritgerðir* III: 47, 49-50. To Rögnvaldur Pétursson March 31 and April 23, 1922.
2. *Bréf og ritgerðir* III: 66-77. To Grímur Grímsson December 5, 1922. Lbs 4585 4to. Letter to Jón Jónsson November 22, 1922.
3. David C. Jones. *Feasting on Misfortune*: 45-50. *Bréf og ritgerðir* III: 35. To Jón Jónsson from Sleðbrjótur January 24, 1922.
4. *Bréf og ritgerðir* III: 30-31. To Rögnvaldur Pétursson January 3, 1922.
5. "Kveldórar" (Evening ramblings). *Bréf og ritgerðir* IV: 248-253.
6. Ágúst H Bjarnason. "Frá Vesturheimi. Stephan G. Stephansson sóttur heim" (From the West. A visit to Stephan G. Stephansson). *Iðunn* 8 (1923-4): 21-31 This section is mainly based on this source.
7. Lbs 548 fol. Letter from Jónas Hall to Rögnvaldur Pétursson April 5, 1920.
8. *Bréf og ritgerðir* III: 63-4. To Jakobs J. Normann November 28, 1922.
9. *Bréf og ritgerðir* III: 60-61. To Rögnvaldur Pétursson October 25, 1922.
10. *Bréf og ritgerðir* III: 94-97. To Jakob J. Normann June 21, 1923.

11. Lbs 550 fol. Letter from Jakob J. Normann to Rögnvaldur Pétursson August 30, 1923.
12. *Bréf og ritgerðir* III: 103. To Rögnvaldur Pétursson August 4, 1923.
13. Lbs 545 fol. Letter from Eggert Jóhannson to Rögnvaldur Pétursson August 26, 1923.
14. *Bréf og ritgerðir* III: 111, 110. To Rögnvaldur Pétursson November 11, 1923 and Grímur S. Grímsson October 22, 1923.
15. *Bréf og ritgerðir* III: 118-119. To Jón Jónsson January 28, 1924.
16. Undated, unpublished letter (1924) from Stephan to Hermann Guðnason, owned by Jón Hermannsson.
17. Lbs 549 fol. Letter from Jónas Hall to Rögnvaldur Pétursson October 21, 1923.
18. *Bréf og ritgerðir* III: 113-114. To Rögnvaldur Pétursson January 16, 1924.
19. *Heimskringla* November 21, 1923.
20. *Lögberg* March 13, 1924.
21. Daisy Neijmann, *The Icelandic Voice in Canadian Letters* 188, 201.
22. *Bréf og ritgerðir* III: 134, 139. Til Jóhannesar P. Pálssonar March 20 and 29, 1924.
23. Lbs 2953 4to. Clipping from *Canadian Bookman*.
24. Lbs 2952 4to. Letter to Stephan from Winifred Reeve March 26, 1924.
25. Lbs 2952 4to. Letter from Stephan to Winifred Reeve April 14, 1924.
26. Lbs 4271 4to. Letter from Stephan to Jakobína Johnson July 7, 1924.
27. *Andvökur* IV: 30.
28. *Bréf og ritgerðir* IV: 137.
29. *Bréf og ritgerðir* III: 188. Undated letter to Sigurður Nordal.
30. *Bréf og ritgerðir* III: 205. To Sveinn Björnsson March 31, 1925.
31. Papers of Rosa Benediktson, Red Deer and District Archives, Acc. No. 003-106. Letter to Stephan from Jónas Hall July 2, 1924.
32. *Bréf og ritgerðir* III: 238. To Jónas Hall August 30, 1925.
33. Sigurður Nordal, "Samlagning". *Ritverk. List og lífsskoðun* II: 394.
34. *Bréf og ritgerðir* III: 342. To Sigfús Blöndal November 3, 1926.
35. Lbs without number. Steinn Dofri's diaries.
36. Bréf og ritgerðir III: 163-164. To Baldur Sveinsson August 30, 1924; Lbs 4349 4to. Letter from Stephan to Jóhannes P. Pálsson August 22, 1924.
37. Lbs 4349 4to. Letter from Stephan to Jóhannes P. Pálsson, late in 1924.
38. *Bréf og ritgerðir* III: 189-190. To Rögnvaldur Pétursson January 4, 1925.
39. Lbs 546 fol. Letters from Grímur S. Grímsson to Rögnvaldur Pétursson December 14, 1924 and December 1, 1925.
40. *Bréf og ritgerðir* III: 68, 224. To Jón Jónsson from Sleðbrjótur December 6, 1922 and Sigurður Nordal June 29, 1925.
41. *Bréf og ritgerðir* III: 164. To Jóhann Magnús Bjarnason September 1, 1924.
42. *Bréf og ritgerðir* III: 112-113. To Rögnvaldur Pétursson, 1924.
43. *Andvökur* IV: 34-40.
44. *Bréf og ritgerðir* III: 160-161. To Rögnvaldur Pétursson August 14, 1924.
45. Lbs 3870 4to.
46. *Bréf og ritgerðir* III: 195, 202. To Jakob J. Normann February 27 and March 30, 1925.
47. *Bréf og ritgerðir* III: 231-232. To Jóhannes P. Pálsson August 15, 1925.

48. *Bréf og ritgerðir* III: 255. To Jóhannes P. Pálsson November 11, 1925.
49. Lbs 549 fol. Letter from Jónas Hall to Rögnvaldur Pétursson June 23, 1925.
50. *Bréf og ritgerðir* III: 65. To Jóhannes P. Pálsson November 29, 1922.
51. *Bréf og ritgerðir* III: 189. Undated to Sigurður Nordal [1924].
52. *Andvökur* IV: 67-71; *Andvökur* VI (first edition): 255-259.
53. *Andvökur* III: 392-393.
54. *Andvökur* III: 392. *Bréf og ritgerðir* III: 257. To Theodóra Thoroddsen November 12, 1925.
55. *Bréf og ritgerðir* IV: 390. To Baldur Sveinsson January 27, 1925.

Chapter 18

1. *Bréf og ritgerðir* III: 304-305. To Jóhannes P. Pálsson May 11, 1926.
2. *Heimskringla* April 6, 1927.
3. Letter to the author from Haraldur Bessason, September 2003.
4. *Bréf til Stephans G. Stephanssonar* III: 114-115. From Guttormur J. Guttormsson October 22, 1926.
5. *Bréf og ritgerðir* III: 344-345. To Guttormur J. Guttormsson November 8, 1926.
6. Lbs 4901 4to. Letter from Jónas Hall to Sigtryggur Guðlaugsson August 3, 1926.
7. *Heimskringla* August 11, 1926.
8. "Vökulok" *Bréf og ritgerðir* IV: 253-254.
9. *Bréf og ritgerðir* III: 319. To Helga Stephansson August 9, 1926.
10. *Bréf og ritgerðir* III: 326. To Jón Jónsson October 8, 1926.
11. *Andvökur* IV: 86.
12. Lbs 556 fol. Letter from Helga Stephansson to Rögnvaldur Pétursson December 18, 1926.
13. *Bréf og ritgerðir* III: 353-354. To Baldur Sveinsson December 20, 1926.
14. *Andvökur* IV: 403.
15. *Bréf og ritgerðir* III: 355. To Jónas Hall January 8, 1927.
16. Lbs 556 fol. Letter from Helga Stephansson to Rögnvaldur Pétursson January 16, 1927.
17. *Bréf og ritgerðir* III: 358-359. To Jónas Hall February 2, 1927.
18. Lbs. 5007 4to. Letter to Stephan from Magnús Jónsson from Fjall February 25, 1927.
19. Lbs 5007 4to. Letter to Stephan from Björgvin Guðmundsson March 19, 1927.
20. *Bréf og ritgerðir* III: 368-369. To Björgvin Guðmundsson April 8, 1927.
21. *Andvökur* IV: 71-80.
22. *Bréf og ritgerðir* III: 372-374. To Grímur S. Grímsson April 12 and Jónas Hall April 25, 1927.
23. *Andvökur* IV: 97.
24. Lbs 4348 4to. Letter from Helga Stephansson to Jóhannes P. Pálsson June 9, 1927.
25. *Bréf og ritgerðir* III: 382. To Grímur S. Grímsson July 1, 1927.
26. *Andvökur* IV: 98.
27. Interview with Edwin Stephenson October 26, 2000.

Bibliography

UNPUBLISHED SOURCES

National and University Library of Iceland, Manuscript Department
Manuscripts relating to Stephan G. Stephansson
Lbs 2180-2183 8vo. Poems compiled by Sigmundur Long, one of them assigned to Stephan G. Stephansson.
Lbs 4495 8vo. Letters, poems, and Guðmundur Stefánsson's travelogue.
Lbs 2950-2952 4to. Correspondence and miscellania. Lbs 1532-1533 4to. Stephan's manuscript to *Andvökur* I-III.
Lbs 2953-2955 4to. Miscellania, drafts, and manuscripts, notebooks etc.
Lbs 3870 4to. Poems and drafts, notebook from 1873.
Lbs 4400 4to Plays and fragments of plays.
Lbs 4585 4to. Letters to Jón Jónsson, Jr.
Lbs 4698 4to. Manuscript fragments of an autobiography.
Lbs 4925 4to. Letters from Stephan and Jónas Hall to Reverend Jón Bjarnason, Skapti Brynjólfsson et. al.
Lbs 5007 4to. Letters to Stephan G. Stephansson.
Lbs 5080 4to. Indriði Einarsson's correspondence.
Lbs 515-519 fol. Scrapbooks.
Lbs 525 fol. The handwritten newsletter *Fjalla-Eivindur*.
Lbs 556 fol. Rögnvaldur Péturssons correspondence relating to Stephan G. Stephansson.

Other manuscripts
Lbs 4258-4259 8vo. The diaries of Jón Jónsson from Mjóidalur.
Lbs 4901 4to. Letters from Jónas Hall to Rev. Sigtryggur Guðlaugsson of Núpur.
Lbs without number. The diaries of Steinn Dofri.

National Archives of Iceland
ÞÍ E 154. Documents from the invitation committee in 1917.
ÞÍ E 243. Hermann Jónasson's papers. Essay on Stephan G. Stephansson.

The Árni Magnússon Institute
Microfilm of a poetry manuscript, including a few from Stephan's youth.

The Local Archive at Húsavík
HHús E/173-11. Stephan's manuscript of the poem „Ég".

Red Deer and District Archives
Papers of Rosa Benediktson, Red Deer and District Archives, Acc. No. 003-106.

Wisconsin Historical Socety Archives
MAD 4 /19/D5-E5. Rasmus B. Anderson Papers.
MAD 4/14/SC 1986. Sarah Schoyen Thompson. "Reminiscences", 1930.
M97-130. Chester H. Thordarson Collection.

Green Bay og Shawano Courthouse
Naturalization Records of Guðmundur Stefánsson, Area Research Center, University of Wisconsin - Green Bay.
Stephan's and Helga's certification of marriage.

Pembina Courthouse
Letters of citizenship for Stephan and his mother, Guðbjörg Hannesdóttir. Preemption no. 4188.
Mortgage records for Pembina County. Book 2: 333; book 32: 164; book 19: 312-315; book 32: 31; book 31: 593-596.

Winnipeg
Records of the Icelandic Cultural Society. Icelandic Collection, Elizabeth Dafoe Library, University of Manitoba.

Privately owned documents
"Skrifbók Guðna Jónssonar á Eyjardalsá". A manuscript belonging to the descendants of Gunnar Guðnason, son of Guðni Jónsson, who was a first cousin to Stephan G. Stephansson. The manuscript contains a number of poems from Stephan G. Stephansson's youth in Iceland as well as his first years in North America.
„Abstract of title to Lot 1 Section 25 Township 28 Range 17. Photocopy in the possession Douglas Yanke, Underhill, Oconto, Wisconsin.

Two letters from Stephan G. Stephansson to Hermann Guðnason at Hvarf in Bárðardalur, son of Guðni Jónsson, Stephan's cousin. Owned by Jón Hermannsson, Hvarf in Bárðardalur.
The papers of Edwin Stephenson, Markerville, Alberta. In the possession of the author.
Kristín Olafson. „Gardar School District No. 26" A typed account, preserved at The State Historical Museum, Pembina County, North Dakota.
Homestead patent and contract of sale for Stephan's land at Gardar, North Dakota, in the possession of John H. Johnson at Gardar, grandson of Stephan's brother-in-law Jón Jónsson (Johnson), Jr.
Jón Jónsson from Mýri. "Minningar" ("Memoirs"). A typed manuscript owned by Heimir Pálsson).
Sigurður Þórólfsson's archive. Letter from Stephan to Þórólfur Sigurðsson.

PUBLISHED SOURCES

Stephan G. Stephansson's writings (in chroniological order, titles translated to English)
"Two letters from Shawano", signed by Stephan and a few others, *Norðanfari*, September 14, 1878 and July 31, 1879.
Úti' á víðavangi, flokkur af tíu smákvæðum (*Out in the Wilderness*, a collection of ten small poems) Winnipeg 1894.
Á ferð og flugi, kvæðabálkur (*En Route*: a cycle of poems) Reykjavík 1900.
Andvökur I-III (*Wakeful Nights*) Reykjavík. 1909-1910.
Kolbeinslag, gamanríma (a humorous ballad) Winnipeg 1914.
[No title nor year] Selected poems reprinted in 1917 intended for fundraising for Stephan's visit to Iceland. Assumed to be edited by Guðmundur Finnbogason and Ágúst H. Bjarnason.
Heimleiðis (*Homeward Bound*) Reykjavík 1917.
Vígslóði (*Trail of War*) Reykjavík 1920.
Andvökur IV-V Winnipeg 1923.
"Nokkrar endurminingar frá Garðar" ("A Few Memoirs from Gardar") in Jackson, Thorstina. *Saga Íslendinga í Norður Dakota* (*A History of Icelanders in North Dakota*), Winnipeg 1926: 297-299.
Andvökur VI Reykjavík 1938.
Bréf og ritgerðir I-IV (*Letters and Essays*). Ed. Þorkell Jóhannesson. Reykjavík 1938-1948.
Andvökur (selected poems). Ed. Sigurður Nordal with an introductory essay.

Reykjavík 1939.
Úrvalsljóð (*Selected Poems*). Ed. by Unnur Benediktsdóttir Bjarklind. Reykjavík 1945.
Guðmundsson, Þóroddur. *Guðmundur Friðjónsson. Ævi og störf* Reykjavík 1950 (includes 3 letters from Stephan, pp. 171-175).
Andvökur I-IV. Þorkell Jóhannesson editor. Reykjavík 1953-58.
Gullregn úr ljóðum Stephans G. Stephanssonar (*Rain of Gold from Stephan G. Stephansson's Poems*). The poet Jóhannes úr Kötlum compiled the poems and wrote and essay on Stephan. Reykjavík 1967.
Frá einu ári Kvæði, bréf og erindi frá árinu 1891 (*From one year. Poems, Letters and Speeches from the year 1891*). Ed. by Finnbogi Guðmundsson. Reykjavík 1970.
"Fjögur sendibréf frá Stephani G. Stephanssyni" ("Four letters from Stephan G. Stephansson") *Árbók Þingeyinga* 16 (1973): 109-117.
Finnbogi Guðmundsson. "Tvö gömul erfiljóð Stephans G. Stephanssonar" ("Two old elegies by Stephan G. Stephansson") *Árbók Landsbókasafns Íslands* 1989: 104-111.
Finnbogi Guðmundsson. "Bætt um betur" ("An Addition"). *Ritmennt* 1(1996): 148-150.
„Bréf til Jóns Kjærnested" (Letters to Jóns Kjærnested) ed. Kirsten Wolf. *Skírnir*, 166 (vor 1992): 41-61.
Böðvar Guðmundsson. "Þrjú óbirt bréf frá Stephani G." ("Three unpublished letters from Stephan G.") *Andvari* 39 (Nýr flokkur 1997): 148-159.
Andvökur Nýtt úrval. (A new selection) Finnbogi Guðmundsson valdi. Reykjavík 1998.

Translations

"Motes in a Sun-Beam", in *Western Icelandic Short Stories*. Translated by Kirsten Wolf and Árný Hjaltadóttir, Winnipeg 1992 (Nine pieces of prose that originally appeared in *Heimskringla* 1894-1901, reprinted in *Bréf og ritgerðir* IV, pp. 41-76, entitled "Buried Alive", "The Morning Breeze", "Greybeard", "Charity and Fairness", "Foreboding", "The Last Plover", "The Death of Old Guðmundur the Student: Half-stolen and Half-created", "The New Hat", "The Seventh Day").
Selected Translations from Andvökur, edited by Jane Ross. Edmonton 1987.
Selected Prose & Poetry. Translated by Kristjana Gunnars. Red Deer 1988.
In Finnbogi Guðmundsson's collection of essays, *Stephan G. Stephansson in Retrospect*, a number of quotations are translated by Kristjana Gunnars.
Two lands, One Poet. An anthology edited by Mooréa Gray, forthcoming.

Bibliography

Several translations by Bernard Scudder are accessible on the Stephan G. Stephansson website: *http://www.stephangstephansson.com/*.

Other printed publications

Adler, Felix. *Creed and Deed. A Series of Discourses*. New York 1977.

Alberta Horse and Cattle Brands. Being brands allotted for the first time and old brands renewed or changed during the years 1919 and 20. Published by the authority of Hon. Duncan Marshall, Minister of Agriculture. Edmonton 1921.

The Great West Before 1900. Alberta in the 20th Century I. Edmonton 1991.

Almanak Ólafs S. Thorgeirssonar. Winnipeg 1895-1954.

Along the Burnt Lake Trail. Red Deer 1977.

Arendt, Hannah, *The Human Condition*. Chicago 1998 [1953]

Bakthtin, M. M. *Speech Genres and Other late Essays*. Austin 1986.

Bakthtin, M. M. *Toward a Philosophy of the Act*. Austin 1993.

Balle, N. E. *Lærdómskver í evangelisk-kristilegum Trúarbrögðum handa Unglingum*. Reykjavík 1869.

Beck, Richard (ed). *Icelandic Poems and Stories. Translations from Modern Icelandic Literature*. New York 1943.

Beck, Richard. *History of Icelandic Poets 1800-1940*. Islandica 34. Ithaca 1950.

Benediktsson, Rósa. "Stephan G. Stephansson & Helga Jónsdóttir". Translated by Nina Campbell, in *My Parents. Memoirs of New World Icelanders*. Ed. Birna Bjarnadóttir and Finnbogi Guðmundsson. Winnipeg 2007: 17-31. Also in Joanne White: *Stephan's Daughter*: 19-30.

Benediktson, Rosa. "From Wisconsin to North Dakota to Alberta", in Joanne White: *Stephan's Daughter*. Calgary 2003: 11-12.

Benediktson, Rosa. "Speech for an Anniversary of Gudbjorg Hannesdottir", in Joanne White: *Stephan's Daughter*. Calgary 2003: 7-10.

Benediktson, Rosa. "My Old Home", in Joanne White: *Stephan's Daughter*. Calgary 2003: 127-129.

Bergmann, Friðrik. "Skyldur vorar við Ísland". *Sameiningin*, May 1888: 33-40.

Bessason, Haraldur. "Where the Limitations of Language and Geography Cease to Exist". *The Icelandic Canadian* 25, 4 (1967): 47-53, 72-76.

Biographical Review of Dane County, Wisconsin. Chicago 1893.

Birkiland, Jóhannes. *Harmsaga æfi minnar* III. Reykjavík 1946.

Bjarnason, Ágúst H. "Frá Vesturheimi. Stephan G. Stephansson sóttur heim". *Iðunn* 8 (1923-1924): 21-31.

Bjarnason, Jóhann Magnús. "Endurminning um Stephan G. Stephansson." *Tímarit Þjóðræknisfélags Íslendinga* 9 (1927): 46-49.

Bréf til Stephans G. Stephanssonar I-III (Letters to Stephan G. Stephansson). (Ed.) Finnbogi Guðmundsson. Reykjavík 1971-1975.

Brooks, Van Wyck. *America's Coming-of-Age*. New York 1958 [1934]

Brown, Craig (ed.). *The Illustrated History of Canada* Toronto 2000 [1987].

Bumsted, J. M. *The Peoples of Canada. A Post-Confederation History*. Toronto 1992.

Carleton, Peter. "Tradition and Innovation in Twentieth Century Icelandic Poetry". Doctoral thesis, Berkeley University 1967.

Cawley, F. Stanton. „The Greatest Poet of the Western World: Stephan G. Stephansson" *Scandinavian Studies and Notes* 15 (1938-39): 99-109.

Clark, Neil M. "The Flare of the Northern Lights Started Thordarson on his Quest" *The American Magazine*. December 1926.

Cook, Ramsay. "The Triumphs and Trials of Materialism." *The Illustrated History of Canada*, ed. by Craig Brown, Toronto 2000 [1987]: 375-266.

Crane, Stephen. *Maggie, a Girl of the Streets*. San Francisco 1968 [1893].

Emerson, Ralph Waldo. *Essays and Lectures*. New York 1983.

Friesen, Gerald. *The Canadian Prairies - A History*. Toronto 1987.

Geirdal, Vigfús. "Foreigners they Will be no Longer in this Country". MA thesis, Uppsala University 1998.

Gilbert, Armida. "Emerson in the Context of the Woman's Rights Movement" in Joel Myerson (ritstjóri) *A Historical Guide to Ralph Waldo Emerson* New York 2000: 211-249.

Gray, James H. *Red Lights on the Prairies*. Calgary 1995 [1971].

Gray, James H. *Booze: When Whisky Ruled the West*. Calgary 1995 [1972].

Grub-Axe to Grain. Calgary 1973.

Gudmundson, V. Emil. *The Icelandic Unitarian Connection - Beginnings of Icelandic Unitarianism in North America 1885-1900*. Winnipeg 1984.

Guðmundsson, Finnbogi. *Stephan G. Stephansson in Retrospect*. Reykjavík 1982.

Gunnars, Kristjana. "Preface", in Stephan G. Stephansson. *Selected Prose and Poetry* Red Deer 1988: vii-xi.

Gunnars, Kristjana. "Translating the Subaltern". *Canadian Ethnic Studies* 29.3 (1997): 75-82.

Gunnlaugsson, Björn. *Njóla eða hugmynd um alheimsáformið*. Reykjavík 1884 [1842]

Hobsbawm, Eric. *The Age of Empire 1875-1914*. London 1987.

Hobsbawm, Eric. *The Age of Extremes. A History of the World, 1914-1991*. London 1994.

Hreinsson, Viðar. "The Power of the Word: Some Reflections on 'The

Icelandic Academy'" *The Icelandic Canadian* 51, 2 (1992): 90-104.
Hreinsson, Viðar. "The Barnyard Poet. Stephan G. Stephansson (1853-1927)" *Nordic Experiences: Exploration of Sandinavian Cultures.* (ed. Berit I Brown) Westport 1997: 97-113.
Hreinsson, Viðar. "Metaphors of Care and Growth: The Poetic Language of Stephan G. Stephansson." *Canadian Ethnic Studies* 29.3 (1997): 51-63.
Hreinsson, Viðar. "Unheard Thunder: Stephan G Stephansson" *Rediscovering Canadian Difference. Ed.* Guðrun Guðsteinsdóttir. The Nordic Association for Canadian Studies Text Series 17. Reykjavík 2001.
Hreinsson, Viðar. "The Poet in the Pigpen: Stephan G. Stephansson" *Rustica Nova. The New Countryside and Transformations in Operating Environment.* Eds. Kalle Pihlainen and Erik Tirkkonen. Turku 2002: 179-194.
Hreinsson, Viðar. "The Icelanders in North America" in *Nordic Immigration to North America. Ed.* Faith Ingwersen. Madison: Nordic Culture Curriculum Project 2002: 49-58.
Houser, George A. *Pioneer Icelandic Pastor: The Life of the Reverend Paul Thorlaksson.* Winnipeg 1990.
Hreinsson, Viðar. "Stephan G. Stephansson" *Dictionary of Literary Biography,* Vol 293 Detroit 2004: 328-343.
Hunford. Jónas. "Stutt ágrip af Landnámssögu Íslendinga í Albertahéraði". *Almanak Ólafs S. Thorgeirssonar.* Winnipeg 1909-1914.
Indriðason, Indriði. "Endurminning frá sumrinu 1917" *Andvari.* Nýr flokkur 100 (1975): 116-123.
Ingersoll, Robert G. *The Works of Robert G. Ingersoll* I-XII. New York 1903.
Jackson, Thorstina. *Saga Íslendinga í Norður Dakota.* Winnipeg 1926.
Jensdóttir, Sólrún. „Books Owned by Ordinary People in Iceland 1750-1830" Saga-Book 19, 2-3 (1975-1976): 264-92
Jochumsson, Matthías. *Bréf Matthíasar Jochumssonar.* Reykjavík 1935.
Johnson, Raelene. "Individual Idealism in the Realistic Poetry of Stephan G. Stephansson." *The Icelandic Canadian* 49 (1990-91): 9-19.
Johnson, Skuli. "Stephan G. Stephansson" *The Icelandic Canadian* 9 (1950): 9-12, 44-56. Reprinted in *The Icelandic Canadian* 50,4 (1992): 268-284.
Johnson. Sveinbjörn. "The Icelandic Settlement of Pembina County". *Collections of the State Historical Society of North Dakota* I. Bismarck 1906: 89-131.
Johnson, Thorvaldur. "Stephan G. Stephansson and Thomas Hardy - a Comparison" *The Icelandic Canadian* 33 (1974): 39-44.
Jones, David C. *Feasting on Misfortunes. Journeys of the Human Spirit in Alberta's Past.* Edmonton 1998.

Jónasson, Jónas. *Hofdala Jónas. Sjálfsævisaga, frásöguþættir, bundið mál.* Editors Hannes Pétursson and Kristmundur Bjarnason. Akureyri 1979.

Jónsson, Björn B. "Vestur-Íslendingar og stríðið". *Minningarbók íslenskra hermanna 1914-1918.* Winnipeg 1923: 41-46.

Jónsson, Jón (John Johnson). "Mylluferð í marz 1881", in Stephan G. Stephansson. *Bréf og ritgerðir* IV: 108-110.

Jónsson, Stefán. *Ritsafn* III. Sauðárkrókur 1986.

Kealey, Gregory S. and Whitaker, Reg (eds.). *R.C.M.P. Security Bulletins. The Early Years 1919-1929.* St. John's Canadian Committe on Labour History (1994).

Literary History of Canada I-II. Ed. Carl F. Klinck. Toronto and Buffalo 1965.

Watson Kirkconnell. "Canada's Leading Poet: Stephan G. Stephansson (1853-1927)". *University of Toronto Quarterly* 5,2 (1936): 263-77.

Kristinsson, Júníus H. *Vesturfaraskrá 1870-1914.* Reykjavík 1983.

Kristjanson, Wilhelm. *The Icelandic People in Manitoba.* Winnipeg 1965.

Kristjánsson, Andrés. *Af lífi og sál, Andrés Kristjánsson ræðir við Ásgeir Bjarnþórsson.* Reykjavík 1975.

Mardiros, Anthony. *William Irvine, The Life of a Prairie Radical.* Toronto 1979.

Maurer, Konrad. *Íslandsferð 1858.* Translated from German by Baldur Hafstað. Reykjavík 1997.

McCracken, Jane. *Stephan G. Stephansson: The Poet of the Rocky Mountains* (Historic Sites Service Occasional Paper No. 9) Edmonton 1982.

Melnyk, George. *The Literary History of Alberta.* Volume One. From Writing-on-Stone to World War Two. Edmonton 1998.

Merk, Frederick. *Econonic History of Wisconsin During the Civil War Decade.* State Historical Society of Wisconsin, Madison 1916: 103-104.

Milnes, H. "Stephan G. Stephansson." *New Frontiers* (1953) 1-7.

Minningarbók íslenskra hermanna 1914-1918. Winnipeg 1923: 41-46.

Moede, Ila Hill. *Grandma's Footprints: A History of Shawano, Wisconsin 1843-1918.* Shawano 1991.

Morkeberg, Carl. *Markerville Story.* Offprint from *The Innisfail Province*, stories that appeared 1967-1971. Innisfail, no date.

Mowat, Carol. "Stephan G. Stephansson's Affirmation of Human Resilience in the Poem 'Sól-laukur'". *The Icelandic Canadian* 48,3 (1990): 9-11.

Mowat, Carol. "Stephan G. Stephansson. An Idealist or a Materialist". M. A. thesis, University of Manitoba, Winnipeg 1990.

My Parents. Memoirs of New World Icelanders. Edited by Birna Bjarnadóttir and Finnbogi Guðmundsson. Winnipeg 2007.

Myerson, Joel. (ed.) *A Historical Guide to Ralph Waldo Emerson*. New York 2000.
Neijmann, Daisy. *The Icelandic Voice in Canadian Letters*. Ottawa 1997.
Nordal, Sigurður. "Samlagning" in *Ritverk. List og lífsskoðun* II. Reykjavík 1987: 394 (originally published in 1927).
Olafson, Magnus. "Gardar Township." *Heritage 89. Pembina County North Dakota* Cavalier 1988.
Parrington, Vernon Louis. *Main Currents in American Thought. An Interpretation on American Literature from the Beginnings to 1920*. I-III. New York 1958 [1927, 1930].
Plat Book of Grand Forks, Walsh & Pembina Co's North Dakota 1893.
Pálsson, Gestur. *Ritsafn. Sögur – kvæði – fyrirlestrar – blaðagreinar*. Reykjavík 1927.
Pálsson, Jóhannes P. "Stephan G. Stephansson. (nokkur orð um skáldið og manninn)". *Tímarit Þjóðræknisfélags Íslendinga* 9 (1927): 37-45.
Pétursson, Rögnvaldur. *Fögur er foldin*. Reykjavík 1950
Ricoeur, Paul. *Time and Narrative* I. Chicago 1984.
Ruff, Allen, and Tracy Will. *Forward! A History of Dane: the Capital County*. Cambridge, Wisconsin 2000.
Robinson, Elwyn B. *History of North Dakota*. Lincoln, Nebraska 1966.
Ruland, Richard and Bradbury, Malcolm. *From Puritanism to Postmodernism. A History of American Literature*. New York 1991.
Sod Shacks and Wagon Tracks. Red Deer 1987.
Service, Robert. *Collected Poems of Robert Service*. Toronto, Montreal 1960.
Sigurðsson, Ólafur. "Stephan G. Stephansson. Nokkrar minningar og viðtöl við hann sumarið 1917" *Heima er bezt* 11, 7 (1961).
Stefánsson, Davíð. "kynni mín af séra Matthíasi". *Mælt mál*. Reykjavík 1963: 24-38.
Susman, Warren I. *Culture as History* New York 1984 [1973].
Thor, Jonas. *Icelanders in North America: the first Settlers*. Winnipeg 2002.
Thoreau, Henry David. *Walden*. Oxford 1997 [1854].
Undína [Helga Steinvör Baldvinsdóttir]. *Kvæði*. Reykjavík 1952.
Vagnsson, Stefán. *Úr fórum Stefáns Vagnssonar frá Hjaltastöðum. Frásöguþættir, þjóðsögur og bundið mál*. Editor Hannes Pétursson. Reykjavík 1976.
Veblen, Thorstein. *The Theory of the Leisure Class*. New York 1934 [1899].
Vermeyden, Paula. "Um hinn eldri kveðskap Stephans G Stephanssonar". *Árbók Landsbókasafns Íslands* 3 (Nýr flokkur 1978): 50-75.
Vilhjálmsson, Konráð. "Af blöðum Konráðs Vilhjálmssonar". *Árbók*

Þingeyinga (1964): 87-91.

Vilhjálmsson, Vilhjálmur S. *Tak hnakk þinn og hest. Minningaþættir Páls Guðmundssonar á Hjálmsstöðum*. Reykjavík 1954.

Vídalín, Jón Þorkelsson. *Vídalínspostilla*. Edited by Gunnar Kristjánsson and Mörður Árnason. Reykjavík 1995 [1720]

Waite, Peter. "Between Three Oceans: Challenges of a Continental Destiny 1840-1900". *The Illustrated History of Canada*, ed. by Craig Brown, Toronto 2000 [1987]: 278-374.

Walz, Gene. *Cartoon Charlie. The Life and Art of Animation Pioneer Charles Thorson*. Winnipeg 1998.

White, Joanne. *Stephan's Daughter. The Story of Rosa Siglaug Benediktson*. Calgary 2003.

Whitman, Walt. *Leaves of Grass*. The First (1855) Edition. New York 1959.

Whitman, Walt. *Leaves of Grass*. (The Deathbed Edition). Oxford 1998 [1891-2].

Whyte, Bertha Kitchell. *Wisconsin Heritage* Boston 1954.

Wiebe, Robert H. *The Search for Order. 1877-1920*. New York 1967.

Woodsworth, James S. *Strangers Within our Gates*. Toronto 1972.

Ziff, Larzer. „Introduction" in *Selected Essays by* Ralph Waldo Emerson. New York 1982: 7-27.

Papers

Framfari (Lundur, Icelandic River, Manitoba) 1877-1880.

Heimskringla (Winnipeg) 1886-1959.

The Index (Boston) 1885-1886.

Leifur (Winnipeg)1883-1886.

Lögberg (Winnipeg) 1888-1959.

The Northern Express (Pembina, Dakota Territories) 1882.

The Pioneer Express (Pembina, Dakota Territories) 1882-1884.

The Province (Innisfail) 1906-1927.

Websites

Hreinsson, Viðar. „Folly in Tailcoat or Multiculturalism" in the cultural website Kistan: *http://kistan.is/default.asp?sid_id=28001&tre_rod=004|&tId=2&FRE_ID=39447&Meira=1.*

Hreinsson, Viðar and Helgason, Jón Karl (editors). "The Icelandic Emigration" a website at the Icelandic National Broadcasting Service: *http://servefir.ruv.is/vesturfarar/*. This website contains some material by and related to Stephan G. Stephansson, such as his fathers travel account: *http://servefir.ruv.is/vesturfarar/e/FyrGudmund.html.*

Index

Icelanders are indexed by first name.

Abel, in the Bible, 318
Adler, Felix, American freethinker, 193, 204, 211
Ahasuerus, the wandering Jew, 410
Anderson, Rasmus B., Professor of Norwegian descent, 117, 121
Andrés Gíslason, in Manitoba, 382
Andri the earl, fictional character, 50, 51, 199
Angantýr, Old Norse legendary character, 290
Anna Hannesdóttir, Stephan's great grandmother, 31
Anna Hannesdóttir, Stephan's maternal aunt, 34, 53
Arngrímur Gíslason, painter in Iceland, 73, 85
Arngrímur Jónsson, in British Columbia, 387
Arthur, Chester A., President of the United States (1881-1886), 186
Arthur, Legendary King, 276
Athugull, pseudonym in *Heimskringla*, 373
Ágúst H. Bjarnason, Icelandic professor, 432, 436, 439, 440, 461, 508-510
Árni Bardal, husband of Fanny, Stephan's daughter, 425, 434, 495
Árni Sveinsson, Argyle, Manitoba, 357, 367, 482, 483
Árni Þórðarson, in Dakota, 150
Ársæll Árnason, Icelandic printer and publisher, 463
Ásgeir Bjarnþórsson, Icelandic painter and artist, 438
Ásgeir Líndal, in Dakota and Victoria BC, 204, 217, 325, 387, 389
Áslaug Hannesdóttir, Stephan's maternal aunt, 39
Baldur Olson, physician in Winnipeg, 540
Baldur Stephansson, Stephan's son, 140, 149, 150, 182, 200, 226, 227, 238, 272-274, 297, 299, 319, 320, 329, 330, 340, 382, 389, 426, 434, 495, 539, 555
Baldur Sveinsson, editor, 356, 370, 376, 377, 381, 394, 438, 458, 459, 462, 463, 474, 475, 513, 526, 527, 533, 538, 548, 549
Baldvin L. Baldvinsson, editor, 344, 345, 381
Baldvin Helgason, pioneer in Dakota, 150, 156, 175, 176
Ball, B.W., American poet, 194
Balle, N.E., Danish bishop, 50, 51, 194, 336
Balthasarsen, fictional character in a play by Stephan, 158
Balzac, Honore de, French writer, 288
Bardal, see Benedikt Jónsson Bardal
Bardal, bookseller in Winnipeg, 350
Benedikt Gröndal, Icelandic poet and teacher, 130, 131, 150
Benedikt Jónsson Bardal, from Mjóidalur, 70, 91, 106, 146, 149, 224, 225, 229, 235, 236, 238, 246, 273, 330

Benedikt Ólafsson, pioneer in Alberta, 224, 395, 396
Benedikt Sveinsson, member of the Icelandic parlament, 438
Bergmann, cousins, i.e. Eiríkur, Friðrik and Sigfús, 177, 185, 190
Bergur, character in a short story by Stephan, 316
Bessi Eiríksson, ferryman in Iceland, 65
Bjarni Thorarensen, sub-governor in North Iceland and poet, 111, 252
Björgvin Guðmundsson, composer, 550
Björn Gunnlaugsson, teacher and poet, 56, 57
Björn Halldórsson, carpenter in Dakota, 189, 198, 210, 221
Björn Jónsson, editor in Akureyri, 96
Björn Jónsson, pastor of Miklibær, 450
Björn B. Jónsson, pastor in Winnipeg, 407, 418
Björn Oddsson, hired man in Mjóidalur, 82
Björn Pétursson, Unitarian pastor in Winnipeg, 192, 202, 203, 210, 231
Blavatsky, Helen Petrovna, writer and theosophist, 270
Borden, Robert, Prime Minister of Canada, 380, 467, 468
Bólu-Hjálmar Jónsson, poet, 54, 62, 63
Bósi, Old Norse legendary character, 54
Brandes, George, Danish literary critic, 174, 250, 253, 278
Brandur, farmhand in Alberta, 487
Brandur J. Brandsson, physician in Winnipeg, 477
Bríet Bjarnhéðinsdóttir, woman's rights activist and editor, 469
Brown, James, in Alberta, 236
Bruno, Giordano, Italian philosopher, 214
Brynjólfsson brothers, see Skafti and Magnús Brynjólfsson,
Brynjólfur Brynjólfsson, in Dakota, 198, 205
Buckmaster, English politician, 499
Burns, Robert, Scottish poet, 399
Byron, lord, English poet, 271
Böðvar, Old Norse legendary character, 412
Börtel, Norwegian farmer in Wisconsin, 113
Cain, in the Bible, 318, 491, 492, 535
Castelo, Jack, lumberjack in Wisconsin, 129
Christ (Jesus), 50-52, 248, 253, 258, 292-294, 315, 410, 499, 501-504
Christian IX, King of Denmark, 426
Cochrane, in Alberta, 281
Columbus, Christopher, explorer, 117
Conway, Moncure D., American Unitarian Minister, 194
Courmont, André, French Consul in Reykjavík, 529-532, 542
Cowshed-Gunna, fictional character in a play by Stephan, 158, 159
Coynbeare, Charles P., lawyer and poet in Alberta, 276
Crane, Stephan, American writer, 310, 311
Cromwell, Oliver, Lord Protector of England, 480
Crusoe, Robinson, fictional person, 269
Curly, little girl in Wisconsin, 131, 133, 134
Dagbjört Anna Jónsdóttir, relative of Stephan, 35, 39
Daisy, character in a poem, 310
Daníel Árnason, at Mikley in Iceland, 451
Darwin, Charles, English naturalist, 193

Davíð Stefánsson, Icelandic poet, 447-449, 461, 462, 546
Dicke, German Pastor in Wisconsin, 120
Dickens, Charles, English novelist, 271, 311
Dolly, horse, 159
Dreyfus, Alfred, French officer, 378
DuBois, W.E.B., civil rights activist, 421
Edwin Stephansson, grandson of Stephan, 554, 555
Eggert Gunnarsson, from Laufás, 93
Eggert Jóhannsson, editor in Winnipeg, 231, 236, 237, 251, 342, 343, 345-347, 349-352, 355, 356, 361, 363, 364, 367, 373, 375, 376, 381, 385-387, 389, 426, 493, 513
Eggert Stefánsson, Icelandic opera singer, 507
Egill Gottskálksson at Vellir, 29, 54
Egill Sigvaldason, Stephan's cousin, 39
Egill Skallagrímsson, a saga hero and poet, 298, 364, 366, 536-538
Einar, character in a short story by Stephan, 316
Einar Benediktsson, Icelandic poet, 535, 536
Einar Hannesson, farmer at Víðimýri and Mælifellsá, 34, 41, 42
Einar Hjörleifsson, poet and editor, 250, 252, 311, 312, 348
Einar Jónsson, Icelandic sculptor, 478, 479, 539
Einar Páll Jónsson, editor in Winnipeg, 517
Einar Stefánsson, farmer at Reynistaður, 32, 33, 41
Eiríkur Hjálmarsson Bergmann, merchant in Dakota, 127, 150, 152-154, 156, 159-163, 167, 169-171, 176, 177, 184, 186-188, 195, 196, 217, 351
Elg-Fróði, Old Norse legendary character, 291
Eliot, George, English writer, 311
Eliot, Thomas S., American poet, 528, 529, 531
Elín Gunnarson, running a guesthouse in Akureyri, 65
Elín Hjörleifsdóttir, wife of Eggert Jóhannsson, 342, 356
Elínborg Pétursdóttir, wife of Reverend Sigurður Arnórsson, 42
Emerson, Ralph Waldo, American writer and freethinker, 111, 165, 166, 172, 192, 193, 194, 204, 215, 249, 266, 323
Emil V. Sommerleaf, pseudonym for Jóhannes Birkiland, 472
Emilía Sigurbjörg Jónsdóttir, in Dakota, 195
Erik, Prince of Denmark, 426
Erna Eggertsdóttir, daughter of Eggert Jóhannsson, 356, 361
Fjalla-Eyvindur Jónsson, Icelandic outlaw, 162
Flaten, Christian, Norwegian pastor in Dakota, 161
Frank, pharmacist in Dakota, 116
Franz Ferdinand, Austrian Archduke, 406
Freud, Sigmund, Austrian psychologist, 528
Friðgeir Jóakimsson Bardal, husband of Sigríður Jónsdóttir, 81
Friðrik J. Bergmann, pastor in New Iceland, 86, 87, 127, 130, 167, 170, 175-177, 187, 191, 207, 216, 230, 231, 238, 251, 309, 312, 347-349, 354-356, 359, 370, 435
Friðrika Baldvinsdóttir, in Dakota, 98
Friðþjófur, Old Norse legendary character, 55
Frímann B. Arngrímsson, Electrical engineer, 203
Frosti, Old Norse semi-god, 314

Fróði, legendary Danish King, 178
Fuller, Margaret, American womens rights advocate, 165
Gaetz, Hezekiel, in Alberta, 239, 282
Garðar Svavarsson, Norse Viking Age explorer, 153
Garrison, William Lloyd Jr., American writer, 193
Garrison, William Lloyd Sr., American journalist and reformer, 193
Geary, William, pharmacist in Alberta, 409, 410
Gertrud, fictional character in a play by Stephan, 158, 159
Gestur Cecil Stephansson, 264, 272, 319, 320, 361-365, 367, 381, 403, 510
Gestur Pálsson, Icelandic poet and editor, 246, 250-254, 264, 275, 278, 288, 311
Gillingham, Rich, in Alberta, 259, 260, 264
Gísli Jónsson Dalmann, brother of Jón Jónsson from Mjóidalur, 70, 87, 91, 106, 122, 123, 125, 149, 177, 184, 224, 225, 229, 235, 238, 241, 259, 261
Gísli Konráðsson, farmer and writer, 38, 50, 53, 54, 56, 111, 199
Glámur, a ghost in The Saga of Grettir the Strong, 290
Glæsir, Stephan's horse, 279, 280
Goodman, see Ólafur and Sigfús Goodman.
Grettir Ásmundarson the Strong, a saga hero, 47, 58, 61, 62, 280, 290, 313, 454, 536
Grímur, pseudonym in *Lögberg*, 535
Grímur Grímsson, in Alberta, 367, 429, 434, 469, 496, 500, 501, 513, 528, 553
Grímur Thomsen, poet and member of parlament (alþingi), 252
Grímur Þórðarson, in Dakota, 127, 150

Gróa Sigurðardóttir, wife of Skafti Brynjólfsson, 362, 413, 414
Grundtvig, N.F.S., pastor and writer in Denmark, 465
Gröndal, see Benedikt Gröndal.
Guðbjörg Guðmundsdóttir, wife of Jón Jónsson junior, 195
Guðbjörg Hannesdóttir, Stephan's mother, 30-33, 35, 36, 38, 40, 42, 44, 56, 58, 67, 79, 86, 89, 91, 96, 97, 101, 108, 113, 150, 182, 228, 232, 244, 299, 319, 374, 376, 377, 510
Guðbjörg Lilja Kristinsdóttir, daughter of Sigurlaug, Stephan's sister, 189, 226, 486, 496, 505
Guðfinna Jónsdóttir from Mjóidalur, 89, 91, 106, 195
Guðmundur Finnbogason, Director of the Icelandic National Library, 91, 416, 427, 428, 431-433, 439, 459, 460, 490, 497
Guðmundur Friðjónsson, poet and farmer, 332, 347, 372, 435, 443
Guðmundur Stefánsson, Stephan's father, 30-33, 35, 37-42, 45, 46, 53, 60, 63, 66, 67, 86, 89, 91, 92, 95, 96, 99-101, 106, 108-110, 113, 114, 117, 121-124, 134, 135, 139, 144, 145, 150, 152, 159-161, 195, 222
Guðmundur Stephansson (Mundi), Stephan's son, 161, 182, 200, 226, 227, 272-274, 297, 299, 319, 320, 330, 331, 336, 362, 381, 427-429, 434, 495, 508, 554, 555
Guðmundur stúdent, character in a short story by Stephan, 315, 316
Guðmundur the Good, Bishop in Holar, 315, 453, 454

Guðni Jónsson, from Eyjardalsá,
  Stephan's cousin, 66, 75,
  444, 446
Guðný Stefánsdóttir, Stephan's
  paternal aunt, 64, 66, 90,
  362, 444-446
Guðrún Grímsdóttir, widow of Þórður
  Árnason, 112, 127, 144,
  149, 150
Guðrún Ólöf Magnúsdóttir, wife of
  Friðrik Bergmann, 187
Gunnar Hámundarson, at Hlíðarendi,
  a saga hero, 313, 402
Gunnlaugur Ólafsson Briem, fostered
  at Halldórsstaðir, 87, 88
Guttormur J. Guttormsson, poet and
  farmer, 358, 359, 500, 516,
  543, 544
Halldór Briem, pastor and editor, 91
Halldór, fictional character in a play by
  Stephan, 158, 159
Halldóra Pétursdóttir, from Valadal, 60
Halldóra Þorbergsdóttir Fjeldsted,
  wife of Sigurður Júlíus
  Jóhannesson, 409
Hallgrímur Gíslason, in Dakota, 91,
  106, 110, 113, 114, 117, 121,
  122, 126, 144, 154, 155, 160,
  161, 171, 177, 219, 220, 388
Hallgrímur Pétursson, poet and pastor,
  364, 366, 396
Hamlet, character in Shakespeare's
  drama, 488
Hannes Frost Kristinsson, son of
  Sigurlaug, Stephan's sister,
  226, 496
Hannes Hafstein, Icelandic minister
  and poet, 173
Hannes Hannesson, brother of
  Guðbjörg Hannesdóttir, 32,
  38, 39, 44, 351
Hannes Jónsson, pastor at Glaumbær,
  34, 39, 40, 46, 51, 58-60, 452
Hannes Marinó Hannesson, lawyer
  in Winnipeg and relative
  of Stephan, 351, 428, 429,
  477, 545
Hannes Þorvaldsson, from
  Reykjarhóll, Stephan's
  maternal grandfather, 31, 42
Hans B. Thorgrimsen, pastor in New
  Iceland, 84, 160, 161, 176,
  177
Haraldur Þorláksson, from
  Stórutjarnir, 84, 109, 119
Harboe, Ludvig, Danish bishop, 51
Haywood, D. (Big Bill), leader of
  Miners Union, 388
Hákon, character in a short story by
  Stephan, 315, 316
Hálfdan Guðjónsson, pastor in
  Sauðárkrókur, 454, 455
Hegel, G.W.F., German philosopher,
  193
Heine, Heinrich, German poet, 382
Helga Davíðsdóttir, wife of Jón Strong,
  335, 336
Helga Guðmundsdóttir, Stephan's
  paternal grandmother, 30,
  31
Helga Jónsdóttir, from Eyjardalsá,
  Stephan's cousin, 66
Helga Sigríður Jónsdóttir, wife of
  Stephan, 71, 72, 88, 89, 92,
  113, 114, 125, 135, 137-140,
  150, 156, 160, 171, 174, 177,
  180, 182, 189, 195, 198, 201,
  202, 219-221, 224, 228, 229,
  232, 233, 235, 236, 238, 244,
  258, 261, 264, 267, 270, 273,
  280, 296, 297, 299, 319-322,
  328-330, 340, 356, 361-363,
  367, 372, 376, 381-384, 389,
  406, 416, 424, 426, 436, 452,
  459, 466, 472, 484, 485, 487,
  495-497, 505, 506, 508, 509,
  515, 526, 533, 541, 542, 547-
  549, 553-555
Helga Stefánsdóttir, Stephan's paternal
  aunt, 64, 66, 67, 80, 114

Helga Steinvör Baldvinsdóttir (Undína), poet, 97, 98, 156, 157, 176, 221
Helgi Jónasson, in Alberta, 281, 297
Hercules, Greek mythological character, 373
Herdís Jónsdóttir, wife of Hallgrímur Gíslason, 91, 106
Hermann Jónasson, fostered at Mýri, 67, 68
Herod, in the Bible, 208
Hervör, Old Norse legendary character, 290, 499
Hjalti, Old Norse legendary character, 412
Hjörtur J. Leó, pastor in British Columbia, 387
Hjörtur Þórðarson (Chester Thordarson), Electrical engineer, 112, 127, 145, 149, 150, 163, 372, 528
Hlér, Old Norse semi-god, 314
Holberg, Ludvig, Danish playwright and historian, 74
Holmes, Oliver Wendell, American poet, 121
Homme, Norwegian pastor, 120, 124, 126, 140
Hólmfríður Guðnadóttir, wife of Sigfús Goodman, 238
Hólmfríður Pétursdóttir, wife of Rögnvaldur Pétursson, 513
Hulda (Unnur Benediktsdóttir Bjarklind), Icelandic poet, 432, 443, 513, 549
Húsavíkurskotta, Icelandic ghost, 449
Ibsen, Henrik, Norwegian playwright, 253, 379
Illugi Ásmundarson, saga hero, brother of Grettir the Strong, 454
Illugi Helgason, from Nesvellir in the Mývatn District, poet, 488
Indriði Einarsson, economist and playwright, 55, 56, 461

Indriði Indriðason, from Fjall, writer and genealogist, 442, 443
Indriði Þorkelsson, at Fjall, farmer and poet, 442, 443
Inga Þórðarson, see Ingibjörg Þórðardóttir,
Ingersoll, Robert Green, American freethinker, 142, 193, 194, 207, 214
Ingibjörg Benediktsdóttir, Icelandic poet, 439
Ingibjörg Pétursdóttir Thorlacius, wife of Eiríkur Bergmann, 187
Ingibjörg Þórðardóttir in Wisconsin, 127, 143, 144
Irvine, William (Bill), socialist leader in Alberta, 434, 452, 469, 500
Jackson, in Alberta, 235
Jackson, Thorstína Canadian writer, 554
Jakob Líndal, in Dakota, 156, 157, 162, 171, 191, 204, 205, 210, 211, 219, 221, 387
Jakob J. Normann in Wynyard, 512, 513, 514, 534, 554
Jakob (Jake) Stephansson, 197, 200, 226, 227, 272, 319, 320, 331, 361, 363, 367, 381, 382, 391, 425, 426, 485, 487, 495, 496, 505, 515, 554, 555
Jakobína Johnson (Sigurbjörnsdóttir), poet in Seattle, 334, 388, 390, 513, 521
Jefferson, Thomas, President of the United States, (1801-1809) 200
Jensen, Lauritz H., running a guesthouse in Akureyri, 65
Johnson, Chris (Kristján Jónsson), in Duluth, 359, 367, 515, 533
Johnson (Grímur Einarsson), merchant in Markerville, 329, 331
Johnson, Pauline, poet in Canada,

Index 599

388-390
Johnson, Thomas H., Attorney
　General of Manitoba, 387,
　428, 434, 477, 493
Jóhann V. Austmann, Canadian
　soldier, 414
Jóhann Björnsson, settler in Alberta,
　245, 327, 328, 337, 494
Jóhann Magnús Bjarnason, teacher,
　poet and writer, 285-288,
　316, 332, 343, 356, 357, 386
Jóhannes P. Pálsson, physician and
　writer, 430, 516, 519, 521,
　527, 534, 540, 553
Jóhannes Stefánsson Birkiland,
　vagabond and writer, 472
Jón Austmann, pastor at
　Halldórsstaðir, 67, 78-80,
　86, 88
Jón Árnason, farmer of Víðimýri, 46,
　54-56, 59
Jón Ásgeirsson, farmer of Þingeyrar,
　48
Jón Benedictson (Benediktsson),
　merchant in Markerville,
　281, 282, 297, 328, 329, 362
Jón Bergmann, from Laugaland,
　Friðriks Bergmann's father,
　160
Jón J. Bíldfell, editor in Winnipeg, 482,
　491-495, 542, 546
Jón Bjarnason, pastor in Winnipeg,
　117, 134, 135, 140, 144, 161,
　176, 177, 189, 190, 202, 207-
　210, 216, 218, 230, 231, 301,
　312, 331, 347, 348, 354, 355,
　404, 405, 413
Jón Einarsson, wrote about Stephan in
　Heimskringla, 288
Jón Eldon, in Alberta, 320
Jón Gíslason Dalmann, 241
Jón Guðmundsson, teacher in Alberta,
　273, 274
Jón Halldórsson, in Mjóidalur, 70
Jón hrak (the Outcast) character in a
　folktale and poem by SGS,
　291, 440, 472, 524, 531
Jón Ingjaldsson, farmer at Eyjardalsá,
　66, 67
Jón Ingjaldsson, farmer at Mýri, 79
Jón Jónasson, physician in Dakota, 155
Jón Jónsson (John Johnson) Junior,
　from Mjóidalur, 71, 72, 89,
　114, 127, 135, 139, 140, 144,
　147, 148, 154-156, 195, 204,
　205, 219, 220, 351, 359, 381,
　389, 424, 425, 541, 542, 544
Jón Jónsson from Sleðbrjótur, in
　Manitoba, 392, 433, 469,
　472, 522, 524
Jón Jónsson, from Kolgröf, 155, 280,
　281
Jón Jónsson Senior, from Mjóidalur,
　68, 70-73, 78, 79, 82, 83, 85-
　89, 91, 92, 94, 101, 106, 110,
　113, 114, 121-125, 127, 134,
　135, 138, 139, 144-146, 149,
　152, 153, 159, 161, 178, 195,
　219, 238, 359, 545
Jón Jónsson, from Mýri, 86, 89, 360
Jón Jónsson Strong, farmer in Alberta,
　320, 322, 330, 335, 336, 363
Jón Kristinsson, first Icelandic baby
　born in Canada, 106
Jón Ólafsson, poet and editor, 245,
　250-252, 269, 271, 275-277,
　286, 295, 296, 304, 362, 372
Jón Pétursson, from Kolgröf, 231, 232
Jón Sigurðsson, philologist, Icelandic
　national hero, 478
Jón Stephansson, 189, 200-202, 222,
　333, 363
Jón Sveinsson, farmer in Alberta, 494
Jón Þorláksson, from Stórutjarnir, 123
Jón Þorláksson, of Bægisá, pastor and
　poet, 65
Jón Vídalín, bishop in Skálholt, 34, 40,
　53, 58, 232
Jóna Jónsdóttir, from Mjóidalur, 72
Jónas A. Sigurðsson, pastor in

Winnipeg, 545
Jónas Hall (Hallgrímsson), from Fremstafell, 151, 156, 170, 171, 189-191, 199, 204, 207, 219, 228, 236, 238, 244, 264, 281, 284, 351, 355, 359, 362, 385, 389, 430, 467, 511, 513, 516, 517, 524-526, 535, 536, 541, 542, 544, 545, 548-550, 552, 553
Jónas Hallgrímsson, Icelandic national poet, 65, 396, 402
Jónas Jónsson Hunford, settler in Alberta, 224, 225, 230, 267, 269, 270, 322, 493, 497, 499, 522, 523
Jónas Jónsson, at Vaglir, 450, 451, 454, 455, 457
Jónas Kortsson, in Dakota, 214
Jónatan Hallgrímsson, in Dakota, 114
Jónína Jónsdóttir, wife of Pétur Hjálmsson, 331
Jóný Sigurbjörg Stephansson, Stephan's daughter, 233, 272, 319, 320, 362, 381, 383, 425, 426, 485-487, 495, 496, 505, 506, 555
Jórunn Hannesdóttir, wife of Pétur Pálmason, 59
Jósefína Baldvinsdóttir, in Dakota, 98
Kant, Immanuel, German philosopher, 193, 204, 369
Karólína Jónsdóttir Dalmann, wife of Gísli Jónsson, 87, 91, 106, 122, 125, 156, 159, 165, 166, 184, 238, 241, 242, 258-263, 381
Kate, cow, 486
Káinn (Kristján Níels Júlíus Jónsson), poet and worker, 359, 467
Kipling, Rudyard, English writer, 400
Kitchener, Lord, British Secretary of State for War, 407
Kolbeinn, semi-historical poet and a character in a poem by Stephan, 396-403, 450
Kolgröf, see Jón Jónsson, from Kolgröf.
Konráð Gíslason Dalmann, 241
Konráð Gíslason, professor, 56
Kristian IX, King of Denmark, 123
Kristinn Kristinsson, husband of Sigurlaug, Stephan's sister, 127, 136, 148, 149, 162, 164, 166, 171, 177, 205, 220, 226, 240, 241, 244, 245, 264, 269, 273, 280, 281, 285, 286, 319, 322, 330, 364, 367, 384, 389, 425, 510, 514, 533, 535
Kristinn Stefánsson, from Egilsá, poet, 160, 171-174, 180, 183, 246
Kristjana Baldursdóttir, daughter of Baldur Sveinsson, 458
Kristján "Nuff" Benediktsson, in Mjóidalur, 72, 73, 79
Kristján Gíslason, in Seattle, 388
Kristján Ingjaldsson, at Mýri, 67, 96
Kristján Jónsson, see Johnson, Chris
Kristján Geiteyingur Jónsson, 404
Kristján Stefánsson, in Winnipeg, 352
Lambertsen, Guðmundur, merchant in Reykjavík, 93, 94
Laurenz, son of Eggert Jóhannsson, 363, 367
Laurier, Wilfred, Prime Minister of Canada, 324, 380, 367, 468
Lárus Guðmundsson, editor in Winnipeg, 389, 517-519, 527
Lárus H. Bjarnason, member of the Icelandic parliament, 440
Leifur Eiríksson, Norse Viking Age explorer, 117, 124
Lillie, daughter of Eggert Jóhannsson, 356
Lincoln, Abraham, President of The United States (1861-1865), 200, 204
Lindal, Walter, Judge in Winnipeg, 477
Linse, in Wisconsin, 125

Index 601

Lína, see Sigurlína Bardal.
Loftur Jónsson, carpenter, 127
Longfellow, Henry W., American poet, 121, 142
Louis, piglet, 486
Lovísa (Henrietta Lovísa) Níelsson, wife of Þorlákur Gunnar Jónsson, 91, 106, 121
Luther, Martin, German reformer, 270, 373, 379
Macdonald, John A., Prime Minister in Canada, 224, 228
Mackintosh, Governor-General in Alberta, 280
Maggie, character in a novel by Stephen Crane, 311
Magnús Brynjólfsson, in Dakota, 198, 204, 206, 349-351, 413
Magnús Gíslason, in Dakota, 106, 110, 113, 121, 123, 125
Magnús Hinriksson, in Churchbridge in Saskatchewan, 360, 367
Magnús Jónsson, the blind, from Fjall, 388, 483, 524, 549, 550
Magnús J. Skaftason, pastor in Winnipeg and editor, 408, 412, 413, 545
Mamie, ewe, 486
Maren Ragnheiður Pétursdóttir, wife of Baldur Sveinsson, 463
Margrét J. Benediktsson (Benedictson), poet and editor of *Freyja*, 313, 354
Margrét Sigurbjörg Bjarnadóttir, wife of Jónas Hunford, 270, 522-524
Margrét Björnsdóttir, wife of Jóhann Björnsson, 337
María Sigurðardóttir, wife of Haraldur Þorláksson, 84
Marker, C.P., in Alberta, 297, 328
Martin, Doctor in Milwaukee, 110
Marx, Karl, German philosopher, 193, 379, 501, 502
Matthías Jochumsson, pastor and poet, 54, 368, 369, 385, 387, 447-450
Maurer, Konrad, German law professor, 52, 53
McKenzie, contractor in Alberta, 239
McKenzie, postmaster in Dakota, 154
McKinney, Louise, American women's rights activist, 469
Miller, merchant in Dakota, 155
Morrison, Dan, in Alberta, 236
Moses, in the Bible, 51, 106, 142, 336
Möller, merchant in Akureyri, 65
Mörkeberg, Daniel Joachim, in Alberta, 297, 426
Nana, character in a novel by Emile Zola, 310
Nellie, mare, 284
Nietzsche, Friedrich, German philosopher, 192, 400, 528
Níels skáldi Jónsson, poet and farmhand, 75
Níels Steingrímur Þorláksson, pastor in New Iceland, 127, 130
Norna-Gestur, Old Norse legendary character, 289
Northfield, Theodore, character in a short story by Stephan, 142
O'Hara, character in a poem by Stephan, 308
Oftelie, Ole, Norwegian farmer in Wisconsin, 110, 113
Oldham, in Alberta, 383
Oliver, Frank, in Alberta, 280
Onoto Watanna, pseudonym of Winifred Reeve, 519
Otur (Otter), Stephan's dog, 294, 295
Ólafur Björnsson, physician in Winnipeg, 542
Ólafur Goodman (Guðmundsson), in Alberta, 224, 225, 238, 258
Ólafur Ólafsson, from Espihóll, 150, 151, 156, 160, 163, 171, 191, 198, 204-206, 210, 216, 224, 225, 229, 238, 259
Ólafur S. Thorgeirsson, printer in

Winnipeg, 347, 349, 434
Ólafur Tryggvason, King of Norway, 289
Ólöf Sigurðardóttir from Hlaðir, poet, 432, 450
Paine, Thomas, English American writer, 214
Parker, Theodore, American freethinker, 111, 193, 194
Parson, physician in Alberta, 376
Paul, in the Bible, 270
Páll Bjarnason, Icelandic poet, 489
Páll Gíslason Dalmann, 241
Páll Guðmundsson, farmer at Hjálmsstaðir, 432, 459, 460, 463
Páll Ólafsson, poet and farmer, 276
Páll Þorláksson, pastor in New Iceland, 84, 104, 105, 108-110, 115, 117, 119-122, 124, 126, 127, 130, 131, 134, 135, 138-141, 144, 146, 147, 150, 152, 160, 161, 174, 176, 178
Pétur Hjálmsson, pastor in Alberta, 331, 361, 364, 382, 394, 452, 481, 487, 494, 506, 523
Pétur Pálmason, of Valadalur, 59, 60
Pétur Thorlacius, from Stokkahlaðir, 117
Polly, horse, 159
Potter, W.J., American freethinker, 193, 194
Powell, J., in Alberta, 281
Ragnheiður (Rænka) Baldursdóttir, daughter of Baldur Sveinsson, 458, 459, 463, 474, 475, 477, 502
Ragnheiður (Sally), character in a poem by Stephan, 304-311, 333
Reeve, Winifred, Canadian novelist, 519, 520, 521
Regina Strong, wife of Guðmundur Stephansson, 330, 336, 362
Riel, Louis David, Canadian politician and rebel, 481
Ríkarður Jónsson, Icelandic sculptor, 302, 460
Ross, contractor in Alberta, 239
Rouleu, judge in Canada, 280
Rousseau, Jean-Jacques, French philosopher, 45
Rósa Jónsdóttir, Stephan's maternal grandmother, 39
Rósa Siglaug Stephansson, Stephan's daughter, 319-322, 330, 340, 362, 381, 382, 384, 388, 425, 426, 485-487, 495, 496, 505, 506, 515, 526, 541, 544-546, 548-550, 553-555
Runólfur Marteinsson, pastor in Manitoba, 274
Rænka, see Ragnheiður Baldursdóttir.
Rögnvaldur Pétursson, pastor in Winnipeg and editor, 342, 344, 352, 356, 363, 364, 373, 376, 379, 395, 397, 408, 430, 443, 469, 471, 477, 478, 481, 484, 493, 494, 504, 505, 508, 511-514, 516, 527, 528, 532-535, 540-544, 546-548, 550
S. Jónsdóttir (probably Sigríður Jónsdóttir), 116
Sage, in Alberta, 225, 235, 236, 239
Salverson, Laura Goodman, writer, 518-521
Satan, 396-402
Schiller, Friedrich, German poet, 181
Schiöth, baker in Akureyri, 65
Scolen, Jerome, in Wisconsin, 113
Scolen, Kristin, in Wisconsin, 113
Scott, Walter, Scottish writer, 101
Service, Robert, Canadian poet and journalist, 385, 470
Sesselja (Cecilia) Jónsdóttir, wife of Benedikt Bardal, 91, 106, 233, 264, 269
Shakespeare, William, English playwright, 74, 165, 488, 489

Index 603

Siegfried, old Norse legendary character, 289
Sifton, Clifford, Minister of Interior in Canada, 324
Sigfús Benediktsson, printer and poet, 313
Sigfús Bergmann, in Dakota, 177
Sigfús Goodman (Guðmundsson), in Alberta, 224, 258, 280, 281
Sigfús Halldórs, editor, 522, 546
Sigga (Sigríður Jónsdóttir), wife of Magnús Gíslason, 123, 124
Sigríður Hall, wife of Steingrímur Hall, singer, 355
Sigríður Jónsdóttir, wife of Ágúst H. Bjarnason, 508
Sigríður Jónsdóttir, Stephan's cousin, 66, 74, 80, 81, 116
Sigríður Herdís Kristjánsdóttir, wife of Jónas Hall, 151, 526
Sigurást Daðadóttir, wife of Jóhann Björnsson, 328
Sigurbjörg Stefánsdóttir, Stephan's paternal aunt, wife of Jón Jónsson at Mjóidalur, 64, 66, 68, 70, 71, 74, 80, 81, 89, 92, 108, 139, 196, 336
Sigurbjörn Hansson, in Dakota, 155
Sigurbjörn Jóhannsson, in Argyle, poet, 334, 335, 388
Sigurður Arnórsson, pastor of Mælifell, 42
Sigurður Jósúa Björnsson, in Dakota and Alberta, 224
Sigurður Baldvinsson, of Garður, 332, 443, 444
Sigurður Christophersson, in British Columbia, 388
Sigurður Helgason, composer, 382
Sigurður Jónsson, from Víðimýri, 56, 237, 246, 322, 341, 342, 554
Sigurður Jónsson, of Arnarvatn, farmer and poet, 441
Sigurður Júlíus Jóhannesson, physician and editor in Winnipeg, 409, 468, 477
Sigurður Kristjánsson, husband of Jenny, Stephan's daughter, 425, 426, 505, 506
Sigurður Nordal, professor, 522, 524, 525, 535, 536
Sigurður trölli (Sigurd the Giant), character in a poem by Stephan, 291, 292
Sigurjón Sveinsson, carpenter, 162, 167, 169
Sigurjóna Sigurbjörnsdóttir, first cousin of Helga, 180, 181
Sigurlaug (Lauga) Einara Guðmundsdóttir, Stephan's sister, 42, 58, 63, 67, 86, 89, 101, 108, 113, 114, 135, 136, 150, 160, 164-166, 177, 189, 220, 226, 228, 233, 245, 264, 273, 319, 363, 364, 367, 376, 384, 389, 391, 486, 510, 534, 535, 541
Sigurlaug Eyjólfsdóttir, wife of Einar Hannesson, 42, 44
Sigurlína Bardal, wife of Baldur Stephansson, 330, 434
Sigvaldi Jónsson, poet and teacher, 38, 39, 41, 42, 44, 45, 55, 111, 273
Sigvaldi Kaldalóns, physician and composer, 507
Simpson, J.M., in Alberta, 280
Sinbad, character from the Arabian Nights, 85
Skafti Brynjólfsson, in Dakota, 198, 204-206, 208, 210, 237, 349, 351-354, 356, 362, 373, 412-414
Snúður, character in a poem by Stephan (Jón Bjarnason), 216
Snæbjörn Steingrímsson, an errand boy, 171, 182, 184
Solómon (Salomon), in the Bible, 186-188, 199

Sophie, wife of Leo Tolstoy, 375
Sören Hjaltalín, in Alberta, 243
Sól, Old Norse semi-god, 314
Spencer, Herbert, English philosopher, 193, 270, 379
Spinoza, Baruch, Dutch philosopher, 214
Stefán Björnsson, pastor and editor, 345
Stefán Einarsson, professor, 517, 522
Stefán Guðmundsson, at Kroppur, Stephan's paternal grandfather, 30, 31
Stefán Hannesson, Stephan's uncle, 227
Stefán Jónsson, from Eyjardalsá, Stephan's cousin, 66, 444, 446
Stefán Kristinn Ólafur Kristinsson, son of Sigurlaug, Stephan's sister, 189, 226
Stefán Stefánsson, in Fagraskógi, member of Icelandic parliament, 462
Steingrímur Grímsson, in Dakota, 184
Steingrímur K. Hall, in Winnipeg, 355
Steinn Dofri, worker and genealogist, 496, 497, 505, 506, 526
Stephan (Stefán, Stebbi) G. Stephansson, 30, 34-65, 67- 82, 85-99, 101- 118, 121-127, 129-144, 147-157, 159-181, 183-186, 188-206, 208-222, 224- 233, 235-307, 309-323, 325-400, 402-407, 409-414, 416, 418, 421, 424- 475, 477, 479-497, 499-555
Stephaný Guðbjörg Stephansson (Bardal by marriage), 233, 272, 319, 320, 362, 381-383, 385, 425, 434, 495, 555
Story, W.W., American sculptor and poet, 194
Sunday, Billy, American evangelist, 435
Sveinbjörn Hallgrímsson, pastor and editor, 75
Sveinbjörn Johnson, lawyer in Dakota, 470, 471
Sveinbjörn Sveinbjörnsson, composer, 507
Sveinn Björnsson, in Dakota and Seattle, 148, 166, 202, 247-249, 388
Tegnér, Esajas, Sweedish poet, 55
Teitur, fictional person, 158, 159
Theódóra Thoroddsen, poet in Reykjavík, 432, 438, 440, 460, 466, 538
Thorarensen, pharmacist in Akureyri, 65
Thoreau, Henry David, American writer, 111, 179, 192
Thorson, Charles, Canadian artist, 380
Thorson, Harald, Norwegian merchant, 147
Todle, see Þórður Árnason, 143
Todleson, Ida see Ingibjörg Þórðardóttir.
Tolstoy, Leo, Russian writer, 286, 375, 426
Tómas Jónasson, peasant playwright, 73, 74, 87, 90, 444
Tóta, Stephan's mare, 295, 340, 341
Tryggvi Gunnarsson, director and member of the Icelandic parliament, 88, 93, 101
Turgenev, Ivan, Russian writer, 311
Týr, Old Norse god, 530
Underwood, B.F., American freethinker, 193, 232
Urt, cow, 426
Valdimar Gíslason Dalmann, 241
Vargur, ram, 486
Vereshchagin, Vasily, Russian painter, 378
Victoria, Queen of British Empire, 148
Vilhelmína Lever, running guesthouse in Akureyri, 38, 65, 92
Vilhjálmur Stefánsson, polar explorer, 394

Vídalín, Jón, (bishop in Skálholt), 34, 40, 53, 58, 232
Völundur, Old Norse legendary character, 230
Wagner, physician in Alberta, 527, 547-549, 555
Walker, livestock merchant in Scotland, 88, 94, 95, 99
Walters, Emilie, Canadian painter, 479
Wardell, F.A., in Dakota, 151
Whaley, physician in Winnipeg, 504, 505
Wheeler, Ella, American poet and teacher, 112
Whitman, Walt, American poet, 111, 114, 167, 192, 194, 220, 268, 297
Whittier, John Greenleaf, American poet, 121
Wilhelm H. Paulson, member of Saskatchewan legislature, 356
Wilhelm II., German Kaiser, 411, 482
Wood, Henry Wise, farmer's leader in Alberta, 500, 506
Woods, W.L., in a survey crew in Alberta, 282
Zola, Emile, French writer, 286, 310, 311
Þiðrandi, character in a poem by Stephan, 551, 552
Þorgeirsboli, ghost, 449
Þorgils Gjallandi (Jón Stefánsson), poet and farmer, 288, 372
Þorgrímur Laxdal, from Akureyri, 116
Þorlákur Gunnar Jónsson, from Stórutjarnir, 84, 85, 88, 91, 104, 106, 119-123, 125, 127, 171, 190, 198
Þorsteinn Erlingsson, poet and editor, 289, 362, 370, 372
Þórður Árnason, from Hrútafjörður, 127, 143, 144
Þórhallur, character in a poem, 551
Þórólfur Sigurðsson, at Baldursheimur, farmer and editor, 441-443, 488, 489
Þórólfur Skallagrímsson, Egill Skallagrímsson's brother, 536
Ægir, Old Norse semi-god, 314
Önundur Tree-leg, character in The Saga of Grettir the Strong, 255, 256

Image Credits

Byggðasafn Skagfirðinga, Sauðárkrókur/Glaumbær, Skagafjörður, Iceland/Nelson Gerrard (photographs of sites and buildings): 29, 32, 39.

Cassel's Old and New Edinburgh Illustrated, James Grant, Cassell & Co. London, Paris, New York, 1890: 100.

Eyrarbakki Icelandic Heritage Centre Library & Photo Archive/Nelson Gerrard, Eyrarbakki, Manitoba, Canada (original and scanned photographs/images): 40, 50, 98, 120, 121, 131, 134, 154, 157, 160, 164, 173, 175, 176, 187, 190, 192, 198, 203, 214, 227, 236, 238, 241, 243, 245, 247, 251, 259, 268, 270, 276, 277, 282, 283, 287, 296, 312, 313, 328, 329, 331, 334, 336, 343, 345, 348, 350, 352, 355, 363, 368, 369, 373, 380, 387, 388, 395, 399, 408, 409, 413, 415, 424, 428, 432, 435, 436, 442, 448, 456, 462, 467, 471, 473, 478, 481, 489, 491, 492, 494, 509, 510, 514, 519, 533, 550.

Glenbow Archives, Calgary: NA-1940-5; NA-303-116; 229, 260.

Handritadeild Landsbókasafns Íslands/Háskólabókasafns/Nelson Gerrard (images of archival material held in this collection): 89, 102, 162, 212, 255.

Héraðsskjalasafn Skagfirðinga (Archives of Skagafjörður), Sauðárkrókur, Iceland: 35, 549.

Iris (Benediktson) Bourne: 81, 195, 341, 377.

John H. Johnson, Gardar, North Dakota: 186, 220, 544.

Library and Archives Canada, Ottawa, Ontario: 231 (1960-125: PA-018755), 240 (1973-275: NPCC-056985).

Listasafn Íslands/National gallery of Iceland, Reykjavík, Iceland: 85.

Ljósmyndasafnið, Reykjavík, Iceland: 437.

Ljósmyndasafn Íslands í Þjóðminjasafni (Icelandic Museum of Photography/National Museum), Reykjavík, Iceland: 53, 84 (v4720), 126 (v4334), 127 (v19828), 139 (v19832), 185 (c19822).

Manitoba Provincial Archives, Winnipeg, Manitoba: 170, 226, 228, 324, 358, 543.

Minjasafnið á Akureyri (Akureyri Museum), Akureyri, Iceland: 59 (M1-B86, Hallgrímur Einarsson), 78 (vk 4686), 83 (M1-A-18, Hallgrímur Einarsson), 90.

Minjasafn/Héraðsskjalasafn Austfirðinga, Egilsstaðir, Iceland/Nelson Gerrard (photograph of interior and artifacts): 92.

National Media Museum/SSPL, Bradford, United Kingdon BD1 1NQ: 104 (SSPL 10440056).

Image Credits

Nelson Gerrard, Eyrarbakki, Manitoba, Canada (original photographs taken on site for this publication): *28, 31, 32, 39, 41, 47, 57, 58, 66, 71, 76, 79, 92, 148, 222, 279, 302, 444, 460.*

Skógasafn (Skógar Museum), Skógar, Austur-Eyjafjöll, 861 Hvolsvöllur, Iceland/Nelson Gerrard (photographs of artifacts): *41, 61.*

Stephansson Family Archive: *233, 235, 272, 320, 362, 383, 392, 421, 425, 501, 506, 515, 523, 534, 539, 541, 545, 547, w553.*

Wisconsin Historical Society, Madison: *112, 128.*

Viðar Hreinsson, private collection: *140.*

Other photos:
Almanak Ólafs S. Thorgeirssonar 1918, facing page 36: *458*

Stephan G. Stephansson. *Bréf og ritgerðir* III, Reykjavík 1947, facing title page: *468.*

Maps and charts:
Maps are made by Jonnathan Tinoco. The following are based on maps Bjarni Hinriksson made for the Icelandic version of the biography: *37, 43, 64, 123, 147, 225, 360, 386, 441, 518.*

State Archives in Bismarck: *151.*

Dolly Stephansson: *374.*

Auður Viðarsdóttir

Viðar Hreinsson, an independent literary scholar, grew up on a farm in the North of Iceland. A lecturer on various aspects of Icelandic literary and cultural history at universities in Iceland, Denmark, and Canada, he also acted as general editor of the acclaimed five-volume series *The Complete Sagas of Icelanders*, published in 1997.

Viðar's two-volume biography of Icelandic-Canadian literary giant Stephan G. Stephansson was published in Icelandic in 2002 and 2003. *Volume I* was nominated for the Icelandic Literary Prize in 2002 and the completed work received the 2003 Award for Excellence in Scholarly Writing.

An outspoken environmental and political activist and former Director of the Reykjavík Academy, Hreinsson has since written two biographies and worked on developing new and critical approaches to Icelandic literary and cultural history.

www.ingramcontent.com/pod-product-compliance
Lightning Source LLC
Chambersburg PA
CBHW071640160426
43195CB00012B/1316